Lecture Notes in Artificial Intelligence 3620

Edited by J. G. Carbonell and J. Siekmann

Subseries of Lecture Notes in Computer Science

Héctor Muñoz-Avila
Francesco Ricci (Eds.)

Case-Based Reasoning Research and Development

6th International Conference
on Case-Based Reasoning, ICCBR 2005
Chicago, IL, USA, August 23-26, 2005
Proceedings

Springer

Series Editors

Jaime G. Carbonell, Carnegie Mellon University, Pittsburgh, PA, USA
Jörg Siekmann, University of Saarland, Saarbrücken, Germany

Volume Editors

Héctor Muñoz-Avila
Lehigh University, Department of Computer Science and Engineering
19 Memorial Drive West, Bethlehem, PA 18015, USA
E-mail: munoz@cse.lehigh.edu

Francesco Ricci
Electronic Commerce and Tourism Research Laboratory, ITC-irst
Via Solteri 38, Trento, Italy
E-mail: ricci@itc.it

Library of Congress Control Number: 2005930340

CR Subject Classification (1998): I.2, J.4, J.1, F.4.1

ISSN 0302-9743
ISBN-10 3-540-28174-6 Springer Berlin Heidelberg New York
ISBN-13 978-3-540-28174-0 Springer Berlin Heidelberg New York

Springer is a part of Springer Science+Business Media

springeronline.com

Printed in Germany

Typesetting: Camera-ready by author, data conversion by Scientific Publishing Services, Chennai, India
Printed on acid-free paper SPIN: 11536406 06/3142 5 4 3 2 1 0

Preface

The International Conference on Case-Based Reasoning (ICCBR) is the preeminent international meeting on case-based reasoning (CBR). ICCBR 2005 (`http://www.iccbr.org/iccbr05/`) was the sixth in this series of biennial international conferences highlighting the most significant contributions to the field of CBR. The conference took place during August 23–26, 2005 at the downtown campus of DePaul University, in the heart of Chicago's downtown "Loop." Previous ICCBR conferences were held in Trondheim, Norway (2003), Vancouver, Canada (2001), Seeon, Germany (1999), Providence, Rhode Island, USA (1997), and Sesimbra, Portugal (1995).

Day 1 of ICCBR 2005 was Industry Day, which provided real-world experiences utilizing CBR in fielded applications. Day 2 featured various workshops on CBR in the health sciences, textual case-based reasoning, computer gaming and simulation environments, and similarities – Processes – Workflows. Days 3 and 4 comprised presentations and posters on theoretical and applied CBR research, as well as invited talks from three distinguished scholars: Derek Bridge, University College Cork, Craig Knoblock, University of Southern California, and Colleen Seifert, University of Michigan.

The presentations and posters covered a wide range of CBR topics, including adaptation, applications, case base maintenance, computer games, creative reasoning, knowledge representation, interactive systems, knowledge management, knowledge acquisition, multiagent collaborative systems, similarity, tutoring systems, bioinformatics, and textual CBR.

This volume comprises papers for all of the presentations and posters. These 45 papers were chosen after a highly selective process. Of a total of 74 submissions, the Program Committee selected 19 papers for oral presentation and 26 papers for poster presentation. Each submission was identified as being in one of three categories and judged using the following criteria: 1. Theoretical/methodological research paper (scientific significance; originality; technical quality; and clarity). 2. Applied research paper (significance for scientific research or innovative commercial deployment; originality; technical quality; and clarity). 3. Deployed application paper (demonstrated practical, social, environmental or economic significance; originality; treatment of issues of engineering, management and user acceptance; and clarity).

Many people participated in making ICCBR 2005 a success. Robin Burke, DePaul University, served as Local Chair, with Héctor Muñoz-Avila, Lehigh University, and Francesco Ricci, ITC-irst, as Program Co-chairs. We would especially like to thank Stefanie Brüninghaus, University of Pittsburgh, for serving as Workshop Coordinator, and Mehmet H. Göker, PricewaterhouseCoopers, and Bill Cheetham, GE Research, for chairing Industry Day. We thank the Program Committee and the additional reviewers for their thoughtful and timely participation in the paper selection process. Finally, we gratefully acknowledge the generous support of the sponsors of ICCBR 2005 and of Springer for its continuing support in publishing the proceedings of ICCBR.

May 2005

Héctor Muñoz-Avila
Francesco Ricci

Organization

Program Chairs

Héctor Muñoz-Avila, Lehigh University, USA
Francesco Ricci, ITC-irst, Italy

Local Chair

Robin Burke, DePaul University, USA

Industry Day Coordinator

Mehmet H. Göker, PricewaterhouseCoopers, USA
Bill Cheetham, GE Research, USA

Workshop Coordinator

Stefanie Brüninghaus, University of Pittsburgh, USA

Program Committee

Agnar Aamodt	Norwegian University of Science and Technology, Norway
David W. Aha	Naval Research Laboratory, USA
Vincent Aleven	Carnegie Mellon University, USA
Klaus-Dieter Althoff	Fraunhofer IESE, Germany
Kevin Ashley	University of Pittsburgh, USA
Paolo Avesani	ITC-irst Trento, Italy
Brigitte Bartsch-Spörl	BSR Consulting, Germany
Carlos Bento	University of Coimbra, Portugal
Ralph Bergmann	University of Trier, Germany
Enrico Blanzieri	University of Trento, Italy
L. Karl Branting	LiveWire Logic, Inc., USA
Derek Bridge	University College Cork, Ireland
Stefanie Brüninghaus	University of Pittsburgh, USA
Robin Burke	DePaul University, Chicago, USA
Hans-Dieter Burkhard	Humboldt University Berlin, Germany
Bill Cheetham	General Electric Co., USA
Michael T. Cox	Wright State University, Dayton, USA
Susan Craw	Robert Gordon University, UK
Pádraig Cunningham	Trinity College Dublin, Ireland

Boi Faltings	EPFL Lausanne, Switzerland
Peter Funk	Mälardalen University, Sweden
Ashok Goel	Georgia Institute of Technology, USA
Mehmet H. Göker	Kaidara Software, Los Altos, USA
Andrew Golding	Lycos Inc., USA
Pedro A. González-Calero	Univ. Complutense de Madrid, Spain
Igor Jurisica	Ontario Cancer Institute, Canada
David Leake	Indiana University, USA
Ramon López de Mántaras	IIIA-CSIC, Spain
Michel Manago	Kaidara Software, Paris, France
Cindy Marling	Ohio University, USA
Bruce McLaren	Carnegie Mellon University, USA
Lorraine McGinty	University College Dublin, Ireland
Bruce McLaren	CMU, USA
David McSherry	University of Ulster, UK
Erica Melis	DFKI, Saarbrücken, Germany
Bart Netten	TNO TPD, The Netherlands
David Patterson	University of Ulster, UK
Petra Perner	IBaI Leipzig, Germany
Enric Plaza	IIIA-CSIC, Spain
Luigi Portinale	University of Eastern Piedmont, Italy
Lisa S. Purvis	Xerox Corporation, NY, USA
Michael M. Richter	University of Kaiserslautern, Germany
Edwina Rissland	University of Massachusetts, USA
Thomas Roth-Berghofer	DFKI, Germany
Rainer Schmidt	Universität Rostock, Germany
Barry Smyth	University College Dublin, Ireland
Raja Sooriamurthi	Indiana University, USA
Henry Tirri	University of Helsinki, Finland
Brigitte Trousse	INRIA Sophia Antipolis, France
Manuela Veloso	Carnegie Mellon University, USA
C. Gresse von Wangenheim	Univ. do Vale do Itajai, Brazil
Ian Watson	AI-CBR, University of Auckland, New Zealand
Rosina Weber	Drexel University, USA
Stefan Wess	empolis, Germany
David C. Wilson	Univ. of North Carolina at Charlotte, USA
Qiang Yang	Hong Kong University of Science & Technology, China

Additional Reviewers

Steven Bogaerts
Sarah Jane Delany
Conor Hayes
John Loughrey
Ana G. Maguitman
Paolo Massa
Stewart Massie
Jens Mänz
Stefania Montani
Thomas Reichherzer
Ke Xu

Sponsoring Institutions

ICCBR 2005 was supported by Kaidara Software, empolis, the Naval Research Laboratory, and PricewaterhouseCoopers. ICCBR 2005 was held in cooperation with AAAI.

Table of Contents

Invited Talks

Scientific Papers

The Virtue of Reward: Performance, Reinforcement and Discovery in Case-Based Reasoning

Derek Bridge

Department of Computer Science, University College, Cork, Ireland
d.bridge@cs.ucc.ie

Agents commonly reason and act over extended periods of time. In some environments, for an agent to solve even a single problem requires many decisions and actions. Consider a robot or animat situated in a real or virtual world, acting to achieve some distant goal; or an agent that controls a sequential process such as a factory production line; or a conversational diagnostic system or recommender system. Equally, over its life time, a long-lived agent will make many decisions and take many actions, even if each problem-solving episode requires just one decision and one action. In spam detection, for example, each incoming email requires a single classification decision before it moves to its designated folder; but continuous operation requires numerous decisions and actions.

Reasoning and acting over time is challenging. A learner's experiences may prove unrepresentative of subsequent problems; a changing environment can render useless the system's knowledge. A system that tries to solve hard combinatorial problems, for example, may find, through exploration in the space of solutions, that earlier training examples are suboptimal. Concept drift in spam detection is another example: spammers send new kinds of unwanted email or find new ways of disguising spam as ham. Agents must be highly adaptive if, over time, they are to attain and maintain high standards of, for example, accuracy, coverage and efficiency.

To address these challenges in case-based agents, I have been drawing ideas from another field, that of *classifier systems*. Classifier systems, first proposed by John Holland, are rule-based systems. They comprise a performance component, a reinforcement component and a discovery component. The performance component chooses the agent's actions. The other two components enable classifier systems to exhibit two kinds of plasticity, parametric plasticity and structural plasticity. The reinforcement component uses feedback from the environment to update rule quality parameters. The discovery component uses genetic operators and other techniques to propose new rules, which may displace existing rules.

I will describe my attempts to build a case-based counterpart to Stewart Wilson's XCS, which is one of the most popular, modern classifier systems. I will describe each of its three components. In discussing the reinforcement component, I will offer reflections on the relationship between Case-Based Reasoning and reinforcement learning. In discussing the discovery component, I will offer reflections on automatic case discovery and case base maintenance.

H. Muñoz-Avila and F. Ricci (Eds.): ICCBR 2005, LNAI 3620, p. 1, 2005.

Learning to Optimize Plan Execution in Information Agents

Craig A. Knoblock

University of Southern California, Information Sciences Institute,
4676 Admiralty Way, Marina del Rey, CA 90292
knoblock@isi.edu

Overview

We can build software agents to perform a wide variety of useful information gathering and monitoring tasks on the Web [1]. For example, in the travel domain, we can construct agents to notify you of flight delays in real time, monitor for schedule and price changes, and even send a fax to a hotel if your flight is delayed to ensure that your hotel room will not be given away [2,3].

To perform each of these tasks, an agent is given a plan and its needs to be able to efficiently execute this plan. In the Web environment, sources can be quite slow and the latencies of the sources are also unpredictable since they can be caused by heavy loads on both servers and networks. Since the primary bottleneck of most agent plans on the web is retrieving data from online sources, an agent should execute information requests as early as possible. To address these issues, we have developed a streaming dataflow language and executor, called Theseus [4], which is optimized for the Web environment in three ways. First, since the executor is based on a dataflow paradigm, actions are executed as soon as the data becomes available. Second, Theseus performs the actions in a plan in separate threads, so they can be run asynchronously and in parallel. Third, the system streams the output from one action to the next so that sequential operations can be executed in parallel.

Theseus is similar to network query engines, such as Telegraph [5] or Tukwila [6], in that they are also streaming dataflow execution systems. However, the network query engines focus on the efficient execution of XML queries, while Theseus provides an expressive language for expressing information gathering and monitoring plans. The Theseus language supports capabilities that go beyond network query engines in that it supports recursion, notification operations, and writing and reading from databases to support monitoring tasks.

We developed an approach to increase the potential parallelism in a streaming dataflow execution system. This optimization technique, called speculative execution [7,8], predicts the results of an operation based on data and patterns that it has seen in the past. The predicted results can then be used to speculate about the operations that will need to be performed later in the plan. The system decides where to speculate by analyzing a plan and determining the critical paths. On these paths it then inserts a "speculate" operation, which uses

H. Muñoz-Avila and F. Ricci (Eds.): ICCBR 2005, LNAI 3620, pp. 2–3, 2005.

input to earlier operations to predict the input to later operations. The system also inserts a "confirm" operation, which ensures that the final result is correct regardless of whether the prediction is correct. This approach to optimizing streaming dataflow plans can achieve arbitrary speedups by speculating on the speculations. If the system is able to make accurate predictions, the executor could speculate on all of the input, execute the entire plan in parallel, and then confirm all of the results.

The effectiveness of the speculation technique depends on making accurate predictions. We have developed a learning system that combines caching, classification, and transduction to learn value predictors [9]. The system uses transducer learning to discover patterns in Web navigation paths, decision tree learning to make predictions on similar inputs, and caching when the first two learning methods are not applicable. Our experiments on a number of real-world examples show that learning the value predictors for speculative execution can provide significant performance improvements over the same plans without any learning.

References

1. Knoblock, C.A.: Deploying information agents on the web. In: Proceedings of the 18th International Joint Conference on Artificial Intelligence (IJCAI-2003), Acapulco, Mexico (2003)
2. Ambite, J.L., Barish, G., Knoblock, C.A., Muslea, M., Oh, J., Minton, S.: Getting from here to there: Interactive planning and agent execution for optimizing travel. In: Proceedings of the Fourteenth Conference on Innovative Applications of Artificial Intelligence (IAAI-2002), AAAI Press, Menlo Park, CA (2002)
3. Chalupsky, H., Gil, Y., Knoblock, C.A., Lerman, K., Oh, J., Pynadath, D.V., Russ, T.A., Tambe, M.: Electric elves: Applying agent technology to support human organizations. In: Proceedings of the Conference on Innovative Applications of Artificial Intelligence. (2001)
4. Barish, G., Knoblock, C.A.: An expressive and efficient language for software agents. Journal of Artificial Intelligence Research (2005)
5. Hellerstein, J.M., Franklin, M.J., Chandrasekaran, S., Deshpande, A., Hildrum, K., Madden, S., Raman, V., Shah, M.A.: Adaptive query processing: Technology in evolution. IEEE Data Engineering Bulletin **23** (2000)
6. Ives, Z.G., Halevy, A.Y., Weld, D.S.: An XML query engine for network-bound data. VLDB Journal **11** (2002)
7. Barish, G., Knoblock, C.A.: Speculative execution for information gathering plans. In: Proceedings of the Sixth International Conference on Artificial Intelligence Planning and Scheduling (AIPS 2002), AAAI Press, Menlo Park, CA (2002)
8. Barish, G., Knoblock, C.A.: Learning value predictors for the speculative execution of information gathering plans. In: Proceedings of the 18th International Joint Conference on Artificial Intelligence (IJCAI-2003), Acapulco, Mexico (2003)
9. Barish, G.: Speculative Plan Execution for Information Agents. PhD thesis, Department of Computer Science, University of Southern California (2003)

Cased-Based Reasoning by Human Experts

Colleen M. Seifert

University of Michigan, 530 Church Street, Ann Arbor, MI 48109-1043
seifert@umich.edu

Abstract. The central insight that led to the field of Case-Based Reasoning was that human memory appears to be organized around individual episodic experiences (Schank, 1982; Kolodner, 1980). At the time, there were few empirical findings available that shed light on how humans encode, retrieve, and reason about complex experiences. In the twenty years since then, researchers in cognitive science have investigated both everyday autobiographical memory and the performance of human experts who process many individual cases within a domain, such as medical diagnosis. The results identify some important features of the case-based reasoning process in humans, and suggest new approaches to building computational models that may display similar capabilities.

1 Introduction

The important role of cases in memory is both intuitive and compelling. Our phenomenological experience confirms that memories for distinct episodes from our pasts come to mind effortlessly, and appear to guide our reactions to new events. Within domains of expertise, these memories for specific past cases appear to separate the true expert from one who has learned only the "rules" of a domain. However, is there any scientific evidence about what human experts can recall about cases, and how their processing of cases leads to the ability to draw on past experiences?

1.1 Aspects of Cognitive Processes in Expert Case Memory

A survey of the current findings in cognitive science draws attention to several features of human case-based reasoning:

1 Elaborative, social processing of interesting cases at the time of learning
2 Domain space "construction:" Rapid identification of novel, never-seen items
3 Cases as schematic, yet unique representations of domain knowledge

1.2 Proposals for Processes in Case-Based Reasoning Systems

The empirical findings suggest that case-based reasoning in human experts is characterized by several distinctive, important processes. By determining how these processes facilitate successful use of cases, we develop proposals for improvements in CBR systems.

H. Muñoz-Avila and F. Ricci (Eds.): ICCBR 2005, LNAI 3620, p. 4, 2005.

Learning to Win: Case-Based Plan Selection in a Real-Time Strategy Game

David W. Aha[1], Matthew Molineaux[2], and Marc Ponsen[3]

[1] Navy Center for Applied Research in Artificial Intelligence,
Naval Research Laboratory (Code 5515), Washington, DC 20375
[2] ITT Industries, AES Division, Alexandria, VA 22303
[3] Department of Computer Science and Engineering,
Lehigh University, Bethlehem, PA 18015
[1,2] {first.last}@nrl.navy.mil [3]mjp304@lehigh.edu

Abstract. While several researchers have applied case-based reasoning techniques to games, only Ponsen and Spronck (2004) have addressed the challenging problem of learning to win real-time games. Focusing on WARGUS, they report good results for a genetic algorithm that searches in plan space, and for a weighting algorithm (*dynamic scripting*) that biases subplan retrieval. However, both approaches assume a static opponent, and were not designed to transfer their learned knowledge to opponents with substantially different strategies. We introduce a plan retrieval algorithm that, by using three key sources of domain knowledge, removes the assumption of a static opponent. Our experiments show that its implementation in the Case-based Tactician (CAT) significantly outperforms the best among a set of genetically evolved plans when tested against random WARGUS opponents. CAT communicates with WARGUS through TIELT, a testbed for integrating and evaluating decision systems with simulators. This is the first application of TIELT. We describe this application, our lessons learned, and our motivations for future work.

1 Introduction

Research on artificial intelligence (AI) and games has an extraordinary history that dates from 1950. Several luminaries have contributed to this field, and automated game-playing programs now exist that outperform world champions in classic games such as checkers, Othello, and Scrabble (Schaeffer, 2001). These efforts brought about significant advancements in search algorithms, machine learning techniques, and computer hardware. As a barometer of continued strong interest, several conferences (e.g., *International Game-On Conference on Computer Games: AI, Design and Education*, *AI and Interactive Digital Entertainment*) and journals (e.g., *Journal of Intelligent Games and Simulation*, *Journal of Game Development*) are devoted to AI and games.

In recent years, AI researchers (e.g., Laird & van Lent, 2001; Buro, 2003) have begun focusing on complex strategy simulation games that offer a variety of challenges, including partially observable environments that contain adversaries who

H. Muñoz-Avila and F. Ricci (Eds.): ICCBR 2005, LNAI 3620, pp. 5 – 20, 2005.

modify the game state asynchronously, and whose decision models are unknown. Among these, games that simulate the evolution of civilizations are particularly intriguing due to their enormous state spaces, large decision spaces with varying abstraction levels, multiple decision threads (e.g., economy, combat), and their need for resource management processes.

Although many studies exist on learning to win classical board games and other games with comparatively smaller search spaces, few studies exist on learning to win complex strategy games. Some argue that agents require sophisticated representations and reasoning capabilities to perform competently in these environments, and that these representations are challenging to construct (e.g., Forbus *et al.*, 2001). Fortunately, sufficiently good representations exist for a small number of gaming environments. In particular, Ponsen and Spronck (2004) developed a lattice for representing and relating abstract states in WARGUS, a moderately complex real-time strategy game. They also sharply reduced the decision space by employing a high-level language for game agent actions. Together, these constrain the search space of useful plans and state-specific subplans (i.e., *tactics*). This allowed them to focus on an ambitious performance task: winning real-time strategy games. They reported good results for a genetic algorithm that learns complete plans, and for a weight-learning algorithm (*dynamic scripting*) that learn policies for selecting tactics that combine into successful plans. However, both approaches assume a fixed adversary, and were not designed to transfer learned knowledge so as to defeat opponents that use dissimilar strategies.

In this paper, we relax the assumption of a fixed adversary, and develop a case-based approach that learns to select which tactic to use at each state. We implemented this approach in the Case-based Tactician (CAT), and report learning curves that demonstrate its performance quickly improves with training even though the adversary is randomly chosen for each WARGUS game. CAT is the first case-based system designed to win against random opponents in a real-time strategy game.

We briefly review case-based approaches in games research and introduce WARGUS in Section 2. We detail our approach and CAT in Section 3. We review our empirical methodology and CAT's results in Section 4, and close with a discussion in Section 5 that mentions several future research objectives.

2 Background

2.1 Case-Based Reasoning Research in Games

Many taxonomies exist for distinguishing computer games. For example, Laird and van Lent (2001) distinguish game genres into action (e.g., WOLFENSTEIN™), adventure, role-playing (e.g., BALDUR'S GATE™), strategy, god (e.g., SIMCITY™), team sports (e.g., MADDEN NFL FOOTBALL™) and individual sports games. Fairclough et al.'s (2001) taxonomy differs slightly, in that they classify god games as a sub-type of strategy games, and place THE SIMS™ in a different category. We instead adopt a taxonomy that is biased by our reading of case-based reasoning (CBR)

Table 1. A partial summary on applying CBR to games

Genre	Examples	Description	Approaches	Performance Task
Classic board	chess (Kerner, 1995), checkers (Powell *et al.*, 2004), Othello (De Jong & Schultz, 1988)	n^2 board, 2-person, no uncertainty	rote learning, min-max, case acquisition	learn evaluation function, move selection, win
Adventure	Bonji's Adventures in Calabria (Fairclough & Cunningham, 2004)	puzzle-solving	planning & dialogue generation	storyline/plot generation and management
Team Sports	RoboCup Soccer (Wendler & Lenz, 1998; Gabel & Veloso, 2001; Wendler *et al.*, 2001; Karol *et al.*, 2003)	real-time multi-agent coordination and planning	various	identify preference location, passing, action selection, select team members
Real-time individual	Bilestoad™ (Goodman, 1994), Space Invaders™ (Fagan & Cunningham, 2003)	real-time single character planning	projective visualization, plan recognition	inflict/avoid damage, plan recognition
Real-time God	SimCity™ (Fasciano, 1996)	real-time single city management	plan adaptation	planning
Discrete Strategy	Freeciv (Ulam *et al.*, 2004)	turn-based civilization management	reflection-guided plan failure recovery	defend a city
Real-time strategy	**Wargus** (Cheng & Thawonmas, 2004; this paper)	**real-time limited civ. management**	hierarchical cases, **plan selection**	manage sub-tasks, **win**

research in games. In particular, we add categories that reflect more traditional games, ignore some that have not attracted strong CBR interest (e.g., action games), and refine categories of real-time games.

Many researchers have published work on CBR in games. We distinguish a subset of this research according to task characteristics (i.e., game genre, state and decision space complexity, adversarial presence, timing constraints, performance task) and CBR approach. Table 1 summarizes some of this work.

Several researchers have addressed classic board games, beginning with Arthur Samuel's (1959) rote learning approach for playing checkers. De Jong and Schultz's (1988) GINA instead memorized a partial game tree for playing Othello. Chess has been a popular topic. For example, Kerner (1995) described a method for learning to evaluate abstract patterns. More recently, Powell et al.'s (2004) CHEBR learned to play checkers given only a paucity of domain knowledge. While these efforts focused on adversarial games, they are turn-based rather than real-time, and have comparatively small decision complexities (see Section 2.2).

Case-based approaches have rarely been used in adventure games. However, this genre may become a rich focus for automated story plot generation. For example, Fairclough and Cunningham (2004) described OPIATE, which uses a case-based planner and constraint satisfaction to provide *moves* for a story director agent so as to ensure that characters act according to a coherent plot. Also, Díaz-Agudo et al. (2004) described a knowledge-intensive approach that extracts constraints from a user's interactively-provided specification, uses them to guide case retrieval and adaptation, and then creates a readable plot using natural language generation techniques. These projects extend earlier CBR work on story generation (e.g., Meehan, 1981).

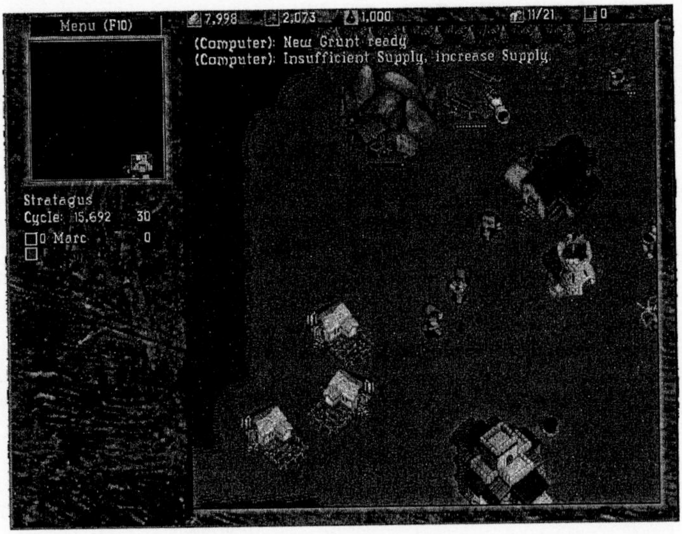

Fig. 1. A screen shot of a WARGUS game

ROBOCUP SOCCER is a popular CBR focus. Wendler and Lenz (1998) described an approach for identifying where simulated agents should move, while Wendler et al. (2001) reported strategies for learning to pass. Gabel and Veloso (2001) instead used a CBR approach to select (heterogeneous) members for a team. Karol et al. (2003) proposed a case-based action selection algorithm for the 4-legged league. While these real-time environments are challenging strategically, they do not involve complicating dimensions common to strategy games, such as economies, research, and warfare.

Some researchers have addressed real-time individual games. Goodman (1994) applied a projective visualization approach for BILESTOAD, a personal combat game, to predict actions that would inflict damage on the adversary and/or minimize damage to oneself. Fagan and Cunningham (2003) instead focused on a plan recognition task; they acquire cases (state-action planning sequences) for predicting the next action of a human playing SPACE INVADERS™. In contrast, CAT does not perform projective modeling, and does not learn to recognize adversarial plans. Instead, it acquires cases concerning the application of a subplan in a given state, learns to select subplans for a given state, and executes them in a more complex gaming environment.

Fasciano's (1996) MAYOR learns from planning failures in SIMCITY™, a real-time city management game with no traditional adversaries. MAYOR monitors planning expectations and employs a causal model to learn how to prevent failure repetitions, where the goal is to improve the ratio of successful plan executions. In contrast, CAT does not employ plan monitoring or causal goal models, and does not adapt retrieved plans. Rather, it simply selects, at each state, a good tactic (i.e., subplan) to retrieve. Also, our gaming environment includes explicit adversaries.

Ulam et al. (2004) described a meta-cognitive approach that performs failure-driven plan adaptation for FREECIV, a complex turn-based strategy game. While they employed substantial domain knowledge in the form of task models, it was only enough to address a simple sub-task (defending a city). In contrast, CAT performs no adaptation during reuse, but does perform case acquisition. Also, CAT focuses on winning a game rather than on performing a subtask.

2.2 Reducing the Decision Complexity of WARGUS: A Real-Time Strategy Game

In this paper, we focus on WARGUS (Figure 1), a real-time strategy (RTS) game that is a clone of the popular commercial game WARCRAFT II™. WARGUS uses STRATAGUS, an open-source engine for building RTS games. WARGUS is an excellent environment for AI research because its fairly mature code can be modified for experimentation.

RTS games usually focus on military combat (versus one or more adversaries), although they also include decision dimensions concerning tasks such as exploration, economic development, research advancement, and limited diplomacy. For example, WARCRAFT™, AGE OF EMPIRES™, and EMPIRE EARTH™ require players to control armies (of multiple unit types) and defeat all opponents in real-time.

Humans and adversaries can use any available *action* to form their game *strategy*, which is a plan. Typical actions include selecting a building to construct, researching a specific new technology, setting a destination for a selected group, and assigning a task to a group (e.g., construct a building). Humans are limited to executing a single new action at any one moment, while existing actions continue to execute simultaneously. Typically, RTS games provide users with a varying set of opponent strategies, each encoded as a *script*. A subplan in these scripts is called a *tactic*.

In addition to having relatively a large state space (e.g., we experiment with a 128x128 map that can involve dozens of units and buildings), WARGUS' decision space is comparatively large. An analysis of this complexity requires some understanding of the game. Winning (i.e., by destroying all the enemy units and buildings) requires managing three key resources: buildings, the workforce, and an army. Spending too little time on the army can lead to a crushing defeat at the hands of a strong neighbor, while spending too much time will cause a lag in research accomplishments, which prevent you from creating army units that are as strong as your neighbors. A balance must be maintained among these three resources. To do this, successful WARGUS players execute orders in one location, hurry to another, and try to return attention to the first location before its orders have terminated.

The decision space is the set of possible actions that can be executed at a particular moment. We estimate this as $O(2^W(A*P) + 2^T(D+S) + B(R+C))$, where W is the current number of workers, A is the number of assignments workers can perform (e.g., create a building, gather gold), P is the average number of workplaces, T is the number of troops (fighters plus workers), D is the average number of directions that a unit can move, S is the choice of troop's stance (i.e., stand, patrol, attack), B is the number of buildings, R is the average choice of research objectives at a building, and C is the average choice of units to create at a building. For the simple early game scenario shown in Figure 1 (which includes some off-screen troops and an off-screen building), this estimate yields a decision complexity of 1.5×10^3, which is substantially higher than the average number of possible moves in many board games (e.g., for chess, this is approximately 30).

Standard domain knowledge (e.g., cannot attack now, need more wood for building) could reduce the number of sensible choices for a WARGUS player in Figure

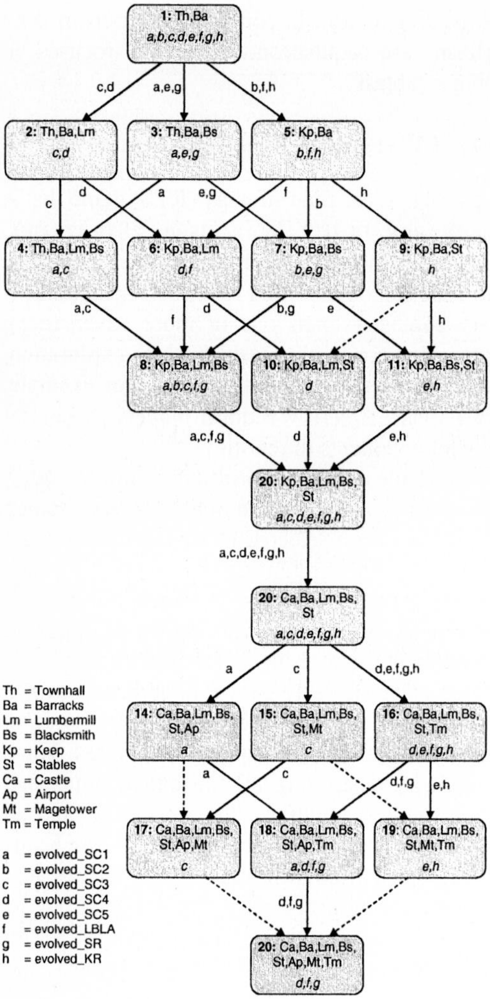

Fig. 2. A building-specific state lattice for WARGUS, where nodes represent states (defined by a set of completed buildings), and state transitions involve constructing a specific building. Also displayed are the evolved counter-strategies (a-h) that pass through each state

1's scenario to roughly ten. However, acquiring, encoding, and using this knowledge is challenging. Thus, existing research efforts on RTS games often focus on simpler tasks. For example, Guestrin et al. (2003) applied relational Markov decision process models for some limited WARGUS scenarios (e.g., 3x3 combat). They did not address more complex scenarios because their planner's complexity grows exponentially with the number of units. Similarly, Cheng and Thawonmas (2004) proposed a case-based plan recognition approach for assisting WARGUS players, but only for low-level management tasks. Their state representation is comprehensive and incorporates multiple abstraction levels. In contrast, CAT employs a simple case representation yet focuses on the complete task of winning the game.

To do this, CAT employs three significant sources of domain knowledge, the first two of which were developed by Ponsen and Spronck (2004), who used dynamic scripting to learn to win WARGUS games against a static opponent from a fixed initial state. The first source, *a state lattice*, is an abstraction of the state space, while the second source, *a set of tactics for each state*, is an abstraction of the decision space.

Figure 2 displays their building state lattice. Consisting of 20 states, it defines sequences of building constructions that can occur during a WARGUS game, where each state corresponds to the types of constructed buildings, which in turn determine the unit types that can be trained and technologies that can be researched. State changes occur when a tactic creates a new building. For example, starting with a Town Hall and a Barracks, the next building choices are a Lumber Mill, a Blacksmith, and a Keep, which replaces the Town Hall. Building these cause transitions from State 1 to States 2, 3, and 5, respectively.

Table 2. Features used in the case Descriptions

Feature	Description
$\Delta Kills_{i-1}$	Number of opponent combat & worker units killed minus the same for oneself, in the preceding state
$\Delta Razings_{i-1}$	Number of opponent buildings destroyed minus same for onself, in the preceding state
$Buildings_o$	Number of opponent buildings ever created
$CombatUnits_o$	Number of opponent combat units ever created
$Workers_o$	Number of opponent worker units ever created
$Buildings_{p,i}$	Number of own buildings currently existing
$CombatUnits_{p,i}$	Number of own combat units currently existing
$Workers_{p,i}$	Number of own worker units currently existing

Ponsen and Spronck (2004) manually designed their tactics and then improved them by searching the space of strategies using a genetic algorithm, where each chromosome is a complete plan (*counter-strategy*). Tactics were manually extracted from chromosomes. They used dynamic scripting to learn weights on tactics, and reported good learning performances versus four opponent strategies. In contrast, Ponsen et al. (2005) automatically acquired tactics by extracting them from the chromosomes based on the building states (i.e., all actions in a building state comprise one tactic). We used this same automatic approach for CAT.

In this paper, we also rely on this state lattice and a set of state-specific tactics. However, we add a third knowledge source: cases that map game situations to tactics and their performance. We will use all three to test how well CAT can play in games against a single, randomly selected WARGUS opponent.

3 Case-Based Strategy Selection

Our case-based approach for selecting which subplan (tactic) to use in each state employs the state lattice and state-specific tactics libraries described in Section 2. By doing this, the decision space (i.e., the number of tactics per state) becomes small, and an attribute-value representation of game situations suffices to select tactics. We define a case C as a tuple of four objects:

$$C = \langle \text{BuildingState, Description, Tactic, Performance} \rangle$$

where BuildingState is an integer node index in the state lattice, Description is a set of features of the current situation (see Section 3.1), Tactic is a counter-strategy's sequence of actions for that BuildingState, and Performance is a value in [0,1] that reflects the utility of choosing that tactic for that BuildingState, where higher values indicate higher performance (see Section 3.3). We next use Aamodt and Plaza's (1994) task decomposition model to detail our approach.

3.1 Retrieval

CAT retrieves cases when a new state in the lattice is entered (i.e., at the game's start, and when a transition building is finished). At those times, it records values for the eight features shown in Table 2, which we selected because they were available and are intuitively informative. They also balance information on recent game changes (i.e., the first two features), the opponent's situation (e.g., Workers_o), and the player's situation (e.g., $\text{Workers}_{p,i}$). When games begin, the value of the first two features is 0 (i.e., because no units have yet been killed and no buildings have yet been razed), while the others have small values (e.g,. only a few workers exist at the game's start, as exemplified in Figure 1). About 50 units are created, per side, in a short game, and a player's limit is 200. In addition to the ten in the state lattice, buildings include farms, towers, and a few others that do not cause state transitions.

Cases are grouped by BuildingState, and, after each game ends, at most one case is recorded per BuildingState. Our experiments involve repeated trials of only 100 games. Therefore, CAT does not require a fast indexing strategy for our evaluation.

CAT's function for computing the similarity between a stored case C and the current game description S is defined as:

$$\text{Sim}(C, S) = (C_{Performance}/\text{dist}(C_{Description}, S)) - \text{dist}(C_{Description}, S)$$

where dist() is the (unweighted, unnormalized) Euclidean distance among the eight features. This simple function emphasizes distance, and prefers higher-performing cases (i.e., those whose Tactic has performed well when selected in previous games) among those whose distance to S is similar (i.e., if two cases are at approximately the same distance from S, then the higher performer among them will have greater similarity). This function is particularly useful for BuildingState 1 (i.e., the game's start), where case Descriptions are all identical, and thus equally distant to the game's initial state. We will consider more elaborate similarity functions in future work.

CAT uses a modified k-nearest neighbor function to select case Tactics for retrieval. Among the k most similar cases, it retrieves one with the highest Performance. However, to gain experience with all tactics in a state, case retrieval is not performed until each available tactic at that state is selected e times, where e is CAT's *exploration* parameter. During exploration, CAT randomly retrieves one of the least frequently used tactics for reuse. Exploration also takes place whenever the highest Performance among the k-nearest neighbors is below 0.5.

3.2 Reuse

CAT's reuse process is given the retrieved case Tactic. While adaptation takes place, it is not controlled by CAT, but is instead performed at the level of the action primitives in the context of the WARGUS game engine (e.g., if an action requests the creation of a building, the game engine decides its location and which workers will construct it, which can differ in each game situation).

3.3 Revision

Revision involves executing the reused tactic in WARGUS, and evaluating the results. No repairs are made to these tactics; they are treated as black boxes.

Evaluation yields the Performance of a case's Tactic, which is measured at both a local and global level. That is, CAT records the WARGUS game score for both the player and opponent at the start of each BuildingState and at the game's end, which occurs when one player eliminates all of the other's units and buildings, or when we terminate a game if no winner has emerged after ten minutes of clock time.

We define the Performance for a Tactic *t* of case *C* with BuildingState *b* as a function of its "global" ($\Delta Score_i$) and "local" ($\Delta Score_{i,b}$) impact on the game score, where the former focuses on relative changes between the time that *t* begins executing in *b* and when the game ends, while the latter focuses only on changes during state *b*:

$$C_{Performance} = \sum_{i=1,n} C_{Performance,i}/n$$

$$C_{Performance,i} = \tfrac{1}{2}(\Delta Score_i + \Delta Score_{i,b})$$

$$\Delta Score_i = (Score_{i,p} - Score_{i,p,b})/((Score_{i,p} - Score_{i,p,b}) + (Score_{i,o} - Score_{i,o,b}))$$

$$\Delta Score_{i,b} = (Score_{i,p,b+1} - Score_{i,p,b})/((Score_{i,p,b+1} - Score_{i,p,b}) + (Score_{i,o,b+1} - Score_{i,o,b}))$$

where *n* is the number of games in which *C* was selected, $Score_{i,p}$ is the player's WARGUS score at the end of the ith game in which *C* is used, $Score_{i,p,b}$ is player *p*'s score before *C*'s Tactic is executed in game *i*, and $Score_{i,p,b+1}$ is *p*'s score after *C*'s Tactic executes (and the next state begins). Similarly, $Score_{i,o}$ is the opponent's score at the end of the ith game in which *C* is used, etc. Thus, *C*'s performance is updated after each game in which it is used, and equal weight is given to how well the player performs during its state and throughout the rest of the game.

3.4 Retention

During a game, CAT records a Description when it enters each BuildingState, along with the score and Tactic selected. It also records the scores of each side when the game ends, along with who won (neither player wins a tie). For each BuildingState traversed, CAT checks to see whether a case *C* exists with the same <Description, Tactic> pair. If so, it updates *C*'s Performance. Otherwise, CAT creates a new case *C* for that BuildingState, Description, Tactic, and Performance as computed in Section 3.3 (this counts as *C*'s first application). Thus, while duplicate cases are not created, CAT liberally creates new ones, and does not employ any case deletion policy.

4 Evaluation and Analysis

Our evaluation focuses on examining the hypothesis that CAT's method for selecting tactics significantly outperforms (1) a uniform selection strategy and (2) simply using the best counter-strategy. We report evidence that supports this hypothesis.

4.1 Competitors: WARGUS Players

Eight opponent scripts (see Table 3) were available for our experiments; some were publicly available and others we manually developed. For each opponent, we used Ponsen and Spronck's genetic algorithm to evolve a set of counter-strategy scripts. We use the best-performing counter-strategies among these (i.e., one per opponent) as a source of tactics, which are sequences of actions within a single building state of a counter-strategy. The names of the counter-strategies are shown in the lower left of Figure 2, which indicates that, for example, the evolved_sc1 counter-strategy includes tactics for building states 1, 3, 4, and 8, among others.

Table 3. WARGUS opponents used in the experiments

Opponent	Description
LBLA	This balances offensive actions, defensive actions, and research.
SR	Soldier's Rush: This attempts to overwhelm the opponent with cheap offensive units in an early state of the game.
KR	Knight's Rush: This attempts to quickly advance technologically, launching large offences as soon as strong units are available.
SC1-SC5	The top 5 scripts created by students, based on a class tournament.

The first WARGUS competitor, *Uniform*, selects tactics at each BuildingState according to a uniform distribution. Uniform should perform poorly because its selection is not guided by performance feedback. Uniform performs identically to CAT during its early stages of an experiment when, due to exploration, it randomly selects a tactic to use at each building state. To compute its results, we ran Uniform 48 times, six times per opponent script, and report its percentage of wins in Figure 4.

The next eight competitors are the counter-strategies. At each building state, they must use the tactic that defines them. Because they were evolved from different manually-generated scripts, we expect their performance to vary. Also, they should outperform Uniform, at least against the opponent on which they were trained. We ran each counter-strategy 10 times per opponent script, recorded the percentage of games that each won among their 80 games, and report the best performer in Figure 4.

The final competitor is CAT, which, after an initial exploration period during which it selects tactics using a uniform distribution, learns to intelligently select tactics at each building state. It should outperform Uniform because it learns to map game situations to a state's tactics, where selected tactics have performed well under similar game situations. Again, the counter-strategies supply the tactics for CAT to select. Thus, it might always select tactics from the same (e.g., best-performing) counter-strategy. Ideally, it should instead select tactics from *different* counter-strategies throughout a game, and across different games, to outperform the best performing counter-strategy. This is feasible: as shown in Figure 2, each counter-strategy traverses a unique sequence of building states. Thus, CAT may learn to select different tactics, for different game situations, from the same building state.

4.2 TIELT Integration

Integrating AI systems with gaming simulators can be a difficult and arduous task. Also, the resulting interface may not be reusable for similar integrations that a researcher may want to develop. Therefore, we used TIELT (Testbed for Integrating and Evaluating Learning Techniques) to perform this integration. TIELT (Aha & Molineaux, 2004) is a freely available middleware tool (http://nrlsat.ittid.com) that facilitates the integration of decision systems and simulators. It provides specific support for machine learning systems, and for complex gaming simulators. We actively support its users, and will use it in a few 2005 workshops and competitions.

TIELT integrations require constructing or reusing five knowledge bases, as shown in Figure 3. The Game Model is a (usually partial) declarative representation of the

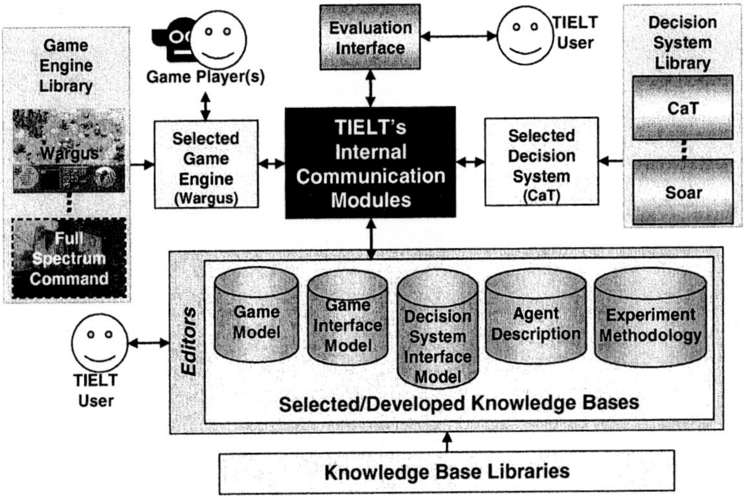

Fig. 3. TIELT's functional integration architecture

game. The Game Interface and Decision System Interface Models define the format and content of messages passed between TIELT, the selected game engine, and the decision system. The Agent Description includes an executable task structure that distinguishes the responsibilities of the decision system from those of game engine components. Finally, the Experiment Methodology encodes how the user wants to test the decision system on selected game engine tasks. Our knowledge bases will be available at TIELT'S www site for others to use (e.g., in future comparison studies).

We created a set of knowledge bases for integrating CAT with WARGUS using TIELT. This required several modifications of STRATAGUS so that it could provide access to subroutines that are germane to our investigation. Also, we increased the speed of WARGUS by a factor of 10 to run games more quickly. (A typical game still required an average of over 3-4 minutes to execute.)

This integration introduced a degree of non-determinism; while Ponsen and Spronck's (2004) earlier work involved updating WARGUS' code directly, our TIELT integration of CAT involves multiple threads and subsequent communication latencies. Thus, although two WARGUS games may have the same initial state and decision system, their results may differ greatly. This is the same that we might expect of a human playing the game, or any external process giving commands.

TIELT'S Game Model for this integration includes operators for key game tasks like building armies, researching technology advances, and attacking. Other operators obtain information about the game (e.g., the player's score). It also contains information about key events such as when a building or unit is completed. This information is maintained by the Game Interface Model, which contains information about the interface format. Future research using STRATAGUS can reuse these models.

The Agent Description links CAT to the abstractions of the Game Model. TIELT retrieves instructions from CAT and executes them using operators. When events recognized by the Game Model occur, it notifies CAT, using information from the

Decision System Interface Model to communicate. For example, when a building is finished, WARGUS sends a message to TIELT. The Game Interface Model interprets this, and fires a Game Model event. The Agent Description, listening for this event, notifies CAT and asks for further instructions. This Agent Description would need to be rewritten to work with another decision system, but the abstractions available from the Game Model simplify this task.

The Experiment Methodology defines the number of runs, when to stop the game, and resets CAT's memory when experiments begin. Also, it records game data into an EXCEL file for post-experiment analyses. It permits us to repeat experiments overnight, and record any data passing from STRATAGUS to CAT, or vice versa.

4.3 Empirical Methodology

We compared CAT versus its competitors for its ability to win WARGUS games. We used a fixed initial scenario, on a 128x128 tile map, involving a single opponent. The opponent was controlled by one of the eight scripts listed in Table 3. With the exception of the student scripts, these were all used in (Ponsen & Spronck, 2004).

Our only independent variable was the approach used to play against WARGUS opponents (i.e., Uniform, one of the eight counter-strategies, or CAT). We fixed CAT's two parameters during the experiment. The value of *k* (the number of nearest neighbors to consider when retrieving cases) was set to 3, as was the value of *e* (the exploration parameter, which determines the number of times that tactics in each state are used prior to permitting case reuse). We have not tuned either parameter setting.

For dependent variables, we collected average statistics on the percentage of games won, lost, and tied, along with the average final game scores for both players.

We ran Uniform on 48 games – six times for each of the eight opponents. We also tested each of the eight counter-strategies versus each opponent ten times. Averaging over multiple games helps to ameliorate the effects of non-deterministic game play.

However, the non-determinism introduced by TIELT's integration prevents testing the competitors on the same problems. Furthermore, it prevents us from periodically testing CAT on the same test set at different points during its training process. Therefore, we report CAT's average results across a sliding window, corresponding to the preceding *n* games, during training. We set *n* to 25 in the experiments (i.e., the measure after 100 games is the percentage of wins in games 76-100), and tested CAT in five trials of 100 games each. (Time limitations prevented us from running additional studies.) Cases are acquired throughout each trial, and the opponent for each game was randomly selected from a uniform distribution on the eight available.

4.4 Results

Figure 4 summarizes our results. As expected, Uniform performs poorly, winning an average of 22.9% of its games. CAT begins at this level, and after 100 games its average winning percentage is 82.4%, while saving an average of 302.4 cases. The best performer among the counter-strategies is evolved_SC5, which won 72.5% of its games. We compared the results (i.e., whether the player had won) for evolved_SC5 versus the final 25 games for CAT's five trials. A one-tail t-Test (2-sample assuming

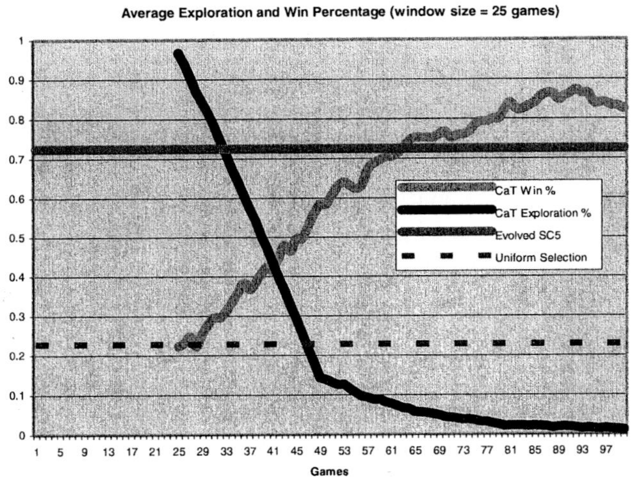

Fig. 4. Comparison of average winning percentages of CAT (across 5 runs) vs. the non-learning Uniform and best performing counter-strategy (Evolved SC5). Also shown is CAT's average exploration percentage. CAT's plots are across a window of the 25 preceding games

unequal variances) does not quite reveal a significant difference (p=0.053). However, there is a significant performance difference (p=0.00004) for the same test when examining the ratios of the final game scores (i.e., player_score/(player_score + opponent_score)), where CAT's average ratio was 0.65 while evolved_SC5's was 0.59. Also, CAT shows signs of overtraining, having peaked at 87.2%. Thus, CAT clearly outperforms the best individual counter-strategy, and correcting for overtraining should further increase its performance.

Also shown in Figure 4 is the average percentage of explorations performed by CAT. This starts at 100% through 24 games and quickly drops to 1%. With this setting for *e*, CAT relies almost exclusively on cases after 100 games.

5 Discussion

The results described in Section 4.4, although encouraging, are somewhat premature. We have not analyzed whether correlations among the eight features motivate using a more structured and informative case representation, such as the ones proposed in (Muñoz-Avila & Aha, 2004). Perhaps features should be differentially weighted, or normalized in distance computations. Also, CAT cheats; we will replace the three opponent-focused features (Table 2) with ones that a human player can observe (e.g., opponent score, observed opponent buildings) to determine whether CAT required them to obtain its good performance.

We have not yet tuned CAT's parameters, and it probably needs a management policy (e.g., for case filtering, deletion) to prevent overfitting, which may be the cause of CAT's final dip in performance in Figure 4. Moreover, CAT does not yet perform plan adaptation, which, given an appropriate domain model, may substantially improve performance. Finally, opponent modeling or plan recognition techniques could also prove useful (e.g., they may increase CAT's learning rate).

Our empirical methodology could be improved by training on a subset of opponent scripts and testing on the remainder, thus better assessing for generalization and transfer. A larger set of opponent scripts (e.g., created using Ponsen and Spronck's (2004) genetic algorithm) would be handy for this type of evaluation.

Ponsen and Spronck's (2004) dynamic scripting algorithm also learns to select which tactic to use at each building state. Its results could be compared with CAT's, for a specific opponent, but this requires that they use the same set of tactics. In their experiments, dynamic scripting selected from an average of 40 tactics per building state level, while in our experiments CAT needed to select among eight per building state level (in the lattice). We will compare these approaches in our future work.

CAT builds on Ponsen and Spronck's (2004) work by relaxing the need to train separately for each opponent. However, we have not tested its ability to work with random initial states, or multiple simultaneous opponents. Also, CAT'S knowledge sources provide no opportunity for online learning, which requires a topology of abstract game states that can recur within a game play, and a means for recognizing them. Thus, we will consider such state topologies for WARGUS and other games.

Dynamic scripting learns weight settings for plans in a plan retrieval process. Like CAT, it exploits plan performance data. However, it does not identify game situations in which those plans should be selected. We expect that dynamic scripting could be enhanced by providing it with game situation information, which may help it to increase its learning rate, and allow it to train on multiple opponents simultaneously.

6 Conclusion

We introduced an approach for case acquisition and tactic (subplan) selection, and its implementation in CAT (Case-based Tactician). We described its application to winning games against WARGUS opponents. CAT is the first case-based reasoning system designed to win real-time strategy (RTS) games against randomly selected opponents. Using Ponsen and Spronck's (2004) state lattice, CAT selects a tactic for each state transition, where the tactics were automatically extracted from a set of genetically evolved counter-strategies. Our experiments showed that CAT learns to perform significantly better than the best performing counter-strategy against WARGUS opponents. In particular, after 100 games, it wins over 80% of its games.

This is the first significant application of TIELT, a tool that assists with integrating decision systems (e.g., CAT) with simulators (e.g., WARGUS). Our experience provided us with key lessons for its continued development (e.g., on how to integrate RTS games, and the evaluation methodologies it should support).

CAT's algorithm has not yet been tailored for this application; its performance can probably be further improved. Also, many interesting research issues require further attention, such as how to enhance dynamic scripting, CAT's applicability to online learning tasks, and learning to win in other gaming engines.

Acknowledgements

This research was supported by DARPA's Information Processing Technology Office and the Naval Research Laboratory.

References

Aamodt, A., & Plaza, E. (1994). Case-based reasoning: Foundational issues, methodological variations, and system approaches. *AI Communications,* **7**, 39-59.

Aha, D.W., & Molineaux, M. (2004). Integrating learning in interactive gaming simulators. In D. Fu & J. Orkin (Eds.) *Challenges in Game AI: Papers of the AAAI'04 Workshop* (Technical Report WS-04-04). San José, CA: AAAI Press.

Buro, M. (2003). Real-time strategy games: A new AI research challenge. *Proceedings of the Eighteenth International Joint Conference on Artificial Intelligence* (pp. 1534-1535). Acapulco, Mexico: Morgan Kaufmann.

Cheng, D.C., & Thawonmas, R. (2004). Case-based plan recognition for real-time strategy games. *Proceedings of the Fifth Game-On International Conference* (pp. 36-40). Reading, UK: University of Wolverhampton Press.

De Jong, K., & Schultz, A.C. (1988). Using experience-based learning in game playing. *Proceedings of the Fifth International Conference on Machine Learning* (pp. 284-290). Ann Arbor, MI: Morgan Kaufmann.

Díaz-Agudo, B., Gervás, P., & Peinado, F. (2004). A case based reasoning approach to story plot generation. *Proceedings of the Seventh European Conference on Case-Based Reasoning* (pp. 142-156). Madrid, Spain: Springer.

Fagan, M., & Cunningham, P. (2003). Case-based plan recognition in computer games. *Proceedings of the Fifth International Conference on Case-Based Reasoning* (pp. 161-170). Trondheim, Norway: Springer.

Fairclough, C.R., & Cunningham, P. (2004). AI structuralist storytelling in computer games. *Proceedings of the International Conference on Computer Games: Artificial Intelligence, Design and Education.* Reading, UK: University of Wolverhampton Press.

Fairclough, C., Fagan, M., Mac Namee, B., Cunningham, P. (2001). Research directions for AI in computer games. *Proceedings of the Twelfth Irish Conference on Artificial Intelligence & Cognitive Science* (pp. 333-344). Maynooth, Ireland: Unknown publisher.

Fasciano, M.J. (1996). *Everyday-world plan use* (Technical Report TR-96-07). Chicago, Illinois: The University of Chicago, Computer Science Department.

Forbus, K., Mahoney, J., & Dill, K. (2001). How qualitative spatial reasoning can improve strategy game AIs. In J. Laird & M. van Lent (Eds.) *Artificial Intelligence and Interactive Entertainment: Papers from the AAAI Spring Symposium* (Technical Report SS-01-02). Stanford, CA: AAAI Press.

Gabel, T., & Veloso, M. (2001). *Selecting heterogeneous team players by case-based reasoning: A case study in robotic soccer simulation* (Technical Report CMU-CS-01-165). Pittsburgh, PA: Carnegie Mellon University, School of Computer Science.

Goodman, M. (1994). Results on controlling action with projective visualization. *Proceedings of the Twelfth National Conference on Artificial Intelligence* (pp. 1245-1250). Seattle, WA: AAAI Press.

Guestrin, C., Koller, D., Gearhart, C., & Kanodia, N. (2003). Generalizing plans to new environments in relational MDPs. *Proceedings of the Eighteenth International Joint Conference on AI* (pp. 1003-1010). Acapulco, Mexico: Morgan Kaufmann.

Karol, A., Nebel, B., Stanton, C., & Williams, M.-A. (2003). Case based game play in the RoboCup four-legged league: Part I the theoretical model. In D. Polani, B. Browning, A. Bonarini, & K. Yoshida (Eds.) *RoboCup 2003: Robot Soccer World Cup VII*. Padua, Italy: Springer.

Kerner, Y. (1995). Learning strategies for explanation patterns: Basic game patterns with applications to chess. *Proceedings of the First International Conference on Case-Based Reasoning* (pp. 491-500). Sesimbra, Portugal: Springer.

Laird, J.E., & van Lent, M. (2001). Interactive computer games: Human-level AI's killer application. *AI Magazine,* **22**(2), 15-25.

Meehan, J. R. (1981). Tale-spin and micro tale-spin. In R.C. Schank & C.K. Riesbeck (Eds.) *Inside computer understanding*. Hillsdale, NJ: Erlbaum.

Muñoz-Avila, H., & Aha, D.W. (2004). On the role of explanation for hierarchical case-based planning in real-time strategy games. In P. Gervás & K.M. Gupta (Eds.) *Proceedings of the ECCBR 2004 Workshops* (Technical Report 142-04). Madrid, Spain: Universidad Complutense Madrid, Departamento di Sistemos Informáticos y Programación.

Ponsen, M.J.V., Muñoz-Avila, H., Spronck, P., & Aha, D.W. (2005). Automatically acquiring domain knowledge for adaptive game AI using evolutionary learning. To appear in *Proceedings of the Seventeenth Conference on Innovative Applications of Artificial Intelligence*. Pittsburgh, PA: AAAI Press.

Ponsen, M., & Spronck, P. (2004). Improving adaptive game AI with evolutionary learning. *Computer Games: Artificial Intelligence, Design and Education* (pp. 389-396). Reading, UK: University of Wolverhampton.

Powell, J.H., Hauff, B.M., & Hastings, J.D. (2004). Utilizing case-based reasoning and automatic case elicitation to develop a self-taught knowledgeable agent. In D. Fu & J. Orkin (Eds.) *Challenges in Game Artificial Intelligence: Papers from the AAAI Workshop* (Technical Report WS-04-04). San Jose, CA: AAAI Press.

Samuel, A. (1959). Some studies in machine learning using the game of checkers. *IBM Journal of Research and Development,* **3**(3), 210-229.

Schaeffer, J. (2001). A gamut of games. *AI Magazine*, **22**(3), 29-46.

Ulam, P., Goel, A., & Jones, J. (2004). Reflection in action: Model-based self-adaptation in game playing agents. In D. Fu & J. Orkin (Eds.) *Challenges in Game Artificial Intelligence: Papers from the AAAI Workshop* (Technical Report WS-04-04). San Jose, CA: AAAI Press.

Wendler, J., Kaminka, G. A., & Veloso, M. (2001). Automatically improving team cooperation by applying coordination models. In B. Bell & E. Santos (Eds.) *Intent Inference for Collaborative Tasks: Papers from the AAAI Fall Symposium* (Technical Report FS-01-05). Falmouth, MA: AAAI Press.

Wendler, J., & Lenz, M. (1998). CBR for dynamic situation assessment in an agent-oriented setting. In D.W. Aha & J.J. Daniels (Eds.), *Case-Based Reasoning Integrations: Papers from the AAAI Workshop* (Technical Report WS-98-15). Madison, WI: AAAI Press.

An Ensemble of Case-Based Classifiers for High-Dimensional Biological Domains

Niloofar Arshadi[1] and Igor Jurisica[1,2]

[1] Department of Computer Science, University of Toronto,
10 King's College Road, Toronto, Ontario M5S 3G4, Canada
niloofar@cs.toronto.edu

[2] Ontario Cancer Institute, Princess Margaret Hospital,
University Health Network, Division of Cancer Informatics,
610 University Avenue, Toronto, Ontario M5G 2M9, Canada
juris@ai.utoronto.ca

Abstract. It has been shown that an ensemble of classifiers increases the accuracy compared to the member classifiers provided they are diverse. One way to produce this diversity is to base the classifiers on different case-bases. In this paper, we propose the mixture of experts for case-based reasoning (MOE4CBR), where clustering techniques are applied to cluster the case-base into k groups, and each cluster is used as a case-base for our k CBR classifiers. To further improve the prediction accuracy, each CBR classifier applies feature selection techniques to select a subset of features. Therefore, depending on the cases of each case-base, we would have different subsets of features for member classifiers.

Our proposed method is applicable to any CBR system; however, in this paper, we demonstrate the improvement achieved by applying the method to a computational framework of a CBR system called *TA3*. We evaluated the system on two publicly available data sets on mass-to-charge intensities for two ovarian data sets with different number of clusters. The highest classification accuracy is achieved with three and two clusters for the ovarian data set 8-7-02 and data set 4-3-02, respectively. The proposed ensemble method improves the classification accuracy of *TA3* from 90% to 99.2% on the ovarian data set 8-7-02, and from 79.2% to 95.4% on the ovarian data set 4-3-02. We also evaluate how individual components in MOE4CBR contribute to accuracy improvement, and we show that feature selection is the most important component followed by the ensemble of classifiers and clustering.

1 Introduction

Case-based reasoning (CBR) has been successfully applied to a wide range of applications such as classification, diagnosis, planning, configuration, and decision-support [1]. CBR can produce good quality solutions in weak theory domains such as molecular biology, where the number and the complexity of the rules affecting the problem are very large, there is not enough knowledge for formal knowledge representation, and our domain understanding evolves over time [2].

H. Muñoz-Avila and F. Ricci (Eds.): ICCBR 2005, LNAI 3620, pp. 21–34, 2005.

Protein expression profiling using mass spectrometry is a recent method for profiling cancer cases to measure thousands of elements in a few microliters of serum [3], and also an example of high-dimensional molecular biology domain. The data obtained are mass-to-charge ratios (m/z values) of varying intensities. Mass spectrometry data sets are represented by two-dimensional matrices, where each row contains the mass-to-charge intensities (known as biomarkers) for cancer and control (normal) samples. In addition, clinical information is used to label and further describe individual samples.

Using principles of case medicine for diagnosis and prognosis, CBR naturally fits this application domain. However, (ultra) high-dimensionality of mass spectrometry data sets (tens of thousands of biomarkers with only few hundreds of samples) poses a challenge that needs to be addressed. One solution is to combine CBR classifiers with other machine learning techniques to improve the prediction accuracy and overcome the "curse of dimensionality". Ensembles improve the accuracy of CBR classifiers [4, 5]; however, since k-nearest neighbor (kNN) and CBR classifiers are categorized under *stable* classifiers, having diverse classifiers is essential to improve the accuracy [6]. Stable classifiers are stable with respect to small changes in the training data.

One way to have diversity for stable classifiers is to select different subsets of features for each classifier [4, 5]. In this paper, in addition to selecting a different subset of features for each member classifier, we cluster the case-base into smaller groups. Data clustering means to group items (data points or attributes) into classes such that items within a cluster are similar to one another and dissimilar to items in other clusters. Thus, by grouping the whole case-base into smaller clusters, different classifiers would have different case-bases.

The goal of feature selection is to identify "informative" features among thousands of available features, i.e., relevant features that improve CBR performance for a given reasoning task. For mass spectrometry data sets, mining a subset of features that distinguishes between cancer and normal samples can play an important role in disease pathology and drug discovery. Early detection of cancer can reduce mortality, and identified biomarkers may also be useful drug discovery targets that may lead to new therapeutical approaches. Moreover, removing "non-informative" features helps overcome the "curse of dimensionality", and improves the prediction accuracy of classifiers.

Our hypothesis can be summarized as follows. Combining an ensemble of CBR classifiers with feature selection and clustering techniques not only helps overcome the "curse of dimensionality", but also leads to diverse classifiers, which is essential for improving the accuracy of ensembles. Our approach has three main components: (1) an ensemble of CBR systems, (2) clustering, and (3) feature selection. In principle, any CBR system, clustering, and feature selection algorithm can be used. However, the choice has to satisfy our performance criteria, which is to maximize prediction accuracy, and be applicable to high-dimensional domains.

We use an ensemble of CBR systems, called the *mixture of experts* (MOE) to predict the classification label of an unseen data (query). A gating network calculates the weighted average of votes provided by each expert. We apply spectral clustering [7] to cluster the data set (case-base) into k groups. Each cluster is considered as a case-base for the k CBR experts, and the gating network learns how to combine the responses provided by each expert. The performance of each CBR expert is further improved by using feature selection techniques. We use logistic regression [8] to select a subset of features in each cluster.

Although the proposed method is applicable to any CBR system, we demonstrate the improvement achieved by applying it to a specific implementation of a CBR system, called *TA3* [9]. *TA3* is a computational framework for CBR based on a modified NN technique and employs a variable context, a similarity-based retrieval algorithm, and a flexible representation language.

The rest of the paper is organized as follows. Section 2 reviews ensembles, clustering, and feature selection techniques. In Section 3, we present MOE4CBR, a method that uses the mixture of CBR experts to classify high-dimensional data sets. Section 4 introduces the *TA3* CBR system, which is used as a framework for evaluating MOE4CBR. In Section 5, we demonstrate the experimental results of the proposed method on two publicly-available ovarian data sets.

2 Related Work

Ensembles improve the stability and accuracy of classifiers if there is diversity in the classifiers [6, 5]. If small changes in training data produces quite different models and thus different predictions, the learner is called an unstable learner [5]. Neural networks and decision trees are examples of unstable learners. For such classifiers, diversity can be achieved if classifiers are trained on different subsets of training data. However, since lazy learners such as kNN and CBR classifiers are relatively stable in the face of changes in training data [6], other sources of diversity must be employed. One way of achieving diversity is to consider a different subset of features for each classifier. Ricci and Aha [4] create various NN classifiers, each one considers a different subset of features and then their predictions are combined using error-correcting output codes (ECOCs). Cunningham and Zenobi [5] show that an ensemble of kNN classifiers based on different feature subsets can classify more accurately than a single kNN classifier based on the best feature subset available.

Clustering and *feature selection* techniques have been applied to many domains including high-dimensional biological domains [10, 11, 12]. Clustering groups samples (cases) into partitions such that samples within a cluster are similar to one another and dissimilar to samples in other clusters. Clustering techniques can be categorized into *partitional* and *hierarchical* methods [13]. Partitional-based clustering techniques attempt to break a data set into k clusters such that each cluster optimizes a given criterion, e.g., minimizes the sum of squared distance from the mean within each cluster. Hierarchical clustering proceeds successively by either merging smaller clusters into larger ones (agglomerative approach), or by splitting larger clusters (divisive approach).

Clustering and feature selection techniques have been applied to CBR systems as well. Yang and Wu [14] propose a method that groups the case-base into smaller case-bases, and then each case-base is maintained individually. They use *density-based* clustering technique [15] in which a cluster is a region with a higher density of points than its surrounding region.

Shiu and Yeung [16] cluster the case-base into smaller partitions and select representative cases for each cluster in order to reduce the size of case-base. In their clustering approach, the similarity matrix of cases is formed, and two cases will be placed in the same cluster if their weighted Euclidean distance is smaller than a predetermined threshold.

Smyth and McKenna [17] cluster the case-base by finding the *related set* of each case. The related set of each case is the union of the set of cases that can be solved by this case and the set of cases that this case can solve. Two cases will be in the same cluster if the intersection of their related sets is not empty. Common problem types are typically represented by large and densely packed clusters, while smaller clusters, or even lone cases, generally represent more unusual problem types. Those cases that do not make critical competence contribution could be deleted. In their case-base editing approach, the size of case-base is minimized, while the range of problems that can be solved remains unchanged.

Feature selection techniques are classified into *filter* and *wrapper* methods [18]. The filter approach selects feature subsets that are independent of the induction algorithm, while the wrapper approach evaluates the subset of features using the inducer, itself. Aha and Bankert [19] discuss how using filter and wrapper techniques improve the classification accuracy of case-based classifiers on the cloud data set with 204 features and a few thousand data points. Their results show that a wrapper feature selection method (called BEAM) applied to an NN classifier improves its prediction accuracy by $\sim$20%.

3 The MOE4CBR Method

The goal of our method is to improve the prediction accuracy of CBR classifiers using the mixture of experts. The performance of each expert in MOE4CBR is improved using clustering and feature selection techniques. Using the results of our earlier performance evaluation [20], we selected spectral clustering [7] for clustering the case-base, and the logistic regression model [8] as a filter feature selection for the *TA3* classifier. Given a labeled training data set, predicting labels of the unseen data (query), is performed in two steps: (1) each CBR experts retrieves l similar cases from its respective (non-overlapping) case-base; (2) the class label for the query is predicted by assigning weights to each expert. We discuss the process in details in the next section.

3.1 Mixture of Experts

The mixture of experts approach is based on the idea that each expert classifies data points (cases) separately, and individual responses are combined by the gating network to provide a final classification label [21]. A general idea of the mixture of experts approach is depicted in Figure 1. In the first step, for an unseen query case, each expert of CBR retrieves l similar cases from its case-base (l can be chosen by the user). It should be noted that experts do not share their case-bases, rather the case-base of each expert is obtained by clustering the whole case-base into k non-overlapping clusters (k can be chosen by the user or estimated by other analysis).

After retrieving l similar cases from the case-base, the expert applies the weighting vote algorithm (see Section 4.3) to predict the class label of the query case, i.e., performs weighted case adaptation. More precisely, let $\{C_1, \ldots, C_k\}$ denote the clusters (or the k case-bases of our k experts), x the unseen data, y a class label, S_j the number of similar cases that belong to C_j, and T_j the number of similar cases with class label y that belong to C_j, $Pr(Y = y|C_j, x)$ is then computed as $\frac{T_j}{S_j}$.

We use CBR to assign weights to each expert – represented by g_j, $1 \leq j \leq k$. Briefly, g_j represents the probability that the unseen data x belongs to the case-base of the jth expert. More precisely, in order to compute g_j that can be shown as $Pr(C_j|x)$ as well, we perform the following steps. Let m represent the number of similar cases retrieved from the whole initial case-base by the gating network (m can be chosen by the user), R_j the number of similar cases to x belonging to C_j (the case-base of the jth expert), g_j then is calculated by dividing R_j by m. Finally, in order to combine the responses of k experts, following formulas are used [8]:

$$Pr(Y = y|x) = \sum_{j=1}^{k} g_j \times Pr(Y = y|C_j, x), \tag{1}$$

with the constraint that:

$$\sum_{j=1}^{k} g_j = \sum_{j=1}^{k} Pr(C_j|x) = 1, \tag{2}$$

As Figure 2 depicts, the MOE4CBR method has two main steps: First, the case-base of each expert is formed by clustering the case-base into k groups. Second, each case-base selects a subset of features "locally". Each of the k obtained sets is considered as a case-base for our k experts of CBR. We use Equations 1 and 2 to combine the responses of the k experts. Each expert applies the *TA3* classifier to decide on the class label, and the gating network uses *TA3* to assign weights (represented by g_j) to each classifier as explained above.

3.2 Clustering

Of the many clustering approaches that have been proposed, only some of the algorithms are suitable for domains with (ultra) high number of features and a low number of samples. The two widely used clustering approaches in (ultra) high-dimensional DNA microarrays [22, 23] are k-means clustering [13] and

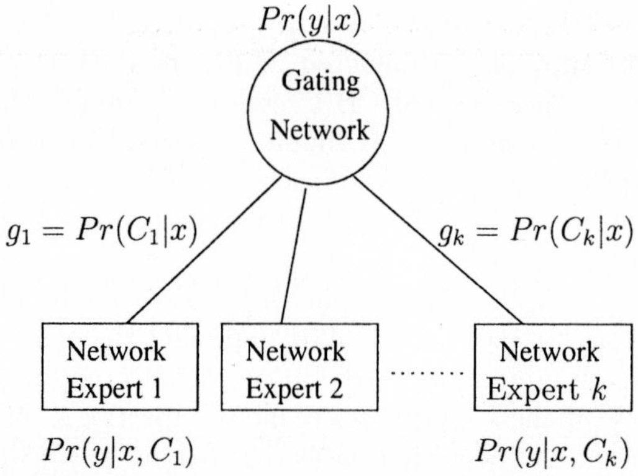

Fig. 1. Mixture of Experts: Terminal nodes are experts, and the non-terminal node is the gating network. The gating network returns the probability that the query x belongs to class Y

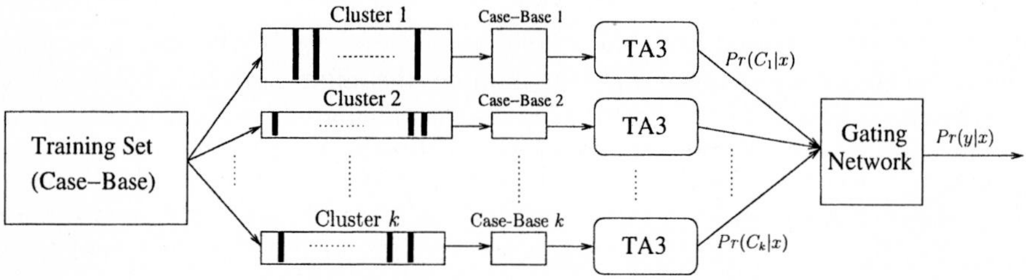

Fig. 2. Mixture of Experts for Case-Based Reasoning: Training set is grouped into k clusters, and after selecting a subset of features for each group (shown with vertical bars), each group will be used as a case-base for the k CBR experts. The gating network combines the responses provided by each *TA3* expert considering the weights of each expert (weights are shown on the arrows connecting *TA3* experts to the gating network)

self-organizing maps (SOMs) [24]. Our earlier evaluation suggests that spectral clustering [7] outperforms k-means clustering and SOMs [20].

Spectral clustering is based on the approach where data points are mapped to a new space, prior to being clustered. More precisely, first, a matrix X holding the Euclidean distance between any two data points (i.e., a transformation of the *affinity* matrix) is formed. Second, matrix Y is formed from X by stacking the k eigenvectors associated with the k largest eigenvalues of matrix X in columns. Each row of Y is treated as a point in $\mathcal{R}^k$ and is clustered into k clusters using k-means algorithm , where k represents the number of clusters and is set by the user. In the next step, data point s_i is assigned to cluster j if and only if row i of the matrix X was assigned to cluster j, where $1 \leq i \leq N$, $1 \leq j \leq k$, and N is the number of data points. This clustering technique has been successfully used in many applications, including computer vision and VLSI [7].

3.3 Feature Selection

The goal of feature selection is to improve the quality of data by removing redundant and irrelevant features, i.e., those features whose values do not have meaningful relationships to their labels, and whose removal improves the prediction accuracy of the classifier.

Fisher's criterion and standard t-test are two statistical methods that have been successfully applied to feature selection problem in (ultra) high-dimensional data sets [25]. In order to select a suitable feature selection approach, we evaluated the performance of Fisher's criterion, t-test, and the *logistic regression* model [8] when used in a CBR classifier [20]. We applied the three feature selection techniques to the *TA3* classifier, and measured the improvement in *accuracy* and *classification error*. Accuracy measures the number of correctly classified cases, and classification error counts the number of misclassified cases. Based on our evaluation, logistic regression as a feature selection method outperforms Fisher and standard t-test techniques [26].

Assuming that classifier x is the logistic of a linear function of the feature vector, for two classes, the logistic regression model has the following form:

$$Pr(y = 0|x, w) = \frac{1}{1 + e^{-w^T x}}, \tag{3}$$

where w is a $p + 1$ column vector of weights, and p is the number of features [8]. Logistic regression has been successfully applied to classifying (ultra) high-dimensional microarrays [27]. However, we use the logistic regression classifier as a filter feature selection method. In order to select a subset of features (genes), the logistic regression classifier is trained using the above Equation on the training set, and features corresponding to the highest ranking magnitude of weights are selected. The data sets are normalized such that all features (regressor variables) have the same mean and variance.

4 An Introduction to the TA3 Case-Based Reasoning System

Although our method can be applied to any CBR system, we used the *TA3* CBR system as a framework to evaluate our method. The *TA3* system has been applied successfully to biology domains such as *in vitro fertilization* (IVF) [28] and protein crystal growth [29]. This section briefly describes the system.

4.1 Case Representation in *TA3*

A case C corresponds to a real world situation, represented as a finite set of attribute/value pairs [28]. Using the information about the usefulness of individual attributes and information about their properties, attributes are grouped into two or more Telos-style categories [30]. In classification tasks, each case has at least two components: problem description and class. The problem description characterizes the problem and the class gives a solution to a given problem. Additional categories can be used to group attributes into separate equivalence partitions, and treating each partition separately during case retrieval.

4.2 Case Retrieval in *TA3*

The retrieval component is based on a modified NN matching [31]. Its modification includes: (1) grouping attributes into categories of different priorities so that different preferences and constraints can be used for individual categories during query relaxation; (2) using an explicit context (i.e., set of attribute and attribute value constraints) during similarity assessment; (3) using an efficient query relaxation algorithm based on incremental context transformations [9].

Similarity in *TA3* is determined as a closeness of values for attributes defined in the *context*. Context can be seen as a view or an interpretation of a case, where only a subset of attributes are considered relevant. By selecting only certain features for matching and imposing constraints on feature values, a context allows for controlling what can and what cannot be considered as a partial match: all (and only) cases that satisfy the specified constraints for the context are considered similar and are relevant with respect to the context.

4.3 Case Adaptation in *TA3*

The adaptation process in CBR manipulates the solution of the retrieved case to better fit the query. We adopt distance-weighted nearest neighbor [32] to determine the classification label of the query based on the labels of similar retrieved cases. Let $x_1, ..., x_k$ denote the k cases retrieved from the case-base that are similar to the query x_q. In order to predict the label of x_q shown with $\hat{f}(x_q)$, following equations are used [32]:

$$\hat{f}(x_q) \leftarrow \underset{v \in V}{argmax} \sum_{i=1}^{k} \omega_i \delta(v, f(x_i)),$$

where

$$\omega_i \equiv \frac{1}{d(x_q, x_i)^2},$$

and V is the finite set of class labels $\{v_1, ..., v_s\}$, $f(x_i)$ the class label of case x_i, and $\delta(a, b) = 1$ if $a = b$ and $\delta(a, b) = 0$ otherwise.

5 Experimental Results

Here we demonstrate the results of applying the MOE4CBR method to the *TA3* classifier. In [33], we showed MOE4CBR improves the prediction accuracy of high-dimensional microarrays. In this study, we show the improvement in the classification accuracy of two publicly mass spectrometry data sets by applying MOE4CBR. Also, we experiment MOE4CBR with different number of experts and evaluate its components separately.

5.1 Data Sets

The experiments have been performed on the following mass spectrometry data sets. The two mass spectrometry data sets [34, 35] discussed in this paper, are both provided online at the National Institutes of Health and Food and Drug administration Clinical Proteomics Program Databank. [1]

1. *Ovarian data set 8-7-02*: Ovarian data set 8-7-02 comprises 162 mass spectra from ovarian cancer patients and 91 individuals without cancer (control group) with 15,154 mass-to-charge ratios (m/z values) measured in each serum.
2. *Ovarian data set 4-3-02*: Ovarian data set 4-3-02 contains spectra from 100 patients with ovarian cancer and 116 individuals without cancer (control group). The serum mass spectrum for each subject consists of 15,154 mass-to-charge ratios.

These two ovarian data sets have been previously analyzed [34, 35, 26, 20]. Sorace et al. [34] evaluate their extracted rules for selecting biomarkers on data set 8-7-02 when it is randomly split into training and test data. Although they achieve 100% sensitivity and 100% specificity, our results are not comparable, as they evaluated their method on randomly selected training and test sets, while we used 10-fold cross-validation. Also, their rules are extracted in an "ad hoc" way, and might not be applicable to other similar data sets.

Ovarian data set 4-3-02 has also been analyzed by Zhu et al. [35]. They achieve 100% specificity and 100% sensitivity. Our results are not comparable, since we used 10-fold cross-validation, while they split the data set randomly into training and test set. Furthermore, it had been recently reported that their results cannot be replicated and the overall best performance achieved using the proposed 18 markers is 98.42% [36].

Similarly, these two ovarian data sets have been analyzed using a *TA3* classifier combined with logistic regression [26]. This approach resulted in 98% accuracy and 2% error for the ovarian data set 8-7-02, and 95.4% accuracy and 4.6% error for the ovarian data set 4-3-02, evaluated using 10-fold cross-validation.

Each of the studies have selected a different set of "informative" biomarkers, and further biological validation, which is beyond the scope of this paper, will be able to determine which list of biomarkers is clinically more "informative" for diagnosis or drug discovery of ovarian cancer samples.

5.2 Evaluating MOE4CBR with Different Number of Experts

Table 1 depicts the results of applying MOE4CBR to our two ovarian data sets with different number of experts. When there is a tie, the *TA3* classifier cannot decide on the label; resulting cases are categorized as "undecided" in the Table. We used 10-fold cross-validation for validation, and the Table shows the average over the 10 folds. In each iteration, MOE4CBR was trained using 9 folds, and

[1] `http://home.ccr.cancer.gov/ncifdaproteomics/ppatterns.asp`

Table 1. Accuracy of MOE4CBR with different number of experts(shown with n) on ovarian data sets. In all experiments, 15 biomarkers were selected by logistic regression, and the whole case-base was clustered into smaller groups using spectral clustering

Ovarian Data Set 8-7-02				
	$n = 1$	$n = 2$	$n = 3$	$n = 4$
Accuracy	98%±2.8%	98.4%±2%	99.2%±1.6%	96.4%±2.9%
Error	2%	1.2%	0.8%	2.8%
Undecided	0%	0.4%	0%	0.8%
Ovarian Data Set 4-3-02				
	$n = 1$	$n = 2$	$n = 3$	$n = 4$
Accuracy	95.4%±4.3%	95.4%±4.8%	94.9%±5%	90.3%±4.9%
Error	4.6%	4.1%	5.1%	7.8%
Undecided	0%	0.5%	0%	1.9%

was tested on the remaining fold, i.e., the test set was quite unseen until the test time, and clustering and feature selection techniques were applied only to the training set.

When there is only one expert – *TA3* classifier – the case-base does not split into groups, and the size of the case-base is reduced by selecting 15 biomarkers out of 15,154 biomarkers. For the ovarian data set 8-7-02, the minimum classification error is achieved when the number of experts equals 3, while for the ovarian 4-3-02, the minimum classification error is realized with 2 experts (Table 1).

5.3 Evaluating Components of MOE4CBR

We used 10-fold cross-validation to evaluate our proposed method in terms of accuracy, classification error, and "undecided" rate, and the results are averaged over 10 folds. We evaluated the components of MOE4CBR as follows:

- This is our base line, where a single instance of *TA3* classifies the query case without being integrated with any FS or clustering technique, and only a single classifier predicts the label.
- In order to evaluate the FS component, we use logistic regression to select 15 biomarkers out of 15,154 biomarkers, and then we apply *TA3* as a CBR classifier.
- In order to evaluate the clustering component, we split the case-base randomly into two groups, and use MOE4CBR to classify the query case. In this case, the number of experts equals 2, logistic regression selects 15 biomarkers, and the results are averaged over 5 iterations.
- Finally, we apply MOE4CBR when logistic regression as a filter FS method selects 15 biomarkers, and spectral clustering groups the case-base into two clusters (i.e., there are only two experts).

As the Table 2 shows, the FS component contributes the most in improving the accuracy of the classifier, while spectral clustering has the least contribution. As is typically found in most studies, kNN and CBR classifiers are

Table 2. Accuracy of MOE4CBR with different components

Ovarian Data Set 8-7-02			
Method	Accuracy	Error	Undecided
Single TA3	90%	9.2%	0.8%
TA3 with LR	98%	2%	0%
MOE4CBR with LR and RC	97.4%	2.6%	0%
MOE4CBR with LR and SC	98.4%	1.2%	0.4%
Ovarian Data Set 4-3-02			
Method	Accuracy	Error	Undecided
Single TA3	79.2%	18.5%	2.3%
TA3 with LR	95.4%	4.6%	0%
MOE4CBR with LR and RC	94.6%	5.2%	0.2%
MOE4CBR with LR and SC	95.4%	4.1%	0.5%

Note. LR: Logistic Regression; RC: Random Clustering; SC: Spectral Clustering

very "sensitive" to the selected features and the "curse of dimensionality" problem. Therefore, removing "non-informative" features helps improve the accuracy. On the other hand, although spectral clustering outperforms k-means and self-organizing maps in terms of precision, recall, and Dunn's index [20], it still does not perform much better than random clustering. This can be due to the ultra high-dimensionality of data sets. Applying FS techniques before clustering may help improve the performance of clustering techniques.

6 Conclusions

Molecular biology is a natural application domain for CBR systems, since CBR systems can perform remarkably well on complex and poorly formalized domains. Although high dimensionality poses a challege and reduces system performance, the classification accuracy improves by using an ensemble of classifiers. Also, removing "non-informative" features from the case-base of each member classifier helps overcome the "curse of dimensionality".

In this paper, we proposed the mixture of experts for case-based reasoning (MOE4CBR) method, where an ensemble of CBR systems is integrated with clustering and feature selection to improve the prediction accuracy of the *TA3* classifier. Spectral clustering groups samples, and each group is used as a case-base for each of the k experts of CBR. To improve the accuracy of each expert, logistic regression is applied to select a subset of features that can better predict class labels. We also showed that our proposed method improves the prediction accuracy of the *TA3* case-based reasoning system on two public ovarian data sets.

Although we have used a specific implementation of a CBR system, our results are applicable in general. Generality of our solution is also not degraded by the application domains, since many other life sciences problem domains are characterized by (ultra) high-dimensionality and a low number of samples.

Further investigation may take additional advantage of Telos-style categories in *TA3* for classification tasks. The system may also benefit from new clustering approaches, and other feature selection approaches such as wrapper and hybrid approaches.

Acknowledgments

This work is supported by IBM CAS fellowship to NA, and the National Science and Engineering Research Council of Canada (NSERC Grant 203833-02) and IBM Faculty Partnership Award to IJ. The authors are grateful to Patrick Rogers, who implemented the current version of *TA3*.

References

[1] Lenz, M., Bartsch-Sporl, B., Burkhard, H., Wess, S., eds.: Case-Based Reasoning: experiences, lessons, and future directions. Springer (1998)
[2] Jurisica, I., Glasgow, J.: Application of case-based reasoning in molecular biology. Artificial Intelligence Magazine, Special issue on Bioinformatics **25(1)** (2004) 85–95
[3] Petricoin, E.F., Ardekani, A.M., Hitt, B.A., Levine, P.J., Fusaro, V.A., Steinberg, S.M., Mills, G.B., Simone, C., Fishman, D.A., Kohn, E.C., Liotta, L.A.: Use of proteomic patterns in serum to identify ovarian cancer. Lancet **359(9306)** (2002) 572–577
[4] Ricci, F., Aha, D.W.: Error-correcting output codes for local learners. In Nedellec, C., Rouveirol, C., eds.: Proceedings of the 10th European Conference on Machine Learning, Springer (1998) 280–291
[5] Cunningham, P., Zenobi, G.: Case representation issues for case-based reasoning from ensemble research. In Aha, D.W., Watson, I., eds.: Case-Based Reasoning Research and Development:4th International Conference on Case-Based Reasoning, Springer (2001) 146–157
[6] Breiman, L.: Bagging predictors. Machine Learning **24** (1996) 123–140
[7] Ng, A.Y., Jordan, M.I., Weiss, Y.: On spectral clustering: Analysis and an algorithm. In G. Dieterich, S. Becker, Z.G., ed.: Advances in Neural Information Processing Systems 14, MIT Press (2002)
[8] Hastie, T., Tibshirani, R., Friedman, J.: The elements of statistical learning. Springer (2001)
[9] Jurisica, I., Glasgow, J., Mylopoulos, J.: Incremental iterative retrieval and browsing for efficient conversational CBR systems. International Journal of Applied Intelligence **12(3)** (2000) 251–268
[10] Xing, E.P.: Feature selection in microarray analysis. In Berrar, D., Dubitzky, W., Granzow, M., eds.: A practical approach to Microarray data analysis. Kluwer Academic publishers (2003) 110–131
[11] Quackenbush, J.: Computational analysis of microarray data. Nat Rev Genet **2** (2001) 418–427
[12] Molla, M., Waddell, M., Page, D., Shavlik, J.: Using machine learning to design and interpret gene-expression microarrays. AI Magazine **25** (2004) 23–44
[13] Han, J., Kamber, M.: Data Mining: Concepts and Techniques. Morgan Kauffmann Publishers (2000)

[14] Yang, Q., Wu, J.: Keep it simple: a case-base maintenance policy based on clustering and information theory. In Hamilton, H., ed.: Advances in Artificial Intelligence, In Proceedings of the 13th Biennial Conference of the Canadian Society for Computational Studies of Intelligence, Montreal, Canada, Springer (2000) 102–114
[15] Ester, M., Kriegel, H.P., Sander, J., Xu, X.: A density-based algorithm for discovering clusters in large spatial databases with noise. In: Proceedings of the 2nd international Conference on knowledge discovery and data mining, Portland, OR, USA, AAAI Press (1996) 226–231
[16] Shiu, S.C., Yeung, D.S.: Transferring case knowledge to adaptation knowledge: An approach for case-base maintenance. Computational Intelligence **17** (2001) 295–314
[17] Smyth, B., McKenna, E.: Building compact competent case-bases. In Althoff, K.D., Bergmann, R., Branting, K., eds.: Proceedings of the 3rd International Conference on Case-Based Reasoning Research and Development (ICCBR-99), Seeon Monastery, Germany, Springer (1999) 329–342
[18] John, G., Kohavi, R., Pfleger, K.: Irrelevant features and the subset selection problem. In: Machine Learning: Proceedings of the eleventh international conference, Morgan Kauffmann (1994) 121–129
[19] Aha, D.W., Bankert, R.: Feature selection for case-based classification of cloud types: an empirical comparison. In Aha, D.W., ed.: Proceedings of the AAAI-94 workshop on Case-Based Reasoning, Menlo Park, CA: AAAI Press (1994) 106–112
[20] Arshadi, N., Jurisica, I.: Data mining for case-based reasoning in high-dimensional biological domains. IEEE Transactions on Knowledge and Data Engineering (2005) To appear
[21] Jacobs, R.A., Jordan, M.I., Nowlan, S.J., Hinton, G.E.: Adaptive mixture of local experts. Neural Computation **3** (1991) 79–87
[22] Golub, T., Slonim, D., Tamayo, P., Huard, C., Gassenbeek, M., Mesirov, J., Coller, H., Loh, M., Downing, J., Caligiuri, M., Bloomfield, C., Lander, E.: Molecular classification of cancer: class discovery and class prediction by gene expression monitoring. science **286** (1999) 531–537
[23] Tamayo, P., Slonim, D., Mesirov, J., Zhu, Q., Dmitrovsky, E., Lander, E., Golub, T.: Interpreting patterns of gene expression with self-organizing maps: methods and application to hematopoietic differentiation. In: Proceedings of the National Academy of Science of the United States of America. Volume 96(6). (1999) 2907–2912
[24] Kohonen, T.: Self-Organizing Maps. Springer (1995)
[25] Jaeger, J., Sengupta, B., Ruzzo, W.: Improved gene selection for classification of microarrays. In: Pacific Symposium on Biocomputing. (2003) 8:53–64
[26] Arshadi, N., Jurisica, I.: Feature selection for improving case-based classifiers on high-dimensional data sets. In: FLAIRS 2005 - The 18th International FLAIRS Conference, AAAI Press (2005) To appear
[27] Xing, E.P., Jordan, M.L., Karp, R.M.: Feature selection for high-dimensional genomic microarray data. In Brodley, C.E., Danyluk, A.P., eds.: Proceedings of the Eighteenth International Conference on Machine Learning, Williamstown, MA, USA, Morgan Kauffmann (2001) 601–608
[28] Jurisica, I., Mylopoulos, J., Glasgow, J., Shapiro, H., Casper, R.F.: Case-based reasoning in IVF: prediction and knowledge mining. Artificial Intelligence in Medicine **12** (1998) 1–24

[29] Jurisica, I., Rogers, P., Glasgow, J., Fortier, S., Luft, J., Wolfley, J., Bianca, M., Weeks, D., DeTitta, G.: Intelligent decision support for protein crystal growth. IBM Systems Journal **40(2)** (2001) 394–409

[30] Mylopoulos, J., Borgida, A., Jarke, M., Koubarakis, M.: Telos: Representing knowledge about information systems. ACM Transactions on Information Systems **8(4)** (1990) 325–362

[31] Wettschereck, D., Dietterich, T.: An experimental comparison of the nearest neighbor and nearest hyperrectangle algorithms. Machine Learning **19(1)** (1995) 5–27

[32] Mitchell, T.M.: Machine Learning. McGraw-Hill (1997)

[33] Arshadi, N., Jurisica, I.: Maintaining case-based reasoning systems: a machine learning approach. In Funk, P., González-Calero, P.A., eds.: Advances in Case-Based Reasoning: 7th European Conference, Springer (2004) 17–31

[34] Sorace, J.M., Zhan, M.: A data review and re-assessment of ovarian cancer serum proteomic profiling. BMC Bioinformatics **4:24** (2003) 14666–14671 available at `http://www.biomedcentral.com/1471-2105/4/24`.

[35] Zhu, W., Wang, X., Ma, Y., Rao, M., Glimm, J., Kovach, J.S.: Detection of cancer-specific markers amid massive mass spectral data. Proceedings of the National Academy of Sciences of the United States of America **100(25)** (2003) 14666–14671

[36] Baggerly, K.A., Morris, J.S., Edmonson, S.R., Coombes, K.R.: Signal in noise: Evaluating reported reproducibility of serum proteomic tests for ovarian cancer. Journal of National Cancer Institute **97(4)** (2005) 307–309

Language Games: Solving the Vocabulary Problem in Multi-Case-Base Reasoning

Paolo Avesani, Conor Hayes, and Marco Cova

ITC-IRST, Via Sommarive 18 - Loc. Pantè, I-38050 Povo, Trento, Italy
{avesani,hayes,cova}@itc.it

Abstract. The problem of heterogeneous case representation poses a major obstacle to realising real-life multi-case-base reasoning (MCBR) systems. The knowledge overhead in developing and maintaining translation protocols between distributed case bases poses a serious challenge to CBR developers. In this paper, we situate CBR as a flexible problem-solving strategy that relies on several heterogeneous knowledge containers. We introduce a technique called *language games* to solve the interoperability issue. Our technique has two phases. The first is an eager learning phase where case bases communicate to build a shared indexing lexicon of similar cases in the distributed network. The second is the problem-solving phase where, using the distributed index, a case base can quickly consult external case bases if the local solution is insufficient. We provide a detailed description of our approach and demonstrate its effectiveness using an evaluation on a real data set from the tourism domain.

1 Introduction

Case-based reasoning (CBR) is a powerful problem-solving strategy that utilises a repository of past problem-solving episodes to search for solutions to new problems. Although CBR has conventionally used a single local case base to solve problems for a particular task domain, it has been recognised that it must adapt to cater towards problem solving where the solution space may be distributed amongst several case bases [15,14,25,17,20]. A key motivation for this is that each case base may specialise in a particular part of the problem space.

Previous research on distributed case-based reasoning is based on the premise of *standardised* case representation across distributed case bases where the domain problems are homogeneous and well defined [10,16,17]. Leake & Sooriamurthi argue the benefits of a broader view for distributed CBR termed *multi-case-base reasoning* (MCBR) in which case base containers may contain knowledge collected in different contexts and for different tasks [13,15]. Such alternative sources of knowledge have the advantage of providing solutions, albeit imperfect, when none are found locally. Furthermore, it may not be practical or beneficial to merge multiple, heterogeneous case bases into a single unified case base for reasons of ownership, retrieval efficiency, maintenance and standardisation [13]. In this paper we consider the role of CBR in the trend towards

H. Muñoz-Avila and F. Ricci (Eds.): ICCBR 2005, LNAI 3620, pp. 35–49, 2005.

decentralised, *heterogeneous* information and service providers on the Internet as exemplified by the Blogger and P2P services [18,23].

A problem that stands out in this analysis is the *vocabulary problem* [9,14]. In single case base systems, the definition of the basic symbolic entities that will be manipulated by the reasoning system is one of the primary development stages [11,22]. In MCBR systems, unless the vocabulary elicitation process is coordinated and agreed between case authors, there will be an interoperability problem between case base containers. Thus, case base designers must either agree a global schema to be shared between all case bases *ex post*, thus negating the benefits of a locally maintained case problem space; or they can adopt a lazy approach whereby the case base is designed independently but will later require mappings or translations to be accessible from other case bases. The first proposal is the type of eager approach being promoted by researchers developing the semantic web protocols [7]. However, the key advantage of interoperability is counterbalanced by the difficulty of producing *ex ante* agreement on a shared schema and of encouraging widespread adoption. An example of the lazy approach is the widely used RSS[1] format, an XML protocol for publishing website information, which does not require shared agreement on the semantics of the content.

In this paper, we present the results of our work on the vocabulary problem where case authors represent their cases independently. We introduce a technique called *language games* that has been used to explore the problem of learning and communication among distributed, autonomous robots [26]. More generally, however, a language game is a computational model that allows convergence on a shared lexicon in a fully distributed framework. We address the problem of case base interoperability by enabling the emergence of a shared lexicon between case base peers. The technique involves the eager computation of case-to-case similarity where each agent locally builds up a global view without having to compromise local vocabulary. The effect of this technique is that participating case bases converge on a commonly agreed indexing lexicon. The proposed solution respects the autonomy principle inherent in the MCBR model: case bases do not have a global view of the solution space represented by external case bases. Instead, they incrementally learn a global perspective.

In particular, our research addresses a key problem in MCBR: *case dispatching* – deciding when and where to dispatch the problem [25,13]. Using the language game technique, each case base builds a local index of the distributed solution space. As such, we adopt the view that there exists a continuum between single and MCBR systems [15]. Our technique clearly has an analogue with indexing in single case bases. However, it differs in that each case base learns to index the relevant cases found in the distributed peer case bases.

The original contribution of this paper is to demonstrate how the language games model can address the vocabulary problem in MCBR. Using a learned lexicon, peer case bases implicitly learn the competences of remote case bases. As well as overcoming the interoperability issue, the advantages of this approach

[1] RSS stands for Really Simple Syndication.

lie in reducing query time computation and bandwidth requirements. This is because remote cases can be retrieved by issuing an indexing label, rather than a full problem description. We demonstrate a proof of concept of our approach on a real dataset from the tourism domain where the problem of mapping between alternative representations has previously had to be solved by hand [8].

In section 2 we describe related work in the area of CBR, information retrieval and machine learning. Section 3 analyses in more detail the vocabulary alignment problem in distributed CBR systems and provides an example of the benefits of our automated indexing approach. In section 4 we give a detailed explanation of the language games technique and in section 5 we demonstrate and evaluate the technique on a real dataset from the tourism domain. In sections 6 and 7 we present a discussion and the conclusion related to our findings.

2 Related Works

CBML, an XML application for exchanging case data in standard form in distributed systems, has previously been proposed [10,3]. However, this initiative is hampered by lack of support and dissemination among developers of CBR systems. Prasad et al. [19] describe a CBR system in which heterogeneous agents, each with access to a case base, cooperate in solving a parametric design task. However, although the agents may have different problem-solving strategies, they share a common schema relating to the design problem. Martin et al. [16] introduced a competence model for distributed case bases. The focus of this work is on cooperative problem-solving and thus, unlike the model we present, agents have a homogeneous representation language and the competence models of external agents are given in advance. McGinty & Smyth [17] demonstrate, with an application in the route planning domain, how expertise from multiple case bases can help plug gaps in knowledge in the local case base. Unlike the work described here, the problem solving competence of the peer agents is determined at query time by broadcasting to all peers in the network. Furthermore, the agents share a common representation model so that cases can be transferred between case bases without the need for translation.

The work of Leake & Sooriamurthi on MCBR bears the most relevance to our paper. MCBR is a problem-solving paradigm where the knowledge from multiple distributed knowledge containers is used, whenever necessary [13,25]. In [13,14], an analysis is presented of the issues involved in supplementing a local case base with knowledge from external 'idiosyncratic' case base containers, where knowledge may have been collected in different contexts. Two central issues relating to MCBR are identified: *case dispatching*, deciding when and from where to supplement the local case base; and *cross-case-base adaptation*, a technique for adapting solutions retrieved from one case base for use in another. In [13], an experimental evaluation demonstrated the benefits of lazily drawing from another case base when solution quality in the local case base was not high enough, even when the external case base reflected a task difference. However, in relation to our approach, the case bases used in the evaluation had differences in solution bias rather than case representation. In [14], a case-based dispatching strategy is introduced whereby each case base learns the problem-solving utility of external case bases for a range of test problems. Thus, each case base also employs a *dispatching case base* method to decide where to dispatch a problem that cannot be solved locally. This technique clearly has resonance with the competence indexing described in this paper. However, as in [13], this work is based on the premise of similar case representation in each case base.

2.1 Relationship to Semantic Web

We can view the vocabulary problem in MCBR systems as a subset of the problems of heterogeneous catalogue alignment being addressed by the Semantic Web community [1]. An open issue is how to preserve local representation while at the same time enabling communication between autonomous peers. The conventional view is that a common ontology for the domain should be established and then mappings produced between the local representation and the shared ontology [6]. Although intuitive, this approach poses difficulties in terms of ex ante agreement on the common ontology and on how the mappings will be constructed. In the European project, Harmonise, for example, a mediator is in charge of managing a shared representation of tourism concepts. Local subscribers then are in charge of *manually* mapping their local encodings to the predefined ontology [8].

Recently, research has been focused on the issues specifically related to the mapping between schemas or shallow representations like taxonomies [5]. The automation of the mapping process would enable pervasive interoperability without the constraint of a mediator, which in distributed applications becomes the "single point of failure". In such a scenario, each peer would autonomously manage the mapping with respect to the other peers. Unfortunately, automatic schema matching has proven to be a complex problem and a general solution is still not available.

2.2 Relationship to Information Retrieval

The issue of vocabulary mismatch has been addressed in information retrieval using techniques such as latent semantic analysis or cross-language indexing to solve the synonymy or translation problems [4,2]. However such techniques assume global access to the document corpus and are useful for providing a centralised indexing on a single server. In contrast, the language games methodology has an inherent communication methodology that allows the development of distributed indexing over autonomous, heterogeneous peers.

3 The Vocabulary Problem

The definition of the fundamental units of meaning that will be manipulated by the reasoning system is the first step required of any developer working in AI. In CBR, Richter has suggested that the term *vocabulary knowledge* describes the basic symbolic entities used to build cases, e.g., attributes, predicates and the schema structure [22]. Although, typically, domain experts are the source of this knowledge, CBR has less problems with the knowledge elicitation bottleneck than rule-based or model-based systems.

The *vocabulary problem* originally referred to a problem in human–computer interaction whereby users were not able to guess the required input terms for a computer programme [9]. The key observation was that programme designers failed to take into account the variety of words people use to refer to the same concept. The *vocabulary problem* in MCBR is similar. It refers to the problem posed where cases in one case base may not be available to another case because the case authors have used heterogeneous case representations. Of course, it is reasonable to expect case authors to make representational choices that reflect the type of problems they need to solve. Furthermore, the design choices may be influenced by the IT infrastructure of which the CBR component is only one part [24].

3.1 Possible Solutions

There are three possible solutions to this problem:

1. Case authors in a particular domain agree in advance a common schema with which to mark up each case base.
2. Each case author encodes the case base using a local representation but provides translations to the representations used in external case bases or to a common schema.
3. Each case author encodes the case base using a local representation and an automated process determines the relationship between cases/case bases.

Solution 1 is difficult to engineer because case authors may not be willing to invest time in developing an ex ante agreement that might limit their independence in modelling their perspective on the problem space. It will fail if developers choose to opt out. For solution 2, the work involved in providing a mapping or translation layer may be greater than the benefits that would be gained. Also, the development and maintenance overheads of this approach are considerably higher, reducing the advantages of CBR over a model-based system. Solution 3 has the advantage of respecting the autonomy of the case base while at the same time enabling interoperability. The drawback is that such automation has proven to be a very challenging task.

3.2 Types of Alignment

We can consider the problem of case base alignment as having three types of solution, as shown in Table 1. The first is a *schema matching policy* where, for example, two case base schemas are matched on a feature by feature basis. Typically, this type of mapping would be done by hand although there are some research initiatives to automate the process [21]. The negative impact of this is the degree of investment required in terms of expert knowledge and maintenance. Rather than aligning features, *the identifier matching policy* involves

Table 1. Types of case base alignment

Alignment	Mapping	Technique
Schema mapping	Feature-to-feature	Manual/semi-automated encoding
Similarity mapping	Case-to-case using a similarity measure	Automated process using a measure of 'aggregate' similarity
Identifier mapping	Case-to-case	Exact matching using a global identifier

matching cases using a global identifier such as an ISBN number. Clearly, there are advantages if cases with heterogeneous representations can be unambiguously identified. The disadvantage, however, is that few domains have global identifiers although this is a key proposal of the Semantic Web project. We identify *similarity based alignment* as occupying a middle ground between the two preceding techniques. With this technique, alignment is based on assessing the similarity between remote cases. In the next subsection, we introduce our similarity based alignment strategy.

3.3 Lexical Indexing

Rather than aligning heterogeneous case representations at a feature by feature level, our solution is to identify similar cases stored in remote case bases and to have the distributed case bases learn how to index these cases using a learned shared lexicon. The process has two stages:

1. **Indexing stage:** An eager learning stage in which external case bases communicate to assess similarity between their cases. During this phase a shared indexing lexicon emerges. We will briefly discuss this in the next subsection but we will leave a detailed explanation until section 4.
2. **Problem-solving stage:** Each case base can quickly retrieve relevant cases by consulting its indexing lexicon and issuing a label identifier.

3.4 Introduction to Case-Based Language Games

Figure 1 provides a simple illustration of a pair of case bases *after* the language games process. The objective of the process is to automatically produce a shared label set, T, which is then used to index similar cases in external case bases. In the diagram, the label l_1 refers to case c_{i1} in case base CB_i and case c_{j9} in case base CB_j. The alignment between cases c_{i1} and c_{j9} occurred during the indexing stage of the language games process. As the figure also illustrates, although the label set that emerges is shared, case bases do not have to compromise their local representation.

The language game itself is a simple process whereby the reference between a case in a local case base and a label is incrementally reinforced through a series of exchanges with other case bases. Let us briefly consider a single language game between two autonomous case bases, CB_i and CB_j. The goal of the game is for peer CB_j to respond correctly to a lexical 'hint' sent by CB_i. The basic methodology involves CB_i, selecting a case, c_i, and then sending the corresponding label l_k to CB_j. CB_j looks up label l_k in its local lexicon and returns a local case c_j to CB_i. CB_i then ranks the cases in its case base in relation to the case c_j. If the most similar case to c_j is the probe case, c_i, the language game is a success and CB_i reinforces the relationship in its lexicon between case c_i and label l_k. The language games methodology is described in detail in section 4.

3.5 The Problem-Solving Stage

In the following example an MCBR strategy allows the user to solve problems by drawing on various information sources. After the eager learning phase, the network of distributed case information can be consulted. Figure 1 illustrates the process. In this scenario, a case base is made up of a set of descriptions of different entertainment itineraries. The solution part of each case description consists of reviews and comments posted by a set of users on the quality of the proposed entertainment package. In our example, each case base contains reviews that are pertinent to a particular interest group. Let us take the scenario where, after querying case base CB_i, the user provides relevance feedback to the case base engine that the solution of the retrieved case c_{i1} was not adequate: in our example, the itinerary is not reviewed in sufficient detail. In response, the engine looks up the case being inspected by the user in its local lexicon. It finds that it corresponds to the lexical label l_1. It then issues a request for solutions for l_1 to the other case bases. Each case base looks up label l_1 in its local lexicon and decodes it to retrieve the local case(s) associated with it. In the example shown in Fig. 1, the solution for case c_{j9} from case base CB_j is returned to the user.

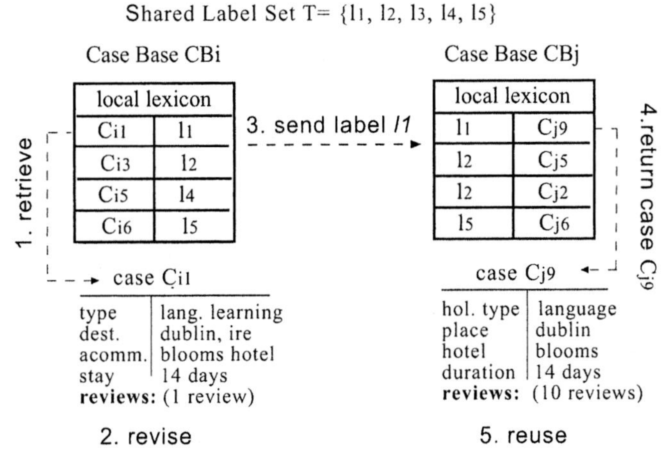

Fig. 1. An example of the distributed indexing produced using the language games model

Thus, the lexical indexing methodology allows the user to *quickly* query external resources when necessary. Furthermore, as similarity computation has been eagerly computed and indexed during the language games stage, the bandwidth and computation overheads involved in sending and decoding a label are very low, entailing fast query time response.

4 Language Games

As we have discussed in the previous section, the goal of the language games model is to enable communication about shared concepts between autonomous peer case bases. In the following we will focus our attention on a specific model of language games known as *naming games* [26]. A naming game is defined by a set of peers $\mathcal{P}$, a set of objects $\mathcal{O}$, and a set of labels $\mathcal{L}$. A peer $p \in \mathcal{P}$ is then defined as a pair $p =< \mathcal{L}_p, \mathcal{O}_p >$.

Each peer $p \in \mathcal{P}$ has its own lexicon drawn from the Cartesian product $\mathcal{L}_p = \mathcal{O}_p \times \mathcal{L}_p \times \mathcal{N} \times \mathcal{N}$, where $\mathcal{O}_p$ are the objects referenced by p (represented as cases), $\mathcal{L}_p$ is the local label set of p, and $\mathcal{N}$ are the natural numbers used to represent the degree of association between $\mathcal{O}_p$ and $\mathcal{L}_p$.

Table 2 illustrates the lexicon of case-base CB_j from Figure 1 *during* the learning phase. In the table, u refers to the number of times the label has been used in different language games by this agent while, a refers to how often it has been successfully used. We can see that the relationship between label l_1 and case c_{j9} has been successfully used 8 times in 10 different language games while the relationship between l_1 and case c_{j6} has been successful only once in 8 games.

Table 2. The lexicon of case base CB_j during the learning phase

$\mathcal{O}_p$	$\mathcal{L}_p$	u	a
cj9	l_1	10	8
cj9	l_2	3	0
cj5	l_3	5	4
cj6	l_1	8	1

The ultimate goal of the game is to bring the local lexica of the peers towards the same association structure. If all the peers converge on the same label to denote the same object the lexica will enable effective communication among peers.

4.1 Let the Games Begin

A naming game involves an iterative process based on pairwise sessions. The basic interaction involves two peers with different roles: a speaker and a listener. We will denote a speaker as p_s and the listener as p_h (The subscript 'h' will always refer to the listener). Figure 2 illustrates the interaction model.

In the beginning, the lexicon of each peer only contains a set of locally defined labels, one for each case in the case base, and the values of u and a are set to zero. The speaker p_s selects an object representation $o_s \in \mathcal{O}_s$ at random and

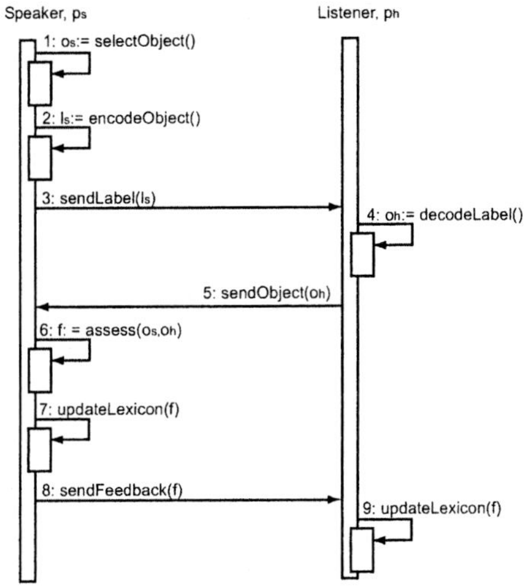

Fig. 2. An illustration of the interaction between the speaker and the listener

encodes it using its local label l_s. The speaker sends the label to the listener. The listener p_h decodes the label by looking it up in its lexicon and, given that this is the first game of the process, finds it is not associated with any object $o_h \in \mathcal{O}_h$. Therefore it creates a new lexicon entry for l_s and associates it with an object representation o_h, selected at random from $\mathcal{O}_h$: $\langle o_h, l_s, 0, 0\rangle \in \mathcal{L}_h$.

The listener sends the object representation to the speaker. The speaker then begins the assessment step. The speaker must verify that the object representation received from the listener refers to o_s, the object selected at the beginning of the communication session. If the object referred to by the listener is the same as that selected by the speaker, the speaker reinforces the relationship between o_s and o_l in its lexicon. It then sends feedback to the listener that the language game was successful. Likewise, the listener reinforces the relationship between l_s and o_h in its lexicon.

4.2 Updating the Lexicon

Based on the assessment phase, the speaker and the listener update their lexica. If the game was successful ($o_s \equiv o_h$) both of them positively reinforce their lexica by updating the corresponding label–object association as follows: $\langle o_s, l_s, u_s + 1, a_s + 1\rangle \in \mathcal{L}_s$ and $\langle o_h, l_s, u_s + 1, a_s + 1\rangle \in \mathcal{L}_h$. If the listener replies with a reference to a different object $o_s \neq o_h$, it means that the communication failed and the peers' lexica are negatively reinforced by only increasing u, the count of the number of times the association was used, while the success count of the association remains the same: $\langle o_s, l_s, u_s+1, a_s\rangle \in \mathcal{L}_s$ and $\langle o_h, l_s, u_s+1, a_s\rangle \in \mathcal{L}_h$.

4.3 Subsequent Games

Encoding. In subsequent games, the speaker p_s again selects an object o_s to encode. The label l_s is chosen according to the associations expressed in the current version of the local lexicon $\mathcal{L}_s$ (local to speaker p_s). The encoding of object o_s is obtained by looking at the most successful label. A label l_j is more successful than a label l_k iff $\langle o_s, l_j, u_j, a_j \rangle \in \mathcal{L}_s$, $\langle o_s, l_k, u_k, a_k \rangle \in \mathcal{L}_s$, $u_j \geq u_k$ and either $a_j/u_j > a_k/u_k$ or $a_j/u_j = a_k/u_k$ and $u_j > u_k$, where u_j represents how many times the label l_j has been used and a_j represents how many times there was an agreement on label l_j with other peers. In case of a tie, a random choice is performed.

Decoding. Likewise, when the listener p_h receives a label l_s from the speaker it looks up the label in its lexicon $\mathcal{L}_h$. It selects the object o_h with the most successful label using the same criteria described for encoding. If the label l_s has zero score association ($a_s = 0$) in the lexicon or is not found at all, the listener creates a new lexicon entry by selecting $o_h \in \mathcal{O}_h$ at random: $\langle o_h, l_s, 0, 0 \rangle \in \mathcal{L}_h$. As before, the entry is initialised with a zero association score. The listener then returns the object o_h to the speaker p_s.

4.4 Assessment

Clearly, the critical point of the game is the assessment step, given that objects can be referenced by heterogeneous representations. In our example, a cultural event is an object that can be referenced by case instances from different schemas. One type of assessment strategy would be to exploit the mapping between the two schemas. An alternative strategy is to assess the equivalence of the object representations by looking directly at the data. In the next section we present how we implement this strategy using similarity assessment.

5 Experimental Evaluation

The current section aims to show how the game model illustrated above can be deployed in a real world scenario. For this purpose we refer to the example scenario we sketched in section 3.5. As before, the user consults a website with a case base back end in order to search for a specific event. An event matching his requirements is retrieved from the local case base. However, the solution part, containing reviews by other users, is not detailed enough. He indicates that the retrieved information is not satisfactory. The second stage involves the case base retrieving alternative reviews from external case bases. However, as Figure 3 demonstrates, the heterogeneity between case base representations poses critical limitations to this approach. Our evaluation will demonstrate how, using the language games approach to produce a distributed index, the user is enabled to quickly retrieve an alternative set of reviews.

Figure 3 illustrates data collected from Harmonise, a European initiative to align data from tourism and destination management companies. To enable interoperability between different representations of the same event, the Harmonise consortium proposes a manual mapping of the RDF schemas to an intermediate schema [8]. In the following we will try to apply the language game approach working at the level of examples rather than schemas.

```
<!--- TIS --->
<event>
  <produniqueid>1</produniqueid>
  <eventplace>Locale Antenna Pressa
    Via Domenico Mascio</eventplace>
  <endingdate_d>21</endingdate_d>
  <endingdate_m>05</endingdate_m>
  <endingdate_y>2004</endingdate_y>
  <startingdate_d>21</startingdate_d>
  <startingdate_m>11</startingdate_m>
  <startingdate_y>2003</startingdate_y>
  <eventtype>1</eventtype>
  <proddescription>
    Orari: dal martedi alla domenica
    ore 9.00-12.00 e ore 16.00-19.00
  </proddescription>
  <prodname>
    La Siri.La fabbrica della ricerca.
    Luigi Casale e l'ammoniaca sintetica
    a Terni - Mostra Storico Documentaria
  </prodname>
</event>
```

```
<!--- WoW --->
<event>
  <title>
    La Siri.La fabbrica della ricerca. Luigi
    Casale e l'ammoniaca sintetica a Terni -
    Mostra Storico Documentaria
  </title>
  <description>
    Orari: dal martedi alla domenica ore
    9.00-12.00 e ore 16.00-19.00
  </description>
  <loc>
    <name>Locale Antenna Pressa Via Domenico
    Mascio</name>
  </loc>
  <date>
    <date.from>20031121</date.from>
    <date.to>20040521</date.to>
  </date>
</event>
```

Fig. 3. Two heterogeneous representations of the same case

For our simulation we will refer to the Harmonise partners as distributed case base providers. Each case base is designed as a collection of cases where the events are represented according to the local RDF schema. For simplicity, we can assume that user annotations, i.e., the solution part of the case, can be homogeneously represented with the RSS format.

The competence of the providers is defined by the events covered by their case bases. Therefore, searching for a given event in remote case bases can be conceived as a task of competence assessment. In the language games model, competence is assessed eagerly by calculating the similarity between two heterogeneous event instances. In this evaluation, we have defined a similarity metric based on the notion of bipartite string matching [12]. First, a linearization preprocessing is performed where the structural information of the schema is dropped and the the event data tokenised. A bipartite graph-matching algorithm is then used, with a distance function, to find the optimal matching of tokens.

We design a language game where players are represented by the case base providers and the events represent the competence that has to be denoted by common labels. Each player is configured with an initial lexicon where the labels are autonomously defined. As the language game is not "linguistic" in terms of natural language, the choice of candidate labels can be arbitrary.

The simulation is arranged as an iteration of pairwise communication sessions. At each iteration, two case base 'players' randomly choose to play. They are randomly assigned the roles of speaker and listener. Therefore, each player meets every other player without any specific bias. The same random strategy is also adopted by the single player in selecting what kind of competence to focus on.

In this evaluation, we extracted 6 different records from the Harmonise dataset, each encoded in 4 different case representations. We then initiated the language games process for a few hundred iterations without any specific stopping criteria.

6 Discussion

The experimental setup described above simulates a scenario with 4 case bases, each having a different representation of the same 6 cases. The evolution of the learning phase of our method is presented in Figure 4 which shows the plot of a sample language game session.

The x axis is used to represent the number of language games between case base pairs. The y axis shows the percentage of lexica convergence: 0% convergence means that there is no label on which all case bases agree; while 100% indicates that all case bases have reached an agreement on how to reference the common cases. At the early stage, as the distributed case bases autonomously define their own lexicon, the probability of choosing the same label to denote the same competence is very low. The steps in the plot represent the increasing agreement in the lexicon: each step means that a competence has been denoted with the same label by all the case bases. After a while, agreement is reached for all competences. When the rate of successful communication reaches 100%, the distributed case bases share a common lexicon.

Three conclusions can be drawn from the evaluation. Firstly, by using the language games approach, it is possible to achieve a convergence on a common lexicon, without the need for ex ante agreement among case bases. Secondly, once the case bases have reached an agreement on a common lexicon, it can be used as an index to encode case base competences. The retrieval of a case from remote case bases can be performed by simply transmitting the corresponding label in the common lexicon. This contrasts with retrieval methods usually employed in distributed case-based systems, where large cases are broadcast to all the remote

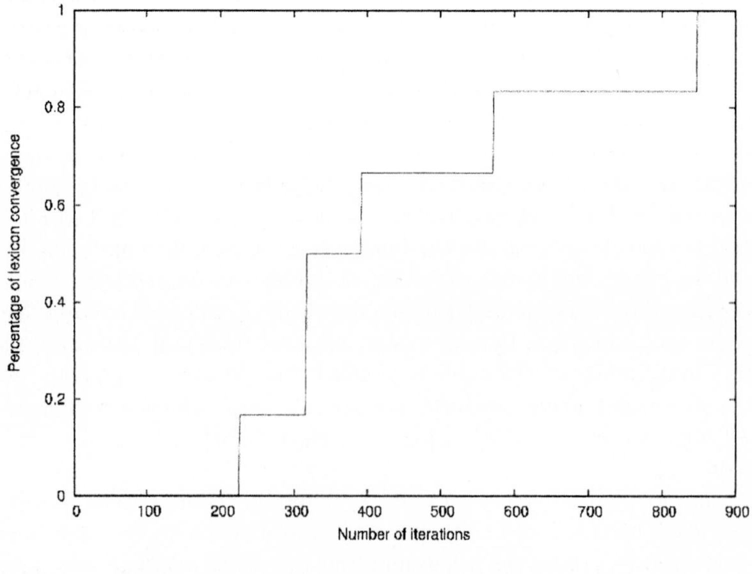

Fig. 4. Formation of an indexing lexicon

case bases and where similarity computations take place on-the-fly, ensuring poor query time response for the user.

A third, more general result is concerned with the design and deployment of distributed case-based reasoning systems. While previous work explores heterogeneity at the level of case-base competence or similarity assessment, we enable heterogeneity during the case authoring stage. We consider this point crucial to the development of an open architecture for distributed case-based reasoning systems that support the deployment of new case bases without constraints on their design.

We recognise that many issues have been neglected in this simulation. First of all, the experimental evaluation involves a small number of case bases and cases. However, we felt that, at this point of the research on distributed case bases, the most critical factor to address was heterogeneity. As such, we decided to demonstrate our approach on a dataset from a real world application rather than on an artificial dataset. We have postponed an analysis of the issues related to scaling for later work. There are other issues related to the deployment of this technique in a real world application. For example, in a real scenario, new case bases can be added to the system at any time. The addition of case bases can affect the process of lexicon agreement and produce a temporary degradation of the communication and problem-solving quality. Furthermore, we still have to develop a fully distributed stopping criteria for the games process. Nevertheless, we believe that our approach based on the language games technique opens a new perspective for research in case-based reasoning.

7 Conclusion

In this paper we analysed the vocabulary problem in MCBR systems. Case-base heterogeneity poses a considerable bar to developing real MCBR systems. For instance, the solution of mapping between containers raises questions about whether there are sufficient benefits in return for the knowledge and maintenance investment required. At the same time, there are clearly situations when knowledge from external sources would improve the solutions provided by a local case-base. We suggest an innovative approach to this problem. Using a technique called *language games*, we eagerly build a distributed lexicon, whereby local cases index the competence of external case-bases. When solutions cannot be found locally the lexicon can be consulted to provide access to similar cases in remote case-bases. We suggest that this work makes three contributions to research in MCBR: firstly, it enables external, heterogeneous sources to be used to solve problems. Secondly, it does so by providing an efficient retrieval method for external cases whereby the query time calculation of similarity on multiple case bases is avoided by broadcasting a single label. Thirdly, it enables autonomous case authoring and maintenance, which is one of the key benefits of the distributed CBR approach.

Acknowledgements

We would like to thank Mirella Dell'Erba and the Harmonise Consortium who kindly provided us with a real world example of a heterogeneous data collection.

This work was partially funded by the DiCA project, thanks to a grant from INRM (Istituto Nazionale Ricerca Montagna) and PAT (Provincia Autonoma di Trento).

References

1. T. Berners-Lee, J. Hendler, and O. Lassila. The Semantic Web. *Scientific American*, 279, May 2001.
2. R. Chau and C.-H. Yeh. A multilingual text mining approach to web cross-lingual text retrieval. *Knowledge Based Systems - Special Issue on Web Intelligence*, 17(5-6):219–227, 2004.
3. L. Coyle, D. Doyle, and P. Cunningham. Representing Similarity for CBR in XML. In P. Funk and P. A. Gonzalez-Calero, editors, *Advances in Case-Based Reasoning, 7th European Conference on Case Based Reasoning (eccbr 2004)*, volume 3155 of *Lecture Notes in Computer Science*, pages 119–127. Springer, 2004.
4. S. Deerwester, S. T. Dumais, G. W. Furnas, T. K. Landauer, and R. Harshman. Indexing by latent semantic analysis. *Journal of the Society for Information Science,*, 41(6):391–407, 1990.
5. A. Doan, P. Domingos, and A. Y. Halevy. Reconciling schemas of disparate data sources: a machine-learning approach. In *SIGMOD '01: Proceedings of the 2001 ACM SIGMOD international conference on Management of data*, pages 509–520. ACM Press, 2001.
6. J. Euzenat. An API for ontology alignment. In *3rd International Semantic Web Conference (ISWC), Lecture notes in computer science 3298*. Springer, 2004.
7. D. Fensel, F. van Harmelen, I. Horrocks, D. L. McGuinness, and P. F. Patel-Schneider. Oil: An ontology infrastructure for the semantic web. *IEEE Intelligent Systems*, 16(2):38–45, 2001.
8. O. Fodor, M. Dell'Erba, F. Ricci, and H. Werthner. Harmonise: a solution for data interoperability. In *Proceedings of the 2nd IFIP Conf.on E-Commerce, E-Business & E-Government*, Lisbon, Portugal, October 2002.
9. G. W. Furnas, T. K. Landauer, L. M. Gomez, and S. T. Dumais. The Vocabulary Problem in Human-System Communication. *Communications of the ACM*, 30(11):964–971, 1987.
10. C. Hayes, P. Cunningham, and D. Michelle. Distributed CBR using XML. In *Workshop: Intelligent Systems and Electronic Commerce, Bremen*, September 1998.
11. J. L. Kolodner. *Case Based Reasoning*. Morgan Kaufmann, San Mateo, 1993.
12. H. Kuhn. The hungarian method for the assignment problem. In *Naval Research Logistic Quarterly*, pages 83–97, 1955.
13. D. B. Leake and R. Sooriamurthi. When Two Case Bases Are Better than One: Exploiting Multiple Case Bases. In *ICCBR '01: Proceedings of the 4th International Conference on Case-Based Reasoning*, pages 321–335. Springer-Verlag, 2001.
14. D. B. Leake and R. Sooriamurthi. Automatically Selecting Strategies for Multi-Case-Base Reasoning. In *ECCBR '02: Proceedings of the 6th European Conference on Advances in Case-Based Reasoning*, pages 204–233. Springer-Verlag, 2002.
15. D. B. Leake and R. Sooriamurthi. Managing Multiple Case Bases: Dimensions and Issues. In *15th FLAIRS conference*, 2002.
16. F. Martin, E. Plaza, and J.-L. Arcos. Knowledge and experience reuse through communications among competent (peer) agents. *International Journal of Software Engineering and Knowledge Engineering*, 9(3):319–341, 1999.

17. L. McGinty and B. Smyth. Collaborative Case-Based Reasoning: Applications in Personalised Route Planning. In *ICCBR '01: Proceedings of the 4th International Conference on Case-Based Reasoning*, pages 362–376. Springer-Verlag, 2001.
18. A. Oram, editor. *Peer-to-Peer, Harnessing the Power of Disruptive Technologies.* O'Reilly & Associates, 2001.
19. M. Prasad, V. R. Lesser, and S. Lander. On retrieval and reasoning in distributed case bases. In *IEEE International Conference on Systems Man and Cybernetics*, October 1995.
20. M. Prasad and E. Plaza. Corporate memories as distributed case libraries. In *Dieng and Vanwelkenhuysen.* 1996.
21. E. Rahm and P. A. Bernstein. A survey of approaches to automatic schema matching. *The VLDB Journal*, 10(4):334–350, 2001.
22. M. Richter. The knowledge contained in similarity measures, 1995.
23. D. J. Schiano, B. A. Nardi, M. Gumbrecht, and L. Swartz. Blogging by the Rest of Us. In *CHI '04: Extended abstracts of the 2004 conference on Human factors and computing systems*, pages 1143–1146. ACM Press, 2004.
24. A. Sengupta, D. C. Wilson, and D. B. Leake. On Constructing the Right Sort of CBR Implementation. In *IJCAI-99 Workshop on Automating the Construction of Case Based Reasoners*, 1999.
25. D. L. R. Sooriamurthi. Case dispatching versus case-base merging: when mcbr matters. *International Journal on Artificial Intelligence Tools: Architectures, Languages and Algorithms (IJAIT)*, 13, No 1:237–254, 2004.
26. L. Steels and A. McIntyre. Spatially Distributed Naming Games. *Advances in Complex Systems*, 1(4):301–323, January 1999.

Evaluation and Monitoring of the Air-Sea Interaction Using a CBR-Agents Approach

Javier Bajo[1] and Juan M. Corchado[2]

[1] Universidad Pontificia de Salamanca, C/ Compañía 5,
37002 Salamanca, Spain
jbajope@upsa.es

[2] Departamento Informática y Automática, Universidad de Salamanca,
Plaza de la Merced s/n, 37008, Salamanca, Spain
corchado@usal.es

Abstract. This paper presents a model constructed for the evaluation of the interaction of the atmosphere and the ocean. The work here presented focuses in the development of an agent based architecture that has been constructed for the evaluation of the interaction, between the atmosphere and the ocean waters, of several parameters. Such evaluation needs to be made continuously in a dynamic environment and therefore requires the use of autonomous models that evolve with the time. The proposed architecture incorporates CBR-agents whose aim is to monitor the evolution of the interaction of parameters and facilitate the creation of an explanation model. The system has been tested and this paper presents the results obtained.

1 Introduction

The agent paradigm is gaining relevance in the development of applications for flexible and dynamic environments, such as the web, personalized user interfaces, oceanography, control systems or robotic environments. Agents are often characterized by their capabilities such as autonomy, reactivity, pro-activeness, social ability, reasoning, learning, and mobility, among others. These capabilities can be modelled in different ways and with different tools [26], one of the possibilities is the use of CBR systems. This paper presents a CBR-agent based architecture that is the core of a distributed system developed for the analysis and evaluation of the interaction between ocean water masses and the atmosphere. The aim of this paper is to present a successful architecture that allows the construction of dynamic systems capable of growing in dimension and of adapting their knowledge to environmental changes. In this work we are mainly interested in the modelling of deliberative agents with CBR systems, as they can be used for implementing adaptive systems. Agents must be able to respond to events, which occur within their environment, take the initiative according to their goals, interact with other agents (even human), and to use past experiences to achieve current goals. Several architectures have been proposed for building deliberative agents, most of them based on the BDI model [21]. In this

H. Muñoz-Avila and F. Ricci (Eds.): ICCBR 2005, LNAI 3620, pp. 50–62, 2005.

model, agents have mental attitudes of Beliefs, Desires and Intentions. In addition, they have the capacity to decide what to do and how to get it according to their attitudes. The beliefs represent its information state, what the agent knows about itself and its environment. The desires are its motivation state, what the agent is trying to achieve. And the intentions represent the agent's deliberative states. Intentions are sequences of actions; they can be identified as plans. These mental attitudes determine the agent's behaviour and are critical in attaining proper performance when the information about the problem is scarce [2, 15].

A BDI architecture has the advantage that it is intuitive and relatively simple to identify the process of decision-making and how to perform it. Furthermore, the notions of belief, desire and intention are easy to understand. On the other hand, its main drawback lies in finding a mechanism that permits its efficient implementation. There are several approaches to formalise and implement BDI agents, among them, dMARS [8], PRS [18], JACK [4], JAM [14], and AgentSpeak(L) [20]. One of the problems for an efficient implementation lies in the use of multi-modal logic for the formalisation and construction of such agents, because they have not been completely axiomatised and they are not computationally efficient. Rao and Georgeff [21] state that the problem lies in the great distance between the powerful logic for BDI systems and practical systems. Another problem is that this type of agent is not able to learn, a necessary requirement for them since they have to be constantly adding, modifying or eliminating beliefs, desires and intentions. It would be convenient to have a reasoning mechanism that would enable the agent to learn and adapt in real time, while the computer program is running, avoiding the need to recompile such an agent whenever the environment changes.

In order to overcome these issues, we propose the use of a case-based reasoning (CBR) system for the development of deliberative agents [5, 8]. The proposed method facilitates the automation of their construction. Implementing agents in the form of CBR systems also facilitates learning and adaptation, and therefore a greater degree of autonomy than with a pure BDI architecture [13]. If the proper correspondence between the three mental attitudes of BDI agents and the information manipulated by a CBR system is established, an agent with beliefs, desires, intentions and a learning capacity will be obtained. Our approach to establish the relationship between agents and CBR systems differs from other proposals [1, 10, 17, 19, 25], as we propose a direct mapping between the agent conceptualisation and its implementation, in the form of a CBR system.

The next section reviews the relationships that can be established between CBR and BDI concepts. Section three describes the environmental problem that motivates most of this research. Section four describes the multiagent based system developed paying special attention to the CBR-BDI agents constructed. Finally the conclusions and the some preliminary results are presented.

2 CBR-BDI Agents

The purpose of case-based reasoning (CBR) is to solve new problems by adapting solutions that have been used to solve similar problems in the past. The deliberative agents, proposed in the framework of this investigation, use this concept to gain in autonomy and improve their problem solving capabilities. Figure 1 shows the activity diagram of a CBR-BDI agent for one of the possible actions, which is composed of a reasoning cycle that consists of four sequential phases: retrieve, reuse, revise and retain.

An additional activity, revision of the expert's knowledge, is required because the memory can change as new cases appear during this process. Each of these activities can be automated, which implies that the whole reasoning process can be automated to a certain extent [6]. According to this, agents implemented using CBR systems could reason autonomously and therefore adapt themselves to environmental changes.

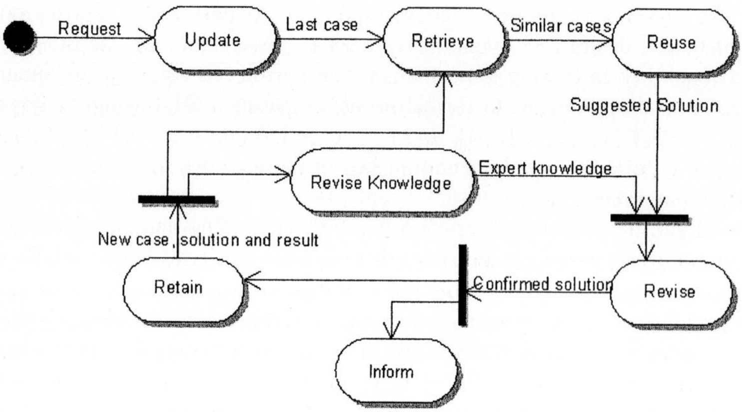

Fig. 1. Activity diagram describing a set of activities, including a CBR-BDI agent reasoning cycle

The CBR system is completely integrated into the agents' architecture. The CBR-BDI agents incorporate a "formalism" which is easy to implement, in which the reasoning process is based on the concept of intention. Intentions can be seen as cases, which have to be retrieved, reused, revised and retained. This makes this model unique in its conception and reasoning capacities. The structure of the CBR system has been designed around the concept of a case. A straight relationship between CBR systems and BDI agents can also be established if the problems are defined in the form of states and actions.

The relationship between CBR systems and BDI agents can be established implementing cases as beliefs, intentions and desires which led to the resolution of the problem. As described in [8], in a CBR-BDI agent, each state is considered as a belief; the objective to be reached may also be a belief. The intentions are plans of actions that the agent has to carry out in order to achieve its objectives [2], so an intention is an ordered set of actions; each change from state to state is made after carrying out an action (the agent remembers the action carried out in the past when it was in a specified state, and the subsequent result). A desire will be any of the final states reached in the past (if the agent has to deal with a situation, which is similar to a past one, it will try to achieve a similar result to the previously obtained result). In [8] can be seen a diagram with a representation of the relationship between BDI agents and CBR systems.

3 Quantification of the Ocean Interaction Budget

An understanding of the natural sources and sinks of atmospheric carbon dioxide is necessary for predicting future atmospheric loading and its consequences for global climate. Present estimates of emissions and uptake do not balance, and although some have attributed the imbalance to a terrestrial sink, the magnitude of the oceanic sink remains undefined [22]. The vast amount of new data on atmospheric CO_2 content and ancillary properties that have become available during the last decade and the development of mathematical models to interpret this data have lead to significant advances in our capacity to deal with such issues. However, a continuing major cause of uncertainty is the role played by photosynthesis in providing a sink for anthropogenic emissions [22]. The solution to these types of problems requires the use of dynamic systems, capable of incorporating new knowledge and facilitating the monitoring and estimation work carried out by oceanographers. The rapid increase in atmospheric CO_2 resulting from atmospheric changes in the carbon cycle has stimulated a great deal of interest.

The need to quantify the carbon dioxide valence and the exchange rate between the oceanic water surface and the atmosphere has motivated us to develop a distributed system that incorporates CBR-BDI agents capable of estimating such values using accumulated knowledge and updated information. The CBR-BDI agents receive data from satellites, oceanographic databases, oceanic and commercial vessels. The information received is composed of satellite images of the ocean surface, wind direction and strength and other parameters such as water temperature, salinity and fluorescence.

The goal of our project is to construct a model that calculates the global budgets of CO_2, a mean CO_2 flux for the whole oceanographic basin. The oceans contain approximately 50 times more CO_2 in dissolved forms than the atmosphere, while the land biosphere including the biota and soil carbon contains about 3 times as much carbon (in CO_2 form) as the atmosphere [24]. The CO_2 concentration in the atmosphere is governed primarily by the exchange of CO_2 with these two dynamic reservoirs. Since the beginning of the industrial era, about 2000 billion tons of carbon have been released into the atmosphere as CO_2 from various industrial sources including fossil fuel combustion and cement production. This amounts to about 35% of the pre-industrial level of approximately 590 billion tons as carbon. At present, atmospheric CO_2 content is increasing at an annual rate of about 3 billion tons which corresponds to one half of the annual emission rate of approximately 6 billion tons from fossil fuel combustion. Whether the missing CO_2 is mainly absorbed by the oceans or by the land and their ecosystems has been debated extensively over the past decade.

It is important, therefore, to fully understand the nature of the physical, chemical and biological processes which govern the oceanic sink/source conditions for atmospheric CO_2 [16, 24]. Satellite-borne instruments provide high-precision, high-resolution data on atmosphere, ocean boundary layer properties and ocean biogeochemical variables, daily, globally, and in the long term (Figure 2). All these new sources of information have changed our approach to oceanography and the data generated needs to be fully exploited. Wind stress, wave breaking and the damping of turbulence and ripples by surface slicks, all affect the air-sea exchange of CO_2. These processes are closely linked to the "roughness" of the sea surface, which can be measured by satellite radars and microwave radiometers. Sea surface roughness consists of a hierarchy of smaller waves upon larger waves (photograph, left, and close-up, below). Different sensors give subtly different measurements of this roughness.

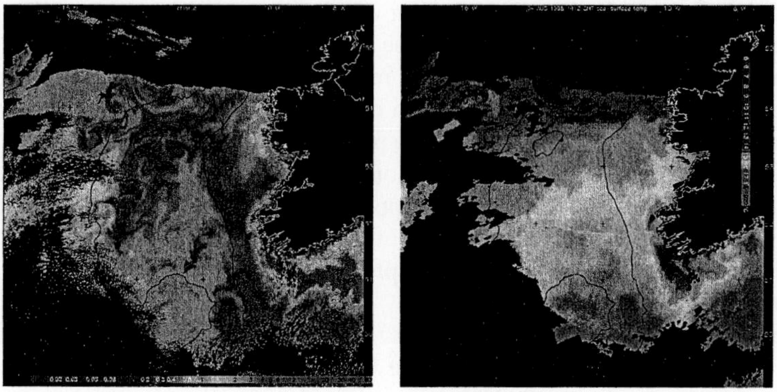

Fig. 2. Satellite colour pictures

Our final aim is to model both the open ocean and shelf seas, and it is believed that by assimilating Earth Observation (EO) data into artificial intelligence models these problems may be solved. EO data (both for assimilation and for validation) are vital for the successful development of reliable models that can describe the complex physical and biogeochemical interactions involved in marine carbon cycling. Satellite information is vital for the construction of oceanographic models, and in this case, to produce estimates of air-sea fluxes of CO_2 with much higher spatial and temporal resolution, using artificial intelligence models than can be achieved realistically by direct in situ sampling of upper ocean CO_2. To handle all the potentially useful data to create daily models in a reasonable time and with a reasonable cost it is necessary the use of automated distributed systems capable of incorporate new knowledge. Our proposal is presented in the following section.

4 Multi Agent System

Our scientific focus is on advancing the science of air-sea interactions and reducing the errors in the prediction of climate change. The primary goal is to quantify accurately the global air-sea fluxes of carbon dioxide. Over the past few years several models have been constructed and experiments carried out. Finally a distributed system has been constructed for solving the previously described problem. Gaia [27] has been initially used for the design of the distributed system, then AUML (Agent-based Unified Modelling Language) has been used for the low level design.

This system incorporates several agents each of them in charge of a different task. Figure 3 presents an extension of the acquaintance model of a Gaia diagram and represents the multiagent architecture, its components and interactions. It incorporates reactive agents, in charge of repetitive tasks, and more complex deliberative CBR-BDI agents in charge of monitoring, modelling and evaluating the interaction between the water surface and the atmosphere.

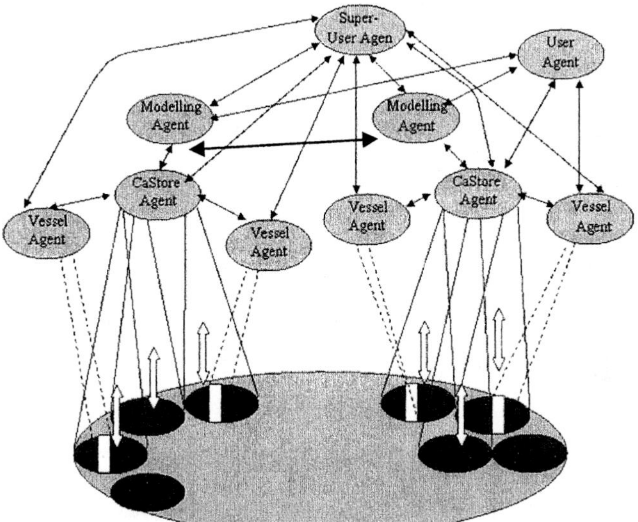

Fig. 3. Multiagente architecture

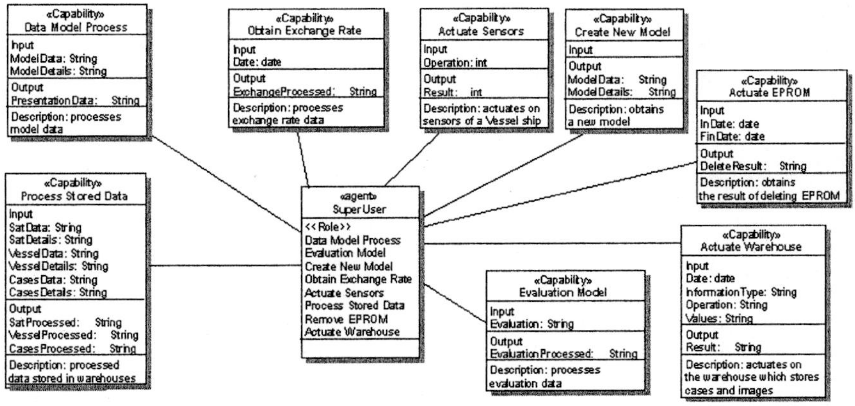

Fig. 4. Super User agent class diagram

The system includes a Super-user agent and several user agents, Modelling agents, CaStore agents and Vessel Agents. The User and Super-user are interface agents that facilitate the access to the system. Figure 4 and 5 show their AUML class diagrams.

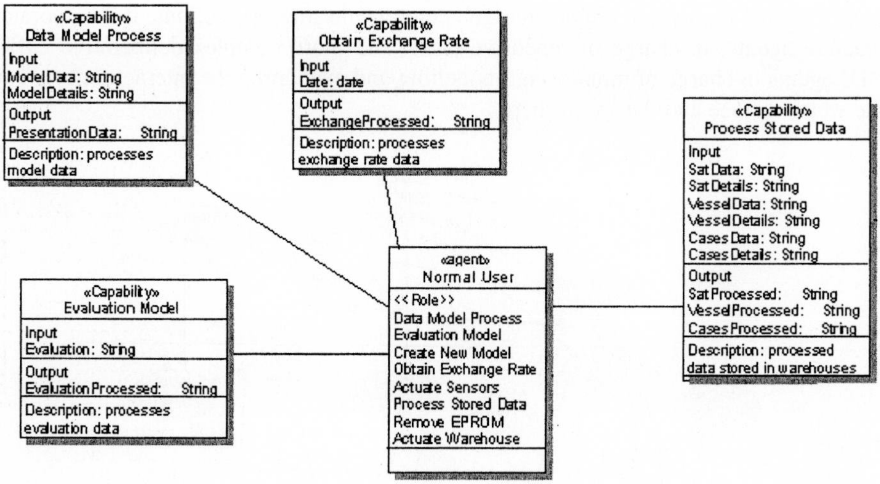

Fig. 5. User agent class diagram

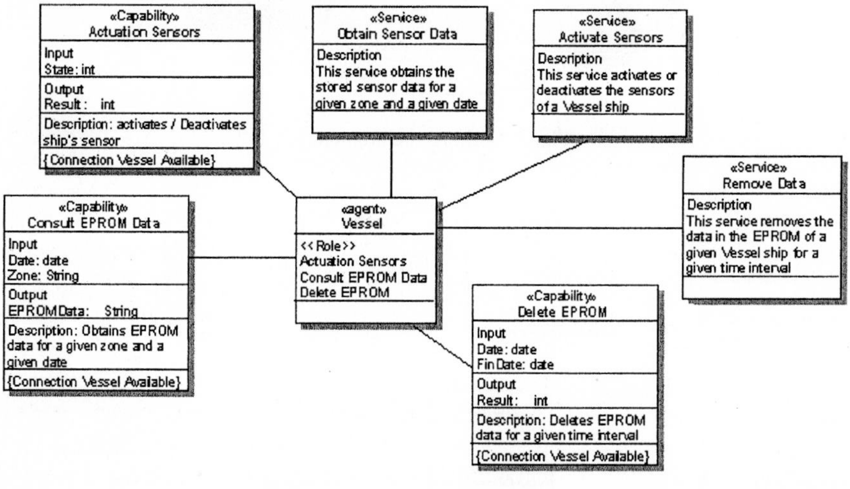

Fig. 6. Vessel agent class diagram

For example the Super-user agent facilitates the interaction between the super user and all the agents of the systems, as shown in Figure 4. These agents also facilitate the access to the data and to the constructed models. They also allow the users to follow and to modify the modelling process.

The vessel agents are installed in the oceanographic and commercial ships that collaborate with the research project. They receive information from different sensors

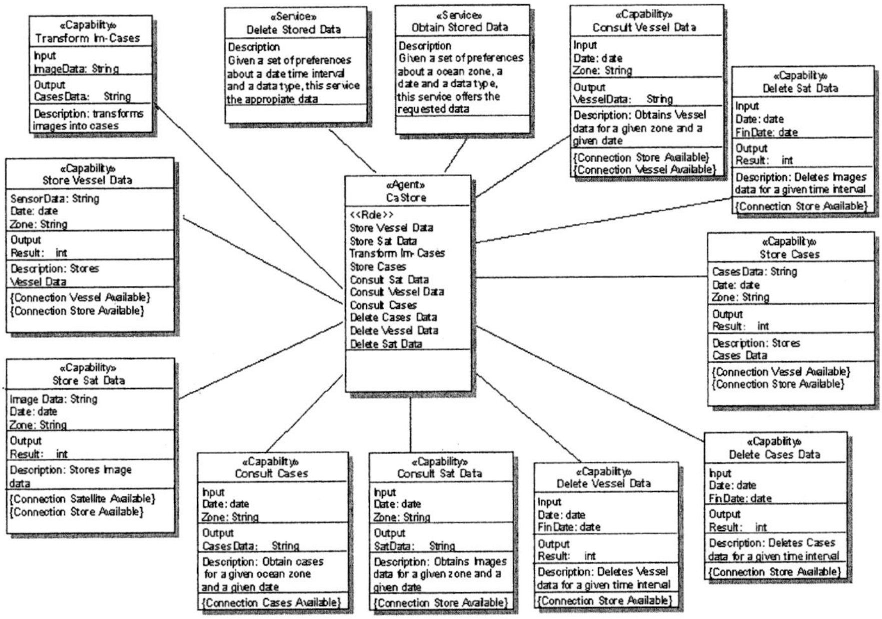

Fig. 7. CaStore agent class diagram

and store it. They can send their stored data to the CaStore agents on demand. The vessel agent may act on the boat sensors and EPRONS. They can also initiate an evaluation process of a given model. Models are always constructed by the Modelling agents. The CaSrore agents transform the satellite images and the data received form the vessel agents in cases. When new cases are constructed the Modelling agents are informed so the model in use may be improved. These agents also facilitate the user the access to the case store. The CaStore agents store historical and updated information incoming form the Vessel agents and from satellites. This data is sent to the Modelling agents, which have the goal of monitoring the ocean evolution and of evaluating the carbon dioxide interaction between the water surface and the atmosphere. The Modelling agents are CBR-BDI agents that use a CBR system to achieve their goals. Figure 8 shows the class diagram of these Modelling agents. The Modelling agents use CoHeL IBR system to achieve their goals [7]. The Cooperative Maximum Likelihood Hebbian Learning (CoHeL) method is a novel approach that features both selection, in which the aim is to visualize and extract information from complex, and highly dynamic data. The model proposed is a mixture of factor analysis and exploratory projection pursuit based on a family of cost functions proposed by Fyfe and Corchado [12] which maximizes the likelihood of identifying a specific distribution in the data while minimizing the effect of outliers. It employs cooperative lateral connections derived from the Rectified Gaussian Distribution [23] in order to enforce a more sparse representation in each weight vector. This method is used for the clustering of instances, and during the retrieval stage of the IBR cycle,

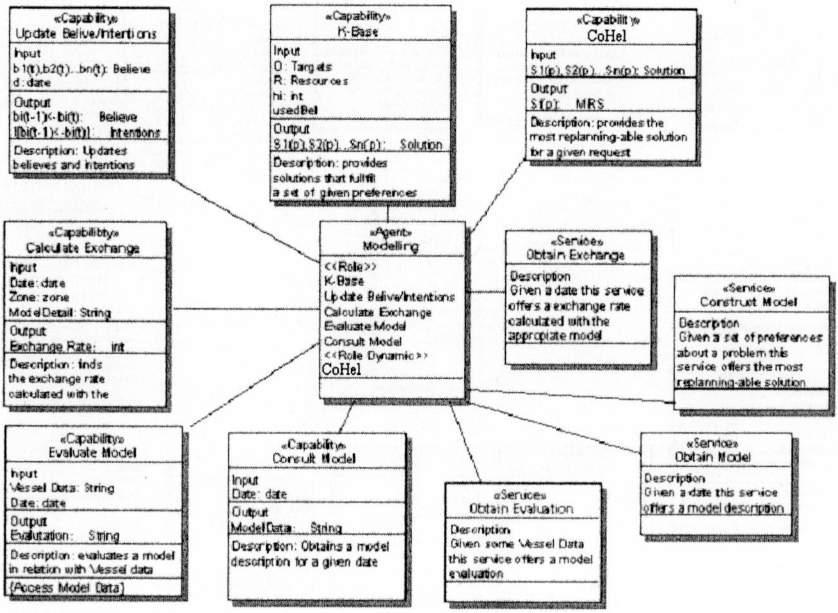

Fig. 8. Modelling agent class diagram

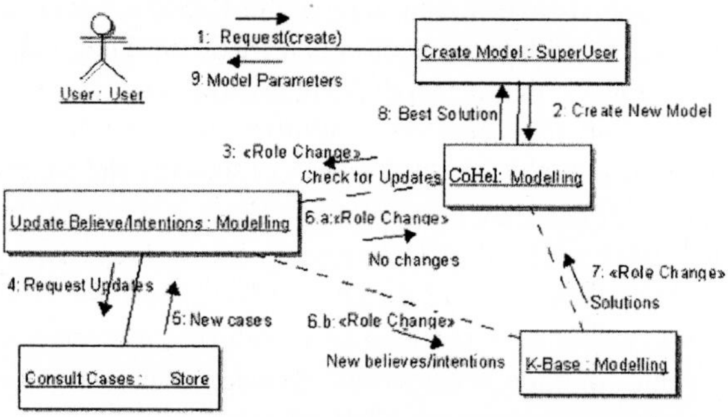

Fig. 9. Modelling agent interaction model, user request

the adaptation step is carried out using a radial basis function network. Finally, the system is updated continuously with data obtained from the CaStore agents. The CoHeL IBR system is described in [7].

Figure 9 shows one of the possible collaboration diagrams of the interaction model between the Modelling agent and the user of the system. This sequence of actions facilitates the construction of a model of the ocean surface – atmosphere interaction of a particular area of the ocean. Each Modelling agent is in charge of a particular

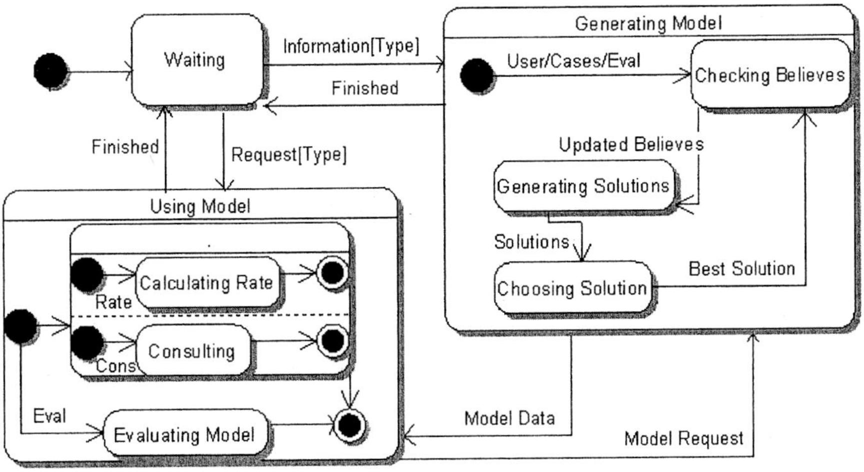

Fig. 10. State diagram for the Modelling agent

oceanic area, for example the North Atlantic Ocean. The relationship between CoHel IBR systems and the BDI agent in which it is embedded can be established implementing instances such as beliefs, intentions and desires which lead to the esolution of the problem. When the Modelling agent starts to solve a new problem, with the intention of achieving a goal (identifying the carbon dioxide rate), it begins a new IBR reasoning cycle, which will help to obtain the solution. The retrieval, reuse and revision stages of the IBR system facilitate the construction of the agent plan. The agent's knowledge-base is the instance-base of the IBR system that stores the instances of past beliefs, desires and intentions. The agents work in dynamic environments and their knowledge-base has to be adapted and updated continuously by the retention stage of the IBR system. Figure 10 presents the state diagram for the Modelling agent. It shows how the agent is continually working and using the IBR life cycle for reasoning and achieving its goals. Figure 2 shows the activity diagram describing a CBR-BDI agent reasoning cycle, which can be applied to this agent too.

5 System Evaluation and Conclusions

The previously described system was tested in the North Atlantic Ocean during 2004. During this period of time the multiagent system has been tuned and updated and the first autonomous prototype started to work in may 2004. Although the system is not fully operational and the aim of the project is to construct a research prototype and not a commercial tool, the initial results have been very successful from the technical and scientific point of view. The construction of the distributed system has been relatively easy using previously developed CBR-BDI libraries [5, 6, 7, 8]. From the software engineering point of view AUML and Gaia [27] provide an adequate framework for the analysis and design of distributed agent based systems. The formalism defined in [13] facilitates the straight mapping between the agent definition and the CBR construction. The user can interact with the Modelling agent (via his/her user agent) following the interaction model described in Figure 10 and obtain information about the carbon dioxide exchange rate of a given area.

Table 1. Instance values

Instance Field	Measurement
DATE	Fecha
LAT	Latitude
LONG	Longitude
SST	Temperature
S	Salinity
WS	Wind strength
WD	Wind direction
Fluo_calibrated	fluorescence calibrated with chlorophyll
SW pCO2	surface partial pressure of CO2

The Modelling Agents have their own interface and can also be accessed via the User or Super user agents. These agents handle beliefs, desires and intention from a conceptual point of view and cases from an implementation point of view. A case is composed of the attributes described in Table 1. Cases can be viewed, modified and deleted manually or automatically by the agent (during its revision stage). The agent plants (intentions) can be generated using different strategies since the agent integrates different algorithms.

Table 2. Million of Tones of C02 exchanged in the North Atlantic

	October 04	November 04	December 04
Multiagent System	-18	19	**31**
Casix manual models	**-20**	**25**	**40**

The interaction between the system developers and oceanographers with the multiagent system has been continuous during the construction and pruning period, from December 2003 to September 2004. The system has been tested during the last three months of 2004 and the results have been very accurate. Table 2 presents the results obtained with the Multiagent systems and with mathematical Models [16] used be oceanographers to identify the amount of CO2 exchanged. The numerical values represent the million of Tonnes of carbon dioxide that have been absorbed (negative values) or generated (positive value) by the ocean during each of the three months.

The values proposed by the CBR-BDI agent are relatively similar to the ones obtained by the standard technique. In this case the case/instance base has been constructed with over 100,000 instances, and includes data since 2002. The multiagent system has automatically incorporated over 20,000 instances during these three months and eliminated 13% of the initial ones. While the CBR-BDI Modelling Agent generates results on a daily basis without any human intervention, the Casix manual modelling techniques require the work of one researcher processing data during al least four working days. Although the proposed system requires further improvements and more work the initial results are very promising. The CoHel IBR systems embedded within the Modelling agent has provided relatively accurate results in the North Atlantic Waters as well as in the Pacific Ocean [7]. The generated framework facilitates the incorporation of new agents using different modelling techniques and learning strategies so further experiment will allow to compare these initial results with the ones obtained by other techniques.

References

1. Bergmann, R. and W. Wilke (1996). On the role of abstraction in case-based reasoning. Lecture Notes in Artificial Intelligence, 1186, pp. 28-43. Springer Verlag.
2. Bratman M.E., Israel D., and Pollack M.E. (1988). Plans and resource-bounded practical reasoning. Computational Intelligence, 4. pages 349-355.
3. Bratman, M.E. (1987). Intentions, Plans and Practical Reason. Harvard University Press, Cambridge, M.A.
4. Busetta, P., Ronnquist, R., Hodgson, A., Lucas A. (1999). JACK Intelligent Agents Components for Intelligent Agents in Java. Technical report, Agent Oriented Software Pty. Ltd, Melbourne, Australia, 1998.
5. Corchado J. M. and Laza R. (2003). Constructing Deliberative Agents with Case-based Reasoning Technology, International Journal of Intelligent Systems. Vol 18, No. 12, December. pp.: 1227-1241
6. Corchado J. M. and Lees B. (2001). A Hybrid Case-based Model for Forecasting. Applied Artificial Intelligence. Vol 15, no. 2, pp.105-127.
7. Corchado J. M., Aiken J., Corchado E. Lefevre N. and Smyth T. (2004) Quantifying the Ocean's CO2 Budget with a CoHeL-IBR System. 7th European Conference on Case-based Reasoning, Lecture Notes in Computer Science, Lecture Notes in Artificial Intelligence 3155, Springer Verlag. pp. 533-546.
8. Corchado J. M., Pavón J., Corchado E. and Castillo L. F. (2005) Development of CBR-BDI Agents: A Tourist Guide Application. 7th European Conference on Case-based Reasoning 2004. Lecture Notes in Artificial Intelligence 3155, Springer Verlag. pp. 547-559.
9. D'Iverno, M., Kinny, D., Luck, M., and Wooldridge, M. (1997). A Formal Specification of dMARS. In: Intelligent Agents IV, Agent Theories, Architectures, and Languages, 4th International Workshop, ATAL '97, Providence, Rhode Island, USA, July 24-26, 1997, Proceedings. Lecture Notes in Computer Science 1365, Springer Verlag, pp. 155-176.
10. Feret M. P. and Glasgow J. I. (1994). Explanation-Aided Diagnosis for Complex Devices, Proceedings of the 12th National Conference an Artificial Intelligence, (AAAI-94), Seattle, USA, August 94.
11. Freedman J. and Tukey J. (1974) A Projection Pursuit Algorithm for Exploratory Data Analysis. IEEE Transaction on Computers, (23): 881-890, 1974.
12. Fyfe C. and Corchado E. S. (2002) Maximum Likelihood Hebbian Rules. European Symposium on Artificial Neural Networks. 2002.
13. Glez-Bedia M., Corchado J. M., Corchado E. S. and Fyfe C. (2002) Analytical Model for Constructing Deliberative Agents, Engineering Intelligent Systems, Vol 3: pp. 173-185.
14. Huber, M. (1999). A BDI-Theoretic Mobile Agent Architecture. AGENTS '99. Proceedings of the Third Annual Conference on Autonomous Agents, May 1-5, 1999, Seattle, WA, USA. ACM, pp. 236-243.

15. Kinny, D. and Georgeff, M. (1991). Commitment and effectiveness of situated agents. In: Proceedings of the Twelfth International Joint Conference on Artificial Intelligence (IJCAI'91), Sydney, Australia, pp. 82-88.
16. Lefevre N., Aiken J., Rutllant J., Daneri G., Lavender S. and Smyth T. (2002) Observations of pCO2 in the coastal upwelling off Chile: Sapatial and temporal extrapolation using satellite data. Journal of Geophysical research. Vol. 107, no. 0
17. Martín F. J., Plaza E., Arcos J.L. (1999). Knowledge and experience reuse through communications among competent (peer) agents. International Journal of Software Engineering and Knowledge Engineering, Vol. 9, No. 3, 319-341.
18. Myers, K. (1996). A Procedural Knowledge Approach to Task-Level Control. Proceedings of the Third International Conference on Artificial Intelligence Planning Systems,, pp. 158-165.
19. Olivia C., Chang C. F., Enguix C.F. and Ghose A.K. (1999). Case-Based BDI Agents: An Effective Approach for Intelligent Search on the World Wide Web, AAAI Spring Symposium on Intelligent Agents, 22-24 March 1999, Stanford University, USA.
20. Rao, A. S. (1996). AgentSpeak(L): BDI Agents speak out in a logical computable language. Agents Breaking Away, 7th European Workshop on Modelling Autonomous Agents in a Multi-Agent World, Eindhoven, The Netherlands, January 22-25, 1996, Proceedings. Lecture Notes in Computer Science 1038, Springer Verlag, pp. 42-55.
21. Rao, A. S. and Georgeff, M. P. (1995). BDI Agents: From Theory to Practice. First International Conference on Multi-Agent Systems (ICMAS-95). San Franciso, USA.
22. Sarmiento J. L. and Dender M. (1994) Carbon biogeochemistry and climate change. Photosynthesis Research, Vol. 39, 209-234.
23. Seung H.S., Socci N.D. and Lee D. (1998) The Rectified Gaussian Distribution, Advances in Neural Information Processing Systems, 10.
24. Takahashi T., Olafsson J., Goddard J. G., Chipman D. W. and Sutherland S. C. (1993) Seasonal Variation of CO2 and nutrients in the High-latitude surface oceans: a comparative study. Global biochemical Cycles. Vol. 7, no. 4. pp 843-878.
25. Wendler J. and Lenz M. (1998). CBR for Dynamic Situation Assessment in an Agent-Oriented Setting. Proc. AAAI-98 Workshop on CBR Integrations. Madison (USA) 1998.
26. Wooldridge, M. and Jennings, N. R. (1995) Agent Theories, Architectures, and Languages: a Survey. In: Wooldridge and Jennings, editors, Intelligent Agents, Springer-Verlag, pp. 1-22.
27. Wooldridge, M. and Jennings, N. R. and Kinny, D. (2000) The Gaia Methodology for Agent-Oriented Analysis and Design. Journal of Autonomous Agents and Multi-Agent Systems, 3 (3). pp. 285-312.

A Comparative Analysis of Query Similarity Metrics for Community-Based Web Search

Evelyn Balfe and Barry Smyth

Smart Media Institute, Department of Computer Science,
University College Dublin, Belfield, Dublin 4, Ireland
{Evelyn.Balfe, Barry.Smyth}@ucd.ie*

Abstract. Collaborative Web search is a community-based approach to adaptive Web search that is fundamentally case-based: the results of similar past search sessions are reused in response to new target queries. Previously, we have demonstrated that this approach to Web search can offer communities of like-minded searchers significant benefits when it comes to result relevance. In this paper we examine the fundamental issue of query similarity that drives the selection and reuse of previous search sessions. In the past we have proposed the use of a relatively simple form of query similarity, based on the overlap of query-terms. In this paper we examine and compare a collection of 10 alternative metrics that use different types of knowledge (query-terms vs. result-lists vs. selection behaviour) as the basis for similarity assessment.

1 Introduction

None of the major Web search engines really consider context, at least in any meaningful way, when responding to typical user queries, even though many searches can be usefully informed by different search contexts. For example, searches that originate from a search box on a motoring Web site are likely to relate to motoring topics and searchers with queries like *beatle* will probably be looking to select results that are car-related. Similarly, searches that originate from the employees of a software company, for queries like *tomcat*, will probably relate to application servers instead of wild cats. There are two important points to make here. First, Web queries are often very vague or ambiguous. Second, many queries originate from ad-hoc communities of like-minded searchers (eg. the visitors to a motoring Web site or the employees of a software company).

When we examined the behaviour of searchers, especially those that relate to community-based search scenarios, we found a high degree of repetition in the types of queries submitted and a high degree of regularity in the types of pages that are selected for these queries [1]. This repetition and regularity motivates our case-based approach to Web search, which works to re-order the search results of a base-level search engine according to the preferences of the

* The support of the Informatics Research Initiative of Enterprise Ireland is gratefully acknowledged.

H. Muñoz-Avila and F. Ricci (Eds.): ICCBR 2005, LNAI 3620, pp. 63–77, 2005.

community. To do this we record the community's search histories as a case-base of search cases and when faced with a new target query we retrieve a set of these cases that have similar queries and then reuse their selected results to adapt the results returned from the base-level search engine.

Previously we have presented a range of evaluation results to show that this so-called *collaborative search* technique can deliver significant benefits to users [1,2]. In the past we have adopted a straightforward *term-based* model of query similarity, one that measures the relative overlap between the terms of two queries. In this paper, after reviewing the collaborative Web search approach, we describe and evaluate 10 new similarity metrics that use a range of different sources of knowledge to inform the similarity judgement. In addition to new term-based metrics, we also propose a family of *result-based* metrics (which estimate the similarity between two queries by examining the result-lists returned by the base-level search engine) and a family of *selection-based* metrics (which compare the selection behaviours of users for the two queries).

2 A Review of Collaborative Web Search

Figure 1 outlines the basic I-SPY architecture which implements collaborative Web search. I-SPY is a meta-search engine, drawing on the results produced by a set of underlying search engines; I-SPY can be found online at *'http://ispy.ucd.ie'*. When I-SPY receives a new query, q_T, from some user, it submits this query to each of its underlying search engines $(S_1, ..., S_n)$ and combines the result-lists that are returned $(R_1, ..., R_n)$. To do this I-SPY must adapt both the new query, to match the format of each underlying search engine, and also the result-lists that are returned to produce a modified result-list R_m.

I-SPY's key innovation stems from its ability to personalize search results by re-ranking results based on the selection history of previous searchers, effectively transforming the meta-search result-list R_m in to a modified result-list, R_T. Further detail is available in [1].

2.1 Profiling Search Histories

The *hit-matrix*, H, maintains a record of the results selected in past search sessions. Each time a searcher selects page (p_j) for some target query (q_T) the value of H_{Tj} is incremented. Thus, H_{Tj} is the number of times that p_j has been selected as a result for query q_T. The row of H that corresponds to q_T provides a complete account of the relative number of all previous page selections for this query, where each page selection is represented by a unique column in H. In essence the hit-matrix is a case-base and each row is a search case that contains, as its specification part, a query, and, as its solution part, a record of the number of selections for different pages in response to this community.

2.2 Reusing Similar Queries

When a searcher submits a new target query (q_T) we use I-SPY to locate all search cases (rows of the hit-matrix) whose queries (q_c) are similar to the target

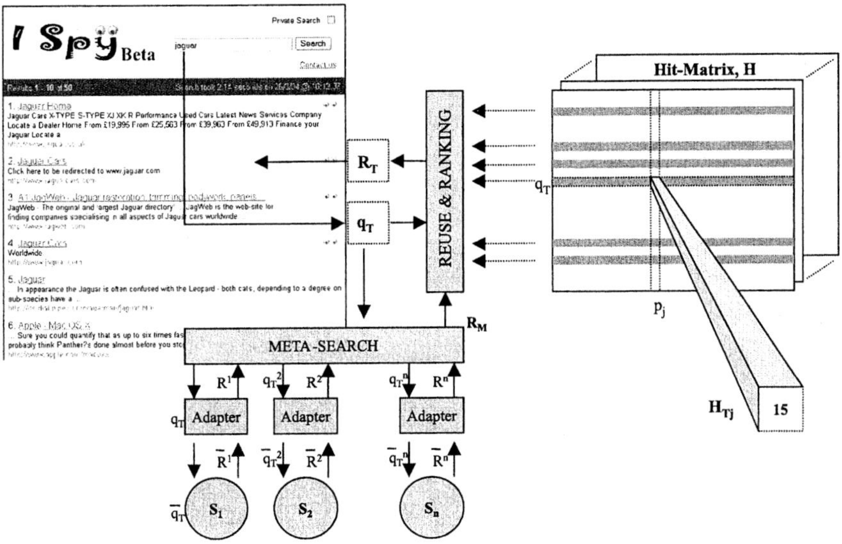

Fig. 1. The I-SPY system architecture

query. To do this we compute the overlap between the terms in q_T and the terms in each candidate query q_c, as shown in Equation 1. I-SPY then selects all search cases, whose queries exceed a given similarity threshold, to produce its list of related search cases. If no similar queries exist or if the hit-matrix is empty then I-SPY performs at least as well as the underlying search engines.

$$Sim(q_T, q_c) = TermOverlap(q_T, q_c) = \frac{|q_T \cap q_c|}{|q_T \cup q_c|} \tag{1}$$

2.3 Result Relevancy

Next we must calculate the relevance scores for the result pages from the retrieved search cases. The relevance of a result-page, p_j, to some query, q_T, can be estimated directly from the hit-matrix entries for q_T. Equation 2 calculates relevance as the number of page selections that have occurred for p_j in response to query q_T (that is, H_{Tj}) as a proportion of the total number of page selections that have occurred for all pages selected in response to q_T (that is, $\sum_{\forall j} H_{Tj}$). For example, a relevance of 0.25 for p_j and q_T, means that 25% of the page selections from result-lists for q_T have been for this page, p_j.

$$Relevance(p_j, q_T) = \frac{H_{Tj}}{\sum_{\forall j} H_{Tj}} \tag{2}$$

Of course if multiple similar search cases (and their queries) are selected for a target query, then there are potentially multiple search histories to inform the relevance of a given page. For example, the page *www.sun.com* may have a high relevance value (let's say, 0.8) for a past query 'java language' but it may have a lower relevance for another past query 'java' (let's say 0.33). It is then a matter of combining these individual relevance values to produce a single relevance score for this page relative to the target query, say 'java inventor'.

We propose a normalised weighted relevance metric that combines the relevance scores for individual page-query combinations. This is achieved using the weighted-sum of the individual relevance scores, such that each score is weighted by the similarity of its corresponding query to the target query. Thus, in our example above, the relevance of the page *www.sun.com* to 'java inventor' is 0.516: the sum of 0.264 (that is, 0.8 page relevance to query 'java language', multiplied by the 0.33 query similarity between this query and the target, 'java inventor') and 0.165 (0.33*0.5 for the past query, 'java'), divided by 0.83, the sum of the query similarities. Equation 3 provides the details of this weighted relevance metric with respect to a page, p_j, a target query, q_T, and a set of queries $q_1, ..., q_n$ from the retrieved search cases. $Exists(p_j, q_i)$ is simply a flag that is set to 1 when p_j is one of the result pages selected for query, q_i.

$$WRel(p_j, q_T, q_1, ..., q_n) = \frac{\sum_{i=1...n} Relevance(p_j, q_i) \bullet Sim(q_T, q_i))}{\sum_{i=1...n} Exists(p_j, q_i) \bullet Sim(q_T, q_i)} \tag{3}$$

The notion of relevance is driven by user's previous page selections and so is dependent on the reliability of the users selection behaviour. However, [3] shows that I-SPY's collaborative search method is robust to high levels of selection noise.

2.4 Communities and Collaboration

The above approach is likely to work as long as the query-space is limited to a relatively narrow and uniform context. One of the fundamental ideas in I-SPY, and the reason for the term 'collaborative search', is that a given hit-matrix should be populated with queries and selections from a community of users operating within a specific domain of interest. As such, I-SPY facilitates the creation of multiple hit-matrices. This affords different communities of users access to a search service that is adapted for their query-space and its preferred pages. For example, a motoring Web site might configure a hit-matrix for its users. I-SPY facilitates this through a simple form-based Web interface and, in doing so, provides the motoring Web site with access to a search interface that is associated with this new hit-matrix. As the community uses its search service, their queries and page selections will populate the associated hit-matrix and I-SPY's ranking metric will help to disambiguate vague queries by promoting previously preferred pages.

A large Web portal might create a range of different hit-matrices, and place corresponding search boxes in different parts of the portal (e.g. News, Sports, Business sections) on the grounds that searchers are more likely to submit queries that are related to the content that is found within this portal section. Alternatively, more formal communities of searchers can be formed by setting up private I-SPY groups that are only made accessible to individuals by invitation.

3 Query Similarity Metrics

Our interest in this paper lies in the role of query similarity. Not only is query similarity pivotal when it comes to the selection of similar search cases, it is also intimately involved in the weighting of relevant results from these cases. So far we have assumed a straightforward model of query similarity, namely the term-overlap metric as shown in Equation 1. Detailed experiments using this metric have been described in [2].

The apparent simplicity of the term-overlap metric begs the question as to whether more sophisticated metrics might deliver further improvements. And so in this paper we compare term-overlap to a number of alternative metrics that fall into three basic categories. First, *term-based* techniques estimate query similarity by examining the differences between the terms used in two queries; obviously the standard overlap metric is one example of this type. A less direct way to compare two queries is to examine the pages that are returned by the base-level search engine in response to them. Thus our second category of metric looks for similarities between the result-lists of the base-level search engine that are returned for the two queries. Finally, our third category of metric measures query similarity by comparing queries in terms of the behaviour of the searchers that have used them; specifically, we compare the result pages that were selected in previous search sessions for the queries.

3.1 Term-Based Approaches

The standard term-overlap metric is certainly an obvious and computationally simple way to measure the similarity between two queries but it appears to have some shortcomings. For example, it views individual terms as atomic units and as such cannot cope with minor term variations such as plurals; for example, "Inventor of internet" is deemed to be only 33% similar to "Inventors internet". And while this problem can be relieved by stemming query terms it is symptomatic of a deeper underlying problem.

Edit-Distance. To address these problems we propose the use of the *Levenshtein Distance* (LD) metric; also known as *edit-distance* (see [4]). The LD of two strings is the minimum number of edit operations needed to transform one string into the other where an operation is either an element insertion, deletion or substitution of a character in the string. For example, the LD between "Inventor of internet" and "Inventors internet" is 3. We propose the use of a normalised version of LD to compare two query strings, as shown in Equation 4, which measures the similarity between a target query, q_T, and a related query, q_i, relative to a set of queries, $q_1, ..., q_n$.

$$EditDistance(q_T, q_i) = \frac{1 - LD(q_T, q_i)}{maxLD(q_T, (q_1, ..., q_n))} \tag{4}$$

In fact we consider two variations of edit-distance similarity. The first calculates the edit-distance similarity between the target query and all other search cases whose corresponding queries, $q_1, ..., q_n$, share at lease one term with the target query , we label this EditDist. In our ModifiedEditDist metric we extend the range of $q_1, ..., q_n$ to refer to the set of all search case queries regardless of whether they meet this minimal term-overlap constraint; that is every query in the hit-matrix, H. This modified metric is likely to be inefficient as it will retrieve many unrelated queries. However it is included for completeness.

Combining Overlap & Edit-Distance. Of course it is possible to combine the similarities produced by the overlap and edit-distance similarity metrics. We propose to combine them using the harmonic mean so as to give preference to those queries that enjoy high overlap values and high edit-distance similarity values – see Equation 5 – whilst penalising those queries that present with contrasting overlap and edit-distance scores.

$$HarmonicMean(q_T, q_i) = \frac{Overlap(q_T, q_i) \bullet EditDistance(q_T, q_i)}{(Overlap(q_T, q_i) + EditDistance(q_T, q_i)/2} \tag{5}$$

3.2 Result-Based Approaches

Sometimes queries are related even though they have no terms in common. For example, *jaguar* and *OS X* both refer to the Macintosh operating system, and we might expect searchers using these queries to be looking for similar types of results. By comparing the result-lists returned by the base-level meta-search engine in response to these queries, we can detect the fact that these queries are similar even though their terms do not suggest it. Of course for efficiency reasons this approach would require the caching of past search results, but assuming that this is feasible then we can propose the following result-based similarity metrics.

Result Overlap. Equation 6 is the simplest option. It calculates the percentage overlap between the result URLs (we look at the top 20 results) from the result-list for the target query ($ResultSet(q_T)$) and the result-list for a candidate query, ($ResultSet(q_i)$), in much the same way that term overlap is calculated.

$$ResultOverlap(q_T, q_i) = \frac{|ResultSet(q_T) \cap ResultSet(q_i)|}{|ResultSet(q_T) \cup resultSet(q_i)|} \tag{6}$$

Result Position Correlation. Of course two result-lists might contain lots of the same results but they may order these shared results differently, indicating potentially important differences between their queries. The *ResultOverlap* metric is blind to this but Equation 7 is not. It calculates similarity based on the Pearson's correlation coefficient between the positions of the shared results from each query's result-list; $\{r_1, ..., r_n\} = ResultSet(q_T) \cap ResultSet(q_i)$ and $Pos_{i,k}$ is the position of the kth shared result for query q_i.

$$ResultPosCorrel(q_T, q_i) = Correl(\{Pos_{T,1}, ..., Pos_{T,n}\}, \{Pos_{i,1}, ..., Pos_{i,n}\}) \quad (7)$$

Result Position Differences. An alternative way to consider the positions of results in the result-list is to calculate the positional difference between corresponding shared results in the result-lists for q_T and q_i. Equation 8 shows how this can be converted into a normalised similarity metric; note that n is the number of shared results and m is the union of the two result-lists.

$$ResultPosDiff(q_T, q_i) = 1 - \frac{\sum_{\forall k=1...n} |Pos_{T,1} - Pos_{i,1}|}{n \bullet m} \quad (8)$$

3.3 Selection-Based Approaches

Our final family of metrics takes advantage of the selection data that I-SPY collects. These selection-based techniques attempt to evaluate query similarity by looking for similarities in the selection patterns of searchers. For instance, we might consider two queries to be similar if users tend to select the same results from their respective result-lists.

Selection Overlap. Once again we start with a straightforward overlap metric. The similarity of two queries is estimated by the percentage overlap between the sets of pages that have been selected for these queries during past search sessions. We call this the *SelectionOverlap* metric and it is presented as Equation 9 between a target query, q_T, and a related query, q_i, from some similar search case. Note that, $SelectionSet(q)$ refers to the set of pages that have been previously selected for query q; that is the set of pages that have hit values in the hit-matrix for q.

$$SelectionOverlap(q_T, q_i) = \frac{|SelectionSet(q_T) \cap SelectionSet(q_i)|}{|SelectionSet(q_T) \cup SelectionSet(q_i)|} \quad (9)$$

Selection Hits Correlation. As with our previous overlap metrics, this new one has its obvious shortcomings. In particular, it gives no credit to the relative number of times that individual result pages have been selected for two queries. Hence, we propose an alternative metric that uses the correlation between the number of times that overlapping pages have been selected for two queries as a measure of query similarity. We call this the *Selection Correlation* metric as shown in Equation 10. In this formula *Correl* refers to the standard Pearson's correlation formula, the set $p_1, ..., p_n$ refers to the set of result pages that have been selected for both q_T and q_i and $H_{i,k}$ refers to the number of hits that p_k has received for q_i.

$$SelectionHitsCorrelation(q_T, q_i) = Correl(\{H_{T,1}, ..., H_{T,n}\}, \{H_{i,1}, ..., H_{i,n}\}) \quad (10)$$

Selection Position Correlation. As with the result-based metrics, we also consider the positions of selected results from a result list. Equation 11 calculates the similarity from Pearson's correlation coefficient between the positions of the shared selections from $p_1, ..., p_n$, the set of selected results from each query; where $Pos_{i,k}$ is the position of the kth shared selection for query q_i.

$$SelectionPosCorrel(q_T, q_i) = Correl(\{Pos_{T,1}, ..., Pos_{T,n}\}, \{Pos_{i,1}, ..., Pos_{i,n}\}) \tag{11}$$

Selection Position Differences. Once again we calculate the positional difference between corresponding shared selections in the result-lists for q_T and q_i. Equation 12 shows how this can be converted into a normalised similarity metric; note that n is the number of shared selections and m is the union of the two result lists.

$$SelectionPosDiff(q_T, q_i) = 1 - \frac{\sum_{\forall k=1...n} |Pos_{T,1} - Pos_{i,1}|}{n \bullet m} \tag{12}$$

4 Evaluation

At this point we have 10 new similarity metrics, 3 that are term-based, 3 that are result-based and 4 that are selection-based. Many of these are designed to improve upon the standard term-based overlap benchmark and in this section we will evaluate each of these metrics using live-user data.

4.1 Live-User Data

The data used in this evaluation was collected during a live-user experiment that involved 92 computer science students from the Department of Computer Science at University College Dublin and took place in October 2003. The original experiment was designed to evaluate the benefits of the standard I-SPY system, relative to a standard meta-search engine, in the context of a fact-finding or question-answering exercise. In this implementation our underlying search engines for our meta-search were Google, HotBot, WiseNut and AllTheWeb. To frame the search task, we developed a set of 25 general knowledge AI and computer science questions, each requiring the student to find out a particular fact (time, place, person's name, system name etc.).

The students were randomly divided into two groups. Group 1 contained 45 students and Group 2 contained the remaining 47. Group 1 served as the *training group* for I-SPY, in the sense that their search histories were used to populate the I-SPY hit-matrix but no re-ranking occurred for their search results. This group also served as a control against which to judge the search behaviour of the second group of users, who served as the *test group*. In total the Group 1 users produced 1049 individual queries and selected a combined total of 1046 pages, while the Group 2 users used 1705 queries and selected 1624 pages. The question of bias within the user groups is examined in [1].

4.2 Methodology

The data from this earlier live-user experiment provides the following key information to form the basis of our current evaluation: the queries submitted by each user; the pages that they selected from the subsequent result-lists; the position of these pages within the result-list; the pages where they located a correct answer to a particular question; and the hit-matrix produced by the Group 1 users. We also have a set of test problems (the Group 2 queries), and a set of correct solutions to these problems (the pages that are known to contain the correct answer to a particular question, verified by manual inspection). In previous experiments we considered a solution, or correct answer, to be associated with an individual query. This time we have altered our methodology slightly by considering a solution set that is associated with a question. This question itself contains a set of related queries $q_1,...,q_n$. In other words, our notion of relevance is with respect to the question and covers the set of queries used by searchers in trying to answer a particular question.

For our experiment we can "re-run" the live-user experiment by responding to Group 2 queries with the new result-lists that are recommended by I-SPY using the 11 query similarity metrics. In addition we also consider the result-lists that are produced prior to promotion. These result-lists correspond to the results of a standard meta-search engine and help us to understand the relative impact of I-SPY's result promotion and re-ranking.

We test our metrics for 3 different query selection thresholds, in each case limiting I-SPY to the selection of the top Q related queries, where Q is set to 5, 10 or 20. Note that this does not actually mean that this number of related queries will always be retrieved for every search session, rather it indicates the maximum number of related queries that can be retrieved. This will allow us to understand the relative performance of each metric for different levels of query similarity. If $Q = 5$ then I-SPY will focus on only the top related queries and thus will have access to limited result selection information. On the other hand if $Q = 20$ then many more queries can be considered but some of these may not be closely related to the target query and so may not contribute useful results to the final result-list.

Thus, each Group 2 user query is replayed and the results (for the different Q thresholds) are computed and compared against a ground-truth of known correct results for each question. This ground-truth (the pages that are known to contain the correct answer to a particular question) is a strong measure of relevance in the sense that we only consider a page to be relevant for a query if it contains the correct answer to the test question that the query was designed to satisfy. Obviously weaker notions of relevance might have been considered. Nevertheless, we believe that it is appropriate to focus on this stronger measure of relevance, given the search task used in our evaluation.

4.3 Precision vs. Recall

The standard objective test of search engine accuracy is the precision and recall test: the former computes the percentage of returned results that are relevant while the latter computes the percentage of relevant results that are returned. We measure the percentage precision and recall values for each of the techniques under review for different result-list sizes (k=5 to 30).

The results are presented as precision vs. recall graphs, for each value of Q, in Figure 2(a, b & c). Each graph presents the plot of precision against recall for the 11 similarity metrics, along with Meta. Each point on a given curve refers to a different result-list size, k. As expected we find that precision tends to fall-off with increasing result-list sizes, while recall improves; typically the number of relevant results is much less than k, and the majority of these relevant results should be positioned near the top of result-lists.

In general we notice that the term-based metrics tend to dominate in terms of their precision and recall performance. For example, at $Q = 5$, the performance of the term-based metrics is significantly better than any of the other techniques with the standard term-overlap metric performing the best. In Figure 2(a) we see that $TermOverlap$ precision at k=5 is 40%. This is compared to precision values of between 28% for $Meta$, 30% for $ResultOverlap$ (the best of the result-based methods) and 31% for $SelectionPositionDifference$ (the best of the selection-based methods). The recall results tell a similar story with a noted improvement in performance for $TermOverlap$ compared to the other techniques.

As Q increases, the performance benefits of the term-based metrics tend to reduce in comparison to some of the competing result-based and selection-based methods, for low values of k. Mostly these competing methods appear to either increase slightly in performance or remain stable as we increase Q. This suggests that at low values of Q, genuinely similar queries are being retrieved by the term-based methods whereas the result-based and selection-based metrics provide little additional related information compared to Meta. We have to retrieve either 10 or 20 similar cases in order for these metrics to perform well. However it is worth noting that when $Q = 10$ and $Q = 20$, if the result-based and selection-based methods are preforming better than the term-based metrics they are only doing so for a result-list size of 5. For example when $Q = 20$ the loss in precision for the term-based metrics between k=5 and k=10 is on average 2% compared to an average loss of 10% for the result-based and selection-based metrics.

As expected the $ModifiedEditDistance$ performed poorly and this performance diminishes greatly as we increased Q. It is an inefficient technique as it retrieves far too many unrelated cases. So much so that the performance, even at $Q = 5$ is not as good as Meta. As we will show in the following section this poor performance is also reflected in other aspects of these experiments.

4.4 Efficiency Concerns

Query similarity plays a pivotal role in collaborative Web search and it is obviously important to use a similarity metric that facilitates the retrieval of search cases that are likely to contribute positively to the relevance of promoted results. Certainly, in the experiments so far it is clear that term-based techniques (with the exception of the modified edit-distance metric) offer greater reliability than

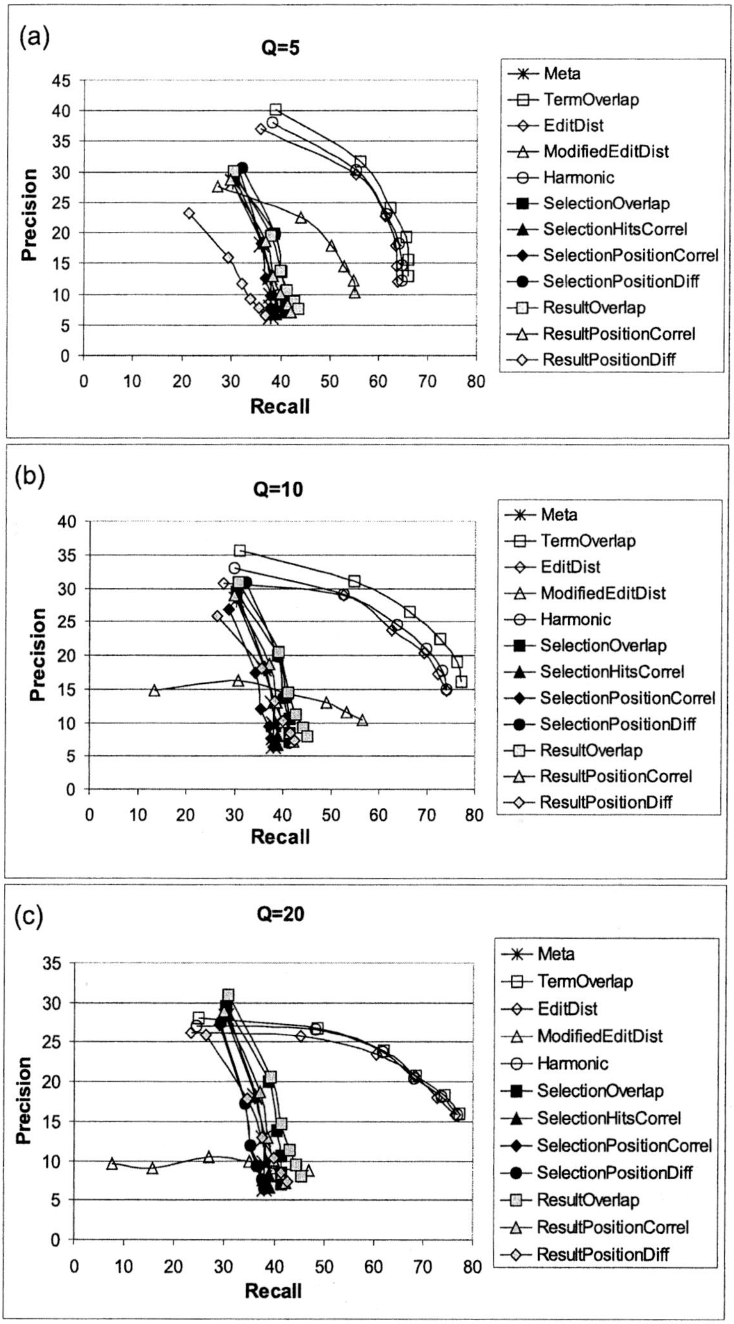

Fig. 2. Precision vs. Recall for (a) Q=5 (b) Q=10 (c) Q=20

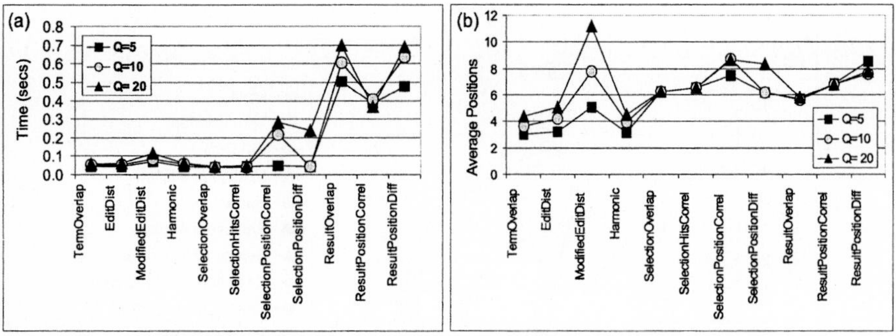

Fig. 3. (a) Average Time per Query (b) Average Position of the First Correct Answer

result-based or selection-based methods, with the term-overlap metric performing best overall. Of course, when choosing between competing similarity metrics we must also consider their efficiency characteristics. This is especially important in I-SPY and collaborative Web search because the chosen metric will be applied repeatedly during every search session and users are unlikely to accept appreciable increases in search time.

Figure 3(a) presents the results of timing studies carried out during our experiments for each of the different similarity metrics under review. Each time-value corresponds to an average over the 1705 test queries. Instead of measuring the actual time taken to compute a single query similarity, we instead measured the average time taken for I-SPY to produce a set of promoted results from its hit-matrix using each of the metrics. Since the only difference between the techniques is their query similarity metric, the timing differences must relate to differences in query similarity calculation times. The results indicate that the result-based techniques perform the worst by taking roughly 10 times longer than the other techniques. The selection-based methods are slightly quicker than the term-based techniques, mainly because the term-based techniques tend to retrieve more similar queries than the selection-based methods, and hence lead to additional relevance calculations. For example, at $Q = 10$ the term-based techniques retrieve on average 8.78 similar queries. This is in comparison to 2.17 similar queries being retrieved by the selection-based techniques. The timings, for both the term-based metrics and the selection-based metrics, are obviously directly dependent on the number of similar cases being retrieved.

4.5 Result Position

Before concluding our evaluation section we examine one final statistic that is again related to the accuracy of the result-lists. Result position is an extremely important factor when it comes to evaluating Web search techniques. For instance, many researchers have highlighted how users are often reluctant to venture beyond the first few results, regardless of how many results are presented to them [5]. Hence in our final experiment we investigate the average position of the first correct answer within the result-lists returned by the various techniques.

The results are presented in Figure 3(b). Once again it is clear that there is a significant benefit for the term-based metrics. *TermOverlap*, *EditDistance* and *Harmonic* are the only metrics to consistently return the first correct answer in the top 5 results across all values of Q. The average position for these 3 metrics for all values of Q is 3.91, in comparison to 6.85 for the result-based techniques and 7.0 for the selection-based metrics. Once again the ModifiedEditDist performs the worst with an average position of 8.04.

4.6 Summary

This paper was motivated by the observation that the simplicity of our existing query-similarity metric might be limiting the performance of our collaborative Web search technique. In fact, our results indicate that this is not so, at least in relation to a comprehensive list of 10 alternative similarity models. We have found that in general the term-based metrics offer superior performance when compared to the result-based and selection-based methods. Significantly, we have also shown that our original term-based overlap metrics offer the best all-round performance when retrieval efficiency and accuracy are considered.

5 Related Work

This work is perhaps most closely related with recent work in the area of query reuse and query refinement and expansion techniques, as a means to improve search-engine performance. Cui et al [6], for example, take advantage of the information contained in Web search-logs as the basis for query expansion. Traditionally, query expansion techniques extract terms from a subset of the top documents returned in response to an initial query. However, Cui et al. exploit the relationship between query terms and document terms which are extracted from user search logs. Frequently occurring, high-quality query terms that lead to result selections are used to expand the initial queries; see also [7] for related work. On the CBR front the *Broadway* recommender system [8] is also focused on query refinement but, it applies case-based techniques to recommend query refinements to a user based on the successful refinements of similar users. Also, the work of [5] applies CBR techniques to Web search. Briefly their PersonalSearcher agent combines user profiling and textual case-based reasoning to dynamically filter web documents according to a user's learned preference.

The core focus in this paper is on evaluating different models of query similarity as a form of case similarity. Alternative approaches to query similarity have mostly centered on the more traditional IR-based techniques. For instance, [9] use past query similarity metrics and document relevance to expand the current query. Their technique relies on term-based similarity methods similar to our own, with past queries selected as similar if they exceed a given similarity threshold. These selected queries are then used to rebuild the new query. One difference, compared to our term-based metrics, however, is the use of term frequency information as term weights during similarity assessment; we will consider weighting options as a matter for future work.

Both [10] and [11] discuss the use of query similarity metrics based on result-set overlaps, again as a guide for automatic query expansion. Raghavan et al. [10], in particular, highlight the importance of query-query similarity metrics during query expansion and argue that existing query-document metrics are inappropriate in this context. Fitzpatrick et al. [11] again focus on the reuse of past queries. They concluded that query reuse based methods can outperform more conventional document-based methods in terms of precision-recall performance. Interestingly in both cases result-overlap metrics were found to be better than term-overlap metrics as a measure of establishing query-query similarity. In our experiments, our result-based metrics performed poorly in comparison to the term-based techniques.

6 Conclusions

The history of Web search has mostly been dominated by term-based IR approaches to document retrieval. Recently researchers have developed new approaches to Web search to solve problems with these term-based methods. Link analysis [12] and query reuse [6,8] techniques are good examples. Even though there are obvious similarities between case-based reasoning and Web search, the case-based reasoning community has largely steered clear of Web search as an application domain. In our own work we have shown how the reuse-based approach of CBR has much to offer in the Web search task.

We have previously described the I-SPY case-based Web search engine [1,2] that is designed to operate with existing search engines. Our basic approach involves the reuse of past search sessions as a source of relevant results. The central contribution of this paper concerns the development of a range of alternative case similarity metrics to drive this reuse. In particular, we have compared families of term-based, selection-based and result-based similarity models. Through a comprehensive evaluation we have shown that the former offer significant advantages, and, in particular, our original term-based metric offers the best overall performance despite its apparent simplicity. While some of the other techniques perform well in certain conditions, for example the selection-based ones in terms of timing, the term-based techniques and in particular the term-overlap metric perform consistently well in all conditions.

References

1. Smyth, B., Balfe, E., Freyne, J., Briggs, P., Coyle, M., Boydell, O.: Exploiting Query Repetition & Regularity in an Adaptive Community-Based Web Search Engine. User Modeling and User-Adapted Interaction: The Journal of Personalization Research ((In Press))
2. Balfe, E., Smyth, B.: Case Based Collaborative Web Search. In: Proceedings of the 7th European Conference on Cased Based Reasoning. (2004) 489–503
3. Boydell, O., Smyth, B.: A Study of Selection Noise in Collaborative Web Search. In: Proceedings of the 19th International Joint Conference on Artificial Intelligence, IJCAI-05. (2005) In Press Edinburgh, Scotland.

4. Masek, W., Paterson, M.: A Faster Algorithm Computing String Edit Distances. Journal of Computer and System Sciences **20** (1980) 18–31
5. Godoy, D., Amandi, A.: PersonalSearcher: An Intelligent Agent for Searching Web Pages. In: IBERAMIA-SBIA. Volume 1952., Springer (2000) 62–72
6. Cui, H., Wen, J.R., Nie, J.Y., Ma, W.Y.: Probabilistic Query Expansion Using Query Logs. In: Proceedings of the 11th International Conference on World Wide Web. (2002) 325–332
7. Balfe, E., Smyth, B.: Improving Web Search Through Collaborative Query Recommendation. In: Proceedings of the 16th European Conference on Artificial Intelligence. (2004) 268–272
8. Kanawati, R., Jaczynski, M., Trousse, B., J-M, A.: Applying the Broadway Recommendation Computation Approach for Implementing a Query Refinement Service in the CBKB Meta-search Engine. In: Conférence Française sur le Raisonnement á Partir de Cas (RáPC'99). (1999)
9. Hust, A., Klink, S., Junker, M., Dengel, A.: Query Reformulation in Collaborative Information Retrieval. In: Proceedings of the International Conference on Information and Knowledge Sharing, IKS 2002. (2002)
10. Raghavan, V.V., Sever, H.: On the Reuse of Past Optimal Queries. In: SIGIR'95, Proceedings of the 18th Annual International ACM SIGIR, Conference on Research and Development in Information Retrieval. (1995)
11. Fitzpatrick, L., Dent, M.: Automatic Feedback Using Past Queries: Social Searching? In: SIGIR '97: Proceedings of the 20th Annual International ACM SIGIR Conference on Research and Development in Information Retrieval, July 27-31, 1997, Philadelphia, PA, USA, ACM (1997) 306–313
12. Brin, S., Page, L.: The Anatomy of a Large-Scale Web Search Engine. In: Proceedings of the 7th International World Wide Web Conference. Volume 30(1-7)., Networks and ISDN Systems (1998) 107–117

A Case-Based Approach for Indoor Location

Carlos Bento, Joao Peixoto, and Marco Veloso

Centro de Informatica e Sistemas da Universidade de Coimbra,
Departamento de Engenharia Informatica,
Polo II da Universidade de Coimbra, Portugal
bento@dei.uc.pt, joao.peixoto@coimbra.ccg.pt
mveloso@student.dei.uc.pt

Abstract. Location is an important dimension for context-awareness in ubiquitous devices. Nowadays different techniques are used alone or together to determine the position of a person or object. One aspect of the problem concerns to indoor location. Various authors propose the analysis of Radio Frequency (RF) footprints.

In this paper we defend that case-based reasoning can make an important contribution for location from RF footprints. We apply an empirical dissimilarity metric for footprint retrieval and compare this approach with the results obtained with a neural network and C5.0 learning algorithms. The RF footprints are obtained from a Global System for Mobile Communications and General Packet Radio Service (GSM/GPRS) network. Signals from these networks are particularly complex when compared to the ones obtained from WiFi or Bluetooth networks.

1 Introduction

A problem of crucial importance in ubiquitous computing is the determination of place for persons and objects. Many proactive decisions are mainly, or in part, dependent on location determination.

Although the problem of open air positioning is, in general, well addressed by Global Positioning System (GPS) technologies, indoor location is a much more challenging one and various approaches have been adopted in the past.

Some of these approaches comprise a specific infrastructure for location. It is the case of active badge systems based on infrared technology [1], or active bats supported on RF and ultrasound signals [2]. Both solutions provide good results in terms of accuracy and precision under adequate conditions.

Another approach to indoor location is indoor GPS. In this approach RF emitters placed in buildings produce signals similar to GPS emitters [3].

Active badges and indoor GPS have in common the need for a dedicated infrastructure which makes these systems expensive and time consuming in terms of implementation.

A different approach is followed by systems that support location on the analysis of RF footprints provided by radio stations, wireless Local Area Networks (LAN), GSM infrastructures or Bluetooth ad-hoc networks.

H. Muñoz-Avila and F. Ricci (Eds.): ICCBR 2005, LNAI 3620, pp. 78–90, 2005.

A system that scans radio stations is RightSPOT [4]. In this program the location of a device is supported on signal strengths from FM radio stations. RADAR is another system for location based on a WiFi structure [5]. In this system signals are received from various WiFi base stations. Triangulation is used to determine user's coordinates. Other approaches comprise, for instance, the use of Bluetooth signals [6].

The RF footprint produced by GSM/GPRS networks can also be the basis for indoor location, similarly to what is performed on WiFi scenarios. Notwithstanding, it is much harder to work with GSM scenarios. In general, indoor GSM signals are instable due to complex reflection mechanisms and to the variance resultant from weather and other fluctuations on the propagation conditions. This characteristic of GSM signals has as a consequence that classical classification by feed forward networks and decision tree algorithms does not seem to be the best approach for this problem.

It happens that when comparing a footprint in memory with a new probe the dissimilarities between them seem to confuse these algorithms.

We think that an algorithm that incorporates empirical and theoretical knowledge in the function that calculates the dissimilarities/similarities that can occur between footprints can help improving this task. It is in this way that we are exploring how case-based reasoning (CBR) can assist achieving better results for indoor location based on GSM footprints.

In this paper we present our starting work on this area and the first results we obtained with a dissimilarity metric for retrieval of RF footprints. We use this metric in the context of a case-based reasoning system for indoor location. We tested our approach at our Department, a six floor building, with an heterogeneous structure.

Section two describes the problem of indoor location from RF footprints. In the next section we describe why we think CBR can help and present our approach. In section four we describe the experimental data. Section five reports the results achieved using a neural network, C5.0, and our CBR approach. Section six outlines the main points for this paper and future work.

2 Propagation of RF Signals

The radio frequency signal is an electromagnetic phenomenon. RF propagation refers to how well a radio signal travels in free space. The RF coverage is mainly determined by three key factors: the height and type of the antenna at the Base Station (BS) and the RF power level radiation. The propagation of RF signals is primarily supported on direct beams. Although, it does not mean that signals are limited to line of sight. However, depending on the orientation, we have different propagation values for the same distance between receiver and antenna (see Figure 1). Propagation of signal from the BS to the Mobile Unit (MU) is affected by many factors. Until the signal finds the first physical obstacle, the propagation takes place in the atmosphere, where it is subject to ducting (a refraction of the signal propagation caused by differences of temperature between

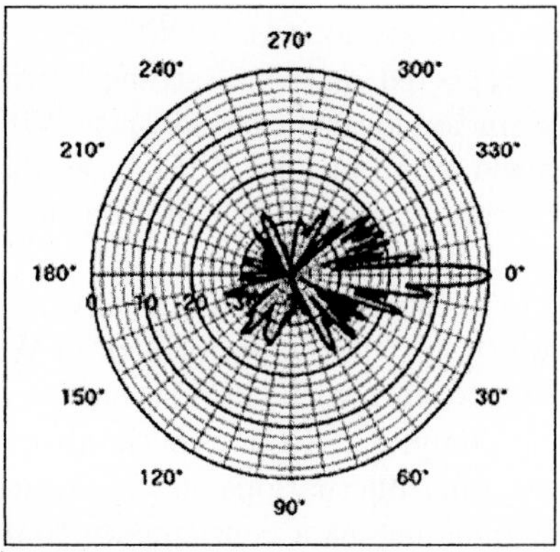

Fig. 1. Antenna's Radio Channels Propagation

two air masses) and attenuation. Ducting is undesirable in RF propagation, but also unavoidable. Normally, the refraction of air decreases as the temperature increases. In free-space, the propagation is attenuated by dense vegetation, precipitation and distance. The attenuation in free-space is determined in terms of distance and is calculated using the following formula:

$$L[dB] = 32.44 + 20logD + 20logf \ . \tag{1}$$

where D is the distance (in kilometers), between the antenna and the receiver, and f is the frequency (in megahertz). Because the antennas are directional, this is an approximate value.

When a signal hits a solid object, like a building, it may be reflected, diffracted and absorbed. Reflection is an abrupt change in direction of a beam and creates a phenomenon called Multipath Fading or Rayleigh Fading, an interference between a direct beam and the reflected beam, which can be added to or subtracted from the received direct beam. The duration of the effect may vary from seconds to minutes. Fading is a random increase in signal loss along a path [7,8]. Diffraction is the bending and spreading of beams when they meet an obstruction. Absorption is a process in which signal is absorbed by particles of solid objects, increasing signal loss. The more solid objects are found between the BS and the MU, the higher is the interference suffered by RF propagation. All these factors influence RF propagation in buildings and are cause of indoor attenuation. For networks, operating at the 2.4GHz radio frequency, indoor attenuation for the received signal can be calculated using the following formula [1] [9]:

$$\overline{Pl}(d_{j,k})[dB] = Pl(d_0) + 10 * \alpha * log(d_{j,k}/d_0) \ . \tag{2}$$

where $\overline{Pl}(d_0)$ is the free-space path loss, α is the path loss exponent, $Pl(d_0)$ is the reference distance, and $(d_{j,k})$ is the physical distance between receiver and

[1] Unfortunately, it is common that, real values vary significantly from the ones produced from the theoretical approach.

transmitter. Concerning the GSM network, there are no studies that allow us to determine indoor attenuation. However, with reference to the 900Mhz to 4.0Ghz radio frequency, Seidel's work [10] shows that the attenuation has nearly the same profile.

Although this model gives us a pattern for indoor attenuation it cannot be directly applied as the distance between the MU and the BSs in the vicinity of the MU are unknown. Another factor of uncertainty concerns the α coeficient that can vary from 1 to 6, with the value dependent on the number and type of obstructions between transmitter and receiver plus the number of building floors. Notwithstanding this formula gives us an important argument for the statement that indoor attenuation is quite diverse along different building zones. This is a starting point for assuming that RF footprints can be good predictors for indoor location.

We consider RF footprints at the channel level. Different base stations communicate with the MU on different channels. Each operator settles its base stations in an hexagonal disposition. Our Country is served by three operators. Base stations have different locations relatively to a building. Because the propagation of the signal is influenced by the path between the various BSs and the MU, and by the configuration of the building, we assume that the various radio channels (transmitting at different frequencies) will have different signal strengths at different zones, making possible to infer location based on this information. This makes quite suggestive to learn cases representing the RF scenarios at the channel level for the different positions and create suitable retrieval and selection algorithm that incorporates theoretical and empirical knowledge to perform the selection of the footprint(s) in memory that better predicts the current position.

3 Opportunities for Case-Based Reasoning

Case-based reasoning is a lazy learning method that supports a decision on previous observations saved in a case library [11].

The CBR cycle comprises gathering the data for a probe, comparing this probe with cases in memory, retrieving the most similar cases, reusing these cases, revising them in order to generate a new case (solution for the new problem represented by an RF footprint), and possibly retaining the new case in the case library [12].

The main goal of our work is to study the advantages of CBR for indoor location, supported on RF footprints, and compare with other approaches like neural networks and decision tree generation algorithms. Our point is that indoor location accommodates, quite naturally, the CBR paradigm.

The type of disturbances that can occur in the signals that were in the origin of the RF footprints and probe suggest the need for a complex similarity function for case retrieval. The similarity function must incorporate domain knowledge and empirical knowledge on the mechanisms concerning line of sight (LOS) and non-line of sight (NLOS) propagation.

Another characteristic that makes CBR an appealing choice is that it is quite suitable for cooperative location in the sense that different explorers can contribute with cases to a shared case library that incrementally improves the location capabilities of a community of "navigators". This gives space for the study of adequate mechanisms for collaborative CBR [13].

RF footprints change also with time, due to periodical adjustments of the signal power in the Base Stations (BT), modification in the network structure, city landscape - buildings that are constructed or demolished can change the footprints for various locations. This is an opportunity for the study and application of suitable case-base maintenance algorithms [14].

Sometimes we cannot determine indoor location at a pre-defined level of accuracy [15], but it is possible , and acceptable, to relax accuracy constraints. In terms of CBR an hierarchical structure for cases (footprints) would be an interesting approach for accuracy acomodation, which is another opportunity for the study and application of hierarchical case-based reasoning [16].

The use of domain knowledge for case-adaptation, specially when a probe fires cases from different locations and an interpolation process are necessary. This is also another opened topic of research in the context of CBR [17].

In summary, we defend that various aspects of CBR can contribute to solve the complex problem of indoor location using GSM footprints[2]. In the next subsections we describe, case representation, dissimilarity metric, and present a global picture for the process as it is currently defined within our framework.

3.1 Case Representation

A case resembles cases in Figure 2. A case comprises a vector of channel numbers. Each channel number has associated with it the mean value of the signal strength obtained with five readings along 15 seconds [3], the standard deviation for these readings, and a relevance factor that is calculated by the following formula:

$$Relevance = MeanRx - StandardDeviation^2 \ . \tag{3}$$

with $MeanRx$ the mean value of the five signal readings along 15 seconds and $StandardDeviation$ the standard deviation for these readings. This formula assigns importance to channels with higher mean signal level and lower standard deviation. It is an empirical formulation that is supported on the theoretical and simulation work from [9] that states that for channels with a large standard deviation, the probability of the probe being close to the respective mean is small, also this implies that the probe has a similarity that is not very different

[2] We stress the context of GSM as for other RF scenarios like WiFi and Bluetooth various solutions with good accuracy and precision are available nowadays. In fact, as we explained before, it is the use of GSM signals that is a much more challenging and a not yet solved problem. Finding a good approach for indoor location using GSM signals is of great impact considering the number of GSM terminals that are currently available.

[3] We use XPanelLog, a program for signal scanning in Qtek smartphones.

CASE N.	Place	Channel	Mean	St Dev	Channel Relevance
001	1.1	1	51.6	3.13	41.8
	1.1	5	40.8	1.3	39.1
	1.1	7	18.4	1.14	17.1
	1.1	499	8.8	1.79	5.6
	1.1	19	11	2.65	4
002	1.1	1	51.6	6.27	12.3
	1.1	5	33.2	4.66	11.5
	1.1	21	14.8	2.28	9.6
	1.1	19	10.8	2.05	6.6
	1.1	500	7	1	6
003	1.2	1	52	1	51
	1.2	5	25.2	3.11	15.5
	1.2	21	1.2	0.45	1
	1.2	23	-2	0	-2
	1.2	9	-1.8	0.84	-2.5

CASE N.	Place	Channel	Mean	St Dev	Channel Relevance
004	1.3	1	51.2	2.68	44
	1.3	5	28.4	4.72	6.1
	1.3	17	1	1	0
	1.3	11	0.2	0.84	-0.5
	1.3	25	-0.6	0.89	-1.4
005	1.4	1	50	0	50
	1.4	5	33.4	0.55	33.1
	1.4	21	0.4	0.55	0.1
	1.4	19	-1.6	0.89	-2.4
	1.4	23	-2.4	0.55	-2.7
PROBE	??	1	60.2	0.84	59.5
		5	37	1	36.0
		7	15.8	1.79	12.6
		19	14	1.22	12.5
		21	13.2	1.64	10.5

Fig. 2. Cases and a probe (only with five channels per case for simplicity reasons)

to all the cases in memory. For each footprint we have the signal strength for about 16 channels, but we exclude from the channel vectors these channels with highest and lowest mean signal strength. The reason to do this comes from our observation that the signals with the highest signal although being more stable, due to a lower multipath fading effect are not good predictor, they tend to have the same mean value along all the building. The signals with the lowest strength are, in general, very instable and in this way are also bad predictors. This vector is sorted by decreasing relevance value calculated by formula (3) as can be observed in Figure 3.

To generate a probe we produce a signal strength sample along 15 seconds which corresponds approximately to five readings for each channel. We calcule the mean strength, standard deviation, and channel relevance for each channel, sort channels by decreasing relevance and discard the signals with highest and smallest mean signal strength.

The vector of channels in the probe and the corresponding vector for each case are then compared according to our similarity metric.

3.2 Dissimilarity Metric

After generating the probe vector this vector is compared with all vectors of the cases in memory. Figure 3 shows the two vectors for a case and a probe. Two factors contribute to the similarity metric that, in fact, is a dissimilarity metric. One is the distance concerning the position of the channels in each vector. For instance, if the same channel is present in the same position in the case and probe vectors, the distance for this channel is 1. If a channel is in the second position in the probe vector and in the fifth position in the case vector then its distance is 4. For channels present in the probe that do not match channels in a case vector we empirically assign a distance of 10. Currently, we do not consider channels in a case that do not match channels in the probe. We think that this is something that needs further consideration in the future.

Another factor that is taken into account for the dissimilarity metric is the difference of strength between matching channels in probe and case vectors. For a

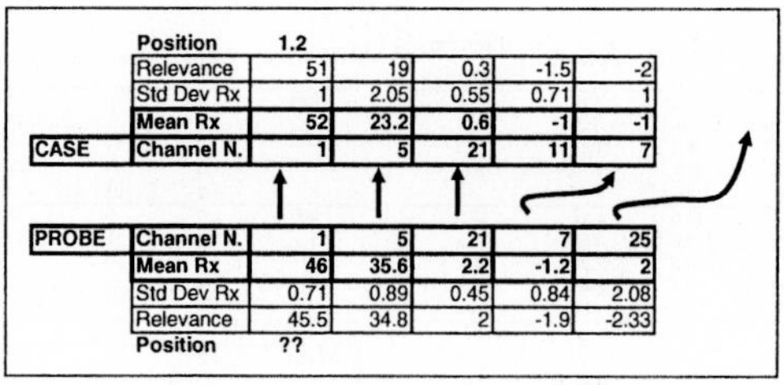

Fig. 3. Matching between a probe and a case

channel in the probe that does not match a case we cannot calculate a difference, so we use the strength of the channel present in the probe.

These two metrics are combined in the following dissimilarity formula:

$$Dissim(p, c) = \sum_{i=1}^{5}(distance_{p_i} * ABS(Rx_{p_i} - Rx_{c_i})) . \tag{4}$$

with p a probe, c a case, i the position of the channel in the probe vector, $distance_{p_i}$ the distance between a channel in the probe vector and the case vector, ABS the absolute value function, and Rx_{p_i}, Rx_{c_i}, respectively, the signal strengths of the ith channel in the probe and case vectors.

As an example, considering vectors in Figure 3 the dissimilarity value for this probe and case is:

$$Dissim(p, c) = |46.0-51.0|+|35.6-23.2|+|2.2-0.6|+2*|-1.2+1|+10*|2| = 39.4 . \tag{5}$$

3.3 Putting All Together

In this section we present the CBR cycle. The first step is the acquisition of seed cases. It is important to stress that later the equipment can acquire new cases by applying revision mechanisms and generating new cases from the old ones, provided a suitable validation process is performed.

In the acquisition phase readings are made at different points and transformed into cases by making the calculations described above.

In the localization phase new probes are acquired each 15 seconds and processed in background mode. This processing comprises sorting the channels in the probe, accordingly to the channel relevance, and calculating the dissimilarity metric for this probe against each case in memory.

Then the case with the lowest dissimilarity value, plus the cases with a dissimilarity value not higher than 30% of the value for the best case are retrieved.

If all retrieved cases suggest the same symbolic position it means there is no conflict and this position is assigned to the probe. If this is not the situation, then the system enters into a voting process in which the best case contributes with 3 votes for its position suggestion, and the other cases with one vote for the respective position suggestion. The position with more votes is the one assigned to the probe.

4 Acquisition of RF Footprints

Our work took place on data acquired at the Department of Informatics Engineering along the six floors of the building. In this paper we only consider the data and results concerning floors one and two. Data from floor one was acquired from a long open area, and data from floor two from a sequence of rooms. The points where data were gathered are presented in Figure 4.

The reason for the different strategy concerning first and second floor has to do with considerations on the literature, and the intuitive feeling that making accurate predictions at indoor open spaces is much more difficult then at closed spaces.

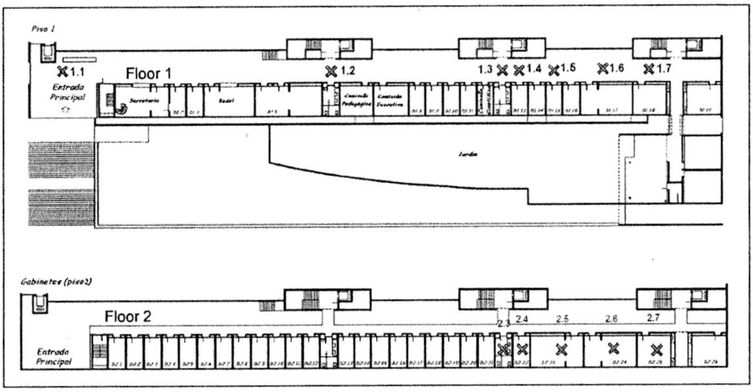

Fig. 4. Floor 1 and 2 of the Department of Informatics Engineering

XPanelLog program was integrated into another program that produces a trace of the RF scenario. This trace comprises the Received Signal level (Rx) along the various channels accessed by our mobile equipment (we used a Qtek 9090 smartphone for tests). In Figure 5 we present the evolution of Rx along three channels with very different mean signal levels. It is evident from these histograms that some signals are very instable. Another observation that we made, is the signal tends to more instable at the higher places in a building. We think these are the strongest challenges in dealing with these signals for indoor location.

In Figure 6 we show the row data produced by XPanelLog, and in Figure 3 we present the transformation of these row data into cases plus a new probe for location determination.

For these tests we used data from seven points at floor one and five points at floor two. From each point we collected 8 cases. Each case is the result of 15 seconds of tracing. Altogether we have 56 cases for floor one and 40 cases for floor number two.

From the total of 96 cases we inserted 56 older ones in memory and used the other 40 as probes.

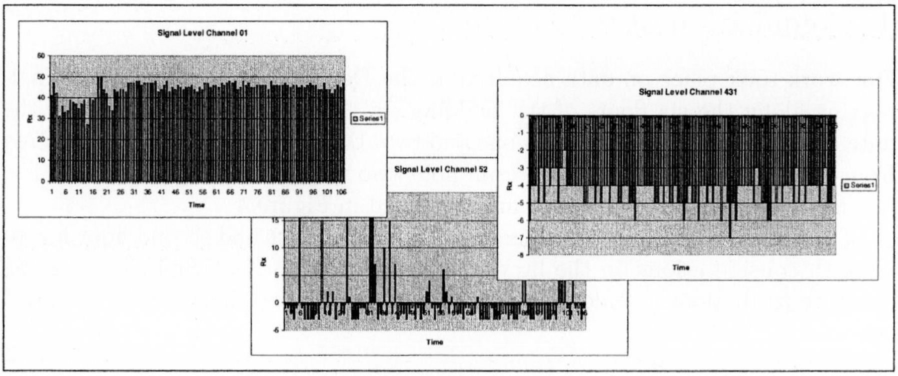

Fig. 5. Signals acquired along 5 minutes for three channels at place 1.2

Place	Channel	Rx 001	Rx 002	Rx 003	Rx 004	...	Average	St Dev
1.2	1	41	47	42	31		44.24	3.97
1.2	5	23	34	18	24		25.32	4.33
1.2	21	1	2	1	1		4.02	2.65
1.2	7	1	3	5	1		1.99	2.81
1.2	17	-1	-1	-2	-3		0.16	5.25
1.2	19	-2	0	-1	2		-0.57	2.69
1.2	29	-3	-2	-3	-3		-0.77	5.63
1.2	25	-2	-3	-3	-2		-0.80	5.20
1.2	31	-2	-3	-4	-5		-1.44	4.94
1.2	11	1	-2	-3	-2		-1.56	3.59
1.2	9	-2	-4	-1	-1		-1.70	2.67
1.2	23	-2	5	-3	-3		-2.08	2.64
1.2	499	-4	-1	0	-2		-3.15	1.15
1.2	500	-6	-3	-2	-3		-3.71	0.99
1.2	424	-5	-3	-4	-4		-4.20	0.80
1.2	431	-6	-4	-4	-5		-4.44	0.81

Fig. 6. Sample of signal data acquisition for place 1.2

5 Experimental Results

For tests we used separately the case library and probes for floor 1 and 2. With the cases in floor 1 we made two other tests, one with all the points and another with more spaced points (1.1, 1.2, 1.3, and 1.7).

We run the three groups of examples separately. Figures 7 and 8 show the results obtained using these cases to train a neural network and C5.0[4]. Results are presented in terms of a coincidence matrix. The topology of the neural networks comprised 15 neurons in the input layer, 20 in the hidden layer and n nodes in the output layer, being n the cardinality of the location variable. For the neural network we used the RBFN method with preventive overtraining. For C5.0 we favored accuracy which means that we accepted a low level of punning. It is clear from these results that using a feed forward network or C5.0 does not drive to good location classifiers, and the results are in fact quite poor when we use the same attributes we used for CBR.

[4] C5.0 is a commercial version of the C4.5 algorithm.

Comparing $N-Place with Place

Correct	11	64,71%
Wrong	6	35,29%
Total	17	

Coincidence Matrix for $N-Place (rows show actuals)

	1.1	1.2	1.3	1.4	1.5	1.6	1.7
1.1	2	0	1	0	0	0	0
1.2	0	2	0	0	0	0	0
1.3	0	0	0	0	0	0	2
1.4	0	0	0	3	0	0	0
1.5	1	0	0	0	1	0	0
1.6	0	0	0	0	0	1	1
1.7	0	0	1	0	0	0	2

Comparing $N-Place with Place

Correct	7	70%
Wrong	3	30%
Total	10	

Coincidence Matrix for $N-Place (rows show actuals)

	1.1	1.2	1.3	1.7
1.1	2	0	1	0
1.2	0	2	0	0
1.3	0	1	1	0
1.7	0	0	1	2

Comparing $N-Place with Place

Correct	6	46,15%
Wrong	7	53,85%
Total	13	

Coincidence Matrix for $N-Place (rows show actuals)

	2.3	2.5	2.7
2.3	0	0	3
2.4	1	1	1
2.5	0	3	0
2.6	0	1	0
2.7	0	0	3

Fig. 7. Coincidence matrices for the NN trained with data from floors 1 and 2

Comparing $C-Place with Place

Correct	10	58,82%
Wrong	7	41,18%
Total	17	

Coincidence Matrix for $C-Place (rows show actuals)

	1.1	1.2	1.3	1.4	1.5	1.6	1.7
1.1	1	1	0	0	0	1	0
1.2	0	2	0	0	0	0	0
1.3	0	2	0	0	0	0	0
1.4	0	0	0	2	0	1	0
1.5	0	0	0	0	1	1	0
1.6	0	0	0	0	0	2	0
1.7	0	0	1	0	0	0	2

Comparing $C-Place with Place

Correct	5	50%
Wrong	5	50%
Total	10	

Coincidence Matrix for $C-Place (rows show actuals)

	1.1	1.2	1.3	1.7
1.1	2	0	0	1
1.2	0	2	0	0
1.3	0	1	0	1
1.7	1	0	1	1

Comparing $C-Place with Place

Correct	7	53,85%
Wrong	6	46,15%
Total	13	

Coincidence Matrix for $C-Place (rows show actuals)

	2.3	2.4	2.7
2.3	2	1	0
2.4	1	2	0
2.5	0	0	3
2.6	0	0	1
2.7	0	0	3

Fig. 8. Coincidence matrices for the C5.0 trained with data from floors 1 and 2

Correct	15	88.24%
Wrong	2	11.76%
Total	17	

Probe	Case Library						
	1.1	1.2	1.3	1.4	1.5	1.6	1.7
1.1	3	0	0	0	0	0	0
1.2	0	2	0	0	0	0	0
1.3	0	0	2	0	0	0	0
1.4	0	0	0	3	0	0	0
1.5	0	0	0	0	1	1	0
1.6	0	0	0	0	0	1	1
1.7	0	0	0	0	0	0	3

Correct	10	76.92%
Wrong	3	23.08%
Total	13	

Probe	Case Library				
	2.5	2.6	2.4	2.3	2.7
2.5	1	0	0	2	0
2.6	0	1	0	0	0
2.4	0	0	3	0	0
2.3	1	0	0	2	0
2.7	0	0	0	0	3

Correct	10	100.00%
Wrong	0	0.00%
Total	10	

Probe	Case Library			
	1.1	1.2	1.3	1.7
1.1	3	0	0	0
1.2	0	2	0	0
1.3	0	0	2	0
1.7	0	0	0	3

Fig. 9. Coincidence matrices for the CBR with data from floors 1 and 2

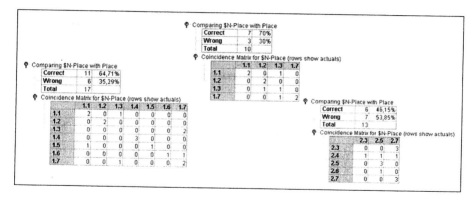

Figure 9 presents the results obtained with our case-based system. From these results it is evident that the CBR system performs acceptably for the group of all points in floor one (correctness: 88.24%), very well when points are more distant between them (correctness: 100%), not as well for points in floor 2 in contiguous rooms (correctness: 77.92%).

Although it is necessary to look with care to these results - we need to acquire more cases and more probes in different days to make this experiment significant, we think that there is an opportunity for a deeper study of this approach and the mechanisms that are provided by CBR for this task. In fact the CBR approach introduces a dramatic improvement versus the neural network and C5.0 experimental results.

Surprisingly to our previous intuition the CBR approach did not work very well for points in contiguous closed spaces as was our expectation. Further work and understanding on this aspect is necessary in the future.

6 Summary and Future Work

Performing indoor location based on footprints of GSM/GPRS signals is a challenging task due to the variability of the received signals. Those signals are quite sensitive to changes due to movements of people and objects, weather conditions, changes in the physical path from the base stations to the receiver, and building structures. In this way, although the task is similar to the one performed by other systems like RADAR, in fact GSM systems have to deal with a much more complex RF scenario.

We defend that an approach supported on CBR is worth pursuing. We can incorporate theoretical and empirical knowledge in the similarity/dissimilarity metric. Also a case-based approach is quite suitable for symbolic location as cases naturally embody the discrete points that must be considered for location. Cases can be organized into an hierarchical structure making the process of case retrieval to go as deeply in the case hierarchy as it is permitted by the quality of these cases. Also a case-based approach is quite suitable for location in a cooperative way. Various systems can contribute with cases along their navigation to a shared case base. Due to changes on the environment along time the RF scenario can change gradually or sometimes abruptly. This is an opportunity for applying the work performed along years of research on case base maintenance. Finally, it is important to stress that according to its nature this is an incremental learning process, that can start with a set of seed cases that when not able to make good classifications can improve itself by incorporating new cases.

A drawback of this kind of approach has to do with the fact that these systems need a learning phase to associate symbolic points to RF footprints. Also changes in the network imply the refreshment of the case base. This is something common to system based on the analysis of RF scenarios.

The present work is at its beginning and a lot of things have to be done to improve results. First we think that it is important to extend the tests and to improve the dissimilarity metric. Things like how long should be the case and probe vectors? What can we do to improve the relevance metric? The present metric gives attention to the channels with the highest mean level discounted by the standard deviation, and discarding the channels in the extremes of the ranking. It is this the best approach?

Another aspect concerns creation of conflict resolution rules - what to do when two or more cases exhibit similar dissimilarity values? Also it is important to investigate revision mechanisms as they are understood by the CBR community. It is possible that when two cases are in conflict the best practice be not to choose one of them but to use both to construct a new case. Also it will be interesting to study how a community of "navigators" can cooperate producing cases to a common library.

We need to produce further work on which are the factors that maintain relatively stable along space and those that are discriminant for a place in order to understand which are the CBR mechanisms that are suitable for indoor location.

Acknowledgements. We would like to thank the anonymous reviewers for their valuable comments, suggestions, and insightful suggestions for future work.

References

1. Roy Want, Andy Hopper, Veronica Falcao, and Jonathan Gibbons. The active badge location system. ACM Transaction on Information Systems, 10(1):91102, January 1992.
2. Andy Ward, Alan Jones, and Andy Hopper. A new location technique for the active office. IEEE Personal Communications, 4(5):4247, October 1997.
3. Frank van Diggelen and Charles Abraham. Indoor GPS Technology. CTIA Wireless-Agenda, Dallas, May 2001.
4. John Krumm, Gerry Cermak, and Eric Horvitz. RightSPOT: A Novel Sense of Location for a Smart Personal Object, in Proceedings of UbiComp 2003: Fifth International Conference on Ubiquitous Computing, Lecture Notes in Computer Science volume 2864, USA, October 2003.
5. Paramvir Bahl and Venkata N. Padmanabhan. RADAR: An In-Building RF-based User Location and Tracking System, in IEEE INFOCOM 2000. Tel-Aviv, Israel, 2000.
6. Abhishek Pramod Patil. Performance of Bluetooth Technologies and Their Applications to Location Sensing. Master of Science Dissertation. Department of Electrical and Computer Engineering, 2002.
7. Beddel, P., Cellular/PCS Management, McGraw-Hill, New York, USA, 1999.
8. Freeman, R., Telecommunications Transmission Handbook, John Wiley and Sons, Inc., USA, 1998.
9. K. Kaemarungsi and P. Krishnamurthy, "Modeling of Indoor Positioning Systems Based on Location Fingerprinting", IEEE INFOCOM 2004, IEEE, 2004.
10. S. Seidel and T. Rappaport, "914 MHz Path Loss Prediction Models for Indoor Wireless Communications in Multifloored Buildings", IEEE Transactions on Antennas and Propagation, IEEE, February 1992, pp. 207-217.
11. D. B. Leake, editor. Case-Based Reasoning: Experiences, Lessons, and Future Directions. Menlo Park, CA: AAAI Press/MIT Press, Menlo Park, CA, 1996.

12. Aamodt A. and Plaza E. (1994). Case-Based Reasoning: Foundational Issues, Methodological Variations, and System Approaches. Pages 39-59 in AICom - Artificial Intelligence Communications 7(1), March 1994.
13. Ontanon, P. Collaborative case retention strategies for CBR agents. in 5th International Conference on Case-Based Reasoning, ICCBR 2003. 2003. Trondheim, Norway: Springer Verlag, Heidelberg, Germany.
14. Zhong Zhang and Qiang Yang, Towards Lifetime Maintenance of Case Base Indexes for Continual Case Based Reasoning. In Proceedings of the 1998 International Conference on AI Methodologies, Systems and Applications (AIMSA98), Bulgaria, October 1998.
15. Sirin Tekinay, Ed Chao, and Robert Richton. Performance Benchmarking for Wireless Location Systems. IEEE Communications Magazine, April 1998.
16. Barry Smyth, Mark T. Keane, and Pdraig Cunningham. Hierarchical Case-Based Reasoning Integrating Case-Based and Decompositional Problem-Solving Techniques for Plant-Control Software Design. IEEE Transactions on Knowledge and Data Engineering archive Volume 13, Issue 5 (September 2001).
17. Wolfgang Wilke, Ralph Bergmann. Techniques and Knowledge Used for Adaptation During Case-Based Problem Solving. IEA/AIE (Vol. 2) 1998: 497-506.

P2P Case Retrieval with an Unspecified Ontology

Shlomo Berkovsky[1], Tsvi Kuflik[2], and Francesco Ricci[3]

[1] University of Haifa, Computer Science Department
slavax@cs.haifa.ac.il
[2] University of Haifa, Management Information Systems Department
tsvikak@is.haifa.ac.il
[3] ITC-irst, Trento
ricci@itc.it

Abstract. Traditional CBR approaches imply centralized storage of the case base and, most of them, the retrieval of similar cases by an exhaustive comparison of the case to be solved with the whole set of cases. In this work we propose a novel approach for storage of the case base in a decentralized Peer-to-Peer environment using the notion of Unspecified Ontology. In our approach the cases are stored in a number of network nodes that is comparable with the number of cases. We also develop an approximated algorithm for efficient retrieval of most-similar cases. The experiments show that the approximated algorithm successfully retrieves the most-similar cases while reducing the number of cases to be compared.

1 Introduction

Peer-to-Peer (P2P) networks provide a distributed computing platform with theoretically unlimited storage, communication and processing capabilities. P2P systems, however, lack any notion of centralized management, depending rather on distributed autonomous management of the resources contributed by the connected peers. Storage resources of P2P systems were used until now for data sharing and distribution, mainly multimedia files. P2P is a fast growing research area that is producing interesting applications [9].

This paper proposes using the resources of a P2P network as a case-based reasoning tool for the purposes of distributed storage of a case base and to support distributed retrieval of similar cases. Since a P2P system does not require central management, and in fact this is the primary motivation for P2P solutions, the cases inserted autonomously by a community of users are described in a fully distributed way, possibly using different features for the same type of cases. This implies that similar cases might be not only different with respect to certain feature values, as in classical CBR approaches, but also capable of being described in different ways (different features, different names for the same concept). Thus, efficient management of the case base requires a stable semantic infrastructure allowing the identification of similarities between these heterogeneous cases. Moreover, this infrastructure should support a retrieval process that: i) maintains decentralized retrieval with low communication overhead, and ii) guarantees discovery of the most similar cases or at least a reasonably good approximation.

H. Muñoz-Avila and F. Ricci (Eds.): ICCBR 2005, LNAI 3620, pp. 91 – 105, 2005.

We used the hypercube-based approach of UNSO (UNSpecified Ontology) [1] to maintain P2P storage of the case base and we developed an approximated algorithm for case retrieval that copes with the constraints of such a distributed storage structure (e.g. reduction of node to node communication). The algorithm is based on the notion of implicit clustering in UNSO, i.e., on the fact that similar cases are inherently located in a relatively close vicinity. Thus, an approximated retrieval algorithm over UNSO is performed through a localized search. This means that the case most similar to a given probe is not searched in the whole case base, but rather that the search focuses on the nodes (storing cases) closer to the node storing the probe, thus decreasing the number of target cases that are compared with the case to be solved. Moreover, since the underlying network consists of distributed connected peers, the computation effort needed to assess the case similarity might also be spread among the peers, eliminating a single computation bottleneck in traditional centralized CBR systems.

The above approach was evaluated in five case bases storing E-Commerce advertisements from five different domains. We have compared the proposed approximated retrieval algorithm with a traditional exhaustive algorithm, and we showed that the former significantly decreases the number of cases that are compared during the retrieval stage, while preserving the essential quality of the retrieved cases. In particular, we measured the recall of the proposed algorithm and the number of case similarity computations performed. We achieved high recall results while still keeping the number of similarity computations smaller than that required by an exhaustive linear search.

The ideas of distributed problem solving in CBR arose in multi-agent CBR systems such as those proposed in [10] and [11], and more recently in [7] and [8]. In [10] the task was solved by iterative negotiations between the agents, targeted to resolve the constraints' conflicts, while in [11] the agents exploited the past experience of other agents. Our approach is quite different, since we assume that the agent/nodes of the P2P network jointly contribute to a single retrieval rather than participating in the problem solving process by performing independent retrievals or exchanging problem solving knowledge.

Thus, the contributions of this work are two-fold. First, we propose a novel notion of pure decentralized storage of the case base in a P2P mode. Second, we develop and evaluate an efficient approximated algorithm for the retrieval of the most similar cases over the above platform.

The rest of this paper is structured as follows. In Section *2* we present semantic approaches to P2P data management. In Section *3* we describe our case model and the UNSO distributed storage. In Section *4* we define the distance metric we have used in our evaluation, and we present the approximate case retrieval algorithm. Finally in Section *5* we present the results of the empirical evaluation, and we conclude in Section *6* summarizing the obtained results and mentioning future lines of research.

2 P2P and Semantic Data Management

Peer-to-Peer (P2P) computing refers to a subclass of distributed computing, where functionality is achieved in a decentralized way by using a set of distributed resources, such as computing power, data and network traffic. P2P systems usually lack a dedicated centralized infrastructure, but rather depend on the voluntary contribution of resources by the connected peers. Systems based on the P2P approach are usually characterized by one or more of the following advantages: cost sharing/reduction, improved scalability/reliability, resource aggregation and operability, increased autonomy, dynamism, and high levels of anonymity/privacy [9].

A number of content-addressable P2P systems for data sharing, such as CAN [12] and Pastry [13] were recently developed. These applications implement a highly scalable self-organizing infrastructure for fault-tolerant routing using distributed hash tables (DHT) [6]. In DHT-based systems users and resources are assigned unique identifiers (called *nodes* and *resources*, respectively) from a sparse space. As accepted in the P2P system, the resources are distributed and stored at the user-side, i.e, each user $node_i$ manages a set of resources $R_i=\{resource_1, resource_2, ..., resource_n\}$. The resources are inserted into the system through $put(user_i, resource_j)$ operation that uses globally-known hashing functions that assign $user_i$ as a provider of $resource_j$ by coupling their identifiers in the DHT. As such, DHT is also partitioned and stored distributively at the user-side. This setting facilitates further discovery of key_j's provider by other users through $get(key_j)$ operation exploiting the same global hashing mechanism.

DHT-based systems are highly scalable, and provide a robust, self-organizable, and completely decentralized structure. Due to an effective routing algorithm that routes the messages to the relevant peers only instead of expensive network flooding, their overall traffic is significantly lower [12,13]. However, DHT-based systems basically rely on hashing-based *put()* and *get()* operations. This results in two major limitations:

- Support for exact-matching lookups only. Similar, but not identical keys key_1 and key_2, will be treated as two diverse resources. Hence, just the searches, specifying the same term used at the insertion of a *key*, will succeed to locate it.
- Support for single-key lookups only. The above *put()* and *get()* primitives handle a single key only, i.e., a resource is described by a single string. Although the key might be represented as a concatenation of the substrings representing parts of the key, any minor change in one of them will prevent identifying the matching.

This has lead to the development of a more complex kind of P2P network, built upon peers using their own, not shared, schemas to describe the objects. This approach is further referred to as semantic or ontology-based data management. A key concept in semantic data management is ontology, i.e., a formal shared conceptualization of a particular domain of interest [5]. It acts as a standardized reference model, providing both human-understandable and machine-processable semantic mechanisms, allowing enterprises and application systems to collaborate efficiently. Techniques for ontology-based data management in P2P networks were initially proposed in HyperCup [14] and further extended in UNSO [1].

HyperCup [14] proposes a flexible ontology-based P2P platform generating a hypercube-like graph of users, where each user is treated as a data source. HyperCup needs predefined ontology of the domain, such that the dimensions of the hypercube match the concepts (features characterizing the domain) of the ontology. According to the above ontology, each user is categorized as the provider of particular data. This categorization determines the location of the user within the hypercube. Thus, the hypercube is virtually constructed of the connected users, whereas each user maintains a data structure of its respective neighbors. For example, in *3*-dimensional hypercube a node located in coordinates (x,y,z) will be connected to 6 neighbors: $(x+1,y,z)$, $(x-1,y, z)$, $(x,y+1,z)$, $(x,y-1,z)$, $(x,y,z+1)$ and $(x,y,z-1)$. The user providing data from a number of domains will maintain a set of hypercube locations, i.e., a separate data structure of neighbors for each location.

Due the fact that the ontology is predefined, and remains unchanged, data sources providing the same content are mapped to the same location. Moreover, if the possible values for ontology concepts (features) can be ordered a priori (as for instance in the feature "quality of the paper") then providers of similar contents are mapped to close locations. This implies causes the formation of so-called "concept clusters", which facilitate multiple-key search by efficient semantic routing of queries constructed as a logical combination of ontology concepts. However, such a setting where data providers share a single global ontology would require central management of the ontology, contradicting the decentralized spirit of a P2P network.

3 Case Representation and Storage in UNSO

UNSO (UNSpecified Ontology) [1] extends the above ideas by assuming that the domain ontology is not fully defined and that parts of it can be dynamically specified by the peers. The description of the resource is relatively free and is represented as an "unspecified" vector $<f_1:v_1, f_2:v_2,..., f_n:v_n>$, where f_i corresponds to a feature of the resource being described, and v_i to the value of the respective feature.

To manage pure distributive storage and retrieval of cases, we adopt the UNSO representation of a case as an unspecified vector. Hence, the cases are represented as a dynamic list of features and their respective values. Different domains may exploit different features or values to describe a case. For example, a medical case may contain features describing the patient and the disease, whereas, a weather forecasting case base could include various geographical and climatic features. Note that when operating in a pure decentralized environment without any form of central management and any predefined ontology, different data sources might represent cases from the same domain in different ways. As such, neither the set of features specified when describing a particular case, nor their respective values can be anticipated. Thus, the main target of UNSO is to manage ontologies that can grow and support updating in a fully distributive way.

In detail, the UNSO generalization of a regular notion of ontology is performed in the following manner:

- The ontological vector description can dynamically grow by allowing it to be formulated by the users as a list of pairs $feature_i{:}value_i$. Two hash functions are used to map the "unspecified" vector to its location in the hypercube: one maps the feature $feature_i$ to a dimension of the hypercube, while another maps the value $value_i$ to a coordinate value within that dimension. For example, consider a case describing E-Commerce advertisement: *<manufacturer:BMW | engine volume:3000 | year of production:1987>*. This is inserted into the hypercube by applying $hash_1$*(manufacturer)*, $hash_1$*(engine volume)*, and $hash_1$*(year of production)* to obtain the relevant dimensions of the hypercube, while $hash_2$*(BMW)*, $hash_2$*(3000)*

and *hash*$_2$*(1987)* will determine the coordinate values in the above dimensions. We note that using two hash functions allows the order of *feature*$_i$*:value*$_i$ pairs appearing in the case model to be ignored.

- The description can be organized in a "hierarchical" multi-layered structure (instead of a single "flat" vector), constructing a hypercube, the vertices of which recursively contain other hypercubes. This is regarded as a multi-layered hypercube (MLH). For example, a 2-layered ontology with three vectors *<manufacturer | color | year of production>* + *< engine volume | transmission | ABS>* with two possible values for each slot will generate a hypercube with *8* recursive nodes, containing "inner" hypercubes of up to *8* nodes. For example, if *ABS* feature might be present only in cars of production years *1970* and after, there is no sense in entering this dimension in the inner hypercubes of cars produced before *1970*. This would be compared to a fixed size *64*-nodes hypercube, had we used one flat vector for the whole ontological case model.

The conversion of a fixed specified ontology to the Unspecified Ontology is summarized in figure *1*. In the case of fixed ontology, a predefined set of features and values is mapped to a location in the underlying hypercube graph. Conversely in UNSO the number of *feature*$_i$*:value*$_i$ pairs in the description of a case is unlimited and their order is insignificant. Thus, UNSO dynamically generates a hypercube-like graph structure, where each vertex is recursively made of another hypercube. Note that the ontology of inner hypercubes is also dynamic and depends on the properties characterizing the cases which correspond to the location in the upper-level hypercube.

To address the problem that cases may have different terms with the same semantic meaning (synonyms), the *feature*$_i$ names are standardized using WordNet [3]. In WordNet, English nouns, verbs, adjectives and adverbs are organized into synonym sets, each representing one underlying lexical concept. For each concept, the set of synonyms can be sorted according to the frequency of usage. To eliminate possible ambiguity and improve the precision, the terms mentioned by the user in the description of a case undergo a simple semantic standardization, substituting the original terms with its most frequent synonyms. Thus, similar, but not identical terms specified by the user as *feature*$_i$ names, are replaced by a single 'representative' term.

As a negative effect of the hashing used in UNSO, the order relations on the stored resources are lost, since neither are the keys anticipated, nor do hashing primitives keep the distance relation. Despite this, UNSO supports the notion of concept clusters due to the fact that contents whose categorizations are identical with respect to a subset of ontology concepts are mapped to locations, whose coordinates have a common identical subset of coordinates. For example, two cases *<manufacturer:BMW | color:red | year of production:1987>* and *<manufacturer:BMW | color:green | year of production:1987>* will obviously be located closer than two arbitrary vectors, as two features (coordinates in UNSO) do overlap.

Thus, UNSO provides a hypercube-based dynamic infrastructure for distributed and fully decentralized management of the case base. The cases, modeled as unspecified ontological vectors, are organized in the hypercube in such a way that similar cases are located in close locations, thus facilitating efficient answering of semantic queries. Moreover, the connectivity maintenance protocols developed in [14] keep the hypercube stable despite sporadic joinings and departures of cases.

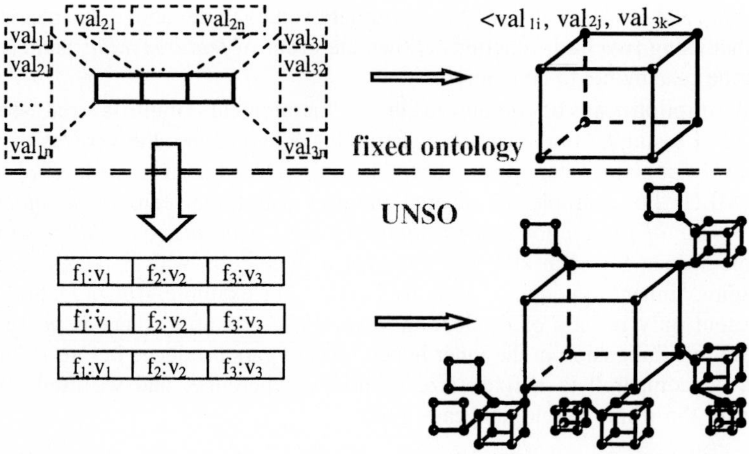

Fig. 1. Generalization of the Fixed Ontology to the Unspecified Ontology

In this paper we consider a case base that stores E-Commerce advertisements (in short, ads). Ads can be divided to two categories: supply ads where users offer products or services in exchange for payment, and demand ads where users seek products or services provided by other users. The system is required to provide a matching functionality between appropriate demand and supply ads. In a decentralized setting, where the users do not use any predefined forms when inserting demand and supply ads into the system, matching functionality is harder to achieve, as the system should be capable of finding the relevant ads basing on possibly partial and incomplete descriptions of the items.

In CBR terms, the case base is a collection of supply ads, stored in a distributed manner and containing a set of descriptions of the products the users are interested in selling. Each case (ad) is formulated as a list of <*$feature_i$:$value_i$*> pairs, while neither properties nor values being known a priori. Hence, the descriptions of demand ads might be incomplete in comparison to the existing supply ads. The demand ad serves as a problem to be solved, whereas the supply ads in the case base provide possible solutions. Since the main target is providing matching functionality, the system should implement the search of the most-similar supply ads, i.e., cases. In the next section we shall describe the similarity metrics on possibly incomplete cases, and the retrieval algorithm.

4 Case Similarity and Retrieval

Retrieving the most-similar cases is one of the primary goals of a CBR system. The more accurate and efficient the similarity assessment, the more quickly the system will indicate the most useful cases. Two policies for case retrieval are typically implemented:

- Retrieve a set of K most-similar cases - calculates the similarity for each target case, ranks the cases according to their similarities and returns K highest cases from the ranked list.
- Retrieve a set of cases whose similarity is above a given threshold β - calculates the similarity for each target case and returns the case if the similarity is higher than β.

Each of the above-mentioned policies requires that the similarity function to be explicitly defined. In this paper we compute the similarity of two cases c_1 and c_2 as $1\text{-}dist(c_1,c_2)$, where *dist* is a distance metrics. When cases are represented as a list of <*feature$_i$:value$_i$*> pairs, in order to compute the distance between the cases, we consider each feature separately. Hence, for the homogeneous cases (all the cases contain the same set of features), and assuming a linear dependency between the features and the distance, the distance metrics $dist(c_1, c_2)$ is defined by:

$$dist(c_1,c_2)=\sum_{i=1}^{|d|} w_i \cdot dist(c_1^i,c_2^i),$$

where d denotes the set of features specified in the cases, w_i is the normalized ($\Sigma w_i=1$) relative weight of the feature f_i, and $dist(c_1^i,c_2^i)$ is the local distance metrics between c_1 and c_2 with respect to the same feature f_i.

To compute the local distance between the values of two features we consider the possible types of values [2]. For Boolean values (true or false), the distance is a trivial comparison between two values, giving 0 if the two values are equal or 1 otherwise. For numeric features, the distance is the difference between them normalized by dividing it by the maximal possible difference (range). Moreover, the distance between two locations in a tree-like taxonomy is defined as the shortest path distance between the two nodes on the tree.

For symbolic or free-language values the distance can be computed as the difference between the numeric representations of the values. Although in particular domains the translation between symbolic and numeric values can be performed manually by a human expert, it is not clear whether it is feasible in any domain, especially if the features are not anticipated by the system. As the current work focuses on distributed retrieval of similar cases, feature distance metric for symbolic and free-language values is defined similarly as for the Boolean features, by:

$$dist(c_1^i,c_2^i) = \begin{cases} 0 & c_1^i = c_2^i \\ 1 & \text{otherwise} \end{cases}$$

Note that both k-nearest neighbor and above threshold retrieval techniques require that the case to be solved be compared with the whole set of the cases in the case base. Given a case base containing descriptions of N cases, the number of case distance computations needed for these retrievals is $O(N)$. More efficient multidimensional retrieval techniques, such as those based on K-d trees [4], were proposed in [15]. K-d tree uses a multi-dimensional tree for management and retrieval of cases. This technique requires $O(N \log N)$ to build the tree and $O(\log N)$ to retrieve the most-similar case (for $N>>2^d$). However, these techniques are applicable when cases are described only with numeric features and they do not resolve the issue of cases with symbolic or free-language feature values. Moreover, it is not obvious how this algorithm could be implemented in a distributed environment, as that described here, where case feature values are retrieved exploiting node-to-node communication.

As we noted above, in a P2P environment with no predefined ontology, users can describe their cases in a relatively free form, hence cases will differ in terms of mentioned features. Therefore, we define a distance metrics for cases with an arbitrary set of features. But, since we are interested in retrieving similar cases (certainly, from the same domain), we can assume that there will be a set of overlapping features that are mentioned both in c_1 and c_2. Thus, we modify the distance function to compute the distance between two cases c_1 and c_2 exploiting only the set of overlapping features:

$$dist'(c_1, c_2) = \sum_{i=1}^{|d'|} w_i \cdot dist(c_1^i, c_2^i),$$

where d' denotes the set of overlapping features, w_i is their normalized relative weight, and $dist(c_1^i, c_2^i)$ is the local distance metrics between the features. We note that similarity ranges between *0* and *1* since also the distance is normalized.

We have exploited the P2P infrastructure of UNSO and the implicit clustering of similar cases for improving the efficiency of case retrieval. Figure *2* presents the pseudo-code of the algorithm we propose for the retrieval of cases whose similarity with the case to be solved is above a threshold β.

Initially, the algorithm determines the location of the case to be solved using a hashing mechanism similar to that used while inserting cases into the hypercube (steps *1-3*). Two functions are used to map the case. The first determines the dimensions of the hypercube and the second the coordinate values within the dimensions. Then the algorithm analyzes the cases stored in adjacent locations by assessing the similarity between each candidate case and the case to be solved (steps *4-7*). The rationale is that in UNSO similar cases are located in close vicinity and therefore to find similar cases we can check only a small portion of the case base. In other words UNSO provides an implicit indexing of the case base. The similarity between each one of the cases and the case to be solved is calculated using the distance metrics discussed above. If the similarity value is higher than the threshold β, then the retrieved case is added to the set of cases with required similarity (steps *8-9*). Finally, the whole set of appropriate cases is returned (step *10*).

For example, consider the following representation of a case to be solved c_s=*<manufacturer:Ford | doors:2 | color:red>* and a flat 3-dimensional hypercube. Assume that the case c_s is mapped to a location *(2,3,4)* in the hypercube. Then the search will compare the c_s with the cases located at *(*,3,4)*, *(2,*,4)*, and *(2,3,*)*, where * denotes any possible value in the respective dimension. In simple words, c_s will be compared against all the cases describing either *2*-door red cars, or red Fords, or *2*-door Fords.

The search for top-*K* similar users is performed in a similar manner; however, the length of the set of *retrieved_cases* is limited to *K* and every appropriate case is added to *retrieved_cases* in such a way that the whole set remains sorted.

```
Retrieve (target_case, β)
(1)  map target_case to the hypercube of dimension n
(2)  assume the location of target_case is (c_1,…,c_n)
(3)  let retrieved_cases be a set of cases, initially empty
(4)  for i=1 to n
(5)  for each possible value x of the i^th coordinate
(6)    let current be the set of cases stored in
       the location (c_1,…,c_{i-1},x,c_{i+1},…,c_n)
(7)     for each test_case∈ current
(8)     if sim(target_case, test_case) > β
(9)       retrieved_cases = retrieved_cases ∪ test_case
(10) return retrieved_cases
```

Fig. 2. Algorithm for retrieving cases with similarity metrics above β

Note that the above algorithm will compute an approximated solution since it checks only cases with one modified feature with respect to the original case to be solved. Intuitively, this is motivated by the fact that the higher number of modified features will be reflected in a lower similarity. Thus, the probability of discovering a similar case decreases with the number of modified features. However, in sparse case bases, or for the retrieval of the *K* most-similar cases (for large *K*), it might be necessary to search cases with more modified features. In order to adapt the algorithm to this constraint, the loop in step *4* is replaced by a nested loop that will retrieve cases from locations with a higher number of modified coordinates.

For the sake of simplicity, the above algorithm discusses the retrieval of similar cases over a flat hypercube. Converting a flat hypercube to MLH will have a minor impact on the retrieval process. The search for modified coordinates will partially take place in another hypercubes. For example, for *2*-leveled *3*-dimensional cubes $<f_1:v_1, f_2:v_2, f_3:v_3>+<f_4:v_4, f_5:v_5, f_6:v_6>$ the searches for the modified values of f_4, f_5, and f_6 will take place in the current secondary-level hypercube, while the searches for f_1, f_2, and f_3 will require cases stored in another secondary hypercubes (siblings of the current hypercube) to be accessed.

As already noted above, the number of comparisons in a naïve retrieval algorithm is $O(N)$, where N is the number of cases in the case base. Intuitively, the complexity of UNSO-based retrieval is significantly lower, as the case to be solved is compared with only a subset of the cases in the case base. The complexity of the above algorithm is $O(nk)$, where n is the dimension of the hypercube, and k is the maximal number of values for each dimension. Insertion of a case into the hypercube will require routing it to its proper location and connecting it to the neighbors in $O(nk)$ steps. Thus, total computational complexity of managing and retrieving cases in UNSO-based structure is lower than the complexity of naïve exhaustive retrieval for a sufficiently large case base.

Moreover, in this setting the retrieval stage is parallelized and the required computational effort is decreased, as the similarity of cases might be computed in parallel in each node (i.e., processed by the user managing a particular node of the hypercube). To implement this, the query with the description of the case to be solved is sent in parallel over all the dimensions. Upon receiving a query, each node forwards the query to the next neighbor in a pipeline manner and initiates local computations. Upon discovering cases with the required similarity, nodes asynchronously send them back to the neighbor from which the query was received.

In summary, the semantic mechanism of Unspecified Ontology facilitates maintaining the case base as a distributed hypercube-like graph with a stable structure. The proposed approximated algorithm allows efficient retrieval of the most similar cases that spreads the required computational effort among the users comprising the hypercube.

5 Experimental Results

To validate the proposed retrieval algorithm, five corpuses of real-life E-Commerce ads from different domains were collected from *http://www.recycler.com* Web-site (*61* refrigerator ads with *10* different features mentioned, *65* camera ads with *13* different features, *76* television ads with *11* different features, *94* printer ads with *11* different features, and *130* mobile phone ads with *9* different features), giving in total *426* ads. Most of the ads contain three to four features. Before inserting the ads into the system, each ad was manually converted to the form of an ontological vector. For example, an ad "Philips 50FD995 50" plasma television, new in box, $4800" was converted to the following ontological description: *<price:4800, manufacturer:Philips, model:50FD995, size:50, screen:plasma, condition:new>*. The conversions were done keeping as close as possible to the original contents of the ads to mimic the insertions by naïve users.

The above UNSO-based model for storage and retrieval of cases was implemented. The number of dimensions in the hypercubes was not limited, i.e., it was equal to the number of different features mentioned by the users in their ads. The cardinality of cube dimensions (the range of coordinates in each dimension) was chosen to be *7*. Version *2.0* of WordNet was used during the insertions of ads to standardize the names of the features and to decrease the semantic ambiguity.

5.1 Retrieval Capabilities

In this experiment we retrieved the cases from the hypercube in two ways. Initially we retrieved the set R_e of the most similar cases using a regular CBR approach. This approach exhaustively compares the case to be solved with each one of the cases stored in the case base and retrieves only those cases whose similarity is above a given threshold β. Then we retrieved the set of the most-similar cases R_u using the above retrieval algorithm over the UNSO hypercube. The efficiency of our approach was quantified by dividing the cardinality of the set retrieved using the UNSO retrieval method by the cardinality of the set retrieved by the exhaustive search. As R_e is the true set of cases with the required similarity, this metrics is notated as the recall of the retrieval.

$$recall = \frac{|R_u|}{|R_e|}$$

Recall values are always less than *1* because the set of cases checked by the approximate retrieval algorithm is a subset of the whole case base; hence we can only miss some case that could be in the exact retrieval set.

Figure *3* shows the measurements of the recall as a function of the similarity threshold β and the maximal allowed number of modified features Δ (i.e., the number of nested loops in step *4* of the algorithm). The experiments were conducted on the corpus of *94* printer ads. In each execution a single case to be solved was chosen, and the total recall was computed as an average of recall values for each chosen case (the number of executions is equal to the size of the corpus).

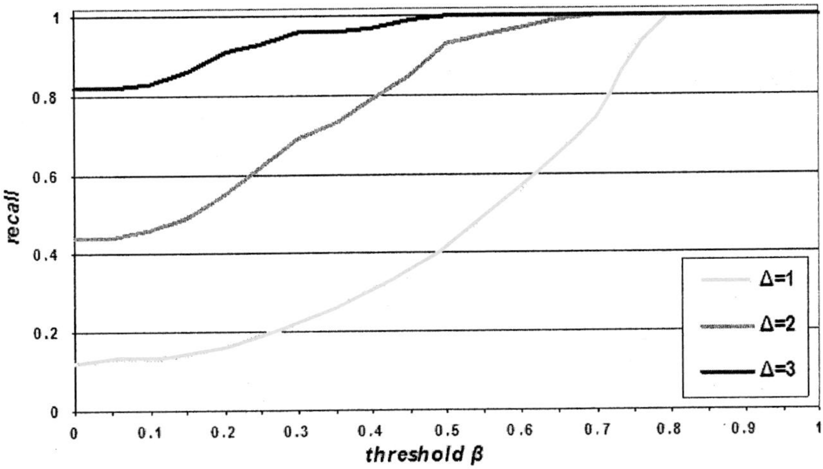

Fig. 3. Recall of the retrieval vs. similarity threshold β for different values of Δ

The results show that for high values of β (similarity close to 1) the recall converges to *1*, i.e., the cardinalities of both sets tend to be equal. This means that for high values of β (for retrieval of relatively similar cases) the set of cases retrieved using the UNSO approach is roughly equal to the set of cases retrieved by the traditional exhaustive approach. For low values of β the recall is low; however, this search might retrieve many cases with low similarity, that are inapplicable in the further adaptation stage of the CBR process. Increasing the value of Δ increases the number of pairs of cases that are compared. Thus, for higher values of Δ the recall converges more quickly and optimal recall is obtained even for relatively low values of β.

The same observation is true also for the other domains. The recall increases with β and the curve converges more quickly to *1* with the increase in Δ. Figure *4* shows the recall for different domains as a function of β for Δ=*2*. Certainly, the origin of the different behavior of the curves is in the different types of data in the domains. For example, recall might be influenced by the number of different features in the ads, their density and so forth. Elaborate analysis of the data is beyond the scope of this work.

A similar behavior could be observed when comparing the results of both retrieval approaches for top-K retrieval. R_e denotes the set of cases retrieved by exhaustive CBR search, and R_u the set of cases retrieved using UNSO. We gradually increase K – the number of cases to be retrieved. The goal of the experiment was to measure the

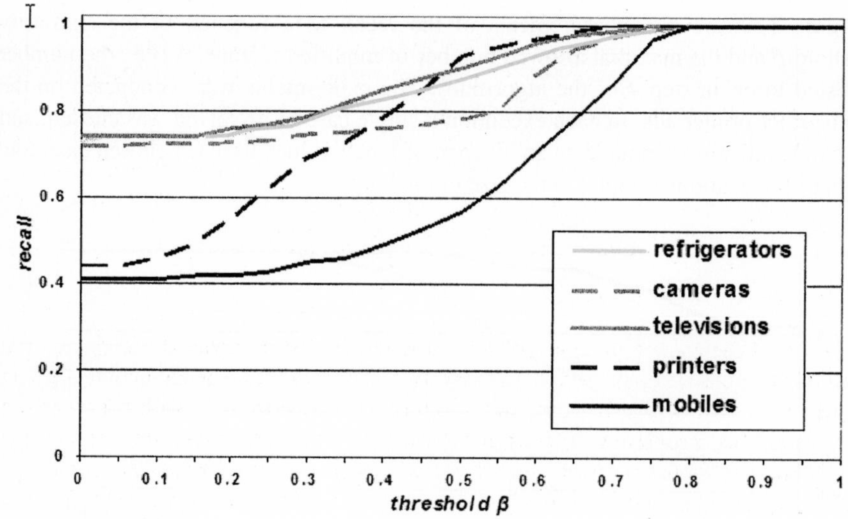

Fig. 4. Recall of the retrieval vs. similarity threshold β for different domains of cases (Δ=2)

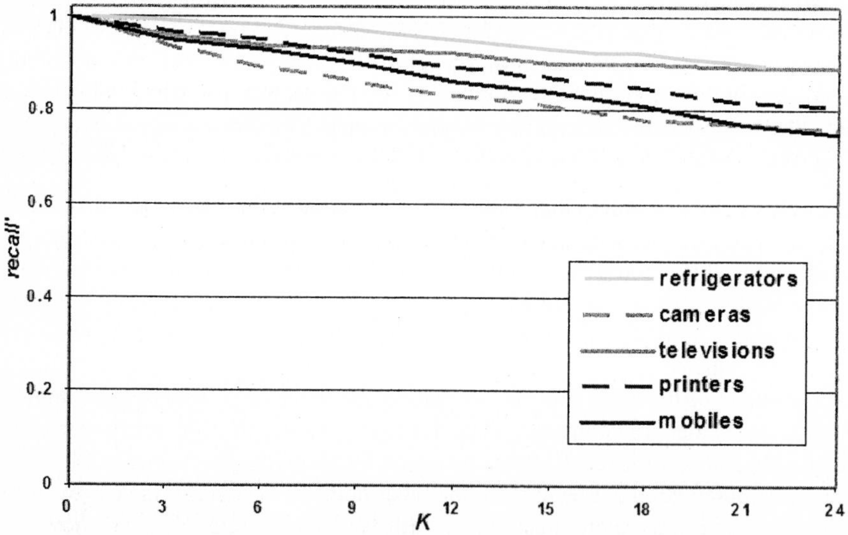

Fig. 5. Recall of top-*K* retrieval vs. *K* for different domains of cases

quality of UNSO retrieval, i.e., to verify that the cases retrieved using UNSO really belong to the set of *K* most-similar cases. We modified the recall metrics to be

$$recall' = \frac{|R_u \cap R_e|}{|R_e|}$$

Figure *5* shows the results of *recall'* measurements for different domain as a function of *K,* with Δ=*2*. It can be seen that for low values of *K* (retrieval of highly similar cases only) there is a high correlation between the set retrieved using UNSO and the real set of *K* most-similar cases found by the exhaustive search. For higher values of *K* (and lower threshold of similarity), *recall'* decreases, as R_e contains fewer similar cases that might not be retrieved using UNSO. Note that for high values of *K* (not illustrated in the figure) *recall'* rises and finally will converge to *1* for *K* equal to the size of the case base. Thus, in the experiment *K* was limited to *24*.

5.2 Computational Optimization

The result of the approximation applied in the UNSO-based retrieval is a decrease in the number of cases compared during the retrieval process. The needed computational effort is reduced because the case to be solved is compared only with cases with at most Δ modified properties, instead of with the whole set of cases stored in the case base. Moreover, as the cases are stored distributively, the comparisons are performed at the user-side, thus not involving central processing. This resolves a possible computational bottleneck of central processing and allows additional spreading of the computational effort.

In this experiment we performed over the threshold retrieval and compared the number of evaluated pairs of cases for both exhaustive and UNSO-based retrieval. In each execution a single case to be solved was chosen, and the total number of compared cases was calculated as an average of the number of comparisons for each chosen case. In this experiment the number of executions was also equal to the size of the relevant corpus.

Figure *6* shows the average number of comparisons in a single UNSO-based retrieval as a function of Δ (the first triplet of bars in each quadruplet), and compares it with the average number of comparisons in the exhaustive retrieval (the fourth bar). The experiments were performed for all the available domains of cases.

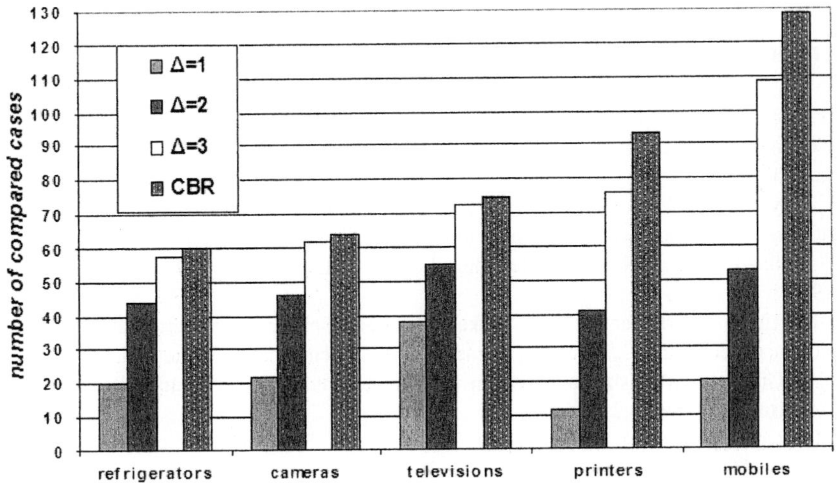

Fig. 6. Average number of comparisons vs. Δ for different domains of cases

The results clearly show that, although in every domain the number of comparisons increases with Δ, even for $\Delta=3$ it is still lower than in the regular exhaustive retrieval. The ratio of the number of comparisons in UNSO-based retrieval divided by the number of comparisons in the exhaustive search varies as a function of the domain. We hypothesize that this factor depends heavily on the characteristics of data in the domain (density, number of mentioned features and so forth).

6 Conclusions and Future Research

In this paper we presented a novel approach to P2P storage of cases using a hypercube-like graph built using UNSpecified Ontology (UNSO). This facilitates the use of an approximated search algorithm for similar cases retrieval.

The experiments showed that the approximated search succeeds in retrieving the most-similar cases. The results are pleasing both for *K*-nearest neighbor and threshold retrieval techniques. The sets of cases retrieved by the exhaustive technique and UNSO tend to be equal for low values of *K* or high thresholds, while the number of comparisons is significantly lower compared to the traditional exhaustive search.

We plan to extend our work by using a more precise distance metrics that computes similarity of heterogeneous cases using different sets of features, takes into account the relative size of the matched case with respect to the total case, and handles local similarity distance for the values of symbolic or free-language features. We are also interested in exploiting different learning algorithms for determining the relevance metrics for the features and identifying their weights w_i.

Moreover, we plan to investigate the influence of different domains and different types of data (for example, the density of the ads in the hypercube, the average number of features used in the ads, the total dimension of the hypercube, and so forth) on the performance of the approximated algorithm. We also plan to conduct large-scale experiments with real-life case bases containing a high number of cases.

References

1. Y. Ben-Asher, S. Berkovsky, "UNSO: Unspecified Ontologies for Peer-to-Peer E-Commerce Applications", In Proc. of the International Conference on Informatics, Turkey, 2004.
2. L. Coyle, D. Doyle, P. Cunningham, "Representing Similarity for CBR in XML", In Proc. of European Conference on Advances in Case-Based Reasoning, Spain, 2004.
3. C. Fellbaum, "WordNet - An Electronic Lexical Database", The MIT Press Publishers, 1998.
4. J.H. Friedman, J.H. Bentley, R.A. Finkel, "An algorithm for finding best matches in logarithmic expected time", in ACM Transactions in Mathematical Software, vol.3(3), 1977.
5. T.R. Gruber, "A translation approach to portable ontology specifications", Knowledge Acquisition Journal, 6(2), pp. 199–221, 1993.
6. M. Harren, J.M. Hellerstein, R. Huebsch, B.T. Loo, S. Shenker, I. Stoica, "Complex queries in DHT-based Peer-to-Peer networks", In Proc. of the International Workshop on Peer-to-Peer Systems (IPTPS'02), MA, 2002.

7. D.B. Leake, R. Sooriamurthi. "When Two Case Bases are Better then One: Exploiting Multiple Case Bases". In Proc. of International Conference on Case-Based Reasoning, Canada, 2001.
8. L. McGinty, B. Smyth. "Collaborative Case-Based Reasoning: Applications in Personalised Route Planning", In Proceedings of International Conference on Case-Based Reasoning, Canada, 2001.
9. D.S. Milojicic, V. Kalogeraki, R. Lukose, K. Nagaraja, J. Pruyne, B. Richard, S. Rollins, Z. Xu, "Peer-to-Peer Computing", Technical Report HPL-2002-57, HP Labs, 2002.
10. M.V. Nagendra Prasad, V. Lesser, S. Lander, "Retrieval and Reasoning in Distributed Case Bases", in Journal of Visual Communication and Image Representation, Special Issue on Digital Libraries, vol.7(1), 1996.
11. E. Plaza, J.L. Arcos, F. Martin, "Cooperative Case-Based Reasoning, In Proc. of the Workshop Distributed Artificial Intelligence Meets Machine Learning, Hungary, 1996.
12. S. Ratnasamy, P. Francis, M. Handley, R. Karp, S. Shenker, "A Scalable Content-Addressable Network", In Proc. of ACM SIGCOMM, CA, 2001.
13. A. Rowstron, P. Druschel, "Pastry: Scalable, distributed object location and routing for large-scale Peer-to-Peer systems", In Proc. of International Conference on Distributed Systems Platforms (Middleware), Germany, 2001.
14. M. Schlosser, M. Sintek, S. Decker, W. Nejdl, "A scalable and ontology-based P2P infrastructure for semantic Web services", In proc. of IEEE International Conference on Peer-to-Peer Computing, Sweden, 2002.
15. S. Wess, K-D. Althoff, G. Derwand, "Using K-d Trees to Improve the Retrieval Step in Case-Based Reasoning", In Proc. of European Workshop on Case-Based Reasoning, Germany, 1993.

Autonomous Internal Control System for Small to Medium Firms

M. Lourdes Borrajo[1], Juan M. Corchado[2], J. Carlos Yáñez[3], Florentino Fdez-Riverola[1], and Fernando Díaz[4]

[1] Dept. Informática, University of Vigo, Escuela Superior de Ingeniería Informática, Edificio Politécnico, Campus Universitario As Lagoas s/n, 32004 Ourense, Spain
{lborrajo, riverola}@uvigo.es
[2] Departamento de Informática y Automática, University of Salamanca, Plaza de la Merced s/n, 37008 Salamanca, Spain
corchado@usal.es
[3] Department of Financial Accounting, University of Vigo, Campus as Lagoas, s/n, 32004 Ourense, Spain
jcyanez@uvigo.es
[4] Dept. Informática, University of Valladolid, Escuela Universitaria de Informática, Plaza Santa Eulalia, 9-11, 40005 Segovia, Spain
fdiaz@infor.uva.es

Abstract. Small to medium enterprises require an internal control mechanism in order to monitor their modus operandi and to analyse whether they are achieving their goals. A tool for the decision support process has been developed based on a case-based reasoning system that automates the internal control process. The objective of the system is to facilitate the process of internal auditing. The system analyses the data that characterises each one of the activities carried out by the firm, then determines the state of each activity, calculates the associated risk, detects the erroneous processes, and generates recommendations to improve these processes. The developed model is composed of two case-based reasoning systems. One is used to identify the activities that may be improved and the other to determine how the activities could be improved. Each of the two subsystems uses a different problem solving method in each of the steps of the reasoning cycle. The system has been tested in 22 small and medium companies in the textile sector, located in the northwest of Spain during the last 29 months and the results obtained have been very encouraging.

1 Introduction

Small to medium enterprises require an internal control mechanism in order to monitor their modus operandi and to analyse whether they are achieving their goals. Such mechanisms are constructed around series of organizational policies and specific procedures dedicated to giving reasonable guarantees to their executive bodies. This

H. Muñoz-Avila and F. Ricci (Eds.): ICCBR 2005, LNAI 3620, pp. 106 – 121, 2005.

group of policies and procedures are named "controls", and they all conform to the structure of internal control of the company. As a consequence of this, the need for periodic internal audits has arisen. Nevertheless the evaluation and the prediction of the evolution of these types of systems, characterized by their great dynamism, are, in general, complicated. It is necessary to construct models that facilitate the analysis of work carried out in changing environments, such as finance.

The processes carried out inside a firm are grouped in functional areas [7] denominated "Functions". A Function is a group of coordinated and related activities, which are necessary to reach the objectives of the firm and are carried out in a systematic and iterative way [14]. The functions that are usually carried out within a firm are: Purchases, Cash Management, Sales, Information Technology, Fixed Assets Management, Compliance to Legal Norms and Human Resources. In turn, each one of these functions is broken down into a series of activities. For example, the function Information Technology is divided in the following activities: Computer Plan Development, Study of Systems, Installation of Systems, Treatment of Information Flows and Security Management.

Each activity is composed of a number of tasks. For example, the activity Computer Plan Development, belonging to the function Information Technology, can be divided in the following tasks:

1. Definition of the required investment in technology in the short and medium time.
2. Coordination of the technology investment plan and the development plan of the company.
3. Periodic evaluation of the established priorities on the technology investment plan to identify their relevance.
4. Definition of a working group focused in the identification and control of the information technology policy.
5. Definition of a communication protocol, in both directions: bottom-up and top-down, to involve the firm employees in the maintenance strategic plan.

Control procedures have also to be established in the tasks to ensure that the established objectives are achieved.

The developed system is composed of two fundamental subsystems [5]:

- Subsystem ISA (Identification of the State of the Activity) whose objectives are: to identify the state or situation of each one of activities of the company and to calculate the risk associated with this state.
- Subsystem GR (Generation of Recommendations), whose goal is to generate recommendations to reduce the number of inconsistent processes in the firm.

Both subsystems are implemented using a case-based reasoning (CBR) system [1, 12, 17, 13]. The CBR system associated with each subsystem uses different problem solving techniques and shares the same case memory [11, 15].

The rest of this article is structured as follows: first, the proposed CBR based model is presented. Then, its results are evaluated. Finally the conclusions are presented.

2 Neuro-symbolic System for Internal Control

This section describes the internal control system in detail. Although the aim is to develop a generic model useful in any type of small to medium enterprise, the initial work has focused in the textile sector to facilitate the research and its evaluation. The model here presented may be extended or adapted for other sectors. Twenty two companies from the North-west of Spain have collaborated in this research, working mainly for the Spanish market. The companies have different levels of automation and all of them were very interested in a tool such as the one developed in the framework of this investigation. After analyzing the data relative to the activities developed within a given firm, the constructed system is able to determine the state of each of the activities and calculate the associated risk. It also detects any erroneous processes and generates recommendations for improving these processes. As shown below the problem solving mechanism developed takes its decision using the help of a couple of CBR systems whose memory has been fed with cases constructed with information provided by the firm and with prototypical cases identified by 34 internal control experts who have collaborated and supervised the model developed.

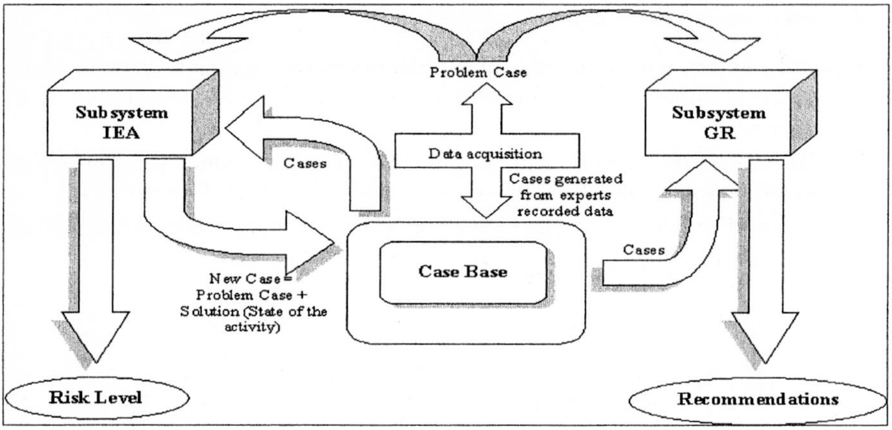

Fig. 1. System reasoning process

The cycle of operations of the developed case based reasoning system is based on the classic life cycle of a CBR system [1, 18]. This cycle is executed twice, since the system bases its operation on two CBR subsystems (subsystem ISA-Identification of the State of the Activity and subsystem GR-Generation of Recommendations), as can be seen in Figure 1. Both subsystems share the same case base (Table 1 shows the attributes of a case) and a case represents the "shape" of a given activity developed in the company.

Every time that it is necessary to obtain a new estimate of the state of an activity, the hybrid system evolves through several phases. This evolution allows the system, on the one hand, (i) to identify the latest situations most similar to the current situation, (ii) to adapt the current knowledge to generate an initial estimate of the risk of the activity being analysed, and on the other hand, (iii) to identify old situations that serve as a basis to detect the erroneous processes developed within the activity and (iv) to select the best of all possible activities. The activity selected will then serve as a guide for the establishment of a set of recommendations that allow the activity, its function and the company itself to develop in a more positive way. The retention phase guarantees that the system evolves in parallel with the firm, basing the corrective actions on the calculation of the error made previously. The following sections describe the different phases of the proposed model.

2.1 Data Acquisition

The data used to construct the model were obtained from a set of surveys:

1. External auditors' surveys. Through the results of the surveys, each one of the functions and activities of a firm is assigned a level importance. This information allows the system to calculate the control risk associated with an activity. Also, it allows the system to prioritise the recommendations for improving the business processes. This data is stored in the system database.
2. Experts' surveys on the different functional areas. The second type of survey was carried out among several experts in the different functional areas of various firms. This type of survey attempts to reflect the experience of the experts in their different fields. For each activity, the survey presents two possible situations: the first one tries to reflect the situation of an activity with an incorrect activity state and the second one tries to reflect the situation of an activity with a satisfactory activity state. Both situations will be valued by the expert using a percentage. The data acquired by the surveys have been used to build the prototype cases for the initial case base.

Table 1 shows the case structure that constitutes the case base.

Table 1. Case structure

PROBLEM						SOLUTION
Case number	Input vector	Function number	Activity number	Reliability	Degree of membership	Activity State

Each case is composed of the following attributes:

- *Case number:* Unique identification: positive integer number.
- *Input vector:* Information about the tasks (n sub-vectors) that constitute an industrial activity: $((IR_1,V_1),(IR_2,V_2),\ldots,(IR_n,V_n))$ for n tasks. Each task sub-vector has the following structure (GI_i,V_i):
  - IR_i: importance rate for this task within the activity. It can only take one of the following values: VHI (Very high importance), HI (High Importance), AI (Average Importance), LI (Low Importance), VLI (Very low importance)
  - V_i: Value of the realization state of a given task: a positive integer number (between 1 and 10).

- *Function number:* Unique identification number for each function
- *Activity number:* Unique identification number for each activity
- *Reliability:* Percentage of probability of success. It represents the percentage of success obtained using the case as a reference to generate recommendations.
- *Degree of membership:* ((n_1 ,μ_1), (n_2, μ_2), …, (n_k, μ_k))
  - n_i: represents the i^{st} cluster
  - μ_i: represents the membership value of the case to the cluster n_i
- *Activity State*: degree of perfection of the development of the activity, expressed by percentage.

2.2 Subsystem ISA (Identification of the State of the Activity)

The subsystem ISA (Identification of the State of the Activity) identifies the state or situation of each of the firm's activities and calculates the risk associated with this situation. The system uses the data for the activity, introduced by the firm's internal auditor, to construct the problem case. For each task making up the activity analyzed, the problem case is composed of the value of the realization state for that task, and its level of importance within the activity (according to the internal auditor).

In this way, a problem case for an activity of *n* tasks, will be composed of a vector such as: ((IR_1,V_1),(IR_2,V_2),...,(IR_n,V_n)) where:

- IR_i: importance rate for this task within the activity. It can only take one of the following values: VHI (Very high importance), HI (High Importance), AI (Average Importance), LI (Low Importance), VLI (Very low importance).
- V_i: Value of the realization state of a given task. It is a positive integer number (between 1 and 10).

2.2.1 Retrieval Phase

This phase has as its objective the retrieval of K cases – the most similar cases to the problem case. This is carried out by means of a technique of cluster-based similarity.

Using the fuzzy C-means method [3,4], the most similar cases belonging to the case base are grouped together. With this clustering method, *n* clusters are obtained, each of them containing cases exclusively from the case base. Each case will have associated a degree of membership for each cluster, expressed by a percentage. A representative case or centre is identified for each cluster.

The object of the following step is to identify the cluster containing the cases nearest to the problem case in order to reduce the size of the problem space. Thus, the problem case is compared with the centre of each cluster. The cluster selected will be the one whose centre is located closest to the problem case. The distance between the problem case and the cluster centres was calculated using the Mahalanobis:

$$d_M\left(x_i, x_j\right) = \left(x_i - x_j\right)\sum^{-1}(x_i - x_j)^T \tag{1}$$

Since a precise estimate, provided by the system, is necessary, only those cases with a high degree of membership to the cluster and a high reliability will be retrieved. The reliability indicates the percentage of probability of success using this case in the process of generating recommendations. In our system, only those K cases with a degree of membership to the cluster greater than 65% and with a reliability higher than 50% will be retrieved. These two percentages have been established by the auditors interviewed.

Figure 2 shows the pseudocode for this retrieval phase. X represents the set of cases that introduces the knowledge about an activity, v_p represents the vector of characteristics (attributes) that describes a new problem, *n_cluster* represents the amount of clusters that the system is looking forward to obtaining (in this case *n_cluster*=3 has been chosen), *max_iter* represents the highest number of iterations of the algorithm and it has been initialized at 100, P represents the set of centres of the *n_cluster* clusters, U is the matrix of memberships, u_{mi} represents the degree of membership of the case i to the cluster m whose center is c_m and K is the set of retrieved cases.

```
procedure retrieve_ISA (input: X,vp, n_cluster, max_iter; output: K)
{
    begin
        calculate_fuzzy_clusters: (P,U) ← FCM(X, n_cluster, max_iter)
        for each center c ∈ P do
            calculate_distance: dc ← DIS(vp, vc)
            assign_couple_center_distance: CD ← (c,dc)
        obtain_nearest_center: cm ← min (CD)
        for each case i ∈ X do
            if umi > 0.65 then
                if reliability(i) > 0.5 then
                    K ← K + i
    end.
}
```

Fig. 2. Pseudocode of the retrieval phase of the subsystem ISA (Identification of the State of the Activity)

Fuzzy clustering techniques are used because of the size of the database and the need to group the most similar cases together in order to help retrieve the cases that most resemble the given problem.

Fuzzy clustering techniques are especially interesting for non-linear or ill-defined problems, making it possible to treat tasks involved in the processing of massive quantities of redundant or imprecise information. It allows the available data to be grouped into clusters with fuzzy boundaries, expressing uncertain knowledge.

2.2.2 Re-use Phase

This phase aims to obtain an initial estimation of the state of the activity analysed. In order to obtain this estimation, RBF networks are used [9, 6, 8]. As in the previous stage, the number of attributes of the problem case depends on the activity analyzed. Therefore it is necessary to establish an RBF network system, one for each of the activities to be analysed.

When the new problem case is presented, the cluster whose centre is closest to the case is identified and a set of K cases is retrieved from the system. These cases are used by the RBF network as a training group that allows it to adapt its configuration to the new problem encountered before generating the initial estimation.

The topology of each of the RBF networks used in this task consists of: an input layer with as many neurons as attributes possessed by the input vector which constitutes the problem descriptor $((IR_1,V_1),(IR_2,V_2),...,(IR_n,V_n))$, a hidden layer with 50 centres, and an output layer with a single neuron corresponding to the variable to be estimated (correction level or state of activity analysed in x percent).

Figure 3 shows the pseudocode of the algorithm that roughly illustrates the steps that need to be followed in order to obtain an initial estimate, using the *K* cases retrieved in the previous phase and the descriptor of the problem for which an estimate needs to be made. In the algorithm, v_p represents the vector of characteristics (attributes) that form the problem case, *K* is the group of most relevant retrieved cases, *confRBF* is the group of neurons that make up the topology of the RBF network and s_i represents the initial solution generated for the current problem.

```
procedure reuse_ISA (input: vp, K, confRBF; output: si)
{
  begin.
   while TRUE do /* infinite loop */
        for each case c ∈ K do /* network adaptation using K cases */
             retrain_network: error ← annRBF(c)
             move_centers: annRBF.moveCenters(c)
             modify_weights: annRBF.learn(c) /* delta rule */
        if (error / |K|) < error_threshold then
             go_to_line 8 /* end of infinite loop and adaptation */
   generate_initial_solution: si ← annRBF(vp)
  end.
}
```

Fig. 3. Pseudocode of the reuse phase of the ISA (Identification of the State of the Activity) subsystem

The RBF network is characterized by its ability to adapt, to learn rapidly, and to generalize (especially in interpolation tasks). Specifically, within this system the network acts as a mechanism capable of absorbing knowledge about a certain number of cases and generalizing from them. During this process, the RBF network, interpolates and carries out predictions without forgetting part of those already carried out. The system's memory acts as a permanent memory capable of maintaining many cases or experiences while the RBF network acts as a short term memory, able to recognize recently learnt patterns and to generalize from them.

2.2.3 Revision Phase

The objective of the revision phase is to confirm or refute the initial solution proposed by the RBF network, thereby obtaining a final solution and calculating the control risk.

In view of the initial estimation or solution generated by the RBF network, the internal auditor will be responsible for deciding if the solution is accepted. For this it is based on the knowledge he/she retains, specifically, knowledge about the company with which he/she is working. If he/she considers that the estimation given is valid, the system will take the solution as the final solution and in the following phase of the CBR cycle, a new case will be stored in the case base consisting of the problem case and the final solution. The system will assign the case an initial reliability of 100%. If on the other hand, the internal auditor considers the solution given by the system to be invalid, he will give his own solution which the system will take as the final solution and which together with the problem case will form the new case to be stored in the case base in the following phase. This new case will be given a reliability of 30%. This value has been defined taking into account the opinion of various auditors in terms of the weighting that should be assigned to the personal opinion of the internal auditor.

From the final solution: state of activity, the system calculates the control risk associated with the activity. Every activity developed in the business sector has a risk associated with it that indicates the negative influence that affects the good operation of the firm. In other words, the control risk of an activity measures the impact that the current state of the activity has on the business process as a whole. In this study, the level of risk is valued at three levels: low, medium and high. The calculation of the level of control risk associated with an activity, is based on the current state of the activity and its level of importance. This latter value was obtained after analysing data obtained from a series of questionnaires (98 in total) carried out by auditors throughout Spain. In these questionnaires the auditors were asked to rate subjects from 1-10 according to the importance or weighting of each activity in terms of the function that it belonged to. The higher the importance of the activity, the greater its weighting within the internal control system.

The level of control risk was then calculated from the level of importance given to the activity by the auditors and the final solution obtained after the revision phase. For this purpose, if-then rules are employed.

2.2.4 Retention Phase

The last phase of the ISA (Identification of the State of the Activity) subsystem is the incorporation of the system's memory of what has been learnt after resolving a new problem. Once the revision phase has been completed, after obtaining the final solution, a new case *(problem + solution)* is constructed, which is stored in the system's memory. Apart from the overall knowledge update involving the insertion of a new case within the system memory, the hybrid system presented carries out a local adaptation of the knowledge structures that it uses.

The fuzzy cluster system contained within the prototypes related to the activity corresponding to the new case is reorganised in order to respond to the appearance of this new case, modifying its internal structure and adapting itself to the new knowledge available.

In this way, the RBF network uses the new case to carry out a complete learning cycle, updating the position of its centres and modifying the value of the weightings that connect the hidden layer with the output layer.

The learning process is continuous whereby the RBF acts as a mechanism capable of absorbing knowledge of a certain number of cases, and to use them as a base with which to generalise. During this process the RBF network interpolates and makes predictions without forgetting part of predictions that have already been made. The system's memory acts as a permanent memory capable of maintaining many cases or experiences while the RBF network acts as a short term memory, capable of recognising recently learnt patterns and generalising on them.

2.3 GR Subsystem (Generation of Recommendations)

The objective of this subsystem is to carry out recommendations to help the internal auditor decide which actions to take, once the stages of the previous subsystem have concluded, in order to improve the company's internal and external processes. This subsystem is totally dependent on the previous subsystem as it begins its work from the case (problem+solution) generated in the ISA – Identification of the State of Activity – Subsystem (see Figure 1).

2.3.1 Retrieval Phase

The second subsystem (GR-Generation of Recommendations) is used to generate recommendations that can guide the internal auditor in his task of deciding the actions to be taken in order to improve the state of the activity analysed. In order to recommend changes in the execution of the business processes it is necessary to compare the current situation in the activity, represented by the *problem case + solution*, generated by the ISA (Identification of the State of the Activity) Subsystem, with those cases from the case base which best reflect the business management.

To this end, only cases most similar to the problem case are worked on. Given that the cluster whose centre was closest to the case problem was identified during the retrieval phase of the ISA (Identification of the State of the Activity) Subsystem, the cases of this cluster will be used in the next reuse phase. The process followed in this retrieval phase is based on the use of *query relaxation* [10] so that initially the cases retrieved from the case base meet the following conditions:

1. The solution or state of activity must be 15-20% superior to the final solution generated by the previous subsystem. If enough cases are not retrieved (25 is considered to be enough) the percentages are relaxed further, increasing in range by 5%.
2. Furthermore, they should possess a degree of membership to the cluster higher than 75% and a level of reliability of over 50%. These two constant values have been established by the auditors.

Figure 4 shows the retrieval process adopted, where X stands for the case group which represents the knowledge of a determined activity that exists within the memory of the system, v_p represents the vector of attributes that describes the problem case, s_f is the final solution generated in the ISA subsystem as a solution to the problem case, s_i is the solution to case i, m is the identifier of the cluster whose centre is closest to the problem case, U is the matrix of memberships, u_{mi} is the level of membership of case i to cluster m and K is the set of the most relevant retrieved cases.

```
procedure retrieve_GR (input: X, v_p, s_f, m, U; output: K)
  {
        begin
              increment ← 0;
              repeat
                    for each case i ∈ X do
                    dif ← s_i - s_f
                    if (dif ≥ 0.15 and dif ≤ (0.20+ increment))
                              and (u_mi > 0.75)
                              and (reliability(i) > 0.5) then
                                    K ← K + i
                    increment ← increment +0,5;
              until |K|>25;
        end
  }
```

Fig. 4. Pseudocode of the retrieval phase in the Generation of Recommendations subsystem

2.3.2 Re-use Phase

Given that the objective of this subsystem is to generate a series of recommendations from the problem case, it is necessary to search for a case from the case base (or a combination of various cases) which serve as a guide to generate recommendations, comparing this/these case/s with the problem case. This comparison will allow the company to detect which processes need to be modified – in other words, which tasks need to be improved.

As already explained above, in the retrieval phase, the cases obtained are those which reflect a most favourable state of the activity, when compared to the state presented by the analysed activity. From all these cases, in this phase of adaptation, the subsystem should select the case which maximises the value of each of the tasks (V_i) taking into account the level of importance (IR_i) or weighting that each task has for the overall activity. This way, the problem of selecting a case from all those retrieved can be made similar to a multi-criteria decision-making problem where the alternatives are the different cases retrieved and the objective is to maximise the values of these tasks (which will then represent the attributes).

In this study, the initial version of the Electre method [2, 16] has been used in order to tackle the problem of choosing one of the alternatives. The Electre method proposes a strategy for reducing the size of all the possible solutions, through the segregation of the most favourable case group from another group which encapsulates the least favourable cases. The application of such a method will produce the selection of one or various cases from among those retrieved.

The Electre method is based on the fact that the vector of preferential weightings subjectively associated with each attribute is known. As in this study, the weighting of an attribute (represented by its level of importance) is different for each alternative, and it is necessary to obtain a single weightings vector for the attributes of the group of alternatives or retrieved cases. In this case, the weighting vector is obtained by calculating, for each attribute, the median weightings for the attribute in question, for all the different alternatives.

On the other hand, as a solution, Electre returns the best alternative, or group of alternatives in the event that there is no single prevalent alternative. Given that for the generation of recommendations it is necessary to begin with a single alternative, where an output to a multicriteria decision method gives various alternatives, their combination will be used, taking the median value for each attribute.

Figure 5 shows the pseudocode for the reuse phase where K is the group of most relevant cases retrieved in the previous phase, v_{el} is the case or alternative obtained after the adaptation phase from group of cases K, $v_{el(j)}$ is the value of the attribute j of the case v_{el}, C is the group of alternatives or cases obtained as output by the Electre method.

The case obtained as a result of the Electre method represents the objective to be reached for the activity analysed or the standard to be followed in order to meet the objectives of the company or, specifically, the objective associated with the activity. In this way, the recommendations which are generated retrospectively, will be used to ensure that the various tasks that make up the problem case achieve a situation which is as similar as possible to the case obtained at the output of the Electre method.

```
procedure reuse_GR (input: K; output: v_el)
{
    begin
        (C,n) ← ELECTRE (K)
        if n > 1 then
            for each attribute j do
                v_el_j ← (Σ_{i=1}^{n} C_ij) / n
    end
}
```

Fig. 5. Pseudocode of the reuse phase of the GR (Generation of Recommendations) subsystem

In this way, in order to generate the recommendations, the output from the Electre method is compared to the problem case, comparing the values (V_i) of each of the attributes or tasks in each case. The objective is to detect which tasks should be improved, establishing an order of priorities in terms of weighting (IR_i) of each task over the overall weighting of the activity. In other words, to identify the possible deviations of the activity and to appreciate the extent of deviations in terms of the tasks' level of importance (IR_i). In this way, the system generates recommendations related to the inconsistent processes found, that is, the differences between the values of the attributes in the problem case and those in the objective case (considered as the standard) obtained by the Electre method, representing the potential recommendations of the auditor.

The group of attributes of stored cases in the case base represent the overall values that both experts in each activity and the auditors have judged to be effective (from the surveys carried out) given the characteristics of the company. Since the characteristics of the current case (problem) are similar to the objective case obtained, the auditor can argue that the values of the attributes must also be similar. This provokes a more convincing argument than basing it on probabilities and estimated losses or risks.

The generation of control recommendations by comparing the values of the current case with those of past cases has also eliminated other problems such as the lack of outputs or pre-defined results. Many possible values exist as well as a large number of combinations that could be included in the recommendations of the auditor. But not all the combinations are valid; some combinations may not be feasible or make sense. In contrast to the CBRs, both the expert systems and the neuron networks will need to have possible outputs specified for them previously.

Based on the predictions and recommendations generated by the system, the internal auditor may inform the company of inconsistent processes and the measures that should be adopted to resolve them. This is a decision support system that facilitates the auditing process for internal auditors.

2.3.3 Retention Phase

After the time necessary for correcting the errors detected, the firm is evaluated again. Auditing experts consider that three months are enough to allow the evolution of the company towards a more favourable state. If it is verified that the erroneous processes and the level of risk have diminished, the retention phase is carried out, modifying the case used to generate the recommendations. The reliability (percentage of successful identifications) of this case is thereby increased by 10%. In contrast, when the firm happens not to have evolved to a better state, the reliability of the case is decreased in 10%. Furthermore, those cases whose level of reliability is smaller than 15% are eliminated, and the remaining cases are regrouped into fuzzy clusters.

3 Results

The hybrid system developed has been tested over 29 months in 22 small to medium companies (12 medium-sized and 10 small) in the textile sector, located in the northwest of Spain. The data employed to generate prototype cases, in order to construct the system's case bases, have been obtained after performing 98 surveys with auditors from Spain, as well as 34 surveys from experts within different functional areas of the firms within the sector.

In order to test this system, various complete operation cycles were carried out. In other words, for a given company, each one of its activities were evaluated, obtaining a level of risk and generating recommendations. These recommendations were communicated to the company's internal auditor and he was given a limit of three months in order to elaborate and apply an action plan based on those recommendations. The action plan's objective was to reduce the number of inconsistent processes within the company. After three months, a new analysis of the company was made and the results obtained were compared with those of the previous three months. This process was repeated every three months.

Results obtained demonstrate that the application of the recommendations generated by the system causes a positive evolution in firms. This evolution is reflected in the reduction of erroneous processes. Results obtained demonstrate that the application of the recommendations generated by the system causes a positive evolution in firms. The indicator used to determine the positive evolution of the companies was the state of each of the activities analysed. If, after analysing one of the company's activities, it is proven that the state of the activity (valued between 1 and 100) has increased over the state obtained in the previous three month period, it can be said that the erroneous processes have been reduced within the same activity. If this improvement is produced in the majority of activities (above all in those of most relevance within the company), the company has improved its situation.

In order to reflect as reliably as possible the suitability of the system for resolving the problem, the results from the analysis of the 22 companies were compared with those of 5 companies in which the recommendations generated by the system have not been applied. In these five companies, the activities were analysed from the beginning of the three month period until the end, using the ISA (Identification of the State of the Activity). The recommendations generated by the second subsystem were not presented to the firm managers (and consequently, the recommendations were not applied).

In order to analyse the results obtained, it is necessary to consider that some of the recommendations implied costs that the companies were not able to afford or that involved a long term implementation. Therefore, companies are considered to have followed the recommendations if they applied more of a 70% of them. On the other hand, the evaluation process was ceased in two of the companies analysed at the request of the companies themselves. Specifically, only one year's data is available for one company while in the case of the other, only data from the first 21 months is available.

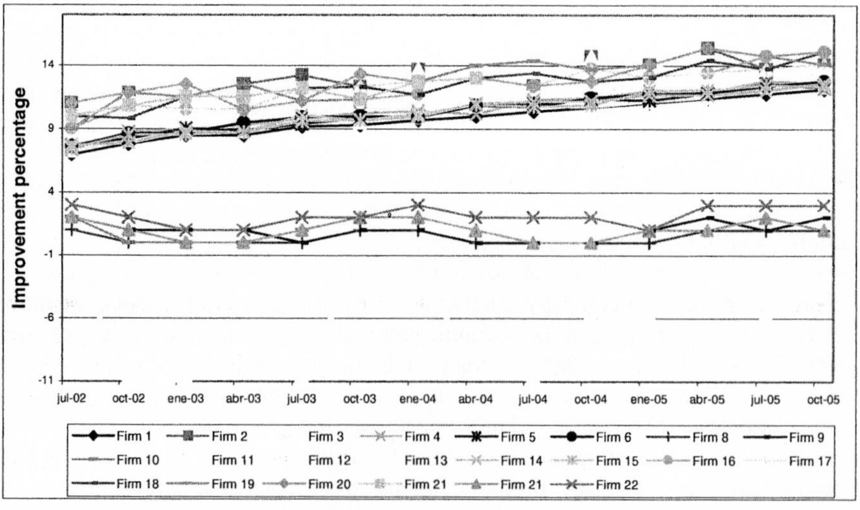

Fig. 6. Firms' evolution

The results obtained were as follows:

1. Of the 22 companies analysed, in those in which the recommendations generated by the system were applied, the results were (see Fig. 6):

a) In 15 companies, the number of inconsistent processes was reduced, improving the state of activities by an average of 11.5%.
b) In 5 of these companies, no improvement was detected in the state of activities. In other words, the application of the recommendations generated by the system did not have any effect on the activities of the company. In two of these companies, the experiment had to be aborted after one year, and 21 months, respectively, because the companies themselves did not allow us to complete the analysis. In the other three companies (in which the system was applied for the full 29 month period), after studying the possible reasons for the results, it has been concluded that the recommendations given were not completely followed, with only certain measures applied and the majority of recommendations ignored.
c) In two companies the inconsistent processes increased, in other words, the application of recommendations generated by the system, prejudiced the positive evolution of the company. Once the situation in each of the companies had been analysed, it was concluded that in both there was a high level of disorganisation, without a clearly defined set of objectives. This means that any attempt to change the business organisation actually will lead to a worse situation.

In general, it could be said that these results demonstrate the suitability of the techniques used for their integration in the developed intelligent control system. The best results occurred in the companies of smaller size. This is due to the fact that these firms have a greater facility to adapt and adopt the changes suggested by the system's recommendations.

2. On the other hand, for the 5 companies in which the recommendations generated by the system were not applied, the results were as follows: four of them improved their results, though reaching an average productivity that was 4% below the same measurement for other companies that did use the system. The fifth company analysed ceased operations before the end of the first year of evaluation.

4 Conclusions

This article presents a neuro-symbolic system that uses two CBR systems employed as a basis for hybridization of a multicriteria decision-making method, a fuzzy clustering method, and an RBF net. As such, the model developed combines the complementary properties of connectionist methods with the symbolic methods of Artificial Intelligence.

The used reasoning model can be applied in situations that satisfy the following conditions:

1. Each problem can be represented in the form of a vector of quantified values.
2. The case base should be representative of the total spectrum of the problem.

3. Cases must be updated periodically.
4. Enough cases should exist to train the net.

The prototype cases used for the construction of the case base are artificial and have been created from surveys carried out with auditors and experts in different functional areas. The system is able to estimate or identify the state of the activities of the firm and their associated risk. Furthermore the system generates recommendations that will guide the internal auditor in the elaboration of action plans to improve the processes in the firm.

Estimation in the environment of firms is difficult due to the complexity and the great dynamism of this environment. However, the developed model is able to estimate the state of the firm with precision, and propose solutions that make it possible to improve each state. The system will produce better results if it is fed with cases related to the sector in which it will be used. This is due to the dependence that exists between the processes in the firms and the sector where the company is located. Future experiments will help to identify how the constructed prototype will perform in other sectors and how it will have to be modified in order to improve its performance.

Although the defined model has not been tested in big firms, it is believed that it could work adequately, although changes would take place more slowly than in small and medium firms. Steps toward this direction have been taken and it is expected that an evaluation of the system will soon be possible in a major international company from the textile sector.

References

1. Aamodt A. and Plaza E. (1994). Case-Based Reasoning: foundational Issues, Methodological Variations, and System Approaches. AICOM. Vol. 7. Nº 1, Marzo 1994.
2. Barba-Romero, S. y Pomeral, J. (1997). Decisiones Multicriterio. Fundamentos teóricos y utilización práctica. Colección de Economía. Servicio de publicaciones Universidad de Alcalá.
3. Bezdek J. C. (1981). Pattern Recognition with Fuzzy Objective Function Algorithms. Plenum Press, New York.
4. Bezdek, J.C., Keller, J.M., Krishnapuram, R. and Pal, N.R. (1999). Fuzzy Models and Algorithms for Pattern Recognition and Image Processing. Kluwer Academic Publishers, Norwell.
5. Borrajo, L.(2003). Sistema híbrido inteligente aplicado a la auditoría de los sistemas internos. Phd Thesis. Teses de doutoramento da Universidade de Vigo. Universidade de Vigo (Spain). ISBN: 84-8158-274-3. December, 2003.
6. Corchado, J.M., Díaz, F., Borrajo, L. and Fdez-Riverola F. (2000). Redes Neuronales Artificiales: Un enfoque práctico. Departamento de publicaciones de la Universidad de Vigo.
7. Corchado, J.M., Borrajo, L., Pellicer, M.A. and Yáñez, J.C. (2004). Neuro-symbolic System for Business Internal Control. LNCS Volume 3275/2004. Springer-Verlag. ISSN:0302-9743.

8. Fdez-Riverola, F. and Corchado, J.M. (2004). FSfRT: Forecasting System for Red Tides. Applied Intelligence. Special Issue on Soft Computing in Case-Based Reasoning. ISSN 0924-669X. Vol 21, num 3, pp 251-264.
9. Fritzke, B. (1994). Fast Learning with Incremental RBF Networks. Neural Processing Letters. Vol. 1. No. 1. pp. 2-5.
10. Gardingen, D. & Watson, I. (1998). A Web Based Case-Based Reasoning System for HVAC Sales Support. In, Applications & Innovations in Expert Systems VI. Milne, R., Macintosh, A. & Bramer, M. (Eds.), pp. 11- 23. Springer, London. ISBN 1-85233-087-2
11. Hunt, J. and Miles, R. (1994). Hybrid case-based reasoning. The Knowledge Engineering Review. Vol. 9:4. pp. 383-397.
12. Kolodner J. (1993). Case-Based Reasoning. San Mateo. CA, Morgan Kaufmann. 1993.
13. Lenz M., Bartsch-Spörl B., Burkhard D. and Wees S. (eds.) 1998. Case-based Reasoning Technology: From Fundations to Applications, Springer Verlag, LNAI 1400.
14. Mas, J. and Ramió, C. (1997). La Auditoría Operativa en la Práctica. Ed. Marcombo, Barcelona.
15. Medsker L. R. (1995). Hybrid Intelligent Systems. Kluwer Academic Publishers.
16. Romero, C. (1993) Teoría de la decisión multicriterio: Conceptos, técnicas y aplicaciones. Alianza Editorial. ISBN: 84-206-8144-X
17. Watson I. (1997). Applying Case-Based Reasoning: Techniques for Enterprise Systems. Morgan Kaufmann.
18. Watson, I. and Marir, F. (1994). Case-Based Reasoning: A Review. The Knowledge Engineering Review. Vol. 9. No. 4. pp. 355-381.

The Application of a Case-Based Reasoning System to Attention-Deficit Hyperactivity Disorder

Donald Brien[1], Janice Glasgow[2], and Douglas Munoz[1]

[1] Center for Neuroscience Studies, Department of Physiology, Queen's University, Kingston, Ontario K7L 3N6, Canada
donald@biomed.queensu.ca, doug@eyeml.queensu.ca
[2] School of Computing, Queen's University, Kingston, Ontario K7L 3N6, Canada
janice@cs.queensu.ca

Abstract. Attention-deficit hyperactivity disorder (ADHD) is a prevalent neuropsychiatric disorder. Diagnosis is currently made using a collection of information from multiple sources, many of which are subjective and not always correlated. This highlights the need for more objective tests of ADHD. We address this need with the development of a system for differentiation based on altered control of saccadic eye movements. Our hypothesis is that there is sufficient predictive information contained in eye movement data to allow for the application of a case-based reasoning (CBR) system capable of identifying meaningful groups of ADHD subjects. An iterative refinement methodology was used to incrementally improve a CBR system, resulting in a tool that could distinguish ADHD from control subjects with over 70% accuracy. Moreover, the incorrectly classified ADHD subjects demonstrated a decreased benefit from medication when compared to correctly classified subjects.

1 Introduction

Attention-Deficit Hyperactivity Disorder (ADHD) is a prevalent neuropsychiatric disorder in children, adolescents and adults, affecting about 5% of school children in North America [4,29]. ADHD is currently defined by symptoms of inattention, hyperactivity and impulsivity [3]. In particular, ADHD subjects lack inhibitory control; that is, they have difficulty suppressing reflexive, and often inappropriate, behavioral responses [28,23]. Diagnosis is generally made using a collection of information from parent and teacher interviews, rating scales of hyperactivity and impulsivity, clinical history, cognitive assessments, and complete neurological and physical examinations [4]. Many sources are needed because they are subjective and often not significantly correlated [4]. The diagnostic process is further complicated by comorbidity (i.e., the presence of other disorders in addition to ADHD) and the fact that the classical symptoms are often situation dependant [5]. This brings into question the reliability and consistency of the current diagnostic process, and highlights the need for more objective tests [22].

Research into the etiology of ADHD has revealed some potential objective diagnostic tests. One possibility is to use the altered control of saccadic eye

H. Muñoz-Avila and F. Ricci (Eds.): ICCBR 2005, LNAI 3620, pp. 122 – 136, 2005.

movements. Saccades are rapid eye movements that bring new visual targets onto the fovea of the retina (the region of highest visual acuity). They can be generated volitionally or automatically in response to sensory stimuli that appear suddenly. Studies have shown that subjects with ADHD have difficulties suppressing automatic, visually-triggered saccades [23,26,30]. Tasks have been developed that can measure the characteristics of saccades precisely [20]. In particular, the pro-saccade and anti-saccade tasks are used to investigate automatic and volitional saccade generation, respectively (see Fig. 1 A and B).

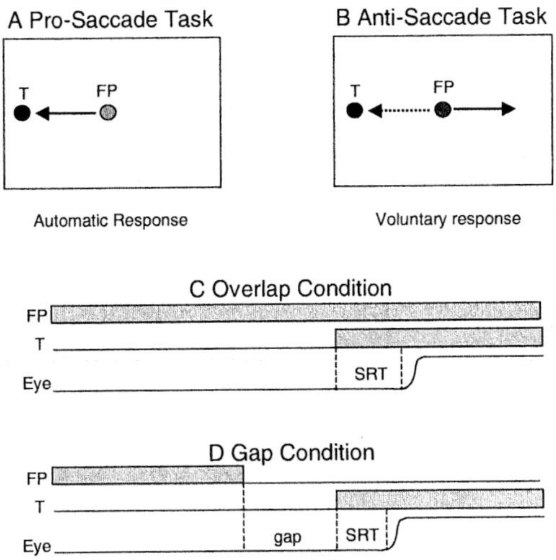

Fig. 1. The behavioral paradigms used to measure saccade performance. Eye represents a trace of the eye movement with time. T = Target. FP = Fixation Point. SRT = Saccadic reaction time

Both tasks begin with the subject looking at a central fixation point (FP) on a large screen in front of them. A visual target (T) then appears to the left or right of the fixation point. The subject is instructed (via the colour of FP) to either look toward the target (pro-saccade) or away from target (anti-saccade). Measurements of saccadic reaction time (SRT – time from target appearance to the onset of eye movement), intra-subject variability in SRT, and direction errors are used to compare the performance of subjects. Compared to age-matched controls, ADHD subjects make significantly more direction errors in the anti-saccade task (i.e., they generate the erroneous automatic pro-saccade) and generally have longer, more variable SRTs in all tasks [23,26]. Some ADHD subjects cluster with the control groups in terms of performance, while others differ significantly, suggesting that subgroups of the disorder may also be present [26]. These results suggest that a subset of ADHD subjects have difficulty suppressing automatic pro-saccades during the anti-saccade test and generally have poor voluntary control over saccade production [26].

The goal of the research described in this paper is to develop a reasoning system for making meaningful groupings of ADHD subjects based on differences in saccade performance. The difficulty in developing such a system lies in the high complexity, high dimensionality, and weakly understood theory of this domain (i.e., causality and interactions are not well defined). This makes traditional artificial intelligence approaches, that rely on first principles and a thorough understanding of the domain to construct a model, impractical. However, the saccade data that have been collected can be viewed as a case base of experiences to which a case-based reasoning (CBR) system can be applied. In CBR, a novel problem (e.g., does a child have ADHD?) is solved by retrieving and adapting similar problem/solution pairs within a case database [19]. Each problem and its corresponding solution can be entered into the database to provide immediate evolution and learning. Re-using the specific knowledge contained in cases compensates for incomplete general domain knowledge.

CBR is appealing in medical domains because a case base is often already present (symptoms, diagnosis, treatment, and outcome for each patient). Furthermore, the CBR cycle fits well with the approach that a health-care worker takes when presented with a new case, making its incorporation into a clinical setting natural. As such, several CBR systems for medical diagnosis and decision support have been implemented (e.g., [2,12,16]). These systems are increasingly using a methodology involving knowledge engineering techniques [32]. As more complex domains are tackled by CBR systems, where representing cases and adapting the solutions of retrieved cases becomes difficult, systematic approaches to CBR development using knowledge engineering are needed [1,7]. This is important in these domains because it elucidates knowledge that aids in the construction of a meaningful case representation; meaningful, in that it allows for retrieved cases to be matched as closely as possible to the target case in order that their solutions can be reused with little adaptation. CBR still has clear benefits in these domains as long as the knowledge engineering efforts required to construct such a case representation are less than would be required to construct an entire general model [7]. This paper describes the application of an iterative refinement scheme involving knowledge engineering in a complex, weak theory domain. It is hypothesized that there is sufficient predictive information contained in the ADHD saccade performance data to allow the development of a CBR system capable of making meaningful groupings.

2 Methods

2.1 The TA3 Decision Support System

Jurisica and colleagues have provided a novel intelligent decision support system that incorporates CBR and is directed at solving problems in biology and medicine [15,16,17]. This system, known as TA3 (pronounced tah-tree), has a flexible design and proven record in medical domains, making it an appealing system for use with the saccade performance data.

The TA3 system uses a novel CBR paradigm [15]. Cases are represented as attribute/value pairs. The attribute/value pairs and their domains are defined in what is called a case description. There are three classes of data defined in a case description: 1) *Description* is the non-predictive data, 2) *Problem* is the predictive data, and 3) *Solution* is the classification, diagnosis, or outcome. Focusing on the Problem class, attributes are grouped into categories. The advantage of grouping attributes is that it allows the assignment of different constraints and priorities depending on an attribute's, or collection of attributes', relevance (i.e., their value in matching similar cases). This minimizes the effect that irrelevant or less relevant attributes may have when trying to match similar cases. Category membership can either be assigned by an expert with domain knowledge of the relevance of different attributes or by a machine learning approach.

The retrieval process uses modified nearest neighbour matching: predictive attributes are grouped to allow different priorities/constraints as explained, an explicit context is used during similarity assessment, and the retrieval algorithm is guided by incremental transformations of the context. A context is simply a subset of the Problem class data of the case description with constraints applied to the attribute/value pairs. Case retrieval proceeds by attempting to satisfy these constraints. The similarity of cases is defined as the closeness of values defined in the context. A case is said to satisfy a context if every attribute value in the case satisfies the constraints imposed on those attributes in the context. Two cases are then said to be similar if they both satisfy the same context [16].

Context based retrieval allows for specialization by the user or system in considering what constitutes a match. To retrieve more or fewer similar cases, the user or the system iteratively applies transformations to the context. Two transformations are possible: *relaxation* and *restriction*. Relaxation can be broken down into two implementations: *reduction* and *generalization*. Reduction, also called m_of_n matching, reduces the number of attributes in a category needed for a match. Generalization increases the range of allowable values that an attribute may take. Similarly, restriction can be broken down into *expansion* and *specialization*, which have the opposite effects of reduction and generalization, respectively. Lower priority categories are relaxed before higher priority categories. Relaxation and restriction are applied iteratively to control the number of cases retrieved. Typically, the retrieval process is user guided and TA3 allows for complete control of the transformations. For example, the user can specify which relaxation technique is used first, how many times each technique should be called, whether or not they should be applied in a round-robin fashion, whether one transformation should be favoured over another, and how much relaxation or restriction should be applied at each iteration.

The flexible nature of TA3 means that its responsibility ends at the retrieval process. It is up to the user to appropriately reuse the set of cases returned based on the problem being solved. Similarly, there is no specific adaptation module in the system. There is support for knowledge mining in TA3 through a context refinement function. Given two or more test sets representing different classes of cases, this function uses Genetic Algorithms to manipulate a context. This function maximizes the distances between different classes and minimizes the distances within the same class. The distance between two cases is defined as the amount of relaxations needed to make the two cases similar. The Genetic Algorithm function works by iteratively creating, mutating and evaluating the fitness of several hundred contexts (where fitness is proportional to distance as defined above). Mutations include altering the priorities of categories, reorganizing categories, or altering how much and the type of transformations that can be applied to categories and attributes. The context with the maximum fitness is output at the end. The information gained by this process may not only determine previously unknown relations in the data, but may provide a new context with which to guide the retrieval process with greater prediction accuracy.

2.2 Data

Cases were compiled from the pro-saccade and anti-saccade tasks performed on children and adults by Munoz and colleagues [26] as well as additional cases tested since then. These tasks are outlined in Fig. 1. Note that during the tasks the fixation point can either remain lit during the appearance of the target (overlap condition; Fig. 1 C) or disappear 200 ms before its appearance (gap condition; Fig. 1 D). The disappearance of the fixation point in the gap paradigm leads to faster SRTs [8] and facilitates the generation of express saccades [9,24,27], which have a latency of approximately 90 to 140 ms. This range of SRTs represents the shortest possible time in which a visually-triggered saccade can be initiated under the restrictions of sensory-motor control [25]. The percentage of express saccades may represent another means of differentiating ADHD and control subjects.

The child cases consisted of 76 children diagnosed in the community with ADHD and 76 normal control children, ages 6 to 16. Diagnosis was confirmed using the traditional multiple source criteria outlined in the Diagnostic and Statistical Manual of Mental Disorders 4th Edition (DSM-IV) [3]. ADHD subjects did not take medication on the day of the experiment. Each subject performed 1 block of 80-120 pro-saccade trials followed by 2 blocks of 80-120 anti-saccade trials. Horizontal eye movements were measured and descriptive/experimental data collected (see [24,26]). The data collected for each subject and each trial are shown in Table 1.

Table 1. Data collected for each subject and trial of the saccade performance tasks

Attribute	Value
Paradigm	The saccade task paradigm – pro or anti
Age	Subject age at time of experiment
Sex	Male or female
Handedness	A numerical handedness score (left/right)
Hyperactivity	Integer hyperactivity score used in diagnosis
Impulsivity	Integer impulsivity score used in diagnosis
Trial	The trial number
SRT	The saccadic reaction time
Correct	Subject moved correctly or incorrectly

In addition, data were collected for many of the ADHD child subjects on separate days while on medication. The off-medication data sets were complete, with no missing values. Not all subjects for the on-medication data had corresponding off-medication trials. Two of the on-medication cases had missing values. In total, 53 off-medication cases with matching on-medication trials were available.

2.3 Iterative Refinement

While one of the strengths of CBR is the ability to apply reasoning in weak theory domains, knowledge engineering is becoming fundamental to building a proper system as the problems tackled become more complex and less well understood [1,7]. This is particularly important in domains where adaptation is difficult or the information necessary to develop a proper adaptation strategy is absent. In these domains, a clear case representation and similarity metric need to be developed in order that cases are matched as closely as possible and solutions can be reused with little change [7]. A knowledge engineering approach was taken in developing a proper case representation, indexes, and retrieval scheme in the saccadic performance domain. This domain can be referred to as a weak theory domain in that the causal relationships and interactions are not well understood. It has been shown that some characteristics of saccade performance of ADHD subjects differ significantly from controls [26], but it is not known what performance attributes are most/least predictive or if these data can be used for discrimination at all. There is certainly not enough understanding of the disorder and its relation to saccadic eye movements to allow for the construction of a general model for diagnosis.

Previous work involving the development of systematic methodologies for managing the knowledge components (case representation, retrieval, and solution adaptation) has been summarized by Aamodt [1]. A model construction view for CBR was described, emphasizing modeling at the knowledge level – the level above the implementation level where only the domain knowledge, tasks, and methods are dealt with. These knowledge components are examined separately so that interactions between them are more apparent and thus more relevant models can be built. Such a knowledge-level view led to the CommonKads methodology for Knowledge-Based Systems [32], a methodology used in weak theory domains where the requirements and interactions of a domain are poorly known or poorly specified. It involves starting with a simple prototype model that is iteratively refined using analysis, design, develop, and test phases until an acceptable level of performance (which is application specific) is achieved. In this way, a workable system can be developed without the need for a clearly defined model. Cunningham and Bonzano successfully applied this strategy to the Air Traffic Control Domain [7]. At each cycle of development, they proposed new case features and then assessed the relevance of these features. The generation of these features (what they call the abductive process) was driven by an error analysis of the previous model by domain experts and knowledge engineers. The iterative refinement scheme used here is based on this approach.

2.4 Evaluation

The accuracy of the TA3 retrieval system in classifying cases (i.e., predicting diagnosis) was determined by dividing the control and ADHD (off-medication) data sets randomly into equally sized testing and training sets. This was necessary because a case representation and context were built incrementally based on exploration of the case base as described above. Case-base systems were constructed by analyzing the training set and the test set was used to assess the performance of the system using leave-one-out testing. Each case in the test set was removed from the case base in turn and a context was created based on the current case description. The system was then directed to retrieve at least one similar case from the case base using the transformation parameters assigned to the current system. If more cases than one were retrieved in an iteration, those cases were also considered valid. The diagnosis for each retrieved case was examined and the proportion of ADHD and control was determined. If the proportion of ADHD or control was higher than what would be expected at random, that proportion was used as the final diagnosis.

3 Experiment and Results

3.1 Model 1 – Initial Prototype

In order to build a proper case base from the data and decide on a case description, the goals and sub-goals were specified and the data were analyzed. The main goal of the CBR system was to provide decision support in the diagnosis of ADHD based on altered saccadic eye movements. One sub-goal was to elicit patterns and relationships within the data. Initially, a checklist/difference-based approach [19] was used to identify not only the potential indexes to be used for retrieval, but the representation of the individual cases (i.e., what a case should look like).

The first step in the checklist-based approach was to identify the specific task(s) of the reasoner. The task of this reasoner was to use saccade performance data as a similarity measure between cases so that a suggested classification could be assigned to a target case based on the classifications of a retrieved set. The next step was to determine what features are predictors of classification. The hypothesis was that saccade performance metrics are good predictors in this domain. These include mean SRT and direction errors during specific tasks. Another good predictor is age, because saccade performance varies greatly with subject age [10, 24]. Some studies [14] indicate that sex may also be a discriminating factor since boys present more severe symptoms than girls in respective age groups. The third step was to make useful generalizations from these predictors. Summarizing statistics used to create the default case representation were those identified important by Munoz and colleagues [26]: mean SRT, coefficient of variation in SRT for correct trials (i.e., the Standard Deviation/Mean * 100), percentage of direction errors (i.e., looking towards the target in an anti-saccade task or away from target during a pro-saccade test – see Fig. 1) and percentage of express saccades.

Table 2. Comparison of the performance of progressive CBR models. G.A. = Genetic Algorithms

	Model 1 Benchmark	Model 2 Age Constraint	Model 3 Statistical	Model 4 Clustering/G.A.
Sensitivity (%)	44.21	55.26	61.32	63.16
Specificity (%)	60.58	65.79	70.52	81.58
Accuracy (%)	52.90	60.53	65.92	72.37

Note that there are 8 tasks when considering all possible conditions and 4 variables measured in each task for a total of 32 task variables. These variables were placed in one default category with no constraints for the prototype case description. Table 2 displays the leave-one-out evaluation results using this case description as well as for subsequent models. As expected from such a basic model, relatively low sensitivity and specificity were found. The system was more accurate, by about 15%, at classifying control subjects than ADHD subjects in the test group.

3.2 Model 2 – Context Constraint

All of the attributes used in Model 1 were not equally predictive and their context parameters needed to be modified to reflect this. One of the problems with Model 1 was that too many cases were being retrieved during a query. The retrieval was not specialized enough. This suggested the need for constraining attributes. Saccade performance varies greatly with age suggesting that it would be a constraint. While there is evidence that sex has an affect on the severity of disorder [14], it has not been shown to affect saccade performance. Therefore, sex was not considered in this model, while age was given its own high priority category. During retrieval, the system was directed to generalize the age category by 10% only once. For example, if the test subject was 11 years old, the age category would be generalized to 10-12 years old.

This manipulation of the case description allowed for increases in sensitivity (over 10%) and specificity (5%) for the test set (see Table 2).

3.3 Model 3 – Statistical

Applying constraints to Model 1 so that fewer and more relevant cases could be retrieved had a benefit to system performance. However, analysis of the remaining summary attributes was not as straightforward as age because less is understood about their relative predictive power. Less predictive attributes were still having a negative effect on retrieval performance by allowing dissimilar cases to be retrieved. In the same manner, more predictive attributes were not being given high enough priority. In order to aid in organizing the performance data into a more effective case-description and context, the following statistical analysis was performed on the experimental data, in addition to that done previously [26]. In order to inspect the variability and overlap of attributes, histograms were created to compare each of the 32 for control and ADHD cases. In addition, a t-test was done on the same attributes.

Through this simple statistical analysis, it was revealed that there were no significant differences between the percentage of express saccades for the ADHD and the control groups. There were also no significant differences for the percentage of direction errors in the pro-saccade tasks. Hence, these attributes are not good differentiators for ADHD and control and were assigned low priority. However, the largest separations (i.e., greatest separation of their distributions) between the two groups and the least variability were found in the percentage of direction errors in the anti-saccade task and in the coefficient of variation in SRT, suggesting they were strong predictors. Less separation was observed in mean latencies, but the difference was still significant. Using this analysis, a new case description and context was developed. SRTs were grouped into a priority 0 category, percentages of direction error in the anti-saccade task were grouped into a priority 6 category, and coefficients of variation in SRT were grouped into a priority 8 category. These priorities are relative and in general represent the number of relaxations that are required before that particular category is relaxed. Age was also placed in a separate category as in the previous model. Percentages of direction error in the pro-saccade task and percentages of express saccades were not included in this case description since they would be placed in a low priority category, which would be fully relaxed during each retrieval.

The accuracy of the system using this new case description (referred to as statistical) was again determined by leave-one-out testing (Table 2). Further increases of over 5% in sensitivity and specificity were realized using this new case description and the test set.

3.4 Model 4 – Genetic Algorithms

The previous model demonstrated that the performance attributes were not equally predictive and simply placing them in their own categories with different priorities increased system performance. Due to the high dimensionality and complexity of the domain, further increases in performance would need increasingly complex forms of analysis. The context refinement tool of the TA3 system was used to aid in more complex knowledge discovery.

Using the training set, this tool was applied to the context of the previous model (statistical) for 400 generations. The resulting context was used to create a new case description. However, no significant increase in performance could be discovered using this method, even with repeated runs. The failure of this tool was likely due to the heterogeneity of the ADHD or control groups. Are there natural subgroups within the ADHD and control groups, which were making it difficult to separate the groups further in a meaningful way? In support of this hypothesis, ADHD is known to be a multidimensional disorder, covering a symptomatic spectrum, where factors of inattention, impulsivity, and hyperactivity may be present in not only different combinations, but to different severities [3]. Furthermore, previous studies involving other tests of ADHD symptoms [11, 13, 22] showed that, while they could not be used reliably in diagnosis, they were useful for identifying subgroups (such as extreme cases of hyperactivity).

One method of discovering naturally occurring subgroups in a database is known as cluster analysis, or unsupervised learning. In this type of analysis, components (or cases) are separated into naturally occurring clusters where intra-group similarity is maximized and inter-group similarity is minimized. This was the approach taken here. Specifically, a probabilistic (Autoclass C [6]) tool was used to visualize the data and determine the appropriate number of clusters or outliers present in the training set. Autoclass C was chosen for its demonstrated ability to automatically determine the appropriate number of clusters present and its comprehensive statistical summary of those clusters. It was found that the ADHD training group subdivided into three groups – two main groups differentiated on mean SRT and percentages of direction errors and one group of outliers. The control group subdivided into four groups, again differentiated on mean SRT and percentages of direction errors. The ADHD and control groups were separated into these seven groups and the context refinement tool was applied under the same conditions as before.

DESCRIPTION

Subject code: aba Hyperactivity: 87 Sex: Male
Handedness: 10 Impulsivity: 76

PROBLEM

Priority 9 – Only generalize once by 10%

Age: 8

Priority 8 – Coefficient of Variation

Anti/Gap/Left: 39.35	Pro/Gap/Left: 59.82
Anti/Gap/Right: 50.01	Pro/Gap/Right: 58.70
Anti/Over/Left: 42.07	Pro/Over/Left: 46.88
Anti/Over/Right: 44.50	Pro/Over/Right: 44.73

Priority 6 – Direction Error (%)

Anti/Gap/Left: 93.33	Anti/Over/Left: 77.78
Anti/Gap/Right: 75.76	Anti/Over/Right: 62.50

Priority 0 – SRT (ms)

Anti/Gap/Left: 363.00	Anti/Over/Right: 483.33
Anti/Gap/Right: 458.00	Pro/Gap/Right: 343.06
Anti/Over/Left: 351.67	Pro/Over/Right: 471.24

Priority -13 – SRT (ms)

Pro/Gap/Left: 338.00	Pro/Over/Left: 431.50

SOLUTION

Diagnosis: ADHD

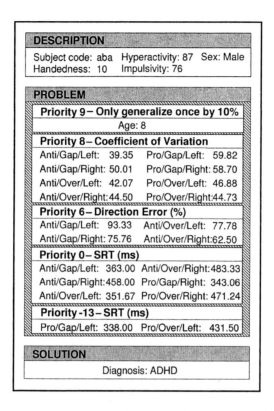

Fig. 2. Final case description. SRT = Saccadic reaction time. CV = coefficient of variation in SRT. Dir. Error = Percentage of Direction Error. Anti = Anti-saccade task. Pro = Pro-saccade task. Over = Overlap condition. Gap = Gap condition

Further increases in specificity and sensitivity were realized, with specificity now reaching over 80% (Table 2). Upon inspection of the new case description (Fig. 2), it was found that categories were left with the same priorities, but the individual attributes had range modifiers applied to them which altered the amount of generalization and reduction that was applied. In addition, a new category was created with low priority and two of the SRT variables were placed in it (pro-saccade gap left and pro-saccade overlap left), suggesting that they were not as predictive. These are the types of complex and attribute specific alterations in the context transformation that would be difficult to discover without a tool like this.

3.5 Final Error Assessment Using on/off Data

Having apparently reached a plateau in performance in the system (given the tools used), a final error assessment was done comparing the performance of incorrectly and correctly classified ADHD subjects while on and off medication. It was hypothesized that if some of the false negatives represented a real sub-group within the data, they might demonstrate an altered performance benefit from medication. In order to test this hypothesis, a paired t-test was done to compare the coefficient of variation in SRT data for each incorrectly and correctly classified subject in the test group (as classified by the system using the case description derived in Model 4) while on and off medication (for those subjects which had data collected in both conditions). The coefficient of variation in SRT data were used because, by the earlier statistical analysis, it was demonstrated to be the most predictive attribute (i.e., it was the least variable and most separated between the ADHD and control groups).

Indeed, significant increases in performance, as demonstrated by significant ($p<0.05$) decreases in coefficient of variation in SRT (Table 3), were observed for the correctly classified ADHD subjects while on medication, while this effect was absent among the incorrectly classified ADHD subjects. Incorrectly classified subjects had non significant changes in coefficient of variation in SRT.

Table 3. The average coefficient of variation in SRT during each test paradigm for correctly and incorrectly classified ADHD subjects while on and off medication. The p-value from a paired t-test is also given and represents the likelihood that the difference in performance between on and off medication would arise by chance. Anti = Anti-saccade task. Pro = Pro-saccade task. Over = Overlap condition. Gap = Gap condition

Test paradigm	Correctly Classified (N=15)			Incorrectly Classified (N=11)		
	ON (avg.)	OFF (avg.)	p-value	ON (avg.)	OFF (avg.)	p-value
Anti/Gap/Right	34.30	41.07	0.046	29.95	27.25	0.584
Anti/Gap/Left	35.29	40.20	0.200	29.00	33.67	0.293
Anti/Over/Right	35.30	41.29	0.072	31.68	31.24	0.935
Anti/Over/Left	34.47	37.67	0.047	26.67	31.82	0.032
Pro/Gap/Right	40.99	52.04	0.047	43.22	37.47	0.198
Pro/Gap/Left	41.04	50.04	0.025	43.41	36.13	0.203
Pro/Over/Right	42.33	47.69	0.103	41.37	41.54	0.968
Pro/Over/Left	36.87	47.86	0.018	37.83	39.57	0.710

4 Discussion and Conclusions

In the study outlined here, an iterative refinement methodology was used to develop a CBR system that could distinguish ADHD from normal control subjects, based on saccade performance, with increasing accuracy. It was further shown that many of the false negatives represented a significant subgroup within the ADHD group.

Saccade performance variables were able to distinguish ADHD from control children with an accuracy of over 70% (Table 2). The relative importance of these variables was assessed and coefficient of variation in SRT was determined to be most useful for predicting ADHD and distinguishing ADHD subjects from controls, while SRT and percentage of direction errors in the anti-saccade task had moderate utility. These results agreed with previous work [26] and support the hypothesis that impulse inhibition in ADHD subjects can be measured through saccade performance and can be used as a means of partially differentiating them from controls. Investigation of the false negatives revealed that those subjects displayed no significant increase in saccade performance while on medication, while the increases displayed by the true positives while on medication were significant. The CBR system was successful at distinguishing meaningful subgroups within the case base and could potentially have clinical utility. These subgroups could either be misdiagnosed cases (by current clinical methods) or naturally occurring subgroups within the disorder that do not respond as well to medication. The fact that the test set is segregated into meaningful subgroups also supports the results from the iterative refinement methodology. Because the data set had to be separated into two groups to use this approach (one for training/exploring and one for testing), there was a danger of selection effects. As the data set grows, this will become less of a concern. The already large number of subjects and the ability of the system to recognize significant subgroups within the current ADHD group suggest that the increases in performance achieved through this methodology were meaningful.

The results of this study are comparable to that of studies on the Continuous Performance Test (CPT) [31], which is likely the most popular objective laboratory test used to assess attention and vigilance. The utility of the CPT remains controversial: studies have shown that ADHD subjects perform poorer than normal controls (e.g., [21]) while others have found that it cannot distinguish ADHD subjects from referred controls (e.g., [22]). However, several studies have found that CPTs may be useful for identifying significant subgroups within the disorder such as subjects that are significantly overactive [22] or subjects that achieve higher conduct scores [11]. The utility of tests such as the CPT and the CBR system developed here will be their ability to provide useful information to a comprehensive neuropsychological assessment, not their use in isolation.

The concentration of the iterative refinement methodology was on the use of knowledge acquisition techniques to develop a more relevant case description and similarity assessment. This allowed the TA3 system to take advantage of more complex relationships, in the form of contexts, in order to compensate for the lack of adaptation strategies. As mentioned, Cunningham and Bonzano [7] used a similar approach to develop the ISAC (Intelligent System for Aircraft Conflict Resolution) system in the air traffic control domain. As with the system developed here, even though the development was not straight forward, CBR still had benefits over a general model approach due to the fact that it circumvented much of the need to understand the underlying causal relationships in the domain. The main difference between ISAC and the system developed here is that ISAC is used for planning tasks, while this system is used for classification tasks in a medical domain. The iterative refinement strategy to CBR development appears applicable across domains and tasks. Further evidence for its applicability in medical decision support is provided by systems developed by Frize and Walker [12] and Althoff and colleagues [2]. Frize and Walker used such a strategy in the development of a system to determine patient status, diagnosis, and therapy in an intensive care setting. Althoff and colleagues used the Inreca (Induction and Reasoning from Cases) approach, along with an incremental development strategy, to develop a system that could quickly aid in the diagnosis and treatment of intoxication cases. One added difficulty in the development of this ADHD system was the lack of feedback by experts (e.g., clinicians) on each model. The use of saccade parameters in diagnosis of ADHD is unproven and it would therefore be difficult for a clinician to comment on the usefulness of returned cases at this time. However, system evaluation was still possible through research, simple statistical approaches and more complex, automated knowledge discovery methods.

The performance of this system will likely increase significantly with the addition of new cases and new knowledge. One problem identified when working with this case base was the need for more cases within each respective age group. With a larger case base, subjects could be restricted to individual ages, instead of groups, and perhaps even sub-year categories in the case of younger children whose performance scores change greatly and quickly. This would also allow for other constraints to be applied, such as sex. In addition, more complex relationships in the data may be discovered to allow more complex contexts to be used for retrieval. This new knowledge could be elucidated through more sophisticated statistical and data acquisition techniques. As a greater understanding of the domain unfolds, the use of more advanced adaptation strategies and prototypical cases may become feasible. The use of more complicated knowledge acquisition techniques will become more prevalent in the field of CBR as more complex domains are tackled. This study provides good support for that notion. Finally, performance could be increased with the addition of an outcome category to cases. This outcome could be based on the diagnosis given by the system. For example, cases that were correctly classified would be given more weight when diagnosing new cases. In this way, the system could also give a weight to the final diagnosis, which would be more useful in decision support than a binary output.

In addition to continuing the refinement strategy with new and more complicated techniques, this system could be applied to other related fields (such as Parkinson's, Tourette Syndrome, and Huntington's) and in conjunction with other objective tests of attention, impulsivity and hyperactivity. The multi-source diagnosis currently being used for ADHD diagnosis is also a good candidate for CBR. Experts could provide valuable feedback and justification to partially automate and perhaps remove some subjectivity from the process. CBR could consolidate the myriad of information currently used to diagnose ADHD, with that obtained from more objective tests such as saccade performance and the CPT, into a database that could be used by clinicians to review and compare cases. While no brief test is likely to diagnosis ADHD conclusively, with its demonstrated ability to detect meaningful groups of ADHD subjects, this system could provide a clinically useful contribution to multi-source ADHD diagnosis.

Acknowledgements

Funding for this research has been provided by the Natural Science and Engineering Research Council of Canada (NSERC), the Institute for Robotics and Intelligent Systems (IRIS) Network Center of Excellence, the Canadian Institutes for Health Research and the Canada Research Chair Program. We thank Igor Jurisica and Patrick Rogers for their input and for providing the TA3 system. We also thank Irene

Armstrong, Andrew Bell, Susan Boehnke, Norah Brien, Brian Coe, Jillian Fecteau, Joanna Gore, Karen Hampton, Ann Lablans, Robert Marino, and Kip Rogers for their invaluable comments and support.

References

1. Aamodt, A.: Modeling the knowledge contents of CBR systems, In: Proceedings of the Workshop Program at the Fourth International Conference on Case-Based Reasoning. Naval Research Lab Technical Note AIC-01-003 (2001) 32-37
2. Althoff, K.D., Bergmann, R., Wess, S., Manago, M., Auriol, E., Larichev, O.I., Bolotov, A. et al.: Case-based reasoning for medical decision support tasks: The Inreca approach. Artif Intell Med. 12 (1998) 25-41
3. American Psychiatric Association, Diagnostic and Statistical Manual of Mental Disorders 4th edition. American Psychiatric Association, Washington, DC. (1994)
4. Barkley, R.A.: ADHD and the Nature of Self-Control. Guilford, New York (1997)
5. Cantwell, D.P.: Attention deficit disorder: a review of the past 10 years. J Am Acad Child Adolesc Psychiat. 35 (1996) 978-987
6. Cheeseman, P., Kelly, J., Self, M., Stutz, J., Taylor, W., Freeman, D.: AutoClass: A Bayesian Classification System. In: Proceedings of the Fifth International Conference on Machine Learning. Morgan Kaufmann Publishers, Ann Arbor, Michigan (June 12-14 1988) 54-64
7. Cunningham, P., Bonzano, A.: Knowledge engineering issues in developing a case-based reasoning application. Knowl-Based Syst. 12 (1999) 371-379
8. Dorris, M.C., Munoz, D.P.: A neural correlate for the gap effect on saccadic reaction times in monkey. J Neurophysiol. 73 (1995) 2558-2562
9. Fischer, B., Weber, H.: Express saccades and visual attention. Behav Brain Sci. 16 (1993) 553-610
10. Fischer, B., Biscaldi, M., Gezeck, S.: On the development of voluntary and reflexive components in human saccade generation. Brain Res. 754 (1997) 285-297
11. Fischer, M., Newby, R., Gordon, M.P: Who are the false negatives of the continuous performance tests? J Clin Child Psychol. 24(4) (1995) 427-433
12. Frize, M., Walker, R.: Clinical decision-support systems for intensive care units using case-based reasoning. Med Eng Phys. 22 (2000) 671-677
13. Halperin, J.M., Sharma, V., Greenblatt, E., Schwartz, S.T.: Assessment of the Continuous Performance Test: Reliability and Validity in a Nonreferred Sample. J Consult Clin Psychol. 3(4) (1991) 603-608
14. Hartung, C.M., Willcutt, E.G., Lahey, B.B., Pelham, W.E., Loney, J., Stein, M.A., et al.: Sex differences in young children who meet criteria for attention deficit hyperactivity disorder, J Clin Child Adolesc Psychol. 31(4) (2002) 453-64
15. Jurisica, I., Glasgow, J.: Applying case-based reasoning to control in robotics. In: 3rd Robtics and Knowledge-Based Systems Workshop. St. Hubert, Quebec (1995).
16. Jurisica, I., Mylopoulos, J., Glasgow, J., Shapiro, H., Casper, R.F.: Case-based reasoning in IVF: prediction and knowledge mining. Artif Intell Med. 12 (1998) 1-24
17. Jurisica, I., Rogers, P., Glasgow, J.I., Fortier, S., Luft, J.R., Wolfley, J.R., et al.: Intelligent decision support for protein crystal growth. IBM Syst Jl. 40(2) (2001) 394-409
18. Kim, K., Han, I.: Maintaining case-based reasoning systems using a genetic algorithms approach. Expert Syst Appl. 21 (2001) 139-145

19. Kolodner, J.: Case-Based Reasoning. Morgan Kaufmann Publishers Inc., San Mateo, California (1993)
20. Leigh, R.J., Kennard, C.: Using saccades as a research tool in the clinical neurosciences, Brain. 127(3) (2004) 460-477
21. Losier, B.J., McGrath, P.J., Klein, R.M.: Error patterns on the continuous performance test in non-medicated and medicated samples of children with and without ADHD: A meta-analytic review. J Child Psychol Psyc. 37 (1996) 971-987
22. McGee, R.A., Clark, S.E., Symons, D.K.: Does the Conners' Continuous Performance Test Aid in ADHD Diagnosis? J Abnormal Child Psychol. 28(5) (2000) 415-424
23. Mostofsky, S.H., Lasker, A.G., Cutting, L.E., Denckla, M.B., Zee, D.S.: Oculomotor abnormalities in attention deficit hyperactivity disorder. A preliminary study, Neurology. 57 (2001) 423-430
24. Munoz, D.P., Broughton, J.R., Goldring, J.E., Armstrong, I.T.: Age-related performance of human subjects on saccadic eye movement tasks. Exp Brain Res. 121 (1998) 391-400
25. Munoz, D.P., Dorris, M.C., Paré, M., Everling, S.: On your mark, get set: Brainstem circuitry underlying saccadic initiation. Can J Physiol Pharocol. 78 (2000) 934-944
26. Munoz, D.P., Armstrong, I.T., Hampton, K.A., Moore, K.D.: Altered Control of Visual Fixation and Saccadic Eye Movements in Attention-Deficit Hyperactivity Disorder. J Neurophysiol. 90 (2003) 503-514
27. Paré, M., Munoz, D.P.: Saccadic reaction time in the monkey: advanced preparation of oculomotor programs is primarily responsible for express saccade occurrence. J Neurophysiol. 76 (1996) 1-23
28. Quay, H.C.: Inhibition and Attention Deficit Hyperactivity Disorder. J Abnormal Child Psychol. 25(1) (1997) 7-13
29. Rapoport, J.L., Castellanos, F.X.: Attention deficit hyperactivity disorder. In: J.M. Weiner, ed., Diagnosis and Psychopharmacology of Childhood and Adolescent Disorders, 2nd edn. Wiley & Son, New York (1996) 265-280
30. Ross, R.G., Hommer, D., Breiger, D., Varley, C., Radant, A.: Eye movement task related to frontal lobe functioning in children with attention deficit disorder. J Am Acad Child Adolesc Psychiatry. 33(6) (1994) 869-874
31. Rosvold, H.E., Mirsky, A.E., Sarason, I., Bransome, E.D.J., Beck, L.H.: A continuous performance test of brain damage. J Consult Clin Psychol. 20 (1956) 343-350
32. Schreiber, G., Wielinga, B., de Hoog, R., Akkermans, H., Van de Velde, W.: CommonKADS: a comprehensive methodology for KBS development. IEEE Expert 9. 6 (1994) 8-37

Reasoning with Textual Cases

Stefanie Brüninghaus and Kevin D. Ashley

Learning Research and Development Center,
Intelligent Systems Program, and School of Law,
University of Pittsburgh,
3939 O'Hara Street, Pittsburgh, PA 15260, USA

Abstract. This paper presents methods that support automatically finding abstract indexing concepts in textual cases and demonstrates how these cases can be used in an interpretive CBR system to carry out case-based argumentation and prediction from text cases. We implemented and evaluated these methods in SMILE+IBP, which predicts the outcome of legal cases given a textual summary. Our approach uses classification-based methods for assigning indices. In our experiments, we compare different methods for representing text cases, and also consider multiple learning algorithms. The evaluation shows that a text representation that combines some background knowledge and NLP combined with a nearest neighbor algorithm leads to the best performance for our TCBR task.

1 Introduction

The goal of researchers investigating Textual CBR (TCBR) has been to enable traditional CBR systems to deal directly and intelligently with cases described as text. So far, the work has focused on retrieving cases to help a human solve textually-described problems, or on assigning indices to or highlighting passages in textual cases humans will use in solving problems. An essential difference between TCBR and Information Retrieval (IR) has been that IR methods tend not to take into account much semantic information or background domain knowledge about problem-solving. By contrast, TCBR methods attempt to leverage domain knowledge. Their indexing and retrieval mechanisms apply domain-specific, problem-solving knowledge, as well as more general knowledge, to process texts to help readers solve specific problems (Lenz 1999, p. 298; Burke 1998, pp. 13-14). IR researchers tend to dismiss such domain-specific techniques as *ad hoc*; textual CBR systems "eschew flexibility and generality for precision and utility for a given group of users." (Burke 1998).

In the relatively brief history of TCBR research, it is a human reasoning agent who solves the textually described problem using the cases returned by the program. However, in the work reported here, an automated reasoning agent solves the problems inputted as texts. Specifically, we describe a program called SMILE+IBP that uses CBR to predict the outcomes of legal disputes inputted directly as text and to explain those predictions. Fig. 1 shows an example of an annotated case text, the squib summarizing the facts of National Rejectors v. Trieman, 409 S.W.2d 1 (Mo.1966), and Fig. 2 shows SMILE+IBP's output for this case. The inputs to its predictive component, the Issue-Based Prediction program IBP, are representations of the problem facts in terms

H. Muñoz-Avila and F. Ricci (Eds.): ICCBR 2005, LNAI 3620, pp. 137–151, 2005.

Since the 1940's, National was practically the sole supplier of coin-handling devices, which are used in vending machines, amusement machines, and coin-operated washing machines. [F15] National developed its products (rejectors and changers) through "many years of trial and error, cut and try and experimentation." In 1957, National employees including defendant Trieman, a sales manager, and Melvin, an engineer, started their own business for producing coin-handling devices. ... Melvin, working at his home, designed two rejectors that were as close as possible to the comparable National rejectors. [F18] ... He also used some National production drawings, as well as a few parts and materials obtained, without consent, from National.[F7] However, none of defendants' drawings was shown to be a copy of a drawing of National. The resulting rejector improved on the National product in certain ways. Melvin and Trieman resign from National. National's vice-president testified that the National rejectors could be taken apart simply and the parts measured by a skilled mechanic who could make drawings from which a skilled modelmaker could produce a handmade prototype. [F16] The shapes and forms of the parts, as well as their positions and relationships, were all publicized in National's patents as well as in catalogs and brochures and service and repair manuals distributed to National's customers and the trade generally.[F27] National did not take any steps at its plant to keep secret and confidential the information claimed as trade secrets. [F19] It did not require its personnel to sign agreements not to compete with National. [F19] It did not tell its employees that anything about National's marketed products was regarded as secret or confidential. [F19] Engineering drawings were sent to customers and prospective bidders without limitations on their use. [F10] ...	F15, Unique-Product(p) F18, Identical-Products(p) F7, Brought-Tools (p) F16, Info-Reverse-Engineerable (d) F27, Disclosure-In-Public-Forum (d) F19, No-Security-Measures (d) F10, Secrets-Disclosed-To-Outsiders (d)

Fig. 1. Summary of the *National Rejectors* case, annotated with applicable Factors

```
Prediction for NATIONAL-REJECTORS
  Factors favoring plaintiff: (F18 F7 F6)
  Factors favoring defendant: (F25 F19 F16 F10)

Issue raised in this case is SECURITY-MEASURES
  Relevant factors in case: F19(D) F10(D) F6(P)
Theory testing did not retrieve any cases, broadening the query.

For SECURITY-MEASURES, query can be broadened for
DEFENDANT.
Each of the pro-D Factors (F10 F19) is dropped for new theory testing.
  Theory testing with Factors (F10 F6) gets the following cases:
  [11 cases won by plaintiff, 2 cases won by defendant]
Trying to explain away the exceptions favoring DEFENDANT
  MBL can be explained away with unshared ko-factor(s) (F20).
  CMI can be explained away with unshared ko-factor(s) (F27 F20 F17).
Therefore, PLAINTIFF is favored for the issue.
  In this broadened query, PLAINTIFF is favored.
  Theory testing with Factors (F19 F6) still does not retireve any cases.
There is no resolution for SECURITY-MEASURES, even when
broadening the query.

Issue raised in this case is INFO-USED
  Relevant factors in case: F25(D) F18(P) F7(P)
Theory testing did not retrieve any cases, broadening the query.

For INFO-USED, the query can be broadened for PLAINTIFF.
Each of the pro-P Factors (F7 F18) is dropped for new theory testing.
  Theory testing with Factors (F7 F25) still does not retrieve any cases.
  Theory testing with Factors (F18 F25) gets the following cases:
  (KG PLAINTIFF F6 F14 F15 F16 F18 F21 F25)
  (MINERAL-DEPOSITS PLAINTIFF F1 F16 F18 F25)
  In this broadened query, PLAINTIFF is favored.
By a-fortiori argument, PLAINTIFF is favored for INFO-USED.

Issue raised in this case is INFO-VALUABLE
  Relevant factors in case: F16(D)
  The case has only one weak factor related to the issue,
  which is not sufficient evidence to include this issue in the prediction.

Outcome of the issue-based analysis:
  For issue INFO-USED, PLAINTIFF is favored.
  For issue SECURITY-MEASURES, ABSTAIN is favored.

=> Predicted outcome for NATIONAL-REJECTORS is ABSTAIN
```

Fig. 2. Case-based analysis of *National Rejectors* text by SMILE+IBP

of abstract features, called Factors. These are prototypical fact patterns that tend to favor plaintiff's (p) or defendant's (d) position (Aleven 2003; Ashley 1990). The classification component, SMILE (SMart Index LEarner) assigns these features automatically to the textual description of the problem's facts using classifiers learned from a database of marked-up case texts. This integration of IBP and SMILE, as shown in Fig.3, allows us to assess the quality of SMILE's index assignments and particularly to test two hypotheses about the best way to represent case texts for learning classifiers. The text representation techniques are alternative means for capturing the kind of domain-specific, problem-solving knowledge and more general knowledge that enable a traditional CBR system to process case texts. In this way, we use enhanced text representations and machine learning to make TCBR techniques more general and automatic while preserving their focus on domain-specific problem-solving.

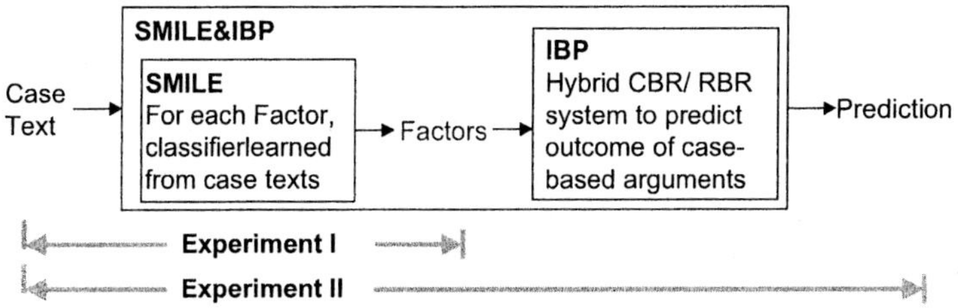

Fig. 3. Setup of the SMILE+IBP system, and outline of the experiments

2 Text Representation for TCBR

The most widely used text representation in TCBR has been a bag-of-words, in which the text is tokenized into single words, thereby doing away with word order. One of the first projects aimed at indexing textual cases, SPIRE (Daniels & Rissland 1997), used a small collection of excerpts related to its indexing concepts to locate the most promising text passages in a new unseen text. SPIRE relied on the passage retrieval module of an IR system, which represents texts as a bag-of-words, to find those sections in a new case that are most similar to its sample excerpts. The experiments compared different weighting schemes and variations of a bag-of-words representation. Other TCBR projects focused on the retrieval of text cases, rather than assigning indices. (Burke *et al.* 1997) and (Lenz 1999) showed that adding semantic information from WordNet can lead to better performance in retrieval-oriented TCBR systems. Recent work in TCBR has considered other, more advanced representations. (Cunningham *et al.* 2004) present a promising approach, which maintains some syntactic information by translating text into a network structure. An evaluation in the legal domain remains somewhat inconclusive, and further experiments will be necessary to show whether this intuitively appealing approach will lead to better performance. SCALIR was developed before the term TCBR was introduced. It also relied on representing legal cases texts in a network structure, with favorable results (Rose 1994). A promising and highly ambitious approach, using natural language processing (NLP) to derive a deep, logical representation, has been proposed for the FACIT project (Gupta & Aha 2004).

As this overview suggests, representation remains a central issue for TCBR; many researchers are exploring better representations for text cases. Our research carries this a step further, in that we incorporate shallow NLP, and in that our CBR application actually reasons with the automatically indexed cases.

Our approach to representing text cases was motivated by three observations and intuitions we gained from indexing text cases manually. First, our collection of legal cases comprises cases from many different jurisdictions and procedural settings, covering a period of about 50 years. This variety is reflected in the texts. The authors follow different stylistic conventions and often use a different vocabulary, as well. For instance, some judges, especially in older cases, tend to use "covenant," whereas others prefer the terms "contract" or "agreement." Adding some form of semantic knowledge to a lexicon may help an indexing program to find commonalities between examples that use a different vocabulary. In past experiments (Brüninghaus & Ashley 1999), we found that adding a thesaurus can lead to performance improvements.

Second, the names of the parties involved in a lawsuit are of little use for indexing, especially in long and complex cases. Keeping track of different names can be hard for humans, and is beyond today's computer systems. Instead, replacing names by their roles in the case makes cases more readable and enables a learning algorithm to better generalize from cases. Moreover, the same name can occur in different cases, sometimes even in different roles. Our collection has two cases involving IBM as plaintiff. Any inferences based on the name IBM would be erroneous, however, because the cases are completely unrelated and involve different scenarios. We hypothesize that replacing the names of parties and products by their roles in the case will lead to better indexing because it allows learning algorithms to generalize more accurately from examples.

Third, word order and other syntactic features are crucial for assigning some more complex indexing concepts. Consider "Plaintiff sent a letter to defendant," which often is related to Factor F1, Disclosure-In-Negotiations (d). A sentence with almost the same words, "A letter was sent to plaintiff by defendant," is not related to F1. In order to distinguish these two instances, at least some level of linguistic analysis and representation of syntactic features are required, like passive voice and the relations between constituents.

More formally, these intuitions inspired the following research hypotheses:

Hypothesis I. Abstracting from names and individual entities in a case text to their roles in the case allows a learning algorithm to better generalize from training examples.

Hypothesis II. Using some linguistic analysis to capture (1) patterns of actions and (2) negation preserves crucial information from the text and thereby leads to better classification.

In order to test our intuitions empirically, we implemented two representations that correspond to adding the knowledge as per the above hypotheses, as well as a baseline.

Bag-of-words/BOW. Our baseline representation, against which all measures will be compared, is the basic bag-of-words. The text is tokenized into single words, whose relative position to each other is lost in the process. We do not eliminate stopwords, and we do not remove suffixes with a stemmer. For instance, consider this sentence from the *ICM* case, which is evidence for Factor F7, Brought-Tools (p): "Newlin copied some files from ICM and brought them with him to DTI." In BOW, it would be represented as AND BROUGHT COPIED DTI FILE FROM HIM ICM NEWLIN SOME THEM TO WITH.

Roles-Replaced/RR. In this representation, names and references to individual entities in the text are replaced by their roles in the lawsuit. The sentence above would become "Defendant copied some information from plaintiff and brought them with him to defendant." Then, this example is tokenized as a bag-of-words, AND BROUGHT COPIED DEFENDANT HIM INFORMATION PLAINTIFF SOME THEM TO WITH. While this representation is still limited to the degree that it is a bag-of-words, it contains more relevant information about the case facts than the previous representation as BOW.

For our evaluation, we assumed there is a program that can automatically replace names by roles with high accuracy, as suggested in (Brüninghaus & Ashley 2001). In the experiments, we relied on texts where this substitution had been carried out manually by experts. With error-free replacements, all observed differences in performance, or their absence, could be attributed to the representation, rather than to an implementation for role replacements.

Propositional-Patterns/ProP. Propositional patterns are intended to capture more of the meaning contained in a sentence and thereby overcome some of the problems of a bag-of-words (Brüninghaus & Ashley 2001). They are powerful features and combine two terms that are in a specified syntactic relation with each other. ProPs differ from bigrams, pairs of adjacent words sometimes used as features in IR, in that we use syntax, and not adjacency, as a criterion. ProPs were inspired by the automatically generated caseframes in the AutoSlog-TS system (Riloff 2003).For SMILE, we are using Ellen Riloff's AutoSlog tools, which include Sundance, a robust partial parser that can be easily configured and adapted for new domains.

Roughly speaking, ProPs combine the headword of the trigger, the most relevant word of the "if" part, and headword of the filler, the most relevant word of the "then" part, of the extraction rules in an IE system. In addition to the syntactic knowledge, ProPs also capture some of the semantic knowledge from Sundance's lexicon, similar to the integration of a thesaurus presented in (Brüninghaus & Ashley 1999), by adding a new ProP for each synonym of the constituent words. Thus, for the sentence from *ICM*, one would get (DEFENDANT COPY) (PERSON COPY) (COPY INFORMATION) (COPY_FROM PERSON) (COPY_FROM PLAINTIFF) (DEFENDANT BRING) (PERSON BRING) (BRING THEM) (BRING_TO DEFENDANT) (BRING_TO PERSON) (BRING_WITH HIM). While this representation is still fairly simple, it is much more likely to allow the inference that Factor F7 applies than the RR representation. In our experiments, this sentence was correctly classified as F7 by RR and ProP, but not by BOW.

Generating the RR representation from the original text corresponds to Hypothesis I, replacing names by roles. We therefore expect that, according to Hypothesis I, the results with cases represented as RR in our experiments will be better than with BOW, or RR > BOW. Deriving ProPs from text where the names are replaced by roles corresponds to Hypothesis II. Consequently, if Hypothesis II applies, ProP > RR. Since ProPs are derived from text in which names are replaced by roles, we also expect that the Hypotheses are transitive and that ProP > BOW.

3 Integration of Indexing and Reasoning in SMILE+IBP

We tested these hypotheses in the context of our SMILE (Brüninghaus & Ashley 2001) and IBP (Brüninghaus & Ashley 2003) programs.

3.1 Classification-Based Indexing in SMILE

For the task of assigning indices, our case base with manually indexed cases together with the textual representation of these cases can be viewed as a set of examples for

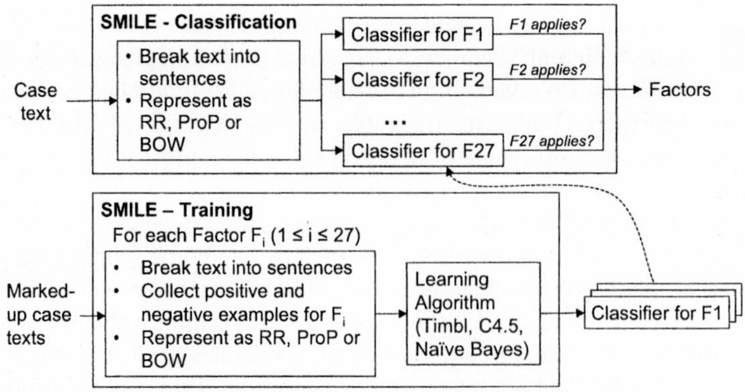

Fig. 4. Architecture of the SMILE system

"how indexing should be done." Following this characterization of the problem, we take a classification-based approach to indexing in SMILE, treating our existing case base as training set, and the Factors as target concepts.

As a machine learning (ML) approach, SMILE has two phases, classification and training; see Fig. 4. In the classification phase, SMILE works in a very modular way. It has 26 separate classifiers, one for each Factor F1 to F27 (for historical reasons, there is no F9).[1] Unlike many other text learning approaches, we treat the text cases as a set of example sentences, rather than one example document. Evidence for Factors is usually found in sentences, as illustrated in the *National Rejectors* squib in Fig. 1. SMILE first splits a new case, which does not have any mark-ups, into a set of sentences and represents them as BOW, RR or ProP. These sentences are then given as input to each of the classifiers. SMILE assigns a Factor if at least one sentence from the case text is labeled as a positive instance. The applicable Factors from all classifiers are then collected for SMILE's output.

In the training phase, the training set consists of the squibs from our collection, marked up with the applicable Factors similar to the *National Rejectors* squib in Fig. 1. As noted, SMILE learns separate classifiers for each Factor. It takes the cases where the Factor applies, and collects the sentences marked up with the Factor as positive training examples. All other sentences, those not marked up from a case where the Factor applies as well as the sentences from the cases without the Factor, are collected as negative training examples. The training examples are represented as BOW, RR, or ProP, and given as inputs to the learning algorithm. The learned classifiers are used as illustrated in Fig. 4.

3.2 Issue-Based Prediction in IBP

IBP is hybrid case-based/rule-based algorithm that predicts the outcome of legal cases. Due to space limitations, we can only give a brief description of IBP, it is discussed in

[1] Strictly speaking, although NN implements classification based on past cases, it does not explicitly learn a classifier in the sense that the other ML approaches do. For this paper, we ignore that difference, and treat NN like other ML algorithms.

Prediction for NATIONAL-REJECTORS, which was won by DEFENDANT
Factors favoring plaintiff: (F18 F15 F7)
Factors favoring defendant: (F27 F19 F16 F10)

Issue raised in this case is INFO-USED
Relevant factors in case: F18(P) F7(P)
The issue-related factors all favor the outcome PLAINTIFF.

Issue raised in this case is SECURITY-MEASURES
Relevant factors in case: F19(D) F10(D)
The issue-related factors all favor the outcome DEFENDANT.

Issue raised in this case is INFO-VALUABLE
Relevant factors in case: F27(D) F16(D) F15(P)
Theory testing did not retrieve any cases, broadening the query.

For INFO-VALUABLE, the query can be broadened for DEFENDANT.
Each of the pro-D Factors (F16 F27) is dropped for new theory testing.
Theory testing with Factors (F16 F15) gets the following cases:
[8 cases won by plaintiff]
In this broadened query, PLAINTIFF is favored.
Theory testing with Factors (F27 F15) gets the following cases:
(DYNAMICS DEFENDANT F4 F5 F6 F15 F27)
In this broadened query, DEFENDANT is favored.
There is no resolution for INFO-VALUABLE, even when broadening the query.

Outcome of the issue-based analysis:
For issue INFO-VALUABLE, ABSTAIN is favored.
For issue SECURITY-MEASURES, DEFENDANT is favored.
For issue INFO-USED, PLAINTIFF is favored.

=> Predicted outcome for NATIONAL-REJECTORS is DEFENDANT

Fig. 5. IBP's analysis of *National Rejectors*, Factors manually assigned by an expert

detail in (Brüninghaus & Ashley 2003) and (Ashley & Brüninghaus 2003). IBP combines a weakly-predictive domain model, which was derived from authoritative legal sources, and a CBR module. The domain model captures the general structure of the domain, the issues and their relations. It relates Factors to issues, but does not include rules to resolve conflicting Factors. For instance, the domain model captures that plaintiff has to show that the information was a trade secret in order to win a claim for trade secret misappropriation. This requires that the information was valuable and that measures were taken to keep it a secret. Based on Hypo, IBP's CBR module supports a form of scientific hypothesis testing to resolve conflicting evidence related to an issue.

Fig. 5 shows IBP's analysis, given an expert's manual interpretation of the *National Rejectors* case. Factors F27, Disclosure-In-Public-Forum (d), F16, Info-Reverse-Engineerable (d) and F15, Unique-Product (p) are related to the issue whether the information is valuable. IBP can conclude that the issue is raised, but needs to rely on its CBR module to find which side is favored on the issue. If the CBR module fails to resolve conflicting evidence, as in *National Rejectors*, IBP abstains on the issue.

We evaluated IBP and compared its predictions to several other ML and CBR-based methods. We found that IBP's predictions are most accurate, with a significant margin (Brüninghaus & Ashley 2003).

3.3 Combination of Indexing and Prediction

Our approaches to indexing in SMILE and prediction in IBP can be combined into SMILE+IBP by using the Factors assigned by SMILE as input to IBP as illustrated in Fig. 3. Thereby, we are in a position to generate a case-based analysis and prediction for cases from case texts, without manual intervention beyond converting and copying files. By combining SMILE and IBP, we have created a TCBR system that can carry out real reasoning beyond just retrieval.

4 Evaluation

Using SMILE and SMILE+IBP, we ran a set of experiments to test the above hypotheses to find out what makes a good text representation. We tried different representations for the cases to be indexed, and measured performance for Factor assignments as well as prediction using the automatically assigned Factors.

4.1 Experimental Design

In these experiments, we used 146 cases from the CATO case database (Aleven 2003) in two forms, represented as a set of applicable Factors and the squibs. The cases represented as Factors were used as the case base for IBP. The squibs summarize the courts' written opinions and help students infer which Factors apply in a case. The full-text opinions tend to be fairly long; *National Rejectors'* is 48 pages. In writing the squibs, the authors were encouraged to copy-and-paste from the opinions' descriptions of case facts. Only a relatively small part of the text of the squibs was written from scratch. The squibs were manually marked up for inclusion in SMILE.

While the manual mark-up for SMILE usually corresponds to CATO's list of Factors, there are some differences. For SMILE, we require that the evidence for a Factor is explicit in the text, and that no indirect inferences are needed even if they are based on common-sense interpretations of the text. As a result, some examples of the harder-to-find Factors were not included in the mark-up, especially Factors F3, Employee-Sole-Developer (d) and F5, Agreement-Not-Specific (d). We also decided not to follow CATO's conventions for Factors F6, Security-Measures (p) and F19, No-Security-Measures (d). In CATO's cases, Factor F6 is assigned whenever there are any security measures. F19 will not apply, even when there is overwhelming evidence that the plaintiff neglected security measures as long as it took some measures. For SMILE, however, F19 is marked up whenever the court explicitly focuses on instances where the plaintiff neglected to take certain security measures, even if plaintiff took some other measures.

The experiments were conducted as a leave-one-out cross-validation over all cases in the collection. For instance, when the *National Rejectors* case was the test example, its squib was included neither in the training set for SMILE, nor in IBP's database for testing predictions; in this run, *National Rejectors* played no role in training SMILE's classifiers or in IBP's predictions.

While the focus of our work is primarily on finding the best text representation, we included three learning algorithms with very different characteristics and learning biases. We considered multiple algorithms because it was not clear *a priori* how suitable these algorithms would be for our task. These algorithms are commonly used in text classification experiments and include Nearest Neighbor (NN), Decision Trees, and Naive Bayes. We selected respectively: Timbl (Daelemans *et al.* 2004), C4.5 (Quinlan 2004) and Rainbow (McCallum 2004). All are suitable for learning from text, freely available implementations from reliable sources. We used default parameters for Timbl, which in particular means k = 1 (i.e., 1-NN). We explored other parameter settings, but found that 1-NN was preferable. In C4.5, we set pruning to 100% confidence level.

Our experiments were run for three algorithms, three representations, 146 iterations of cross-validation, and 26 Factors, for an overall of about 35,000 experiment runs. The data included about 2,000 example sentences, with about 2,000 features for each representation. The experiments for this in-depth evaluation on rather complex data ran around the clock for several weeks. After our experiments, the most suitable representation and algorithm can be identified to learn one classifier for each Factor, which will be more efficient by three orders of magnitude.

In analyzing the results, we applied statistical tests to find whether the observed differences are statistically significant, or merely caused by random effects. Because our experiments were run as cross-validation, the commonly used T-test may not lead to reliable results (Dietterich 1996; Salzberg 1997). Based on the recommendations in (Dietterich 1996), we used Wilcoxon's Signed-Rank test, a so-called non-parametric test. A common pitfall in comparing multiple algorithms (or in our case, representations) is the repeated, pairwise comparison of results. However, this requires that a significant difference among all alternatives is shown first. We used Friedman's test for this purpose. Following convention, we say that results with $p < 0.05$ are statistically significant (Cohen 1995).

4.2 Experiment I

In our first set of experiments, we compared the effect of representation and learning algorithm on Factor assignment. We kept everything fixed; the only change was the combination of learning algorithm and representation. As a result, all observed differences can be attributed to these conditions.

We followed the evaluation commonly carried out for text classification. As illustrated in Fig. 3, the input in Experiment I is a raw case text, without any annotations, the output a set of Factors. Performance for each Factor was measured in terms of the F-measure, which is defined as the harmonic mean of precision and recall (Cohen 1995) as follows: $F = \frac{2*\mathrm{precision}*\mathrm{recall}}{\mathrm{precision}+\mathrm{recall}}$.

The averaged results over all Factors in Fig. 6 show two major results: Timbl is the best learning algorithm for the task, and RR and ProP outperform BOW.

First, let us consider the differences between the representations, focusing on the best algorithm in the experiments, the Timbl implementation of NN. Friedman's test indicates that the differences among all nine variants are statistically significant. For the results with Timbl, in the top of both the chart and the table in Fig. 6, Wilcoxon's Ranked-Sign test shows that scores for ProP and RR are significantly higher that BOW. These results provide evidence for Hypothesis I. RR has a higher score than ProP, which is not consistent with Hypothesis II; however, the difference is not statistically significant. The second experiment discussed in Section 4.3 provides additional evidence concerning Hypothesis II.

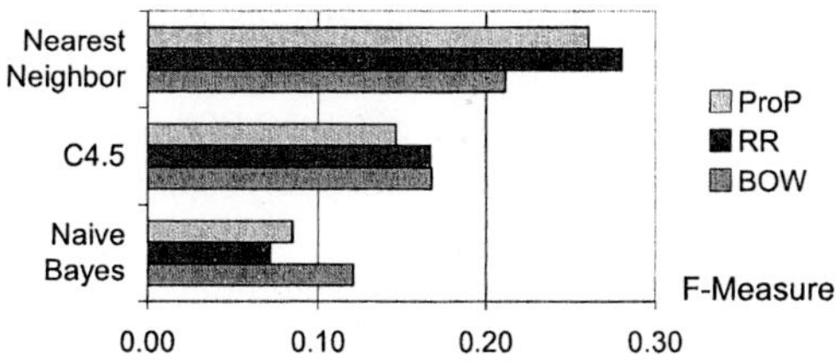

F-Measure	ProP	RR	BOW
Nearest Neighbor	0.261	0.280	0.211
C4.5	0. 147	0.167	0. 168
Naïve Bayes	0.085	0.072	0.121

Fig. 6. Average F-measure for Experiment I

One reason that Hypothesis II could not be confirmed here is that NLP remains one of the main problems with generating ProPs. Even though Sundance is a very robust state-of-the-art parser, its outputs are not always accurate enough for high-performance indexing from complex texts. In *National Rejectors*, ProP does not find Factor F27, Disclosure-in-Public-Forum (d). The relevant sentence is "The shapes and forms of the parts, as well as their positions and relationships, were all publicized in plaintiff's patents as well as in catalogs and brochures and service and repair manuals distributed to plaintiff's customers and the trade generally." This sentence has several constructs that are notoriously difficult to parse. In the first clause, Sundance gets confused by the verb phrase "were all publicized," and parses it as an active verb construction, with "all" as the subject. As a consequence, the ProPs generated for the sentence are hardly of any use for assigning indices, and Factor F27 is missed. In order to show that the problem is not a general limitation of ProPs, but rather caused by language too complex for the parser, we modified the grammar to "The shapes and forms of the parts and their positions and relationships were publicized in plaintiff's patents, catalogs and brochures and manuals, which were distributed to plaintiff's customers and the general trade." When we manually added the ProPs for this sentence's parse, it was correctly classified as an instance of F27. The sentence retrieved as most similar comes from the *Dynamics* case: "The first two of these features were publicized in a conference paper and an advertizing brochure." This example shows how minor grammatical adjustments can lead to correct Factor assignments. It indicates that our experiments are a lower bound on the performance of ProPs, which most likely will increase with more accurate parsing.

When we focus on the relative strengths of ProP and RR, we find that RR tends to have an advantage for Factors that favor plaintiff, while ProP tends to have an advantage for Factors that favor defendant. It appears that a number of pro-plaintiff Factors capture situations or features of the product, like Factor F15, Unique-Product (p). Such Factors can be represented fairly well through single words, and thus RR often suffices. Several of the pro-defendant Factors, on the other hand, describe defendant's actions, like F27. This requires more information about "who did what" and lends itself to representation with ProPs. Experiment II will further investigate how these relative strengths of ProP and RR have an impact on reasoning with the cases.

Second, with regard to the best learning algorithm, we found that NN outperforms C4.5 and Naive Bayes. The latter is remarkable because Naive Bayes is often hard to beat for text classification tasks. In our experiments, Naive Bayes had fairly good scores for only one Factor, F6, Security-Measures(p), which has 198 sentences marked-up. For most other Factors, it failed to find any instances.

In our collection, it appears that the conditions are not favorable for Naive Bayes. The distributions are extremely skewed. We have around 2,000 example sentences, yet, for some Factors, fewer than ten sentences are marked up. Thus, the prior probability for a Factor is low. In addition, the relevant vocabulary is large, around 2,000 features for each representation. With such sparse data, there may not be sufficiently many examples to derive reliable probability estimates.

On the other hand, NN does not rely on the prior class probabilities and has an advantage, especially for Factors with very few positive instances. Our experience confirms the reasoning of (Cardie & Howe 1997), who had good results with a NN approach for an information extraction task. They chose NN for an application where the distributions are highly skewed and where the goal is to find the minority class.

Similarly, the experiments show that C4.5 is not ideal for the task. The inductive bias of C4.5 is to learn trees with short branches; it does best when it can find relatively few highly predictive words. However, C4.5 is less suited for more complex concepts, or Factors, where multiple features may have to be weighed in a context-sensitive manner. Another problem is the small number of positive instances for many of the Factors. For instance, apart from the *National Rejectors* case, only *Dynamics* uses "was publicized" in relation to F27. Thus, it would not be possible for C4.5 to correctly find F27 in *National Rejectors*. In general, C4.5 has no way to generalize from singletons. A NN approach, on the other hand, is more suitable for such concepts. Moreover, C4.5 appears to provide evidence against Hypothesis II (see the middle column and line in Fig. 6); the results for ProP are much lower than both BOW and RR. However, this observation is related to the fact that C4.5 is not appropriate for singleton examples. ProPs are a more powerful, but also more specific representation than BOW and RR, which alleviates the problem of rare examples.

4.3 Experiment II

While Experiment I gives some important insights into how different representations have an impact assigning individual Factors, it only considers Factors in isolation. It does not capture the overall gestalt of a case, the interactions among Factors, or how some Factors are more relevant for our CBR task than others. For instance, not assigning Factor F27 to *National Rejectors*, as discussed above, is a critical error that can have a strong impact on prediction. In Experiment II, we therefore push a step beyond the sort of evaluation commonly carried out for text classification experiments by including prediction as an indicator for how well the assigned Factors capture the contents of a case. As before, the inputs in Experiment II are the squibs, but the outputs are the predictions of the cases' outcomes, as illustrated in Fig. 3. As in Experiment I, we kept everything else constant; the only difference was the representation of the text cases. Thus, all observed differences in performance can be attributed to the representation.

The experiments were scored by comparing IBP's predictions to the cases' real outcomes. We recorded accuracy over the cases where IBP made a prediction, as well as coverage, which is the percentage of cases where IBP made a prediction. Then, we combined these by adapting the F-measure for predictions: $F_{pred} = \frac{2*accuracy*coverage}{accuracy+coverage}$.

ProP has the best performance, with an F_{pred}-measure of 0.703, followed by RR, with 0.6 and BOW with 0.585; see "Overall" in Fig. 7. The difference among the representations is statistically significant, using Friedman's test. The difference between ProP and RR, as well as between ProP and BOW is also statistically significant, using a Wilcoxon Ranked-Sign test, the difference between BOW and RR is not significant.

We grouped the cases by outcome in order to find out whether there is a difference in performance between cases won by plaintiff and cases won by defendant. A good prediction method, we would expect, has about equal performance for cases won by either side. A method that always predicts the majority class may have high accuracy and coverage, but would be of relatively little use for a practical application. It would

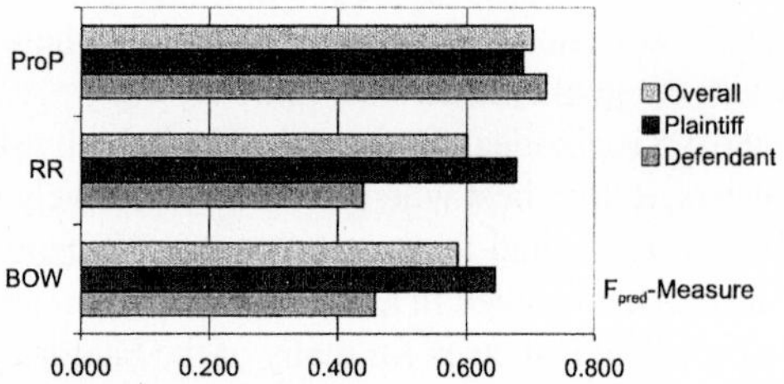

F_{pred}-Measure	ProP	RR	BOW
Overall	0.703	0.600	0.585
Plaintiff	0. 689	0.678	0. 645
Defendant	0. 724	0.440	0. 459

Fig. 7. F_{pred}-measure for the classification by SMILE+IBP as a function of case outcome

correspond to an attorney who always advises the plaintiff to sue, and the defendant to settle, irrespective of the case facts.

Comparing prediction performance for the three representations in our experiment, shown in Fig. 7, we found that only ProP satisfies this requirement. Its F-measure is about the same for the cases won by plaintiff and those won by defendant. RR and BOW, on the other hand, have very good performance for the majority class, cases won by plaintiff, but do poorly for the minority class.

To summarize, ProP has significantly better performance than RR and BOW in Experiment II. In addition, ProP is preferable because its performance does not depend on which side won. ProPs are the better representations in both respects; thus, Experiment II supports Hypothesis II.

5 Discussion

The performance of SMILE and SMILE+IBP leaves considerable room for improvement. The average F-measure in Experiment I is below 0.3, which is clearly not sufficient for a practical application. These results raise the question whether the predictions based on automatic Factor assignments have any utility.

In Experiment II, we therefore compared the outputs of SMILE+IBP to an informed baseline. For purposes of the baseline, we assume that it knows the probability of plaintiff and defendant winning. The baseline flips a biased coin, which predicts "plaintiff wins" with the prior probability for plaintiff. This baseline is preferable to the frequently used prediction of the majority class because it takes additional knowledge about the underlying class distribution into account, and because it will have roughly equal performance for cases won by either side, as required above.

SMILE+IBP with Timbl/ProP performs better than this informed baseline: It has an F-measure of 0.70, the baseline's is 0.66. This difference is statistically significant. In interpreting these numbers, one should note that the F-measure is a derived value and does not correspond to any observable features. In particular, we cannot conclude from the difference of 0.04 that SMILE+IBP is "merely 4% more accurate than the baseline." In fact, SMILE+IBP has more than 15% higher accuracy for those cases where it makes a prediction.

We also tested whether one could make equally accurate predictions as SMILE+IBP directly from the case texts, without going through the Factor representation. In a leave-one-out classification experiment with Timbl/ProP, we treated cases won by defendant as positive examples, cases won by plaintiff as negative examples. In 85% of the cases, the classifier predicted "plaintiff wins." The prediction that defendant wins was equally likely for cases won by either side. In effect, the classifier learned to predict the majority class. As argued above, these predictions are of no practical use. We conclude from this experiment that predicting the case outcome directly from the texts is not possible, and that representing cases in terms of Factors in SMILE+IBP is necessary.

In a more informal analysis, IBP's output also provides evidence that SMILE+IBP can generate useful reasoning, despite the many incorrect decisions it made. Shown in Fig. 1, CATO's "gold standard" representation of *National Rejectors* has Factors F7, Brought-Tools (p), F10, Disclosure-to-Outsiders (d), F15, Unique-Product (p), F16, Info-Reverse-Engineerable (d), F18, Identical-Products (p), F19, No-Security-Measures (d), and F27, Disclosure-In-Public-Forum (d).

According to a legal publisher's succinct summary of the court's reasoning, "evidence established that there were no actual trade secrets with respect to plaintiff's [products] and that, although individual defendants, former employees of plaintiff, had improperly used plaintiff's materials and drawings in production of products to compete with plaintiff's products, where plaintiff had not considered information regarding its products to be trade secrets, no warning had been given against use of information." The corresponding issues in IBP's domain model are whether security measures had been taken (Security-Measures), whether the information was valuable (Info-Valuable), and whether defendants had used the information (Info-Used).

As shown in Fig. 5, IBP's analysis of the manually represented case finds all these issues. It correctly reasons that plaintiff is favored for Info-Used, and that defendant is favored for the issue Security-Measures. However, for Info-Valuable, which has Factors for both sides, IBP cannot find sufficient evidence to conclude which side is favored and abstains on that issue. Overall, this analysis matches the court's opinion and leads to a correct prediction.

SMILE+IBP's automatic analysis identifies the same issues, but does not correspond equally well to the court's reasoning because of incorrect Factor assignments. Fig. 2 shows that SMILE found two extra Factors, F6, Security-Measures (p), and F25, Info-Reverse-Engineered (d). It also missed two Factors, F15, Unique-Product (p), and, especially, F27, Disclosure-In-Public-Forum (d), as discussed in Section 4.2. IBP's analysis of *National Rejectors* correctly identifies the issue Info-Used, and comes to the correct conclusion that the plaintiff was favored on the issue. Related to issue Info-Valuable, SMILE assigned only Factor F16, Info-Reverse-Engineered (d). This Factor tends to give inconclusive evidence on this issue and, therefore, is called a weak Factor. IBP takes a conservative approach in this situation; if it finds only a weak Factor, it not does include the issue in its prediction. SMILE also finds the issue Security-Measures. Because of the incorrectly assigned Factor F6, however, IBP cannot resolve the conflicting evidence, which includes Factors F6 and F19; it abstains for the issue. Based on this analysis of the issues, SMILE+IBP abstains for *National Rejectors*.

In processing the example, SMILE+IBP trips over an inconsistency between CATO's representation and SMILE's mark-up conventions. As noted, cases may have textual evidence for F6 as well as for F19 in SMILE+IBP because SMILE can assign both Factors, F6 and F19, to a case. On the other hand, IBP was developed following CATO's conventions that F6 and F19 are mutually exclusive. As a practical matter, it is difficult to implement a principled strategy for SMILE's choosing between F6 and F19 without deeper reasoning and an even more informative knowledge representation. In order to maintain IBP's accuracy and reliability, we do not attempt to resolve the conflict heuristically and let the program abstain on the issue. In a real-world application, a human could easily be alerted if SMILE assigned both F6 and F19 to a case and could determine manually which Factor should apply. Sometimes, indexing may be best handled by a human. Thus, this example raises a more general question for TCBR systems, whether and how best to keep a human in the loop.

6 Summary and Conclusions

This paper introduced SMILE+IBP, a system that integrates methods for assigning abstract indexing concepts to text cases with an interpretive CBR system for argumentation and prediction. The resulting system can carry out reasoning from text cases that goes beyond text retrieval. The goal of our investigation was to identify a good representation for indexing text cases. The experiments showed that both adding background knowledge to replace names and individual entities by their role for the case and using NLP to generate more powerful features, called Propositional Patterns, leads to performance improvements. While our experiments indicate that adding NLP is beneficial, they also pointed to some limitations. Especially for our complex and hard-to-parse texts, NLP remains a bottleneck to which many errors can be attributed, even though we had a robust, high-performance parser. Further, our experiments suggest that ProPs are most beneficial for Factors that correspond to relatively complex fact situations. On the other hand, for simpler fact patterns, like our F15, a representation like RR, that does not rely on NLP, may be suitable.

Among three different learning algorithms, NN had the best performance. Our data are very skewed and sparse, which makes it difficult to find patterns or generalize from the examples. Under these circumstances, NN did a better job identifying the most relevant examples, especially for the harder-to-find concepts.

SMILE+IBP has not reached the level of performance that would be required by attorneys. It is a step in that direction, however, in that it integrates indexing and reasoning with text cases. Despite all SMILE's limitations, the program does significantly better than an informed baseline. Moreover, as illustrated in the *National Rejectors* example, IBP is fairly robust. IBP+SMILE's analysis of the automatically indexed case is reasonable and identifies the major issues. Due to errors by SMILE, IBP abstains, indicating that human intervention may be required. Indexing text cases is a hard problem; automatic indexing will always be subject to certain limits and a human may need to tackle the harder problems of text interpretation.

Acknowledgements

This research has been supported by the National Science Foundation under award IDM-9987869. We would like to thank Ellen Riloff for giving us access to AutoSlog/Sundance, which have been a relevant resource and inspiration for this project.

References

Aleven, V. 2003. Using Background Knowledge in Case-Based Legal Reasoning: A Computational Model and an Intelligent Learning Environment. *Artificial Intelligence* 150(1-2):183–237.

Ashley, K., and Brüninghaus, S. 2003. A Predictive Role for Intermediate Legal Concepts. In *Proc. 16th Annual Conference on Legal Knowledge and Information Systems.*

Ashley, K. 1990. *Modeling Legal Argument, Reasoning with Cases and Hypotheticals.* MIT-Press.

Brüninghaus, S., and Ashley, K. 1999. Bootstrapping Case Base Development with Annotated Case Summmaries. In *Proc. 3rd International Conference on Case-Based Reasoning.*

Brüninghaus, S., and Ashley, K. D. 2001. The Role of Information Extraction for Textual CBR. In *Proc. 4th International Conference on Case-Based Reasoning.*

Brüninghaus, S., and Ashley, K. D. 2003. Combining Case-Based and Model-Based Reasoning for Predicting the Outcome of Legal Cases. In *Proc. 5th International Conference on Case-Based Reasoning.*

Burke, R.; Hammond, K.; Kulyukin, V.; Lytinen, S.; Tomuro, N.; and Schonberg, S. 1997. Question-Answering from Frequently-Asked Question Files: Experiences with the FAQ-Finder System. *AI Magazine* 18(1):57–66.

Burke, R. 1998. Defining the Opportunities for Textual CBR. In *Proc. AAAI-98 Workshop on Textual Case-Based Reasoning.*

Cardie, C., and Howe, N. 1997. Improving Minority Class Prediction Using Case-Specific Feature Weights. In *Proc. 14th International Conference on Machine Learning.*

Cohen, P. 1995. *Empirical Methods for Artificial Intelligence.* MIT-Press.

Cunningham, C.; Weber, R.; Proctor, J. M.; Fowler, C.; and Murphy, M. 2004. Investigating Graphs in Textual Case-Based Reasoning. In *Proc. 7th European Conference on Case-Based Reasoning.*

Daelemans, W.; Zavrel, J.; van der Sloot, K.; and van den Bosch, A. 2004. TiMBL: Tilburg Memory Based Learner, version 5.02. http://ilk.kub.nl/software.html.

Daniels, J., and Rissland, E. 1997. Finding Legally Relevant Passages in Case Opinions. In *Proc. 6th International Conference on Artificial Intelligence and Law.*

Dietterich, T. 1996. Statistical Tests for Comparing Supervised Classification Learning Algorithms. Oregon State University Technical Report.

Gupta, K., and Aha, D. W. 2004. Towards Acquiring Case Indexing Taxonomies from Text. In *Proc. 6th International Florida Artificial Intelligence Research Society Conference.*

Lenz, M. 1999. *Case Retreival Nets as a Model for Building Flexible Information Systems.* Ph.D. Dissertation, Humboldt University, Berlin, Germany.

McCallum, A. K. 2004. Bow: A toolkit for statistical language modeling, text retrieval, classification and clustering. http://www.cs.cmu.edu/ ~mccallum/bow.

Riloff, E. 2003. From Manual Knowledge Engineering to Bootstrapping: Progress in Information Extraction and NLP. Invited Talk at the Fifth International Conference on Case-Based Reasoning (ICCBR-03), http://www.iccbr.org/iccbr03/invited.html.

Rose, D. 1994. *A Symbolic and Connectionist Approach to Legal Information Retrieval.* Hillsdale, NJ: Lawrence Earlbaum Publishers.

Salzberg, S. 1997. On Comparing Classifiers: Pitfalls to Avoid and a Recommended Approach. *Data Mining and Knowledge Discovery* 1(3):317–328.

Using Ensembles of Binary Case-Based Reasoners

Bill Cheetham and Joe Shultz

General Electric Global Research, 1 Research Circle, Niskayuna,
NY 12309, USA
{cheetham, Shultz}@research.ge.com

Abstract. An ensemble of case-based reasoning systems was created to diagnose unplanned shutdowns of large gas turbines. One case-based reasoning system was created for each of the four most common causes of the shutdowns. Each of these reasoners determines its confidence that the root cause it diagnoses is the actual root cause or not. A fusion module combines these confidence values into a single diagnosis for the shutdown.

1 Introduction

Ensembles of Case-Based Reasoning (CBR) systems can have better results than a single CBR system for many classification and diagnostic tasks. Recent work in multi-classifier systems [7, 12] has shown that a set of binary (i.e. two class) classifiers can improve the accuracy of multi-class (i.e. more than two classes) classifiers, such as a diagnostic system. A set of binary classifiers decreases the complexity of the individual classifiers but increases the complexity of the system by requiring the creation of multiple classifiers and a process for combining the results of the set of classifiers. These increases in complexity can be reduced by using a Genetic Algorithm for tuning the CBR system [1] and a confidence value in the result of the CBR system [5] to facilitate the combination of the classifier results. This paper will show how an ensemble of binary CBR systems that each produces a confidence value can be used for multi-classification tasks, such as diagnostics for a large gas turbine.

1.1 Problem Description – Large Gas Turbines

General Electric (GE) Energy implemented a CBR system for diagnosing unexpected shutdowns (also called trips) of large gas turbines. However, there was a problem with creating the similarity measure for the CBR system. The problem is that there are many causes for the turbine trips and different attributes are important for different trips. The set of attribute weights for the similarity showed the average importance of the attributes, but some causes had specific attributes that were only important for that root cause. The standard sum of weighted attribute distance similarity algorithm did not do a good job of retrieving the cases most appropriate to new problems with these trip causes. A simple example of this problem can be shown in the car diagnostics domain. Imagine a car diagnostic system that determines the reason for a car not starting. In this example we will say that there are only two reasons a car will not start,

H. Muñoz-Avila and F. Ricci (Eds.): ICCBR 2005, LNAI 3620, pp. 152 – 162, 2005.

either the battery is dead or the car is out of gas. A standard CBR system will have cases that have attributes for battery charge and gas gauge reading, see Figure 1a. These attributes would both be important in the similarity calculation, so the battery charge could have an effect on whether or not one out-of-gas case matches another out-of-gas case. A ensemble of two CBR systems could be created for the car not starting problem where one CBR system diagnoses if the battery is dead using the battery charge attribute and another diagnoses if the car is out of gas using the gas gauge attribute, see Figure 1b. Then a fusion module can take the output of the two CBR systems and determine the correct output for the ensemble.

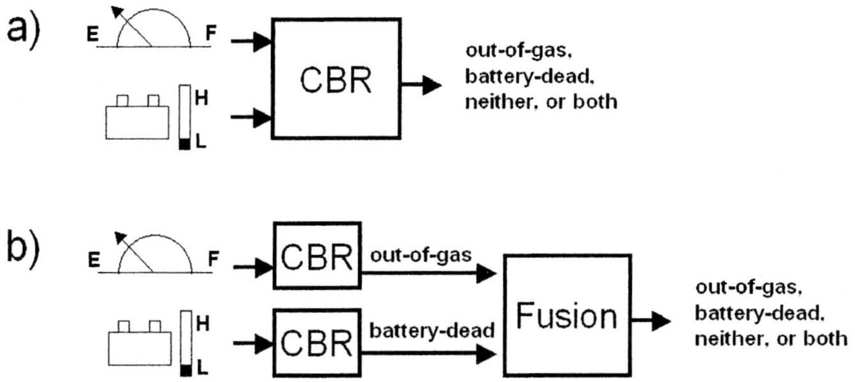

Fig. 1. Car Diagnostic as a) Standard CBR and b) an Ensemble

The car example is similar to our gas turbine diagnostics problem except there are fifty-two ways to trip a turbine and identifying each way depends on a set of attributes and possibly heuristic domain knowledge. This makes a single similarity function for gas turbine diagnostics very complicated. We wanted to make a similarity function that is simple to understand and maintain. In order to diagnose gas turbines we created an ensemble of CBR systems where each system diagnoses if a single root cause was present or not then the results from all CBR systems are combined to give the recommendation for the ensemble.

1.2 Related Work

Using an ensemble of CBR systems is not a new idea. Cunningham and Zenobi described how a diverse set of classifiers would produce a lower error than the member classifiers [4]. They suggest each CBR classifier should have a different subset of the attributes. They select a subset of attributes that does a "good" job as a classifier and tends to disagree with the other classifiers when it is not correct. We are following these guidelines and adding that these subsets can be constructed using domain knowledge where each subset contains the attributes necessary for diagnosing a single fault. Plaza and Ontanon showed how a set of CBRs could be used in a multiagent system [9]. When one CBR agent asks another CBR agent to solve a problem the second agent can say "sorry, it cannot solve the problem" or "yes, it can solve the problem." If it can solve the problem it also says how many cases it has that support the solution provided. We have built a system that can also say "sorry, it cannot solve the problem" or "yes, it can solve it," but when our CBR system can solve the problem it sends back a confidence value that predicts the correctness of the solution based on how many cases it has that support the solution provided and many other confidence indicators, see [5] for a list of confidence indicators. The confidence value maps the outputs to approximate probability estimates [12] in the correctness of the root cause suggested.

Friedman describes the use of a set of two-class classifiers to solve a multi-class problem [7]. He suggests creating a decision boundary between every pair of problems. For example, if there were four classes (F1, F2, F3, F4) then there would be decision boundaries between F1 and F2, F1 and F3, F1 and F4, F2 and F3, F2 and F4, and F3 and F4. We will take this idea but create classifiers that differentiate a class from the union of all other classes. In the example above there would be four classifiers, F1 and the union of F2 + F3 + F4, F2 and the union of F1 + F3 + F4, F3 and the union of F1 + F2 + F4, and F4 and the union of F1 + F2 + F3.

Two methods for combining two class classifiers in solving multiple class problems were described by Tax and Duin [12]. They compared having each two-class classifier vote, using one vote per classifier, with a real valued confidence value for each classification. Their confidence value is a function of the distance from the object being classified to the nearest decision boundary. They found that the confidence value gives at least as good and often better results than the voting strategy. We will also use a confidence value, but as stated above it will be based on a larger set of confidence indicators than just the distance to the nearest decision boundary.

There is no reason to restrict the individual reasoner to being CBR systems. Bonissone [2] describes a system that uses a CBR system, neural net, and regression tree to each solve the problem of determining the value of real estate. The final value for a property is the combination of the values from the three systems.

1.3 Real World Ensemble Processes

Before we discuss the turbine domain we will briefly mention two domains where a problem is solved in multiple ways. One domain is bird identification, where the general impression, size and shape (GISS) technique is used. GISS identifies a bird based on size and shape, plumage, activity, sound, nest, and egg. Each of these methods of identification is done independently then combined to classify the bird. The plumage module would use the attributes about the birds' throat, collar, breast, wings, tail, head, eyes, bill and legs. The eggs module would use attributes about the eggs' length, width, shape, color, texture, weight, and markings. A web site that describes GISS in more detail is http://www.sabirding.co.za/rmm/tour/id.htm. The GISS technique is a modified version of how World War II anti-aircraft gunners identified friendly and enemy aircraft.

As another example, recent research in neurobiology [8] has shown that the human brain acts as a coordinated ensemble. The brain is functionally divided into many competing regions as is described by Koch.

"The cortical areas in the back of the brain are organized in a loosely hierarchical manner, with at least a dozen levels, each one subordinate to the one above it. ... Coalitions of neurons, coding for different objects in the world, compete with each other; that is, one coalition strives to suppress the activity of neurons that code for other objects. ... Usually only a single coalition survives."

The coalitions are organized in columns going up the cortical hierarchy. The firing strength of the neurons in the columns is proportionate to the column's confidence that it has identified the object for which it codes. It is believed that these columns also store explicit memories (i.e., cases), which are retained, retrieved, and reused to allow the neurons to perform their pattern matching function. One goal of the authors is to determine the usefulness of this brain model in solving their real world problems.

The book "Wisdom of Crowds" [11] gives guidelines on how a group can be smarter than a single expert. The group should be diverse, independent, decentralized, and as competent as possible. The individual CBR systems of an ensemble should also follow these guidelines. Independence and decentralization are an easy task for computer algorithms, so developers should strive for the system to be as diverse and competent as possible. If different individual reasoners provide similar functionality then there is little value in having both reasoners. So, each reasoner should perform a different function than all others. You also want each reasoner to be as useful as possible for its function. So, they should be competent with the lowest error rate possible.

2 Existing CBR System

Engineers at GE Energy's monitoring and diagnostics (M&D) center in Atlanta remotely diagnose gas turbine trips many times every day. A diagnostic CBR system has been created to automate a portion of their analysis [6]. When a trip happens, real time data from sensors on the turbines is automatically downloaded from the turbine's controller. The engineers usually look at a subset of the sensor values to make a hypothesis about the root cause then review all data needed to confirm this hypothesis. The CBR system will classify the trip into one of six possibilities. These possibilities are four common trip causes, one bin called "Other" that represents any other trip besides these four, or "Unknown." We are not allowed to disclose the actual four trip causes, but for this paper we can call them problems with Fuel, Controls, Sensors, and Speed. As mentioned earlier, there are 52 ways to trip a turbine so 48 of these are lumped together into the "Other" bin. A classification of "Unknown" means the CBR system could not determine which of the root causes applied to the trip (i.e., could not pick one of the other five choices with confidence). The architecture of the CBR system is shown in Figure 2. When a trip is detected the features needed for diagnosis are automatically calculated from sensor data and placed in the 'New Trip" database table. The CBR decision engine is started and the Retrieval module accesses weights from the configuration file to select cases from a case base. The distance to each case is calculated and the most similar ones are placed in the "Nearest Neighbor" table. These nearest neighbors are used to determine the root cause of the trip and the confidence [5] that the root cause is correct. The root cause and confidence are placed in the "Root Cause" table. Information from the "New Trip," Nearest Neighbors," and "Root Cause" tables are used to display the results of the CBR system to a user. After the turbine is fixed the root cause is verified and the case is added to the case base. The initial architecture of this CBR system and an evolutionary algorithm (EA) that optimizes the configuration parameters are described in [1].

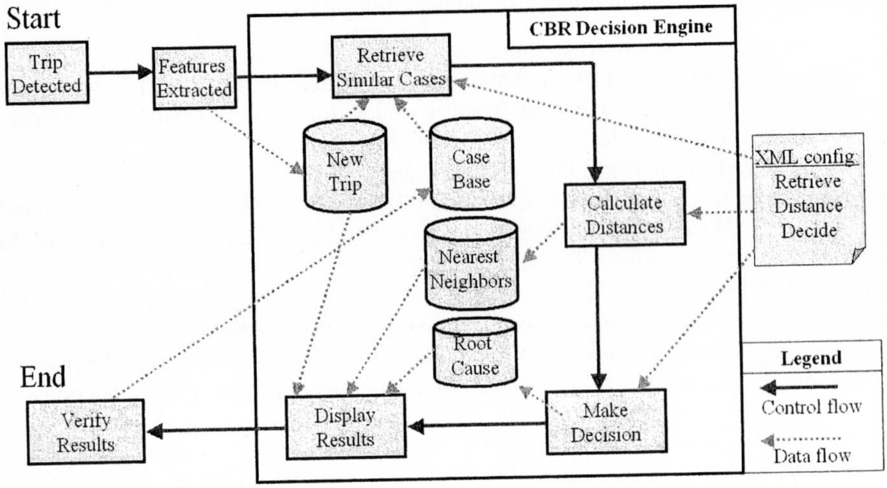

Fig. 2. CBR Process

Each turbine has about two thousand sensors that record control settings, temperatures, pressures, and many other pieces of information. A case consists of about thirty attributes that are calculated from a subset of these sensors and the validated root cause. Not all of these attributes are present in every case because of different turbine configurations. One of the most useful attributes for each type of root cause is listed below. The root cause which uses the attribute is listed first, then a dash, then a short description of the attribute, and then the attribute name in parenthesis.

1) Fuel - Time before trip of last transfer of fuel (last trans)
2) Control - Time before trip of last change in the control setting (last change)
3) Sensors - Difference between high and low temperature sensors (temp diff)
4) Speed - Speed of turbine rotor at trip in revolutions per minute (RPM)

The case base has 456 verified cases. These cases include all root causes that took place during the time data was collected. Only about 20% of the cases have the one of the four root causes that the system can diagnose. There is a separate test set with 302 cases. The parameters of the CBR system were tuned using the EA, which used leave-one-out testing on the case base to evaluate the fitness of a set of parameters. The results of leave-one-out testing on the case base using the final set of parameters is given in Table 1. The rows give the actual root cause and the columns are the root cause suggested by the CBR system. For this paper, we used a simplified version of the confidence calculation that was used in production. If the weighted sum of similarities for a class is greater than 0.6 then that class is the one suggested. If there is no class with a value of 0.6 then the suggested class is “Unknown.” The user interface shows the root cause when it is one of the four classes diagnosed and does not show it when it is "Other" or "Unknown," so Table 1 is functionally identical to Table 2, which has "Other" combined with "Unknown."

Table 1. Confusion Matrix for Training Set

	Fuel	Control	Sensors	Speed	Other	Unknown
Fuel	25	0	0	0	2	1
Control	0	8	0	0	1	2
Sensors	0	0	5	0	12	7
Speed	0	0	0	13	0	2
Other	4	1	0	0	369	1

Table 2. Combined Confusion Matrix for Training Set

	Fuel	Control	Sensors	Speed	Unknown
Fuel	25	0	0	0	3
Control	0	8	0	0	3
Sensors	0	0	5	0	29
Speed	0	0	0	13	2
Other	4	1	0	0	370

A single numeric score for the competency of the case base is obtained by multiplying the cells of the confusion matrix with the corresponding cells of a reward matrix and summing the products. Table 3 shows a reward matrix. The values on the diagonal are correct so they get a positive score. The values not on the diagonal and not in the "Unknown" column are incorrect so they get a negative score. The size of the positive and negative scores depends on the monetary value of being correct and incorrect respectively. The value of the cells in the "unknown" column can be positive, zero, or negative. A positive score would make the ensemble less likely to propose a guess the larger the value (i.e, having more false negatives). A negative score would make the ensemble more likely to take a guess when the correctness is questionable (i.e., having more false positives). The score for the combination of Tables 2 and 3 is 551. The higher this number the better.

Table 3. Reward Matrix for Training Set

	Fuel	Control	Sensors	Speed	Unknown
Fuel	4	-12	-12	-12	1
Control	-12	4	-12	-12	1
Sensors	-12	-12	4	-12	1
Speed	-12	-12	-12	4	1
Other	-12	-12	-12	-12	1

Using this numeric scoring we ran the EA multiple times and obtained some surprising results. The weights returned by the EA were usually quite different from run to run but the score was the same. The EA would usually converge in the first five generations and then never surpass that score. We investigated the reason for this and found two causes. First, when the weight of an attribute useful for one type of trip was increased it would help the accuracy of that trip but could hurt the accuracy of all other trip causes. Secondly, many of the cases that were incorrectly classified as "Other" were surrounded in most dimensions by cases classified as "Other," so no set of weights would be able to correctly classify the case. Additional attributes, which do not currently exist, may be needed to correctly classify some of the incorrect cases.

3 Gas Turbine Ensembles

The ensemble will make all possible hypotheses at once and have an individual CBR system for each hypothesis. The transformation of the existing CBR system into an ensemble of CBR systems involved

- Creating multiple CBR systems that determine if the root cause of the cases is either the root cause being diagnosed by the individual CBR system or one of the 51 other root causes,
- Retuning all parameters for each individual CBR module (including attribute weights and confidence calculation) using the EA, and
- Creating a fusion module to combine the results of the individual CBR modules.

The multiple CBR systems shown in Figure 3 were used to replace the single CBR Decision Engine from Figure 1. We wanted the ensemble of CBR modules to run off the same database structure that was in place for the single CBR system, so adapting the retrieve module was necessary. The retrieve module maps all root causes into just two options, the root cause of the individual CBR system and "Other". For example, the Fuel CBR maps all root causes that are not Fuel to "Other."

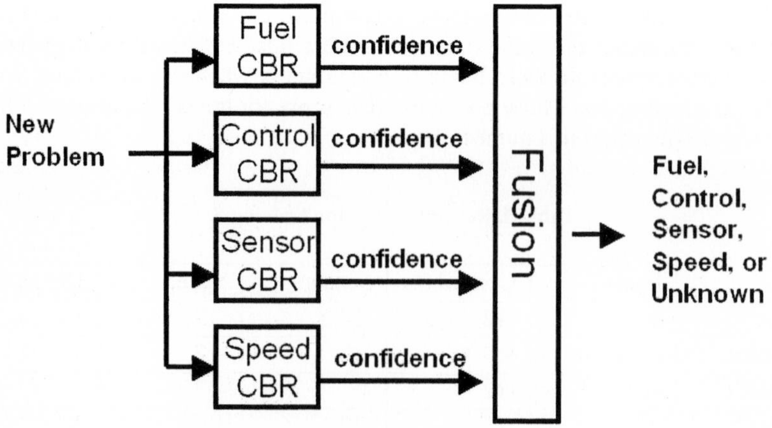

Fig. 3. Ensemble of Case-Based Reasoners

3.1 Tuning the Parameters of the Individual CBR Systems

The EA was used to determine attribute weightings and confidence parameters in each of the individual CBR systems. Table 4 shows the weightings for each individual CBR system in the ensemble. The four attributes listed in section two are the attributes in the first four columns. The last column has the confidence value that needs to be exceeded in order to suggest a root cause instead of "Unknown."

Table 4. Parameter weights

	Last trans	Last change	Temp diff	RPM	Confidence
Fuel CBR	0.5	0.1	0	0.3	0.5
Control CBR	0.1	0.3	0.7	0.7	0.3
Sensor CBR	0	0.1	0.9	0.1	0.7
Speed CBR	0.2	0	0	0.6	0.3

The retrieval, distance, and decide modules of the individual CBR systems could be further differentiated with customizations such as different values of k (from kNN) in retrieval and domain knowledge specific to the individual root cause that changes how the distance and decision calculations are performed. A fifth binary CBR system could be created for the root cause "Other." We have not made any of these changes, but hope to when this project continues.

3.2 Fusion Module

The fusion module takes the confidence values from each individual CBR system and determines a single suggested root cause. Published methods of fusing results range from simple voting techniques to learning combination functions [10]. Burke suggested a variety of methods for combining CBR recommender systems [3] that included a weighted method of numerically combining recommendations and a switching method of having the fusion module select the best recommendation. None of these methods had the advantage of individual classifiers or recommenders that provide a confidence value in the likeliness that they are correct. With this confidence value, we simply selected the root cause with the highest confidence as our recommendation and displayed it to the user. If no individual classifiers were confident in the solution then we return "Unknown." In practice, if more than one individual CBR system had the same highest confidence or confidences within a predefined range then we would display both root causes to the user. The user could choose to view all root causes that had confidence. However, for a fair comparison with the single CBR approach we forced the fusion module to select a single root cause or "Unknown." The result of the ensemble of CBRs is given in Table 5. The evaluation score for this set of results is 567 as compared to 551 for the single CBR approach. The ensemble had slightly better results. But there were more tunable parameters in the ensemble, which increases the risk of over tuning the system. The next section applies both the single CBR systems and the ensemble to a test set.

Table 5. Confusion Matrix for Ensemble

	Fuel	Control	Sensor	Speed	Unknown
Fuel	27	0	0	0	1
Control	0	11	0	0	1
Sensors	0	0	4	0	30
Speed	0	0	0	14	1
Other	4	1	0	0	370

4 Test Results and Conclusion

The single CBR system and Ensemble of CBRs were both applied to a test set of 302 trips that we collected after the ones used for the case based. The confusion matrix for the results of the single CBR system is shown in Table 5 and the results for the ensemble are given in Table 6. The evaluation score for the single CBR is 229 and the ensemble is 230, so the results are very similar. It would have been nice to have had results that more clearly showed one of the techniques to be superior, but these are the results we obtained. For now, we cannot conclude that the ensemble is better than the single CBR system for this one example. However, the slight improvement in the evaluation score coupled with the increased modularity and success of ensembles of binary classifiers in other domains shows that there is enough potential to continue this line of research. As a side note, the results for the test set were worse than those for the case base. One reason for this is that there were some new types of control trips that do not exist in the case.

Table 6. Confusion Matrix for Single CBR on Test Set

	Fuel	Control	Sensor	Speed	Unknown
Fuel	5	0	0	0	4
Control	0	0	1	0	7
Sensors	0	1	2	0	9
Speed	0	0	0	5	4
Other	4	4	2	1	253

Table 7. Confusion Matrix for Ensemble on Test Set

	Fuel	Control	Sensor	Speed	Unknown
Fuel	6	0	0	0	3
Control	0	1	0	0	7
Sensors	0	1	1	0	10
Speed	1	0	0	4	4
Other	4	4	1	1	254

5 Future Work

We plan to continue gathering test data and increase the number of root causes covered by this CBR system. The ensemble technique can be re-evaluated when these test cases and root causes are added. It is possible that the ensemble will be more scaleable than the single CBR system. There are other domains at GE where single CBR systems have been used to automate the diagnostic process [13], so we hope to apply the ensemble technique to these domains. In general, the ensemble technique could work for any decision problem where the problem is decomposable into sub-problems or there are multiple ways of solving the problem.

Finally, we would like to add features that are inspired by neurobiology. Two of these features are augmenting the confidence values sent to the fusion module and having the fusion module provide feedback to the individual CBR systems. First, the confidence values could be more than one crisp number. A variety of explanatory information could be sent from the individual CBR systems to the Fusion module in order to allow the Fusion module to make a more informed conclusion. Second, the neurological connections in the brain go up to fusion modules and down from the fusion modules to lower levels. Individual CBR systems could receive additional attributes that are sent back down from the fusion module to resolve conflicts and prompt another session that continues until a single conclusion is made, a cycle is detected, or a set limit is reached. This feedback might also be used to maintain the weights of the CBR system similar to the way backpropagation is used to train a neural net. Figure 4 shows an ensemble that would include these features.

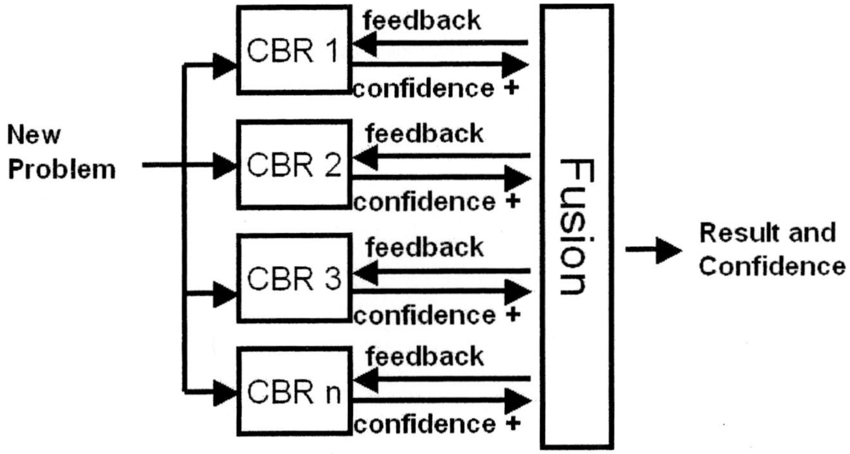

Fig. 4. Ensemble Based on Neurobiological Model of Brain

References

1. Aggour, K., Pavese, M., Bonissone, P., Cheetham, W., SOFT-CBR: A Self-Optimizing Fuzzy Tool for Case-Based Reasoning, The 5th International Conference on Case-Based Reasoning, Trondheim, Norway, June 23 -26 (2003)

2. Bonissone, P., Cheetham, W., Golibersuch, D., Khedkar, P., Automated Residential Property Valuation: An Accurate and Reliable Approach Based on Soft Computing, in Soft Computing in Financial Engineering, R. Ribeiro, H. Zimmermann, R.R. Yager, & J. Kacprzyk (Eds.), Physica-Verlag Springer-Verlag, Heidelberg (1998)
3. Burke, R., Hybrid Recommender Systems with Case-Based Reasoning, Seventh European Conference on Case-Based Reasoning, Madrid, (2004)
4. Cunningham, P., Zenobi, G., Case Representation Issues for Case-Based Reasoning from Ensemble Research, Fourth International Conference on Case-Based Reasoning, Vancouver, Canada, July/August (2001)
5. Cheetham, W., Price, J., Measures of Solution Accuracy in Case-Based Reasoning Systems, Seventh European Conference on Case-Based Reasoning, Madrid, August 30 - September 2 (2004)
6. Devaney, M., Cheetham, W., Case-Based Reasoning for Gas Turbine Diagnostics, The 18th International FLAIRS Conference, Clearwater Beach, Florida, (2005)
7. Friedman, J., Another approach to polychotomous classification, Technical report, Department of Statistics, Stanford University, Stanford, CA, (1996)
8. Koch, C., The Quest for Consciousness: A Neurobiological Approach, Roberts and Company, Engelwood, Colorado, (2004)
9. Plaza, E., Ontanon, S., Ensemble Case-based Reasoning: Collaboration Policies for Multiagent Cooperative CBR, Fourth International Conference on Case-Based Reasoning, Vancouver, Canada, July/August (2001)
10. Roli, F., Giacinto, G., Vernazza, G., Methods for Designing Multiple Classifier Systems, Multiple Classifier Systems: Second International Workshop, MCS 2001 Cambridge, UK, July 2-4, (2001)
11. Surowiecki, J., The Wisdom of Crowds, Doubleday, New York (2004)
12. Tax, D., Duin, R., Using two-class classifiers for multi-class classification. In International Conference on Pattern Recognition, Quebec City, QC, Canada, August (2002)
13. Varma, A., ICARUS: Design and Development of a Case-Based Reasoning System for Locomotive Diagnostics, Third International Conference on Case-Based Reasoning, Seeon Monastery, Germany, July (1999)

Transfer in Visual Case-Based Problem Solving

Jim Davies[1], Ashok K. Goel[2], and Nancy J. Nersessian[2]

[1] School of Computing, Queen's University, Kingston, Ontario, K7L 3N6, Canada
jim@jimdavies.org
[2] College of Computing, Georgia Institute of Technology, Atlanta, Georgia 30332, USA
{nancyn, goel}@cc.gatech.edu

Abstract. We present a computational model of case-based visual problem solving. The Galatea model and the two experimental participants modeled in it show that 1) visual knowledge is sufficient for transfer of some problem-solving procedures, 2) visual knowledge facilitates transfer even when non-visual knowledge might be available, and 3) the successful transfer of strongly-ordered procedures in which new objects are created requires the reasoner to generate intermediate knowledge states and mappings between the intermediate knowledge states of the source and target cases. We describe Galatea, the two models created with it, and related work.

1 Introduction

Experimental evidence shows that visual knowledge often plays a role in case-based reasoning [2,7,11]. Why might this be? What functions do the visual representations serve in retrieval, adaptation, evaluation and storage of cases? These questions are very broad because they pertain to a variety of cognitive phenomena ranging from visual perception to external memory to mental imagery. In order to explore these issues deeply, in the following discussion we focus exclusively on case-based problem solving. Problem solving involves generating a procedure which may contain a number of steps. We will call procedures with the following two properties "strongly-ordered procedures:" 1) two or more steps are involved, and 2) some steps cannot be executed before some other steps have already been executed. Case-based problem solving is taking a solution from a source case and applying that solution or a modification of it to a target case.

Many past case-based systems in problem-solving domains have used visual knowledge and have supported visual reasoning (e.g., ARCHIE [13]. AskJef, [1]). However, these systems typically contain multi-modal cases, i.e., cases that contain both visual (e.g., photographs, drawings, diagrams, animations and videos) and non-visual knowledge (e.g., goals, constraints, plans and lessons). As a result, the precise role of visual knowledge in case-based problem solving remains unclear. In contrast, the present work deals with cases that contain only visual knowledge. Further, past case-based systems such as ARCHIE and AskJef leave the adaptation task to the user and do not automate the transfer of diagrammatic knowledge from a source case to a target problem. The present work directly addresses the transfer task in case-based problem solving.

H. Muñoz-Avila and F. Ricci (Eds.): ICCBR 2005, LNAI 3620, pp. 163 – 176, 2005.

Some domains are replete with visual information (e.g. libraries of CAD files, photograph databases), but others that need not explicitly contain visual information can be visually represented all the same. For example, effectively connecting a battery to wires might be represented, among other ways, functionally (the battery needs to be physically in contact with the wire so it can conduct electricity) or visually (the image of the end of the wire is adjacent to the image of the battery). Even though other kinds of knowledge and representations of these domains might be used to reason, human beings often claim to experience visual imagery when reasoning about them. The first hypothesis of this work is that visual knowledge alone is sufficient for automatic transfer of problem-solving procedures in some domains. The second hypothesis is that visual knowledge facilitates transfer even when non-visual knowledge might be available. One important implication of this hypothesis is that cases that when represented non-visually are semantically distant, could be represented in visually similar ways, thus facilitating transfer.

In this paper we describe the Galatea computational model, which, given a source problem-solving case and a target problem case, both represented visually, can solve the problem by transferring the solution from the source to the target case. We present Galatea and models of two human experimental participants implemented with it. The data we modeled comes from a cross-domain case-based problem-solving experiment [3]. Here we focus on two participants, L14 and L22. The source case (see Figure 1) is about a laboratory that needs to keep contaminated air from entering from the outside through its single door. The solution is to put in an airlock or vestibule, so that air is less likely to blow through both doors at once.

The unsolved target case describes a weed trimmer at the end of an arm that extends from the side of a truck. It clips the grass and weeds along the side of the road. The problem is that street signs get in the way. The task is to make the arm so that it can pass through the street signs. The transferred solution is to make an arm with a vestibule: While one door lets the sign into the vestibule, the other supports the arm. Then the first door closes, supporting the arm, and the second opens to release the sign on the other side. L14 was one of the participants who successfully solved this problem. The marks L14 made on his or her paper can be seen in Figure 2.

In the following section we will describe Galatea, using our model of L14 as a running example.

2 Galatea

The modeling architecture used to model L14 is an implemented LISP computer program called Galatea. The issue is how a case-based problem solver might represent its diagrammatic knowledge of the source case and target problem, and how might it transfer the relevant problem-solving steps from the source to the target?

Galatea represents a source case as a series of knowledge states starting from the initial knowledge state and ending in the final or goal knowledge state. A knowledge state is represented diagrammatically in the form of shapes, their locations, sizes, and motions (if any), and the spatial relationships among the shapes.

Please read the two problems below. At the bottom of the page, please try to solve **Problem 2.** *Draw a diagram to show what you're thinking. The solution to* **Problem 1** *may be helpful in solving* **Problem 2.**

Problem 1: A computer chip manufacturer has designed a special lab for manufacturing microscopic devices. They have taken great care to seal off the lab from the surrounding environment in order to keep the air inside the lab free of dust and undesirable gases. The problem, though, is that whenever lab workers enter or leave the room, the seal is broken and contaminated air is allowed in. The company is trying to design a door that will allow workers to enter and leave the lab easily, while minimizing the amount of contaminated air that is let in.

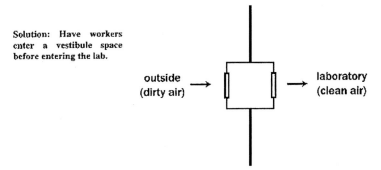

Solution: Have workers enter a vestibule space before entering the lab.

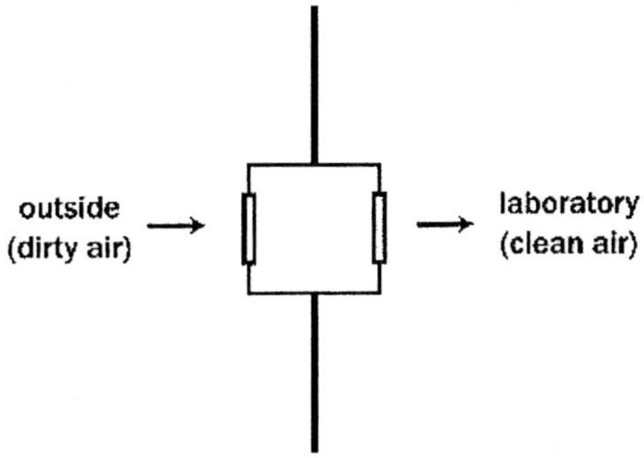

Problem 2: In order to trim the weeds that grow along the side of the road, the Department of Transportation has designed a weed trimmer that attaches to the end of a long pole sticking off the side of a truck. As the truck drives down the highway, the trimmer is extended about 6 feet to the right, perfectly positioned to trim the weeds at the side of the road. The problem is that the 6-foot pole is obstructed by sign posts that are positioned at the curb in certain parts of the city. The weed-trimmer pole, in fact, is exactly 2 feet too long to clear the sign posts. Although the weed-trimmer pole could be retracted or lifted out the way to clear the sign posts, this would interfere with the weed trimming. And although the pole could bend over the top of the sign posts, this would be impractical since in some areas the signs are 15 feet tall. The Department of Transportation is trying to design a pole that can pass *through* the sign posts without stopping or changing the position of the trimmer.

Fig. 1. L14's stimulus

In the space below, try to design a weed-trimmer pole that can pass through sign posts. Draw a diagram to illustrate what you're thinking.

The problem is 2 ft too long, so from 3½ ft to 4½ ft. Have a sliding bar that unlatches (twist) and retracts (Pull), for upcoming signs. And slides back up and latches when sign passes in. Then other arm does same and the sign passes through

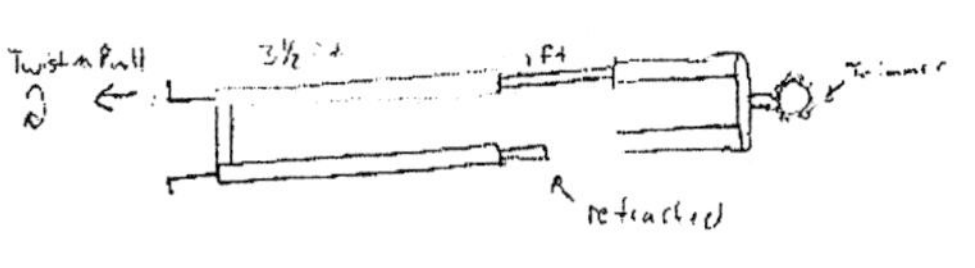

Fig. 2. The inscriptions L14 made on his or her experiment sheet

Succeeding states in the series of knowledge states are related through visual transformations such as move, rotate, scale and decompose. Each transformation relates two knowledge states. Transfer works by applying, step by step, each transformation in the source case to the knowledge states of the target case (See Figure 3).

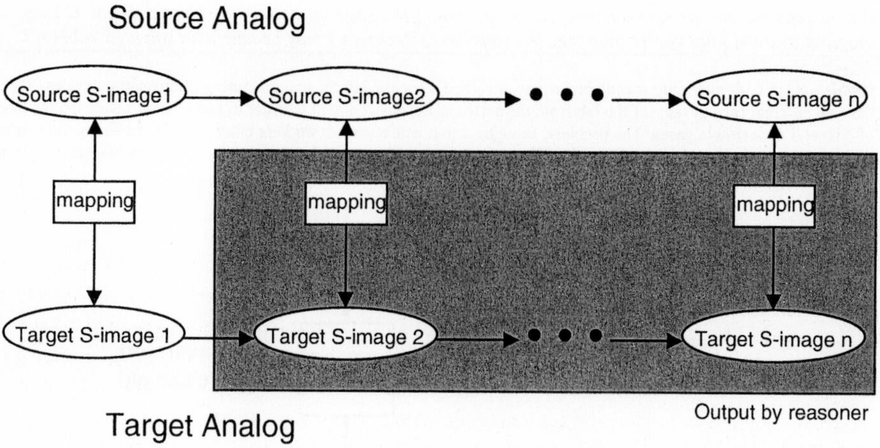

Fig. 3. Galatea's processing in the abstract

2.1 Knowledge Representation

Galatea describes visual cases using Covlan (Cognitive Visual Language), which consists of knowledge states, primitive elements, primitive relations, primitive transformations, general visual concepts, and correspondence and transform representations. In Covlan, all knowledge is represented as propositions relating two elements with a relation.

Knowledge States: Knowledge states in Covlan are symbolic images, or s-images, which contain visual elements, general visual concepts, and relations between them. Cases are represented by a series of s-images, connected with transformations.

Visual Transformations. An s-image in the sequence is connected to other s-images before and after it with transformations. Transformations, like ordinary functions, take arguments to specify their behavior.

These transformations control normal graphics transformations such as translation (*move-to-location*), and rotation (*rotate*). In addition there are transformations for adding and removing elements from the s-image (*add-element, remove-element*). Certain transformations (*start-rotating, stop-rotating, start-translation, stop-translation*) are changes to the dynamic behavior of the system under simulation. For example, *rotate* changes the initial orientation of an element, but in contrast *start-rotating* sets an element in motion.

Primitive Elements are the visual objects in a diagram. The element types are *rectangle, circle, arrow, line,* and *curve.* Each element is represented as a frame with attribute slots, such as *location, size, orientation,* or *thickness.* A particular example of an element is referred to as an *element instance.*

General Visual Concepts. These act as slot values for the primitive elements as well as arguments for the visual transformations. The concepts are *location, size, thickness, speed, direction, length, distance, angle,* and *direction.* Each concept has several values it can take. For example, the *size* can be *small, medium,* or *large,* and *thickness* can be *thin, thick* or *very-thick. Location* specifies an absolute qualitative location in an s-image (*bottom, top, center,* etc.)

Primitive Visual Relations. This class of symbols describes how certain visual elements relate to each other and to the values taken by general visual concepts. The visual relations are *touching, above-below,* and *right-of-left-of.* The motion relation is *rotation*.

Correspondence and Transform Representations. The knowledge of which objects in one s-image correspond to which objects in another is a *mapping,* which consists of a set of alignments between objects. Different sets of alignments compose different mappings. The ith s-image in the source and the ith s-image in the target have a *correspondence* between them; each correspondence (or *map*) can have any number of *mappings* associated with it (determining which mapping is the best is the "mapping problem.") The correspondence and mapping between the initial s-images (i=1) in the source and target is given as part of the input to Galatea; the system generates the subsequent correspondences and mappings.

Similarly, successive s-images in a series have *transform-connections.* These are needed so that Galatea can track how visual elements in a previous knowledge state change in the next.

2.2 Algorithm

Following is the control structure for Galatea's transfer of problem-solving procedures from a source case to the target problem. Figure 4 shows the s-image structure for L14's problem and solution. The Figure references in the algorithm description below refer to Figure 4.

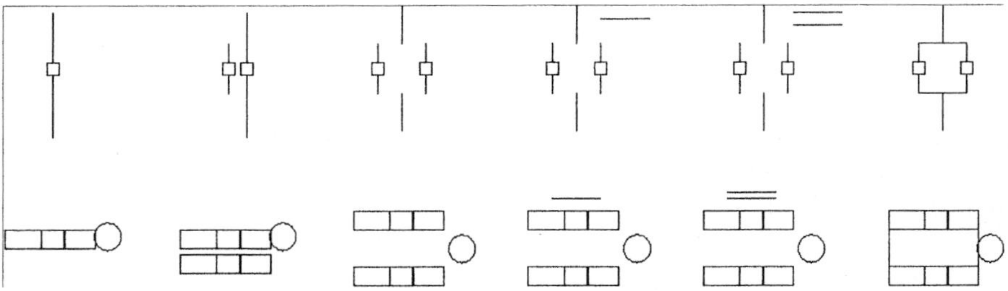

Fig. 4. Outline of our model of L14. The six images along the top represent the source, and the six images along the bottom the target, left to right, are separated by transformations: 1) *replicate*, 2) *add connections*, 3) *add component*, 4) another ad*d component*, and 5) *add connections*

The solution procedure (for the source, and then for the target) is that the doorway mechanism gets replicated, and then moved to the correct positions. Two walls are created to complete the vestibule, and finally they are placed in the correct position so that the vestibule is complete.

1. **Identify the first s-images of the target and source cases.** These are the current source and target s-images.

2. **Identify the transformations and associated arguments in the current s-image of the source case.** This step finds out how the source case gets from the current s-image to the next s-image. The model of L14 involves five transformations (see Figure 4). The first transformation is *replicate*. The second transformation is *add-connections* which places the door sets in the correct position in relation to the top and bottom walls. The third and fourth transformations are *add-component*, which adds the top and bottom containment walls. The fifth transformation, another *add-connections*, places these containment walls in the correct positions in relation to the door sets and the top and bottom walls.

3. **Identify the objects of the transformations.** The object of the transformation is what *object* the transformation acts upon. For L14's first transformation, this object is the parts of the door in the first s-image (we'll call it *door-set-l14s1*).

4. **Identify the corresponding objects in the target problem.** In the target, the trimmer arm's door mechanism is the corresponding object.

5. **Apply the transformation with the arguments to the target problem component.** A new s-image is generated for the target problem (bottom middle) to record the effects of the transformation. Replicate takes two arguments: some *object* and some *number-of-resultants*. In this case the *object* is *door-set-b1s1* (b1s1 means "base one, s-image two") and the *number-of-arguments* is two. The *replicate* is applied to the first L14 s-image, with the appropriate adaptation to the arguments: The mapping between the first source and target s-images indicates that the *door-set-b1s1* maps to the *door-set-l14s1*, so the former is used for the target's object argument. The number *two* is a literal, so it is transferred directly. Galatea generates *door-set1-l14s2* and *door-set2-l14s2* in the next s-image.

The second transformation is *add-connections*. The effect of this transformation is to place the replicated door-sets in the correct spatial relationships with the other element instances. It takes *connection-sets-set-b1s3* as the *connection/connection-set* argument. This is a set containing four connections. Galatea uses a function to recursively retrieve all connection and set proposition members of this set. These propositions are put through a function which creates new propositions for the target. Each proposition's relation and literals are kept the same. The element instance names are changed to newly generated analogous names. For example, *door1-endpoint-b1s3* turns into *door1-endpoint-l14s3*.

Then, similarly to the replicate function, horizontal target maps are generated, and the other propositions from the previous s-image are instantiated in the new s-image.

The inputs to this transformation are *nothing* (a literal denoting that there is not any thing in the previous s-image that is being modified), the connection set *connection-sets-set-b1s3*, the source s-image *lab-base1-simage2*, the current and next target s-images *l14-simage2* and *l14-simage3*, the mapping *l14-simage2—l14-simage3-mapping1,* and the rest of the memory.

6. **Map the original objects to the new objects in the target case.** A transform-connection and mapping are created between the target problem s-image and the new s-image (not shown). Maps are created between the corresponding objects. In this example it would mean a map between door-sets, as well as their component objects. Galatea does not solve the mapping problem, but a mapping from the correspon-

dences of the first s-image enables Galatea to automatically generate the mappings for the subsequent s-images.

7. **Map the new objects of the target case to the corresponding objects in the source case.** Here the parts of the door set in the target s-image are mapped to the parts in the second source s-image. This step is necessary for the later iterations (i.e. going on to another transformation and s-image). Otherwise the reasoner would have no way of knowing which parts of the target s-image the later transformations would operate on.

8. **Check to see if goal conditions are satisfied.** If they are, exit, and the solution is transferred. If not, and there are further s-images in the source case, set the current s-image equal to the next s-image and go to step 1.

We now present the main algorithm in pseudo code, followed by English descriptions of some of its functions.

```
Main
Input:
1. Source
2. Target Problem
3. Vertical mapping between source and target cases
Output:
1. A set of new target s-images
2. Vertical mappings between corresponding source and
           target s-images
3. Horizontal mappings between successive target states
4. Transformations connecting successive target states
Procedure
While more-source-states(goal-conditions, memory) do
         Current-target-s-image <- get-next-target-s-
           image(target problem, current s-image)
         Current-source-s-image <- get-next-source-s-
           image(source, current-s-image)
         Current-transformation <- get-
           transformation(current-s-image)
         Current-arguments <- get-arguments(current-
           source-s-image)
         Source-objects-of-transformation <- get-
           target-object-of-trans(current-source-s-
           image)
         Current-vertical-mapping <- get-
           mapping(current-target-s-image, current-
           source-s-image)
         Target-object-of-transformation <- get-source-
           object-of-transformation(current-vertical-
           mapping, source-objects-of-transformation)
         Target-arguments <- adapt-arguments(get-
           arguments(current-source-s-image)
         Memory <- memory + apply-
           transformation(current-transformation, tar-
           get-object-of-transformation, target-
           arguments)
         Memory <- memory + create-horizontal-
           mapping(current-target-s-image, get-next-
           target-s-image)
```

```
Current-target-s-image <- get-next-target-s-
  image(target problem, current-s-image)
Current-source-s-image <- get-next-source-s-
  image(source, current-s-image)
Memory <- memory + carry-over-unchanged rela-
  tionships(applied-transformation)
Memory <- memory + create-vertical-
  mapping(current-target-s-image, current-
  source-s-image)
```

Adapt Arguments. When an argument needs to be adapted to the target analog, Galatea looks at the argument and determines whether it is a literal, a function, or an element instance component of an s-image. Literals are returned verbatim. If the argument is a function (e.g. the number of people in a group) then Galatea applies the same function to the analogous group in the target and returns that value. If the argument is an element instance, then Galatea returns the analogous object in the target.

Carry Over Unchanged Relationships. The *get-analogous-chunks* sub-function constructs and returns chunks that are identical to the input chunks, except that the symbols that have maps in the input mapping are replaced with those symbols they are associated with in those maps. The vertical map relationships are carried over as well, constituting the vertical maps for unchanged element instances.

Creation of Horizontal Maps Between Changed Components. The *creation-of-horizontal-maps-between-changed-components* is embedded in each of the transformations. The transformation results are obtained from running the transformation. The *target-objects-of-transformation* are known because they are the input to the transformation. The two lists are put in alphabetical order and maps are created between each nth list object.

Creation of Horizontal Maps Between Unchanged Components. Similarly, *creation-of-horizontal-maps-between-unchanged-components* makes maps between old objects (the objects in the old s-image and new objects (from the current-s-image, minus the objects created by the transformation), alphabetizes them, and creates maps between the *n*th item in each list.

Creation of Vertical Maps Between Changed Components. The algorithm for creating vertical maps between changed components takes as input the transformation results in the source and target, alphabetizes them, and creates maps between the *n*th item in each list.

We can now evaluate what made L14's data (Fig. 2) differ from the stimulus drawing (Fig. 1): L14 features a longer vestibule in the drawing than the vestibule pictured in the stimulus. In fact, there is no trimmer arm (analogous to the wall in the lab problem) in the drawing at all that is distinct from the vestibule, save a very small section, apparently to keep the spinning trimmer blade from hitting the vestibule. The entire drawing is rotated ninety degrees from the source. The single lines in the source are changed to double lines in the target. The doors also slide in and out of the vestibule walls. What's interesting about this modification is that it does not appear that this kind of door opening is possible with the diagram given of the lab in the source: Since the door is a rectangle that is thicker than the lines representing the walls, the door could not fit into the walls. In contrast L14 explicitly makes the doors and walls thick (with two lines) and makes the doors somewhat thinner. L14 adds objects to the target not found in the source: a blade and a twisting mechanism to describe how the doors can work. L14 also included numerical parameters to describe the design of the trimmer: to describe length. Finally, L14 includes some mechanistic description of how the trimmer would work.

Of these seven differences, our model successfully re-creates four of them. The *rotation* of the source is modeled by a rotation in the target start s-image. In the s-image, all spatial relationships are defined only relative to other element instances in the s-image. Each instance is a part of a single set which has an orientation and direction. In the case of s-image 1 of the target, it is facing right. Since all locations are relative, there is no problem with transfer and each s-image in the model of L14 is rotated to the right. The *line to double line* difference is accounted for by representing the vestibule walls with rectangles rather than with lines, as it is in the source. Because the mapping between the source and target correctly maps the *side1* of the rectangle to the *startpoint* of its analogous line, the rectangle/line difference does not adversely affect processing transfer. The *long vestibule* difference is accounted for by specifying that the heights of the vestibule wall rectangles are *long*. In the source the vestibule wall lines are of length *medium*, but this does not interfere with transfer. The trimmer head *added object* is accounted for by adding a circle to the first s-image in the target.

Unaccounted for are the two bent lines emerging from the vestibule on the left side, the numeric dimensions and words describing the mechanism. Also, L14 shows one of the doors retracting, and the model does not. The model also fails to capture the double line used to connect the door sections, because the single line is transferred without adaptation from the source. This could be fixed, perhaps, by representing the argument to the *add-component* as a function referring to whatever element is used to represent another wall, rather than as a *line*.

3 The Galatea Model of Participant L22

L22 worked on the same problem as L14 and received in his or her stimuli the image presented in Fig. 5. The marks L22 made on the experiment sheet are reproduced in Fig. 6. Our model of L22 involves five transformations. The first transformation is *replicate*. To *replicate* the door mechanism, the starting state, s-image 1, must have a single door. A portion of the information in the first s-image of the source can be seen in Fig. 7. All of the objects in Fig. 7 are a part of *door-set-s1*. It takes in the *door-set1-s1* as an argument, generating *door-set1-s2* and *door-set2-s2* as output in the second s-image. There are three connected rectangles, corresponding to the top wall, door, and bottom wall. The second transformation is *add-connections* which places the door sets in correct position in relation to one another. The third and fourth transformations are *add-component*, which add the top and bottom containment walls. The fifth transformation, another *add-connections*, places these containment walls in the correct positions in relation to the door sets.

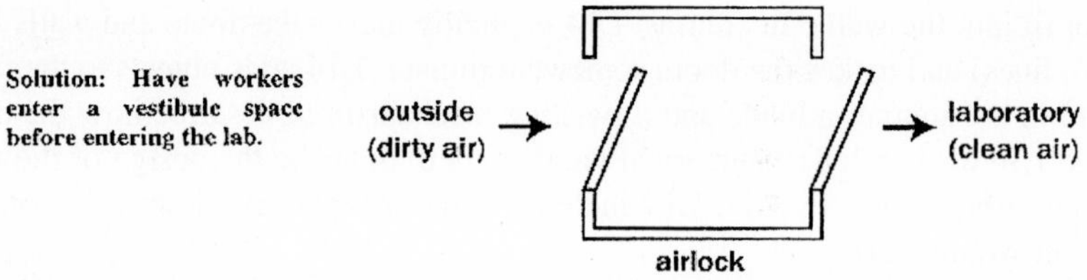

Fig. 5. The image from the source stimulus that L22 received in the experiment. It is a top-down view of the airlock. This stimulus's text (not shown) is identical to that of L14 (Figure 1)

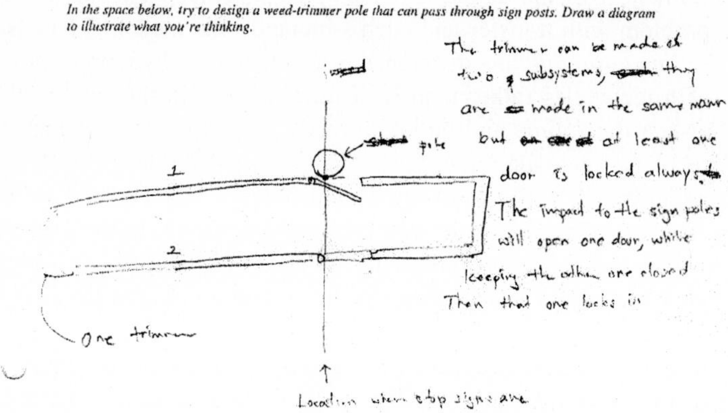

Fig. 6. The marks L22 made on his or her experimental sheet

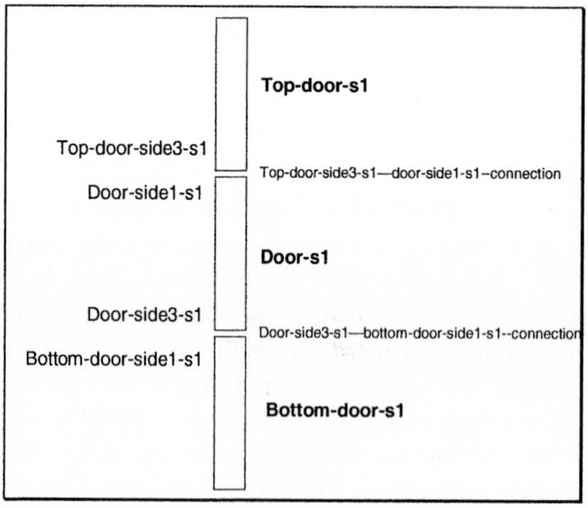

Fig. 7. A portion of the first s-image of the L22 model. S1 refers to the fact that the symbols are in the first s-image. The top-door, door, and bottom-door are all in the door set that gets replicated in transformation one

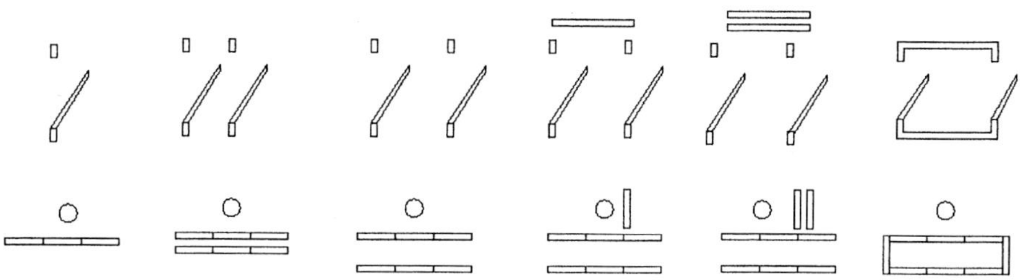

Fig. 8. Outline of our model of L22. The six images along the top represent the source, and the six images along the bottom the target, left to right, are separated by transformations: 1) *replicate*, 2) *add connections*, 3) *add component*, 4) *add component*, and 5) *add connections*

The images along the top of Fig. 8 represent the source s-images. The images along the bottom of Fig. 5 show the sequence of target s-images. Only the first s-image of the target is given as input to the system. The rest are generated by Galatea. The circle depicted represents a cross-section view of the sign that must pass through the arm. The door mechanism in the arm, which gets replicated and connected up properly, is oriented differently than the door in the lab problem, but the transformations are general enough to allow transfer. In the bottom right s-image we can see the solution state, as generated by Galatea. The redundant door mechanism will allow the sign to pass through one, into the vestibule, while the other door keeps the structure in place. Then the first door can close, supporting the structure, while the second door opens to let the sign post out the other side.

We can now examine what made L22 differ from the stimulus drawing: The entire drawing is rotated ninety degrees from the source. An object is added to the target that has no analog in the source: the trimmer. L22 features a proportionately longer vestibule than in the source, and has some explicit simulation diagrammed. Of these differences, all but the last were modeled by changing the nature of the start s-image for L22.

4 Related Work

In the introduction, we noted that the issue of visual knowledge in case-based reasoning is very broad and thus has attracted the attention of many researchers in several areas. In order to look at the issue deeply, we focused our discussion exclusively on case-based problem solving, i.e. case-based transfer of a procedure from a source case to a target case. Below we relate our work to some representative case-based problem solving systems with emphasis on systems use visual knowledge in transferring problem-solving procedures.

FABEL [8] is an example of a case-based system that adapts diagrammatic cases in the domain of architectural design. In FABEL, the source diagram specifies the spatial layout of a building or similar structure. FABEL adapts source diagrams by extracting and transferring specific structural patterns to the target problem. It uses domain-specific heuristics to guide pattern extraction and transfer. Galatea too adapts diagrams by extracting and transferring patterns. Pattern transfer in Galatea is facilitated by three main elements. Firstly, Galatea explicitly represents the knowledge states of its source cases in the form of s-images. Secondly, each s-image is composed of primitive visual elements and relations. Thirdly, succeeding knowledge states in Galatea's source cases are related by primitive visual transformations. In this way, Galatea captures the diagrammatic *problem solving* of the source cases. Given a mapping between the visual elements in the target problem and a source case, this knowledge enables Galatea to extract and transfer the appropriate series of visual transformations from the source case to the target problem. In particular, the knowledge states identify the names and arguments of specific transformations that need to be transferred from the source case to the target problem.

REBUILDER [9] is a case-based reasoner that does retrieval, mapping, and transfer of software design class diagrams. The diagrams are represented structurally, not visually, however. This means that, for example, that the connection is between two nodes is more important than the length and direction of that connection. That is, REBUILDER works with a different level of visual abstraction, a level at which only the structural relationships, such as connectedness, between visual elements are relevant to the task. In contrast, Galatea takes into account additional geometric information such as the length, direction and thickness of lines. What is the right level of visual abstraction for visual case-based problems requires additional research. The choices made by Galatea and REBUILDER depend largely on the specific domains in which they operate. In REBUILDER's domain of software design class diagrams, only the structural relations appear to be important.

FAMING [6] is a case-based reasoning system that uses cases describing physical mechanism parts. FAMING uses the SBF (Structure-Behavior-Function) ontology to describe the cases. The structure is described in terms of a metric diagram (a geometric model of vertices and connecting edges), a place vocabulary (a complete model of all possible qualitative behaviors of the device), and configuration spaces (a compact representation of the constraints on the part motions.) Shape features can involve two objects, expressing, for example, one part's ability to touch another part. Human designers are necessary for FAMING's processing. The designer chooses which cases and functions should be used, which dimensions the system should attempt to modify, and which shape features should be unified. It uses qualitative kinematics to propose design solutions for the desired function following the designer-suggested idea. Though not described as a visual system, the important parts of physical mechanisms of the sort FAMING uses inevitably contain much knowledge that could be construed as visual. However, FAMING modifies cases according to shape substitution, and, unlike Galatea, makes no attempt to transfer strongly-ordered procedures of any sort.

Non-visual case base problem-solving systems, such as CHEF [10] and PRODIGY [14] provide interesting points of comparison regarding the transfer process. CHEF is a case-based reasoner that transfers and adapts cooking recipes from a source to a target. CHEF does not create intermediate knowledge states. This is because it does not transfer procedures that create new objects. The Prodigy case-based reasoning system implements the theory of Derivational Analogy. It models transfer using memories of the justifications of each step, allowing for adaptation of the transferred procedure. Traces, called "derivations," are scripts of the steps of problem solving, along with the justifications for why the steps were chosen over others. PRODIGY too does not store the intermediate steps; instead it stores only a record of the changes made to them. This means that the states can be inferred, but are not explicitly present in the case memory. CHEF and PRODIGY avoid the generation of intermediate knowledge states and mappings because the examples with which they have been implemented do not have procedures that create new objects.

5 Conclusions

In the introduction to this paper, we described the two main hypotheses of this work: (1) visual knowledge alone is sufficient for transfer of problem-solving procedures in some domains, and (2) visual knowledge facilitates transfer even when non-visual knowledge might be available. Both hypotheses were strongly supported by the evidence described above, and we had an unexpected discovery of a third, which makes for three claims.

First, visual knowledge is sufficient for transfer of some problem-solving procedures. There are seven models written in Galatea that support this claim. We described the models of L14 and L22 in this paper. We modeled two additional participants from the Craig *et al.* experiment, a historical example from the scientific thinking of Maxwell [5], the fortress/tumor problem [4] and the cake/pizza problem [4]. Each of these models uses case-based reasoning to solve a problem using only visual knowledge. The fact that four of these models are based on human experimental participant data lend support to the hypothesis that this claim might apply to human problem solving, as well as artificial case-based reasoning systems, although more empirical research would be needed to substantiate this. As shown above, most of the differences between source and target, as displayed in the participant data, were accounted for in our models. In light of this research we can speculate for which domains visual knowledge might be sufficient for transfer of problem-solving procedures: those domains, the solution procedures of which *could* be adequately described with descriptions of changes to visio-spatial properties. A way to think about this is if the important differences between the problem and the solution are reflected in *visual* differences, then that problem is likely to fall in this class.

The second claim is that visual knowledge facilitates transfer even when non-visual knowledge might be available. L22's lab/weed trimmer problem involves physical systems that can be described visually or non-visually. Galatea's visual ontology of primitive elements and transformations allows transfer between systems that, though they may be semantically distant, have visual similarities, which facilitates the transfer. This is also true for the three other lab/weed trimmer participants, as well as for the fortress/tumor example.

In the course of building the models of Galatea, we discovered that the successful transfer of strongly-ordered procedures in which new objects are created requires the reasoner to generate intermediate knowledge states and mappings between the intermediate knowledge states of the source and target cases. Galatea shows why, in detail, this is so. Components of the problem are *created* by the operations, and these components are acted on by later operations. For L22's problem, for example, the door set must be replicated before the two sets can be moved in relation to one another. When the reasoner transfers the second operation of moving the door sets, how does it know what the corresponding objects are in the target? It must have some mapping to make this inference. And since one of the door sets did not exist in the start states of the problems, this mapping cannot be given as input with the initial mapping. The new knowledge state with the duplicated door set must be generated, and then a mapping must be made on the fly between it and the second knowledge state of the source case.

References

1. Barber, J., Jacobson, M., Penberthy, L., Simpson, R., Bhatta, S., Goel, A., Pearce, M., Shankar, M. & Stroulia, E. Integrating artificial intelligence and multimedia technologies for interface design advising. *NCR Journal of Research and Development,* 6(1), 75—85, October 1992.
2. Casakin, H., Goldschmidt, G.: Expertise and the use of visual analogy: Implications for design education. *Design Studies.* (1999)
3. Craig, D. L., Catrambone, R., Nersessian, N. J.: Perceptual simulation in analogical problem solving. In *Model-Based Reasoning: Science, Technology, & Values.* New York: Kluwer Academic / Plenum Pubishers. (2002) 167–191
4. Davies, J., Goel, A. K.: Representation issues in visual analogy. *Proceedings of the 25th Annual Conference of the Cognitive Science Society.* (2003) 300--305.
5. Davies, J., Nersessian, N. J., Goel, A. K.: Visual models in analogical problem solving. *Foundations of Science, Special Issue on Model-Based Reasoning: Visual, Analogical, Simulative.* By Magnani, L. and Nersessian, N.J. (Eds.) (in press)
6. Faltings, B., Sun, K.: FAMING: Supporting innovative mechanism shape design. *Computer-Aided Design,* 28(3) (1996) 207—216
7. Farah, M. J.: The neuropsychology of mental imagery: Converging evidence from brain-damaged and normal subjects. In *Spatial Cognition- Brain Bases and Development.* Erlbaum (1988)
8. Gebhardt, F., Voss, A., Grather, W.: *Reasoning with Complex Cases.* Kluwer (1997)
9. Gomes, P., Seco, N., Pereira, F. C., Paiva, P., Carreiro, P., Ferreira, J. L., Bento, C.: The importance of retrieval in creative design analogies. In *Creative Systems: Approaches to Creativity in AI and Cognitive Science.* Workshop program in *The Eighteenth International Joint Conference on Artificial Intelligence.* (2003)
10. Hammond, K. J.: Case-based planning: A framework for planning from experience. *Cognitive Science.* (1990)
11. Monaghan, J. M., Clement, J.: Use of computer simulation to develop mental simulations for understanding relative motion concepts. *International Journal of Science Education.* (1999)
12. Gebhardt, F., Voss, A. Grather, W. & Schmidt-Belz. *Reasoning With Complex Cases,* Kluwer, 1997.
13. Pearce, M., Goel, A. K., Kolodner, J. L., Zimring, C., Sentosa, L., & Billington, R. Case-based design support: A case study in architectural design. *IEEE Expert: Intelligent Systems & Their Applications.* 7(5): 14-20, (1992)Shepard, R., Cooper, L.: *Mental Images and Their Transformations.* MIT Press. (1988)
14. Veloso, M. M.: Prodigy/analogy: Analogical reasoning in general problem solving. *EWCBR* (1993) 33—52

Generating Estimates of Classification Confidence for a Case-Based Spam Filter

Sarah Jane Delany[1], Pádraig Cunningham[2], Dónal Doyle[2], and Anton Zamolotskikh[2]

[1] Dublin Institute of Technology, Kevin Street, Dublin 8, Ireland
sarahjane.delany@comp.dit.ie
[2] University of Dublin, Trinity College, Dublin 2, Ireland
{padraig.cunningham, donal.doyle, zamolota}@cs.tcd.ie

Abstract. Producing estimates of classification confidence is surprisingly difficult. One might expect that classifiers that can produce numeric classification scores (e.g. k-Nearest Neighbour, Naïve Bayes or Support Vector Machines) could readily produce confidence estimates based on thresholds. In fact, this proves not to be the case, probably because these are not probabilistic classifiers in the strict sense. The numeric scores coming from k-Nearest Neighbour, Naïve Bayes and Support Vector Machine classifiers are not well correlated with classification confidence. In this paper we describe a case-based spam filtering application that would benefit significantly from an ability to attach confidence predictions to positive classifications (i.e. messages classified as spam). We show that 'obvious' confidence metrics for a case-based classifier are not effective. We propose an ensemble-like solution that aggregates a collection of confidence metrics and show that this offers an effective solution in this spam filtering domain.

1 Introduction

One might expect that classifiers that produce numeric scores for class membership would deliver effective estimations of prediction confidence based on thresholds on these scores. Examples of classifiers that produce numeric scores in this manner are; Naïve Bayes, k-Nearest Neighbour [1], Neural Networks [2], Logistic Regression [3] and Support Vector Machines [4]. Our experience with these classifiers suggests that the numeric scores from Logistic Regression are predictive of confidence but those from Naive Bayes, Neural Networks, Support Vector Machines (SVM) and k-Nearest Neighbour (k-NN) are not. We demonstrate that this is the case for k-NN, Naïve Bayes and SVM in Section 3.

In this paper we are concerned with generating estimates of classification confidence for a case-based spam filter called ECUE (Email Classification Using Examples) [5]. ECUE has the advantage of being very effective at tracking concept drift but this requires the user to identify False Positives (FPs) and False Negatives (FNs) so that they can be used to update the case-base. Identifying FNs is not a problem because they turn up in the Inbox (i.e. spam that has been

H. Muñoz-Avila and F. Ricci (Eds.): ICCBR 2005, LNAI 3620, pp. 177–190, 2005.

allowed through the filter). Identifying FPs involves monitoring a spam folder to identify legitimate email that has been classified as spam. Our objective here is to be able to partition this class so that the user need only monitor a subset - the set for which the confidence is low.

A straightforward success criterion in this regard is the proportion of positives for which prediction confidence is high and the prediction is correct (clearly there cannot be any FPs in this set). A mechanism that could label more than 50% of the positive class (i.e. classified as spam) as confident and have no FPs in this set would be useful. The lower-confidence positives could be allowed into the Inbox carrying a *Maybe-Spam* marker in the header or placed in a *Maybe-Spam* folder that would be checked periodically.

In section 2 we provide a brief overview of research on estimating confidence. The basic indicators for confidence that can be used with k-NN are described in section 3 where we show that no single one of these measures is effective in estimating confidence. In section 4 we present some simple techniques for aggregating these basic indicators and present an evaluation on unseen data that shows a simple voting technique to be very effective. The paper concludes in section 5 with a summary.

2 Review

Cheetham and Price have recently emphasised the importance of being able to attach confidence values to predictions in CBR [6,7]. This has been a research issue since the earliest days of expert systems research: it is part of the body of research on meta-level knowledge [8,9], the view being that it is important for a system to 'know what it knows'. TEIRESIAS is a system in this spirit, it was designed to simply admit its ignorance instead of venturing risky advice [10].

More recently, the system SIROCCO from McLaren and Ashely [11] uses meta-rules to determine the system's confidence. Their system operates in an engineering ethics domain, in which incorrect suggestions could be considered sensitive and damaging. In this system, if any one of the meta-rules are fired then the system considers itself inadequate for the task. Their evaluation of SIROCCO shows that allowing the system to produce 'don't know' results reduces the number of incorrectly classified cases, with a small trade off whereby the number of correctly classified cases is reduced.

So while it is clear that it is useful to be able to produce estimates of confidence, it is also clear that that generating reliable estimates is not straightforward. Cheetham and Price [7] describe 12 measures of confidence that can be applicable for a k-NN classifier. Some of these indicators increase with confidence and some decrease. Since no single indicator is capable of producing a robust measure of confidence they explore the use of a decision tree, that is allowed to use all the measures, as a mechanism for aggregating all the available metrics. The authors show that, even using a decision tree to learn a good confidence measure from historic data, it is difficult to avoid the situation where predictions labelled as confident prove to be incorrect. They also emphasise that the confidence estimation mechanism will need to be updated over time as the nature of the problems being solved can change.

Because of this we choose to concentrate on simpler aggregation mechanisms. We engineered all indicators so that they increased in value as confidence increased. This allowed us to consider additive and multiplicative mechanisms as well as various 'voting' alternatives.

2.1 Indirect Methods of Conveying Confidence

It is worth mentioning that there are other more indirect ways of conveying confidence to the user. Rather than conveying confidence as a term or a numeric score it can be conveyed by giving the user some insight into the problem domain. Confidence can be conveyed by presenting explanation cases [12] or by highlighting whether a feature has a negative or positive correlation with respect to the classification [13] or by highlighting features that contribute positively and negatively to the classification [14] Confidence may also be conveyed by using visualisation tools to highlight features that contribute to similarity and to differences [15].

3 Confidence Measures

This section describes a number of confidence measures that could be used to predict confidence in ECUE, a case-based spam filter. We concentrate on using measures appropriate for a k-NN classifier. We evaluate these measures on a number of spam datasets to assess their performance at predicting confidence.

The k-NN measures that we propose evaluating, which are described in Section 3.1, perform some calculation on a ranked list of neighbours of a target case. We do not use the basic classification score of the target case as ECUE uses unanimous voting in the classification process to bias the classifier away from FPs. Unanimous voting requires all the k nearest neighbours retrieved to be of classification *spam* in order for the target case to be classified as *spam*. Therefore there is no classification 'score', as such.

3.1 Proposed k-NN Confidence Measures

The objective of the k-NN measures is to identify those cases that are 'close' (i.e. with high similarity) to cases of the same class as the target case and are 'far' (i.e. low similarity) from cases of a different class. The closer a target case is to cases of a different class, the higher the chance that the target case is lying near or at the decision surface. Whereas the closer a case is to other cases of the same class, the higher the likelihood that it is further from the decision surface.

Similarity is determined by comparing features including the words and letters used in the body of the email and certain header fields including the subject, the 'from' address and addresses in the 'to' and 'cc' header fields [5].

For each k-NN confidence measure discussed in this section the same process occurs. Each target case is classified by ECUE as either spam or non-spam. For those target cases predicted to be spam a ranked list of neighbours of the target case is retrieved. This list of neighbours is a list of all the cases in the case-base ordered by distance from the target case. Those cases with classification equal to that of the target case (i.e. with classification spam) are considered to be *like* cases, while those cases with classification of nonspam are considered to be *unlike* cases. The measures can use

- the distance between a case and its nearest neighbours (let $NN_i(t)$ denote the ith nearest neighbour of case t) or,
- the distance between the target case t and its nearest like neighbours (let $NLN_i(t)$ denote the ith nearest *like* neighbour to case t) and/or
- the distance between a case and its nearest unlike neighbours (let $NUN_i(t)$ denote the ith nearest *unlike* neighbour to case t).

The number of neighbours used in each measure is adjustable and is independent of the number of neighbours used in the initial classification. All measures are constructed to produce a high score to indicate high confidence and a low score to indicate low confidence.

Avg NUN Index

The Average Nearest Unlike Neighbour Index (Avg NUN Index) is a measure of how close the first k NUNs are to the target case t as given in Equation 1.

$$AvgNUNIndex(t, k) = \frac{\sum_{i=1}^{k} IndexOfNUN_i(t)}{k} \tag{1}$$

where $IndexOfNUN_i(t)$ is the index of the ith nearest unlike neighbour of target case t, the index being the ordinal ranking of the case in the list of NNs.

This is illustrated in Figure 1 where NLNs are represented by circles, NUNs are represented by stars and target cases are represented by triangles. For $k = 1$, the index of the first NUN to target case T_1 is 5 whereas the index of the first NUN to target case T_2 is 2, indicating higher confidence in the classification of T_1 than T_2.

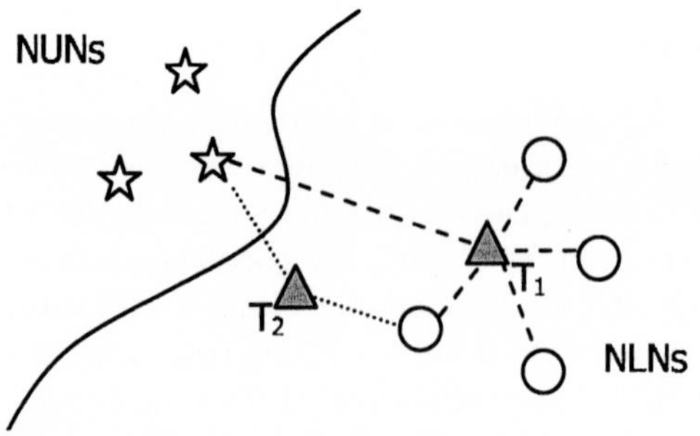

Fig. 1. Average NUN Index Confidence Measure

Similarity Ratio

The Similarity Ratio measure calculates the ratio of the similarity between the target case t and its k NLNs to the similarity between the target case and its k NUNs, as given in Equation 2.

$$SimRatio(t,k) = \frac{\sum_{i=1}^{k} Sim(t, NLN_i(t))}{\sum_{i=1}^{k} Sim(t, NUN_i(t))} \tag{2}$$

where $Sim(a,b)$ is the calculated similarity between cases a and b.

This is illustrated in Figure 2 where, for $k = 1$, the similarity between the target case T_1 and its NLN is much higher than the similarity between T_1 and its NUN. Whereas the similarity between target case T_2 and its NLN is only marginally higher than the similarity between T_2 and its NUN. The ratio of these similarites for T_1 will give a higher result than that for T_2 indicating higher confidence in the classification of T_1 than T_2.

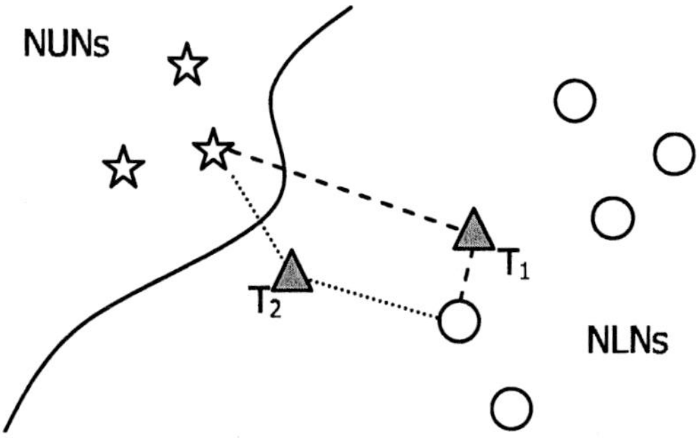

Fig. 2. Similarity Ratio Confidence Measure

Similarity Ratio Within K

The Similarity Ratio Within K is similar to the Similarity Ratio as described above except that, rather than consider the first k NLNs and the first k NUNs of a target case t, it only uses the NLNs and NUNs from the first k neighbours. It is defined in Equation 3.

$$SimRatio(t,k) = \frac{\sum_{i=1}^{k} Sim(t, NN_i(t))1(t, NN_i(t))}{1 + \sum_{i=1}^{k} Sim(t, NN_i(t))(1 - 1(t, NN_i(t)))} \tag{3}$$

where $Sim(a,b)$ is the calculated similarity between cases a and b and $1(a,b)$ returns one if the class of a is the same as the class of b or zero otherwise.

This measure will attempt to reward cases that have no NUNs within the first k neighbours, i.e. are in a cluster of k cases of the same class. This is illustrated in Figure 3 where, considering $k = 3$, the target case T_1 has no NUNs within the first three neighbours whereas target case T_2 has two NUNs and one NLN. The Similarity Ratio Within K will be much larger for T_1 than that for T_2 indicating higher confidence in the classification of T_1 than T_2.

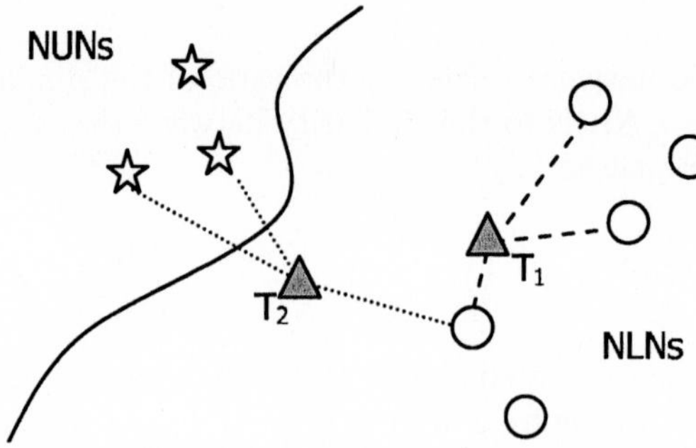

Fig. 3. Similarity Ratio Within K Confidence Measure

If a target case t has no NUNs then Equation 3 is effectively Equation 2 with the denominator set to one.

Sum of NN Similarites

The Sum of NN Similarities measure is the total similarity of the NLNs in the first k neighbours of the target case t, see Equation 4.

$$SumNNSim(t,k) = \sum_{i=1}^{k} 1(t, NN_i(t))Sim(t, NN_i(t)) \quad (4)$$

where $Sim(a, b)$ is the calculated similarity between cases a and b and $1(a, b)$ returns one if the class of a is the same as the class of b or zero otherwise.

For target cases in a cluster of cases of similar class this number will be large. For cases which are closer to the decision surface and have NUNs within the first k neighbours, this measure will be smaller. In fact for target cases with no NUNs within the first k neighbours this measure will be equal to the value of the Similarity Ratio Within K. Although this measure does not reward such cases as strongly as the Similarity Ratio Within K does as the resulting measure for the sum of the NLNs is not reduced by the influence of the NUNs.

Average NN Similarity

The Average NN Similarity measure is the average similarity of the NLNs in the first k neighbours of the target case t, see Equation 5.

$$SumNNSim(t,k) = \frac{\sum_{i=1}^{k} 1(t, NN_i(t))Sim(t, NN_i(t))}{\sum_{i=1}^{k} 1(t, NN_i(t))} \quad (5)$$

where $Sim(a, b)$ is the calculated similarity between cases a and b and $1(a, b)$ returns one if the class of a is the same as the class of b or zero otherwise.

3.2 Assessing k-NN Confidence Measure Performance

In order to assess the performance of these confidence measures we evaluated each of them on a number of spam datasets. Five datasets were used. Each con-

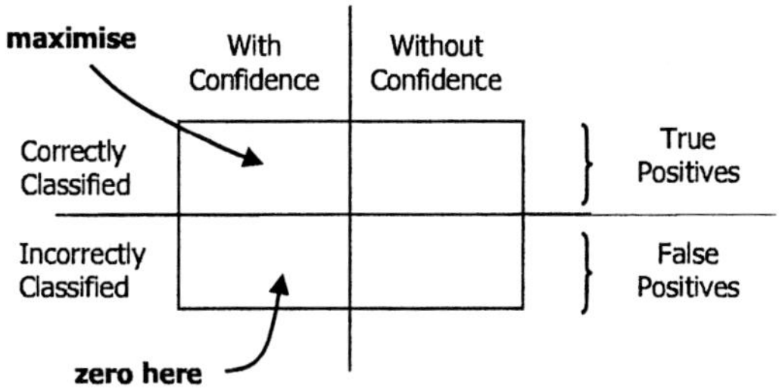

Fig. 4. Criteria used to identify the best confidence threshold level

sisted of legitimate and spam emails received by a single individual over a period of time. Each dataset represents a different period of time for a single individual. Two different individual's mail were used over all datasets. The legitimate emails in the datasets include a mixture of business, personal and mailing list emails. Case-bases were built from each of the five original datasets. Case representation details are available in [5,16].

ECUE's case-base maintenance procedure to handle concept drift in spam filtering [17] has two components; an initial case-base editing stage and a case-base update protocol. In order for the evaluation to closely reflect the operation of ECUE, the case-base from each dataset was edited using the case editing procedure [18]. After editing the datasets averaged 700 emails in size with an average of 45% spam and 55% legitimate emails.

The evaluation involved performing a leave-one-out validation on each dataset for each measure. We evaluated each measure using k neighbours from $k = 1$ upto $k = 15$ and identified the confidence threshold, over all the k values, that gave us the highest proportion of correctly predicted spam emails when there were no incorrect predictions (i.e. FPs). This is illustrated in Figure 4.

This was achieved by recording the confidence measure results for each target case $c_i, i = 1 \ldots N$, that was classified by ECUE as spam. The results recorded included the number of neighbours k used in the measure, whether the target case was classified correctly or not and the measure calculated, m_{ik}. Setting the threshold t_k equal to the minimum value of m_{ik} for a given k and varying the threshold in small units ($t_k = t_k + .01$) up to the maximum value of m_{ik}, the number classified correctly with confidence (CC_k) and the number classified incorrectly with confidence (CI_k) as given by Equations 6 and 7 , were calculated.

$$CC_k = \sum_{i=1}^{N} \mathrm{gte}(m_{ik}, t_k) \tag{6}$$

$$CI_k = \sum_{i=1}^{N} \mathrm{lt}(m_{ik}, t_k) \tag{7}$$

where $\mathrm{gte}(a, b) = 1$ if $a >= b$ and $\mathrm{gte}(a, b) = 0$ otherwise and $\mathrm{lt}(a, b) = 1$ if $a < b$ and $\mathrm{lt}(a, b) = 0$.

Table 1. Best percentage confidence achievable for each dataset using different confidence measures

Confidence Measure	Dataset 1	Dataset 2	Dataset 3	Dataset 4	Dataset 5	Avg
Avg NUN Index	23%	76%	75%	41%	44%	51.8%
Sim Ratio	46%	84%	50%	49%	16%	49.0%
Sim Ratio Within k	21%	29%	71%	91%	57%	54.8%
Sum NN Sim	21%	29%	68%	91%	58%	53.4%
Avg NN Sim	20%	29%	49%	91%	60%	49.8%
Naive Bayes	0%	94%	0%	83%	56%	46.4%
SVM	29%	100%	77%	81%	33%	63.8%
ACM	55.4%	85.4%	83.8%	93.7%	77.3%	79.1%

The selected threshold value was the threshold t_k that maximised CC_k, the number of spam correctly predicted with high confidence when the number of incorrect predictions with high confidence was zero (i.e. $CI_k = 0$).

The results of this evaluation are presented in rows 1 to 5 of Table 1 (the other measures in rows 6 to 8 are described later). It details for each measure the highest percentage confidence that can be achieved on each dataset. This is the proportion of *spam* predictions that are made with high confidence. In all situations no highly confident incorrect predictions were made so no FPs are included in this proportion. In effect, this proportion of the spam can be ignored by the user, whereas the remaining percentage would have to be checked by the user.

Looking at the proportion of spam predictions for which confidence is high across all datasets it is evident that no single measure achieves good percentage confidence across all datasets. If we define "good" performance as having confidence in at least 50% of the spam predictions, none of the measures achieve "good" performance on more than three of the five datasets. The best performing measure is the Similarity Ratio Within K which has good performance on three of the five datasets with an average performance across all datasets of 54.8% but with minimum performance of 21%.

3.3 Naïve Bayes and SVM Confidence Measures

Naïve Bayes is currently the machine learning technique of choice for spam filtering [19,20,21,22,23] although there has been a lot of interest recently in applying SVMs to the problem [23,24,25,26,27]. Naïve Bayes and SVM classifers produce numeric scores; Naïve Bayes produces a 'probability' of spam whereas an SVM produces a 'distance' from the hyperplane separating the spam and non spam classes. These scores can be used to predict confidence in the classifiers' prediction.

We examined confidence measures produced by Naïve Bayes on the five datasets. The implementation used is that described by Delany et al. [5]. The confidence threshold was identified as the highest numeric score returned by the classifier for a FP prediction. This ensured that no incorrectly classified spam emails were considered confident predictions. The 6th row of Table 1 gives the confidence predictions for the five datasets using the Naïve Bayes classifier. It is clear from the results that the Naïve Bayes numeric score cannot be used as a predictor of confidence. In two of the five datasets there are zero confident predictions as there are FPs with the maximum score.

We also evaluated using a SVM on the five datasets. The implementation used is a 2-norm soft-margin SVM as described in [4] with a dot product kernel function. The confidence threshold was identified as the highest postive result returned for nonspam email. This will ensure that no legitimate email will be confidently considered as spam. The 7th row of the Table 1 gives the confidence predictions for the five datasets using an SVM for classification. Although the average score across all datasets of 63.8% is higher than the best of the k-NN measures the SVM confidence measure does not realistically achieve any better overall performance as it also only achieves "good" performance on three of the five datasets but with slightly higher minimum performance of 29%. It is worth noting that the performance of dataset 2 is actually 99.7% but is reported as 100% due to rounding.

3.4 Implications for Predicting Confidence in Spam Filtering

To summarise, it appears that the confidence measures for k-NN, Naïve Bayes and SVMs presented here cannot consistently produce estimates of prediction confidence for spam. The average performance of the k-NN and the SVM measures shows promise however the lack of consistency across all datasets is an issue. The thresholds achieved for each k-NN measure across the five datasets also varies considerably. For example, considering the Similarity Ratio Within K measure which has the best of the k-NN measures performance, Table 2 shows the variation in the threshold across the five datasets.

Table 2. Demonstrating the variation in thresholds for the Similarity Within K Ratio confidence measure across the five datasets

Threshold	**Dataset 1**	**Dataset 2**	**Dataset 3**	**Dataset 4**	**Dataset 5**
k - num neighbours used	11	7	14	1	3
Value	991.07	574.08	717.04	58	214.1

It is important to note that the figures in Table 1 are very optimistic as the test data was used to set the threshold.

4 The Aggregated Confidence Measure

Since none of the individual measures discussed in Section 3 was consistently effective at predicting confidence we evaluated a number of aggregation approaches which involved combining the results from the individual measures. The aggregation approaches we considered included:

(i) Summing the results from each of the 5 individual measures evaluated at the same value of k and comparing the sum against a threshold;
(ii) Using the best threshold for each individual measure and indicating confidence if a certain number of the measures indicate confidence;
(iii) Using a fixed k across all measures and indicating confidence if a certain number of the measures indicate confidence.

We found that the simplest and most effective method of aggregating the results is to assign confidence to a prediction if any of the individual measures indicated that the prediction was confident as in (ii) above. We call this measure the Aggregated Confidence Measure (ACM). The algorithm for the ACM has two stages:

(i) calculation of the constituent measure threshold values in a pre-classification stage,
(ii) determination of the ACM during classification.

The pre-classification stage involves pre-processing of the case-base to identify the best threshold for each individual constituent measure. This is performed in the manner described in Section 3.2. A threshold consists of two values; the k value indicating the number of neighbours to use in the calculation and the actual threshold value above which the prediction is considered confident. These constituent measure thresholds are stored.

The ACM is then determined during classification for each target case that is classified as spam by ECUE. Using the appropriate threshold value of k, the actual score for each individual constituent measure is calcuated for the target case. The ACM specifies that if at least one of the calculated scores for the individual measures is equal to or greater than the stored threshold value for that measure, confidence is expressed in the prediction.

4.1 Assessment of ACM's Performance

We evaluated the ACM on the five datasets already used in Section 3. The results are presented in row 8 of Table 1. It is evident that the ACM is effective across all datasets with an average of 79% of the spam predictions being predicted with high confidence. The ACM also results in more than 50% of each dataset being predicted with high confidence. It is worth noting that the level of high confidence predictions for the ACM is also higher than the best individual measure's performance on each dataset (rows 1 to 5 of Table 1).

4.2 Evaluation on Unseen Data

One limitation of the evaluation performed in Section 4.1 is that the assessment was performed on the datasets which themselves were used to derive the confidence thresholds for the constituent confidence measures. In order to validate the ACM it is necessary to evaluate its performance on unseen data.

Table 3. Performance of ACM on unseen data using Dataset 6

Month	1	2	3	4	5	6	7	8	Overall
Total emails classified	772	542	318	1014	967	1136	1370	1313	7382
Number of Spam	629	314	216	925	917	1065	1225	1205	6496
Number of Non Spam	93	228	102	89	50	71	145	108	886
%FPs classified	4.3%	2.6%	1.0%	1.1%	6.0%	1.4%	0.0%	1.9%	2.0%
%Confident FPs	0.0%	0.9%	0.0%	1.1%	0.0%	0.0%	0.0%	0.9%	0.5%
%Confidence	70%	87%	76%	94%	89%	73%	77%	99%	85%

Table 4. Performance of ACM on unseen data using Dataset 7

Month	1	2	3	4	5	6	Overall
Total emails classified	293	447	549	693	534	495	3011
Number of Spam	142	391	405	459	406	476	2279
Number of Non Spam	151	56	144	234	128	19	732
%FPs classified	0.7%	3.6%	3.5%	2.6%	1.6%	0.0%	2.2%
%Confident FPs	0.0%	3.6%	0.7%	0.4%	1.6%	0.0%	0.8%
%Confidence	95%	95%	87%	64%	89%	88%	85%

To do this we used ECUE along with two further datasets that have been used in concept drift evaluations of ECUE [17]. Each dataset is derived from an individual's email received over the period of approximately one year. The first 1000 emails (consisting of 500 spam and 500 legitimate emails) in each dataset were used as training data to build the initial case-base classifier and the remaining emails were left for testing. These datasets, 6 and 7, include eight and six months of test emails repectively. The monthly class distribution of the test emails is evident in rows 2 and 3 of Tables 3 and 4.

To evaluate the ACM on unseen data involved building confidence thresholds for the ACM constituent measures on the initial case-base and then classifying the remaining emails using the ACM to determine how confident the *spam* predictions are. In this way, the test emails were not used in the determination of the confidence thresholds in any way.

The test emails were presented in date order for classification. Since this email data is subject to concept drift, ECUE's case-base update policy was applied to allow the classifier to learn from the new types of spam and legitimate email presented. The update policy has a number of components; an immediate update of the case-base with any misclassified emails when a FP occurred, a daily update of the case-base with any other misclassifieds emails that occurred that day, and a monthly feature reselection process to allow the case representation to take any new predictive features into account. In order to keep the confidence thresholds in line with the updates to the case-base an update policy for the confidence thresholds was also applied. This policy had two components; the confidence thresholds were updated whenever a confident FP email occurred and also after a monthly feature reselect.

Tables 3 and 4 show the results of testing the performance of the ACM on unseen data using the two datasets 6 and 7. The tables present the accumulated monthly results for each dataset listing the total number and types of emails that were classified, the percentage of incorrect spam predictions (i.e. FPs) made (labeled *%FP classified*) and the percentage of incorrect spam predictions made with high confidence (labeled *%Confident FPs*). The table also gives the total percentage of spam predictions with high confidence (labeled *%Confidence*).

In both datasets predictions of confidence are high, averaging 85% in both cases with a lowest monthly level of 64%. This is the percentage of spam predictions that can be ignored by the user, the remaining spam predictions can either be flagged in the Inbox as *Maybe Spam* or placed in a separate *Maybe Spam* folder for the user to check.

However in some of the months the ACM has resulted in confident incorrect predictions. Although the actual numbers of emails are low (four emails for Dataset 6 and six emails for Dataset 7) the ideal situation is one where all incorrect predictions have low confidence and will be flagged for the user to check. FPs flagged as confident will end up in the *spam* folder and may be missed by the user. Examining the confident FPs, three are emails from mailing lists and two are responses to Web registrations which users may not be too concerned with missing. The remaining five are important, some work related and one even a quotation in response to a online car hire request.

It is clear that we are approaching the limits of the accuracy of machine learning techniques in this domain. We see two possibilities for addressing these FPs. Close examination of such emails may identify domain specific characteristics that could be used as a feature or number of features in the case representation. Secondly, most deployed spam filtering solutions do not rely on one approach for filtering spam, they combine a number of techniques including white and black listing, rules, collaborative and learning approaches. Incorporating additional techniques into ECUE to add to its case-based approach could help in catching these outlier FPs.

5 Conclusions

We have shown that confidence measures based on the numeric scores from Naïve Bayes, SVM or measures based on the k nearest neighbours for a case-based classifier are not consistent at predicting confidence in the spam filtering domain.

We have described an aggregation-based approach to combining individual k-NN confidence measures that shows great promise in confidently predicting spam. We evaluated this aggregated confidence measure by incorporating it into the classification process of a case-based spam filter and showed that it could successfully separate the spam predictions into two sets, those with high confidence of spam which can be ignored by the user and those with low confidence which should be periodically checked for False Positives. The high-confidence set included 85% of the predicted spam reducing the number of spam that the user needs to check.

References

1. Mitchell, T.: Machine Learning. McGraw Hill, New York (1997)
2. Fausett, L.: Fundamentals of Neural Networks: Architectures, Algorithms, and Applications. Prentice Hall (1993)
3. Hosmer, D.W., Lemeshow, S.: Applied Logistic Regression. Wiley Series in Probability and Statistics. Wiley (2000)
4. Christianini, N., Shawe-Taylor, J.: An Introduction to Support Vector Machines: And Other Kernel-based Learning Methods. Cambridge University Press (2000)
5. Delany, S., Cunningham, P., Coyle, L.: An assessment of case-based reasoning for spam filtering. Artificial Intelligence Review (to appear) (2005)
6. Cheetham, W.: Case-based reasoning with confidence. In Blanzieri, E., Portinale, L., eds.: 5th European Workshop on Case-Based Reasoning. Volume 1898 of LNCS., Springer (2000) 15–25
7. Cheetham, W., Price, J.: Measures of solution accuracy in case-based reasoning systems. In Funk, P., González-Calero, P., eds.: 7th European Conference on Case-Based Reasoning (ECCBR 2004). Volume 3155 of LNAI., Springer (2004) 106–118
8. Lenat, D., Davis, R., Doyle, J., Genesereth, M., Goldstein, I., Schrobe, H.: Reasoning about reasoning. In Hayes-Roth, F., Waterman, D.A., Lenat, D.B., eds.: Building Expert Systems. Addison-Wesley, London (1983) 219–239
9. Davis, R., Buchanan, B.: Meta level knowledge. In Hayes-Roth, F., Waterman, D.A., Lenat, D.B., eds.: Rule-Based Expert Systems. Addison-Wesley, London (1985) 507–530
10. Davis, R.: Expert systems: Where are we? and where do we go from here? AI Magazine **3** (1982) 3–22
11. McLaren, B.M., Ashley, K.D.: Helping a cbr program know what it knows. In Aha, D., Watson, I., eds.: 4th International Conference on Case-Based Reasoning (ICCBR-2001). Volume 2080 of LNAI., Springer (2001) 377–391
12. Doyle, D., Cunningham, P., Bridge, D., Rahman, Y.: Explanation oriented retrieval. In Funk, P., González-Calero, P.A., eds.: 7th European Conference on Case-Based Reasoning (ECCBR 2004). Volume 3155 of LNAI., Springer (2004) 157–168
13. Nugent, C., Cunningham, P.: A case-based explanation system for black-box systems. Artificial Intelligence Review (to appear) (2005)
14. McSherry, D.: Explaining the pros and cons of conclusions in cbr. In Funk, P., González-Calero, P., eds.: 7th European Conference on Case-Based Reasoning (ECCBR-2004). Volume 3155 of LNAI., Springer (2004) 317–330
15. Massie, S., Craw, S., Wiratunga, N.: A visualisation tool to explain case-base reasoning solutions for tablet formulation. In: 24th SGAI International Conference on Innovative Techniques and Applications of Artificial Intelligence (AI-2004). LNCS, Springer (2004)
16. Delany, S., Cunningham, P., Coyle, L.: An assessment of case-based reasoning for spam filtering. Procs. of 15th Irish Conference on Artificial Intelligence and Cognitive Science (2004) 9–18

17. Delany, S.J., Cunningham, P., Tsymbal, A., Coyle, L.: A case-based technique for tracking concept drift in spam filtering. In Macintosh, A., Ellis, R., Allen, T., eds.: Applications and Innovations in Intelligent Systems XII, Procs. of AI 2004, Springer (2004) 3–16
18. Delany, S.J., Cunningham, P.: An analysis of case-based editing in a spam filtering system. In Funk, P., P.González-Calero, eds.: 7th European Conference on Case-Based Reasoning (ECCBR 2004). Volume 3155 of LNAI., Springer (2004) 128–141
19. P.Pantel, Lin, D.: Spamcop: A spam classification and organisation program. In: Procs of Workshop for Text Categorisation, AAAI-98. (1998) 95–98
20. Sahami, M., Dumais, S., Heckerman, D., Horvitz, E.: A bayesian approach to filtering junk email. In: Procs of Workshop for Text Categorisation, AAAI-98. (1998) 55–62
21. Androutsopoulos, I., J.Koutsias, Chandrinos, G., Paliouras, G., Spyropoulos, C.: An evaluation of naive bayesian anti-spam filtering. In Potamias, G., Moustakis, V., van Someren, M., eds.: Procs of Workshop on Machine Learning in the New Information Age, ECML 2000. (2000) 9–17
22. Schneider, K.: A comparison of event models for näive bayes anti-spam e-mail filtering. In: 10th Conference of the European Chapter of the Association for Computational Linguistics (EACL'03). (2003) 307–314
23. Zhang, L., Zhu, J., Yao, T.: An evaluation of statistical spam filtering techniques. ACM Transactions on Asian Language Information Processing (TALIP) **3** (2004) 243–269
24. Drucker, H., Wu, D., Vapnik, V.: Support vector machines for spam categorisation. IEEE Transactions on Neural Networks **10** (1999) 1048–1055
25. Androutsopoulos, I., Paliouras, G., Michelakis, E.: Learning to filter unsolicited commercial email. Technical Report 2004/02, NCSR "Demokritos" (2000)
26. Kolcz, A., Alspector, J.: Svm-based filtering of email spam with content-specific misclassification costs. In: TextDM'2001 (IEEE ICDM-2001 Workshop on Text Mining), IEEE (2001) 123–130
27. Michelakis, E., Androutsopoulos, I., Paliouras, G., Sakkis, G., Stamatopoulos, P.: Filtron: A learning-based anti-spam filter. In: 1st Conference on Email and Anti-Spam (CEAS 2004). (2004)

Improving Gene Selection in Microarray Data Analysis Using Fuzzy Patterns Inside a CBR System

Florentino Fdez-Riverola[1], Fernando Díaz[2], M. Lourdes Borrajo[1], J. Carlos Yáñez[3], and Juan M. Corchado[4]

[1] Dept. Informática, University of Vigo, Escuela Superior de Ingeniería Informática, Edificio Politécnico, Campus Universitario As Lagoas s/n, 32004 Ourense, Spain
riverola@uvigo.es

[2] Dept. Informática, University of Valladolid, Escuela Universitaria de Informática, Plaza Santa Eulalia, 9-11, 40005 Segovia, Spain
fdiaz@infor.uva.es

[3] Dept. of Financial Accounting, University of Vigo, Campus Universitario As Lagoas s/n, 32004 Ourense, Spain
jcyanez@uvigo.es

[4] Dept. de Informática y Automática, University of Salamanca, Plaza de la Merced s/n, 37008 Salamanca, Spain
corchado@usal.es

Abstract. In recent years, machine learning and data mining fields have found a successful application area in the field of DNA microarray technology. Gene expression profiles are composed of thousands of genes at the same time, representing complex relationships between them. One of the well-known constraints specifically related to microarray data is the large number of genes in comparison with the small number of available experiments or cases. In this context, the ability to identify an accurate gene selection strategy is crucial to reduce the generalization error (false positives) of state-of-the-art classification algorithms. This paper presents a reduction algorithm based on the notion of fuzzy gene expression, where similar (co-expressed) genes belonging to different patients are selected in order to construct a supervised prototype-based retrieval model. This technique is employed to implement the retrieval step in our new gene-CBR system. The proposed method is illustrated with the analysis of microarray data belonging to bone marrow cases from 43 adult patients with cancer plus a group of three cases corresponding to healthy persons.

1 Introduction and Motivation

Practically all cells in the human body have the same genes, but these genes can be expressed differently at different times and under different conditions. Studying these various states helps scientists understand more about how the cells function and about what happens when the genes in a cell do not work properly. In the past, scientists have only been able to conduct such genetic analyses on a few genes at once. However, in recent years DNA microarray technology has become a fundamental tool

H. Muñoz-Avila and F. Ricci (Eds.): ICCBR 2005, LNAI 3620, pp. 191 – 205, 2005.

in genomic research, making the investigation of global gene expression of all aspects of human disease possible [1-4]. Nowadays, it is possible to monitor simultaneously the expression levels of thousands of genes during important biological processes and across collections of related samples.

Microarray technology is based on a database of over 40,000 fragments of genes called expressed sequence tags (ESTs), which are used to measure target abundance using the scanned intensities of fluorescence from tagged molecules hybridised to ESTs [5, 6]. Since the number of examined genes in an experiment is measured in terms of thousands, different data mining techniques have been intensively used to analyse and discover knowledge from gene expression data [7, 8]. However, having so many fields relative to so few samples creates a high likelihood of finding false positives. This problem is increased if we consider the potential errors that can be present in microarray data, namely *symmetric* and *random* errors [9]. Symmetric (controllable) errors produce approximately similar variations at microarray experiments and it can be handled through normalization techniques [10]. Random (uncontrollable) errors cause different degrees of variations in microarray experiments by chance [11]. Considering a bidimensional matrix containing data from different microarray experiments (from different patients, different times in the same individual, or different tissue types within an individual), we have to deal with the previous commented *intra-experimental* and *inter-experimental* variations. Other issues related with the pre-processing stage within the microarray life cycle are well illustrated in the work of [12].

For several years we have been working in the identification of techniques to automate the reasoning cycle of case based reasoning (CBR) systems [13,14]. In this paper, we propose a fuzzy codification for the gene expression levels of each sample based on the discretization of real gene expression data into a small number of fuzzy membership functions. The proposed method is able to generalize samples as a whole, diminishing the effect of both inter and intra experimental variations. The developed method can be used for different measure platforms (RT-PCR, Affymetrix GeneChip, Rosetta oligoarrays, etc.) and serves as a pre-processing step before gene selection and clustering methods, as we will see later.

We are interested in the development of a robust case-based reasoning system that may be employed in the study of cancer treatment. The goal of the decision support tool is to facilitate the construction of therapies, including the level of aggressiveness of treatment, to more closely match the underlying disease, hopefully reducing side effects in low risk cases and increasing cure rates in high-risk cases.

Input space reduction is often the key phase in the building of an accurate classifier [15]. Based on the fuzzy discretization method presented in this paper, we propose the use of a fuzzy prototype-based retrieval system able to differentiate several kinds of cancer for microarray data. In this case, the goal is the identification of an expression profile that can be used to classify the cancer in our CBR system.

The paper is organized as follows: Section 2 introduces the use of CBR systems and reviews different gene selection approaches, as well as classification techniques for microarray data analysis. Section 3 explains in detail the proposed fuzzy prototype-based retrieval method. Section 4 discusses the experimental results obtained with the new gene-CBR system built with the proposed method. Finally, Section 5 gives out the concluding remarks and future work.

2 Related Work

Case-based reasoning is a computational reasoning paradigm that involves the storage and retrieval of past experiences to solve new problems. It is an approach that is particularly relevant in scientific domains, where there is a wealth of data but often a lack of theories or general principles.

The domain of molecular biology can be characterized by substantial amounts of complex data, many unknowns, a lack of complete theories and rapid evolution, where reasoning is often based on experience rather than general knowledge. Experts remember positive experiences for the possible reuse of solutions while negative experiences are used to avoid potentially unsuccessful outcomes. Similar to other scientific domains, problem solving in molecular biology can benefit from systematic knowledge management using techniques from AI. Case-based reasoning is particularly applicable to this problem domain because it (*i*) supports rich and evolvable representation of experiences/problems, solutions and feedback; (*ii*) provides efficient and flexible ways to retrieve these experiences; and (*iii*) applies analogical reasoning to solve new problems [16].

Several methods derived from machine learning have been applied to reduce dimensions in the field of microarray data. These works include the application of genetic algorithms [17], wrapper approaches [18], support vector machines [19], etc. Other approaches focus their attention on redundancy reduction and feature extraction [20, 21], as well as the identification of similar gene classes making prototypes-genes [22]. One way or another, the selected method has to pursue two main goals: (*i*) reduce the cost and complexity of the classifier and (*ii*) improve the accuracy of the model.

Classical reduction dimension methods applied to microarray data [23] tend to identify differentially expressed genes from a set of microarray experiments. A differentially expressed gene is a gene which has the same expression level for all examples of the same class, but different for those examples belonging to different classes. The relevance value of a gene depends on its capacity of being differentially expressed. However, a non-differentially expressed gene will be considered irrelevant and will be removed from the classification process even though it might well contain information that would improve the classification accuracy.

The task addressed here is slightly different from that of feature selection for gene expression based classifiers [24, 25]. Our proposed method aims to find all genes that are significantly expressed between the existing classes in order to obtain a fuzzy representation of the expression levels belonging to those genes that best explain each class in the form of a fuzzy-prototype. The final goal is the application of the proposed method as a retrieval step for our gene-CBR system.

3 Fuzzy Prototype-Based Retrieval Method for CBR Systems

The proposed method employs a fuzzy codification for the gene expression levels of each case, based on the discretization of real gene expression data into a small number of fuzzy membership functions. The whole algorithm comprises of two main steps. First, we discretize the gene expression levels into binary variables according to a supervised learning process. Then, a fuzzy pattern is generated from the data, which is representative for each specific pathology. To carry out the integration of the proposed method within the CBR life cycle, a measured distance has to be defined in order to determine the distance of a gene expression profile (or new case) to a specific gene expression pattern.

3.1 Fuzzy Discretization of Gene Expression Levels

Given a set of n features or attributes (in this work, gene expression levels), $\boldsymbol{F} = \{F_1, F_2, ..., F_n\}$, the discretization process is based on determining the membership function of each feature to three linguistic labels (Low, Medium, and High). Then, each real value F_j is replaced by its three values of membership to these fuzzy labels (μ_{jL}, μ_{jM} and μ_{jH}, respectively), and so, a new set of $3n$ features, $\boldsymbol{F'} = \{\mu_{1L}, \mu_{1M}, \mu_{1H}, ..., \mu_{nL}, \mu_{nM}, \mu_{nH}\}$ is constructed from the original set of features $\boldsymbol{F}$.

The membership functions to linguistic labels are defined in a similar way to the form that has been used by [26, 27]. These authors used a polynomial function that approximates a Gaussian membership function, where its centre and amplitude depend on the mean and on the variability of the available data respectively. The original membership functions are considered symmetric, but, in this work we have considered asymmetric functions for the linguistic labels in the extremes (labels Low and High). To support this choice, it is assumed that values below the centre of membership function for label Low are *low* values for the feature F_j at a fuzzy degree of 1. The same consideration is made to the label High.

Concretely, the membership function for the label Low is defined by:

$$\mu_{jL}(x)=\begin{cases} 1 & \text{if } x-c_{jL}\leq 0 \\ 1-2\left(\dfrac{x-c_{jL}}{\lambda_{jL}}\right)^2 & \text{if } 0\leq x-c_{jL}\leq \dfrac{\lambda_{jL}}{2} \\ 2\left(1-\dfrac{x-c_{jL}}{\lambda_{jL}}\right)^2 & \text{if } \dfrac{\lambda_{jL}}{2}\leq x-c_{jL}\leq \lambda_{jL} \\ 0 & \text{otherwise} \end{cases} \tag{1}$$

where c_{jL} is the mean of the values of feature F_j below the mean of all values of the feature F_j, (namely, given c_{jM} = E[F_j], the centre c_{jL} is is the mean of the values of feature F_j that are comprised between $\mathtt{min}(F_j)$ and c_{jM}) and the λ_{jL} parameter is the distance between c_{jM} and c_{jL}, $\lambda_{jL} = c_{jM} - c_{jL}$. As it is defined, this function is asymmetric, as is shown in Figure 1.

For the label High the definition of its membership function is made in a similar way,

$$\mu_{jH}(x)=\begin{cases}1 & \text{if } x-c_{jH}\geq 0\\ 1-2\left(\dfrac{x-c_{jH}}{\lambda_{jH}}\right)^2 & \text{if } -\dfrac{\lambda_{jH}}{2}\leq x-c_{jH}\leq 0\\ 2\left(1+\dfrac{x-c_{jH}}{\lambda_{jH}}\right)^2 & \text{if } -\lambda_{jH}\leq x-c_{jH}\leq -\dfrac{\lambda_{jH}}{2}\\ 0 & \text{otherwise}\end{cases} \tag{2}$$

but in this case, the centre c_{jH} is the mean of the values of F_j that are comprised between the mean value of all values, c_{jM}, and the maximum value, $\max\{F_j\}$, whereas the amplitude parameter, λ_{jH}, is given by the difference c_{jH} - c_{jM}. This function extends the right side of the domain of Feature F_j, and it is shown in Figure 1. It is also an asymmetric membership function.

Last, the membership function to the label Medium is a symmetric function defined as:

$$\mu_{jM}(x)=\begin{cases}1-2\left(\dfrac{\left\|x-c_{jM}\right\|}{\lambda_M}\right)^2 & \text{if } 0\leq\left\|x-c_{jM}\right\|\leq\dfrac{\lambda_{jM}}{2}\\ 2\left(1-\dfrac{\left\|x-c_{jM}\right\|}{\lambda_{jM}}\right)^2 & \text{if } \dfrac{\lambda_M}{2}\leq\left\|x-c_{jM}\right\|\leq\lambda_{jM}\\ 0 & \text{otherwise}\end{cases} \tag{3}$$

where the centre parameter, c_{jM}, is the mean of all values of feature F_j, $c_{jM} = \mathrm{E}[F_j]$, and the amplitude parameter λ_{jM} is given by the half of the distance between the centres of the extreme functions, namely, $\lambda_{jM} = ½ (c_{jH} - c_{jL})$. The form of this function is also shown in Figure 1.

Once defined the three membership functions for each feature F_j, a threshold value Θ can be established (for example, 0.5) to discretize the original data in a binary way, according to any linguistic label from the defined labels Low, Medium and High. The discriminatory criterion for any label is simply defined by:

$$F'_{j\bullet}=\begin{cases}1 & \text{if } \mu_{j\bullet}(x)\geq\Theta\\ 0 & \text{if } \mu_{j\bullet}(x)<\Theta\end{cases} \tag{4}$$

As is shown in Figure 1, for concrete values of threshold Θ, specific zones of the feature domain for which none of the labels will be activated can exist (see the neighbour region of the intersection of membership functions of label Medium and High in Figure 1). This fact must be interpreted as the specific value of the feature is not enough to assign it a significant linguistic label at the significance degree of membership fixed by threshold Θ. On the other hand, one value can activate simultaneously two linguistic labels, since at the significance level given by Θ, any assignment of the measure to a linguistic label is significant (see, the neighbour region of the intersection of label MEDIUM and HIGH in Figure 1).

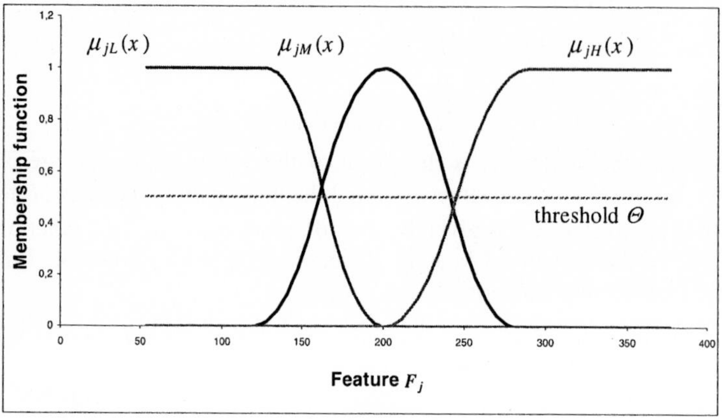

Fig. 1. Membership functions for the linguistic labels: LOW, MEDIUM and HIGH

This section has presented a method used to discretize numeric features into binary variables according to the definition of three linguistic labels, and therefore the method is defined in a fuzzy sets manner. Summarizing, given a data set $\boldsymbol{D}$ with m observations $\{\boldsymbol{x}_1, ..., \boldsymbol{x}_m\}$ about n numeric features $\boldsymbol{F} = \{F_1, ..., F_n\}$, namely, $\boldsymbol{x}_i \in \mathbf{R}^n$, the fuzzy discretization process, defined above, transforms the original data set into another set with the same number of observations but a different number of features. The new data set $\boldsymbol{D'}$ has m observations which are now referred to as a set of $3n$ binary features, namely, $\boldsymbol{x'}_i \in \{0, 1\}^{3n}$. The real value of feature F_j for the observation $\boldsymbol{x}_i$, denoted by x_{ij}, is replaced by the three binary values given by expression (4) for each linguistic label, that is to say, by the tuple $\langle F'_{jL}(x_{ij}), F'_{jM}(x_{ij}), F'_{jH}(x_{ij})\rangle$.

3.2 Generating Fuzzy Patterns from Data

This section explains how to generate a fuzzy pattern from data, which is representative for a specific decision class. The process is carried out according to a supervised learning process from the available data as described below.

Given a subset of observations $\boldsymbol{D}_i = \{\boldsymbol{x}_{i_1}, \boldsymbol{x}_{i_2}, ..., \boldsymbol{x}_{i_m}\} \subseteq \boldsymbol{D}$, which have associated the same class label C_i, for any observation $\boldsymbol{x}_{i_l}$ $(i_1 \leq i_l \leq i_m)$,

- First, it is discretized with regard to the linguistic labels Low, Medium and High associated to each feature, F_j. Namely, the discrete values $F'_{jL}(x_{i_l j})$, $F'_{jM}(x_{i_l j})$, and $F'_{jH}(x_{i_l j})$ are computed using the expression given by (4). Then, the three binary values for each feature are replaced by a single label, $F_j^{''}(\boldsymbol{x}_{i_l}) \in \{\mathrm{L}, \mathrm{LM}, \mathrm{M}, \mathrm{MH}, \mathrm{H}, *\}$. If only one of the three binary values is active, the respective label is assigned: L (Low), M (Medium), and H (High). As mentioned in Section 3.1, a unique real value can activate simultaneously two linguistic labels, so it may occur that two binary values are activated - the possible cases are LM (Low and Medium) and MH (Medium and High). Finally, it is also possible that one value does not fire any linguistic label, and then, the label * is assigned. The assignment criteria is given completely by expression (5).

$$F_j^{''}(\boldsymbol{x}_{i_l}) = \begin{cases} L & \text{if } F'_{jL}(x_{i_l j}) = 1 \wedge F'_{jM}(x_{i_l j}) = 0 \wedge F'_{jH}(x_{i_l j}) = 0 \\ LM & \text{if } F'_{jL}(x_{i_l j}) = 1 \wedge F'_{jM}(x_{i_l j}) = 1 \wedge F'_{jH}(x_{i_l j}) = 0 \\ M & \text{if } F'_{jL}(x_{i_l j}) = 0 \wedge F'_{jM}(x_{i_l j}) = 1 \wedge F'_{jH}(x_{i_l j}) = 0 \\ MH & \text{if } F'_{jL}(x_{i_l j}) = 0 \wedge F'_{jM}(x_{i_l j}) = 1 \wedge F'_{jH}(x_{i_l j}) = 1 \\ H & \text{if } F'_{jL}(x_{i_l j}) = 0 \wedge F'_{jM}(x_{i_l j}) = 0 \wedge F'_{jH}(x_{i_l j}) = 1 \\ * & \text{if } F'_{jL}(x_{i_l j}) = 0 \wedge F'_{jM}(x_{i_l j}) = 0 \wedge F'_{jH}(x_{i_l j}) = 0 \end{cases} \tag{5}$$

- Secondly, the fuzzy pattern (corresponding to the class C_i) is constructed from the discretized and summarized data, selecting those labels of features which are different to the label "*" and have an appearance relative frequency in set $\boldsymbol{D}_i$ equal to or greater than a predefined ratio Π ($0 < \Pi \leq 1$, for example, $\Pi = 2/3$). Formally, for each feature F_j, the appearance frequency of any label $E \in \boldsymbol{E} = \{\mathrm{L}, \mathrm{LM}, \mathrm{M}, \mathrm{MH}, \mathrm{H}, *\}$ in the set $\boldsymbol{D}_i$, $\pi_{ij}(E)$, can be computed according to the expression given by

$$\pi_{ij}(E) = \frac{\sum_{i_1 \leq i_l \leq i_m} \delta_j(\boldsymbol{x}_{i_l}, E)}{i_m}, \text{ where } \delta_j(\boldsymbol{x}_{i_l}, E) = \begin{cases} 1 & \text{if } F''_j(\boldsymbol{x}_{i_l}) = E \\ 0 & \text{otherwise} \end{cases} \tag{6}$$

- Once, the frequency of each label is computed for every feature, a 3-tuple of the form ⟨feature, label, frequency⟩ is included in the fuzzy pattern of class C_i, only if its frequency exceeds the predefined ratio Π. Namely, the fuzzy pattern $\boldsymbol{P}_i$ is given by:

$$\boldsymbol{P}_i = \left\{ \bigwedge_{F''_j \in F''} \left\langle F''_j, E^j, \pi^j \right\rangle : E^j = \arg\max_{E \in \boldsymbol{E}} \{\pi_{ij}(E)\} \wedge E^j \neq * \wedge \pi^j = \pi_{ij}(E^j) \geq \Pi \right\} \tag{7}$$

- The predefined ratio Π controls the degree of exigency for selecting a feature as a member of the pattern, since the higher the value of Π, the fewer number of features which make up the pattern.

The method presented in this section aims to construct a fuzzy pattern which is representative of a collection of observations belonging to the same decision class, namely, the gene expression pattern of a specific kind of cancer. The pattern's quality of fuzziness is given by the fact that the labels, which make it up, come from the linguistic labels defined during the discretization stage. On the other hand, if a specific label of one feature is very common in all the examples (belonging to the same class), this feature is selected to be included in the pattern and, therefore, a frequency-based criteria is used for selecting a feature as part of the pattern.

3.3 Measuring the Distance of a New Case to a Gene Expression Pattern

This section describes how to measure the distance of a gene expression profile to a specific gene expression pattern. This feature is very important to perform different tasks such as clustering, supervised classification, the recovery of similar cases in a CBR system, and so on.

The defined metric is based on the comparison of the similarity of any two of the linguistic labels defined in Section 3.1. It is assumed that the similarity of two linguistic labels is determined by the degree of overlapping between labels and its definition is argued below.

From the traditional theory of sets it is known that the similarity between two sets *A* and *B* (and assuming that set *A* acts as a reference set), can be evaluated by:

$$sim(A, B) = \frac{|A \cap B|}{|A|} \tag{8}$$

Likewise, a similarity metric can be defined between fuzzy sets. In this case, it has been considered that the fuzzy intersection of two fuzzy sets *A* and *B* (represented by its membership functions, μ_A and μ_B, respectively) is given by the application of the `min` operator to the two membership functions, namely, $\mu_{A \cap B} = \texttt{min}\ \{\mu_A, \mu_B,\}$. On the other hand, the cardinality operator can be replaced by the integral operator, and then the similarity between two fuzzy sets can be evaluated by:

$$sim(A, B) = \frac{\int \min\{\mu_A(x), \mu_B(x)\} dx}{\int \mu_A(x) dx} \tag{9}$$

The metric *sim*(*A*, *B*) varies between the values 0 (total dissimilarity) and 1 (total similarity). At this point, the analytical calculation of the integrals that appear in expression (9) must be made. After some calculus, facilitated by the fact that the defined membership-functions are polynomial, a closed form for these integrals has been determined. These calculations are out of the scope of this work, and they do not contribute to the explanation of our proposal.

Now, given a set of data $\boldsymbol{D} = \{\boldsymbol{x}_1, ..., \boldsymbol{x}_m\}$, where $\boldsymbol{x}_i \in \mathbf{R}^n$, is a vector of *n* real values, each one referred to a feature in the set of features provided by a patient's gene expression profile, $\boldsymbol{F} = \{F_1, F_2, ..., F_n\}$. A representative pattern of the data set $\boldsymbol{D}$ can be extracted according to the process described in the previous section, which is an expression of the form:

$$\boldsymbol{P} = \bigwedge_{F''_j \in F''} \left\langle F''_j, E^j, \pi^j \right\rangle = \left\langle F''_{j_1}, E^{j_1}, \pi^{j_1} \right\rangle \wedge \ldots \wedge \left\langle F''_{j_n}, E^{j_n}, \pi^{j_n} \right\rangle \tag{10}$$

where j_n is the number of variables which the pattern has. Given a new observation $\boldsymbol{x} \in \mathbf{R}^n$, we are interested in evaluating the distance between the observation $\boldsymbol{x}$ and the pattern given by $\boldsymbol{P}$. After discretizing and summarizing the novel observation $\boldsymbol{x}$ following the process described in Section 3.1, the original vector $\boldsymbol{x} = \langle F_1(\boldsymbol{x}), ..., F_n(\boldsymbol{x})\rangle$ will be replaced by its discrete version, $\boldsymbol{x}'' = \langle F''_1(\boldsymbol{x}), ..., F''_n(\boldsymbol{x})\rangle$, where $F''_j(\boldsymbol{x})$ is defined by (6).

Then, assuming that the metric given by $sim(A, B)$ is available, the distance between the novel observation $\boldsymbol{x}$ and the pattern $\boldsymbol{P}$, denoted by $d(\boldsymbol{P}, \boldsymbol{x})$, is defined as:

$$d(\boldsymbol{P},\boldsymbol{x}) = \frac{j_n}{\sum_{j_1 \le j_k \le j_n} sim(E^{j_k}, F''_{j_k}(\boldsymbol{x}))\cdot \pi^{j_k}} - 1 \qquad (11)$$

This definition assumes that the similarity of an observation $\boldsymbol{x}$ to a pattern $\boldsymbol{P}$ depends on the sum of the similarity of their individual labels - evaluated by the term $sim(E_j, F''_j(\boldsymbol{x}))$ - and weighted by term π^j - the relative frequency of the pattern's label for the jth feature, E^j, in the original data set $\boldsymbol{D}$. Then, the distance is defined as inversely proportional to this similarity and normalized by the number of terms of the pattern - to allow us to compare the same observation with patterns of different length - and adjusted in such a way, that the range of the defined distance is between 0 (perfect match) to ∞ (complete dissimilarity).

Finally, it may be interesting to have threshold Δ associated to each pattern, so that the distance between an observation (or other pattern) and a reference pattern exceeds this threshold, it must be concluded that the observation is out of the influence area of the reference pattern. To compute this threshold, we must consider the mean of the distances of every observation $\boldsymbol{x}_i \in \boldsymbol{D} = \{\boldsymbol{x}_1, ..., \boldsymbol{x}_m\}$ (which were used to construct $\boldsymbol{P}$) to the pattern $\boldsymbol{P}$, and the threshold is defined as the upper bound of the confidence interval of this mean with a significance level of 5%. Then, the threshold for the pattern $\boldsymbol{P}$, Δ_P, is defined as:

$$\Delta_P = E[d(\boldsymbol{P},\boldsymbol{x}_i)] + \tfrac{1{,}96}{\sqrt{m-1}}\sqrt{\mathrm{Var}[d(\boldsymbol{P},\boldsymbol{x}_i)]} \qquad (12)$$

and so, it depends on the mean distance of all observations (used to construct it) to the pattern $\boldsymbol{P}$, the variability of these distances and the number of available observations.

4 Case Study: Acute Myeloid Leukemia

The study described in this paper was carried out in the context of the FSfRT architecture. FSfRT is a structured hybrid system that can employ several soft computing techniques in order to accomplish the 4-steps of the classical CBR life cycle [28].

The FSfRT architecture is an extension of a previous successful system [29] able to make predictions of red tides (discolourations caused by dense concentrations of microscopic sea plants, known as phytoplankton). The FSfRT architecture allows us the combination of several soft computing techniques in order to test their suitability working together to solve complex problems. The core and the interfaces of FSfRT have been coded in Java language and new capabilities are being developed. The general idea is to have different programmed techniques that are able to work separately and independently in co-operation with the rest. The main goal is to obtain a general structure that could change dynamically depending on the type of problem. Figure 2 shows a schematic view of the system.

The core of the system, which is composed of a *Knowledge Acquisition Module* (KAM), is shown on the left of Figure 2. The KAM is able to store all the information needed by the different techniques employed in the construction of the final gene-CBR system. In the retrieval and reuse stages, several soft computing techniques can be used [30, 31], while in the revise stage, our system employs a set of TSK fuzzy systems [32] in order to perform the validation of the initial solution proposed by the system.

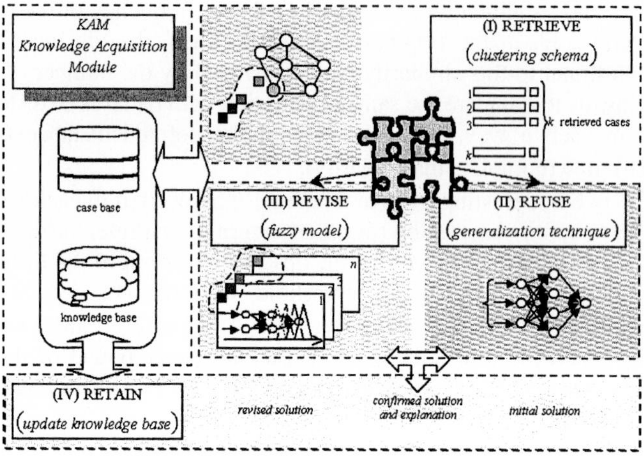

Fig. 2. FSfRT system architecture

The gene-CBR system is being developed, and as a first step, the fuzzy prototype-based retrieval method previously described has been evaluated. The main goal is to reduce the original data set of features while maintaining the classification accuracy of the system classifying the cancer.

Recent studies in human cancer have demonstrated that microarrays can be used to develop a new taxonomy of cancer, including major insights into the genesis, progression, prognosis and response to therapy based on gene expression profiles [33]. Often, cancers that appear histologically similar can have dramatically different responses to standard therapies and different courses of development. Since these differences in behaviour are likely to be reflected in the differences in the set of genes expressed, one promising use for microarrays is to more finely differentiate cancers using gene expression levels to bolster standard histology.

In our experiments, we work with a database of bone marrow cases from 43 adult patients with AML, a particular kind of cancer, plus a group of three samples belonging to healthy persons for test purposes (see Table 1 for a concrete description). The group of ill patients can be divided into four different groups, each of them characterized for having a different type of cancer with a different treatment and outcome. Each case (microarray experiment) stores 22,283 ESTs corresponding to the expression level of thousands of genes. The data consisted of 1,025,018 scanned intensities.

Table 1. Classification of patients taking into account the type of cancer

	healthy	APL	AML-inv()	AML-mono	AML-other
Number of patients	3	10	4	7	22

In the group of patients suffering AML-other, it was detected by the experts that new types of cancer would be able to rise. In our experiments, we randomly select 31 cases for training the method and 12 cases for test purposes (38% of the whole data, including at least one example from each group).

In order to generate a fuzzy pattern for each pathology (as described in Section 3.3) without taking into account the healthy people, the first step carried out was to discretize the expression profiles of all the genes regarding the linguistic labels Low, Medium and High. To do this, several experiments were carried out to select and adequate value for the theta (Θ) threshold (Section 3.1). The next step was to define the minimum appearance frequency, phi (Π), needed to consider a gene for representing a pathology in its corresponding fuzzy pattern (Section 3.2).

Table 2. Percentage of misclassifications using the Fuzzy Prototype-based Retrieval Method

	Π = 0.66	Π = 0.75	Π = 0.80	Π = 0.83	Π = 0.86
Θ = 0.75	41.67%	33.33%	33.33%	25.00%	25.00%
Θ = 0.85	41.67%	25.00%	25.00%	8.33%	25.00%
Θ = 0.95	41.67%	16.67%	16.67%	8.33%	16.67%
Θ = 0.975	33.33%	16.67%	16.67%	8.33%	8.33%
Θ = 0.9875	33.33%	16.67%	16.67%	8.33%	16.67%
Θ = 0.99	25.00%	16.67%	16.67%	8.33%	25.00%
Θ = 0.999	16.67%	8.33%	8.33%	0.00%	25.00%

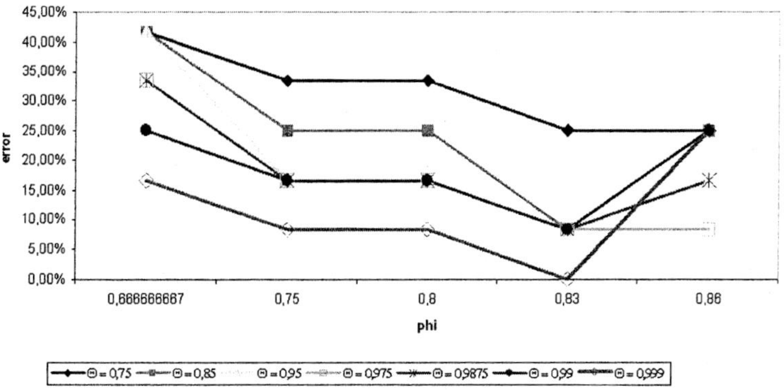

Fig. 3. Classification error varies accordingly phi and theta parameters

Table 2 shows a summary of different values for the theta and phi ratios and the percentage of misclassifications over the test cases while Figure 3 shows a representation of the classification error versus phi and theta values.

From Table 2 and Figure 3 it can be seen that for $\Theta = 0.999$ and $\Pi = 0.83$, the proposed method was able to correct classify the whole test bed. Moreover, the proposed method employs on average only 2% of the whole data for this task (see Table 3).

As we mention above, the main goal of our method was to reduce the original set of features while maintaining the classification accuracy of the system classifying the cancer. In this context, Table 3 shows the gene reduction percentage using the selected phi and theta values. For example, to identify the patients with APL leukemia we only need to analyse 681 variables (genes) out of the 22,283 that compose the whole case (patient descriptor).

Table 3. Reduction percentage obtained over the whole data using optimal values for theta and phi parameters

	APL	AML-inv()	AML-mono	AML-other		
				Sub_1	Sub_2	Sub_3
Original set	22,283	22,283	22,283	22,283	22,283	22,283
Selected set	681	591	292	176	235	817
% reduction	96.9%	97.4%	98.7%	99.2%	98.8%	96.3%

As Table 3 shows, the fuzzy prototype-based retrieval method was able to identify the three subtypes of AML-other as experts previously sensed. In this sense, the outcome generated overcomes those obtained by specific classification techniques such as PAM (*Prediction Analysis of Microarrays*) [34].

The main advantages of the proposed technique are that new subgroups of cancer are correctly identified and that fewer genes are needed in order to classify each case.

These results are very promising considering the reduction percentage of genes done by the proposed technique, especially if this work is compared with the previous one presented in [33]. However, this work that has been developed in the past eight months requires further experimental validation and follow up study. Many current efforts are being directed towards this area of research.

5 Conclusions and Future Work

An advantage of CBR systems as a problem-solving paradigm is that it is applicable to a wide range of problems. It can be used to propose new solutions or evaluate solutions to avoid potential problems. In the work of [35] it is suggested that analogical reasoning is particularly applicable to the biological domain, partly because biological systems are often homologous (rooted in evolution). Also, due to the fact that biologists often use a form of reasoning similar to CBR, where experiments are designed and performed based on the similarity between features of a new system and those of known systems.

In this work, we have presented a fuzzy codification for the gene expression levels of microarray data, based on the discretization of real gene expression data into a small number of fuzzy membership functions. Our proposed method aims to find all genes that are significantly expressed between the existing classes in order to obtain a fuzzy representation of the expression levels belonging to those genes that best explain each class in the form of a fuzzy-prototype. Then the proposed method is able to generalize over all of the samples diminishing drastically the number of genes needed to perform correct classifications. The fuzzy representation technique can be used to implement the retrieval stage of gene-CBR system under construction. Empirical studies show that this reduction technique allows to obtain a more general knowledge about the problem and to gain a deeper insight into the importance of each gene related to each pathology.

The remaining work is geared towards the study of new techniques that can be used for implementing the reuse, revision and retain phases of the gene-CBR life cycle. It is always important to completely define how a case could be represented and how we can maintain clinical and biological characteristics as well as temporary evolution of all the patients stored in the case base.

References

1. Schena, M., Shalon D., Davis, R., Brown, P.O.: Quantitative monitoring of gene expression patterns with a cDNA microarray. Science, Vol. 270. (1995) 467-470
2. DeRisi, J., Penland, L., Brown, P.O., Bittner, M.L., Meltzer, P.S., Ray, M., Chen, Y., Su Y.A., Trent, J.M.: Use of a cDNA microarray to analyse gene expression patterns in human cancer. Nature Genetics, Vol. 14. (4). (1996) 367-370
3. The Chipping Forecast I. Special Supplement. Nature Genetics, Vol. 21. (1999)
4. The Chipping Forecast II. Special Supplement. Nature Genetics, Vol. 32. (2002)
5. Lipshutz, R.J., Fodor, S.P.A., Gingeras, T.R., Lockhart, D.H.: High density synthetic oligonucleotide arrays. Nature Genetics, Vol. 21. (1999) 20-24
6. Golub, T.R., Slonim, D.K., Tamayo, P., Huard, C., Gaasenbeek, M., Mesirov, J.P., Coller, H., Loh, M.L., Downing, J.R., Caligiuri, M.A., Bloomfield, C.D., Lander, E.S.: Molecular classification of cancer: class discovery and class prediction by gene expression monitoring. Science. Vol. 286 (5439). (1999) 531-537
7. Articles on microarray data mining. ACM SIGKDD Explorations Newsletter, Vol. 5 (2). (2003) 1-139
8. Cho, S.B., Won, H.H.: Machine learning in DNA microarray analysis for cancer classification. Proc. of the First Asia-Pacific Bioinformatics Conference, Vol. 19. (2003) 189-198
9. Morrison, N., Hoyle, D.C.: Normalization concepts and methods for normalizing microarray data. In Berrar, D.P., Dubitzky, W., Granzow, M. (eds.). A Practical Approach to MicroArray Data Analysis, Kluwer Academic Publishers, Boston (2003)
10. Bilban, M., Buehler, L.K., Head, S., Desoye, G., Quaranta, V.: Normalizing DNA microarray data. Current Issues in Molecular Biology, Vol. 4 (2). (2000) 57-64
11. Schuchhardt, J., Beule, D., Malik, A., Wolski, E., Eickhoff, H., Lehrach, H., Herzel, H.: Normalization strategies for cDNA microarrays. Nucleic Acids Research, Vol. 28 (10). (2000) e47

12. Rubinstein, B.I.P., McAuliffe, F., Cawley, S., Palaniswami, M., Ramamohanarao, K., Speed, T.S.: Machine learning in low-level microarray analysis. ACM SIGKDD Explorations Newsletter, Vol. 5 (2). (2003) 130-139
13. Corchado, J.M., Corchado, E.S., Aiken, J., Fyfe, C., Fdez-Riverola, F., Glez-Bedia, M.: Maximum Likelihood Hebbian Learning Based Retrieval Method for CBR Systems. Proc. of the 5th International Conference on Case-Based Reasoning, (2003) 107-121
14. Corchado, J.M., Aiken, J., Corchado, E., Lefevre, N., Smyth, T.: Quantifying the Ocean's CO2 Budget with a CoHeL-IBR System. Proc. of the 7th European Conference on Case-based Reasoning, (2004) 533-546
15. Cakmakov, D., Bennani, Y.: Feature selection for pattern recognition, Informa Press (2002)
16. Jurisica, I., Glawgow, J.: Applications of case-based reasoning in molecular biology. Artificial Intelligence Magazine, Special issue on Bioinformatics, Vol. 25 (1). (2004) 85-95
17. Li, L., Darden, T.A., Weinberg, C.R., Levine, A.J., Pedersen, L.G.: Gene assessment and sample classification for gene expression data using a genetic algorithm/k-nearest neighbor method. Combinatorial Chemistry and High Throughput Screening, Vol. 4 (8). (2001) 727-739
18. Blanco, R., Larrañaga, P., Inza, I., Sierra, B.: Gene selection for cancer classification using wrapper approaches. International Journal of Pattern Recognition and Artificial Intelligence, *accepted for publication* (2004)
19. Guyon, I., Weston, J., Barnhill, S., Vapnik, V.: Gene selection for cancer classification using support vector machines. Machine Learning, Vol. 46 (1-3). (2002) 389-422
20. Jaeger, J., Sengupta, R., Ruzzo, W.L.: Improved gene selection for classification of microarrays. Proc. of Pacific Symposium on Biocomputing, (2003) 53-64
21. Qi, H.: Feature selection and kNN fusion in molecular classification of multiple tumor types. Proc. of the International Conference on Mathematics and Engineering Techniques in Medicine and Biological Sciences, (2002)
22. Hanczar, B., Courtine, M., Benis, A., Hennegar, C., Clément, K., Zucker, J.D.: Improving classification of microarray data using prototype-based feature selection. ACM SIGKDD Explorations Newsletter, Vol. 5 (2). (2003) 23-30
23. Zheng, G., Olusegun, E., Narasimhan, G.: Neural network classifiers and gene selection methods for microarray data on human lung adenocarcinoma. Prof. of Critical Assessment of Microarray Data Analysis, (2003) 63-67
24. Hochreiter, S., Obermayer, K.: Feature selection and classification on matrix data: from large margins to small covering numbers. Advances in Neural Information Processing Systems, Vol. 15. (2003) 913-920
25. Weston, J., Mukherjee, S., Chapelle, O., Pontil, M., Poggio, T., Vapnik, V.: Feature selection for SVMs. Advances in Neural Information Processing Systems, Vol. 13. (2001) 668-674
26. Pal, S., Shiu, S.: Foundations of Soft Case-Based Reasoning. John Wiley, New York (2004)
27. Pal, S., Mitra, P.: Case Generation Using Rough Sets with Fuzzy Representation. IEEE Transactions on Knowledge and Data Engineering, Vol. 16 (3). (2004) 292-300
28. Riesbeck, C.K., Schank, R.C.: Inside Case-Based Reasoning, Lawrence Erlbaum Associates, Hillsdale, NJ, US (1999)
29. Fdez-Riverola, F., Corchado, J.M.: FSfRT, Forecasting System for Red Tides. An Hybrid Autonomous AI Model. Applied Artificial Intelligence, Vol. 17 (10). (2003) 955-982
30. Pal, S.K., Dilon, T.S., Yeung, D.S.: Soft Computing in Case Based Reasoning, Springer Verlag, London (2000)

31. Sankar, K.P., Simon, C.K.S: Foundations of Soft Case-Based Reasoning, Wiley-Interscience, Hoboken, New Jersey (2003)
32. Fdez-Riverola, F., Corchado, J.M.: Employing TSK Fuzzy models to automate the revision stage of a CBR system. Current Topics in Artificial Intelligence, LNAI 3040. (2004) 302-311
33. Gutierrez, N.C., López-Pérez R., Hernández, J.M., Isidro, I., González, B., García, J.L., Fermiñán, E., Lumbreras, E., San Miguel, J.F.: Gene expression profile reveals deregulation of new genes with relevant functions in the different subclasses of acute myeloid leukemia. Blood, Vol. 102 (11). (2003)
34. Tibshirani, R., Hastie, T., Narasimhan, B., Chu, G.: Diagnosis of multiple cancer types by shrunken centroids of gene expression. Proc. of the National Academy of Sciences of the United States of America, Vol. 99(10). (2002) 6561-6572
35. Aaronson, J.S., Juergen, H., Overton, G.C.: Knowledge Discovery in GENBANK. Proc. of the First International Conference on Intelligent Systems for Molecular Biology, (1993) 3-11

CBR for State Value Function Approximation in Reinforcement Learning

Thomas Gabel and Martin Riedmiller

Neuroinformatics Group, Department of Mathematics and Computer Science,
Institute of Cognitive Science, University of Osnabrück,
49069 Osnabrück, Germany
{thomas.gabel, martin.riedmiller}@uni-osnabrueck.de

Abstract. CBR is one of the techniques that can be applied to the task of approximating a function over high-dimensional, continuous spaces. In Reinforcement Learning systems a learning agent is faced with the problem of assessing the desirability of the state it finds itself in. If the state space is very large and/or continuous the availability of a suitable mechanism to approximate a value function – which estimates the value of single states – is of crucial importance. In this paper, we investigate the use of case-based methods to realise that task. The approach we take is evaluated in a case study in robotic soccer simulation.

1 Introduction

Case-based Reasoning (CBR) is based on the assumption that similar problems have similar solutions. Systems relying on that paradigm have been successfully used in several application domains, such as diagnosis, classification, prediction, control and action planning. Various reasons have contributed to the attractiveness of employing case-based methods: They are straightforward to implement, help in reducing the knowledge acquisition effort and they are noise-tolerant due to their approximate nature. In this work we will exploit these advantages in the context of Reinforcement Learning and thus, more specifically, in an application field that covers the tasks of prediction and action planning.

Reinforcement Learning (RL) follows the idea that an autonomously acting agent obtains its behaviour policy through repeated interaction with its environment on a trial-and-error basis. The experience the agent gathers that way is then processed and integrated into a mathematical function that tells how much it is worth aspiring to enter a specific state by performing a specific action. So, one central issue in RL represents the learning of that function, which reflects the value of a state and from which a good policy for action choice may be induced. That task is aggravated when the set of states in which the agent can find itself is infinite, i.e. when working with a large, continuous state space. Then, storing states' values explicitly is impossible and, hence, it becomes indispensable to make use of a suitable function approximation mechanism.

In this paper we investigate the use of CBR methods for that task. Their application seems promising insofar as they are considered suitable for handling noisy data and learning and generalising fast from few training examples.

H. Muñoz-Avila and F. Ricci (Eds.): ICCBR 2005, LNAI 3620, pp. 206–221, 2005.

However, the approximation of a state value function in RL bears some inherent difficulties to be coped with: In particular, the function that we want to approximate with maximal accuracy is a moving target, i.e. changes over time, since at the beginning of the learning process only little is known about its shape, whereas at later stages of learning much more experience about its real shape will have been collected. Therefore, we present a systematic compilation of various CBR techniques to deal with this and other important problems and examine the capabilities of a CBR-based state value function approximation compared to a table-based and neural net-based function representation.

In Section 2 we introduce the necessary vocabulary, review some basics of the Reinforcement Learning paradigm and motivate the use of CBR technology to represent and approximate a state value function. Section 3 introduces our CBR-based approach to state value function approximation. We present a specialised RL algorithm, that employs a CBR-based function approximator, as well as necessary methods required for case base management. Furthermore, we discuss benefits and limitations of the ideas given. Section 4 reveals one of the underlying motivations of our work: Our research group participates in the RoboCup championship tournaments in robotic soccer simulation, where one of our main research goals is to realise an increasing part of our soccer-playing agents' behaviour by using machine learning techniques. So, we outline a specific sub-task – the intercept ball problem – of robotic soccer simulation and present results in solving that task with RL which we obtained using CBR methods for approximating the underlying state value function. Finally, Section 5 concludes.

2 The Reinforcement Learning Framework

One of the general aims of Machine Learning is to produce intelligent software systems, sometimes called agents, by a process of learning and evolving. Reinforcement Learning represents one approach that may be employed to reach that goal. In an RL learning scenario the agent interacts with its initially unknown environment, observes the results of its actions, and adapts its behaviour appropriately. To some extent, this imitates the way biological beings learn.

In each time step an RL agent observes the environmental state and makes a decision for a specific action, which, on the one hand, may incur some immediate reward (also called reinforcement) generated by the agent's environment and, on the other hand, transfers the agent into some successor state. The agent's goal is not to maximise the immediate reward, but its long-term, expected reward. To do so it must learn a decision policy π that is used to determine the best action for a given state. Such a policy is a function that maps the current state $s \in S$ to an action a from a set of viable actions A. This idea of learning through interaction with the environment can be rendered by the following steps that must be performed by an RL agent (illustrated and refined in Figure 1):

1. the agent perceives an input state s
2. the agent determines an action a using a decision making function (*policy*)
3. action a is performed

4. the agent obtains a scalar reward r from its environment (reinforcement)
5. information about the reward r that has been received for taking action a in state s is processed

The basic Reinforcement Learning paradigm is to learn the mapping $\pi : S \to A$ only on the basis of the rewards the agent gets from its environment. By repeatedly performing actions and observing resulting rewards, the agent tries to improve and fine-tune its policy. The respective Reinforcement Learning method (step 5) specifies how experience from past interaction is used to adapt the policy. Assuming that a sufficient number of states has been observed and rewards have been received, the optimal decision policy will have been found and the agent following that policy will behave perfectly in the particular environment.

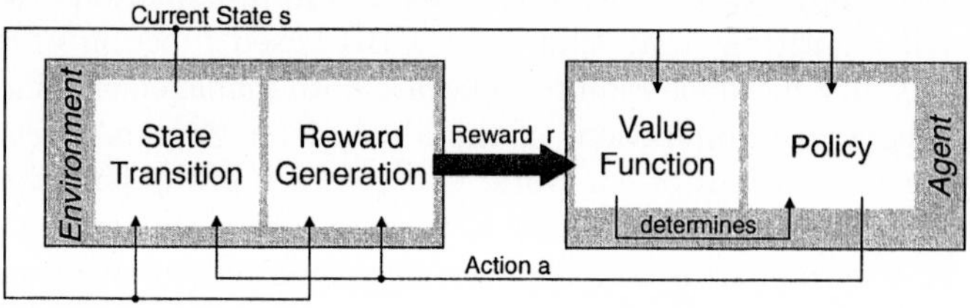

Fig. 1. Schematic View on RL Using State Value Functions

2.1 Learning Value Functions

The Reinforcement Learning problem is usually formalised as a Markov Decision Process (MDP) within the context of Dynamic Programming [3]. An MDP is a 4-tuple $M = [S, A, r, p]$ where S denotes the set of environmental states, A the set of actions the agent can perform, and $r : S \times A \to \mathbb{R}$ the function of immediate rewards $r(s, a)$ (sometimes called costs of actions) that arise when taking action a in state s. The function $p : S \times A \times S \to [0; 1]$ depicts a probability distribution $p(s, a, s')$ that tells how likely it is to end up in state s', when performing action a in state s.

Being in search of an optimal behaviour in an unknown environment, the agent needs a facility to differentiate between the desirability of possible successor states, in order to decide on a good action. A common way to rank states is by computing and using a so-called *state value function* $V^\pi : S \to \mathbb{R}$ which estimates the future rewards that can be expected when starting in a specific state s and taking actions determined by policy $\pi : S \to A$. Thus, $V^\pi(s) = E[\sum_{t=0}^{\infty} r(s_t, \pi(s_t))|s_0 = s)]$, where $E[\cdot]$ denotes the expected value. If we assume we are in possession of an "optimal" state value function $V^\star$, it is easy to infer the corresponding optimal behaviour policy[1] by exploiting that value function greedily according to $\pi^\star(s) := \arg\max_{a \in A}\{r(s, a) + \sum_{s \in S} p(s, a, s') \cdot V^\star(s')\}$.

[1] Note, that often – in particular, in cases where no model p of the environment is available – state-action value functions $Q : S \times A \to \mathbb{R}$ are learnt, which provide an estimation of how desirable it is to choose a specific action in a certain state. The paper at hand, however, deals with state-value functions only.

So, the crucial question is, how to obtain the optimal state value function. To perform that task, Dynamic Programming methods, e.g. value iteration [2], may be employed which converges under certain assumptions to the optimal value function $V^\star$ of expected rewards. Value iteration is based on successive updates of the value function for all states $s \in S$ according to $V_{k+1}(s) := max_{a \in A}\{r(s,a) + \sum_{s' \in S} p(s,a,s') \cdot V_k(s')\}$, where index k denotes the sequence of approximated versions of V, until convergence to $V^\star$ is reached.

Research in Reinforcement Learning, however, has generated a variety of methods that extend those well-known optimisation techniques, aiming at applicability also in situations where large state spaces must be handled or the absence of a transition model p prevents the usage of simple value iteration. Although some details of the RL learning algorithm we use in the scope of this work are given in Section 2.2, a discussion on progress and state of the art in RL goes beyond the scope of this paper; the interested reader is referred to [21].

2.2 Temporal Difference Methods

Temporal difference (TD) methods comprise a set of RL algorithms that incrementally update state value functions $V(s)$ after each transition (from state s to s') the agent has gone through. This is particularly useful when learning along trajectories $(s_0, s_1, \ldots, s_N)$ that start in some start state s_0 and end in some terminal state $s_N \in G$, where G is a set of goal state. This means learning can be performed online, i.e. the processes of collecting (simulated) experience and learning the value function run in parallel. In this work we update the value function's estimates according to the $TD(1)$ update rule [20], where the new estimate for $V(s_k)$ is calculated as $V(s_k) := (1-\alpha) \cdot V(s_k) + \alpha \cdot return(s_k)$ with $return(s_k) = \sum_{j=k}^{N} r(s_k, \pi(s_k))$ indicating the summed rewards following state s_k and α representing a decaying learning rate. The whole episode-based $TD(1)$ learning algorithm to be used in conjunction with a table-based function representation of V (i.e. the state value for each state is stored explicitly) proceeds as in Algorithm 1.

One inherent feature of this learning algorithm – as well as of any algorithm that optimises a state value function – is that at the beginning of learning the estimates for $V(s)$ are typically very coarse. To put it differently, initially V represents a rather noisy estimate of the true optimal value function $V^\star$, steadily converging towards $V^\star$ as long as all criteria for convergence are fulfilled. For the family of $TD(\lambda)$ algorithms convergence is guaranteed, if each state is visited by an infinite number of episodes and if the step size parameter α diminishes towards zero at a suitable rate.

2.3 The Need for Function Approximation

As outlined in the previous sections, the determination of an optimal state value function is crucial to most RL methods. Intending to show the functioning of some new RL technique in principle, one usually chooses typical benchmark problems (grid worlds) that are very limited in terms of state and action space

1. initialise state value function V arbitrarily, let policy π be given by ε-greedy exploitation of V
2. **repeat**
   (a) generate random start situation s_0 for current episode, set $k := 0$
   (b) **while** $s_k \notin G$ **and** $k < maxEpisodeLength$ **do**
      i. choose next action a_k by exploiting V ε-greedily according to $a_k := argmax_{a \in A}(r(s_k, a) + \sum_{s' \in S} p(s_k, a_k, s') \cdot V(s'))$ or choose a random action with probability ε
      ii. perform a_k, entering state s_{k+1} and perceiving immediate reward $r(s_k, a_k)$
   (c) **for all** steps s_k in episode $(s_1, \ldots, s_N)$
      i. $return(s_k) := \sum_{j=k}^{N-1} r(s_j, a_j) + r(s_N)$
      ii. $V(s_k) := (1 - \alpha) \cdot V(s_k) + \alpha \cdot return(s_k)$ with α as learning rate

   until stop criterion becomes true

Algorithm 1. Episode-Based RL Algorithm Using Table-Based State Value Function

size. In those cases, having to deal with only a finite number of states, it is feasible to store $V(s)$ for each single state $s \in S$ explicitly using a tabular function representation with $|S|$ table entries. However, when aspiring to apply RL techniques to real world problems – as we do in this paper – and thus working with high-dimensional and probably continuous state spaces, computational and/or memory limitations inhibit the use of a tabular function representation. Instead, the employment of a function approximator becomes inevitable.

Thus, we deal with "suboptimal" methods that approximate the optimal state value function $V^\star(s)$: We replace the optimal value function by an appropriate approximation $\tilde{V}(s, t)$, where t determines the set of the approximator's parameters. In particular, we focus on the use of Case-Based Reasoning as a suitable technique to approximate $V^\star$ using k-nearest neighbour regression and compare it to other function approximation methods.

3 CBR-Based Value Function Approximation

When approximating some target function $f(x) = y$, the system is usually provided with a set of training data tuples (x_i, y_i) of f's desired input-output behaviour and tries to reconstruct f so that these data pairs are explained best. So, for the case of approximating a state value function, an ideal training data set would be made up of tuples $(s, V^\star(s))$ with s covering some subset of S. Unfortunately, learning the optimal state value function $V^\star$ is the overall learning goal, which is why obtaining such a training set is impossible. In other words, the approximation of the value function must be conducted in parallel to computing $V^\star$, which complicates the function approximator's adjustment heavily. As early estimates of $V(s)$ can be interpreted as noise-afflicted versions of the optimal values $V^\star(s)$, the application of CBR to approximate V appears promising in that respect. Moreover, CBR systems are straightforward to implement and comparatively easy to tune. This argument is striking when comparing CBR as function approximation scheme with the use of neural nets, which are notoriously hard to tune in the context of RL algorithms. The latter advantage of CBR is supported by Gordon [7]: A case-based function approximator can be characterised as a contraction mapping ("averager") whereas neural nets fall into the category of expansion mappings ("exaggerators"), that can exaggerate changes in their training values and cause instability in the respective learning algorithm.

3.1 Related Work

CBR-related (case-based, instance-based, and sometimes so-called memory-based) techniques have been used in the context of Reinforcement Learning at times.

The idea of using instances of stored experience to predict the value of some *solution attribute* of a new unseen example is the main feature of case-based regression algorithms. In [8] the idea of weighted k-nearest neighbour regression is introduced. Here, the numerical prediction of a query's solution attribute is determined as a weighted average of the solution attribute values of the query's nearest neighbours. Peng [13] was one of the first to use a nearest-neighbour approach in the context of value function approximation for RL. In that work, however, the important topic of case-base management is not addressed. Suitable techniques to limit the potentially rapid growth of the case base by remembering too many cases have been presented later on: For example, in [5] the authors apply instance-based regression in a relational RL context and develop strategies to confine the data inflow. Similar ideas are also part of the work of Ratitch [14], though here Sparse Distributed Memories, which are a specialised application of CBR using specific similarity measures, are used as the underlying prediction technique. In both [17] and [6], promising results of approximating value functions in continuous state spaces for dynamic control tasks are presented. Their special focus is, in the case of the former, to learn from a small amount of data, boosting the learning process with initial training examples from a human expert, and, in the case of the latter, relevant extensions that allow their algorithms' application also in more complex domains. A comprehensive article addressing the comparison of several memory-based approaches to function approximation is the one by Santamaria et. al [16]. Using their terminology the ideas we present in this paper ought to be classified as instance-based methods, as they reserve the term "case-based" explicitly for situations where the actions to be chosen represent the cases' solutions. Nevertheless, we proceed using the well-established CBR vocabulary in the following. The contribution of this work lies in a systematic compilation of various CBR techniques in an RL context and their application to tasks with real-time constraints. Moreover, we examine the performance of a CBR-based value function approximation in a case study in robotic soccer and compare it to other function approximation methods.

3.2 Function Approximation with k-Nearest Neighbour Regression

Our approach to CBR-based state value function approximation is based on the following main characteristics, that will be discussed in more detail subsequently:

- an attribute-value based state/case representation,
- the local-global principle for similarity assessment and retrieval, and
- k-nearest neighbour regression to predict the cases' solution attribute.

We assume a continuous, n-dimensional state space $S \subset \mathbb{R}^n$ where each $s = (s_1, s_2, \dots, s_n) \in S$ is a vector of real numbers and each dimension has its individual domain $D_i \subset \mathbb{R}$. Accordingly, we define a *case* c^s for state s to be an $n+1$-dimensional real-valued vector $c^s = (s_1, \dots, s_n, c^s_v)$, where the first n elements represent the case's problem part and correspond to state s. The last entry depicts the case's solution $c^s_v = V(s)$, i.e. the expected reward when the RL agent starts from s.

Using this notation the *global similarity* between two cases is defined as

$$sim(c^{s_1}, c^{s_2}) := \sum_{i=1}^{n} w_i \cdot sim_i(c_i^{s_1}, c_i^{s_2}) \tag{1}$$

The weights w_i, which are normalised so that $\sum_{i=1}^{n} w_i = 1$, are used to strengthen or weaken the relevance of individual dimensions. For all $i \in \{1, \dots, n\}$ a *local similarity measure* $sim_i : D_i \times D_i \to [0,1]$ assesses the degree of similarity along a single dimension. Currently, we use the Euclidian distance for all sim_i. However, as previous research in learning similarity measure has shown [18], the adjustment of feature weights as well as of local measures may have a significant influence on the system's performance. Therefore, we currently plan to incorporate some of these ideas into our RL learning framework.

Case value (or state value, respectively) prediction according to k-nearest neighbour regression is defined as

$$\tilde{V}(s, CB) := \frac{\sum_{c^{s_i} \in NN_k(c^s)} sim(c^s, c^{s_i}) \cdot c_v^{s_i}}{\sum_{c^{s_i} \in NN_k(c^s)} sim(c^s, c^{s_i})} \tag{2}$$

so that $\tilde{V}(s, CB)$ stands for the currently predicted value of $V^\star(s)$ approximated with help of the CBR system's case base CB, where $NN_k(c^s)$ is the set of c^s's k nearest neighbours in CB. Other authors [12] use kernel functions to support the regression task: The weighted contribution of each neighbouring case's value c_v is then computed using the kernel being parameterised by the similarity function. Compared to that approach our regression scheme depicts a simplification, which we chose with regard to the learning of similarity measures we plan.

Working with a CBR-based value function approximation requires slight modifications to our episode-based RL algorithm given in Section 2.2. If that algorithm needs an estimated value for a specific state s it now computes $\tilde{V}(s, CB)$ instead of $V(s)$. However, the update of a state's value, i.e. the assignment of a new value to state s, cannot be realised in such a straightforward manner as in the case of the algorithm using a table-based representation of V. As can be seen in Algorithm 2 we add a new case containing the corresponding state's backed-up value to the case base, but also call appropriate case base management routines.

1. start with case base $CB = \varnothing$, let the approximated state value function be $\tilde{V}(s, CB)$, and policy π be given by greedy ε-exploitation of $\tilde{V}$
2. **repeat**
   (a) generate random start situation s_0 for current episode, set $k := 0$
   (b) **while** $s_k \notin G$ **and** $k < maxEpisodeLength$ **do**
      i. choose next action a_k by exploiting $\tilde{V}$ ε-greedily according to $a_k := \arg\max_{a \in A}(r(s_k, a) + \sum_{s' \in S} p(s_k, a_k, s') \cdot \tilde{V}(s', CB))$ or choose a random action with probability ε
      ii. perform a_k, entering state s_{k+1} and perceiving immediate reward $r(s_k, a_k)$
   (c) **for all** steps s_k in episode $(s_1, \ldots, s_N)$
      i. $return(s_k) := \sum_{j=k}^{N-1} r(s_j, a_j) + r(s_N)$
      ii. create a new case $c^{new} := (s_k, return(s_k))$
      iii. $CB := CB \cup c^{new}$
      iv. **call** case base management routines
   until stop criterion becomes true

Algorithm 2. Episode-Based RL Algorithm Using CBR-based Function Approximation

3.3 Case Base Management

Starting with an empty case base, the learning algorithm steadily increases its competence by storing new experiences. However, there are a number of reasons why the inflow of new cases ought to be limited.

- The more cases the case base contains, the longer the retrieval of the query's nearest neighbours takes. Although there exist techniques to reduce the computational effort during retrieval, e.g. *kd*-trees [6], it is advisable to limit the growth of the case base's size when intending to use the system for real-time control tasks.
- As already noted early estimates of the state value function's values represent rather noisy versions of the optimal values. Thus, it is indispensable to also discard some cases already stored. At this point, the difficulty arises to differentiate between important outliers and simply wrong estimates.
- Simple instance-based learning by just remembering all cases would not be applicable since the amount of data the agent collects would become unmanageable as the agent continues to learn.

There exist a number of approaches to remove "useless" cases during training, e.g. the *IBx* algorithms by Aha [1]. For learning embedded in an RL context, however, more specialised techniques are necessary. In [6] it is pointed out that being selective in adding cases may slow down the learning rate. Furthermore, we need to stress that each new case $c^{new} = (s_k, return(s_k))$ composed by Algorithm 2 contains the currently most up-to-date estimate for the state value $V(s_k)$. these reasons we insist on explicitly storing this piece of brand-new information by adding it to the case base and removing its very nearest neighbour c^j for which it holds $sim(c^{new}, c^j) > 1 - \delta$ with some extremely small $\delta > 0$.

Anyway, when the number of cases stored in CB exceeds some critical value $|CB| > \mu$, so that the realisation of a retrieval/regression within a certain amount of time cannot be guaranteed, it is inevitable to also remove some cases. A first approach to tackle that problem would be to remove the oldest or least frequently used elements of CB. This idea seems intuitive, as old cases usually contain worse estimates of the corresponding state's value than newer ones, but this strategy might lead to a function approximator that easily "forgets" some of its valuable experience made in the past. This danger may become particularly problematic, when some regions of the state space are visited rather rarely during learning and hence eventually good estimates are erased due to infrequent occurrence.

More complex scoring measures calculating which cases are to be removed have been proposed by several authors. In [6] it is suggested to remove those cases that contribute least to the overall approximation. In [5] the authors pursue a more error-oriented view and propose the deletion of cases that contribute most to the prediction error of other examples. A considerable flaw of those more sophisticated measures is their complexity. The determination of the case(s) to be removed involves the computation of a score value for each $c^i \in CB$ which in turn requires at least one retrieval and regression, respectively, for each $c^j \in CB$ $(j \neq i)$. These repeated entire sweeps through the case base induce an enormous computational load, although optimisations may find a partial remedy. Consequently, these approaches are not best suited in systems which are learning with tight time requirements and handling a high-dimensional state space, which necessitates the use of larger case bases.

For these reasons, we employ a heuristic scoring measure that is made up of three components, computationally less demanding, and brought about good results during evaluation. As formalised in Algorithm 3 this measure's components reflect the distribution of cases throughout the state space, the correctness of predictions for values of the state value function as well as the case's age.

3.4 Benefits and Limitations

The main CBR principle, telling similar problems have similar solutions, can also be utilised when employing case-based methods for function approximation, provided that the target function to be approximated can be characterised as locally smooth. So, CBR's robustness against noisy data also applies when approximating state value functions. All experience is stored explicitly so that the negative influence of a wrong state value estimate is only local. In the RL context the function to be approximated is learnt concurrently with acting and thus is not static, but changes over time converging towards $V^\star$. Hence, early experience may be considered as "noise" at later stages of learning.

CBR is an approximate technique by nature. Accordingly, the quality of a case-based value function approximation depends strongly on the number of cases stored. Aiming to tackle high dimensional state spaces, the case base size that is needed to obtain high-quality approximations grows exponentially with the number of dimensions. Then, not only a memory shortage may arise, but also real-time usage of the system becomes impractical, as the time for case

1. **if** $|CB| \leq caseBaseMaxSize$ **return**
2. **for all** $c^i \in CB$
   (a) compute the set $NN_k(c^i)$ of the k nearest neighbours around c^i
   (b) compute the similarity density around c^i as $\varphi(c^i) := \frac{1}{k}\sum_{c^j \in NN_k(c^i)} sim(c^i, c^j)$
   (c) compute the standard deviation of stored state values within c^i's nearest neighbours as $\sigma_v(c^j) := \sqrt{\frac{1}{k}\sum_{c^j \in NN_k(c^i)}(c_v^i - c_v^j)^2}$
   (d) compute the score components
      i. case neighbourhood score: $S_n(c^i) := \varphi(c^i) \cdot \sigma_v(c^i)$
      ii. regress error score: $S_e(c^i) := \sum_{c^j \in NN_k(c^i)} sim(c^i, c^j) \cdot |c_v^j - \hat{c}_v^j|$ where $\hat{c}_v^j$ is the system's prediction for c_v^j using $CB \setminus c^j$
      iii. age score: $S_a(c^i) := \frac{t(c^i)}{2|CB|}$ with $t(c^i)$ telling how many time steps ago c^i has been added to CB
   (e) let the overall score $S(c^i)$ be the sum of its component
3. delete ϱ cases with highest score values

Algorithm 3. Case Base Management: Deletion of Stored Cases

retrieval/regression grows at least logarithmically with the number of stored cases. Thus, a trade-off between approximation quality and real-time constraints has to be found. Another meaningful advantage of CBR systems is the speed at which they learn. As each piece of experience is remembered explicitly, the system is capable of representing a quite good, though far from perfect, function approximation with a rather small number of cases.

To sum up, we can distinguish two main application fields for CBR-based function approximators: If maximal accuracy in approximating V and/or real-time application of the policy are not an issue, an RL agent using a case-based value function representation can become applicable within shortest time. Otherwise, a case-based function approximator might be used for the starting stage of the learning process: That way, average or even good approximation results may be obtained within a very short time and used to initialise and speed up the training of another approximator (e.g. a neural net) with which nearly maximal accuracy can be attained. As for the experiments presented in the following, we focus on the latter use of a case-based state value function approximator.

4 Experimental Evaluation

In the previous section we have introduced a number of methods to apply a CBR-based approach to state value function approximation within a Reinforcement Learning context. Now, we want to investigate the performance and usability of the ideas presented, comparing them to two different approaches to function approximation, viz a table-based representation and neural nets. The application scenario our evaluation is embedded in is robotic soccer simulation and thus, in particular, our research group's RoboCup competition team Brainstormers [10].

4.1 Robotic Soccer Simulation

RoboCup [22] is an international research initiative intending to expedite AI and intelligent robotics research by defining a set of standard problems where various technologies can and ought to be combined to solve them. Annually, there are championship tournaments in several leagues – ranging from rescue tasks to real soccer-playing robots and simulated ones. The focus of the evaluation at hand is laid upon RoboCup's 2D Simulation League, where two teams of simulated soccer-playing agents compete against one another using the Soccer Server [11], a real-time soccer simulation system.

Robotic Soccer represents an excellent testbed for Machine Learning and, particularly, for RL tasks. Several research groups have dealt with the task of learning parts of a soccer-playing agent's behaviour autonomously (e.g. [9]), also relying on case-based methods at times (e.g. [4]). From a learning point of view it is also our long-term goal to realise an agent that obtains its behaviour by entirely employing a Reinforcement Learning methodology: Although we made some progress towards tackling the more complex task of learning a cooperative team behaviour [10], the most convincing learning results have been obtained for smaller sub-problems so far, especially for the learning of basic behaviours, so-called *skills.*

Intercept Ball Task

One of the most important fundamental capabilities of a soccer player – whether simulated or real – is to intercept a running ball as quickly as possible. Since a match's course of action can only be influenced significantly, if a team is in ball possession, this skill is crucial for being competitive. In the scope of this experimental evaluation we focus on the intercept ball task.

The optimal behaviour for ball interception is of course to compute the best interception point and to move to that point along the shortest path. If the physical laws of the environment are known and the simulation is deterministic that calculation may be done exactly. An illustration of the intercept ball task is given in Figure 2. For more details on analytical solutions the reader is referred to [19]. However, as already mentioned, it is our aim to realise a growing part of our agents' behaviour as modules that were learnt using RL. Hence, we formalised the intercept task as an MDP, applied Algorithm 2, and learnt a state value function for this problem. The problem's state space is continuous and 6-dimensional, i.e. $S = \{s = (v_{b,x}, v_{b,y}, v_{p,x}, v_{p,y}, d_{bp}, \alpha_{bp})\}$ where $\boldsymbol{v_b}$ is the ball's and $\boldsymbol{v_p}$ the player's velocity, d_{bp} the distance and α_{bp} the relative angle between ball and player. Viable actions for the player are, as determined by the Soccer Server, turn (real-valued from $[-180°, 180°]$) and dash (with dash power parameter within $[0, 100]$). A ball is considered to have been intercepted successfully, when the player has gained "control" over it, which means the player has moved to the point where the ball is within the player's kickable area. We here only consider a deterministic soccer simulation environment where $\forall s \in S$ and $\forall a \in A$ there is a $s' \in S$ with $p(s, a, s') = 1$, although our algorithms and function approximation techniques work for stochastic environments as well.

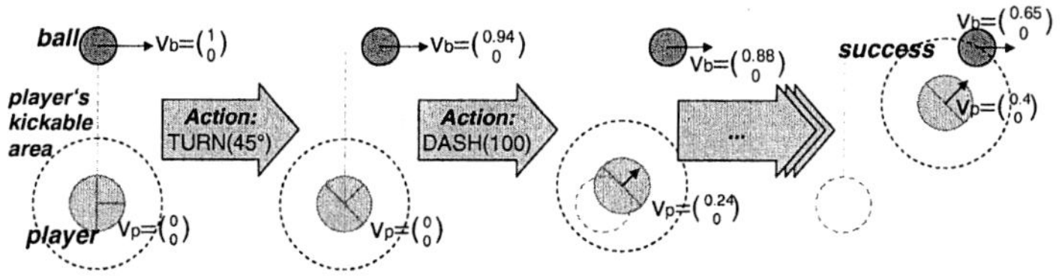

Fig. 2. Illustration of the Intercept Ball Task

4.2 Results

For the purpose of assessing the quality of learnt policies for ball interception, we focus on two evaluation measures: The average success rate measures the percentage of successful episodes, i.e. of those episodes in which the agent managed to intercept the ball in less than $maxEpisodeLength = 80$ simulation cycles. Speed brings about competitiveness. Thus, the more relevant measure are the *costs* (negative rewards) that are incurred during an episode. For the task at hand, those are best expressible in terms of the average episode length, i.e. the number of steps it took the agent to intercept the ball. All evaluation results presented in this section are based on episodes that we obtained using (a) the learnt state value function and the policy induced from it and (b) a fixed set of randomly created starting situations from which the agent had to intercept the ball.

In a first step we wanted to figure out which case base sizes are sufficient to gain satisfactory interception results. As Figure 3 shows surprisingly good results can be obtained with 1000 cases, reaching success rates of more than 90% and average sequence lengths of less than 25 steps. As a trade-off between accuracy and intended retrieval speed (being proportional to case base size) during real-time usage of the system we focus on $|CB| = 2000$ in the following.

Comparison to Other Function Approximation Methods

The most straightforward way to represent a state value function in a continuous space is to discretise the state space along each of its dimensions and to use a table to explicitly store state values. Then, of course each real state has to be mapped into the grid induced and, the other way round, each table entry represents an entire subset of the state space. For the intercept ball problem and the comparison to a CBR-based approach we employed tables of different sizes ($5k$, $100k$, and $600k$ entries). Note, that with the exception of only the smallest table, these approaches exceed the CBR-based approaches' memory requirements by far (Figure 3). As to be expected, finer discretisations yield improved results. Interestingly, the difference between $T100k$ and $T600k$ is only marginal and even the latter does not supersede the results of $CB500/2000$. Secondly, we employed neural nets (feedforward with one hidden layer) to approximate V. After having experienced a certain number of episodes and states, respectively, the net was trained at a time with the collected data using the backpropagation variant *RPROP* [15]. To generate efficient and stable learning results a considerable amount of work had to be invested into tuning relevant parameters. Anyway, as neural nets are capable of representing arbitrarily complex functions, this kind of function approximator reached the best overall results, at least in the long run of learning.

Having a look at the speed of the learning process, it becomes obvious that the CBR-based versions yielded their maximal accuracy after comparatively few training episodes. Thus, a good state value function approximation could be obtained very quickly, in general within less than 2000 training episodes (note the discontinuity in the chart's abscissa). During that time neither a table-based nor a neural net-based function approximation could reach comparable results.

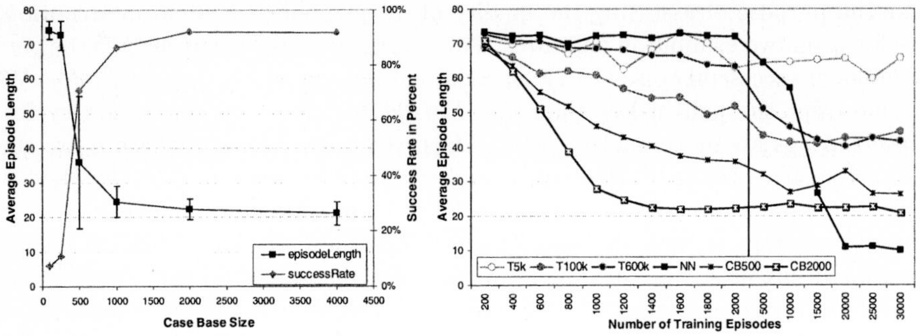

Fig. 3. Intercept Results for Varying Case Base Sizes (left) and for Different Function Approximators (right)

4.3 Discussion

The intercept case study has shown empirically that a CBR-based state value function representation can provide an approximation of good quality within very short learning time. However, it must be acknowledged that there are two important objections that prevent the employment of a completely CBR-based function approximator in a highly competitive domain like robotic soccer. First, the accuracy reached in approximating V is not sufficient when compared to the performance of the neural net as function approximator. Second, the time consumption for case retrieval grows with increasing case base size and, hence, with approximation accuracy. Consequently, it is unrealistic to perform an entire case retrieval and corresponding state value regression once per simulation cycle[2].

Nevertheless, we spot two main application scenarios for a function approximation using CBR in an RL context. On the one hand, its usage appears attractive when a new learning task is tackled: Then, it is usually difficult to figure out and settle upon relevant task-specific parameters appropriately (either when hand-coding or when trying to learn a solution for the task at hand).

[2] As far as a competition soccer team is considered, several agent behaviours will have to be executed (not only a behaviour for ball interception), so the $100ms$ a simulation cycle lasts in RoboCup cannot be reserved for the ball interception exclusively.

Using CBR might help to come to a good, though not optimal, behaviour policy, within little time, for example, when intending to learn more complex and less well-understood behaviours such as team-play.

On the other hand, an existing case base of state value pairs might be employed to boost the training of another function approximator. Investigating this idea, we first trained a CBR-based function approximator for a fixed number of training episodes (750) and then switched to using a neural net to represent the value function. We hereby used all the stored cases including their state values as training examples for the first training of the net and then switched to learning using that net. Figure 4 shows that the learning process could be decisively accelerated.

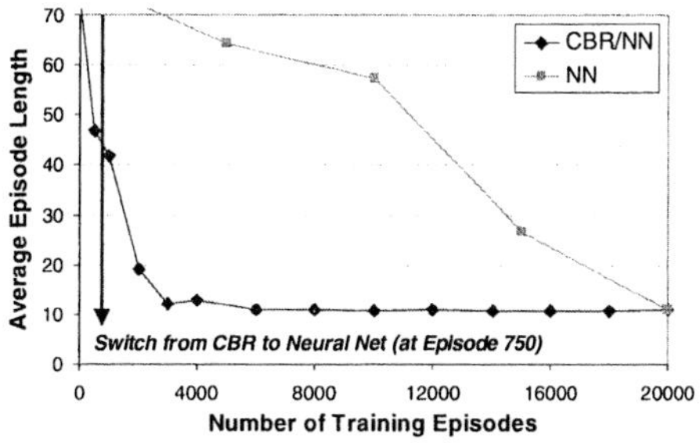

Fig. 4. Usage of CBR to Boost the Neural Net-Based Learning

5 Conclusions

In this paper we applied case-based methods to approximate state value functions over high-dimensional, continuous state spaces, as required in the context of Reinforcement Learning. In so doing, we embedded a CBR-based function approximator into an episode-based $TD(1)$ learning algorithm, developed appropriate procedures to handle the growth of the case base and, for the purpose of evaluation, performed an empirical case study in the context of robotic soccer simulation, where we compared our approach to function approximation with two different ones. The results obtained showed that using a CBR-based state value function representation yields good behaviour policies for the RL agent within a very short time and with comparatively little case data. Almost optimal policies could, however, not be obtained – the quality of policies induced from neural nets representing the value function turned out to be superior, but here more tuning effort was needed to produce stable learning results.

In our view, the major strength of the CBR-enhanced learning approach is the speed with which good, though not optimal, learning results can be achieved. This refers to the fact that little time is needed to tweak a CBR system as well as to the little time needed for the learning process to run; after a few hundred training episodes already good policies are learnt. Furthermore, if one is interested in a near-optimal agent behaviour using, for example, a neural net-based state value function approximation, the learning process can be boosted using CBR as shown in Section 4.3.

An interesting issue for future research is the consideration of more sophisticated similarity measures on the basis of which to perform k-nearest neighbour retrieval and regression. This might increase the case-based function approximator's accuracy, as inherent similarities and dissimilarities of regions within the state space could be exploited better. Therefore, the incorporation of an approach to automatically optimise the CBR-based function approximator's local similarity measures and feature weights [18] seems promising.

References

1. D. Aha. Tolerating Noisy, Irrelevant and Novel Attributes in Instance-Based Learning Algorithms. *Journal of Man-Machine Studies*, 36(2):267–287, 1992.
2. R. E. Bellman. *Dynamic Programming.* Princeton University Press, USA, 1957.
3. D. P. Bertsekas and J. N. Tsitsiklis. *Neuro Dynamic Programming.* Athena Scientific, USA, 1996.
4. H.D. Burkhard, J. Wendler, T. Meinert, H. Myritz, and G. Sander. AT Humboldt in RoboCup-99. In *RoboCup*, pages 542–545, 1999.
5. K. Driessens and J. Ramon. Relational Instance Based Regression for Relational RL. In *Proceedings of ICML 2003*, pages 123–130, Washington, 2003. AAAI Press.
6. J. Forbes and D. Andre. Representations for Learning Control Policies. In *Proceedings of the ICML-2002 Workshop on Development of Representations*, pages 7–14. The University of New South Wales, 2002.
7. G. J. Gordon. Stable Function Approximation in Dynamic Programming. In *Proceedings of ICML 1995*, pages 261–268, San Francisco, 1995. Morgan Kaufmann.
8. J. D. Kelly and L. Davis. A Hybrid Genetic Algorithm for Classification. In *Proceedings of the Twefth International Joint Conference on Artificial Intelligence (IJCAI 1991)*, pages 645–650, Sydney, Australia, 1991. Morgan Kaufmann.
9. Gregory Kuhlmann and Peter Stone. Progress in Learning 3 vs. 2 Keepaway. In *RoboCup-2003: Robot Soccer World Cup VII*, Berlin, 2004. Springer Verlag.
10. A. Merke and M. Riedmiller. Karlsruhe Brainstromers – A Reinforcement Learning Way to Robotic Soccer II. In *RoboCup2001: Robot Soccer World Cup*, 2001.
11. I. Noda, H. Matsubara, K. Hiraki, and I. Frank. Soccer Server: A Tool for Research on Multi-Agent Systems. *Applied Artificial Intelligence*, 12(2-3):233–250, 1998.
12. D. Ormoneit and S. Sen. Kernel-Based Reinforcement Learning. Technical Report TR 1999-8, Statistics Institute, Stanford University, USA, 1999.
13. J. Peng. Efficient Memory-Based Dynamic Programming. In *12th International Conference on Machine Learning*, pages 438–446, USA, 1995. Morgan Kaufmann.
14. B. Ratitch and D. Precup. Sparse Distributed Memories for On-Line Value-Based Reinforcement Learning. In *Machine Learning: ECML 2004, 15th European Conference on Machine Learning*, pages 347–358, Pisa, Italy, 2004. Springer.
15. M. Riedmiller and H. Braun. A Direct Adaptive Method for Faster Backpropagation Learning: The RPROP Algorithm. In *Proceedings of the IEEE International Conference on Neural Networks (ICNN)*, pages 586–591, San Francisco, USA, 1993.
16. J. Santamaria, R. Sutton, and A. Ram. Experiments with RL in Problems with Continuous State and Action Spaces. *Adaptive Behavior*, 6(2):163–217, 1998.
17. William D. Smart and Leslie Pack Kaelbling. Practical Reinforcement Learning in Continuous Spaces. In *Proceedings of the 17th International Conference on Machine Learning (ICML 2000)*, San Francisco, USA. Morgan Kaufmann.
18. A. Stahl and T. Gabel. Using Evolution Programs to Learn Local Similarity Measures. In *Proceedings of the 5th International Conference on Case-Based Reasoning (ICCBR 2003)*, pages 537–551, Trondheim, Norway, 2003. Springer.

19. F. Stolzenburg, O. Obst, and J. Murray. Qualitative Velocity and Ball Interception. In *Advances in AI, 25th German Conference on AI*, pages 283–298, Aachen, 2002.
20. R. S. Sutton. Learning to Predict by the Methods of Temporal Differences. *Machine Learning*, 3:9–44, 1988.
21. R. S. Sutton and A. G. Barto. *Reinforcement Learning. An Introduction.* MIT Press/A Bradford Book, Cambridge, USA, 1998.
22. M. Veloso, T. Balch, and P. Stone et al. RoboCup 2001: The Fifth Robotic Soccer World Championships. *AI Magazine*, 1(23):55–68, 2002.

Using CBR to Select Solution Strategies in Constraint Programming*

Cormac Gebruers[1], Brahim Hnich[1], Derek Bridge[2], and Eugene Freuder[1]

[1] Cork Constraint Computation Centre, University College Cork, Cork, Ireland
{c.gebruers, b.hnich, e.freuder}@4c.ucc.ie
[2] Department of Computer Science, University College Cork, Cork, Ireland
d.bridge@cs.ucc.ie

Abstract. Constraint programming is a powerful paradigm that offers many different strategies for solving problems. Choosing a good strategy is difficult; choosing a poor strategy wastes resources and may result in a problem going unsolved. We show how Case-Based Reasoning can be used to select good strategies. We design experiments which demonstrate that, on two problems with quite different characteristics, CBR can outperform four other strategy selection techniques.

1 Introduction

Organisations, from factories to universities, must daily solve hard combinatorial problems. *Constraint programs*, which reason with declaratively-stated hard and soft constraints, are one of the most expressive, flexible and efficient weapons in the arsenal of techniques for automatically solving these hard combinatorial problems. They have been successfully employed in many real-life application areas such as production planning, staff scheduling, resource allocation, circuit design, option trading, and DNA sequencing [21].

Despite the broad applicability of constraint programs, constraint programming is a skill currently confined to a small number of highly-experienced experts. For each problem instance, a constraint programmer must choose an appropriate *solution strategy* (see Sect. 2). A poor choice of solution strategy wastes computational resources and often prevents many or all problem instances from being solved in reasonable time. The difficulty of choosing a good solution strategy is compounded by the growing number of strategies. Our understanding of when it is appropriate to use a strategy has not kept pace. Improvements in the quality of decision-making would have considerable economic impact.

In this paper, we use decision technologies to support the choice of solution strategy. That is, for a given problem, such as the Social Golfer Problem (defined later), we try to predict good solution strategies for instances of that problem

* This material is based upon work supported by Science Foundation Ireland under Grant No. 00/PI.1/C075.

H. Muñoz-Avila and F. Ricci (Eds.): ICCBR 2005, LNAI 3620, pp. 222–236, 2005.

which differ in size, constraint density, and so on. In Sect. 2, we introduce constraint programming and define what we mean by a solution strategy. Sect. 3 shows how CBR and decision trees can be used to select solution strategies; we also define three benchmark approaches. Sect. 4 explains our experimental methodology. Experiments are reported in Sect. 5.

2 Constraint Programming

A solution strategy S comprises a model M, an algorithm A, a variable ordering heuristic V_{var} and a value ordering heuristic V_{val}: $S =_{\text{def}} \langle M, A, V_{var}, V_{val} \rangle$ [1]. We will look at each component in turn.

2.1 Models

The task of modelling is to take a problem and express it as a Constraint Satisfaction Problem (CSP). We define a CSP to be a triple $\langle X, D, C \rangle$. X is a finite set of *variables*. D is a function that associates each $x \in X$ with its *domain*, this being the finite, non-empty set of values that x can assume. C is a finite set of *constraints* which restrict the values that the variables can simultaneously assume. A simple example is given in Fig. 1. A solution to a CSP is an assignment of values to variables such that every variable has exactly one value from its domain assigned to it and all the constraints are satisfied. For example, $\{x_1 = 1, x_2 = 3\}$ is one solution to the CSP in Fig. 1.

There are often multiple ways of taking an informally-expressed problem and expressing it as a CSP. We refer to each formulation as a model. To exemplify, we consider an example problem known as the Social Golfers Problem:

> *"The coordinator of a local golf club has come to you with the following problem. In her club, there are 32 social golfers, each of whom play golf once a week, and always in groups of 4. She would like you to come up with a schedule of play for these golfers, to last as many weeks as possible, such that no golfer plays in the same group as any other golfer on more than one occasion."* Problem 10 in [6]

The problem is generalised with its instances being described by four parameters $\langle w, m, n, t \rangle$: the task is to schedule $t = m \times n$ golfers into m groups each of n golfers over w weeks so that no golfer plays any other golfer more than once. The Social Golfer Problem has elements in common with many real-world scheduling problems. A factory needing a daily schedule might need to solve different instances of such a problem (i.e. with different parameter values) every 24 hours. Savings in solution time could be of considerable value.

X	D	C
x_1	$\{1, 2, 3\}$	$x_1 \leq x_2$
x_2	$\{2, 3, 4\}$	

Fig. 1. A simple CSP

We will briefly describe three possible models for the Social Golfers Problem. In the *set-based* model [15], there are $m \times w$ variables. Each variable MW_i^j represents the ith group of players in the jth week. Hence, the values these variables take on are sets, each containing n player identifiers.

In the *integer total-golfer* model [18], there are $t \times w$ variables. Each variable TW_i^j represents the ith golfer in the jth week. Hence, the values these variables take on are integers between 1 and m, identifying which of the m groups golfer i belongs to in week j. In fact, this model is not used in practice, because no efficient way has been found of expressing the constraint that groups from different weeks share at most one golfer.

However, even the integer total-golfer model does have a use, because there is a practical model which combines the set-based model with the (incomplete) integer total-golfer model [2]. Combining models is a commonplace and productive technique in constraint programming. The combined model contains both the $m \times w$ set-valued variables and the $t \times w$ integer-valued variables. Additional constraints, known as *channelling constraints*, ensure that, when a golfer is assigned to a group in the integer total-golfer model, the set-based model makes that golfer a member of the appropriate set-valued variable, and vice-versa.

2.2 Algorithms

Solving a CSP involves *search*. Each variable is assigned a value in turn and the legality of that assignment is tested. If any constraints involving that variable have been violated, the value is retracted and another tried in its place. Suppose, for the CSP in Fig. 1, that $x_1 = 3$; if we now try to assign $x_2 = 2$, we violate the constraint $x_1 \leq x_2$. Hence, we would backtrack: we would retract $x_2 = 2$ and try, e.g., $x_2 = 3$ instead.

When, during search, a legal assignment has been made, certain values in the domains of *other* variables may no longer be able to participate in the solution under construction. These unsupported values can be removed from further consideration, a process known as *propagation*. In Fig. 1, suppose we assign $x_1 = 3$; then 2 can be removed from the domain of x_2: it cannot participate in any solution where $x_1 = 3$ as it would violate the constraint $x_1 \leq x_2$. The constraint programming community has devised numerous algorithms that give different trade-offs between the relative degrees of search and propagation.

2.3 Variable and Value Ordering Heuristics

The efficiency of search and propagation may be influenced significantly by the order in which variables are instantiated and the order in which values are chosen. The constraint programming literature lists numerous heuristics for guiding these choices; see, e.g., [20].

2.4 Strategy Selection

We have presented above the four components of a solution strategy, $S =_{\text{def}} \langle M, A, V_{var}, V_{val} \rangle$. Defining solution strategies in this modular way is convenient but may be misleading. It is not meant to imply that each component of a strategy can be chosen independently of the other components. Some components may be incompatible with others; and good performance from a strategy will require that the chosen components perform as a cohesive unit. Hence, we do not treat strategy selection as four independent decisions, nor four cascaded decisions. Instead, we treat each solution strategy, of which there are many, as if it were an atomic entity. Strategy selection is then a single decision: choosing, if possible, the best strategy from this large set of atomic strategies.

2.5 Related Work

CBR has previously been used to support software development tasks. There is work, for example, on design reuse and code reuse, of which [7] and [8] are representative. More in the spirit of the work we report in this paper, however, is the use of CBR to choose data structures for storing matrices in scientific problem-solving environments [22].

While many synergies between constraint technology and CBR have been reported (with a review in [19]), the only work we know of in which CBR is used to make constraint programming decisions is our own. In [12], we use CBR to choose models for logic puzzles; in [5], we use CBR to choose between integer linear programming and constraint programs for bid evaluation problems.

There is related work that does not use CBR. For example, Borret and Tsang develop a framework for systematic model selection [3], building on Nadel's theoretical work [14]. Minton dynamically constructs constraint programs by performing an incomplete search of the space of possible programs [13]. The contrast between his work and ours is that we seek to re-use existing strategies, rather than construct new programs.

Rather different again is the system reported in [4], which executes multiple strategies, gathers information *at runtime* about their relative performance and decides which strategies to continue with. The focus in that system is domains where optimisation is the primary objective, rather than constraint satisfaction.

Finally, we note that, outside of constraint programming, machine learning has been used in algorithm selection tasks, e.g. sort algorithm selection [9].

3 Strategy Selection Techniques

We describe here how we have applied CBR and decision trees to strategy selection. We also describe three benchmark approaches.

3.1 Case-Based Reasoning

Each case represents one problem instance. The 'description' part of a case is a feature vector that characterises the instance (see below for a discussion of the features). The 'solution' part of a case identifies the solution strategies that have performed well on this instance. This needs a little more explanation.

Our decision to treat a solution strategy, although it is made up of four components, as an atomic entity means that the 'solution' part of a case needs only contain solution strategy labels. Thus, our task has become one of case-based classification. In fact, as we will explain in detail in Sect. 4.2, it may be appropriate to regard more than one solution strategy as appropriate for a particular instance. Hence, the 'solution' part of a case is a *set* of solution strategy labels. In summary, each case $\langle \mathbf{x}, S \rangle$ comprises feature vector $\mathbf{x} = \langle v_1, \ldots, v_i \rangle$ and a set S of strategy identifiers.

With strategy selection reduced to a classification task, simple CBR techniques suffice. We retrieve the k-nearest neighbours (we use $k = 3$) and we use majority voting to to choose a strategy.

It remains to discuss the features we use. For three reasons, we have chosen to use *surface features* in our work to-date:

- The over-riding reason is that, as a matter of good methodology, we need to discover just how predictive surface features are before turning to other approaches.
- A lesser reason is that, anecdotally, surface features (if anything) would appear to be what human programmers use when selecting an initial strategy.
- Finally, surface features are cheap-to-extract and cheap-to-compare in the similarity measure. By contrast, the main alternative is to compare the constraint graphs of problem instances. For reasons of computational complexity, this is to be avoided, if possible.

The features we use might also be described as *static features*: they can be obtained *prior* to execution; an example is the constraint density of the problem instance. We are not using *dynamic features*, that are only obtainable during execution, e.g. the number of backtracks at a certain point.

Finally, it has turned out that all our features are numeric, and so we compute similarity as the inverse of Euclidean distance with range normalisation [23].

However, prior to using case bases for strategy selection, we use the *Wrapper method* to select a predictive subset of the features [11] and these are the ones used in the CBR.

3.2 Decision Trees

The decision trees we use are induced by C4.5 [17] from the same problem instances that make up the case bases in our CBR approach. The tests that label the interior nodes of the trees are drawn from the same features as used in the CBR systems. Leaves are labelled by solution strategies. We use C4.5 with all its default settings, also allowing it to prune the trees to avoid over-fitting.

3.3 Benchmark Approaches

We have used three benchmark approaches for strategy selection:

Random: A strategy is selected randomly, with equal probability, from among the candidates.

Weighted Random: A strategy is selected randomly, but the probability that a candidate is selected is proportional to how often that strategy is a winning strategy in the dataset.

Use Best: In this approach, the same strategy is selected every time: the one that is a winner most often in the dataset.

4 Experimental Methodology

4.1 Candidate Strategies

As Sect. 2 shows, for any given problem instance, there is a vast number of possible strategies, combining different models, algorithms and heuristics. In practice, human programmers entertain very few strategies. Similarly, in our experiments it is not feasible to choose among all possible strategies. Instead, we use around ten candidate strategies. Lest we be accused of thereby making the prediction task too easy, we use candidates that informal experimentation shows to be competitive on the different problem instances and which give, as much as possible, a uniform distribution of winners because this maximises the difficulty of strategy selection.

4.2 Winning Strategies

We have to define what it means for a candidate strategy to be a winner on a problem instance. Surprisingly, it is not easy to obtain a consensus within the constraint programming community on this.

To exemplify this, suppose the execution times of two strategies s_1 and s_2 on a problem instance are 1000ms and 990ms respectively. While s_2 is the winner, some might argue that s_2 exhibits no material advantage: the difference is 10ms, which is only 1% of the faster execution time. Similarly, if s_3 takes 505000ms and s_4 takes 500000ms, s_4 is the winner; but in percentage terms the difference between them is also 1%, the same as that between s_2 and s_1. In some domains, where time is critical, any advantage may be worth having; in other domains, performance within, e.g., an order-of-magnitude of the fastest strategy may be regarded as acceptable. In the latter case, if a strategy selection technique were to pick any of the high-performing strategies, it could be regarded as having made a correct choice.

Our resolution to this lack of consensus is to use different definitions of *winner*: we parameterise the definition of winning strategy and plot results for different parameter values. We define a winning strategy using a window of execution time. The best execution time recorded for an instance constitutes the window's lower bound. The upper bound is determined by a multiplication factor. We denote different winning strategy definitions by their multiplication factor, e.g. $\times 1.0$, $\times 10.0$, etc. If a strategy's execution times falls within the window, it is considered one of the joint winners.

4.3 Dataset Generation

For each problem, we generate a dataset of problem instances. We need to label each instance with its set of winning strategies. So we solve each instance with each of the candidate strategies in turn and record the execution times. Since some strategies perform unreasonably poorly on certain instances, execution is done subject to a timeout of 6000ms. We do not admit into a dataset instances where all strategies time out and instances where all strategies are joint winners. These instances are of no use in prediction experiments.

4.4 Evaluation

The dataset is randomly partitioned into a training set and a test set, where the training set is 60% of the instances. For each instance in the test set, we use CBR, decision trees and the benchmark approaches to predict a solution strategy for that instance. We determine, in each case, whether the prediction is one of the winning strategies. Results are subject to 10-fold cross-validation.

We report the following results:

Prediction Rate: This is the number of times a strategy selection technique predicts a winning strategy — the higher the better.

Total Execution Time: This is the total execution time of the predicted strategies over all test instances — the lower the better.

Where the strategy selection technique predicts a strategy that was one of the timeout strategies, we add only the timeout value (6000ms) into the total. This understates the true total execution time, which we would have obtained had we not subjected strategy execution to a timeout. Strategy selection techniques that incorrectly pick strategies that timeout are, therefore, not being penalised as much as they could on these graphs.

Note that prediction rate on its own would be a misleading metric — there would be little utility to a technique that picked the best strategy for 90% of the instances if these were ones where solving time was short but which failed to pick the best strategy for the remaining 10% of instances if these were ones where the solving time exceeded the total for the other 90%. This motivates the use of total execution time as an additional metric which gives a good indication of whether the technique is making the right choices when it matters, i.e. when incorrect choices of strategy lead to very long solving times. For comparison, we also plot the minimum possible total execution time, i.e. the sum of the execution times of the best strategy for each instance.

5 Experiments

For each problem, we describe the features we use, the candidate strategies, the distribution of those strategies in the dataset and we plot the prediction rate and the total execution time.

5.1 The Social Golfer Problem

Features. The features we use are summarised in Table 1. Note how we define some features as ratios of others. One might argue that the feature, e.g., m/w is unnecessary when we already have the features m and w. However, unless we use a non-linear similarity measure [16], similarity on features m and w will not necessarily be the same as similarity on feature m/w. By explicitly including features such as m/w, we avoid the need for a non-linear similarity measure.

Table 1. Social Golfer Problem Features (w : number of weeks; m : number of groups; n : number of golfers per group; t : total number of golfers)

				Predictive?		
Feature	Type	Min.	Max.	CBR	Full DT	Pruned DT
w	*integer*	1	13	✓	depth 1	×
m	*integer*	2	7	✓	×	×
n	*integer*	2	10	×	×	×
t	*integer*	4	70	×	depth 0	×
m/w	*real*	$\frac{2}{13}$	7	✓	depth 1	×
n/w	*real*	$\frac{2}{13}$	10	✓	depth 1	×
t/w	*real*	$\frac{4}{13}$	70	×	depth 1 or 2	×
n/m	*real*	$\frac{2}{7}$	5	✓	×	×

The final three columns of Table 1 attempt to show which of the features are selected by the Wrapper method for use in CBR and at what depth in the full decision trees induced by C4.5 the different features appear. It has to be kept in mind that this is only rough summary information: different outcomes are

Table 2. Social Golfer and Extra Golfer Strategies (Strategies s_1 and s_2 are used only for the Social Golfer Problem)

	Strategy			
ID	Model	Algorithm	Var. Heuristic	Val. Heuristic
s_1	*set model*	*dfs, IlcExtended*	*group set*	*lex (set)*
s_2	*set model*	*dfs, IlcExtended*	*week set*	*lex (set)*
s_3	$fcp_g fcd_g$	*dfs, IlcExtended*	*group set*	*IloChooseMinSizeInt, lex (set)*
s_4	$fcp_g fcd_g$	*dfs, IlcExtended*	*week set*	*IloChooseMinSizeInt, lex (set)*
s_5	$fcp_g fcd_g$	*dfs, IlcExtended*	*static golfer*	*IloChooseMinSizeInt, lex (set)*
s_6	$fcp_g fcd_g$	*dfs, IlcExtended*	*static week*	*IloChooseMinSizeInt, lex (set)*
s_7	$fcp_g fcd_g$	*dfs, IlcExtended*	*min domain*	*IloChooseMinSizeInt, lex (set)*
s_8	$fcp_g fcd_d$	*dfs, IlcExtended*	*group set*	*IloChooseMinSizeInt, lex (set)*
s_9	$fcp_g fcd_d$	*dfs, IlcExtended*	*week set*	*IloChooseMinSizeInt, lex (set)*
s_{10}	$fcp_g fcd_d$	*dfs, IlcExtended*	*static golfer*	*IloChooseMinSizeInt, lex (set)*
s_{11}	$fcp_g fcd_d$	*dfs, IlcExtended*	*static week*	*IloChooseMinSizeInt, lex (set)*
s_{12}	$fcp_g fcd_d$	*dfs, IlcExtended*	*min domain*	*IloChooseMinSizeInt, lex (set)*

possible on the different folds of the cross-validation. The full decision tree has a depth of only 2; the reason that the final column, for the pruned tree, contains no information is that the full tree is pruned to a tree containing just one node, labelled by *use* s_2, i.e. use strategy 2. In fact, this is not a good decision tree for this dataset: in approximately 40% of the instances s_2 is outperformed.

Candidate Strategies. Twelve strategies, summarised in Table 2, are used in our Social Golfer experiments; each is the winner on certain instances. In two strategies, we use the set-based model. In the rest, we use the combined model. Using this combined model, Bessiere et al. investigate different ways of expressing the partitioning and disjointness constraints [2]. They design ways of expressing them 'globally', which we denote fcp_g and fcd_g respectively, and ways of decomposing them into more primitive forms, which we denote by

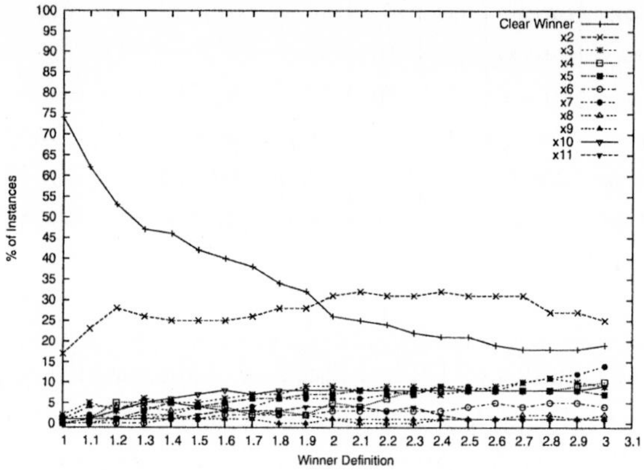

Fig. 2. Ties, Social Golfer Dataset

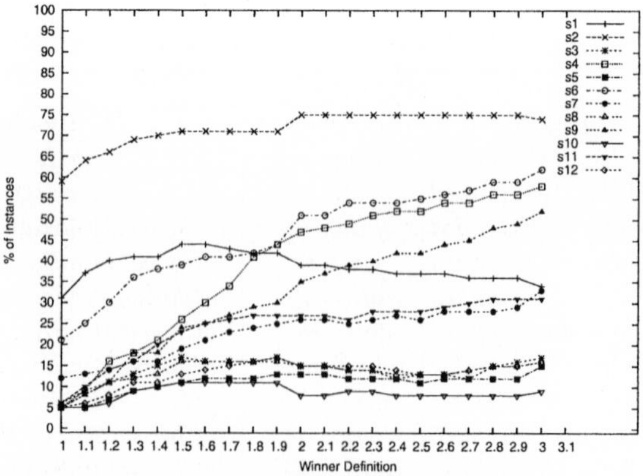

Fig. 3. Strategy Distribution, Social Golfer Dataset

Table 3. Extra Golfer Problem Features (w : number of weeks; m : number of groups; n : number of golfers per group; x : extra golfers; t : total number of golfers)

Feature	Type	Min.	Max.	*Predictive?* CBR	Full DT	Pruned DT
w	*integer*	1	13	✓	depth 3	×
m	*integer*	2	7	×	depth 3	×
n	*integer*	2	10	✓	depth 1 or 3	depth 1
t	*integer*	5	74	×	depth 2 or 3	×
x	*integer*	1	4	×	depth 2 or 3	×
m/w	*real*	$\frac{2}{13}$	7	✓	depth 3	×
n/w	*real*	$\frac{2}{13}$	10	✓	depth 0 or 3	depth 0
t/w	*real*	$\frac{5}{13}$	74	✓	depth 2	depth 2
x/w	*real*	$\frac{1}{13}$	4	×	depth 3 or 4	×
n/m	*real*	$\frac{2}{7}$	5	✓	depth 1 or 2 or 3	depth 2 or 3
t/m	*real*	$\frac{5}{7}$	37	✓	×	×
x/m	*real*	$\frac{1}{7}$	2	✓	depth 3	×
t/n	*real*	$\frac{5}{10}$	37	✓	depth 2 or 3	depth 2
x/n	*real*	$\frac{1}{10}$	2	×	depth 3	×
x/t	*real*	$\frac{1}{74}$	$\frac{4}{5}$	×	depth 3 or 4	depth 3 or 4

fcp_d and fcp_g respectively. So, in fact, there is not a single model here; there are four, depending on which combination of constraints is used: $\langle fcp_g, fcd_g\rangle$, $\langle fcp_g, fcd_d\rangle$, $\langle fcp_d, fcd_g\rangle$ or $\langle fcp_d, fcd_d\rangle$. Experiments reported in [2] reveal that fcp_g and fcp_d perform identically for the Social Golfers Problem, so we can arbitrarily adopt fcp_g. But this still leaves us with two models, $\langle fcp_g, fcd_g\rangle$ and $\langle fcp_g, fcd_d\rangle$.

For algorithms and heuristics, we follow [2], which gives us a good number of competitive strategies. In particular, we use ILOG Solver's Depth-First Search algorithm (*dfs*) with the propagation level parameter for global constraints set to *IlcExtended*, which maximises the propagation [10]. We have used five variable ordering heuristics but just one value ordering heuristic, *IloChooseMinSizeInt, lex (set)* [2]. Space limitations preclude a description of their details.

Dataset Characteristics. Our Social Golfer dataset contains 367 instances prior to filtering. (The exact number of instances after filtering depends on the parameterisation of the winning window.) Fig. 2 shows, for different winner parameterisations, the number of instances where there are ties for first place; we show in how many instances there is a clear winner, in how many two strategies tie, in how many three strategies tie, and so on. More ties and higher cardinality ties make prediction easier. Fig. 3 shows, for different winner parameterisations, the percentage of instances for which each of the twelve strategies is one of the winners. The sum of the percentages exceeds 100% because an instance can have more than one winning strategy.

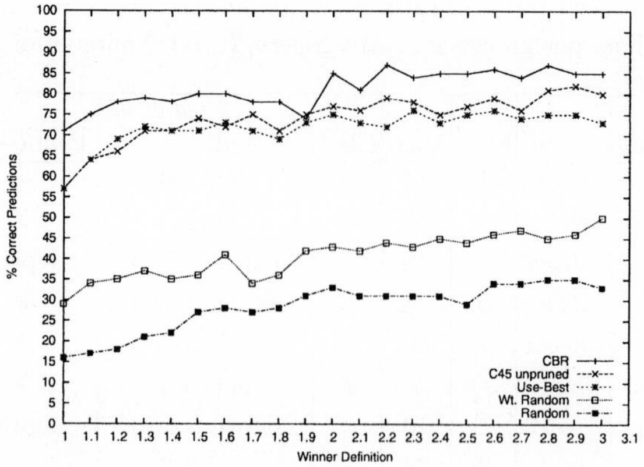

Fig. 4. Prediction Rates, Social Golfer Dataset

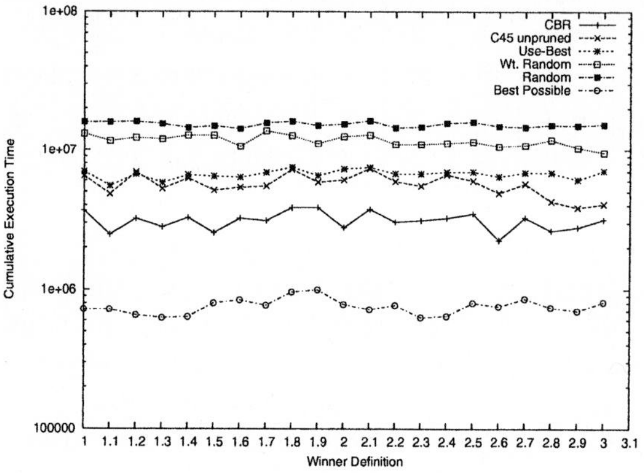

Fig. 5. Total Execution Time, Social Golfer Dataset

Results. Figs. 4 and 5 show the prediction rate and the total execution time for CBR, unpruned decision trees (which gave better results than pruned ones) and the benchmarks, again for different winner parameterisations. The results are discussed in Sect. 5.3.

5.2 The Extra Golfer Problem

The Extra Golfers Problem is a generalisation of the Social Golfers Problem. It introduces x additional golfers (in our experiments $x \in [1..4]$), i.e. $t = m \times n + x$. Thus there is an excess of golfers and some golfers rest each week, i.e. the set of golfers is no longer *partitioned* into groups each week, as there will be some golfers left over. This may not seem like a very different problem. But, in fact, this small change to the problem brings large differences in terms of winning

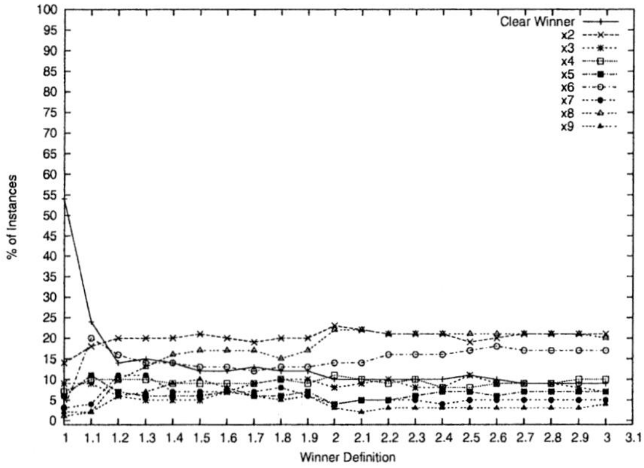

Fig. 6. Ties, Extra Golfer Dataset

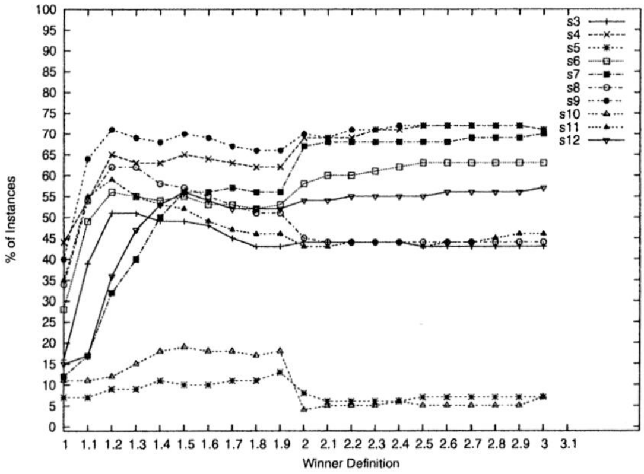

Fig. 7. Strategy Distribution, Extra Golfer Dataset

strategies (compare Figs. 2 and 3 with Figs 6 and 7), and therefore it is an interesting second problem for us.

Features. We summarise the features in Table 3. Compared with the Social Golfer Problem, there are some additional features, and the 'predictiveness' of the features (summarised in the final three columns) is different. In this dataset, there is no dominant strategy (unlike s_2 in the Social Golfers dataset), and so all the decision trees are more complex than they were for the Social Golfers.

Candidate Strategies. Ten of the same strategies that were used for the Social Golfer Problem (Table 2) can be used for the Extra Golfers Problem. The two which use the pure set-based model, s_1 and s_2, are inapplicable because the set-based model assumes that the golfers are partitioned.

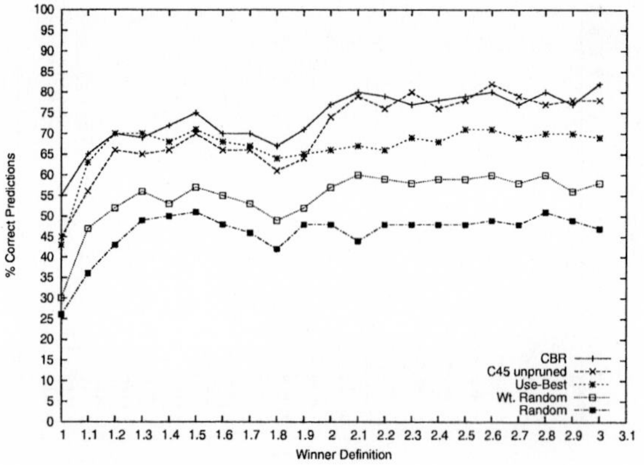

Fig. 8. Prediction Rates, Extra Golfer Dataset

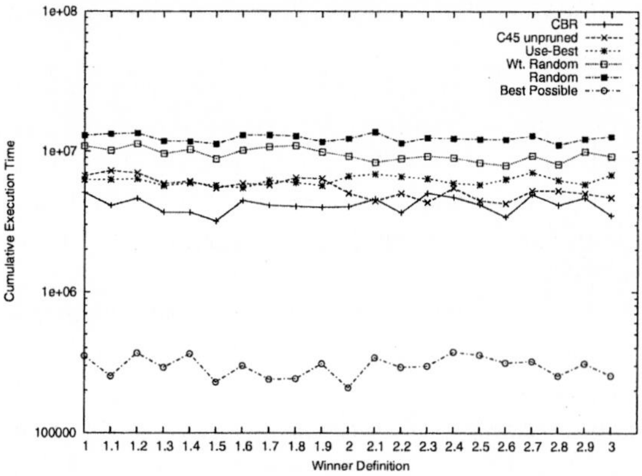

Fig. 9. Total Execution Time, Extra Golfer Dataset

Dataset Characteristics. Our Extra Golfers dataset contains 440 instances prior to filtering. The number of ties and the distribution of the strategies are shown in Figs. 6 and 7. As we mentioned above, these graphs show the Extra Golfer datasets to be quite different from those for the Social Golfer Problem.

Results. Results are shown in Figs. 8 and 9, and are discussed in Sect. 5.3.

5.3 Discussion of Results

As we would expect, the graphs for prediction rate (Figs. 4 and 8) exhibit better performance as the winning strategy definition is relaxed: as the number of joint winners grows, it becomes easier to predict a wining strategy. Of the techniques, for the Social Golfer dataset, CBR outperforms the next best techniques (use-best and decision trees) by about 10%, achieving a prediction rate of between 70 and 80%. For the Extra Golfer dataset, while CBR still has the best prediction rate, use-best and decision trees are not far behind.

The graphs for total execution time (Figs. 5 and 9) give an indication of the quality of a technique, regardless of whether a winning strategy is predicted or not. The Social Golfer dataset is the tougher of the two, because the differences in execution times render the costs of making a wrong decision greater. Here, CBR significantly outperforms the other strategies — note the logarithmic scale. This is largely because it predicts far fewer strategies that time out. The Extra Golfers dataset again brings use-best, decision trees and CBR closer in terms of performance with CBR doing slightly better.

6 Conclusions and Future Work

In this paper, we have demonstrated that CBR outperforms four other strategy selection techniques on two problems with quite different characteristics. We have shown empirically that CBR achieves higher prediction rates than the other techniques, and predicts fewer strategies that fail to find a solution in reasonable time. By using CBR to select solution strategies, we have demonstrated that significant amounts of computation time can be saved; such savings can have considerable economic impact.

We have shown that it is possible to achieve good results using just surface features. We have added clarity to strategy selection methodology by introducing a parameterised definition of winning strategy and determining the impact of different parameterisations.

Future work will involve other datasets for other constraint programming problems; more considered selection of case base size and contents (including consideration of case-base editing); scaling the system to facilitate a broader selection of candidate strategies; deploying a wider range of strategy selection teqhniques (e.g. statistical methods); and further analysis of how dataset characteristics impact strategy selection.

References

1. Beacham, A., Chen, X., Sillito J. and Van Beek, P.: Constraint Programming Lessons Learned from Crossword Puzzles. In *Procs. of 14th Canadian Conference on Artificial Intelligence*, pp.78–87, 2001
2. Bessiere, C., Hebrard, E., Hnich, B. and Walsh, T.: Disjoint, Partition and Intersection Constraints for Set and Multiset Variables. In *The Principles and Practice of Constraint Programming, Procs. of CP-2004*, pp.138–152, 2004
3. Borret, J.E. and Tsang, E.P.K.: A Context for Constraint Satisfaction Problem Formulation Selection. *Constraints*, vol.6(4), pp.299–327, 2001
4. Carchrae, T. and Beck, J.C.: Low-Knowledge Algorithm Control. In *Procs. of the 19th AAAI*, pp.49–54, 2004
5. Gebruers, C., Guerri, A., Hnich, B. and Milano, M.: Making Choices using Structure at the Instance Level within a Case Based Reasoning Framework. In *Integration of AI and OR Technologies in Constraint Programming for Combinatorial Optimization Problems*, Springer Verlag, pp.380–386, 2004

6. Gent, I., Walsh, T. and Selman, B.: *CSPLib: A Problem Library for Constraints.* `http://4c.ucc.ie/{}~tw/csplib/` (Last accessed 02/02/2005)
7. Gomes, P.: *A Case-Based Approach to Software Design*, PhD Dissertation, Universidade de Coimbra, Portugal, 2003.
8. Grabert, M. and Bridge, D.: Case-Based Reuse of Software Examplets. *Journal of Universal Computer Science*, vol.9(7), pp.627-640, 2003
9. Guo, H.: *Algorithm Selection for Sorting and Probabilistic Inference: A Machine Learning-Based Approach.* PhD Dissertation, Dept. of Computing and information Sciences, Kansas State University, 2003
10. *ILOG Solver.* `http://www.ilog.com/products/solver/` (Last accessed 02/02/2005)
11. Kohavi, R. and John, G.: Wrappers for Feature Subset Selection. *Artificial Intelligence*, vol.97(1–2), pp.273–324, 1997
12. Little, J., Gebruers, C., Bridge, D. and Freuder, E.: Capturing Constraint Programming Experience: A Case-Based Approach. In *International Workshop on Reformulating Constraint Satisfaction Problems*, Workshop Programme of the 8th International Conference on Principles and Practice of Constraint Programming, 2002
13. Minton, S.: Automatically Configuring Constraint Satisfaction Programs: A Case Study. *Constraints*, vol.1(1), pp.7–43, 1996
14. Nadel, B.: Representation Selection for Constraint Satisfaction: A Case Study Using n-Queens. *IEEE Expert*, vol.5(3), pp.16–23, 1990
15. Novello, S.: *An ECLiPSe Program for the Social Golfer Problem.* `http://www.icparc.ic.ac.uk/eclipse/examples/golf.ecl.txt` (Last accessed 02/02/2005)
16. Pang, R., Yang, Q. and Li, L.: Case Retrieval using Nonlinear Feature-Space Transformation. In *Procs. of the 7th European Conference on Case-Based Reasoning*, pp.361–374, 2004
17. Quinlan, J.R.: *C4.5: Programs for Machine Learning.* Morgan Kaufmann, 1993
18. Smith, B.: *Reducing Symmetry in a Combinatorial Design Problem.* Technical Report 2001.01, University of Leeds School of Computing Research Report Series, 2001
19. Sqalli M., Purvis, L. and Freuder, E.: Survey of Applications Integrating Constraint Satisfaction and Case-Based Reasoning. In *Procs. of the 1st International Conference and Exhibition on The Practical Application of Constraint Technologies and Logic Programming*, 1999
20. Tsang, E.: *Foundations of Constraint Satisfaction.* Academic Press, 1993
21. Wallace, M.G.: Practical Applications of Constraint Programming. *Constraints*, vol.1(1–2), pp.139–168, 1996
22. Wilson, D. C., Leake, D. B. and Bramley, R: Case-Based Recommender Components for Scientific Problem-Solving Environments. In *Procs. of the 16th International Association for Mathematics and Computers in Simulation World Congress*, CD-ROM, Session 105, Paper 2, 2000
23. Wilson, R. and Martinez, T.: Improved Heterogeneous Distance Functions. *Journal of Artificial Intelligence Research*, vol.6, pp.1–34, 1997

Case-Based Art

Andrés Gómez de Silva Garza and Arám Zamora Lores

Computer Engineering Department, Instituto Tecnológico Autónomo de México (ITAM),
Río Hondo #1, Colonia Tizapán-San Ángel, 01000—México, D.F., México
agomez@itam.mx, aram_n1@hotmail.com

Abstract. While there have been plenty of applications of case-based reasoning (CBR) to different design tasks, rarely has the methodology been used for generating new works of art. If the goal is to produce completely novel artistic styles, then perhaps other reasoning methods offer better opportunities for producing interesting artwork. However, if the goal is to produce new artwork that fits a previously-existing style, then it seems to us that CBR is the ideal strategy to use. In this paper we present some ideas for integrating CBR with other artificial intelligence techniques in order to generate new artwork that imitates a particular artistic style. As an example we show how we have successfully implemented our ideas in a system that produces new works of art in the style of the Dutch painter Piet Mondrian. Along the way we discuss the implications that a task of this nature has for CBR and we describe and provide the results of some experiments we performed with the system.

1 Introduction

While there have been plenty of applications of case-based reasoning (CBR) to different design tasks (e.g., see [1]), rarely has the methodology been used for generating new works of art. If the goal is to produce completely novel artistic styles, then perhaps other reasoning methods that rely less on examples as a source of knowledge offer better opportunities for producing interesting (i.e., original, novel) artwork. However, if the goal is to produce new artwork that fits a previously-existing style, then it seems to us that CBR is the ideal strategy to use.

In this paper we present some ideas for integrating CBR with other artificial intelligence techniques in order to generate new artwork that imitates a particular artistic style. As an example we show how we have successfully implemented our ideas in a system that produces new works of art in the style of the Dutch painter Piet Mondrian. Exemplars of artwork produced by Mondrian are presented to the system in the form of cases. The cases are then adapted in order to produce new artwork, and the new works of art are evaluated to determine if they fit the required style.

The paper is organized as follows. In Section 2 we introduce Mondrian´s artistic style and show the case representation scheme we have used. In Section 3 we discuss issues related to case retrieval and case adaptation for tasks like ours and give the results of some experiments related to these issues. Of particular interest is our case adaptation method, which is based on an evolutionary algorithm, and our evaluation

H. Muñoz-Avila and F. Ricci (Eds.): ICCBR 2005, LNAI 3620, pp. 237 – 251, 2005.

module, which we implemented in two versions, one rule-based and one based on a neural network. Section 4 briefly compares and contrasts our research with other projects that use CBR and/or evolutionary algorithms for design. Finally, in Section 5 we discuss the results and implications of our work and give some conclusions.

2 Piet Mondrian's Artistic Style and Case Representation Used

Piet Mondrian was a Dutch painter active mainly in the first half of the 20th century. Like many other modern painters, Mondrian started his career painting landscapes, human figures, and other realistic subjects, but eventually developed his own distinctive and abstract style (called simply *de stijl*, which is Dutch for "the style"). Paintings in Mondrian's style typically include vertical and horizontal black lines over a white background, with some or all of the primary colors (blue, red, and yellow), plus black, filling in some of the square or rectangular regions (or parts of the regions) separated out from the background by the black lines. It is this style that our system, MONICA (MONdrian-Imitating Computer Artist), tries to emulate. Fig. 1 shows a typical Mondrian painting in his distinctive style.

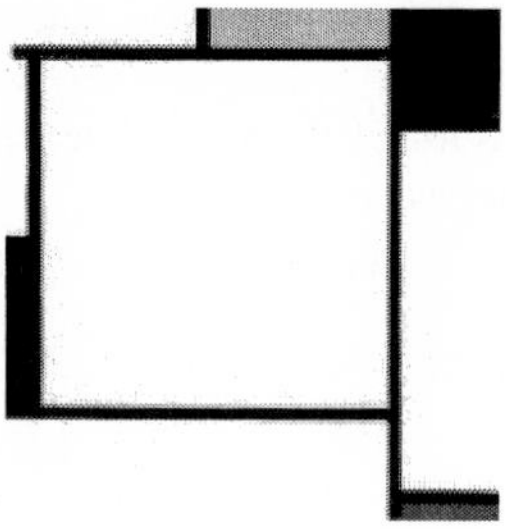

Fig. 1. A typical Mondrian painting

MONICA's reasoning engine is implemented in C++ and its graphical output capabilities in OpenGL. We have gathered 55 cases of Mondrian paintings such as the one shown in Fig. 1 from several Internet sites, and from [2] and [3], and we have represented them as cases in MONICA's case memory. Our cases do not include any of Mondrian´s "lozenges" (rhomboidal paintings employing the same style), only rectangular ones. They also do not include paintings that represent stylistic transitions that Mondrian underwent through his career, only paintings that can truly be said to belong to *de stijl*. After analyzing the 55 Mondrian cases we observed certain patterns, such as the fact that there never seem to be more than 20 lines and colored regions in any painting, and the fact that we can treat lines as if they were extremely thin, black colored regions. These observations led us to come up with the following case representation scheme.

A case is split into twenty parts, each of them corresponding to one of twenty possible colored regions (including lines) permitted in a painting. Fig. 2 illustrates this division of a case at the highest level.

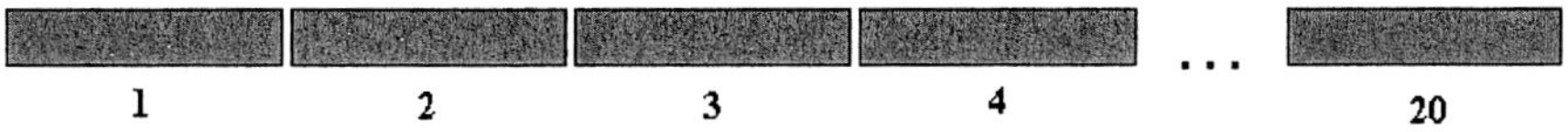

Fig. 2. Case representation used

Fig. 3 shows at an intermediate level how each of the twenty parts of a case is split into five sections in order to represent in them the color, width, height, and x- and y-coordinates (of the center, as per OpenGL standards) of each colored region. These last four measurements are all limited to the same range of values (which again depend on the specifications of OpenGL).

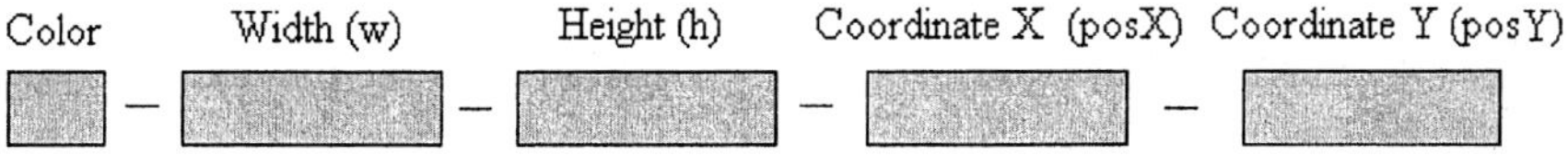

Fig. 3. Representation of each colored region in a case

Fig. 4 shows, at the bit level, the internal details of the representation of the color and one of the four measurements shown in Fig. 3.

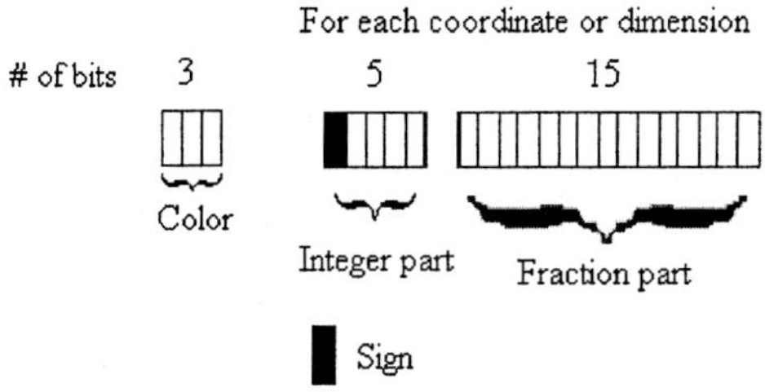

Fig. 4. Bit-encoding of the color and any one measurement in the representation

3 Case Retrieval and Case Adaptation

The specification of the task we are interested in, "producing new artwork that fits a particular style," does not just characterize the class of problems that we would like to solve, but is also the specification given at each problem-solving instance, each execution of the implementation. This specification is vaguer than the tasks that most CBR systems are required to perform (in which, typically, specific values required for particular parameters in a valid solution are given to a system when initiating a problem-solving episode). In fact, if it weren't for the word "new" in our task specification, then in the case of MONICA all the cases in memory already would be valid solutions (as they all fit Mondrian's style, since they are all Mondrian paintings), and new solutions wouldn't need to be generated—the old ones could just retrieved. This observation has implications for both case retrieval and case adaptation.

With respect to case retrieval, in a situation like MONICA's it can't just be a matter of using the problem specification as an index to probe the case memory, because of two reasons mentioned above: first of all the problem specification is too vague and secondly all the cases in memory would match the problem specification. The concept of elaborating on the problem specification (i.e., analyzing it in order to extract a more precise, formal, problem specification), which many researchers (e.g., [4], [5]) have suggested as a prior subtask to case retrieval, also doesn't make sense. There simply isn't any additional, hidden, indirect, information in the problem specification that can be inferred and used to make the specification more precise (and therefore used as a index that will end up retrieving only a subset of the cases in memory). This suggests that either case retrieval is unnecessary or that the system's task has to be specified more precisely. As we don't want to do the latter (since we don't want to bias the resulting paintings to appear more like some of Mondrian's prior paintings than like others by specifying additional requirements on their features), it would seem that the first conclusion is the correct one (i.e., not to perform case retrieval in the traditional sense).

This has implications for case adaptation and raises questions such as: do we use all of the cases in memory or just one for case adaptation, and do we even need so many cases or not? If we were to use only one case and adapt it to produce a new painting (or even try the same with several cases, but adapting them one at a time), we would again be biasing the resulting painting to look too much like the original case, unless we could come up with extremely bizarre (and probably complicated) adaptation procedures. From the point of view of art, it would be more interesting to have the capacity to explore the entire space of paintings that fit Mondrian's style, and from the point of view of CBR, it would be nice to be able to do so without having to spend much time inventing complex (and highly domain-specific) adaptation rules. Thus, it would seem that being able to draw ideas from several cases at a time makes more sense in order for case adaptation to have the capacity to produce Mondrian-like paintings that do not resemble any of the originals too closely (yet still fit his artistic style).

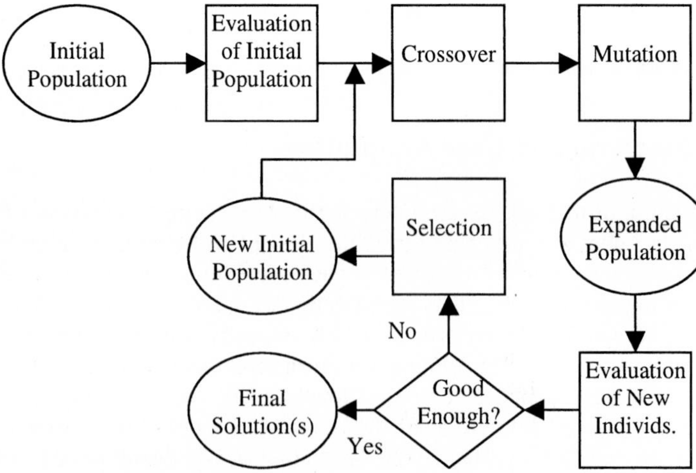

Fig. 5. Flow diagram for evolutionary case adaptation

Drawing ideas from several cases in order to explore the entire space of paintings that fit Mondrian's style can be achieved by ensuring that the case adaptation method can perform not only parametric but also structural adaptation, the two types of case adaptation that exist according to [6]. One general-purpose problem-solving method that can achieve both parametric and structural adaptation is evolutionary algorithms [7], and this is the method we have chosen to perform the case adaptation subtask. We have in the past implemented the evolutionary approach to case adaptation successfully for the design of tall buildings [8] and residential floor plans [9], and we describe it formally in [10]. Fig. 5 shows this approach graphically. The rest of this section discusses several of its characteristics and examines some of them through some experiments.

3.1 Initial Population of the Evolutionary Algorithm

Evolutionary algorithms require a population of individuals (genotypes) to operate on, and generally these individuals are generated at random in order to seed the initial population. By turning to CBR, however, we can use cases to initialize the population, thus giving a head-start to the evolutionary search mechanism by starting the search from known solution states instead of having to randomly search the solution space before converging on the vicinity of good solutions. We showed in [9] that the solution-finding (convergence) time was cut in half by using cases rather than random individuals as the initial population of an evolutionary algorithm. However, in evolutionary algorithms (and biology!) an important issue is that of diversity in the population [11], and there can't be too much diversity if the entire population fits entirely within a specific genetic mold (in this case, Mondrian's artistic style).

One research group that has used cases in the initial population of an evolutionary algorithm [12] has suggested that one way to achieve diversity is to create an initial population that consists of both cases and random individuals, rather than only cases. In fact, they have performed several experiments and have come to the conclusion that only between 10% and 15% of the initial population should consist of cases, and the rest should be random individuals, in order to achieve some diversity while at the same time having some cases to guide the evolutionary search. However, it is our contention that this figure depends largely on the problem-solving domain being addressed (which influences the landscape of the solution space and thus how much diversity is really needed in order to explore all relevant areas of the space while looking for appropriate solutions). It can also depend on the case/genotype representation that is being used in the evolutionary algorithm and on the nature of the results that one is interested in getting (for instance, whether the evolutionary algorithm is being used to obtain one solution to a problem or many different ones, whether or not we already know of some solutions—e.g., the cases—but are interested in finding new ones, whether we are more interested in optimizing the quality of the solution or the efficiency of the algorithm, etc.). In order to test this assertion we performed an experiment with MONICA.

In the experiment, we ran MONICA 10 times on each of 10 combinations of cases and random individuals in the initial population of the evolutionary algorithm. The first combination used 10% of cases in the initial population and 90% of random individuals, the second combination 20% of cases and 80% of random individuals, etc. We ran the system 10 times on each of these combinations in order to get average results because, due to the random nature of some of the evolutionary operators (see Subsection 3.2 below), one run wouldn't be guaranteed to be representative. For each of the 10 runs for a given combination, the same initial population was used, and the cases that were included as part of this initial population were chosen randomly from amongst the 55 MONICA has in its memory. This choice of which cases to include in the initial population could be considered the equivalent of "case retrieval" or "case selection" in our approach, but it is quite different from the traditional notion of case retrieval in CBR. Since the last combination used in the experiment included 100% of cases and no random individuals in its initial population, since we have 55 cases, and since we didn't want the size of the population to vary across different runs (in order for this parameter to not affect the results), we chose 55 as the size of the population for all 100 system executions. We left all other evolutionary algorithm parameters constant across all runs.

In order to compare the results of the experiment we decided that the most important thing for us would be to determine which combination of cases and random individuals in the population seem to maximize the efficiency of case adaptation. The efficiency of an evolutionary algorithm can be measured both in CPU time or in the number of evolutionary cycles (generations) required (see Subsection 3.2 below) in order to obtain an acceptable solution. We measured both parameters, but the corresponding results were analogous, so in Fig. 6 we present a graph showing only the average CPU time needed to produce a good solution (i.e., a new painting fitting Mondrian's style) for each of the 10 combinations of cases and random individuals we tried.

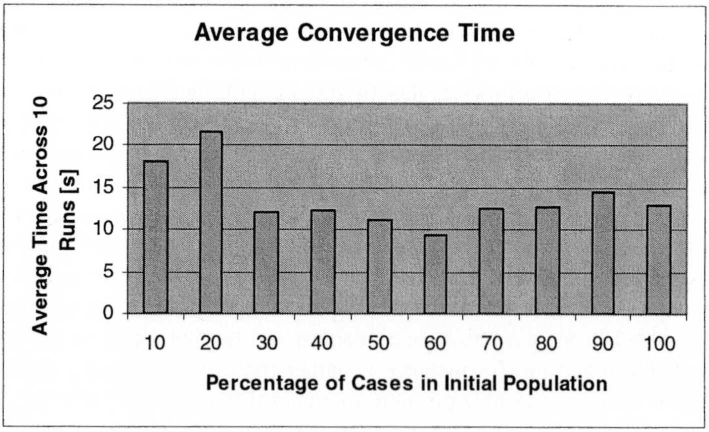

Fig. 6. Graph showing CPU time for different combinations of cases and random individuals in the initial population

As can be seen in Fig. 6, for our particular case/genotype representation and domain, and using speed of convergence as the criterion for comparison, it seems that any percentage higher than or equal to 30% of cases in the initial population is best (with 60% being up to 30% faster than some of the other possibilities). This proves our assertion that the 10%-15% heuristic given in [12] is too simplistic and not necessarily applicable to all situations. The probable reason for our results is that if there aren't enough cases in the initial population to give the system a head start, it may be a long time before Mondrian-like paintings start resulting from the evolutionary algorithm's operations. For this particular domain the cut-off point (above which adding more cases doesn't seem to continue improving convergence time much) seems to be somewhere between 20% and 30%, but there's no reason to presuppose that it would be the same for other domains or if we had used a different case/genotype representation. The slight increase in convergence speed when the percentage of cases is above 60% may be due to the diversity factor—having less than 40% of random individuals in the initial population might not allow the algorithm to produce new Mondrian-like paintings as quickly as with a larger amount of randomness (and thus diversity) in the initial population.

3.2 Crossover and Mutation

The evolutionary operators which are applied cyclically on the individuals in the population are mutation and crossover, both of which involve some random choices, and which achieve parametric and structural adaptation, respectively. Mutation achieves parametric adaptation by modifying the value of one parameter in a previously-known solution to produce a new offspring solution. Which parameter's value will be modified, and what its new value will be, are typically decided at random. Crossover achieves structural adaptation by combining the parameters of two previously-known solutions (thus resulting in two offspring solutions that can have structures that are very different from those of their parents). The combination is achieved by splitting the two original solutions in two and then interchanging their two halves to create the new solutions. In MONICA we allow the split to occur between any two of the bits that can be seen in Fig. 4 (which shows the detailed case representation scheme used). Which two individuals in the population will be combined and where exactly will the split occur in them are decisions that are again typically made at random. If these two operators are applied continuously through several evolutionary cycles, which is what normally occurs in evolutionary algorithms, and the new initial populations (for each cycle) contain some of the new offspring solutions created during the previous evolutionary cycles, then eventually solutions may be produced that combine some features from many, if not all, of the original cases. This mechanism is what allows us to explore the space of Mondrian-like paintings widely, rather than being stuck with tweaking only one at a time, and thus never departing too much from its overall appearance.

Our evolutionary case adaptation method represents a generate-and-test, trial-and-error, brainstorming-like approach [13] in which many possible paintings (entire populations of them) are generated quickly, by using mainly random decisions. Probably most of these paintings are of quite low quality (i.e., do not fit Mondrian's style), but after being generated they are then evaluated to determine how much they "make sense." In the context of our research, making sense would imply being as close as possible to the style of Mondrian. The best paintings (according to the evaluation subroutine of the evolutionary algorithm) are kept for future evolutionary generations, and the others are discarded (so as to keep the size of the population of the algorithm constant across generations). This process is labeled "Selection" in the flow diagram in Fig. 5 and ensures a monotonic increase in the average quality of the paintings in the population between generations (a characteristic known as elitism in the terminology of evolutionary algorithms). Depending on what is desired, either when this average quality or when the quality of just one individual painting is good enough according to the evaluation subroutine, the process is terminated. The evaluation subroutine of the evolutionary algorithm, therefore, is of critical importance to the success of the approach.

3.3 Evaluation of Adapted Cases

Every new solution generated and proposed by the evolutionary case adaptation method is assigned a number between 0 and 1 (known as its fitness value in the evolutionary algorithms literature) which represents its quality. In MONICA's domain, a value of 1 is assigned to paintings that belong to Mondrian's style, and a 0 would be assigned to paintings that are extremely far away from being able to be considered Mondrian-like. In MONICA we implemented two methods for deciding how much a painting fits the style of Mondrian. The first method is rule-based, and the second method is based on a neural network.

In the rule-based evaluation method the rules were programmed based on the authors' observations of the stylistic patterns present in the 55 Mondrian cases used, and the limits of these patterns. While art experts might be able to suggest subtle modifications or additions to these rules, we believe that they do capture the essence of Mondrian's style quite well (and have performed a cognitive experiment to support our claim, the details and results of which can be found in [14]). The rules, if applied to any of the original Mondrian cases, would give a fitness value of 1. If they are applied to the new "cases" generated by the case adaptation algorithm, they give a fitness value that can guide the evolutionary search in the right direction by giving it an idea of how good or how bad each of the paintings it generates is. This influences which individuals survive across evolutionary cycles and which are discarded during the selection step. The eight rules we have implemented are the following:

1. EvaluateColor: Each colored region that is contained in a case must have one of the five valid colors (blue, yellow, red, black, white).
2. EvaluateCoordinates: The height, width, x-coordinate, and y-coordinate of each colored region in a case must all fall between 0 and 3.9999 (as per OpenGL usage).
3. EvaluateLineThickness: Up to two black colored regions are allowed in a case that are not thin, but all other black regions must be either vertically or horizontally thin (and thus represent a line rather than a rectangular region).
4. EvaluateNumberOfVerticalLines: A minimum of two and a maximum of ten vertical lines must be present in a case.
5. EvaluateNumberOfHorizontalLines: A minimum of two and a maximum of ten horizontal lines must be present in a case.
6. EvaluateLimits: Each colored region in a case must be adjacent either vertically (both above and below) or horizontally (both to the left and to the right), or both, to another colored region or to the edge of the "frame" (with some small tolerance).

7. EvaluateFrame: All other colored regions in a case must fall within the coordinates of the "frame" (which is a white colored region with fixed coordinates that doesn't participate in the evolutionary process).
8. EvaluateNumberOfColoredRegions: There must be at least one colored region represented in a case, and at most 13, not counting lines (with a maximum of 20 including lines, as mentioned in Section 2).

Each case is assigned a value between 0 and 1 according to each of these rules. Some rules are either completely satisfied or completely violated by a particular case, and thus can assign only 0 or 1 as values. An example of this is Rule 5: if the number of horizontal lines in a case falls within the acceptable values (2-10, inclusive) then the case has a fitness of 1 according to this rule; otherwise the fitness value is 0. Other rules can be satisfied to different degrees, and can thus return different values between 0 and 1, inclusive. An example of this is Rule 7: if a case contains five colored regions and four of them fall fully within the coordinates of the frame but one doesn't, then the case has a fitness of 4/5=0.8 according to this rule, if only two of the five colored regions lie within the coordinates of the frame then the fitness of the case would be 2/5=0.4, etc. The global fitness value for the case is assigned by finding the average value given to the case according to each of the different rules (i.e., adding the eight individual values and dividing the total by eight). The convergence times shown in Fig. 6 were the result of running MONICA with the rule-based evaluation method. As can be seen, the average time needed to produce a new Mondrian-like painting was most of the time under 20 seconds.

For MONICA's neural evaluation method we tried out a few different network architectures and subsequently ended up implementing a neural network with 100 neurons in its input layer, a hidden layer with 50 neurons, and one neuron in its output layer, with a full set of connections between each neuron of a given layer and each neuron in the next layer. The 100 neurons in the input layer correspond to the five values needed to represent each of the 20 possible colored regions that make up a case (as shown in Figs. 2-4). The one output neuron is due to the fact that the network's task is to simply assign a fitness value (between 0 and 1, as with the rule-based method) that represents how much a painting fits Mondrian's style. The size of the hidden layer was determined empirically after a few trials with different numbers of hidden neurons.

The neural network had to be trained to recognize Mondrian's style. In order to do this, of the 55 Mondrian cases 70% was used for the training procedure, with the remaining 30% of the cases used to test the resulting network. The training procedure took advantage of the already-programmed evolutionary algorithm (seeded with a traditional random initial population) in order to generate possible weight assignments for each of the neural network's connections. Determining convergence (and therefore the end of the training period, leading to the final values for the weights of all the connections) was based on having lowered the mean square error to below 0.03 when using the neural network to classify the cases used for training (and verifying that the error was likewise below that same threshold when classifying the test cases). This error corresponds to a fitness of 0.85 for the set of weight assignments generated.

The neural network in MONICA took 5½ hours to train. Once trained, the weights of its connections are fixed and never have to change again. Using these final weights in the neural network to evaluate new paintings produced by case adaptation typically required 30 minutes (from the beginning of a run to the generation of the first new Mondrian-like painting), as compared to under 20 seconds for the rule-based evaluation method (see Fig. 6). As the difference in time is so large, we decided to stick with the rule-based evaluation method to evaluate the "Mondrianness" of new paintings.

4 Related Work

Our work on MONICA evolves from our previous work on the GENCAD project (see [8], [9], and [10]) in which we proposed the use of evolutionary algorithms for case adaptation and applied our ideas to the domains of structural design of tall buildings and residential floor plan design. In GENCAD, a new problem, triggering the CBR process, was specified by giving specific details about characteristics desired of a solution (e.g., specific values for the dimensions, use, materials, etc., required for a tall building). In contrast, in MONICA there is no need for the user to give any specific problem requirements, since the task is more vague (and the same from one problem-solving episode to the next): to generate new artwork that fits within a particular style. In GENCAD, the evolutionary algorithm's entire initial population consisted of cases retrieved from memory, and the mutation rate was relatively low, so most of the content and structure of most of the solutions proposed by the system was directly contributed by the cases. In MONICA, some of the initial population of the evolutionary algorithm is created at random, as described above, and this factor, together with a higher mutation rate, both contribute to a faster divergence from the initial knowledge in the form of cases as the evolutionary algorithm proceeds. Finally, the potential to produce creative results of GENCAD's (and therefore MONICA's) process model was determined to be high according to two criteria, as reported in [15].

As with GENCAD, MONICA performs transformational rather than derivational analogy: the cases that its evolutionary algorithm adapts are past solutions (Mondrian paintings), not traces of past problem-solving episodes. This contrasts with some of the initial work combining CBR with evolutionary algorithms, such as [16], in which cases represented traces of changes in the parameters of an evolutionary algorithm operating in dynamic environments (therefore having to re-adjust itself periodically). More similar to both GENCAD and MONICA in the way that CBR is combined with evolutionary algorithms is the work of Louis and his collaborators, summarized in [12], which we mentioned with respect to the experiment described in Section 3.1. In both our work and theirs, the evolutionary algorithm operates populations that, at least partially, consist of cases, rather than using the cases exclusively to decide how to initialize (and later on, during execution, to modify) the evolutionary algorithm's parameters, as in [16].

Some previous CBR work on design domains includes Kritik [17], CADSYN [18], CADRE [19], CYCLOPS [20], JULIA [21], and a host of other, similar projects. All of these projects have the disadvantage that usually large amounts of domain-specific knowledge (apart from the cases) is either needed to perform case adaptation and/or to decide which of many generic adaptation methods to use in a given situation. This knowledge can be represented as heuristics, constraints, hierarchies, models, or other formalisms. Domain knowledge is again used in order to evaluate the results of case adaptation to verify if the solution produced meets the requirements of a given set of problem specifications. In contrast, the evolutionary approach to case adaptation does not require any domain knowledge in order to generate potential solutions to a problem. The evolutionary operators of crossover and mutation do not worry about the semantics of the genotypes they operate on, and domain knowledge is only needed for recognition, during the evaluation phase (which is usually much less complex than the generative phase), of whether proposed solutions are satisfactory or not. This has the advantage of reducing the difficulty and slowness of knowledge acquisition that many knowledge-based (including traditional CBR) systems suffer from.

Some previous work on evolutionary algorithms applied to design tasks is collected in [22] and [23]. Several chapters in these collections describe evolutionary systems for artwork generation, and even for the imitation of specific artistic styles (such as Escher's). However, they all rely on the user to provide feedback at each evolutionary cycle in order to decide which new paintings produced by evolution are "good enough" (resemble the style of interest), and therefore should be kept in the population to participate in the next evolutionary cycle, and which ones to discard. In contrast, in MONICA, the desire was to have a fully autonomous method for the imitation of an artistic style. The use of cases as a basis for initiating the generation of new paintings that might fit the desired style, and the use of the same cases in order to come up with a set of evaluation rules and to train a neural network to recognize the style of interest, allowed us to make MONICA an autonomous system instead of having to include the user in the reasoning cycle.

5 Results and Discussion

We have presented our ideas for producing case-based art, exemplifying them in the domain of generating new paintings in the style of the Dutch painter Piet Mondrian. We haven't yet shown any of the new paintings produced by our system, MONICA, so in Fig. 7 we display three of them in order to prove its capabilities. Most people would probably agree that they do belong to the same artistic style as the real Mondrian painting shown in Fig. 1.

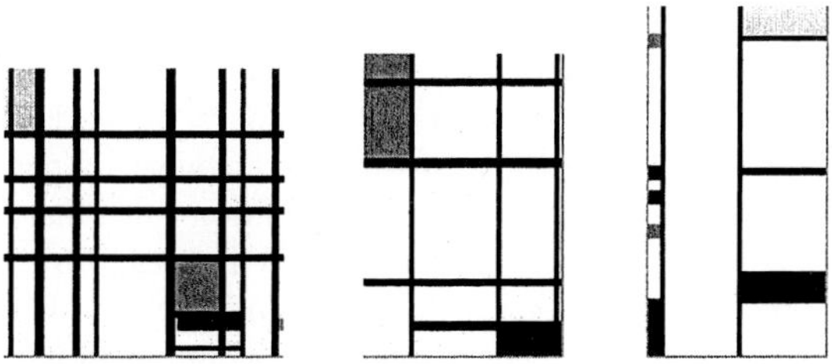

Fig. 7. Three Mondrian-like paintings produced by MONICA at different times

Our approach for case-based art is a hybrid one. CBR is used as the main reasoning method, but additional artificial intelligence techniques, specifically evolutionary algorithms, neural networks, and rule-based reasoning, are used to help perform some of the subtasks required by CBR. These four problem-solving methods are closely integrated in MONICA, reinforcing each other and taking advantage of their individual characteristics.

CBR is used as the overall reasoning method because it uses knowledge in the form of examples, and capturing the essence of an artistic style requires the observation of multiple exemplars. An evolutionary algorithm is used for case adaptation because it provides the capability to perform both parametric and structural adaptation, and it does so without the need to explicitly acquire and code a lot of domain-specific knowledge. The initial population of this evolutionary algorithm is based at least partially on some of the cases representative of the artistic style of interest. We have described and shown the results of an experiment which explores how much of the initial population should be composed of cases (and how much should be random, as with traditional evolutionary algorithms). The experiment shows that for MONICA's task, problem-solving domain, and case representation used, seeding the initial population of the evolutionary algorithm with 60% of cases and 40% of random individuals seems to be the best choice.

The evaluation of new solutions suggested by the evolutionary algorithm in MONICA is performed either in a rule-based fashion or with the aid of a neural network. The rule-based approach implies having to code some explicit domain knowledge, specifically knowledge of how to recognize whether a painting belongs to a given style or not in the form of rules. The rules in MONICA were generated by its programmers based on observing stylistic patterns (and limits on them) in the Mondrian cases in memory. In the case of Mondrian's style, coming up with a set of rules that help determine how much a painting fits his style was not very difficult, but Mondrian's style is quite simple and geometric. More complicated and less abstract artistic styles might be too complex to be able to code explicitly in a rule-based fashion. There might just be too many rules that can be thought of, even a large amount of rules might not constrain the search sufficiently, and there is always the possibility of logical contradictions and similar problems when dealing with large sets of rules.

The neural-network approach to evaluating the new paintings produced by the evolutionary algorithm might be more fruitful for more complex artistic styles. In order to train the neural network the only explicit knowledge that is required is the set of cases that we already have. The training mechanism of the neural network can even use the same evolutionary algorithm as the case adaptation technique (but using it to evolve possible weight assignments for the neural network, rather than to evolve possible new paintings), as we have done. Once the neural network has been trained, the knowledge that it implicitly contains, distributed amongst its connections, would in theory be equivalent to the potential set of recognition rules that embody the artistic style of interest. We have shown that this second approach to evaluation requires a lengthy training time and that using it during the production of new paintings slows the process down considerably. Therefore, for generating imitations of Mondrian's paintings, the rule-based evaluation method makes more sense; however, for more complex artistic styles the neural approach may be the only feasible solution, and we have shown it to work as well, despite its lower efficiency.

Fig. 8 shows our complete process model for case-based art (while the flow diagram shown in Fig. 5 shows additional internal details of the evolutionary cycle that appears in the right side of Fig. 8), with annotations on the different reasoning modalities we have used for separate subtasks. Future work will center on using the same hybrid CBR-based approach to produce new paintings in the styles of other human artists (painters, but perhaps also musicians and writers), not just Mondrian, and on exploring further the benefits and effects of combining CBR with other artificial intelligence techniques. It might also be worth looking into different ways of evaluating the potential solutions produced by the evolutionary algorithm to complement the rule-based and neural-based methods, such as measuring their distance from the cases in memory as a way to determine how closely they fit Mondrian's style. This exploration of alternative forms of evaluating new artwork might be necessary in order to continue using the same process model to imitate more complicated artistic styles.

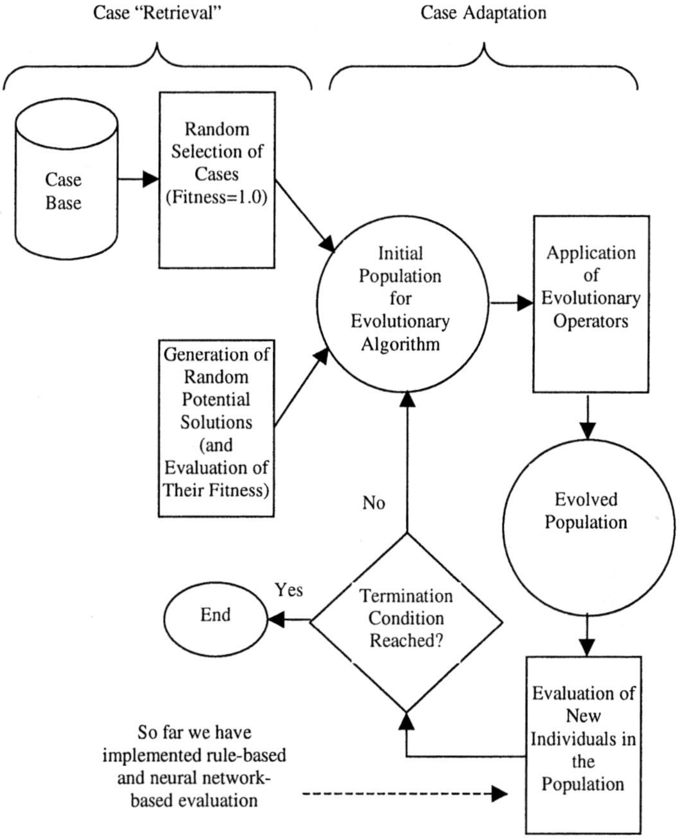

Fig. 8. Process model for case-based art

References

1. Maher, M.L. and Pu, P. (eds.): Issues and Applications of Case-Based Reasoning in Design. Lawrence Erlbaum Associates, Mahwah, New Jersey (1997)
2. Deicher, S.: Mondrian. Benedikt Taschen Verlag GmbH, Cologne, Germany (1999)
3. Bax, M.: Complete Mondrian. Lund Humphries (Ashgate Publishing), Aldershot, United Kingdom (2001)

4. Kolodner, J.L. and Wills, L.: Case-Based Creative Design. Proceedings of the American Association for Artificial Intelligence Spring Symposium on AI and Creativity. AAAI Press, Menlo Park, California (1993)
5. Bhatta, S. and Goel, A.: Model-Based Indexing and Index Learning in Analogical Design. Proceedings of the Seventeenth Annual Conference of the Cognitive Science Society (CogSci-95). Lawrence Erlbaum Associates, Hillsdale, New Jersey (1995)
6. Kolodner, J.L.: Case-Based Reasoning. Morgan Kaufmann, San Mateo, California (1993)
7. Mitchell, M.: An Introduction to Genetic Algorithms (Complex Adaptive Systems Series). MIT Press, Cambridge, Massachusetts (1998)
8. Gómez de Silva Garza, A. and Maher, M.L.: A Knowledge-Lean Structural Engineering Design Expert System. Proceedings of the Fourth World Congress on Expert Systems. Mexico City, Mexico, pp. 178-185 (1998)
9. Gómez de Silva Garza, A. and Maher, M.L.: An Evolutionary Approach to Case Adaptation. In Althoff, K.-D., Bergmann, R., and Branting, L.K., Case-Based Reasoning Research and Development: Proceedings of the Third International Conference on Case-Based Reasoning ICCBR-99 (Lecture Notes in Computer Science Vol. 1650). Springer, Heidelberg, Germany, pp. 162-172 (1999)
10. Gómez de Silva Garza, A. and Maher, M.L.: A Process Model for Evolutionary Design Case Adaptation. In Gero, J.S. (ed.), Artificial Intelligence in Design '00. Kluwer Academic Publishers, Worcester, Massachusetts, pp. 393-412 (2000)
11. Mezura-Montes, E. and Coello Coello, C.A.: Adding a Diversity Mechanism to a Simple Evolution Strategy to Solve Constrained Optimization Problems. Proceedings of the Congress on Evolutionary Computation (CEC-03). IEEE Service Center, Piscataway, New Jersey, pp. 6-13 (2003)
12. Louis, S.J.: Learning from Experience: Case Injected Genetic Algorithm Design of Combinatorial Logic Circuits. In Parmee, I.C. (ed.), Adaptive Computing in Design and Manufacture V. Springer-Verlag, Berlin, Germany, pp. 295-306 (2002)
13. Clark, C.H.: Brainstorming: The Dynamic Way to Create Successful Ideas. Doubleday, Garden City, New York (1958)
14. Gómez de Silva Garza, A. and Zamora Lores, A.: A Cognitive Evaluation of a Computer System for Generating Mondrian-like Artwork. In Gero, J.S. (ed.), Design Computing and Cognition '04. Kluwer Academic Publishers, Worcester, Massachusetts, pp. 79-96 (2004)
15. Gómez de Silva Garza, A. and Maher, M.L.: GENCAD: A Hybrid Analogical/Evolutionary Model of Creative Design. In Gero, J.S. and Maher, M.L. (eds.), Computational and Cognitive Models of Creative Design V. Key Centre of Design Computing and Cognition, University of Sydney, Australia, pp. 141-171 (2001)
16. Ramsey, C.L. and Grefenstette, J.J.: Case-Based Initialization of Genetic Algorithms. Proceedings of the Fifth International Conference of Genetic Algorithms, pp. 84-91 (1993)
17. Goel, A.K., Bhatta, S.R., and Stroulia, E.: KRITIK: An Early Case-Based Design System. In Maher, M.L. and Pu, P. (eds.), Issues and Applications of Case-Based Reasoning in Design. Lawrence Erlbaum Associates, Mahwah, New Jersey, pp. 87-132 (1997)
18. Zhang, D.M.: A Hybrid Design Process Model Using Case-Based Reasoning, Ph.D. Dissertation, Department of Architectural and Design Science, University of Sydney, Australia (1994)
19. Faltings, B.: Case Reuse by Model-Based Interpretation. In Maher, M.L. and Pu, P. (eds.), Issues and Applications of Case-Based Reasoning in Design. Lawrence Erlbaum Associates, Mahwah, New Jersey, pp. 39-60 (1997)

20. Navinchandra, D.: Case-Based Reasoning in CYCLOPS, A Design Problem Solver. In Kolodner, J. (ed.), Proceedings of Case-Based Reasoning Workshop. Morgan Kaufmann, San Mateo, California, pp. 286-301 (1988)
21. Hinrichs, T.R.: Plausible Design Advice Through Case-Based Reasoning. In Maher, M.L. and Pu, P. (eds), Issues and Applications of Case-Based Reasoning in Design. Lawrence Erlbaum Associates, Mahwah, New Jersey, pp. 133-159 (1997)
22. Bentley, P. (ed.): Evolutionary Design by Computers. Morgan Kaufmann Publishers, San Francisco, California (1999)
23. Bentley, P. and Corne, D.W. (eds.): Creative Evolutionary Systems. Morgan Kaufmann Publishers, San Francisco, California (2002)

Supporting Conversation Variability in COBBER Using Causal Loops*

Hector Gómez-Gauchía, Belén Díaz-Agudo,
Pedro Pablo Gómez Martín, and Pedro González-Calero

Dep. Sistemas Informáticos y Programación,
Universidad Complutense de Madrid, Spain
{hector, belend, pedrop, pedro}@sip.ucm.es

Abstract. Conversational Case Based Reasoning (CCBR) is a form of CBR where users initiate conversations with the system to solve a certain problem. Current CCBR solutions are limited to specific domains. In the solutions we find a lack of flexibility to deal with the user's variability: different conversation strategies depending on the user's current mood, computer skills, and domain expertise. We focus our framework, COBBER, in the user's variability during a computer session. COBBER is a CCBR framework to build CCBR applications in a systematic way. The framework offers, independently to the domain, models of different conversation strategies using causal loops.

1 Introduction

Conversational Case Based Reasoning (CCBR) is a form of CBR where users initiate problem solving conversations to solve a certain problem. The whole user query is defined by means of the set of questions and answers provided by the user during the conversation. The CCBR approach is one of the most successful types of CBR and has been typically used in interactive help-desk and WWW diagnostic systems [15].

One of the distinguishing benefits of CCBR is that users are not required to initially provide a complete description of their problem[1]. During each iteration of the conversation the user is prompted with a question or a ranked set of questions. The user answers one or more of these questions and receives suggestions about her problem.

Most previous work in CCBR has focused on minimizing the number or the cost of questions asked by the system. Approaches include: inferring description details from the user's text, and inferring answers to redundant questions (because they have been already implicitly answered) [2], ordering questions according to information gain criteria [5] or recognizing the point in the dialogue at which no more questions are required [12].

In contrast, our research has focused on the dialogue capabilities of CCBR systems, a topic of recent research [4]. We do not consider the natural language

* Supported by the Spanish Committee of Science & Technology (TIC2002-01961).

H. Muñoz-Avila and F. Ricci (Eds.): ICCBR 2005, LNAI 3620, pp. 252–266, 2005.

processing problems associated to dialogue understanding and generation. Instead, our research focuses on enhancing human-machine communication, trying to make up for components that we lose from human-to-human communication, mainly non-verbal cues and changes in conversational strategy. These changes happen when the user needs variations during the conversation, e.g.: domain oriented variations, once user confidence demands shorter, faster answers; in contrast, if the user gets lost, she needs more extended answers. Other variations are oriented to personal characteristics. For example, colorful interfaces and shortcut keys, if the user is a computer expert and likes graphic interfaces; or a GUI adapted for users with poor computer skills. We also allow for variations in the user's mood when she interacts with the system. It reacts differently if the user is experiencing trouble to understand something or, to the contrary, is fluent, improving and happy. The lack of variations like these results in deficient user satisfaction.

We find a lack of CCBR systems regarding that type of communication with the user. Current systems do not take a cognitive approach (created with the user in mind), or take into account the variability of the user: her current state (mood, emotions) together with her skills. Our current research emerges from the study of current CCBR systems and from the difficulties we found in our previous CCBR work [7]:

- Developing CCBR systems have been individually created, where every new CCBR system represents an adhoc solution for the specific problem and domain it solves. The drawback of this way is that building a new CCBR system is an expensive effort.
- It is common that final users abandon good interactive systems because they get frustrated using them. Users reach cognitive dead ends when they do not understand something and the system keeps giving more and more information, until they get lost and abandon the system. A common solution is to model user's knowledge when she is working with the system. But, often, this solution does not help because the system does not react to the user's sensation of being lost or frustrated. The system keeps treating her as if everything were going smoothly. And this frustrates the user more until she abandons the system. This situation is common in the online help applications, where the user gets more and more frustrated as the interaction continues in a hard wired direction.
- The CCBR is guided by questions inside the cases to organize the dialogue. The conversation is a sequence based only on the knowledge of the user obtained by her descriptions and answers about the domain. The system does not know anything about the kind of user, her personal tendencies and tastes. For the system, all the users are the same.
- There is a lack of important dynamic knowledge related to the evolution and the outcome of the conversation. This is unfortunate, because this knowledge would be useful because the reactions of the user to the output of the system determines the success of the conversation.

Our proposed framework, COBBER, has four main objectives:

- To give a flexible framework to build CCBR applications in a systematic way, instead of starting from scratch for each new application. This objective includes reusing knowledge and tasks by making the domain independent from the rest of the conversation tasks and knowledge.
- To have a cognitive approach that includes user variability: her domain knowledge, her computer skills, her personal tendencies.
- To include, throughout the session, the dynamic changes of conversation strategies depending on the current trend of the conversation and the current user's state, i.e.: her domain knowledge, her mood and her personal tendencies or tastes.
- To include a guided process: for ontology conceptualization, for case base authoring and framework instantiation.

To develop COBBER we are working on extending jCOLIBRI [1], a framework for developing CBR systems [3], with a CCBR model. jCOLIBRI promotes software reuse for building CBR systems, and tries to integrate the application of well known Software Engineering techniques with the key idea of separating the reasoning processes (using Problem Solving Methods) from the domain model (ontologies with general knowledge).

This paper focuses on the idea of modeling CCBR system conversation strategies with causal loops from the system dynamics field, that are described in section 3. These loops allow for changing the style and approach of the conversation if the user does not feel confident with it. In section 2 we describe an overview of the COBBER architecture. Section 3 describes the main ideas behind system dynamics and how we apply them to the conversations. In section 4 we give one example in the domain of Help-Desk systems. And in section 5 a case study in a different domain, Intelligent Tutoring Systems, is presented, which is our current ongoing work.

2 The COBBER Architecture

The design of the framework follows the knowledge level paradigm, where the system has a hierarchy of tasks shown in Figure 1. The reasoners solve the tasks that represent the main functions of the framework. Each reasoner includes several subtasks following the AI approach, e.g.: diagnosis, prediction, planning, to obtain its goals. The core reasoners are those that execute the CCBR cycle, while the additional reasoners perform auxiliary tasks, e.g. there is a reasoner used for helping to instate the framework. The control of the activation sequence of the tasks is in the supervisor reasoner. It also eliminates the contradictions of the local actions of the other reasoners and generates the global actions. To improve the reusability, the domain reasoner is independent to the rest of the reasoners. Most of the reasoners are a compound of CBR systems, although

[1] http://sourceforge.net/projects/jcolibri-cbr/

others use other paradigms, such as the rule based system that is used for one of the subtasks in the supervisor reasoner. Other new reasoners may be added or exchanged if needed. In this article we include only the core and the GUI adaptor reasoners.

Static knowledge is modeled with ontologies following the Description Logics paradigm, written in OWL language. Each ontology describes knowledge for a specific aspect of the model. The dynamic knowledge is modeled by case bases, which are instantiations of the concepts described in the ontologies. One of the main ontologies is the CBRonto, used in the jCOLIBRI framework, with the concepts needed for the CBR tasks themselves. There is a CCBRonto that is a conversational extension of the CBRonto.

Cases are indexed and retrieved using a set of concepts that corresponds to the case description and exists in the ontologies. Each reasoner has its own case bases. There is an example in Figure 1 of the three case types used by the system dynamics reasoner. All the cases have the same structure: a name, a description, and a solution. The description contains the concepts used to index the case. The similarity between cases is measured by the proximity of the concepts in the ontology. The description may have some slots that represent a stereotypical situation in the domain. In these slots, we apply a standard similarity.

The solution has several types of slots depending on the reasoner. For example, the domain reasoner has suggestions for the solution; and intentional

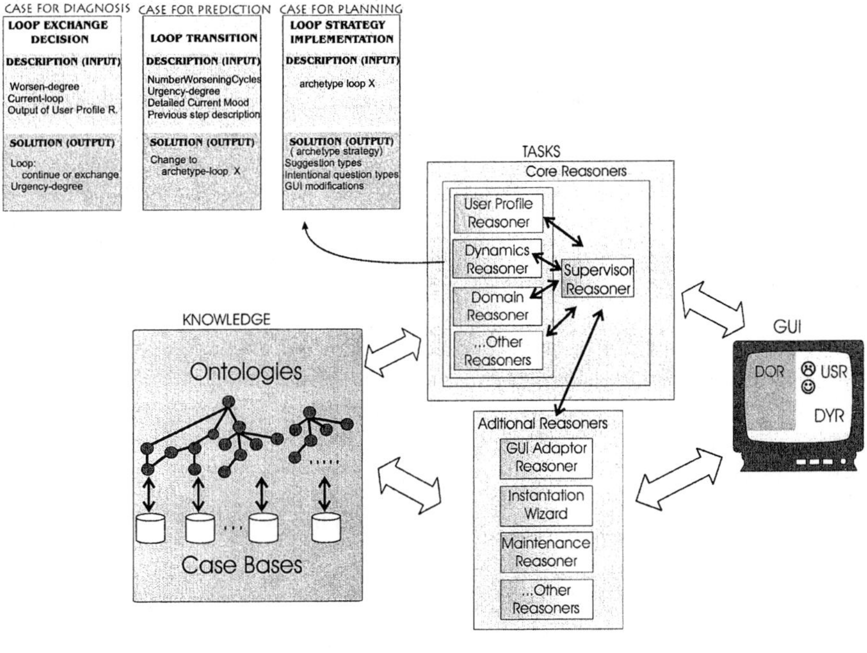

Fig. 1. COBBER Architecture and conversation dynamic cases

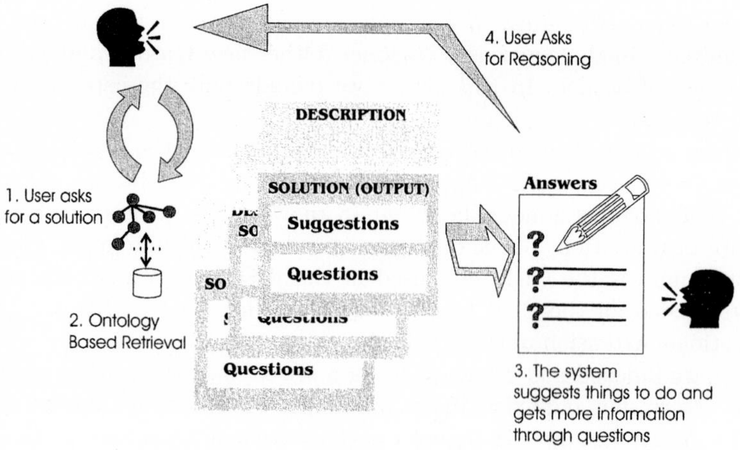

Fig. 2. User interaction model

questions to guide the user to choose one of the possible paths from the current point of the conversation. In opposition to the standard CCBR, these questions are used in the next reasoning cycle, where we retrieve only those cases that the user has shown interest in by answering questions related to them.

The GUI, shown in Figure 1, is divided into three main areas and another one is at the bottom for interactive communication with the system. The three main areas correspond to the three main tasks: the domain, the user profile, and the conversation dynamics reasoners. This layout of the screen makes it possible to communicate without interference among the tasks in any moment of the reasoning cycle. The user may run a new reasoning cycle anytime without answering some of the questions of the reasoners. The user may chose to work only with the domain task, working as it were a standard CCBR system.

Figure 2 shows the interactions between the user and the system. Our approach models the users session with the CCBR system as a learning process: the user needs to learn to solve a problem, like in the case of tutoring systems. The system, throughout the interaction with the user, incrementally gives pieces of knowledge to build the complete solution. The system guides the user at the three views: domain content, user characteristics and conversation strategies. To do so we need a user model. We extend the concept of user model of tutoring systems, that we call *extended user profile*, to include these features:

- Learnt Domain Model: the user's partial view of the domain knowledge at the starting point of the current session. This is equivalent to the user's model in tutoring systems.
- Personal Model: the user's self-identified characteristics provided by herself.
  - The level of domain expertise (novice, experienced, expert)
  - The level of computer skills (computer novice, computer literate, computer expert.)
  - The personality: personal tendencies dealing with the system.

3 System Dynamics Applied to the Conversation

The main goal of managing the conversation dynamics independently from the user profile and the domain model reasoners is to be able to model the strategy of the conversation itself and change it if something goes wrong. This will prevent users from giving up the communication with the system, when it fails to meet their needs. This is known in other works as a *breakdown* [10]. The users show some breakdown symptoms that we capture through simple multiple choice questions. We ask about typical user reactions, which appear in the following order[10]: tiredness, intolerance, anger, confusion, irony, humor, exhaustion, uncertainty, lack of desire to communicate. After the diagnosis of the breakdown symptoms, we apply a conversation strategy in order to correct the failure of communication. The strategy actions will be at a meta-level of the conversation. These strategies create different conversation dynamics when the user plays different roles and assigns to the computer other roles, depending on her appraisal of the situation.

To model the conversation evolution along the time, we represent each conversation's dynamics with a different *causal loop*. It is used in the System Dynamics field [6] and in the Systems Thinking field [13]. A generic loop, applied to the conversation, has four phases in a cycle executed in this order:

1. *Actions* to give some knowledge to fulfill user expectations.
2. *Effects*, i.e., how the action impacts on the user knowledge about the domain and on her personal state, e.g.: mood, breakdown symptoms, etc.
3. *Detection of effects* in the user, through questions.
4. *Corrections* i. e., expected domain knowledge and conversation meta-level corrections to keep the user in the right mood to continue working with the system. These corrections are implemented as new actions. That takes us to the beginning of the loop again.

Our model is based on the conclusion from careful observation of our students' actual behavior working in our laboratories: the breakdown symptoms appear not only due to user's reactions to the system's behavior but also some user's basic needs activated by that behavior, e.g.: having food if she gets fired. When the user, in general, has a system problem, she asks for a solution. But, when she has, let say, the previous example's basic need, she is blocked by the fear, and cannot dare to ask somebody about a solution. There are slight variations among the classification of those unfulfilled basic human needs. The most common is Maslows pyramid[11]. Its main categories are: physiological needs, safety needs, belonging and love needs, esteem needs and fulfillment needs. This classification is commonly used in other areas, such as marketing. The way to help to overcome those needs is by influencing the user through conversation meta-level actions:

1. To help the user to perform an introspection to find out her needs that are active. This is done through answering some *intentional questions*.

2. To encourage the user to overcome the needs. This is done with a set of supporting *suggestions* specific for each need.
3. To adapt the system to the user's needs. This is done by a set of variations of the GUI.

In the conversation dynamics reasoner, the goal of the intentional questions is based on the therapy theories where users relieve their problems by talking about them to somebody, like a friend. [2] These theories have been applied successfully in several well known areas, such as the support groups of the Alcoholic Anonymous [9]. COBBER is not a therapy framework, it just reacts to the mood indicated by the user and provides facilities to overcome some momentary blockages.

3.1 System Dynamics: Archetypes of Causal Loops

The main idea behind these loops is simple: the feedback generated by some actions in a loop can reinforce or counteract other actions. A basic loop, in which the effect of the corrections counteracts the previous effect of the actions, is called a *balancing loop.* On the contrary, when the conversation goes well we want to keep the same trend doing improvement actions, instead of corrections. This is a *reinforcing loop.* To model any system we may combine several of both kinds of loops in infinite manners. But researchers find out that all combinations follow a set of few patterns. They are known as *archetypes* of causal loops. The most accepted archetypes are those that enumerate Senge [13]: AccidentalAdversaries, Balancing, DriftingGoals, FixesThatFail, Reinforcing, and some others. We only describe two loops because the article's extension restriction. The descriptions are applied to our domain, the interaction between the user and the computer, i.e. the conversation:

The *Balancing Loop* shown in Figure 3 attempts to decrease the gap between a current state and a desired state through some actions. The positive/negative sign means that the influence in the target is in the same/opposite direction that the influence that received the origin. In the balancing loop we see that when the action favors the goal, it influences positively the current state. This causes that the gap gets smaller because its sign is negative, i.e. the opposite direction. At the contrary, if the action worsens the goal, the gap gets bigger. This loop represents the usual fluent conversation strategy: the actions that the user does may get smaller or bigger gap to the desired state. It is to have enough knowledge to solve the problem. Then, the user take actions to correct the conversation deviation until she reaches the solution. The problem arises when the user gets tired, disoriented, or just blocked. In that moment the conversation strategy changes completely, and should be modeled by different loops. Let us see one of the most complex one.

The *Accidental Adversaries* loop shown in Figure 4 models a very problematic conversation strategy where the user appraises the situation as if the computer

[2] In fact, the word COBBER, the framework's name, means "friend" in australian english.

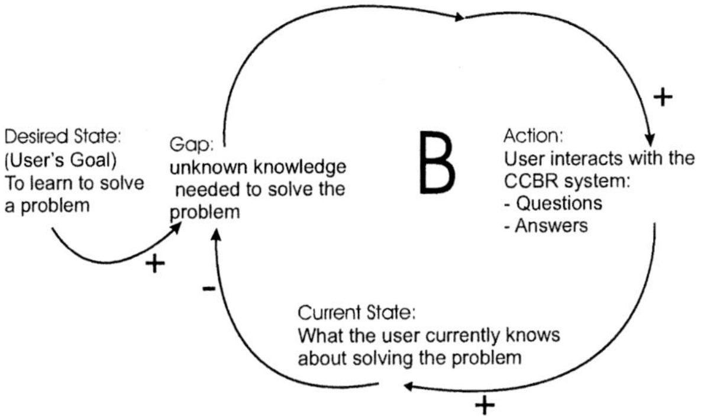

Fig. 3. *Balancing* loop applied to a fluent conversation

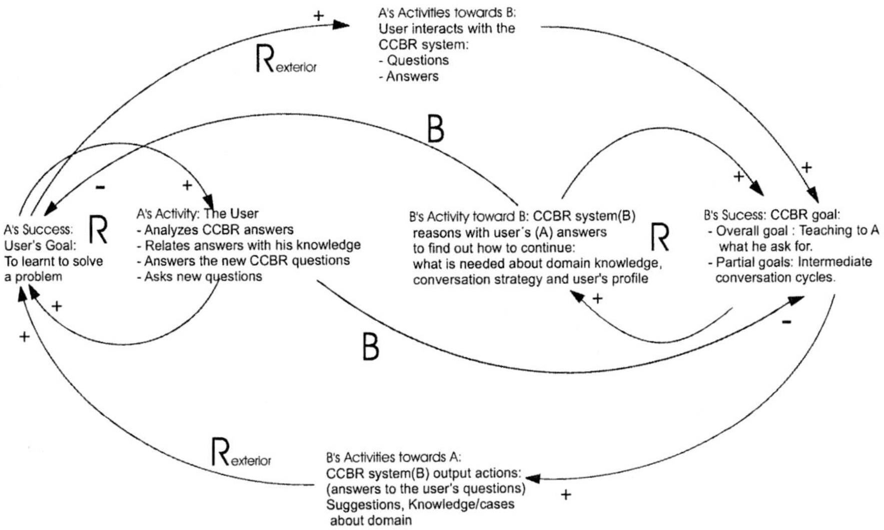

Fig. 4. *Accidental Adversaries* loop applied to a conversation with difficulties

were an enemy against him. Actually, what is happening is that both, the user and the computer, have compatible goals that are favoring each other. But, suddenly, the user feels that the actions of the computer start going against her goal. As a reaction to this appraisal the user performs defensive actions, which are against the computer's goal. This is why it is called accidental adversaries loop. It has three reinforcing loops marked with a big "R" and two balancing loops marked with a big "B". Overall system growth is driven by a global reinforcing loop. Two local reinforcing loops create balancing loops that then limit the growth of the overall system. It is not easy to understand at first sight, but we expect that following the dynamics along the different loops the reader may envision how the whole archetype works.

3.2 Description of the Conversation Dynamics Reasoner

In this section we describe how causal loops are applied in the framework and its tasks. They are supported by three types of cases included in Figure 1. The reasoner has three tasks which follow the CBR paradigm. Each task uses its own case type for the reasoning process. The tasks are:

- Diagnosis : *Loop exchange decision.* The main slots used in this task are:
  - Conversation trend (input): how the conversation is going in respect to the overall goals of the user. This uses the output of the user profile reasoner.
  - Worsening Level (input): how bad the conversation was in the previous cycle.
  - Loop Continuity (output): it is the decision to continue in the same causal loop or to change to another one.
  - Urgency Degree (output): how urgent is to perform the change.
- Prediction: *Loop Transition.* Although this task is a CBR system it acts as a fuzzy finite state automaton, where each state is a loop type and the transition conditions are the input of the cases. The main slots used in this task are:
  - The input of the previous task.
  - Current loop (input) that is active in this reasoning cycle.
  - Urgency Degree (input) that is the output of previous task.
  - Detailed Users Current Mood (input) that is obtained with intentional questions to the user. This mood is used to find out the active basic needs that are affecting the user in relation to the conversation. This is described in the next section.
  - Change to loop X (output): which loop is predicted that will improve the current conversation state.
- Planning: *Loop strategy Implementation.* This task implements the conversation strategy for each loop, i.e.: how to affect the conversation tendency and how to influence the user's state. This is done with the only tool that the system has, the variability of the system, that has these elements:
  - Suggestion types: each type is directed to a different need of the Maslow's classification.
  - Intentional question types: to help the user to explain her appraisal of the situation.
  - GUI modifications: they are the GUI look and behavior, which affect the user's appraisal of the situation.

Wether the second task will be activated depends on the outcome of the first one. If the Loop Continuity says to continue in the same loop the second and third task will not be executed.

4 An Example of COBBER Applied to the Domain of Help-Desk

We introduce the rest of the reasoners within an example. Its domain is a Help-Desk system that solves problems about an invoicing application created by a local software producer, GoldenSoft.

In Figure 5 there is an example of the user's conversation. The order of the steps is just for explanatory purposes. Note that the conversation has been divided into two figures to fit into the article. In the descriptions of the conversation for each reasoner, there are some jumps from one figure to another in order to describe the evolutions of different situations in two reasoning cycles. In the figures, the names "DomainGUI", "C. DynaGUI" and "UserProfGUI" represent the system output to one of the three main parts in the GUI. The same names with the word "user:" mean the input with the user's answer to each of the three parts. The same names ending with an "R" indicate what are the tasks executed by that reasoner.

Let's start with the initial cycle of the user's session. We describe only the CBR retrieve task of the reasoners. The adaptation for the CBR reuse task is mainly on the degree applied to the action slots in the cases, i.e. the level of worsening-degree of the conversation situation or the urgency-degree of exchange of conversation strategy. All the case bases have degrees of intensity.

The Domain Reasoner (DOR). The domain cases are indexed by the concepts in the case description and other additional properties, which create hierarchies of cases. One example of these additional properties is the *complexity degree*, which is used to retrieve cases at the adequate complexity according to the user profile that is currently active. In the initial cycle of the example in Figure 5 the user is novice. Therefore, when she describes her problem in a vague way in step 4, the system retrieves the "easy" and "generic" cases. There is one case that has those characteristics, the *company-chapter*, shown in step 5. The case is found because in the ontology are synonyms of the concept *enterprise*. The solution of the retrieved case is also generic and easy. If the user is not satisfied, she needs to go deeper by answering the intentional questions in step 12 of Figure 6. Then, the domain reasoner retrieves a deeper case, the *create-company* case, which narrows the scope of the problem. The case solution and intentional questions are shown to the user and the process continues until the user is satisfied with the solution.

The User Profile Reasoner(USR). The user answers the questions of step 1 of Figure 5 to establish the user profile used in the current cycle. The profile reasoner retrieves the case *user type NoviceExcited-A.1.3.* Based on the user's properties, the actions of this case modify the behavior of the system: activating an on-line help for novice users in computer skills, giving a "delicate" qualification to the personal suggestions, using a "most-text" GUI and applying a delay of a hundred milliseconds in order to slow down the computer responses. This user's type may change in each reasoning cycle when the user answers the questions of the profile reasoner, e.g.: in the step 14, the user clicks on a angry face.

———— CYCLE 1 (INITIAL) ————

1. (UserProfGUI) *Please introduce your user name and password*
   -- output-- *To serve you better, describe with which properties you identify most today: (profile questions)*
   - *a)- Domain expertise* (novice, experienced, expert)
   - *b)- Computer skills* (low,medium,high)
   - *c)- Mood* (☹ , ☺ , ...)
   - *d)-* personal tendencies (Speed of work, Text - graphics, mouse - control keys)
2. (user: UserProfGUI) *Peter, *****, a) novice, b) low ,c)* ☺, *d)slow, text, mouse*
   -- input--
3. (Domain GUI) *Please write a description of your problem:*
   -- output--
4. (user: DomainGUI) *I have a problem with a new enterprise*
   -- input--
5. (Domain R) `retrieve (with description concepts and DOMAonto + cases)`
   (result)

case 'Company Chapter'
Solution:(actions) - Suggestions: *Company Actions describe the possibilities of the application to manage enterprises..."* - Next Cycle Intentional Questions: *If you describe more your query I can be more specific? Might be a problem with some of these tasks : Create, Duplicate, Delete?*

6. (UserProf. R) `retrieve (with profile answers and USERonto + cases)`
   (result)

case 'user type noviceExcited-A.1.3' :
Solution: (actions) - Turn on : computer skills explanations 'novice' (CBR of computer help) personal suggestions : type 'delicate' - For GUI: general: most-text speed: delayed 100 ms ....

7 (C. Dyna. R) `retrieve`
`step1: loop exchange decision(DYNAonto + cases CB1)`
   (result)

case 'continueBL-BD-RL-INITIAL-A.2.5' :
Solution: (actions) - To do:Continue - Level: High

`Step2: loop transition(DYNAonto + cases CB2 + step1)`
   (result)

No execution because previous step result: "continue in the same loop"

`Step3: loop strategy implementation (DYNAonto + cases CB3 + current-loop)`
   (result)

case 'BalancingLoop-INIT'
Solution:(actions) - Suggestions Type: { } - Next Cycle Intentional Questions Type: { 1.- VerificationOfSatisfaction} - GUI: None

Fig. 5. The conversation example of a Help-Desk system: part 1 of 2

Then, the profile reasoner retrieves the *user type noviceMad-A.1.4*, that includes a solution with a loop property value "very supportive". This property feeds the conversation dynamics reasoner.

The Conversation Dynamics Reasoner (DYR). In the initial reasoning cycle, the balancing loop is active. In the second reasoning cycle the *loop exchange decision* task is activated because the user has changed her mood in the step 14 in Figure 6 and her answer, in step 13, to the VerificationOfSatisfaction-Question has been "no". The output, in the step 17, of this task is to change of loop, which activates the *loop transition* task that decides, based on some input of the previous task and questions to the user, that the appropriate loop for the new conversation strategy is the Accidental Adversaries. The last task *loop strategy implementation* retrieves the case with the actions to implement that strategy: a set of suggestion types, next cycle intentional question types and GUI variations. These types act as a strategic filter when the supervisor decides on the global suggestions and questions to output to the user.

```
------------------------- CYCLE 2 -------------------------
12. (user : DomainGUI)  Yes, my problem is in the insertion of a new enterprise -- input--
13. (user: C. DynaGUI)  no -- input--
14. (user: UserProfGUI)  c) Mood ☹ -- input--
15. (Domain R) retrieve (with description concepts and DOMAonto + cases)
    (result)   | case 'Create Company'
               | Solution:(actions)
               | - Suggestions: "This task includes the creation of files and parameters to
               |   perform invoicing, accounting, encashment, payments, assets management. To
               |   generate the company you need..."
               | - Next Cycle Intentional Questions:
               |   Click where you have the problem: parameters, generation of files, ...."

16. (UserProf. R) retrieve (with profile answers and USERonto + cases)
    (result)   | case 'user type noviceMad-A.1.4' :
               | Solution: (actions)
               | - Turn on :   computer explanations 'novice'
               |               personal suggestions : type 'delicate'
               | - For GUI:    general: most-text
               |               speed: delayed 10 sec
               | - Loop Properties: very supportive

17. (C. Dyna. R) step1: retrieve loop exchange decision(DYNAonto + cases CB1)
    (result)   | case 'changeBL-BD-RL-INITIAL-H' :
               | Solution: (actions)
               | - To do:Change
               | - Level: High
                 Step2: retrieve loop transition(DYNAonto + cases CB2 + step1)
    (result)   | case 'BalancingLoopToAccidentalAdversariesLoop'
               | Solution: (actions)
               | - Change Current-Loop to AccidentalAdversariesLoop

                 Step3: loop strategy implementation
                                        (DYNAonto + cases CB3 + current-loop)
    (result)   | case AccidentalAdversariesLoop
               | Solution:(actions)
               | - Suggestions Type: { 1.- SafetyNeed (2) , 2.- RecognitionNeed(1)
               |                       3.- RealizationOfPotentialsNeed(1)}
               | - Next Cycle Intentional Questions Type:
               |        { 1.- SafetyNeed(2) , 2.- RealizationOfPotentialsNeed (1)
               |          3.- ProblemSolved(1)}
               | - GUI: MoreGraphics, MoreBrightColours, MoreSimplifiedInformation
18. (Supervi . R) RuleSystemTMS (output of previous reasoners + CB + SUPEonto)
    (result)   | Solution:(actions)
               | - global suggestions : NormalGraphics(GUR)
               | - activated rules:
               |   Rules for suggestions: No more than 2 of SafetyNeed type
               |   Rules for contradictions:
               |   <for GUI> If MoreGraphics(loop) & mostText(USR) then
               |             choose NormalGraphics(GUR)
```

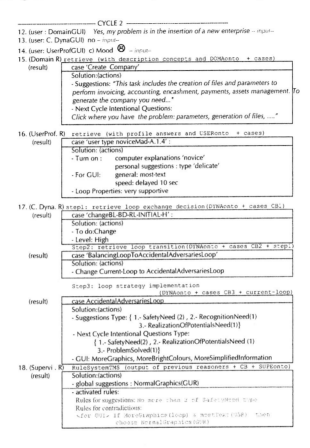

Fig. 6. The conversation example of a Help-Desk system: part 2 of 2

The Supervisor Reasoner(SUR). This task has two main functions: to activate the right reasoner at the right time and to solve the conflicting local actions proposed by the reasoners in order to obtain a set of coherent global actions. The first function is the control of the reasoning flow. In a cycle some steps should not be performed, like the loop transition of the conversation dynamics reasoner in step 7 of Figure 5. Therefore the supervisor skips that activation. The conflict resolution is implemented as a Truth Maintenance System (TMS) with a rule base that decides between the conflicting actions. Some rules are shown in step 18 of Figure 6. The rule base includes filtering rules, like the rule shown in the same figure, that limits the number of suggestions of the same kind to avoid boring the user.

The GUI Adaptor Reasoner (GUR). The GUI has a set of variability features, which are used to adapt to the user's types, personal preferences, and moods. These features are adapted according to the actions proposed by the other reasoners. In the example of Figure 5 the answers to section "d)" in step 2 are processed by this reasoner to adapt to the user personal tendencies. The "for GUI" actions of the case in steps 6 and 16 of the user profile reasoner are processed by the GUI adaptor reasoner as well. It acts again with the loop strategy implementation in step 17. And, again, the GUI adaptor is activated in step 18, when the supervisor decides GUI changes.

5 Ongoing Work: Javy

In parallel to COBBER and jCOLIBRI, we are working on JV^{2}M, an Intelligent Tutoring System that aims to teach the Java source code compilation process[3]. In order to understand the underlying mechanisms, pupils need to know the Java Virtual Machine (JVM) structure and instructions, because the generated object code must be fed to it.

Instead of a boring application, JV^{2}M immerses the student in a 3D virtual environment that represents a metaphorical JVM. This way, pupils are not required to write the resulting object code, but *execute it* in that JVM manipulating the virtual objects. We use COBBER to enrich the previous JAVY-student interaction providing additional knowledge about the personality and the mood of the user.

The recreated world is also inhabited by JAVY, an animated pedagogical agent ([8]) that monitors the student while she is solving the exercises. If the pupil makes a mistake, JAVY offers a hint. The user can also ask him for help when she gets stuck. In that case, a conversation starts between JAVY and the student in a similar way to the example previously shown in the help desk domain.

Conversation is controlled using a case base, with cases arranged as was described in section 2. Specifically, we have a case for each concept of the domain being taught, and for each identified misconception students can suffer. Apart of the explanation to be provided to the user, each case has also a set of intentional questions that are used to drive the conversation to more specific cases. Usually, CCBR systems ask the user to write a first description of her problem using natural language, which is used as an initial case description. However JAVY doesn't let the user introduce any text, because the first case description is *inferred from the context*, avoiding the user's having to manually specify her problem. How this is performed is out of the scope of this paper.

As an example of the current interaction, let suppose the user is solving an exercise where she must run a JVM instruction, concretely the "`imul`". She gets stuck and asks JAVY for help. A fragment of the conversation follows:

- **Javy:** This instruction is used to multiply two numbers. Both values are retrieved from the operand stack, and the result is left in the same place. Does it solve your problem? You can also be wondering what the operand stack is, or the way you can get one operand from it.
- **User:** Could you please explain what the operand stack is?

[3] http://gaia.sip.ucm.es/grupo/projects/javy/index.html

- **Javy:** operand stack is the stack where temporary results of arithmetic logic expressions are stored. It is also used to keep parameters in the method invocation or to deposit the return values of some JVM instructions.
  Now, what do you want to know? You can have problems about what a stack or an operand is, or about how you can manipulate the operand stack in the virtual environment.

The explanations given by JAVY are retrieved from the cases solution in the case base. Intentional questions are also extracted from each case. The student does not write free natural language because the system proposes a set of alternatives and the graphical user interface only lets the user pick one of them.

6 Conclusions

We identified several difficulties to build CCBR systems. To overcome them we propose a framework, named COBBER, that uses a cognitive approach. Cognition refers to mental activity including thinking, remembering, learning, and using language. When we apply a cognitive approach to learning, we focus on the understanding of information and concepts. We centered in two aspects of the criticism to cognitive approach [14] that may be considered in the CCBR systems too. The first one is the emotion challenge: cognitive science neglects the important role of emotions in human thinking and working. And the second one is the dynamic systems challenge: The mind is a dynamic system, not a computational system. We overcame these critics by the idea that the system should react to the variability of the user by the dynamic adaptation, throughout the session, using the variability of the system:

- For the user conversation strategies: modeling them with causal loops.
- For the user mood: influencing her with intentional questions, intentional suggestions, and GUI variations.
- For the user tendencies or tastes: adapting the system to them with GUI variations.
- For the user domain knowledge query: obtaining the domain answers to user questions with a basic CCBR cycle.
- For the user domain knowledge expertise: adapting the level of complexity of the domain knowledge presentation.
- For the user computer skills: simplifying the GUI and with an additional computer help subsystem.

References

1. D. W. Aha and L. A. Breslow. Refining conversational case libraries. In *International Conference on CBR (ICCBR 97)*. Springer-Verlag, 1997.
2. D. W. Aha, T. Maney, and L. A. Breslow. Supporting dialogue inferencing in conversational cbr. In B. Smyth and P. Cunningham, editors, *Advances in Case-Based Reasoning – (EWCBR'98)*. Springer-Verlag, 1998.

3. J. Bello, P. González-Calero, and B. Díaz-Agudo. Jcolibri: An object-oriented framework for building cbr systems. In *ECCBR*, pages 32–46, 2004.
4. K. Branting, J. C. Lester, and B. W. Mott. Dialogue management for conversational case-based reasoning. In *ECCBR*, pages 77–90, 2004.
5. M. Doyle and P. Cunningham. A dynamic approach to reducing dialog in on-line decision guides. In *European Workshop on CBR (EWCBR 2000)*. Springer-Verlag, 2000.
6. J. Forrester. *Industrial Dynamics*. MIT Press, 1956.
7. H. Gómez-Gauchía, B. Díaz-Agudo, and P. A. González-Calero. A case study of structure processing to generate a case base. In *ECCBR*, pages 587–600, 2004.
8. W. L. Johnson, J. Rickel, R. Stiles, and A. Munro. Integrating pedagogical agents into virtual environments. *Presence: Teleoperators & Virtual Environments*, 7(6):523–546, December 1998.
9. K. Makela, I. Arminen, K. Bloomfield, and I. E.-S. et al. *Alcoholics Anonymous As a Mutual-Help Movement: A Study in Eight Societies*. University of Wisconsin Press, 1996.
10. T. D. Martinovski, B. Breakdown in human-machine interaction: the error is the clue. In *ISCA tutorial and research workshop on Error handling in dialogue systems*, pages 11–16, August 2003.
11. A. Maslow. *Motivation and personality*. New York: Harper and Row, 1970.
12. D. McSherry. Increasing dialogue efficiency in cbr without loss of solution quality. In *International Joint Conference on Artificial Intelligence (IJCAI)*. Acapulco, Mexico, 2001.
13. P. M. Senge. *The Fifth Discipline: The Art and Practice of the Learning Organization*. Currency Doubleday, 1990.
14. P. Thagard. Cognitive science. *The Stanford Encyclopedia of Philosophy (Summer 2004 Edition)*.
15. I. Watson. *Applying case-based reasoning: Techniques for enterprise systems*. Morgan Kaufmann, San Francisco, 1997.

Opportunities for CBR in Learning by Doing*

Pedro Pablo Gómez-Martín, Marco Antonio Gómez-Martín,
Belén Díaz-Agudo, and Pedro A. González-Calero

Dep. Sistemas Informáticos y Programación,
Universidad Complutense de Madrid, Spain
{pedrop,marcoa,belend,pedro}@sip.ucm.es

Abstract. In this paper we partially describe JV^{2}M, a metaphorical simulation of the Java Virtual Machine where students can learn Java language compilation and reinforce object-oriented programming concepts. This description is contextualised within an abstract categorization of learning-by-doing tutoring systems intended to identify different activities where CBR can be applied. We concentrate on one of those activities, concretely on the automatic generation of new exercises through retrieval and adaptation of seed cases representing prototypical examples.

1 Introduction

Helping students with learning is a complex, demanding, and often frustrating task. "Learning by doing" or "active learning" is a model of teaching/learning that means engaging all of our senses and attention into discovering something new. It is the counterpart of the traditional educational model or "passive learning" consisting of an instructor lecturing to a big number of students. Research has long shown that people retain information longer when they have explored it with multiple senses. There is an old Chinese proverb that says: *"Tell me - I forget. Show me - I remember. Let me do - I understand."*

Computer interactive knowledge-based learning environments are considered a good solution to instruct students in those domains where "learning by doing" is the best methodology of teaching. Students are faced with more and more complex problems, tailored to their needs depending on their increasing knowledge. Note that learning with a computer does not necessarily imply an active learning. Our goal is that when a student sits in front of a screen, she does not automatically assume a passive intellectual stance.

We are developing one of such learning environments, called JV^{2}M [5]. Students can learn the Java Virtual Machine (JVM) structure [10] and Java language compilation. To avoid passive attitudes, the system presents a metaphorical 3D virtual environment which simulates the JVM. The user is symbolized as an avatar which interacts with the virtual objects. An animated pedagogical agent called JAVY (JavA taught VirtuallY) also inhabits this virtual environment, and is able to monitor the student whilst she is solving a problem, with the purpose

* Supported by the Spanish Committee of Science & Technology (TIC2002-01961).

H. Muñoz-Avila and F. Ricci (Eds.): ICCBR 2005, LNAI 3620, pp. 267–281, 2005.

of detecting errors she makes in order to give her advice or guidance. He can even solve the exercise by himself giving explanation at each step. Figure 3 shows a screenshot of the system[1].

Case-based reasoning (CBR) techniques fit in many ways in those systems that conform to the active learning methodology. For example, recovering previously resolved exercises in order to show them as examples is a marvellous way of feedback. Also, CBR can be used to decide which exercise to practise next. Depending on the taught domain, different degrees of additional knowledge should be incorporated in the traditional CBR cycle.

In the next section we present our vision of the learning by doing approach of teaching, and we identify the points where CBR techniques can fit. Once the big picture has been described, section 3 focuses on our system, JV^{2}M, describing one of the CBR uses, the next exercise selection. Section 4 finishes with some conclusions and future work.

2 Learning by Doing and CBR

Learning-by-doing is an experience-based style of learning where the student is aware what she needs to learn during the resolution of a problem.

We claim that trying to learn skills, abilities or creativity in a comfortable passive position is absolutely useless and ineffective. The learning-by-doing approach attacks this problem giving students exercises that are considered a valuable learning experience. Each problem is selected for a purpose, putting into practise some concepts of the taught domain. In order to be effective, problems selection must be adequate, following a pedagogical direction. A balance is needed between the exercise difficulty and the student knowledge in order to neither overestimate nor bore her.

Our utilisation of the learning-by-doing model unfolds in a cycle, shown in Figure 1. It consists of five steps:

1. *Selection of concepts to practise:* concepts of the taught domain are chosen. As said before, if we want a successful learning, this selection cannot be arbitrary, but depending on the current student knowledge. This selection opens the door for pedagogical decisions. For example, the so called "learning by discover" methodology can be put into practise if always some unknown concept is chosen in order to force the students to investigate and build their own knowledge.
2. *Exercise selection:* using the previous selected concepts, the student is provided with an exercise to put them into practise.
3. *Exercise resolution:* the pupil solves (or tries to solve) the problem she faces.
4. *Solution verification:* the student answer is tested (compared with the system solution) in order to evaluate its correctness.
5. *Feedback:* using the conclusions reached in the previous step, advices are provided to the student. The tutor can give explanations about the mistakes made or even supply theoretical knowledge when needed.

[1] http://gaia.sip.ucm.es/grupo/projects/javy/index.html

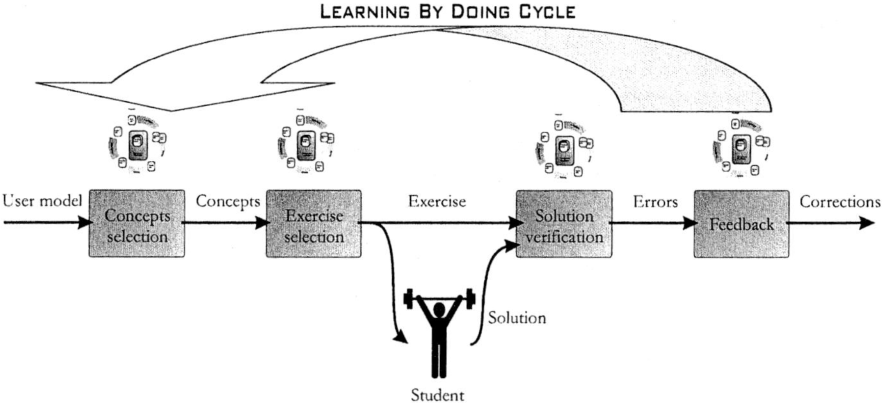

Fig. 1. Workflow between stages

This cycle is valid for both traditional teaching system, driven by human tutors, and for computer stand-alone application where the teacher is an interactive program, such as the Intelligent Tutoring Systems (ITS) [14].

When the student solves the exercise using a computer, the three last stages usually blend. As the system often provides contextualised help, it needs to test continuously the partial solution (stage 4) and to provide feedback before the student entirely finishes her answer (stage 5).

2.1 Where Does CBR Fit in a Learning by Doing Model?

The system must participate in four of the five previous steps (all except the third one). When developing a learning-by-doing ITS, each step can be considered an independent problem to be solved. Figure 1 sumarises this idea, and shows the inputs and outputs of each step.

We claim that in some domains each step in Figure 1 can be solved using CBR techniques:

1. *Selection of concepts to practise:* the common approach ([2] [14]) is to have a hierarchy of concepts classified by the difficulty level, and organized in some kind of chapters and sections. The next concepts to practise are chosen depending on the user model and the previously visited sections. We believe that this task can also be done using a simple CBR cycle. Case descriptions would contain partial user models and the proposed concepts as the solutions. Learning should be the main benefit of using CBR: new cases can be added, taking into account the successes and failures of past pupils trying to overcome the chosen concepts.
2. *Exercise selection:* using the chosen concepts to learn, an exercise must be proposed. Depending on the interaction between this stage and the previous one, more information can be used. For example, not only the concepts to practise can be provided, but also the concepts that should not be used

at all because the student has no idea about them yet. This task can be performed using a CBR approach [14]. If the adaptation capacity is limited (or there is no adaptation at all), the system will demand a big amount of exercises (many of them quite similar), in order to let the user practise the same concept more than once without repeating the same exercise. On the other hand, the system will require fewer but archetypical exercises if it can modify them by itself, creating variations of exercises to avoid user solving the same problem over and over again.

CBR cycle has a *problem description* as its input, and a *solution* as output. Curiously, in this stage the output case is in fact a *problem*, but one that *the student* (instead the system) has to solve.

This paper is dedicated specially to this stage, and how we are putting it into practise in our system, JV^2M.

3. *Solution verification:* once the student has proposed a solution, the system must test its correctness. In some domains, an expert system can be built to correct the answer of the student. This idea is used, for example, in Andes [4], a model tracing tutor for teaching quantitative physics. Other areas are more complex to formalize and require the existence of a correct solution to be compared with the student's one. If a CBR approach was used in the previous stage, the right solution could be attached to the exercise. If adaptability was done, both components (exercise and solution) should have been changed.

   Another choice is to have some CBR subsystem which constructs a valid solution (instead of holding it on the case), and then compare the student answer and the system one.

4. *Feedback:* if it want to be educative, the system should be more communicative than a mere "It's Ok" or a "You're wrong". We need the previous step to give us more information about the errors in order to provide some useful help.

   One alternative is what it is called "Case Based Teaching" [15]. CBR techniques are used to provide the student with previously resolved exercises related in some way to the current one, so she is supposed to realise her own mistakes by herself.

   Another option is to store common problems in a case base using the conversational CBR approach [1]. When a new problem is detected, the system starts a conversation with the pupil until some tip is provided. An improvement to this idea would be to automatically answer some of the questions using the current context of the exercise to focus the conversation. Ideally the system could retrieve a case (containing the feedback) without need a conversation with the student at all.

In this paper we are considering the role that CBR plays within step 2 of the learning by doing cycle (Figure 1), i.e., the election or creation of the next exercise to practise.

3 JV^2M: A Case-Based Intelligent Tutoring System

In this section, we will describe the way we are using Knowledge Intensive CBR to select the next exercise presented to the user. A set of concepts to practise is supposed to have been chosen, and at this stage we select the exercise that matches them.

Case descriptions include the concepts of the discipline which each exercise (case) contains. Case solutions store the exercises themselves. Concretely, in JV^2M they consist on Java compilation exercises that the student must resolve.

The simplest CBR approach would represent cases as plain source code. Unfortunately, adaptation of the recovered exercises would become quite difficult.

Our Knowledge Intensive approach to CBR benefits from the use of an ontology with general knowledge about the domain of compiling Java programs. We claim that the use of additional domain knowledge avoids the use of a big exercise repository, and eases adaptation based on deleting some elements, or substituting them by other related ones.

As we will describe in section 3.5, adaptation benefits from the structured representation of the exercises and from the relations among the individuals through the domain knowledge ontology.

For example, suppose I want to retrieve an exercise that contains multiplicative expressions. The system could retrieve the example shown in Figure 2, which has no multiplicative expression but an additive one and an "`if`" instruction. Adaptation would remove the "`if`" structure –task a bit dirty and error prone if it was performed directly over the plain text– and substitute the "`a + 3`" expression by other one using the multiplicative operator: "`a * 3`". Afterwards, operands could also be replaced: "`a * a`", "`5 * 3`", ...

We will now focus in the exercise selection, the second stage of Figure 1. Before going into the details, we will briefly describe JV^2M in order to clarify the context.

3.1 JV^2M

JV^2M is a learning by doing approach to teach the compilation of object-oriented languages, in particular teaching Java compilation. It includes a metaphorical simulation of the Java Virtual Machine (JVM), where compilation scenarios are explored. The learning environment is complemented with a pedagogical agent, a human-like figure that assists the student in the learning process ([8] [9] [12]). This agent, called JAVY, monitors the user providing help when needed. Interaction is similar to a 3D-graphical adventure game that tries to guarantee student motivation. Figure 3 shows a screen shot of the system running, with the user in the middle of the screen and JAVY in the right down corner.

Actually, real-world compilers need to understand two languages: the source language and the object language. In our domain they are Java and the JVM 'assembler instructions' respectively. Despite the fact that we are assuming our students know how to program in Java, we don't want to force them to understand the JVM in advance. To overcome this limitation, JV^2M actually teaches simultaneously both things: Java compilation and JVM structure.

```
public class IfExample {
    public static void main (String params) {
        int a;
        a = 12;
        if (a < 5) {
            int c;
            c = a + 3;
        }
    }
}
```

Fig. 2. Retrieved case

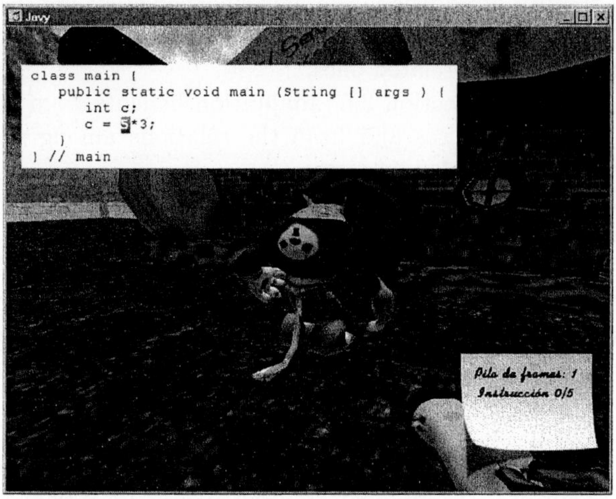

Fig. 3. Student is examining the Java source of the current exercise

It could be argued that learning how to compile Java code is not a very useful task. But the JVM is in fact an advanced *stack machine*, as the majority of the theoretical machines commonly used during compiler courses. It also possesses some high level instructions referring to some basic concepts of the object-oriented programming (OOP), for example dynamic linking. So we claim that teaching these instructions can reinforce the OOP ideas.

During the first interactions with the system, the user is presented with both source and object code. The user needs only worry about *executing* the compiled code provided in the metaphorical JVM shown in the virtual environment. Nevertheless, the student is supposed to pay attention to both of the codes and to understand their relationships because she will be asked to compile the source code by herself (without seeing any object code) in the subsequent exercises.

Interaction in the virtual environment is performed using four actions imported from the entertainment software arena: "look at", "take", "use" and "use with". Also, an inventory is available to temporary store objects. The vir-

Fig. 4. Java compilation elements

tual world is populated with other characters (apart from JAVY and the user's avatar) that represent basic structures of a real JVM. When talking to them and interchanging objects, basic actions ("microinstructions") are executed in the underlying JVM simulation.

3.2 Domain Knowledge

The domain ontology contains knowledge related with the Java language compilation and it is partially based on the Java Language Specification. Figure 4 partially shows this ontology. It has been designed using Protégé 3.0 and formalized in OWL[2]. Concretely we are using OWL-DL sublanguage because we need both the maximum expressiveness and automatic reasoning with that knowledge, so computational completeness is required.

[2] http://www.w3.org/TR/owl-features/

Our first impulse in creating the ontology was to mimic the Java language grammar. We soon realised that this would have been an error. Generally speaking, grammars need a big amount of non-terminal symbols, becoming quite complex. If we had used this option, our ontology would have been populated with a lot of useless concepts as "`FieldModifierOptional`" or "`MethodHeader`".

Actually, grammars are just a tool used by compilers to generate the *syntactic tree*. This tree is then enriched in order to create the *semantic tree*, becoming a key aspect in the compilation process. So it become clear that a more realistic approach was to use concepts based on the *syntactic tree* instead of the grammar, because compilation process depends closer on them.

3.3 The Case Base

Each case represents a Java compilation exercise, i.e., a simple piece of code that the student has to learn to compile.

Lets suppose the system is at the beginning of the second stage of Figure 1. At this point, it has a set of concepts of the discipline that the student must learn.

Each case of the case base of exercises is composed of:

- **Description:** concepts that it puts into practise, and
- **Solution:** one or more exercises the student must resolve to learn the concepts of the case description.

Each Java exercise is not stored as plain source code. Instead we represent it as a structured description in OWL (individual) that is classified and indexed by the ontology concepts. Figure 5 partially shows the instance graph used to represent the exercise of Figure 2 (case solution).

The case description is represented as a simple instance that is classified below the domain concepts that the exercise help to learn (or practise): "`if`" expression, variables, additive expression, and assignment. These index concepts are shown in Figure 6 and belong to the ontology shown in Figure 4.

Note that *the program* of the exercise shown in Figure 2 is quite useless. Fortunately, our domain does not need to retrieve source code that *does* something useful. It is only required to *compile*. This loosening in the exercises restrictions opens the door to a more sophisticated adaptation process. Nevertheless, it is still unclear if this fact has some kind of repercussion in the pedagogical aspects of the application.

Next, we describe the CBR processes over this case base. The goal is to choose the best exercise to be practised next.

3.4 Case Retrieval

As we have described, each case represents a compilation exercise and it is indexed by the domain concepts that the exercise practises.

The query to the CBR system is defined by:

- A set of concepts C_i that the user needs to learn (or practise) in the next exercise.

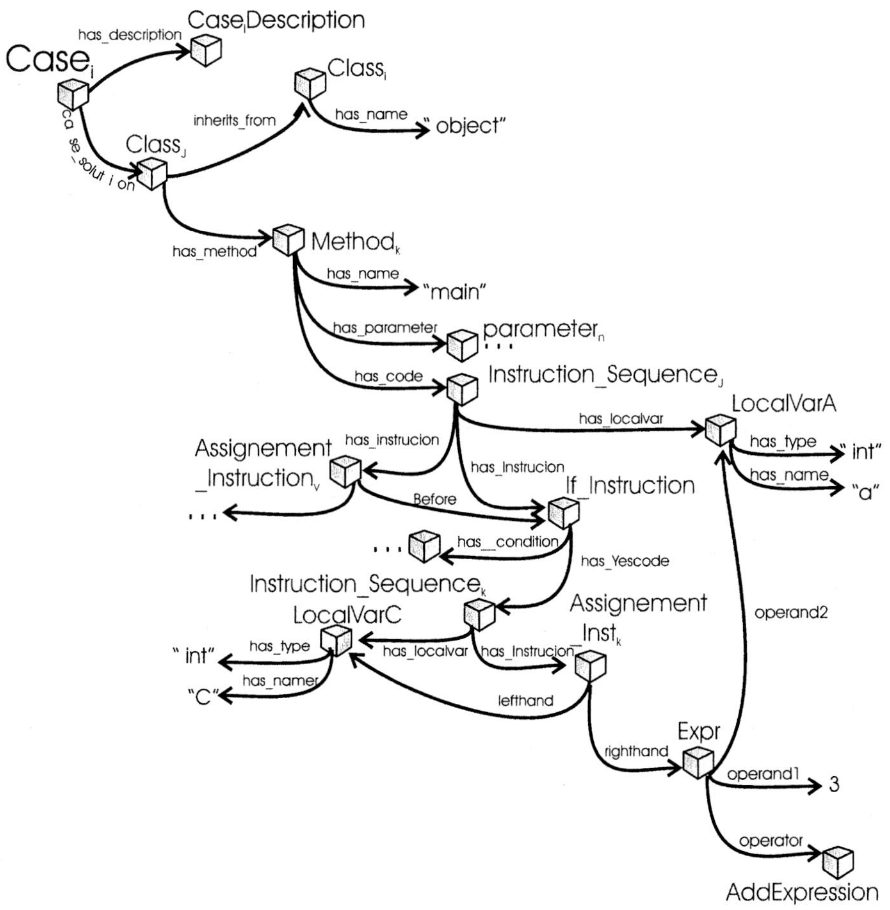

Fig. 5. Instance Graph to represent the if example of Figure 2

- A set of concepts L_j with which the user is already familiarized. The set of L_j are extracted from the user model representation whose description is out of the scope of this paper.
- A set of concepts N_k that should not be practised in the next exercise. The pedagogical module (first step of Figure 1) obtains this set of N_k mainly describing the concepts that the user does not know yet.

The goal of the retrieval task is finding an exercise to help learning concepts C_i without including any concept N_k.

The representational approach to case retrieval [11] assigns similarity meaning to the path joining two individuals in a case organization structure or in the domain terminology (note we use rich domain taxonomies). With this approach A is more similar to B than C to B iff A is closer to B than C is to B.

In this system we have applied this approach using the subsumption links in the domain ontology to define the distance between two individuals. In fact, we are using retrieval operations based on Description Logics instance recognition that have been proposed in the literature [7,13,3]. Retrieval is defined as a classification process where the queries are represented as DL instances.

Given a query individual q the retrieval process has two steps:

1. Filtering
   (a) R = set of instances that belong to the conjunction concept ($and[C_1, \ldots, C_n]$). This process will get instances belonging to all C_i concepts.
   (b) If R is empty, find the set of most specific concepts $[C_1, \ldots, C_n]$, where q is an instance of all concepts in this set, and add their instances to R. This process will get instances belonging to some C_i concepts.
2. Selection
   (a) The retrieved individuals from R will be ranked by a similarity function and the most similar will be returned. The similarity measure will take into account the L_j and N_k concepts.

Note that, even in the best situation (1.a.), adaptation can still be required because the retrieved case could include N_k concepts to be removed. Besides, the pedagogical module can ask for variations of a certain retrieved exercise if the student has already solved it, but she needs more practice of the same concepts.

Figure 6 shows an example where:

- C_1 = Multiplication
- L_1 = Local Variables, L_2 = Assignment Instruction.
- U_1 = If Instruction, U_2 = While Instruction.

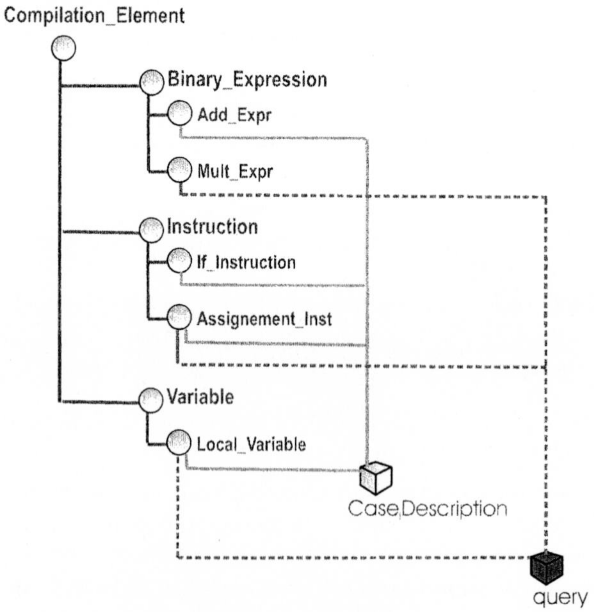

Fig. 6. Case Adaptation Example

3.5 Case Adaptation

Case adaptation plays a fundamental role in the ability of CBR systems to solve new problems. Case adaptation is a knowledge-intensive task and most CBR systems have traditionally relied on an enormous amount of built-in adaptation knowledge in the form of adaptation rules.

Our knowledge intensive approach to CBR relies on the explicit representation of general terminological knowledge about the domain. That way, certain adaptation knowledge is explicitly represented in the domain knowledge taxonomy, as it indicates, for instance, that individuals that are close in the taxonomy are eventually interchangeable.

In [6] we formalize an adaptation scheme based mainly on deletions and substitutions, where:

- Instead of having rules, dependencies within a case are explicitly represented in order to guide the adaptation.
- The search for substitutes is guided by a set of *memory instructions* (a path of relations). The system developer could include some of them, but the rest are learned by the system.

In the ongoing example we distinguish two situations requiring adaptation:

1. Adaptation due to the query, i.e., the retrieved case does not teach all the required concepts, or teaches some concepts that are too advanced. We need to apply the deletion and/or substitution adaptation operators. After adaptation the case will teach a different set of concepts (asked by the query but not included in the retrieved case).
2. Adaptation to generate a variation to practise certain concepts. The retrieved case teaches all the required concepts, but we have to change the arguments and operands.

We propose an adaptation mechanism as a process that propagates changes from description to solution items, as follows:

1. The list $L = L_R \cup L_S$ of items in the solution that need to be adapted is obtained. These items are:
   - L_R: concepts that depend on a feature of the case description which does not appear in the query.
   - L_S: concepts that have been substituted by a different value in the query.
2. Every item in L is deleted or substituted by a proper new item. First, those that only depend on values from the case description, then, those that depend on other items of the solution that have already been adapted. Of course, circularity is not allowed in the dependency relation.

In the example domain there are clear implicit dependencies, for instance, between the declaration of a variable, a parameter or an attribute –static or dynamic– and its uses.

Figure 6 shows an example where the query asks for an exercise to practise multiplication. Lets assume that the best retrieved case is $Case_i$ (sketched in Figure 5. To obtain the list L of items in the solution that need to be adapted:

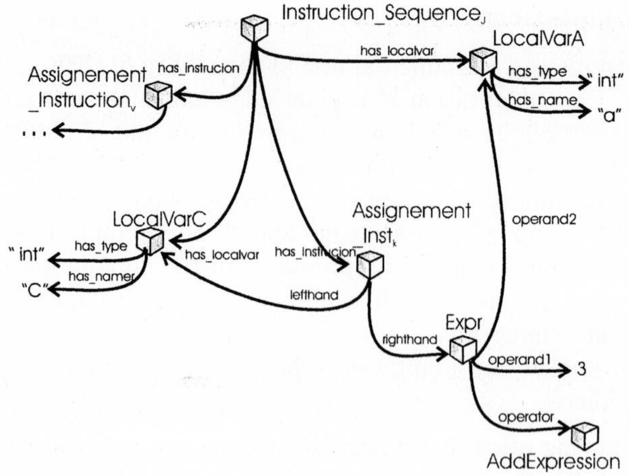

Fig. 7. Case Adaptation Example (Delete If)

```
public class IfExample {
    public static void main (String params) {
        int c;
        c = 5 * 3;
    }
}
```

Fig. 8. Retrieved case

1. Find items to be removed: those items depending on the *If Instruction* concept because it appears in the retrieved case and belong to the unknown concepts (U_1).
   L_R = {If Instruction}
2. Find items to be substituted: those items appearing in the retrieved case and not in the query *and* all the items depending on these ones.
   L_S ={Add Expression}

Which concepts are included in L_R and which are in L_S depends on the query.

Remove Example. Given L_R = {If Instruction} we find the dependent items. In the "`if`" instruction there are clear dependencies with its condition and the item that aggregates its "yes" code (Instruction Sequence K) (see Figure 5).

The inner code (`int c; c = a + 3;`) will be related to the outer code block (Instruction Sequence J). Result is shown in Figure 7.

Substitution Example. Giving L_S ={Add Expression} we are substituting *Add Expression* by *Multiplication Expression* that is required in the query (see Figure 6). Using the domain ontology we can know that these items are similar.

These changes are due to the query, i.e., the retrieved case does not teach all the required concepts, or teaches some too advanced concepts.

As we described, there are other type of adaptation to generate a variation to practise certain concepts. Now that the adapted case teaches all the required concepts we could change the operands. For instance changing the constant 3 for another one.

The final result exercise is shown in Figure 8.

3.6 Revise Solution

Previous sections have described the way we choose the next exercise to practise. Once the complete exercise has been decided, it should be revised in order for the system to be sure about its correctness, in other words, whether the adapted exercise has a solution.

Fortunately, this step becomes quite easy in our domain, because an "expert system" exists which is able to solve all the valid exercises: the Java compiler, `javac`. A tool is needed to translate back the exercise structure modelled in OWL to plain source code to feed the compiler[3]. The same code that has been tested with `javac` will be shown to the user in the virtual environment.

4 Conclusions and Future Work

In this paper we have described our vision of active learning systems, and we have identified some points where CBR techniques match on them.

One of such systems, JV^{2}M, has also been presented. We have detailed how knowledge intensive CBR is applied to it in one of the identified stages of the "learning by doing" cycle: the exercise selection.

The "source code" used throughout the system has only one restriction: it must be correct. The system does not need to propose exercises that execute useful algorithms while they compile without problems. That relaxes the restrictions for the CBR adaptation task allowing us attempt more sophisticated changes.

We plan analyse deeply the use of CBR in the other stages of the active learning cycle. We envision a first step also developed with knowledge intensive CBR, where the additional knowledge will be composed of both pedagogical knowledge and domain curriculum knowledge.

Regarding to the selection of the exercise described in this paper, we will analyse different alternatives to incorporate some kind of difficulty level. Exercise selection currently depends on the concepts to practise but no complexity level for each of them is provided. More work is needed in this area.

The next step in this work is addressing the evaluation of the student solution. We are currently considering some alternatives that will be soon analysed.

[3] We are currently working in this tool.

Some research is still needed in the feedback phase. We think it is promising the use of conversational CBR (CCBR) techniques in order to start a conversation with the user when she gets stuck. This conversation can be contextualised using the user model.

References

1. D. W. Aha, L. Breslow, and H. Muñoz-Avila. Conversational Case-Based Reasoning. *Applied Intelligence*, 14(1):9–32, 2001.
2. P. Brusilovsky, E. W. Schwarz, and G. Weber. Elm-art: An Intelligent Tutoring System on World Wide Web. In C. Frasson, G. Gauthier, and A. Lesgold, editors, *Intelligent Tutoring Systems*, volume 1086 of *Lecture Notes in Computer Science*, pages 261–269. Springer, 1996.
3. B. Díaz-Agudo and P. A. González-Calero. A declarative similarity framework for knowledge intensive CBR. In *Procs. of the (ICCBR 2001)*. Springer-Verlag, 2001.
4. A. S. Gertner and K. VanLehn. Andes: A coached problem solving environment for physics. In G. Gauthier, C. Frasson, and K. VanLehn, editors, *Intelligent Tutoring Systems*, volume 1839 of *Lecture Notes in Computer Science*, pages 133–142. Springer, 2000.
5. P. P. Gómez-Martín, M. A. Gómez-Martín, and P. A. González-Calero. Javy: Virtual Environment for Case-Based Teaching of Java Virtual Machine. In V. Palade, R. J. Howlett, and L. C. Jain, editors, *KES*, volume 2773 of *Lecture Notes in Computer Science*, pages 906–913. Springer, 2003.
6. P. A. González-Calero, M. Gómez-Albarrán, and B. Díaz-Agudo. A substitution-based adaptation model. In *Challenges for Case-Based Reasoning - Proc. of the ICCBR'99 Workshops*. University of Kaiserslautern, 1999.
7. G. Kamp. Using Description Logics for Knowledge Intensive Case-Based Reasoning. In B. Faltings and I. Smith, editors, *Third European Workshop on Case-Based Reasoning (EWCBR'96), Lausanne, Switzerland*, pages 204–218. Springer-Verlag, Berlin, 1996.
8. J. C. Lester, C. Callaway, B. Stone, and S. Towns. Mixed initiative problem solving with animated pedagogical agents. In *Working Notes of the AI & Education Workshop on Pedagogical Agents*, pages 56–62, Kobe, Japan, August 1997.
9. J. C. Lester, S. A. Converse, S. E. Kahler, S. T. Barlow, B. A. Stone, and R. Bhogal. The persona effect: affective impact of animated pedagogical agents. In *Proceedings Human Factors in Computing Systems (CHI'97)*, pages 359–366, Atlanta, March 1997.
10. T. Lindholm and F. Yellin. *The Java Virtual Machine Specification. 2nd Edition.* Addison-Wesley, Oxford, 1999.
11. B. Porter. Similarity assessment: Computation vs. representation. In *Proc. of the CBR Workshop DARPA 1989.*, 1989.
12. J. Rickel and W. L. Johnson. Animated agents for procedural training in virtual reality: perception, cognition and motor control. *Applied Artificial Intelligence*, 13(4):343–382, 1999.
13. S. Salotti and V. Ventos. Study and Formalization of a Case-Based Reasoning System using a Description Logic. In B. Smyth and P. Cunningham, editors, *Advances in Case-Based Reasoning – (EWCBR'98)*. Springer-Verlag, 1998.

14. R. H. Stottler. Tactical Action Officer Intelligent Tutoring System (TAO ITS). In *Proceedings of the Industry/Interservice, Training, Simulation & Education Conference (I/ITSEC 2000)*, November 2000.
15. G. Weber and T. J. Schult. CBR for tutoring and help systems. In M. Lenz, B. Bartsch-Spörl, H.-D. Burkhard, and S. Wess, editors, *Case-Based Reasoning Technology*, volume 1400 of *Lecture Notes in Computer Science*, pages 255–272. Springer, 1998.

Navigating Through Case Base Competence

Maarten Grachten, F. Alejandro García, and Josep Lluís Arcos

IIIA, Artificial Intelligence Research Institute,
CSIC, Spanish Council for Scientific Research,
Campus UAB, 08193 Bellaterra, Catalonia, Spain
{maarten, fgarcia, arcos}@iiia.csic.es
http://www.iiia.csic.es

Abstract. The development of large-scale case-based reasoning systems has increased the necessity of providing tools for analyzing the case base structure. In this paper we present a hierarchical competence model approach based on the solution qualities. Using this hierarchical approach we propose a new method for visualizing case base competence and understanding the way a CBR system behaves in different parts of the problem space. The visualization method has been used in the *Tempo-Express* system, a CBR system for applying expressivity-aware tempo transformations to recordings of musical performances.

1 Introduction

The development of large-scale case-based reasoning systems has increased the necessity of providing tools for analysing the case base structure and its relation with the similarity measures used in the retrieval phase [1,2]. These tools may be used either in the design stage or in the maintenance stage of the CBR systems.

Reinartz and Iglezakis [3] proposed a collection of properties for monitoring the quality of a CBR system. Moreover, they defined a collection of modify operators on cases for improving the quality of the case base. Their proposal is focused on syntactical measures and tries to avoid domain-specific measures.

The competence model introduced by Smyth et al. [4] is a nice contribution of the analysis of case base structure by assessing the local competence contributions of cases and their interactions. The competence model proposes the use of a *Solves* relation between cases (being either true or false for a given pair of cases). This interpretation of the *Solves* concept (being either true or false) is obvious for classification problems but may be inappropriate for other tasks such as design or configuration. In these tasks it seems more natural to define *Solves* as a *function* (indicating the quality of the solution) rather than a relation. In this paper we present the concept of an hierarchical competence model that is based on such a function and allows for a finer analysis of the case base structure.

We believe that, with increasing complexity of CBR systems, the analysis of the case base structure becomes a hard task without the support of tools capable of accurately visualizing the complex case base structure. The navigation through the case base space may play an important role for understanding the similarity

H. Muñoz-Avila and F. Ricci (Eds.): ICCBR 2005, LNAI 3620, pp. 282–295, 2005.

relationships between cases and the quality of the contribution of a given case to the solution of other problems.

Previous work on visualizing the case base structure includes the PROFIL system [5] and the *Picture Perfect* tool [6]. The PROFIL system is a CBR decision support tool for metallic sections design that provides a visualization tool for relating target problem with the collection of retrieved cases. Cases are plotted on a two-dimensional plane where the first dimension represents the similarity of the cases with the target case and the second dimension represents the solution quality. Nevertheless, the visualization is problem centered and only preserves the similarity relationship between the target problem and each case. That is, the similarity relationship among the retrieved cases is lost.

The *Picture Perfect* tool [6] provides an alternative two-dimensional plot where the similarity relationships among all the cases of the case base is preserved. A force-directed graph-drawing algorithm is used for preserving the similarity relationships among cases. The algorithm is an iterative algorithm that uses the case similarities as force vectors. The drawback of the approach is that the quality of solutions is not visualized.

Using the competence model analysis, Smyth et al. [4] proposed a case-authoring tool for visualizing the competence of an evolving case base and help the application designers to identify redundant cases for deletion and useful new cases for addition. Nevertheless, the visualization tool is focused on showing the relationship between the competence group sizes and their coverage.

We propose a new visualization method for case base competence based on the solution qualities. This method allows us not only to draw 'competence islands' in an 'unsolved ocean', but rather to draw the complete surfaces, with hills and valleys.

With respect to the mapping, this poses some new problems. In complex CBR systems, it is usually impossible to find a mapping of the cases to the two-dimensional plane that preserves the case distances. When the distortion is too high, it is impossible to draw a competence map using straight-forward 2D multidimensional scaling (the competence groups would not appear as separated regions). Therefore we propose an alternative way of mapping the cases to the two-dimensional plane, that uses both case distance information and hierarchical competence information.

The paper is organized as follows: In section 2 the competence model is summarized and extended. In section 3 we present a new technique for visualizing competence surfaces using the notion of hierarchical competence groups presented in section 2. In section 4 we exemplify and report the use of the visualization technique in the *TempoExpress* system, a CBR system for applying expressivity-aware tempo transformations to recordings of musical performances. The paper ends with a discussion of the results, and the planned future work.

2 Computation of Case Base Competence

Competence groups were defined by Smyth and McKenna [4] as a proposal for an effective model of case base global competence measure that assesses the local competence contributions of cases and their interactions. Competence groups are defined from the notions of *coverage* and *reachability.* The coverage set of a case c_i is defined as the set of all target problems that can be solved using c_i. The reachability set of a target problem is defined as the set of all cases that can be used to solve it. Formally:

$$CoverageSet(c_i \in CB) = \{c_j \in CB : Solves(c_i, c_j)\} \quad (1)$$

$$ReachabilitySet(c_i \in CB) = \{c_j \in CB : Solves(c_j, c_i)\} \quad (2)$$

where the *Solves* predicate has to be defined for the CBR system under inspection.

From the coverage and reachability definitions, Smyth and McKenna define a *Related Set* of a case c_i as the union of its coverage and reachability sets. Then, a set of cases $G \subseteq CB$ is a competence group if and only if:

$$\begin{aligned} &\forall c_i \in G, \exists c_j \in G - \{c_i\} : SharedCoverage(c_i, c_j) \\ &\wedge \forall c_i \in G, \nexists c_j \in CB - G : SharedCoverage(c_i, c_j) \end{aligned} \quad (3)$$

where two cases have a *SharedCoverage* when their related sets have a non empty intersection.

Using the notion of competence groups, the case base can be organized with a set of case clusters that do not interact from a competence viewpoint.

The use of a *Solves* predicate is possibly a good indicator in analytical tasks (see [7] for a conceptual distinction of CBR tasks). In analytical tasks there is a limited number of solutions and solutions are simple, non-aggregate entities (classification/diagnosis is a typical analytical task). Nevertheless, in synthetic tasks—where the solutions have a composite structure, and as a result the number of possible solutions is usually very large (a typical example of a synthetic task is structural design)—modeling *Solves* as a binary predicate on cases of the case base CB (a subset of $CB \times CB$) is not satisfactory. CBR systems for solving synthetic tasks can be viewed as systems that locally approximate a complex target function. In that context, it is more natural to conceive of the *Solves* notion as a function of type $CB \times CB \rightarrow [0, 1]$ that assesses the quality of the solution. Thus, in synthetic tasks we will say that the solution generated from a case c_j for a target problem c_i is of quality γ.

Then, we can extend the definitions of coverage and reachability in the following way:

$$CoverageSet_\gamma(c_i \in CB) = \{c_j \in CB : \gamma \leq Solves(c_i, c_j)\} \quad (4)$$

$$ReachabilitySet_\gamma(c_i \in CB) = \{c_j \in CB : \gamma \leq Solves(c_j, c_i)\} \quad (5)$$

where γ can take values in the interval [0,1].

Using the above equations (4) and (5), the competence groups defined in a given case base may vary depending on the threshold value used for γ. Then, defining a collection of γ-cuts a hierarchical competence model of the case base can be constructed.

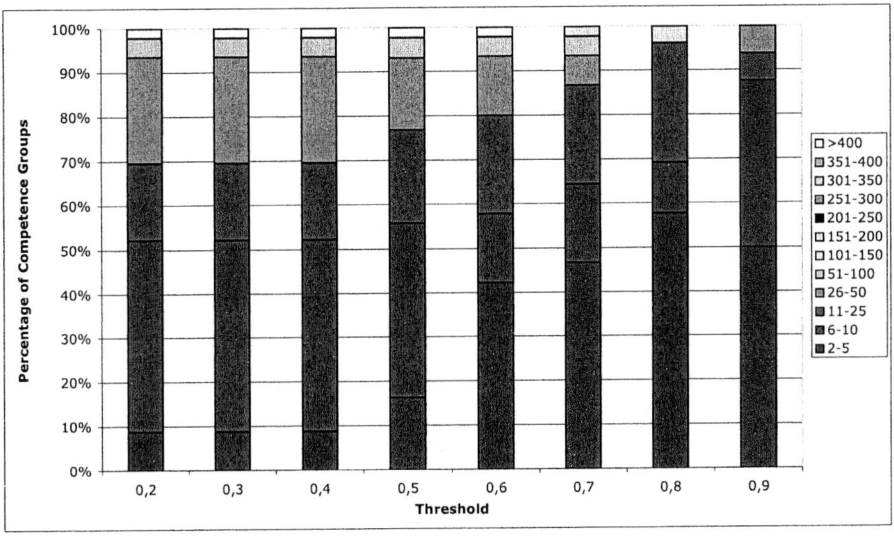

Fig. 1. Competence group sizes in *TempoExpress* for different γ values

This hierarchical competence model allows a finer analysis of the case base competence. The first analysis we can perform is the study of the changes on the sizes of the competence groups when we relax the quality criterion γ.

Figure 1 shows the effect varying the quality threshold in the *TempoExpress* system (see section 4). For a quality threshold of 0.9 (right side column) 50 % of the competence groups are formed by at most 5 cases and 36 % of the competence groups are formed by collections between 6 and 10 cases. On the other side, for a quality threshold of 0.2 there are competence groups with over 400 cases — more than a quarter of the whole case base size.

Given a hierarchical competence model of the case base, it is interesting to analyse the correlation between the case similarities and the quality of the solutions they provide. For this purpose, in the next section we will describe a technique for visualizing the case base taking into account this relationship.

3 Mapping Competence to the Plane

After obtaining the competence partitioning of the cases base at several threshold levels, we can map the cases to a plane, in order to visualize the hierarchical structure of the partitioning. Ideally, the cases would be mapped to the plane so that their mutual euclidean distances are proportional to their real distances. But as mentioned before, there is no guarantee that high dimensional data can be faithfully mapped to a two-dimensional plane. As a consequence, the positioning of the cases according to their real distances do not necessarily provide a good separation of the competence groups. Therefore, a method is needed to alter the case positioning in such a way that the competence groups at each threshold level are spatially separated, preferably with minimal distortion of the real case distances. In this section we propose an algorithm for finding a mapping in the two-dimensional plane that satisfies our requirements. The method is similar to the visualization technique employed by Smyth et al. [6], in the sense that it starts with a random positioning of the cases in the plane and iteratively changes the positions to have the euclidean distances in the plane approach the real distances between the cases. Our method however is more elaborate to accommodate for the additional requirements that are involved to draw the hierarchical competence groups.

The input to the mapping algorithm is the hierarchical structure of competence groups, together with a distance matrix D containing the distances between all pairs of available cases. Rather than considering the competence groups as sets of cases (which they are really), we consider them as nodes in a tree. Nodes at the lowest level in the tree (i.e. with the highest γ-threshold) have as children the cases that are in the corresponding competence groups. But nodes at higher levels have nodes as children rather than cases. To position the set of nodes at a particular γ-level, it is necessary to know something about the way the children of those nodes are arranged. This implies a bottom up traversal of the tree, positioning the nodes level by level.

The first step is thus to position the cases of each node at the lowest level independently. For every bottom-level node, the positioning of its cases is guided by a single (soft) constraint:

- the euclidean distance between two cases in the plane should be equal to the target distance d^t(as defined in D) between the cases

In an iterative process a random positioning of the cases is repeatedly altered to satisfy this constraint as good as possible. If no more progress can be made, the iteration is stopped. The resulting positioning is saved. Note that at this point the cases in the nodes are only positioned internally to the node, not with respect to the cases in the other nodes at the same level. But since we calculated the node internal positionings, we can now compute the positioning of the nodes with respect to each other. To do that, we calculate two values for each node n: the *centroid* and *width*:

$$Centroid(n) = \frac{1}{N} \sum_{c \in Children(n)} p_c = \frac{1}{N} \sum_{c \in Children(n)} \langle x_c, y_c \rangle \tag{6}$$

$$Width(n) = \max_{c \in Children(n)} d(\langle x_c, y_c \rangle, Centroid(n)) \tag{7}$$

where N is the number of children of node n and $p_c = \langle x_c, y_c \rangle$ is the position of case c in the plane. The centroid is the center of gravity of the positioning of the children and the width of the node is the euclidean distance between the centroid and the child furthest away from the centroid.

The positioning of the nodes with respect to each other is then guided by two (soft) constraints:

1. the distance between the centroids of two nodes should not be smaller than the sum of the widths of the two nodes.
2. the euclidean distance between the centroids of two nodes should be equal to the target distance between two nodes.

The target distance between two nodes n_i, and n_j is defined simply as the average target distance between the cases of the corresponding competence groups $CG(n_i)$, and $CG(n_j)$:

$$d^t(n_i, n_j) = \sum_{c \in CG(n_i)} \sum_{c' \in CG(n_j)} d^t(c, c') \tag{8}$$

In the same way as the cases were positioned, the nodes are positioned by iteratively adapting a random positioning to satisfy the constraints. At each iteration, the two constraints are used to calculate two new positionings from the previous positioning. The two positionings are combined linearly to obtain the final positioning for that iteration. As before, when no further improvements can be made to the positioning, the iteration is stopped, the positions of each node are saved, and the process is repeated for the parent nodes.

When the tree has been traversed from bottom to top in this way, we have a positioning for each node in the tree (the position of the root node was not derived but is set to the origin). But note that the positions that were computed for the cases in the initial stage were not updated after computing the positions of the parent nodes. So the final stage is to traverse the tree again in a top down manner to propagate the parent positions down to the children. So for every child n its position p_n is updated as follows:

$$p_n = p_n + p_{Parent(n)} - Centroid(Parent(n))$$

The resulting positioning of cases in the two-dimensional plane will reflect the real distances between the cases as good as possible while at the same time preventing overlap between competence groups at the same γ-level.

3.1 Analysis of Various Competence Scenarios

The mapping obtained in this way provides valuable information about the way a CBR system behaves in different parts of the problem space. Some typical scenarios have been plotted in figure 2. The figure shows the contours of the competence groups for the complete range of γ-values. Dark colors represent regions with low competence without cases (or low competence cases) and light colors represent regions with high competence.

Figure 2(a) shows a part of the problem space where there are many cases that form a single high competence group, without low competence cases (i.e. even with a high solution quality threshold, the cases have shared coverage with each other). This means that in such a region, a case can be solved well even if there is not a very nearby case. Another situation is shown in figure 2(b), which is also a well covered region, but it is composed of separated high competence sub

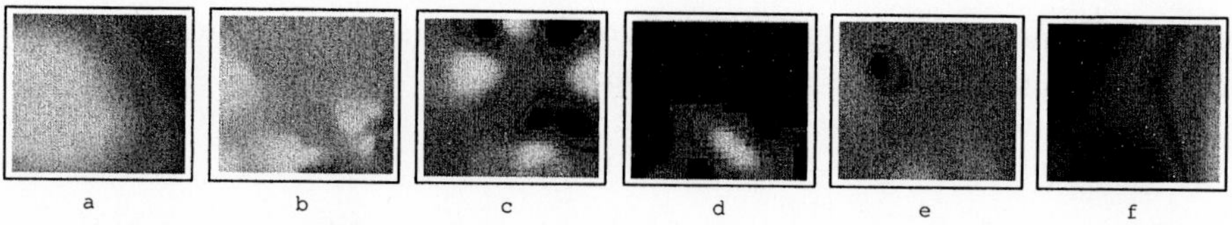

Fig. 2. Some typical competence scenarios

regions. So although cases can be solved well here, the target solutions are not the same for every part of the region. Figure 2(c) shows a situation where high competence and low competence regions are mixed. This means that even though quite similar problems can be retrieved from the case base, they may not provide a good solution for the target problem. In figure 2(d) a region is shown that has only a single dense competence group in an otherwise low competence area. In this scenario, it is probable that the region needs many more cases to provide good competence. The opposite is shown in figure 2(e), where a predominantly high competence region contains single dense low competence area, implying that although the cases in the region can be generally be solved well, there are some similar cases that are hard to solve, and cannot either be used to solve other cases in the region. Finally, figure 2(f) shows a region with low competence. This may indicate that there are either no cases at all in this region, or the cases in this region all have low competence.

4 Experimentation

We have applied the techniques described in this paper in the *TempoExpress* system [8]. *TempoExpress* is a CBR system for applying expressivity-aware tempo transformations to monophonic audio recordings of musical performances. *TempoExpress* has a rich description of the musical expressivity of the performances, that includes not only timing deviations of performed score notes, but also represents more rigorous kinds of expressivity such as note ornamentation, and note consolidation/fragmentation. Within the tempo transformation process, the expressivity of the performance is adjusted in such a way that the result sounds expressively natural for the new tempo. A case base of previously performed melodies is used to infer the appropriate expressivity.

A case is represented as a complex structure embodying three different kinds of knowledge: (1) the representation of the musical score (notes and chords), (2) the musical model of the score (automatically inferred from the score using Narmour's Implication/Realization model and Lerdahl and Jackendoff's Generative Theory of Tonal Music as background musical knowledge [9,10]), and (3) a collection of annotated performances. These annotated performances are acquired automatically from the recordings using a technique explained in detail in [11].

For the case base design, several saxophone performances were recorded from 5 jazz standards, each one consisting of 4–5 distinct phrases. The performances were played by a professional performer, at 9–14 different tempos per phrase. From this, the initial case base was constructed, containing 20 scores of musical phrases, each with about 11 annotated performances (in total more than 5.000 performed notes).

When a new problem has to be solved in *TempoExpress*—i.e. an input phrase performance that must be transformed to another tempo—the problem is solved stepwise by decomposing the input phrase into segments. These segments are sequences of consecutive notes of around five notes and usually correspond to the musical motifs that constitute the musical phrase. The solution for each input melody segment is constructed from the most similar melody segments in the case base.

We have analyzed the *TempoExpress* case base composed of 1310 cases. A case consists of a phrase performance at a particular tempo (the input tempo) and a number representing the desired output tempo. Because an output performance is generated segmentwise for the input case, segments from various retrieved cases are usually involved in the solution of the different segments of the problem. As a consequence, a case may provide only a partial solution to the problem. To represent this relation, we define a solution function as follows:

$$Solves(c_i, c_j) = \frac{||SolvedNotes(c_i, c_j)||}{||Notes(c_j)||} \tag{9}$$

Where $SolvedNotes(c_i, c_j)$ are the notes in the melodic phrase of c_j that were provided with a solution (an expressive interpretation) from the retrieved case c_i (whether a solution for a note can be provided depends on whether segments can be convincingly matched between the input and retrieved phrases). $Notes(c_j)$ is the complete sequence of notes in the melodic phrase of c_j. Rather than representing the true $Solves$ relation, this is a confidence measure for the solution that serves as an approximation. Roughly speaking, the confidence measure is proportional the amount of solution information that could be transferred from the retrieved solutions to the current problem.

The distance function between cases is a linear combination of the pairwise distance of the three case components: phrase, input tempo, and output tempo. The phrase distance is measured as the edit distance between abstract sequential representations of the phrases (using the Implication/Realization model [9], see [12] for details).

With the $Solves$ function as defined above, we computed competence groups at ten different quality threshold values (see section 2). Using the case distance function explained above, the resulting hierarchical competence structure was mapped to the two-dimensional plane, following the method described in section 3. The results are shown as a contour plot in figure 3, and as a 3D surface in figure 4. In both figures, low competence regions are represented by darker colors and high competence regions are represented by lighter colors. In the 3D plot, valleys and hills correspond to low and high competence regions respectively. In the contour plot, the cases are plotted on top of the map as plus signs[1] (the

[1] The plus signs on some shades may be hard to see when printed in black and white. It is recommended to inspect the pdf version of this document which contains colored graphics. Feel free to contact the authors to obtain an electronic copy.

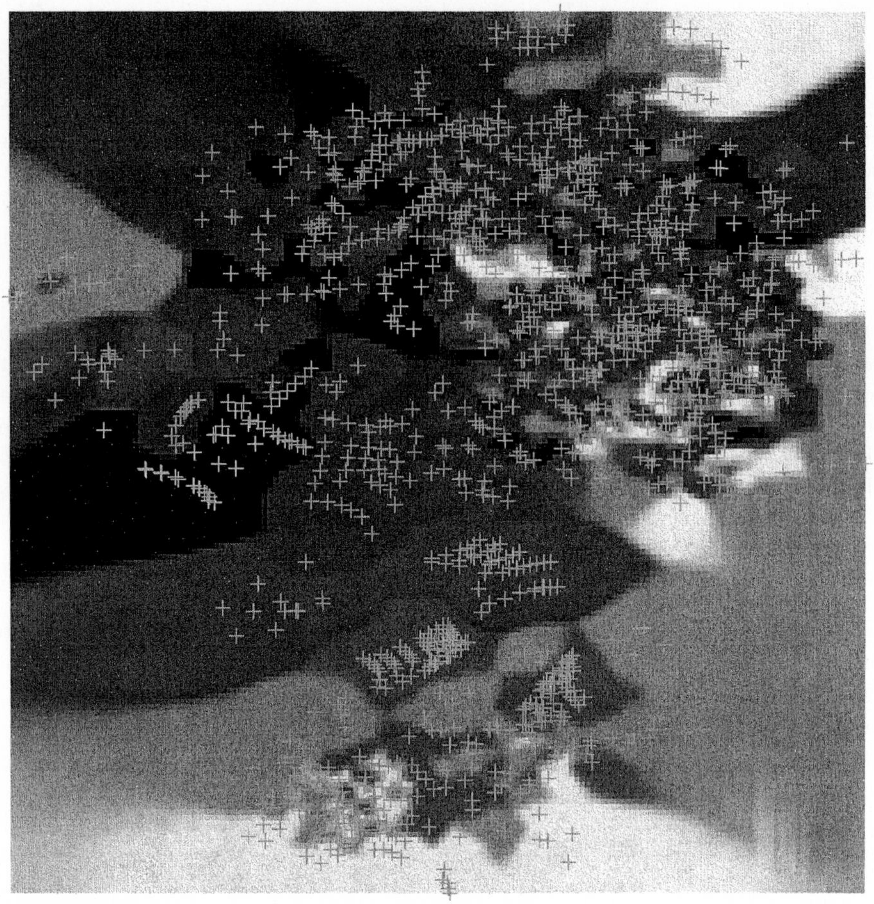

Fig. 3. Contour representation of the competence of *TempoExpress*

colored map was derived from the scattered case information using *gnuplot*'s *dgrid3d* function).

Viewing the contour map at a glance, some comments can be made. The map shows a rather non-homogeneous distribution of cases and competence areas. The lattice-like positioning of some groups of cases (mostly in the lower part of the figure) reflects the fact that the case distance takes into account the input and output tempos of the cases (phrase performances are available at regularly spaced tempos). It makes sense that each of these lattice structures tends to have a single competence level, since the cases within the structures are various tempo transformation tasks of the same phrase, and the major factor determining whether a case is hard to solve is the phrase (i.e. whether the phrase consists of melodic fragments for which examples are known). Note also that the larger single-colored areas at the edges of the figure should be interpreted with some care, since they are unpopulated and the competence estimates mainly result from far-reaching extrapolations of the competence of the nearest-by cases.

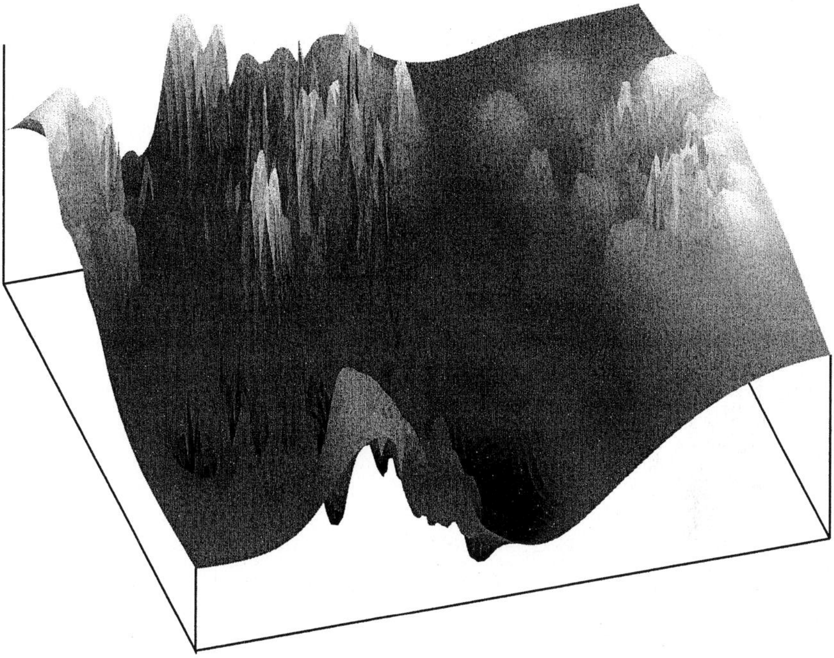

Fig. 4. 3D surface representation of the competence of *TempoExpress*

The contour map shows roughly three distinct areas within the problem space. Firstly, in the upperleft quadrant of the map there is a coherent set of problems for which no good solution could be constructed (conform scenario *f*, section 3.1). Secondly, in the lower part of the map, there is another rather populated area for which generally good solutions are found (conform scenario a/b, section 3.1). Lastly, there is a mixed competence region in the upperright quadrant, that shows scattered high and low competence groups (conform scenario *c*, section 3.1).

A disadvantage of the visualization technique is that the final positioning of the cases is only an approximation of a map that satisfies the constraints of faithful case distances and non-overlapping groups (since usually there is no map that completely satisfies both constraints at the same time). It thus sometimes happens that in the global competence map (figure 3), the shade indicating the competence is an average of partially overlapping competence branches of the hierarchical competence structure. Figure 5 shows this situation schematically for two competence branches mapped on a single dimension. In order to get a better impression of individual competence branches, it is therefore useful to view them in isolation.

The competence tree of the *TempoExpress* case base turned out to consist of 46 competence branches just below the root of the tree. In figure 6, two of such branches are shown. Note that the competence distribution of in these maps is

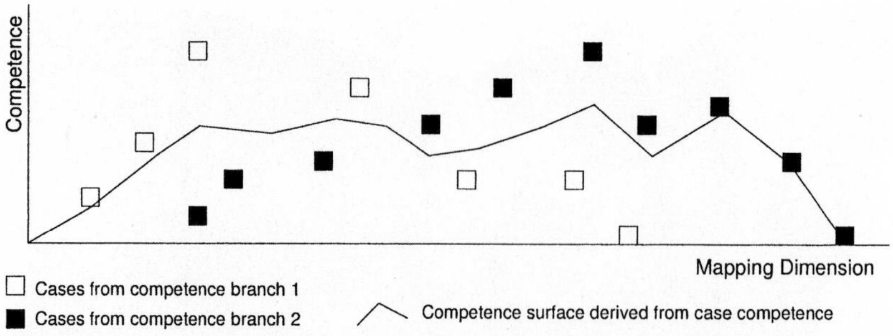

Fig. 5. Problems of non-ideal mapping: Branches from the hierarchical competence structure overlap and the competence surface does not accurately reflect the true competence of the cases

less complex than the distribution of the global map. Apart from the fact that the number of cases is smaller, the relation between the positioning of the cases and their competence is more comprehensible. Figure 6(a), for example shows a pattern of steadily increasing competence from the lowerleft to the upperright corner. Inspection of the individual cases showed that cases clustered at a particular competence level tended to have the same musical phrase. A clear relation between competence and input or output tempo was not found. Additionally, note that the case-distance for this particular subset could be mapped to a single dimension, since the cases are positioned roughly on a straight line.

Figure 6(b) shows another, relatively large branch. Since this branch is well separated spatially, it is easy to locate it in the global contour map. It corresponds to the lower part of the map, that was identified earlier as the major high competence area of the map. As before, particularly for the lower competence levels, a clustering of cases in various competence levels can be noticed, that turns out to be correlated with the musical phrase of the case. There are some phrases, like *Body And Soul [phrase B2]* (Green), and *Like Someone In Love [phrase B2]* (Van Heusen/Burke), that appear in the low competence regions of both branches. Since cases pertaining to those phrases tend to be in low competence areas, regardless of the input and output tempos of the cases, an obvious conclusion is that the case base lacks musical material sufficiently similar to those phrase, and therefore no good tempo transformations can be constructed for those phrases.

On the other hand, the phrases *Like Someone In Love [phrase A1]*, and *Up Jumped Spring [phrase A1]* (Hubbard) occur on the high competence region of both branches. The latter case proves that even distinct phrases can have shared coverage, and that a solution to one can be helpful to construct a solution of the other (this is possible, since the final solution is constructed from *parts* of other solutions).

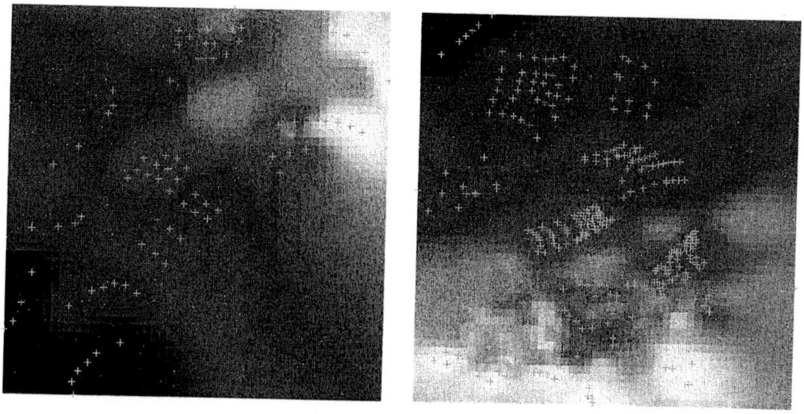

a b

Fig. 6. Two competence branches in isolation

5 Conclusions

We believe that in the design and maintenance of complex CBR systems, the use of tools for analyzing the case base structure become indispensable. Moreover, these analysis tools must be capable of accurately visualizing the complex case base structure in a way that the system designers/users may improve the performance of the CBR system.

In this paper we presented a hierarchical competence model approach, that extends the existing competence model allowing a finer analysis of the case base structure, particularly for CBR systems that perform *synthetic tasks*. Using this hierarchical approach we have proposed a new visualization method for case base competence based on the solution qualities. This method allows us not only to draw 'competence islands' in an 'unsolved ocean', but rather to draw the complete surfaces. The mapping obtained using the proposed method provides valuable information about the way a CBR system behaves in different parts of the problem space. Moreover, some typical competence surfaces have been identified and described.

We wish to add a measure that indicates the faithfulness of the two-dimensional mapping. This is indispensable, since a rigorous reduction in data dimensionality inherently comes with distortion. Especially if more detailed information can be provided about the fidelity/distortion at various regions in the map, this may facilitate the interpretation of the visualized data.

The visualization method has been used for analyzing the case base of the *TempoExpress* system, a CBR system for applying expressivity-aware tempo transformations to recordings of musical performances. Although currently competence maps were only shown as 'snapshot' images, we believe that the approach is very suitable for an interactive case base visualisation tool, where the user can for example zoom in on certain competence areas, or view the effect of raising/lowering the solution-quality threshold on the average case characteristics for a particular competence group.

We plan to use visualization technique presented here in the *T-Air* system, a case-based reasoning application developed for aiding engineers in the design of gas treatment plants [13].

Acknowledgments

This research has been supported by the Spanish project TIC 2003-07776-C2-02 "CBR-ProMusic: Content-based Music Processing using CBR", EU-FEDER funds, and a FPI fellowship.

References

1. Smyth, B., Keane, M.T.: Remenbering to forget: A competence-preserving case delection policy for case-based reasoning systems. In: Proceedings of IJCAI-95. (1995) 377–382
2. Wilson, D.C., Leake, D.B.: Maintaining case-based reasoners: Dimensions and directions. Computational Intelligence **17** (2001) 196–213
3. Reinartz, T., Iglezakis, I., Roth-Berghofer, T.: Review and restore for case-based maintenance. Computational Intelligence **17** (2001) 214–234
4. Smyth, B., McKenna, E.: Competence models and the maintenance problem. Computational Intelligence **17** (2001) 235–249
5. Wybo, J.L., Geffraye, F., Russeil, A.: PROFIL: a decision support tool for metallic sections design using a cbr approach. In Veloso, M., Aamodt, A., eds.: Proceedings of the First International Conference on Case-Based Reasoning (ICCBR-95). Number 1010 in Lecture Notes in Artificial Intelligence. Springer-Verlag (1995) 33–42
6. Smyth, B., Mullins, M., McKenna, E.: Picture perfect - visualization techniques for case-based reasoning. In Horn, W., ed.: ECAI 2000. 14th European Conference on Artificial Intelligence, IOS Press (2000) 65–69
7. Plaza, E., Arcos, J.L.: Constructive adaptation. In Craw, S., Preece, A., eds.: Advances in Case-Based Reasoning. Number 2416 in Lecture Notes in Artificial Intelligence. Springer-Verlag (2002) 306–320
8. Grachten, M., Arcos, J.L., de Mántaras, R.L.: Evolutionary optimization of music performance annotation. In: CMMR 2004. Lecture Notes in Computer Science, Springer (2004)
9. Narmour, E.: The Analysis and cognition of basic melodic structures : the implication-realization model. University of Chicago Press (1990)
10. Lerdahl, F., Jackendoff, R.: An overview of hierarchical structure in music. In Schwanaver, S.M., Levitt, D.A., eds.: Machine Models of Music. The MIT Press (1993) 289–312 Reproduced from Music Perception.
11. Arcos, J.L., Grachten, M., de Mántaras, R.L.: Extracting performer's behaviors to annotate cases in a CBR system for musical tempo transformations. In Ashley, K.D., Bridge, D.G., eds.: Proceedings of the Fifth International Conference on Case-Based Reasoning (ICCBR-03). Number 2689 in Lecture Notes in Artificial Intelligence. Springer-Verlag (2003) 20–34

12. Grachten, M., Arcos, J.L.: Using the Implication/Realization Model for Measuring Melodic Similarity. In: Proceedings of the 16th European Conference on Artificial Intelligence, ECAI 2004, IOS Press (2004)
13. Arcos, J.L.: T-air: A case-based reasoning system for designing chemical absorption plants. In Aha, D.W., Watson, I., eds.: Case-Based Reasoning Research and Development. Number 2080 in Lecture Notes in Artificial Intelligence. Springer-Verlag (2001) 576–588

A Knowledge-Intensive Method for Conversational CBR

Mingyang Gu and Agnar Aamodt

Department of Computer and Information Science,
Norwegian University of Science and Technology, Sem Sælands vei 7-9,
N-7491, Trondheim, Norway
{Mingyang.Gu, Agnar.Aamodt}@idi.ntnu.no

Abstract. In conversational case-based reasoning (CCBR), a main problem is how to select the most discriminative questions and display them to users in a natural way to alleviate users' cognitive load. This is referred to as the question selection task. Current question selection methods are knowledge-poor, that is, only statistical metrics are taken into account. In this paper, we identify four computational tasks of a conversation process: *feature inferencing*, *question ranking*, *consistent question clustering* and *coherent question sequencing*. We show how general domain knowledge is able to improve these processes. A knowledge representation system suitable for capturing both cases and general knowledge has been extended with meta-level relations for controlling a CCBR process. An "explanation-boosted" reasoning approach, designed to accomplish the knowledge-intensive question selection tasks, is presented. An application of our implemented system is illustrated in the car fault detection domain.

1 Introduction

The basic idea underlying case-based reasoning (CBR) is to reuse the old solution to the previous most similar problem in helping solve the current problem. Before we can reuse any existing solution, we have to find the most similar previous problem, corresponding to the retrieve phase in the standard CBR cycle [5].

In the traditional CBR process, users are assumed to be able to give a well-defined problem description (a new case), and based on such a well-defined description a CBR system can find the most appropriate previous case. But this assumption is not always realistic. Users usually only have vague ideas about their problems when beginning to retrieve cases, and often describe them by surface features, while the previous cases have been described by providers using the essential features. Furthermore, even if users understand what their problems are and what aspects they should describe, they do not know exactly what terms to use to express their problems.

In general, the knowledge gap between case users and case providers is a major cause for the difficulty of case retrieval. Users usually input a problem description by "guessing" the appropriate feature terms, and the system either returns too many matched cases or none. Conversational Case-Based Reasoning (CCBR) [6] has been proposed to bridge this knowledge gap.

H. Muñoz-Avila and F. Ricci (Eds.): ICCBR 2005, LNAI 3620, pp. 296 – 311, 2005.

Conversational CBR provides a mixed-initiative dialog for guiding users to refine their problem descriptions incrementally through a question-answer sequence. In the CCBR process, a user's initial problem description is used to retrieve the first set of candidate cases. Subsequent questions, prompted by the CCBR system, will cut down this case set iteratively until a manageable number of cases remain. That is, instead of letting a user guess how to describe her problem, CCBR discovers a sequence of discriminative questions, which help to extract information from the user, and to construct the problem description automatically and incrementally. CCBR applications have been successfully fielded, e.g., in the troubleshooting domain [11, 16] and in the products and services selection in E-Commerce [23].

A core research concern in conversational CBR is how to minimize the cognitive load demanded on users to retrieve their desired cases [23, 22], which requires to select the most discriminative questions [6, 8, 9] and ask them in a natural way in the conversation process [8, 12].

Up to now, several methods, such as the static decision tree [10], the information gain metric [11, 13, 23], the occurrence frequency metric [6], the information quality metric [9], the similarity variance metric[21], and the attribute-selection strategies [20], have been proposed to support question selection in the conversational CBR process. However, all the methods mentioned above are basically knowledge-poor, that is, they only take statistical information into account. The potential that general domain knowledge has for playing a positive role in the question selection process is little explored. For example, if the answer to question B can be inferred from that of question A, or the answer to question A is easier or cheaper to obtain than that to question B, question A should be prompted to users before question B. Such a knowledge-intensive question selection approach can select and display discriminative questions based on their semantic relations rather than only their statistical metrics.

We have identified four tasks in conversational CBR, for which general domain knowledge has a potential to control and improve the process: feature inferencing, question ranking, question clustering, and question sequencing.

Feature Inferencing (FI). If one feature of a problem can be inferred from the current problem description, this feature can be added to the problem description automatically, instead of posing a question to the user. Users are likely not to trust a communicating partner who asks for information that is easy to infer. General domain knowledge (domain rules or domain models) can be used to infer the features implicit in the problem description.

Question Ranking (QR). In the conversation process, the identified discriminative questions need to be ranked intentionally before displaying them to users. An integrated method should be adopted, which uses not only the superficial statistical metrics of the questions, but also the semantic relations among them. For example, if the answer to question C can be inferred from one of the possible answers to question D, it may be better to ask question D first.

Even though an integrated question ranking module outputs a set of sorted questions, their screen arrangement and questioning sequence should not be decided by such a sorted order alone. The main reason lies in that people always hope to inspect or answer questions in a natural way. They would prefer to see a set of questions that are connected by some semantic relations, grouped together, and to answer them in an uninterrupted sequence. These requirements are captured by the following two tasks:

Consistent Question Clustering (CQC). The arrangement of questions on the screen should be consistent, that is, the questions with some semantic relations among them should be grouped and displayed together, and the order of the questions in each group should be decided intentionally. For example, the questions having dependency relations among them should be grouped and displayed together.

Coherent Question Sequencing (CQS). The questions asked in the sequential question-answer cycles should be as related as possible, that is, the semantic contents of two sequential questions should avoid switching too often. For example, if in the previous question-answer cycle a more general question in an abstraction taxonomy is asked, the downward more specific question should be asked in the succeeding cycle rather than inserting other non-related questions between them.

The suggested knowledge-intensive conversational CBR process is illustrated in Fig. 1. The lines in bold are the modules used to complete the tasks identified above.

```
NewCase := New-Case-Formalize(InitialProblemDescription);
SequentQuestions :=null;          //(CQS)
Repeat:
   NewCase := Feature-Inference(NewCase); // (FI)
   SortedRetrievedCases := CBR-Retrieve(NewCase);
   DiscriminativeQuestions := Question-Identify(SortedRetrievedCases, NewCase);
   RankedDiscriminativeQuestions := Integrated-Question-Rank(DiscriminativeQuestions);     // (QR)
   RankedDiscriminativeQuestions :=
        Ranked-Questions-Adjust (SequentQuestions, RankedDiscriminativeQuestions);        // (CQS)
   GroupedRankedDiscriminativeQuestions := Question-Group(RankedDiscriminativeQuestions); // (CQC)
   Display(GroupedRankedDiscriminativeQuestions, SortedRetrievedCases);
   If (users find their desired cases or have no question to answer) then
      Return SelectedCases;
   Else
      SelectedQuestionAndAnswer := User-Select-and-Answer-Question();
      SequentQuestions := Sequent-Question-Identify(SelectedQuestionAndAnswer);          // (CQS)
      NewCase :=NewCase-Update(NewCase, SelectedQuestionAndAnswer);
   End If
```

Fig. 1. The knowledge-intensive CCBR process

In this paper we present an explanation-boosted reasoning approach for support of knowledge-intensive question selection. The use of explanation in case-based reasoning is not new, but the meaning of the term differs. In our approach, the explanation part of the process mainly uses general domain knowledge (rather than specific cases), targeted at system internal reasoning (rather than user understanding). However, the explanations constructed can also be displayed to the user for transparency, justification, and increased understanding. What we mean by explanation-boosted reasoning is a particular method for constructing explanation paths that exploit general domain knowledge for the question selection tasks. The method was briefly introduced in an earlier workshop paper [14], in which only two of the four question selection tasks were described. In the presented paper we extend the description to cover more CCBR tasks, we explicitly relate the tasks with meta-level relations for reasoning, and we present the first implemented version of the system.

The rest of this paper is organized as follows. In Section 2, we identify several semantic relations related to question selection. In Section 3, our explanation-boosted question selection method is described from the perspectives of knowledge representation, explanation construction and reasoning method. The system implementation of this approach, and related research, are summarized in Section 4 and Section 5, respectively. Our conclusion is drawn in Section 6.

2 Semantic Relations for Question Selection

General domain knowledge enables question selection to be based on semantic rather than purely syntactic criteria. Below, we describe a set of semantic relations among features, which influence question selection.

- Feature Abstraction. A feature can be described at different abstraction levels that form a subsumption hierarchy. The lower the level a feature belongs to, the more specifically it can describe the case, but the more difficult it will be to obtain. The appearance of a lower level feature can be used to infer the existence of higher level features. For instance, the feature of "Fuel Transmission Faulty" is a lower level feature than that of "Fuel System Faulty". In [17], Gupta argued that the conversations should follow a downward taxonomic traversal to extract questions from general to specific, which prunes questions deemed irrelevant or implicitly inferred by the taxonomy. Here, we define a relation "subclass of" to express the relation of "feature abstraction". "A is a subclass of B" means A is a lower level feature than B.
- Dependency Relations. A dependency relation between two features exists if the appearance of one feature depends on the existence of the other. For instance, the assertion that the fuel pump can pump fuel depends on that the car has fuel in its fuel tank. We define a relation "depends on" to describe dependency relations. "A depends on B" means B is a necessary condition for A.
- Causality Relations. The causality relation means that one feature can cause the occurrence of another feature. For example, an electricity system fault in a car can cause its engine not to start. Here, we define a relation "causes" to express causality relations. "A causes B" means B is the result of A.
- Co-occurrence Relations. A particular relation, "co-occurs with", is defined to express that two features happen together, even though we cannot tell which one causes the other.
- Answer Acquisition Costs. The costs or difficulties of obtaining answers to different questions are various [11]. For instance, to test whether a switch has a fault is more difficult than to test whether the battery has electricity. The relation "is more costly than" is defined to represent that the answer to one question is more difficult or costly to obtain than the answer to another question.

How the above relations can be used to support the knowledge-intensive question selection tasks is illustrated in Table 1.

Our intention here is not to enumerate all the semantic relations that influence the question selection in conversational CBR, but to give some examples and illustrate how our approach can utilize them to improve the question selection process. System implementors can also define their own semantic relations which they think influence the question selection process. We will show that it is straightforward to add a new semantic relation into the question selection application later in the paper.

Table 1. Semantic relations used in the knowledge-intensive question selection

	Feature Inferencing	Knowledge-Intensive Question Ranking	Consistent Question Clustering	Coherent Question Sequencing
Feature Abstraction (A is a subclass of B)	Inference B from A	Ask A after B	Group A and B together	A succeeds B
Dependency Relations (A depends on B)	Inference B from A	Ask A after B	Group A and B together	A succeeds B
Causality Relations (A causes B)	Inference B from A	Ask B after A	Group A and B together	
Co-occurrence Relations (A co-occurs with B)	Inference B from A; Inference A from B		Group A and B together	
Answer Acquisition Costs (A is more costly than B)		Ask A after B		

3 An Explanation-Boosted Question Selection Approach

In this section, the explanation-boosted question selection approach is described, focusing on three architectural and methodological issues: knowledge representation, explanation construction, and explanation-boosted reasoning method.

3.1 Knowledge Representation

A frame-based knowledge representation model, which is a part of the CREEK system [1, 3, 24], is adopted in our system. In CREEK, both case-specific knowledge and general domain knowledge are captured as a network of concepts and relations, each concept and relation is represented as a frame in a frame-based representation language. A frame consists of a set of slots, representing relationships with other concepts or with non-concept values, e.g. numbers. A relationship is described using an ordered triple $<C_f, T, C_v>$, in which C_f is the concept described by this relationship, C_v is another concept acting as the value of this relationship (value concept), and T designates the relation type, simply called relation. The equation $T = C_v$ can also be used to describe a relationship when C_f is default. Viewed as a semantic network, a concept corresponds to a node and a relation corresponds to a link between two nodes.

In the system presented here, knowledge is represented at two levels. The first is the object-level, in which case-specific knowledge and general domain knowledge are represented within a single representation framework. The second is the meta-level, which is used to express the inter-relations of the semantic relations influencing the question selection tasks.

3.1.1 An Object-Level Knowledge Representation Model

As an illustration of how a case is described, Fig. 2 shows, in a frame view, the contents of a new case in the car fault domain, while Fig. 3 shows, in a semantic network view, a part of the integrated knowledge base for that domain. As can be seen, the semantic relations identified in Section 2 are represented as relations connecting different concepts. Cases are integrated into the general domain model, since all case features are defined as concepts within it.

The relationship values, which have corresponding relationships in the retrieved cases, but do not have the same type relationships in the new case, can be converted into discriminative questions. For example, if the relationship value, "Engine Dose Not Turn", has a relationship in one of the retrieved cases, that is, "has engine status = Engine Does Not Turn", but does not have the same type relationship in the new case, then a discriminative question, "What is the engine status of your car?", is added to the discriminative question list.

We define a function that maps a set of relationship values to a set of questions, Q: relationship value set → question set. On this function, we define the following properties:

– The question transformed from one relationship value is the same as those formed by the relationship values that belong to the same relation type. So we only predefine one question for each relation, which is shared by the relationship values belonging to this relation. For example, Q("Engine Fires") = Q("Engine Turns") = Q("Engine Does Not Fire") = Q("Engine Stops After A Few Seconds") = "What is the engine status of your car?".
– The semantic relations that exist between two relationship values are transferred to the two questions transformed by these two relationship values. For instance, the "causes" relation that "Fuel Pump Damaged" "causes" "Engine Stops After A Few Seconds" is transformed to Q("Fuel Pump Damaged") "causes" Q("Engine Stops After A Few Seconds"). Following the "has question" link to the actual question, "What is the fuel pump status of your car?", it follows that this question "causes" the question "What is the engine status of your car?".

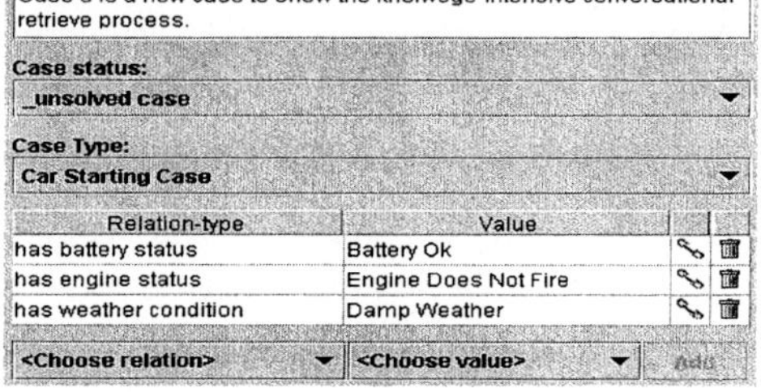

Fig. 2. The frame structure for a car starting case in CREEK

3.1.2 Meta-level Relations and Reflective Reasoning

Four meta-level relations have been defined in order to control the inference processes related to each of the four question selection tasks. For feature inferencing, we define the "*infers*" relation to express that if A infers B, we can get B from the existence of A. This relation has the property of transitivity that if A infers B and B infers C then A infers C. Several semantic relations identified in Section 2, "subclass of", "depends on", "causes" and "co-occurs with" are subclass relations of the "infers" relation since all these relations can be used to infer the existence of the post-condition based on the appearance of the pre-condition.

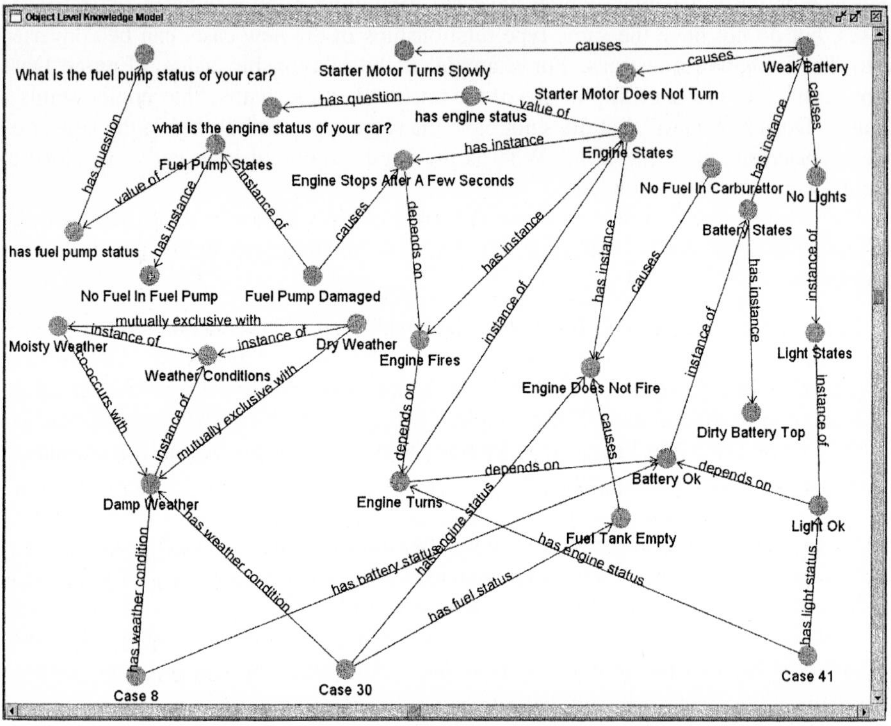

Fig. 3. The "Dialogue" pane in one conversation session

The second metal-level relation, "*appears after*", is defined to complete the question ranking task. "A appears after B" means that Q(A) should be asked after Q(B). This relation also has the property of transitivity that if A appears after B and B appears after C then A appears after C. We define several relations identified in Section 2, "subclass of", "depends on", "caused by" and "is more costly than" as the subclass relations of the "appears after" relation because all these relations can rank the pre-condition question to be asked after the post-condition question.

The third meta-level relation, named "joins", is defined to realize the consistent question clustering task. "A joins B" means that Q(A) should be grouped and displayed together with Q(B). We define several relations identified in Section 2, "subclass of", "depends on", "causes" and "co-occurs with" as subclass relations of the "joins" relation because all the questions connected by these relations should be grouped and displayed together. The transitivity property is not defined on "joins" because we assume that only the questions that have direct "joins" relations between them can be grouped and displayed together.

The last meta-level relation, called "succeeds", is used in the coherent question sequencing task. "A succeeds B" means Q(A) should be asked directly after Q(B) in two sequential question-answer cycles. There are two relations, "subclass of" and "depends on", defined as the subclass relations of this "succeeds" relation. On this basic relation, the transitivity property is also defined, that is, if A succeeds B and B succeeds C, we can get A succeeds C.

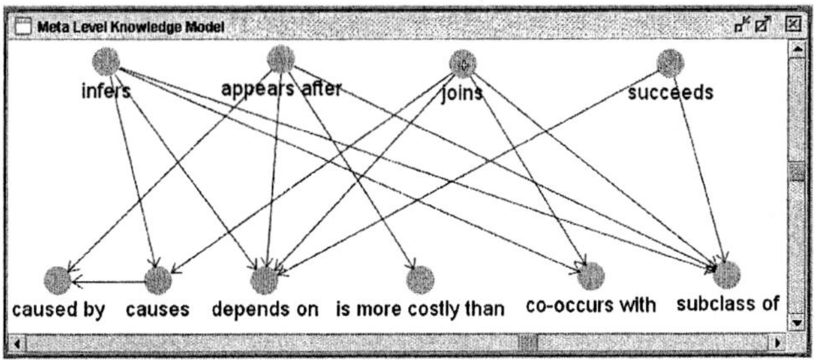

Fig. 4. The structure of the meta-level knowledge representation model

Fig. 4 shows the structure of the meta-level knowledge representation model described above. The top part relations are the meta-level relations defined above, while the bottom part relations are the semantic relations identified in Section 2. The lines from the top part relations to the bottom part relations designate the "has subclass" relations, while the line from "causes" to "caused by" is a "has inverse" relation.

One type of reflective reasoning operation, subclass inheritance, is made explicit in this meta-level knowledge representation model. Subclass inheritance is a special case of the more general "plausible inheritance" mechanism in CREEK [1], and makes subclass relations inherit the properties and reasoning operations (e.g. explanation construction, as introduced in the next sub-section) defined on their parent relation. Thus we need only define the properties and reasoning operations once on the meta-level relations, and all its subclass relations that express much richer domain-specific meanings can inherit them automatically. The other benefit is that new semantic relations can be easily incorporated through defining them as the subclasses of one of the meta-level relations.

3.2 Explanation Construction

Explanation construction is to set up explanation paths between concepts in the semantic network, which are used to explore solutions for particular knowledge-intensive question selection tasks.

We have defined two levels of explanation construction operations. The first level is called "Direct Explanation Construction", which is suitable when there is a direct (local) relation between two concepts. For example, if there are two questions Q(A) and Q(B) and there is a relation "A is a subclass of B", then a direct explanation is constructed that "Q(A) is ranked after Q(B) because A (one possible answer of Q(A)) is a lower level concept than B (one possible answer of Q(B))" in the knowledge-intensive question ranking phase.

The second level is referred to as "Transitive Explanation Construction", which is suitable where there is no direct relation between two concepts in the knowledge base, but we can set up a new semantic relation between them through exploring other relations in the knowledge base.

The transitive explanation construction is based on the transitivity property defined on different relations. In the meta-level knowledge model, we define the transitivity property on the "infers" relation, the "appears after" relation and the "succeeds" relation, and all their sub-class relations can inherit such property from them. So in each relation category (formed by one of these three basic relations and its sub-class relations), all the subclass relations can be transferred on each other to construct new super-class type relations.

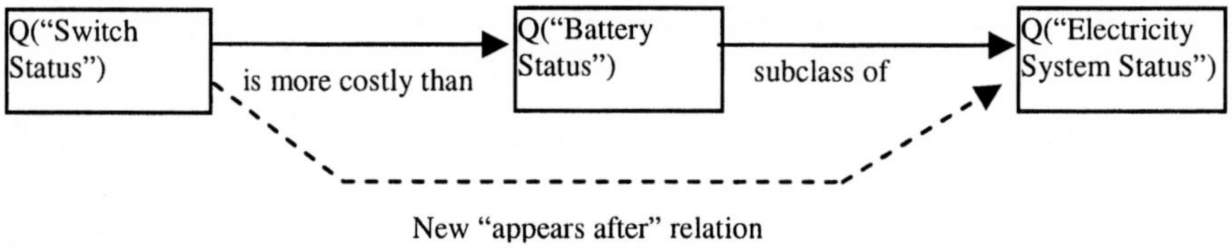

Fig. 5. How to construct a new "appears after" relation

Fig. 5 gives an example of how to build up a new explanation path in the "appears after" relation category through exploring two different subclass relations. In this figure, there are two relations: Q("Switch Status") "is more costly than" Q("Battery Status") and Q("Battery Status") is a "subclass of" Q("Electricity System Status"). Following the "is more costly than" relation and the "subclass of" relation, a new "appears after" relation, Q("Switch Status") "appears after" Q("Electricity System status"), is constructed. Thus if we have two questions Q("Switch Status") and Q("Electricity System Status"), we can rank them through constructing the explanation path that "Q("Switch Status") should be asked after Q("Electricity System Status"), because to answer Q("Switch Status") is more costly than to answer Q("Battery Status"), and Q("Battery Status") is a lower level question than Q("Electricity System Status")" in the concept taxonomy about the electricity system fault.

As discussed in the previous subsection, the "joins" relation does not have the property of transitivity. So we can only use the "Direct Explanation Construction" operation to construct explanations to accomplish the consistent question clustering task.

In the CREEK representation, each relation has a default explanation strength attached to it. The explanation strength of a constructed chain of linked relations, which constitute an explanation path, is calculated on the basis of these defaults (in our implementation introduced in Section 4, we will simply use the product of the defaults to indicate the explanation strength of the constructed explanation path).

3.3 Explanation-Boosted Reasoning Process

The explanation-boosted reasoning process can be divided into three steps: ACTIVATE, EXPLAIN and FOCUS. The three steps, which constitute a general process model for knowledge-intensive CBR, was initially described for the retrieve phase [1], although it applies in principle to all four phases of the CBR cycle. Here this model is instantiated for the different question selection tasks. ACTIVATE determines what knowledge (including case-specific knowledge and general domain knowledge) is involved in one particular task, EXPLAIN builds up explanation paths to explore possible solutions for that task, and FOCUS evaluates the generated explanation paths and identify the best one/ones for that particular task. The operations, done at each step in accomplishing a knowledge-intensive question selection task, are shown in Table 2.

Table 2. Explanation-boosted Reasoning Process in the knowledge-intensive question selection

	Feature Inferencing	Knowledge-intensive Question Ranking	Consistent Question Clustering	Coherent Question Sequencing
ACTIVATE (identify knowledge)	New case features and the related "infers" relations	Discriminative questions and the related "appears after" relations	Sorted questions and the related "joins" relations	Answered questions in the last conversation session and the "succeeds" relations between them and the discriminative questions in current session
EXPLAIN (construct explanation paths)	Feature inferencing explanation paths	Knowledge-intensive question ranking explanation paths	Question clustering explanation paths	Question sequencing explanation paths
FOCUS (evaluate explanation paths and use them to accomplish particular tasks)	The accepted explanations are transformed to new case features	The accepted explanations are combined together with statistical metrics to rank discriminative questions	The accepted explanations are used to group the sorted questions	The accepted explanations are used to re-rank the discriminative question groups

4 System Implementation

We have implemented our proposed approach within the TrollCreek system [2]. TrollCreek is an implementation of CREEK that contains a graphical knowledge model editor and a knowledge-intensive case-based reasoner. Our implementation adds the conversational process with its explanatory mechanism into the retrieve phase.

We are currently exploring two application domains for our CCBR method, car fault detection, and component retrieval for reuse of useful components when developing image processing software [15]. Car fault detection is an example domain adopted in our group for the study of basic knowledge modeling, and representational and reasoning methods, related to particular research directions (e.g. conversational CBR). The knowledge base in this domain incorporates the car fault detection domain knowledge and 29 stored cases. In the graphic window of the knowledge base, we can select an existing case or create a new case to start a knowledge-intensive conversational case retrieve process.

A conversational retrieve process contains one or several conversation sessions (the number of the sessions depends on when the searcher finds her desired case or whether there are still discriminative questions left).

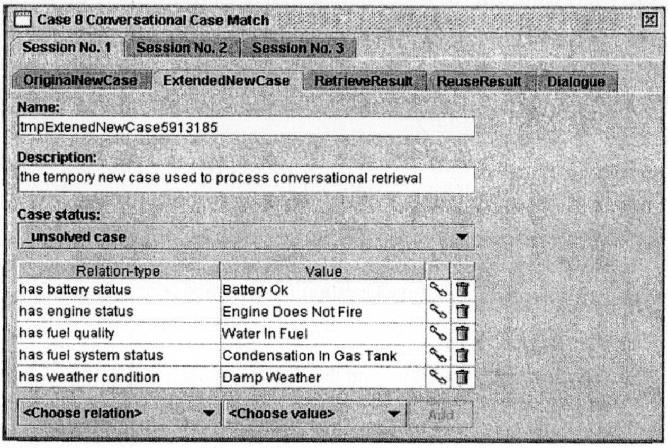

Fig. 6. The "ExtendedNewCase" pane in one conversation session

In the computer interface there are five window panes to move between within each session: The **OriginalNewCase** pane (the example of the content of this pane can be seen in Fig. 2) is used to display the new case in the particular conversation session. The new case extended by the inferred features in the feature inferencing phase is then displayed in the **ExtendedNewCase** pane (as shown in Fig. 6). Based on the extended new case, the CBR retrieve module retrieves a set of sorted cases and displays them in the **RetrieveResult** pane (as illustrated in Fig. 7). In this pane you can inspect the matching details between each retrieved case and the extended new case. The solution for the extended new case is then calculated by the retrieved cases and displayed on the **ReuseResult** pane. If you are not satisfied with the retrieved cases and the reuse result, you can go to the **Dialogue** pane (shown on Fig. 8) to select and answer the discriminative questions, and enter a new conversation session.

The question ranking module divides the identified discriminative questions into two groups: Group one includes the questions that are constrained to be ranked after other questions by some constructed "appears after" explanation paths; Group two contains all the remaining questions. The questions in Group two then gets ranked based on their occurrence frequency metrics [6]. Each question in Group one has one or more "appears after" explanation attached to it. The questions are sorted according to the strongest explanation attached to each questions. Then the ranked questions in Group two are sorted in front of the questions in Group one. If there are some "succeeds" explanation paths between the answered questions in the last conversation session and the current questions, the ranking priority of these involved questions are further increased (putting them in the front of the question queue), and the internal sequence of these "succeeding" questions are decided by their explanation strengths in the "succeeding" explanation paths. The ranked questions are displayed in the Dialogue pane. When each question is selected, its "joined" questions are also displayed in the "Dialogue" pane to prompt the user for further selecting and answering.

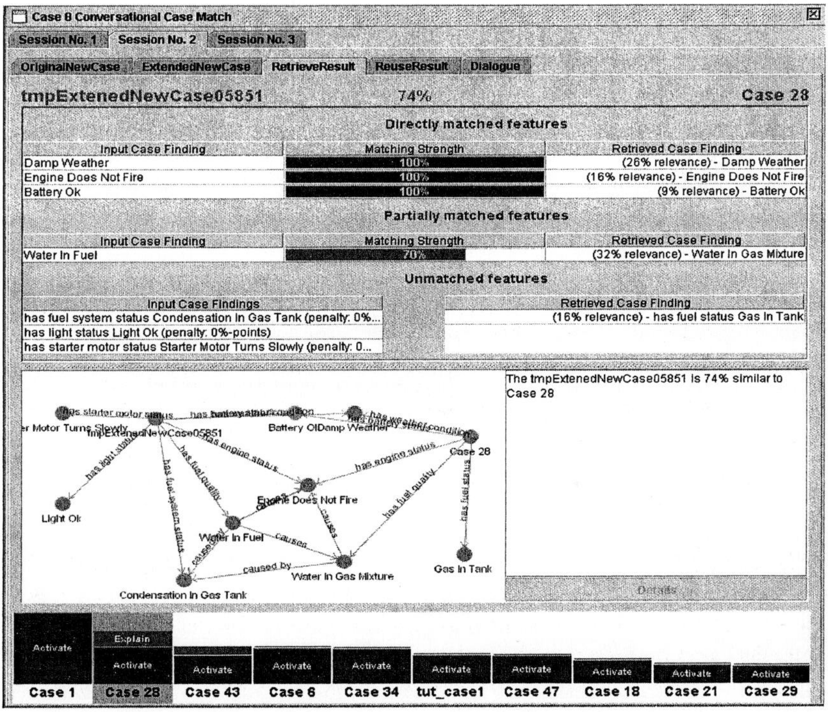

Fig. 7. The "RetrieveResult" pane in one conversation session

Our studies so far indicate that using general domain knowledge as explanatory support in a conversational CBR process improves the focusing of question-asking, and hence reduces the cognitive load needed to identify the best matching case. The target application for empirical testing of our approach will be software component reuse. We are currently building a knowledge base for the components existing in the DynamicImager system [15], a visualization and image processing development environment, in which there are about 200 different image operating components that can be combined in various ways. Our evaluation process will compare component retrieval with and without the explanation method, applied to one-shot vs. conversational CBR retrieval.

5 Related Research

In [22], Schmitt and Bergmann propose a formal model for dialogs between users and a conversation system, in which they identify four important issues in the conversation process: a small number of questions, comprehensible questions, low answering cost of questions and comprehensible question clustering. They also argue that the main reason for the unnatural question sequence during dialogue is due to the ignorance of the relations between different questions. However, they do not give methods about how to incorporate the semantic relations during the dialog process.

In [8], Aha, Maney and Breslow propose a model-based dialogue inferencing (feature inferencing) method. In their method, the general domain knowledge is represented in a library model (including object models and question models) taking the form of a semantic network. At run time, a set of rules are extracted from the library model using an implication rule generator, and the generated rules and the existing problem description are input to a PARKA-DB to infer the implicit knowledge.

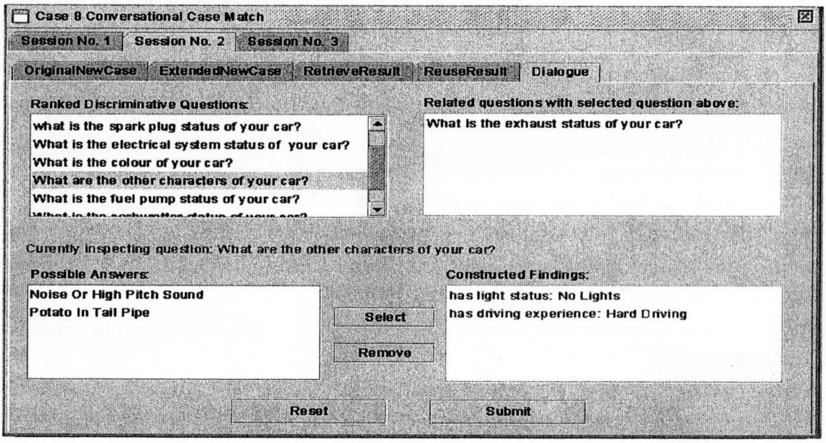

Fig. 8. The "Dialogue" pane in one conversation session

In [17], Gupta proposes a taxonomic conversational CBR approach to tackle the problems caused by the abstraction relations among features. In his approach, cases are described using one or more factors. For each factor, an independent subsumption taxonomy is created by the library designer in advance, and only the most specific feature in each factor taxonomy is selected to describe a case. The similarity between one <question, answer> pair in a case query and one in a case is calculated based on their relative positions in the taxonomy. The question generated from a higher level feature in one factor taxonomy is constrained to be asked before those that come from the lower level features.

Aha, Gupta and Sandhu identify the dependency relation among features [7, 18]. In their method, dependency relations are only permitted to exist between the root nodes among various factor taxonomies and the post-condition node in one dependency relation is excluded from the case representation. In the question ranking step, the question generated from a post-condition node in a dependency relation has higher priority to be asked than the question formalized by the pre-condition node.

Carrick, Yang, Abi-Zeid and Lamontagne try to eliminate the trivial and the repeated questions from users by accessing other information sources to answer them automatically [9]. They take the question answer acquisition costs into account when selecting a task (question) to execute instead of only the information quality metric. In this method, an execution plan is formulated for each question using a hierarchical task network (HTN). The estimated cost for each question is calculated through propagating cost values upward from leaves to the root using the mini-max algorithm.

Comparing with the above knowledge-intensive question selection methods, our approach contributes to the conversational CBR research in two ways: we propose a common integrated framework (including knowledge representation model, explanation construction mechanism and three-step reasoning process) to solve the knowledge-intensive question selection tasks comprehensively (feature inferencing, integrated question ranking, consistent question clustering and coherent question sequencing); and by creating a meta-level knowledge representation model, our approach has the capability to be easily extended to support richer semantic relations that influence the question selection in conversational CBR.

6 Conclusion

The explanation method presented in this paper is based on the CREEK knowledge-intensive CBR approach. The method described extends the existing system with a conversational method and an explanation mechanism targeted at conversational CBR support.

Limitations of the approach include the following two problems. The first is the method's dependence on knowledge engineering. The knowledge base combining both specific cases and general domain knowledge is assumed to exist initially. The construction of this knowledge base puts a significant workload on the development team. However, recent developments in the areas of Knowledge Acquisition and Modeling, as well as Ontology Engineering, provide systematic methods that help reduce this problem [4] . We are also looking into machine learning methods, particularly Bayesian Networks, for solving parts of the problems involved [19] .

The second is conflicting knowledge correction. We store the general domain knowledge in the knowledge base, which explicitly expresses the relations among concepts. However, the knowledge provided by users, including the initial problem description and later answers to discriminative questions, can conflict with this stored general domain knowledge. The problem can be reduced by incorporating an automatic mechanism to detect the knowledge conflicts in order to warn users to revise their new cases, or help knowledge base designers to update the predefined mistaken knowledge.

References

1. Aamodt A. Explanation-driven case-based reasoning. Topics in Case-based reasoning 1994:274-88.
2. Aamodt A. Knowledge-intensive case-based reasoning in Creek. In Funk P, Calero PAG eds. 7th European Conference on Case-Based Reasoning. Madrid, Spain: Spinger, 2004.
3. Aamodt A. A Knowledge Representation System for Integration of General and Case-Specific Knowledge. International Conference on Tools with Artificial Intelligence. New Orleans, 1994:4.
4. Aamodt A. Modeling the knowledge contents of CBR systems. Workshop Program at the Fourth International Conference on Case-Based Reasoning. Vancouver: Naval Research Laboratory Technical Note AIC-01-003, 2001:32 - 7.
5. Aamodt A, Plaza E. Case-Based Reasoning: Foundational Issue, Methodological Variations, and System Approaches. AI Communications 1994;7:39-59.
6. Aha DW, Breslow LA, Munoz-Avila H. Conversational Case-Based Reasoning. Applied Intelligence 2001;14:9-32.
7. Aha DW, Gupta KM. Causal Query Elaboration in Conversational Case-Based Reasoning. International Florida Artificial Intelligence Research Society Conference. Pensacola Beach, Florida, USA, 2002:95-100.
8. Aha DW, Maney T, Breslow L. Supporting Dialogue Inferencing in Conversational Case-Based Reasoning. European Workshop on Case-Based Reasoning. Dublin, Ireland, 1998:262-73.
9. Carrick C, Yang Q, Abi-Zeid I, et al. Activating CBR Systems through Autonomous Information Gathering. International Conference on Case Based Reasoning. Germany, 1999.
10. Cunningham P, Bergmann R, Schmitt S, et al. WEBSELL: Intelligent Sales Assistants for the World Wide Web. KI - Kunstliche Intelligenz 2001;1:28-31.
11. Cunningham P, Smyth B. A Comparison of Model-Based and Incremental Case-Based Approaches to Electronic Fault Diagnosis. Case-Based Reasonging Workshop. Seattle, USA, 1994.
12. Doyle M, Cunningham P. A Dynamic Approach to Reducing Dialog in On-Line Decision Guides. European Workshop on Advances in Case-Based Reasoning. Trento, Italy, 2000:49-60.
13. Göker MH, Thompson CA. Personalized Conversational Case-Based Recommendation. the 5 th European Workshop on Case-Based Reasoning(EWCBR 2000). Trento, Italy, 2000.
14. Gu M, Aamodt A. Explanation-boosted question selection in conversational CBR. ECCBR-04 workshop on Explanation in CBR. Madrid, Spain, 2004:105-14.
15. Gu M, Aamodt A, Tong X. Component retrieval using conversational case-based reasoning. In Shi Z ed. International Conference on Intelligent Information Systems. Beijing, China, 2004.
16. Gupta KM. Knowledge-based system for troubleshooting complex equipment. international Journal of Information and Computing Science 1998;1:29-41.
17. Gupta KM. Taxonomic Conversational Case-Based Reasoning. International Conference on Case-Based Reasoning. Vancouver, BC, Canada, 2001:219-33.
18. Gupta KM, Aha DW, Sandhu N. Exploiting Taxonomic and Causal Relations in Conversational Case Retrieval. European Conference on Case Based Reasoning. Aberdeen, Scotland, UK, 2002:133-47.

19. Langseth H, Aamodt A, Winnem OM. Learning Retrieval Knowledge from Data. In Anand SS, Aamodt A, Aha DW eds. Workshop ML-05: Automating the Consruction of Case-Based Reasoners, in Sixteenth International Joint Conference on Artificial Intelligence. Stockholm, 1999:77 - 82.
20. Mcsherry D. Interactive Case-Based Reasoning in Sequential Diagnosis. Applied Intelligence 2001;14:65-76.
21. Schmitt S. simVar: A Similarity-Influenced Question Selection Criterion for e-Sales Dialogs. Artificial Intelligence Review 2002;18:195-221.
22. Schmitt S, Bergmann R. A Formal Approach to Dialogs with Online Customers. The 14th Bled Electronic Commerce Conference. Bled, Slovenia, 2001:309-28.
23. Shimazu H. ExpertClerk: A Conversational Case-Based Reasoning Tool for Developing Salesclerk Agents in E-Commerce Webshops. Artificial Intelligence Review 2002;18:223 - 44.
24. Sørmo F. Plausible Inheritance: Semantic Network Inference for Case-Based Reasoning. Department of Computer and Information Science. Trondheim: Norwegian University of Science and Technology, 2000:102.

Re-using Implicit Knowledge in Short-Term Information Profiles for Context-Sensitive Tasks

Conor Hayes, Paolo Avesani, Emiliano Baldo[1], and Pádraig Cunningham[2]

[1] ITC-IRST, Via Sommarive 18, 38050 Povo, Trento, Italy
{hayes, avesani}@itc.it
[2] Department of Computer Science, Trinity College Dublin
Padraig.Cunningham@cs.tcd.ie

Abstract. Typically, case-based recommender systems recommend single items to the on-line customer. In this paper we introduce the idea of recommending a user-defined *collection* of items where the user has implicitly encoded the relationships between the items. Automated collaborative filtering (ACF), a so-called 'contentless' technique, has been widely used as a recommendation strategy for music items. However, its reliance on a global model of the user's interests makes it unsuited to catering for the user's local interests. We consider the context-sensitive task of building a compilation, a user-defined collection of music tracks. In our analysis, a collection is a case that captures a specific short-term information/music need. In an offline evaluation, we demonstrate how a case-completion strategy that uses short-term representations is significantly more effective than the ACF technique. We then consider the problem of recommending a compilation according to the user's most recent listening preferences. Using a novel on-line evaluation where two algorithms compete for the user's attention, we demonstrate how a knowledge-light case-based reasoning strategy successfully addresses this problem.

1 Introduction

There have been many research and application initiatives promoting case-based reasoning (CBR) as a suitable recommender methodology for on-line services [27,5]. When a CBR reasoning component is employed to advise on purchasing *configurable* products such as personal computers, holidays and electronic equipment, additional knowledge is required to encode the constraints and dependencies between components. This type of *expert* knowledge is often deployed during the adaptation [24] stage.

In this paper we introduce the concept of recommending a *collection* of items using case-based techniques. A collection is a set of items that have been assembled by a user according to a particular idea or motivation. While it has much in common with a configurable entity, it differs in that the relationships between component parts cannot be described *a priori* in a formal way. Rather, they are *implicitly* encoded by the user during his/her construction of the collection. The recommendation strategies

H. Muñoz-Avila and F. Ricci (Eds.): ICCBR 2005, LNAI 3620, pp. 312–326, 2005.

described in this paper make use of these implicitly encoded *rules of thumb* to provide advice to other users.

Our research is based upon experiments conducted on data from the Smart Radio system, an online streaming music system which allowed users to build collections of music (compilations) which could be recommended to other users with similar tastes [15, 14, 13]. The music domain is a classic example in which an acute knowledge elicitation bottle neck applies [7,9], making it very difficult to extract the expert rules that encode the relationships between music items. However, with the arrival of new on-line music services, consumers are faced with the familiar problem of *information overload* often described for textual material [10,22]. As such, automated collaborative filtering (ACF), a so-called 'contentless' approach to recommendation and personalisation, has dominated in applications in the music domain [14,25,18]. One serious drawback with ACF is that it is not able to make recommendations that are sensitive to the local interests or activities of the user [19].

In this paper we consider two context-sensitive tasks in this domain that cannot be satisfactorily performed using the ACF algorithm.

1. Providing advice to the user when he/she is building a compilation.
2. Recommending a new compilation based on the user's current listening preference.

In previous work Aguzzoli and Avesani proposed a simple case-based recommendation strategy for collections of music items [1]. A key idea here is that long-term user profiles are not used to make recommendations. Instead, each compilation is viewed as representing a short-term, context-specific need. In this paper we reformulate the compilation-building task as an incremental *case completion* exercise. As each track is added to a target compilation, similar compilations are retrieved and the tracks extracted from these compilations are offered to the user to complete the partial compilation. Whereas the experiments in [2] were based on compilations synthesised from a collaborative filtering data set, we present for the first time experiments based on real compilation data collected from users of the Smart Radio system.

We then address the problem of automatically providing a suitable follow-up compilation based on the user's current listening preferences. Using a MAC/FAC [12] approach, compilations retrieved by the ACF algorithm are re-ranked using a knowledge-light, case-based process. In contrast to the evaluation of compilation completion, we demonstrate how an *on-line* evaluation can give a true indication of user satisfaction with one algorithm over another.

Section 2 briefly describes the Smart Radio system operation, and introduces the idea of a compilation, a user-defined collection of music tracks. In Section 3 we describe our solution to the compilation-building task using a case completion strategy, and in Section 4 we introduce the idea of a *context* and the strategy we use to further refine recommendations made by the ACF engine. Section 5 presents an *offline* evaluation of the compilation completion technique. By contrast, Section 6 introduces an *online* evaluation of the context-boosted ACF technique. Finally, we discuss our conclusions and future work in Section 7.

2 Music Recommendation

Although a late starter, the online retail of music has grown rapidly over the past two years. With record companies increasingly making their back catalogues of music available online, consumers are presented with an information overload problem. This problem is exacerbated by the fact that, unlike documents, which can be rapidly downloaded and scanned for relevance, a music file has a longer download time and must be listened to in real time to determine its relevance.

Smart Radio is a web-based client-server application that allows users to build compilations of music that can be streamed to the desktop [15,14,13]. The idea behind Smart Radio is to encourage the sharing of music programmes using automated recommendation techniques (see Figure 1). The unit of recommendation in Smart Radio is the *compilation*, a collection of music tracks assembled on the fly by one listener and recommended to other like-minded listeners.

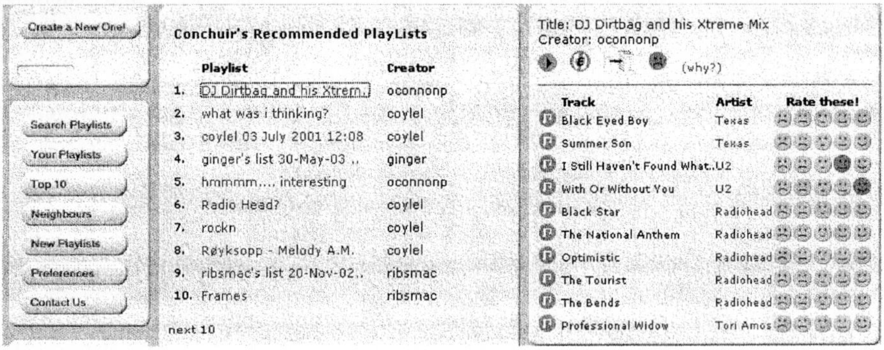

Fig. 1. A screen shot of the Smart Radio recommendation screen

In contrast to text-based information retrieval where a page of text can be automatically parsed into a vector of words, there is great difficulty in extracting fundamental units of meaning equivalent to words from music files [11,7,9]. Typically, some metadata is available such as *genre*, *artist*, *release date*, but this data is sparse, non-standardised and often not useful for prediction purposes.

Thus, music recommender systems such as Smart Radio generally rely upon techniques such as ACF where explicit content mark-up is not required. The key idea in ACF is that users can be clustered together based on their usage patterns. Recommendations can be made to a target user based on the accumulated data in neighbouring user profiles. As similarity between user profiles is calculated based on the intersection of the item ids between profiles and not on content description, ACF allows recommendations to be made in domains like music where there is a *knowledge-elicitation* bottleneck. A second strength of ACF is that it can make recommendations that would otherwise escape content-based recommender strategies. This is because it relies upon *implicit knowledge* expressed in user preferences that may capture the subtle relationship between items that would otherwise escape a content-based system [8]. It is this type of *implicit* knowledge that we wish to explore in this paper.

Recent work in the CBR community has drawn a parallel between ACF and CBR as case completion [16,1]. Despite this, ACF has a weakness that is not apparent in CBR systems. Whereas the CBR case has typically been viewed as capturing a single problem/solution episode, a single ACF user case may capture several heterogeneous episodes reflecting the various interests of the user over time. Thus, the ACF recommender caters to the user's global interests but is unable to make context-sensitive recommendations. In the next section, we describe a solution to this problem by using short-term, task-oriented profiles.

3 Compilation Building as Case Completion

A compilation is a user-defined collection of music, very often made up of a mixture of tracks by different artists, but not necessarily so. We view a compilation as a case that captures a particular short-term music/information requirement. Apart from its component tracks, it also implicitly contains the knowledge and search effort required to assemble the collection. Our hypothesis is that each compilation is built according to an implicitly articulated guiding principle. Thus, each compilation case inherently contains information about the relatedness between component tracks. Indeed, a similar type of 'relatedness' information, useful for accurate recommendation, has been mined from lists of favourite artists posted by music fans on the Web [8].

In Smart Radio, a compilation consists of a collection of 10 tracks that is assembled for *immediate* delivery using streaming protocols. Thus, the user must choose the composition of the compilation with care because once the compilation has started to play, its composition cannot be modified. In the next subsection, we describe how we allow users to reap the benefit of the compilation-building expertise of previous users.

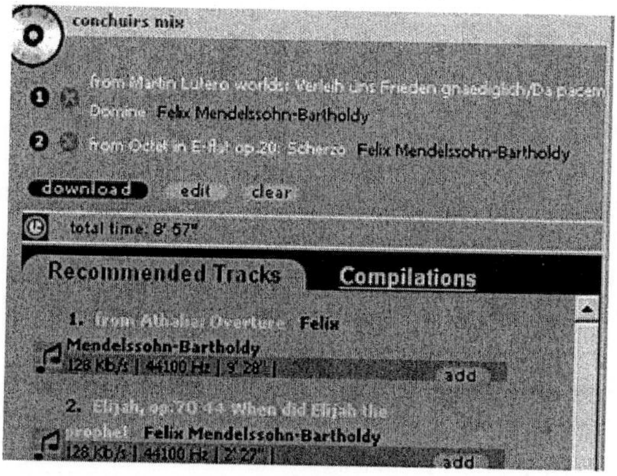

Fig. 2. A screen shot of a compilation advisor system

3.1 The Compilation Completion Advisor

Building a compilation is a context-sensitive task where tracks are selected according to a particular theme or idea of the user. The key to this approach is to realise that a short-term profile can capture a single problem-solving episode that is better able to provide context-sensitive recommendations. Thus, instead of using user profiles to make recommendations we choose to tap the specific knowledge in other compilations.

In earlier work Aguzzoli & Avesani have described the basic mechanism for recommending compilations [1]. The process is akin to the interactive case completion methodology of the NaCoDAE system [2]. As the user adds tracks to a compilation, the retrieval engine retrieves similar compilations by ranking the compilations in the case base according to similarity to the partial compilation. It then offers the user a choice of the top 10 ranked compilations (the top ranked compilation is displayed by default) or a list of tracks ranked by frequency of occurrence from the top 10 ranked compilations (see Figure 2). The process iterates until the maximum number of tracks in a compilation has been achieved. In the case of the Smart Radio system this is 10.

Using a compilation as a short-term profile is problematic in that similarity can only be measured on items shared in common between compilation profiles. As a compilation is made up of 10 out of a possible 2148 tracks, many compilations cannot be compared because they do not have any tracks in common. In contrast, a typical user profile would contain tracks from many sessions and thus have a better chance of intersecting with other profiles. We address this problem using the *agave* algorithm to reduce the sparsity of the compilation data set [1]. Using agave, each compilation is transformed from binary vector (of component tracks) to a vector of *mu* values where each *mu* value represents the degree of relatedness between the compilation and each track in the data set. Thus, compilations can be easily matched using metrics like the Pearson coefficient. In earlier work Avesani & Aguzzoli have demonstrated that agave performs better than singular value decomposition (SVD), another technique for reducing sparsity in ACF data sets [1]. In Section 5, using compilations collected from real users, we evaluate the compilation advisor at different stages of compilation completion.

4 Recommending Compilations in Context

Whereas in section 3 we described how we used the implicit compilation-building knowledge to help the user build a compilation, we now turn our attention to recommending a full compilation. Many of the same issues still apply. Using a typical ACF strategy, recommended compilations may not suit the user's current compilation preferences. Our goal is to make recommendations that are appropriate within the user's listening context.

In the field of user modelling, the objective in isolating context information is that tasks being undertaken by the user may be anticipated and a portion of the work carried out automatically in advance. Applications such as Watson [4] and Letizia [20], which monitor the user's behaviour and attempt to retrieve or predict relevant information, have been termed 'reconnaissance aides'. In both Watson and Letizia the context is represented by a content-based analysis of the topics currently of interest to the user. If the user digresses or switches subject while researching a topic, both reconnaissance aides will require time to respond. However, the advantage of an implicitly generated profile is that it is a "zero input" strategy, i.e. the user does not need to explicitly describe his/her goals [20].

Using a zero input strategy, our goal is to enhance the ACF technique so that compilations based on the user's current context are promoted. We use a MAC/FAC influenced methodology to achieve this:

1. The ACF module selects a subset of the compilation case base.
2. These primed cases are then ranked according to their similarity to the user's listening context.

This process is indicated in Figure 3 where the darker shaded cases to the right represent cases ranked by similarity to the user's listening context.

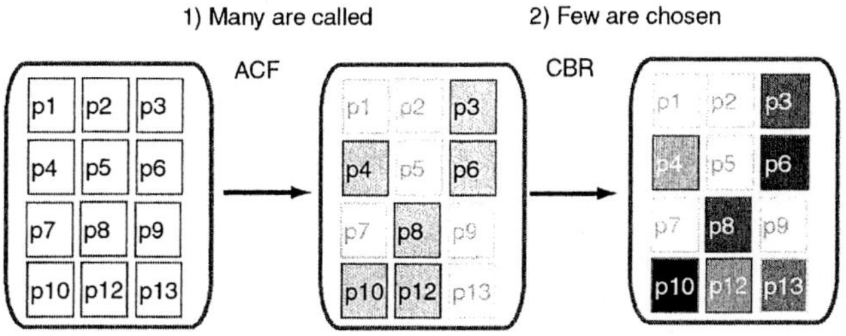

Fig. 3. The two-stage strategy for providing context-sensitive recommendations

4.1 ACF Module

The typical ACF matrix (users X ratings) is based on the ratings (explicit and implicit) that users have assigned tracks. Thus, the correlation between users is calculated based on tracks from compilations users had built or played. A neighbourhood is formed for a target user and a set of candidate compilations that the user has not yet heard is extracted from the neighbour profiles. In order to rank these compilations the ACF module makes a prediction for the component tracks not rated by the user. The overall score for a compilation is a weighted sum of the predictions or real scores for the tracks in a compilation where the weight is a user preference for the fraction of unfamiliar music in a compilation [14].

Unlike typical ACF systems where items are recommended once only (and accepted or rejected by the user), compilations are recycled in Smart Radio. The rationale is that people are receptive to listening again to music they like as long as the time between repeats is not too short. So during the compilation ranking phase, if the top recommended compilation did not meet a threshold, we performed the compilation extraction process again, this time considering compilations (by other users) that the user had already listened to *n* days earlier. We set n = 30.

Furthermore, in order that we do not recommend compilations containing tracks the user has just recently played we employ a 'refractory period' of several hours for each track played by a user. Compilations with a high overall refractory period are not considered for recommendation for the user. However, once the period has expired those compilations can be considered for recommendation again.

4.2 Case Ranking Module

Unlike the examples of the *reconnaissance* aides described above, which used information retrieval analyses to build a short-term user profile, the Smart Radio domain suffers from a deficit of content descriptions. Therefore, the solution is to use a lightweight case-based representation of each compilation using some freely available meta-data. The content descriptors we use are the *genre* and *artist* tags found in a few bytes of information at the end of the mp3 file. Although the information this inexpensive process yielded was not particularly rich, the alternatives in the music domain are expensive. We transform the compilation representation into a *case-based* representation where the case features indicate the *genre/artist* mixture within the compilation. Our goal is to capture the type of music mix, using the available features that would best indicate this property. We have two feature types associated with each track, `genre_` and `artist_`. The case representation we used in Smart Radio is illustrated in Table 1.

Table 1. A case captures the composition of the compilation in terms of the quantity of genres and artists present. For reasons of space only one artist feature is shown

Feat. type	Feature	Value
genre_	Jazz	1
genre_	Blues	2
genre_	Folk	3
genre_	Country	4
artist_	John Coltrane	1

By playing a compilation the user triggers a context event. The contents of the compilation are assumed to indicate the user's current listening preference. We term this *contextualising by instance*. The transformed compilation has two types of features: `genre_` features and `artist_` features. The currently playing compilation is used as the target for which we try and find the most similar cases available from the compilation cases retrieved by the ACF step. Compilation similarity is determined by matching the proportions of genre and artist contained in a compilation [13].

In section 6, we present an online evaluation of this technique where we test user response to recommendations presented from the context-boosted ACF strategy and the standard ACF strategy.

The content-based strategy in Smart Radio evolved through our identification of the problem of insensitivity to user context in version 1.0 of the system. For this reason, the content-based strategy was always designed as an augmentation of the primary ACF strategy. Within the taxonomy of hybrid strategies suggested by Burke, the Smart Radio hybrid is best described as a *Cascading* system [6]. Unlike the *EntreeC* system, another type of Cascading hybrid, the Smart Radio system uses ACF as its primary recommendation strategy and the content-based ranking as a supplemental process. A complete description of the integrated ACF–CBR approach we adopt is beyond the scope of this paper. Readers are directed to [13] for a more in-depth discussion of the similarity techniques and the architecture we use.

5 Off-line Evaluation of Case Completion

As we described in section 3, compilations are built according to the 'expert knowledge' of users. In this section we describe an offline evaluation performed on real compilation data collected from Smart Radio listeners. The evaluation had the following objectives:

1. To demonstrate that short-term information profiles are more successful than typical long-term profiles for a context-sensitive task such as compilation completion.
2. To evaluate whether completion information should be based on individually retrieved compilations or an aggregation of tracks from the *k*-nearest neighbours.

5.1 Compilation Completion

Our evaluation strategy involved simulating a case completion process whereby we measured recall at different stages of case completion. The recall measure represents the probability that a relevant item will be retrieved. Each compilation in the case base is a unique, user-defined collection of music. A *leave-one-out* approach was used whereby we removed a percentage of tracks for each compilation. By retrieving a set of *k*-nearest compilations we then attempted to predict the missing tracks. In order to simulate performance at difference levels of completion, the missing tracks were removed in increments of 10%. In calculating recall at each percentage of the partially completed compilation, the relevant set refers to the set of items removed. The algorithms we used are described below.

- **TopN:** This technique was used as a baseline approach. We recommend the *N* most frequent tracks in the data set.
- **Order-based:** Collections assembled by users are biased in terms of the order in which users are presented with candidate items by the system interface. For instance, the Smart Radio file browser orders tracks alphabetically by artist. Users will have a tendency to include some tracks in their compilations that are 'nearby', such as tracks by the same artist or from the same album. The order-based technique tests the extent of this bias by recommending the next *n* tracks (as presented by the Smart Radio file browser) to the last track in the partial compilation. Tracks already in the compilation are not considered. $n = 10$.
- **Overlap_Userbased_knn_topN:** This is the standard user-based ACF algorithm. We represent the data in the training set as a set of long-term user profiles containing tracks from the compilations that the user has downloaded in the past. Using the overlap method, recommendations are made by firstly retrieving the best matching user profiles (*k*nn) for the target compilation and then choosing the most frequently occurring items in the retrieved profiles (topN) [23]. However, as each user profile has a binary representation in terms of tracks, similarity between the target and candidate profiles is based on the amount of overlapping tracks.

- **Overlap_Comp-based_knn_topN:** We then retrieve compilations rather than user profiles using the *overlap* method as before. Again, track recommendations are made by choosing the most frequently occurring items in the retrieved profiles.

The next three approaches use agave sparsity reduction. We make recommendations based on the first *k* compilations retrieved.

- **Agave_P_knn:** The similarity metric is the Pearson coefficient. Recommended items are presented in the order they occur in the *k* ranked compilations. Items already in the target compilations and any lower ranking duplicate items are removed.
- **Agave_LS_knn_topN:** The similarity metric is based on the Least Squares metric used by Shardanand and Maes [25]. Recommended items are ranked according to their frequency in the *k* compilations.

5.2 Evaluation Methodology

The Smart Radio data set contains 803 compilations built by listeners to the Smart Radio system from a corpus of 2148 tracks. Each compilation has 10 tracks. Each compilation in the data set is evaluated using the *leave-one-out* methodology. When we use the agave approach we recalculate the *mu* scores using the data set minus the compilation being tested. For each compilation test, recall is measured at incremental stages of completion. For example, in the first test we remove 90% of the compilation. The remaining 10% is used as the target and the 90% we removed acts as the relevant set with which we can calculate the recall score for the retrieved tracks. We continue to test in increments of 10% until we finally evaluate recall when 90% of the compilation is present and 10% acts as the relevant set. In each test, the retrieval size is set at 10 compilations. However, the *Agave_P_knn* algorithm only used the track data in the first or second compilation. In measuring recall, we consider the ranked list of tracks produced by each algorithm. Tracks already found in the target compilation or duplicates of tracks already ranked higher in the retrieval list are considered non-relevant items for the purpose of calculating recall.

5.3 Results

Figure 4 illustrates the Recall graph for case completion where the x axis represents the percentage of the compilation used as the target compilation. Clearly, the *topN* and *user-based* approaches perform very poorly when faced with a context-specific task. The *comp-based* approach, which utilises short-term profiles in the form of other compilations, performs significantly better even though the similarity is based only on compilation overlap. The *order-based* approach performs relatively well suggesting that users are influenced by the logical ordering of tracks by artist and album. The order-based approach performs worse than the comp-based approach up to the 60% mark. At the 90% level, however, its performance jumps to match the best performing algorithms. This suggests that at 90% of compilation completion users tend to opt for a nearby track in order to terminate the compilation building process. Clearly, however, the algorithms that use the short-term profiles and the agave sparsity reduction techniques perform best overall.

The difference between the performance of the user-based approach and the approaches based on compilation retrieval seems to be due to the loss of context information in the user profiles.

One of our objectives was to test whether presenting compilations in the order they are ranked by the similarity metric is an adequate recommendation strategy. Our hypothesis is that the first 1 or 2 ranked compilations are likely to contain sufficient track information to complete the test compilation. In fact, *agave_P_knn* perform very well indeed. These algorithms represent the view the user would have when choosing the 'compilations' tab in Figure 2. All the other algorithms aggregate the track data from the *k*-nearest compilations, ranking them by frequency, for example. This is equivalent to the view in the 'tracks' tab of Figure 2. Our evaluation suggests that the knowledge contained in the first two top-ranking compilations is strong enough to compete with the aggregated data from *k* compilations.

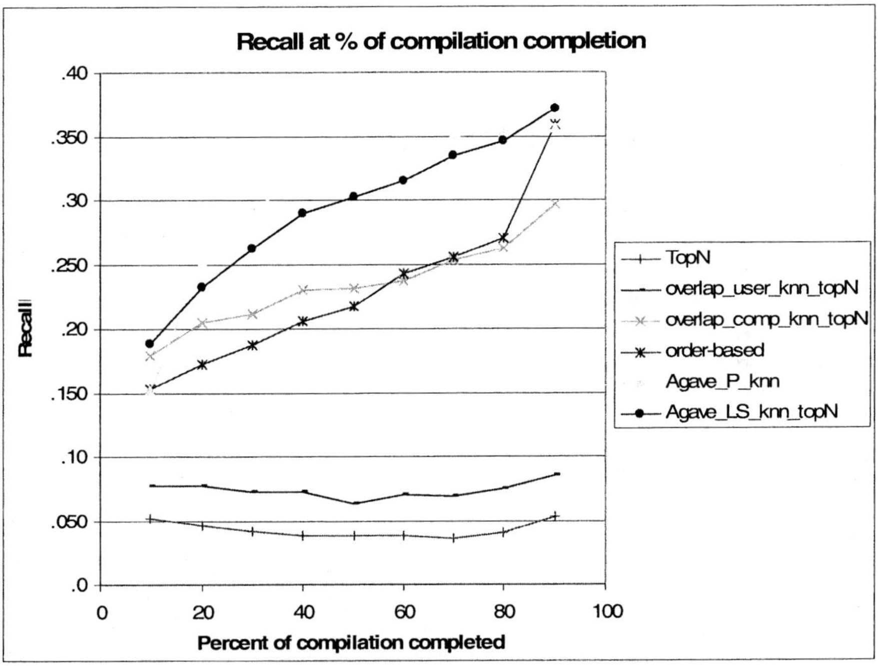

Fig. 4. Recall graph for compilation completion

6 An *Online* Evaluation of Context-Boosted ACF vs. ACF

The evaluation in section 5 is an example of an *off-line* evaluation of a recommender strategy which is typically based on techniques in machine learning and information retrieval [3]. However, it has been regularly observed that off-line evaluations of recommender systems have a number of shortcomings [26,17,19]. For example, it is not at all clear whether users are sensitive to slight improvements in prediction error of one algorithm over another. Secondly, an algorithm can only be evaluated on predictions it makes on items that have been observed by the user, which may be only a fraction of the overall items in the domain. Thus, in an offline evaluation, there is no way of measuring 'true recall' because we are unable to measure the potential relevance of items that have not been rated by the user.

This problem is particularly apparent when evaluating the success of a recommender strategy like the content-boosted ACF where we need to analyse the correctness of the ranking produced in response to a context event. It was not clear how we might perform this in an off-line setting. Therefore, to test our hypothesis we performed a comparative analysis of how the algorithm performs in an *online* setting. Unlike the off-line analysis, this methodology plays one recommendation strategy against the other in a live system and measures the *relative* degree of success of each strategy according to whether the user utilises the recommendations of either system. A more detailed discussion of our on-line evaluation framework for recommender systems is presented in [17].

6.1 Evaluation Environment

The evaluation environment was the Smart Radio system – a live, on-line application used by a community of users, with a well defined recommendation task using a specific user interface. The application was serviced by two competing recommendation strategies: ACF and context-boosted ACF. The ACF implementation was that described in Section 4.1. The context-boosted ACF implementation deployed the same ACF technique described in Section 4.1 but then re-ranked the results using the case-based ranking described in Section 4.2.

In order to be able to gauge a relative measure of user satisfaction with the two strategies, we logged the user interactions with respect to the recommendations made by either strategy. Other aspects of the recommendation process that might have influenced user satisfaction were kept the same (interface, interaction model). The proposed methodology can be seen as a competition between two different approaches to solving the same problem (in this case, winning user satisfaction). In this regard, we define three evaluation policies.

Presentation Policy: The recommended compilations in Smart Radio were presented as a ranked list. For evaluative purposes, we *interleaved* recommendations from each strategy. As a user is most likely to inspect the top-ranked compilation in the recommendation set, this position is alternated between each recommender strategy after each compilation 'play' event.

Evaluation Policy defines how user actions can be interpreted to express a preference for one algorithm over the other. In this evaluation, a preference was registered for one strategy when a user inspected and then played a compilation from his/her recommendation set.

Comparison Policy defines how to analyse the evaluation data in order to determine a winner. Obviously, the simplest way is to count the number of rounds won by the competing systems. However, certain algorithms, such as ACF, may only start to perform well after sufficient data has been collected. Therefore, we analyse the performance of each system over time. As individual users may have different degrees of interaction with the system, we provide a comparative analysis of users based on how intensively they used the system.

6.2 Results

The results refer to the listening data of 58 users who played a total of 1012 compilations during the 101-day period from 08/04/2003 until 17/07/2003. Table 3 gives the breakdown of the sources of compilations played in the system for this period. The recommendation category was by far the most popular means of finding compilations. Building compilations from scratch or explicitly searching for compilations should not be considered 'rival' categories to the recommendation category given that an ACF-based system requires users to find a proportion of new items from outside the recommendation system itself.

Cumulative Score: Table 3 gives the cumulative breakdown between ACF and context-boosted ACF recommendations for the period. From a total of 504 recommended compilations played, 311 were sourced from context-boosted recommendations, while 177 came from normal ACF recommendations. 16 came from bootstrap recommendations, which we haven't discussed here.

Interval-Based Evaluation: In order to check that these results were consistent throughout the evaluation period, we divided the period into 15 intervals of one week. Figure 8 shows the proportions of ACF to context-boosted recommendations analysed on a weekly basis for the period. We can see that the context-boosted ACF outperformed the pure ACF recommendation strategy in all but one of the intervals. We have tested these results using a paired *t*-test and found them to be statistically significant within a confidence level of 99%.

User-based Evaluation: An analysis of our users' behaviour demonstrated considerable variance. During the evaluation period we had users who used the system several times a week, sometimes for hours every day, as well as other users who used the system much less frequently. In order to check that the performance of our recommender holds for different degrees of usage, we split the dataset according to the number of compilations each user listened to. There are 10 categories in which users may fall, representing different degrees of usage of the system. Figure 9 illustrates the comparative success of the two strategies in each usage range.

Whilst ACF is marginally greater in two intervals, if we use a paired *t*-test on the individual user recommendation data we find that the hypothesis, ACF $\leq$ context-boosted ACF, once again holds with a confidence level of 95%. However, Figure 3 would suggest that the preference for context-boosted ACF is more pronounced among regular users of the system. Light users simply might not have used the system enough to have formed a preference for either recommendation strategy. Heavier users, on the other hand, have a much greater chance to explore the facilities of the system and implicitly express preferences for one strategy over another through regular use.

Table 2. Source of compilations played from 24:00 08/04/2003 until 24:00 17/07/2003

Source	Number	Percentage
Top Compilations	87	8
Past Compilations	194	19
Trusted Neighbour	23	2
Recommendations	504	50
Explicit Search	94	9
Compiled from Scratch	110	11

Table 3. The cumulative scores for the ACF vs. context-boosted ACF analysis

Algorithm name	Number of 'play' events	Percentage
Standard ACF	177	35
Context-boosted ACF	311	62

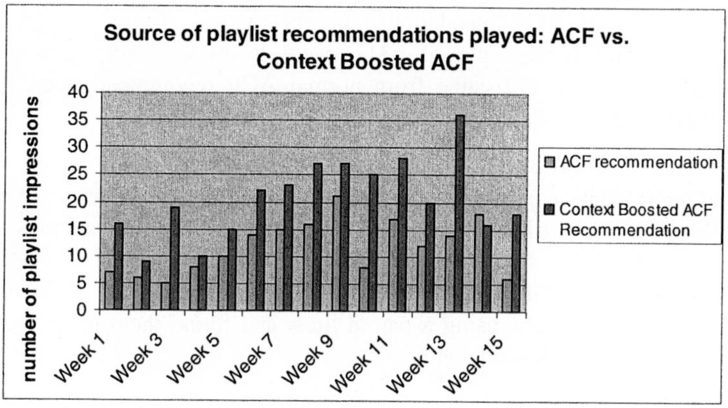

Fig. 5. ACF vs. context-boosted ACF over 15 weekly intervals

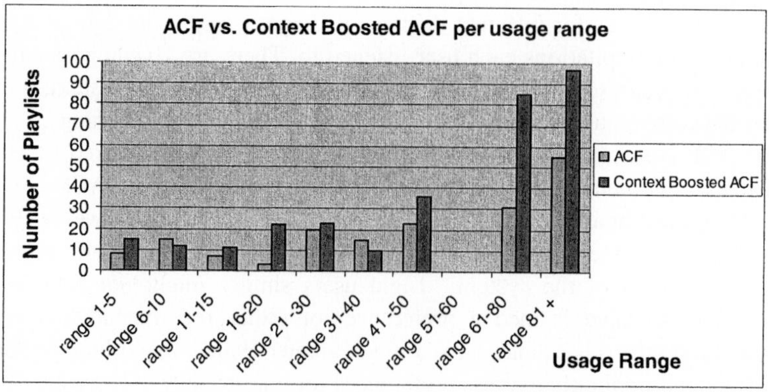

Fig. 6. A user-based analysis of the evaluation

7 Conclusions

In this paper we demonstrate the importance of considering the context of the online user's interests or tasks. In the domain of music, however, there is great difficulty in extracting content or knowledge with which to model user profiles. Conventionally, the ACF technique is used. However, ACF makes recommendations based on a global model of the user's interests. We show how short-term profiles in the form of collections of music are much more successful in providing advice in the compilation-building exercise. The key observation we make is that such short-term collections contain implicit knowledge as to the relatedness of their component tracks. However, we note that typical off-line approaches are limited to evaluating algorithmic performance on items the user has rated in the past. In our second evaluation we demonstrate how an online test gives evidence of user satisfaction with one strategy over another. In particular, we show user preference for a context-enhanced ACF algorithm over a standard ACF algorithm.

We recognize that our concept of context is defined specifically by the music domain. A compilation gives us a convenient, short-term representation of the user's local listening interests. Without such a structure, the division of a user's browsing habits into categories is much more problematic. However, our approach does demonstrate that where a user must make informed choices about assembling related objects, tapping the implicit knowledge from previous user knowledge is helpful.

Furthermore, the knowledge-light approaches in this paper are motivated by the difficulty of extracting rich content description for music. If richer content was available, the possibility of using more sophisticated case-based techniques for music retrieval would be very attractive. Unfortunately, for the moment, several recent reviews in the field of music retrieval would suggest that the problem of capturing and representing the semantics of musical artifacts in a scalable way is far from being solved [7,9].

References

1. Aguzzoli, S., Avesani, P., Massa, P. Collaborative case-based recommender systems. In ECCBR 2002, Aberdeen, Scotland, Springer Verlag, 2002.
2. Aha, D. W., Maney, T., Breslow, L. Supporting dialogue inferencing in conversational case-based reasoning. EWCBR 1998, Dublin, Ireland, pp. 262–273, 1998.
3. Breese, J.S., Heckerman, D., Kadie, C. Empirical analysis of predictive algorithms for collaborative filtering. In Proceedings of the 14th Annual Conference on Uncertainty in Artificial Intelligence, pp. 43–52, July 1998.
4. Budzik, J., Hammond, K. J. User interactions with everyday applications as context for just-in-time information access. In Proc. of the 2000 International Conference on Intelligent User Interfaces, (New Orleans, Louisiana, USA), ACM Press, 2000.
5. Burke, R., (ed). Proceedings of the workshop on Case-based Reasoning in Electronic Commerce. ICCBR, Vancouver, BC. 2001
6. Burke, R., Hybrid Recommender Systems: Surveys and Experiments in User Modelling and User-Adapted Interaction 12(4): 331-370; Kluwer press, Nov 2002..
7. Byrd, D., Crawford, T. Problems of music information retrieval in the real world, Information Processing and Management: an International Journal, v.38 n.2, 2002

8. Cohen, W., Fan, W. Web-collaborative filtering: Recommending music by crawling the web. In Proceedings of the Ninth International World Wide Web Conference, 2000.
9. Downie, J. Stephen. Music information retrieval (Chapter 7), In: Cronin, Blaise (Hg.) Annual Review of Information Science and Technology 37: Information Today Books, pp.295-340, 2003
10. Foltz, P.W., Dumais, S.T. Personalized information delivery: An analysis of information filtering methods. Communications of the ACM 35(12), 51–60, 1992
11. Foote, J., an overview of Audio information retrieval. Multimedia Systems 7: 2–10 Springer Verlag, 1999.
12. Gentner, D., Forbus, K. D., MAC/FAC: A model of similarity based access and mapping. In Proc. of the 13th Annual Conference of the Cognitive Science Society. Erlbaum
13. Hayes, C., Cunningham, P. Context Boosting Collaborative Recommendations. In the Journal of Knowledge Based Systems, Volume 17, Issue 5-6, July 2004, Elsevier, 2004
14. Hayes, C., Cunningham, P., Clerkin, P., Grimaldi, M. Programme-Driven Music Radio. In the proc. of ECAI 2002, Lyons France ed.: Frank van Harmelen, IOS Press, 2002
15. Hayes, C., Cunningham, P., SmartRadio–community based music radio; Knowledge Based Systems, special issue ES2000, Volume 14, Issue3-4, , Elsevier, 2001
16. Hayes, C., Cunningham, P., Smyth, B. A case-based reasoning view of automated collaborative filtering, in: Aha, D.W., Watson, I. (Eds.), Proc. of 4th International Conference on Case-Based Reasoning, LNAI 2080. Springer Verlag, pp. 234–248, 2001
17. Hayes, C., Massa, P., Avesani, P., Cunningham, P., An on-line evaluation framework for recommender systems in the proceedings of the IWorkshop on Recommendation and Personalization Systems, AH 2002, Malaga, Spain, 2002. Springer Verlag.
18. Hayes, C., Smart Radio: Building Community Based Radio. PhD thesis. Department of Computer Science. Trinity College Dublin, 2004
19. Herlocker, J. L., Konstan, J. A., Terveen, L. G., and Riedl, J. T. Evaluating Collaborative Filtering Recommender Systems. In Proceedings of the ACM Transactions on Information Systems, vol. 22, no. 1, pp. 5-53, 2004
20. Lieberman, H., Fry, C., and Weitzman, L., Exploring the Web with Reconnaissance Agents," Communications of the ACM, Vol. 44, No. 8, August 2001.
21. Resnick, P., Iacovou, N., Suchak, M., Bergstrom, P., Riedl, J. An Open Architecture for Collaborative Filtering of Netnews. pp. 175-186. ACM Conference on Computer Supported Co-operative Work, 1994.
22. Resnick, P., Varian, H. R. Recommender Systems. Communications of the ACM 40(3), 56–58, 1997
23. Sarwar, B., Karypis, G., Konstan, J., Riedl, J. Analysis of recommendation algorithms for e-commerce, in: Proceedings of ACM E-Commerce, 2000
24. Schmitt,S., Bergmann, R. Applying Case-Based Reasoning Technology for Product Selection and Customization in Electronic Commerce Environments. In Proc. of 12th International Bled Electronic Commerce Conference, Bled, Slovenia, June 7 - 9, 1999
25. Shardanand, U., and Mayes, P., Social Information Filtering: Algorithms for Automating 'Word of Mouth', in Proceedings of CHI95, 210-217, 1995.
26. Swearingen, K., Sinha, R., Beyond Algorithms: An HCI Perspective on Recommender Systems, ACM SIGIR Workshop on Recommender Systems, 2001.
27. Wilke, W., Lenz, M., Wess, S. Case-Based Reasoning for Electronic Commerce. In: Lenz et al. (Eds.): Case-Based Reasoning Technology from Foundations to Applications, Springer, 1998.

Acquiring Similarity Cases for Classification Problems

Andrew Kinley

Fordham University
kinley@cis.fordham.edu

Abstract. The situation assessment and similarity components of the interpretive case-based reasoning process are integral for a successful case retrieval. However, for classification problems there are domains where it can be difficult to define sets of relevant features to extract from a problem description. Likewise it is not always obvious which of these features to apply to the similarity assessment process and what, if any, weights they should be given. We suggest learning the concept of similarity by training on a set of past situations. Rather then develop a general function, we store the knowledge gained in individual similarity comparisons as similarity cases. These similarity cases define a similarity space that can be searched to identify how new problem situations can be classified. This paper describes our approach of acquiring similarity cases in the context of a straightforward classification task. A proof of concept system was built that creates similarity cases from a repository of known spam email messages and can use the similarity cases to classify unknown messages as positive or negative examples of spam.

1 Introduction

Case-based reasoning (CBR) solves problems by retrieving prior problem solving episodes and reusing the past solutions as basis for solving and or interpreting the current situation. The success of the retrieval is based in large part on accurate situation assessment of the current input problem and employing appropriate similarity criteria. In some problem domains it can be difficult to predefine the most relevant set of features to extract from a problem description for use in similarity assessment. Further, when and how to apply the sets of features to specific problems may require a more complete domain theory than is available. The classification of spam email messages is one such domain that is not only ill-defined but suffers from problems such as *concept drift*[1] and ongoing and deliberate attempts to disguise itself as legitimate email.

In this paper, we present an approach of acquiring similarity knowledge through supervised learning to build specific instances of feature sets that capture the essence of successful similarity assessments. These feature sets are recorded as *similarity cases*. These similarity cases can then be used as a basis for interpretive CBR on classification tasks. Each similarity case is constructed from the subset of features most responsible for the similarity between two training examples. The similarity cases represent different views and interpretations

H. Muñoz-Avila and F. Ricci (Eds.): ICCBR 2005, LNAI 3620, pp. 327–338, 2005.

of examples in the domain and provide several alternatives for examining new classification problems. To explore this idea, a proof of concept system was built that creates similarity cases from a repository of known spam email messages and uses the similarity cases to classify test messages as positive or negative examples of spam.

This paper describes the acquisition of similarity cases in the context of a straightforward classification task. It begins by examining the problem in greater depth, and then identifies characteristics of domains for which this approach might be applicable. Following this, spam-filtering is defined and presented as the experimental domain. Next we describe the approach used to create and deploy similarity cases for reuse in classifying unknown spam messages. Early results from our proof of concept system are reported and discussed along with known challenges. Finally we conclude by examining our work in the context of prior similar work and suggesting some areas requiring additional study.

2 Background

Two important aspects of using case-based reasoning for interpretative classification are situation assessment and similarity assessment. During situation assessment the current problem is examined to determine what information would best match indexes in the case base. This aspect of CBR is well documented by Kolodner's text [2] and many approaches have been described [3, 4, 5, 6, 7]. Situation assessment approaches may make use of all of the information available or extract a subset of the available information using predefined checklists of features. When too much information is maintained a large number of less useful cases may be retrieved or it may be difficult to distinguish between disparate partially matching cases. When too little information is kept, the similarity metric may have incomplete information with which to make useful matches or may have lost a crucial piece of data needed for the classification of the current scenario.

The pitfalls of situation assessment can be illustrated by a simple example. Consider a common problem in academia; the selection of students for acceptance on the basis of applications for admission. An admissions officer studies each application to determine if the individual is the type of student likely to succeed. These determinations are often based on past examples of student success and failure. If the admissions officer only chooses a few aspects of the application to examine – such as grade point average or standardized test scores – he or she may miss relevant and valuable information that has been submitted by the applicant. If, in contrast, the admissions officer considers all aspects of the application then the importance of a single recommendation letter, no matter how strong, may be diminished if it is only considered as one small part of the whole. Ideally an admission officer determines the key aspects of each application on an individual basis. Thus one student with strong scores may be examined differently then a student with strong recommendation letters and still result in a positive outcome for that student. However, there is no a priori way of determining what the relevant features of a given application should be.

Similarity assessment takes over where situation assessment ends. It examines the case-base of stored solutions and, taking the problem description developed during situation assessment, retrieves a case or set of cases that match most closely. Typical approaches take the features and or dimensions identified during situation assessment and use a weighted matching function to compare the features to each case index. Many successful approaches and alternatives to similarity assessment have previously been reported [8, 9, 5, 10, 11, 12]. This process faces many of the same problems as situation assessment where too much, too little or incorrect information can degrade the comparison. Simply because a stored case achieves a high score when compared with a problem description does not guarantee that it is applicable in the current situation.

Consider again the admissions problem. If similarity assessment weighs grade point average and standardized tests scores higher than other features of an application, a past student could be remembered with close if not exact matching features. While the past student may have been rejected, it is perhaps suggestive but not a guarantee that the current student should also be rejected. Other, typically lesser, aspects of the past application may have in fact been the cause of the previous rejection. The problem does not necessarily get easier if all pieces of information are accounted for. The matching past student may have been rejected. The current student while identical in most aspects may require a different and relatively unique interpretation if that student has an influential parent. Examination of the past cases is insufficient to explain this difference at the time of retrieval and thus some other mechanism is required to fill this knowledge gap.

3 Similarity Cases

The problems described in the previous section are not necessarily typical of all or even many case-based reasoning systems. However, interpretive classification tasks are one area in which these problems can arise, particularly in domains that are ill-defined. This paper describes the development of a novel similarity learning approach that attempts to learn a concept theory for similarity in a given domain using a supervised learning algorithm. Our approach can be exemplified by the admissions officer who might record for each student accepted, which aspects of that student were relevant to his or her admission. Thus a student admitted on the basis of grades would have that information recorded, while a child of an influential alumnus would have that fact recorded. We call the recorded relevant similarity features *similarity cases*. Thus when evaluating a new applicant, each stored similarity cases can be examined to determine its applicability to the current situations and use that knowledge to guide the decision making process.

The addition of similarity cases into a case-based reasoning process creates its own set of issues for a system:

- **How can similarity cases be learned?** Given a set of classified cases, similarity cases can quickly be generated by finding similarly classified examples and extracting the relevant features they have in common.
- **How does a new situation handle conflicting similarity cases?** It is possible for one problem description to match or partially match with several similarity cases and this can be problematic if it leads to different proposed classifications. Since different matches can use disparate sets of features, it is entirely reasonable that our applicant for admission has the influential parent that suggests acceptance and a poor GPA which another case suggests rejection. If the similarity cases provide insufficient coverage of the similarity space this can be problematic and perhaps best left for guidance from an expert user. In situations such as this, the similarity cases may suggest reverting to the original complete past problem descriptions and then can be used to guide their processing.
- **What are the added costs of using similarity cases?** The addition of similarity cases to the case-based reasoning process has the potential to add significant overhead to the incremental learning process. However, since the majority of similarity cases are created from seed cases prior to full deployment of the system much to the infrastructure cost is avoided. Otherwise similarity cases have the effect of acting like typical case indexes and should not require large amounts of added time to process.

4 Spam Filtering

A common problem computer users face today is tackling the daily influx of unwanted junk e-mail commonly known as spam. Estimates on the prevalence of spam have indicated that it comprises approximately 55% of all email messages [13]. In fact, certain free email servers indicate that over 90% of all the messages received can be classified as spam. The problem has grown to such an extent that legislation, albeit ineffective, has been created in many places to attempt and reduce the amount of unsolicited email. The prevailing opinion is that technology will need to solve the problem and spam filtering tools have become integral parts of many email servers and end-user email applications.

Several approaches to spam filtering are in wide spread use and include:

- Creating blacklists of spam distributors. This is effective when certain domains or users are frequent contributors of spam. However, most spam distributors vary the names and domains listed within their spam messages. In the long term this may not be a successful approach in reducing spam.
- Using collaborative methods in which users submit *spam signatures* to a central server or share their signatures with other users. When these same messages are distributed in the future they can be quickly removed. Spam distributors circumvent this strategy by varying aspects of the content of the message without changing the primary message.

– Using content based filtering which is by far the largest and currently the most successful approach to spam filtering. In content based filtering, different aspects of each email can be examined. By using an assortment of methods, a determination can be made as to the likelihood of a message being spam. The most successful of the content-based filtering methods is a naive Bayesian algorithm that determines a probabilistic value for each email. Appropriate thresholds on this value can be determined to eliminate the vast majority of incoming spam. By some accounts the Bayesian approach can accurately identify 80% of all spam messages without removing wanted emails. While successful, Bayesian methods are still subject to problems of concept drift and as the spam distributors significantly change their strategies the probabilistic models need to be rebuilt.

One related problem that compounds the identification of spam is that different individuals may classify the same message differently. Thus one person's spam is another's wanted email. In response, many spam- filtering strategies attempt to learn individual user's preferences, but are of limited success as users are not always diligent with providing the necessary feedback to the spam-filtering agent.

We have selected the spam identification domain to study our ideas on similarity learning. Spam has the property that there is no clear definition of what makes message spam other than the "I will know it when I see it" method. Some spam messages closely resemble non-spam messages when using certain comparison criteria. Two spam messages may have little to nothing in common with one another. One strategy of spam distributors is to disguise the message as something a user may want to read or try to "phish" the user into reading the message by providing urgent and seemingly relevant information. This can make it difficult to automatically classify a message as spam if it is not clear which aspects of the message identify it as spam and which aspects are meant to disguise the message. This research with spam filtering is predicated on several assumptions:

– We are not currently attempting to outdo commercial spam filtering approaches, and in fact believe that Bayesian classifiers in combinations with other methods will continue to be the most accurate and quickest approaches to the solving problem.
– We are studying the concept of similarity assessment, and spam filtering provides a readily accessible and practical domain for examining this problem.
– Our goal is to classify messages as spam that are clearly spam to most users. We are not, at this time, concerned with messages that could be classified differently by different users.

5 Knowledge Representation

We initially examine each spam message as the raw text email message. While potentially of great value, we have chosen to ignore all of the information provided in the header of the email. While fields in the header can potentially yield valuable clues as to the classification of a message, spam distributors are capable of framing these headers in ways that would be undetectable by the best current methods. For each message we extract the text as words from its body, removing common words and stemming appropriate terms [14]. From an analysis of many messages we have identified a fixed set of N terms that appear in our corpus. From these N terms we construct, for each message, vectors of length N that store the number appearances of that term in the message.

For example, if our vector stores values for the terms
$< apple, cat, hot, milk, sell >$
and the following message was presented "The cat drank hot milk, but the cat did not like hot apples." The vector for this message would appear as
$< 1, 2, 2, 1, 0 >$.

This vector provides us with an easy way to represent the content of each term. One draw back of this approach is that it loses the context of each term. We hope to develop additional methods to study the question of context in the future.

A traditional CBR approach might store these vectors (or another comparable representation) as cases. Comparisons between this case repository and new problem descriptions could be used to effectively classify large amounts of spam messages. However, these vectors can contain values for many terms that do not contribute to a message's classification. Thus our term "cat" might appear frequently in a given message and yet not be an indicator that a case is spam. Thus we are potentially faced with identifying which features are relevant while avoiding terms that could incorrectly raise or lower a similarity score.

6 Our Approach

We approach this problem by creating similarity cases from a set of known spam messages. In brief, this process is performed by examining each pair of messages and determining what features exist in common between them. The resulting similarity case is a snap shot of which features were most relevant in the comparison of two similarly classified messages. These similarity cases are then used as potential classifiers of new test messages.

Our algorithm can be described more formally as consisting of of two general steps: a pre-processing phase (step 1) and a classification phase (step 2):

1. For each training message:
   (a) Compute the intersection of all features with similar classification.
   (b) Score each computed intersection with respect to relevance and frequency of terms.
   (c) Record the K highest scores intersections as similarity cases.
2. When a test message is presented to the system for classification.
   (a) Retrieve all similarity cases applicable to the test message.
   (b) Compute a likelihood score for the test message based on the the similarity cases retrieved.
   (c) If a predefined threshold is reached then classify the message as spam.

We will now examine each of these steps in greater detail.

6.1 Computing the Intersections (Step 1a)

When comparing two training messages, no assumptions are made about the relative importance of terms in the message. There is a tacit assumption that the filtered terms of the message will act as features in lieu of any other possibly available information.

6.2 Scoring the Intersections (Step 1b)

Each intersection computed from comparisons using each test message is the given a quality score based on the size of the intersection and the importance of the terms in the intersection. Small intersections are generally of less interest since they suggest that the comparison found little in common between messages. Larger intersections can also be troublesome and suggestive of identical messages. This is tempered by weighing the relevance of each individual term based on its frequency in the compared messages and its overall frequency in the test set.

6.3 Building the Similarity Case (Step 1c)

For each of K highest scoring intersections, we construct a similarity case based solely on the relevant intersections.

6.4 Retrieve Similarity Cases (Step 2a)

The step is perhaps misnamed since similarity cases are not retrieved in the traditional sense. Rather all similarity cases are applied to the test problem to find a best fit. A good fit between a similarity case is achieved when all or at least most of the terms stored in the similarity case appear in the test message. We have found that as allowing as few as 50% the terms to match for a "good fit" has produce reasonable results. This process while potentially computationally intensive, the vector representations of terms allow for some speedup in processing. All similarity cases that pass the good fit test are retained for the next step.

6.5 Score the Test Message (Step 2b)

We score the test message based on the number of similarity cases retained from the prior step. The option also exist to create weights for stored similarity cases based on a user defined relevance score or other usability metrics. This later option is useful to account for examples that are rare and for which most similarity cases are not applicable. However, their may be similarity cases that, while infrequently used, provide accurate results and deserve greater weighting.

6.6 Classify Message

Finally, the score from the prior step is taken and if a designated threshold is achieved them classify the message appropriately.

7 Evaluation

We built a small proof of concept system to verify the integrity of our model as a precursor to a much large system currently under development. We wanted to identify whether similarity cases could be successful at driving the spam classification task while identifying potential questions and problems that might arise in its deployment. We selected 50 training spam messages at random from a larger collected repository. From these training message we created similarity cases using our algorithm (K = 4) for a total of 200 similarity cases. These similarity cases were then used to classify a collection of 40 test messages of which 20 were spam and 20 were non-spam. For the purposes of this experiment a "strong classification" of spam was one in which there were over ten similarity case matches. A "weak classification" had fewer then ten similarity case matches. Finally, "no classification" was given if there were no matching similarity cases.

Table 1. Results of similarity cases

Test Case	Number	Strongly Spam	Weakly Spam	No Classification
Spam	20	12	5	3
Non Spam	20	0	5	15

The results of this test, captured in table 1, were mixed. The similarity cases were able to strongly suggest a test message was spam slightly over half of the time. Another quarter of these test message were weakly suggestive of spam. Non-spam cases faired well as about a quarter were weakly suggestive of spam and the remainder found no relevant similarity cases.

An examination of the data introduced an insightful and unfortunately classic AI problem that is present in this approach. Despite the fact the learning is supervised, there is not external influence affecting the causal links that are captured in the similarity cases. One such example of a type that was not uncommon among the similarity cases contained only the terms <http email> neither of which tend to be good indicators of spam messages. However, on further reflection these terms are excellent indicators that a message is email which is yet another trait that the root messages had in common.

Developing similarity cases from a larger training case-base would provide us with broader coverage of the similarity space which may produce better results but perhaps could discover other unintended similarities between messages. Some expert knowledge may be required by the system to better guide it in its initial creation of similarity cases.

8 Related Work

There is a substantial amount of work in both the areas of similarity assessment and spam filtering.

Similarity assessment is a classic problem in Case Base Reasoning. Rissland [8] was one of the earliest to describe using *dimensions* of cases to project cases onto the case base. In fact, the goal of similarity cases can be viewed as trying to discover these dimensions from the cases themselves. The importance of being able to examine existing cases from different perspectives and using different lines of reasoning is critical in interpretive CBR and has played a major role in the legal reasoning systems such as the work on HYPO [5]and GREBE [9]. Those system used expert knowledge to define these dimensions in advance while this approach attempts induce and discover them.

The idea of storing similarity knowledge is not new. Leake et al [15] described recording case adaptation knowledge and using it as the basis of learning new similarity criteria. Their approach suggested doing away with feature assessment altogether and instead evaluated past cases on the basis on their adaptability. These adaptation cases were learned by a separate module of the system. Our approach differs from this in that we are trying to capture the elements of similarity assessment that are contributing to accurate retrievals. We learn what features produce successful results and store the successful feature set as a unique case.

Some early systems like Prodigy/Analogy [10] have advocated refining similarity criteria to focus on goal-relevant portions of the problem description and thus retrieve past cases with the most relevant similarities. Our approach differs from this in that we do not explicitly assign relevance to features but instead store similarity cases that capture prior sets of relevant features.

Our actual approach to similarity assessment is inspired by the K-NN similarity assessment approach which is described in numerous locations including Aha [16]. We extract the relevant features from episodes of applying the KNN approach and store the results as similarity cases. Several approaches have been presented to build a similarity function including decisions trees [17]. However, these attempt to induce a general model of similarity for the system whereas our approach attempts to not define a specific model of similarity but looks to capture those types of similarity comparison that may be indicative of a particular classification. It has also been shown that trying to induce feature weights from examples can lead to overfitting [18].

Prior research that most closely matches our work has involved applying lazy learning methods to vary local weight across the feature space [19, 20]. A similar idea has also been espoused by [21] who created different feature subsets called ensembles to produce diversity in nearest neighbor classifiers. Their approach, however, emphasizes the selection of diverse ensembles while we store similar feature subsets within similarity cases derived from past successful similarity assessment episodes.

Spam filtering has been the subject of several research projects many of which are summarized in [22]. Case-based reasoning has been used for spam filtering by [1], although they paid special attention to how the incremental learning of CBR could more robustly handle the issues of concept drift.

9 Future Work

This project is best classified as early work and there are several aspects of this problem currently under study. We are currently working with a much larger system and intend to perform a far more rigorous cross-validation study using a larger body of test and training messages. In addition, we intend to apply human expertise to rank the similarity cases to compare these rankings to the algorithms rule based rankings.

To improve spam classification there are several augmentations to our system that we could examine. We have previously mentioned that there are several different representations of terms from a given email message that can be studied. In particular we can explore different types of weightings on textual features based of the perceived importance and relevance of a term in a document. Further, we can add textual context to our representation in attempt to capture relationships between terms in a email message, as well as building knowledge hierarchies to capture similar meanings between terms.

Interesting questions on the benefits of similarity cases still have to be answered. We have not yet examined the utility of the "similarity case" case base. How do the stored similarity cases accurately reflect the notion of similarity in the domain? Given that our initial domain was purposely restricted and simple, are the similarity cases effective discriminants to the concept of spam? We intend to expand the domain to examine whether the system can continue to distinguish between message types when negative instances of spam are added. We would also like to examine whether there are any lessons to be learned from examine the meta-reasoning that occurs in the selection and application of similarity cases.

10 Conclusions

We have presented an alternative method for determine similarity in the domain of spam filtering. We create similarity cases to be snapshots of different possible views of similarity among spam messages. Test messages find "best fit" similarity cases and from them determine a likelihood of themselves being classified as spam. Thus the similarity case can store the concept of "spam" in many disparate ways some of which might be applicable at any given time. By storing these concepts of similarity for spam messages, we have the ability to avoid some of the pitfalls that traditional models for spam-filtering might face. Spam messages may become disguised, filled with distractor terms or other clever approaches but at their essence they must still remain spam. Similarity cases are potentially one approach to identify some of these essential characteristics.

Our approach has only been evaluated as a proof of concept but has shown itself to be capable of producing accurate classifications. Additional work will further refine the effectiveness of the method and determine how similarity cases can be exploited as part of other machine learning methods.

References

[1] Cunningham, P., Nowlan, N., Delany, S.J., Haar, M.: A case-based approach to spam filtering that can track concept drift. In: Proceedings of ICCBR-2003. Workshop on Long-Lived CBR Systems. (2003)
[2] Kolodner, J.: Case-Based Reasoning. Morgan Kaufmann, San Mateo, CA (1993)
[3] Kolodner, J., Simpson, R., Sycra-Cyranski, K.: A process model of case-based reasoning in problem-solving. In: Proceedings of the Ninth International Joint Conference on Artificial Intelligence, Los Angeles, CA., IJCAI (1985)
[4] Koton, P.: Smartplan: A case-based resource allocation and scheduling system. In Hammond, K., ed.: Proceedings of the DARPA Case-Based Reasoning Workshop, San Mateo, DARPA, Morgan Kaufmann (1989) 290–294
[5] Ashley, K.: Modeling legal argument: reasoning with cases and hypotheticals. MIT Press, Cambridge (1990)
[6] Yang, Q., Abi-Zeid, I., Lamontagne, L.: An agent system for intelligent situation assessment. In: Artificial Intelligence: Methodology, Systems, and Applications: 8th International Conference, Springer Verlag (1998) 466–474
[7] Leake, D.: Constructive similarity assessment: Using stored cases to define new situations. In: Proceedings of the Fourteenth Annual Conference of the Cognitive Science Society, Hillsdale, NJ, Lawrence Erlbaum (1992) 313–318
[8] Rissland, E., Valcarce, E., Ashley, K.: Explaining and arguing with examples. In: Proceedings of the Fourth National Conference on Artificial Intelligence, Austin, TX, American Association for Artificial Intelligence (1984) 299–294
[9] Branting, K., Porter, B.: Rules and precedents as complementary warrants. In: Proceedings of the Ninth National Conference on Artificial Intelligence, Menlo Park, CA, AAAI Press (1991) 3–9
[10] Veloso, M.: Planning and Learning by Analogical Reasoning. Springer Verlag, Berlin (1994)
[11] Leake, D., Kinley, A., Wilson, D.: Linking adaptation and similarity learning. In: Proceedings of the Eighteenth Annual Conference of the Cognitive Science Society, Mahwah, NJ, Lawrence Erlbaum (1996) 591–596
[12] Smyth, B., Keane, M.: Retrieving adaptable cases: The role of adaptation knowledge in case retrieval. In Wess, S., Althoff, K., Richter, M., eds.: Topics in Case-Based Reasoning, Berlin, Springer Verlag (1994) 209–220
[13] Beaver, K.: The Definitive Guide to E-mail Management and Security. Realtimepublishers.com (2003)
[14] Porter, M.: An algorithm for suffix stripping. Program **14** (1980) 130–137
[15] Leake, D., Kinley, A., Wilson, D.: Case-based similarity assessment: Estimating adaptability from experience. In: Proceedings of the Fourteenth National Conference on Artificial Intelligence, AAAI Press (1997)
[16] Aha, D.: Feture weighting for lazy learning algorithms. In Liu, H., Motoda, H., eds.: Feature Extraction, Construction adn Selection: A Data Mining Perspective. Kluwer, Norwell, MA (1998)
[17] Cardie, C.: Using decision trees ot improve case-based reasoning. In: Proceeding of the Tenth International Confernece on Machine Larninng, Morgan Kaufmann (1993) 25–32
[18] Kohavi, R., Langley, P., Yun, Y.: The utility of feature weighting in nearest neighbor algorithms. In: Proceedings of the European Conference on Machine Learning. (1997)

[19] Aha, D., Wettschereck, D.: Case-based learning: Beyond classification of feature vectors. Call for papers of ECML-97 workshop (1997)
[20] Bonzano, A., Cunningham, P., Smyth, B.: Using introspective learning to improve retrieval in cbr: A case study in air traffic control. In: Proceedings of ICCBR-97, Springer (1997) 291–302
[21] Cunningham, P., Zenobi, G.: Using diversity in preparing ensembles of classifiers bases on different feature subsets to minimize generalization error. In: Machine Learning: EMCL: 12th European Conference on Machine Learning, Springer Verlag (2001) 576–587
[22] Androutsopoulos, I., Paliouras, G., Sakkis, V., Spyropoulos, C., Stamatopoulos, P.: Learning to filter spam-email: A compariosn of a naive bayesian and memory-based approach. In: Workshop on Machine Learning and Textual Information Access, 4th European Conference on Principles and Practices of KDD. (2000) 160–167

A Live-User Evaluation of Incremental Dynamic Critiquing

Kevin McCarthy, Lorraine McGinty, Barry Smyth, and James Reilly

Adaptive Information Cluster*, Smart Media Institute,
University College Dublin, Dublin, Ireland
{kevin.mccarthy, lorraine.mcginty, barry.smyth,
james.d.dreilly}@ucd.ie

Abstract. Feature critiquing has emerged as an important feedback strategy for conversational recommender systems as it offers a useful balance between user effort and recommendation efficiency. Dynamic critiquing has recently been presented as an extension to conventional (single-feature) critiquing that supports the simultaneous critiquing of multiple features. To date, dynamic critiquing has been evaluated through a variety of artificial user trials to demonstrate its *potential* advantages, when it comes to improving recommendation efficiency and quality. However these advantages have never been verified through any large-scale user trial. The contribution of this paper is that we present the results of such an evaluation, which confirms the advantages of dynamic critiquing in a realistic online, e-commerce setting. Furthermore we investigate the impact of implicitly maintaining session specific user models to influence the selection of *compound* critiques. These models are incrementally constructed as the user critiques example recommendations from cycle to cycle. Our live-user evaluation also enabled us to analyse how real users interact with the compound critiques that are produced in this way. The results demonstrate that our incremental critiquing approach has the capability of generating more relevant critique options, and that users frequently recognise the benefits associated with using these as feedback options, leading to significantly shorter recommendation sessions.

1 Introduction

Critiquing has emerged as a important form of feedback in conversational recommender systems especially in e-commerce settings. Shoppers are presented with a sequence of product suggestions and are offered an opportunity to *critique* individual features in order to refine their preferences [2,3,4,10,14]. For example, when shopping for a digital camera, a user might be presented with a suggestion for a *$500, 6M Pixel, Canon* and they might indicate that they are looking for something a little less expensive by selecting the *cheaper* critique; this effectively constrains the *price* of recommendations during the next recommendation cycle.

* This material is based on works supported by Science Foundation Ireland under Grant No. 03/IN.3/I361.

H. Muñoz-Avila and F. Ricci (Eds.): ICCBR 2005, LNAI 3620, pp. 339–352, 2005.

In our work we have been interested for some time in improving the effectiveness of the basic approach to critiquing. In particular, we have proposed an approach known as *dynamic critiquing*, which presents users with a set of so-called *compound* critiques, in addition to the standard (single-feature) *unit* critiques that are normally available. Importantly, these compound critiques are automatically generated by mining the cases that remain during a given recommendation cycle. Essentially each compound critique represents a set of unit critiques that are found to recur in multiple remaining cases. In previous work, [6,12], we have shown that dynamic critiquing has the potential to lead to improved recommendation efficiency by reducing average session length when compound critiques are selected. However since our previous evaluations were limited to the use of artificial-user data, their true significance is unknown without independent confirmation from live-user trials.

As part of this paper we describe a recent extension to dynamic critiquing called *incremental critiquing* [13], which maintains a record of the critiques (unit and compound) that a given user has selected during a recommendation session. This record is then used to influence future recommendations and is designed to provide the user with intelligent recommendations that reflect their previous critiques as well as their most recent critique applications. In addition, and the main contribution of this paper, we describe the results of a comprehensive live-user trial of dynamic critiquing involving more than 1000 live-user recommendation sessions. This data provides, a compelling account of the real benefits of dynamic critiquing and serves to confirm the benefits suggested by previous artificial user trials.

2 From Dynamic to Incremental Critiquing

The novelty of dynamic critiquing stems from its ability to mine the available cases in order to identify frequently recurring feature differences (relative to the currently recommended case). Groups of these differences become the compound critiques that are presented to the user as part of the current recommendation cycle. Figure 1 shows a screen-shot of a conversational recommender system that we have developed to showcase and evaluate the dynamic critiquing approach. It shows a recommended case, its unit critiques and three relevant compound critiques. From here the user can select a critique (i.e., unit or compound) to inform the next recommendation cycle, terminating their session when they see a satisfactory camera.

In [12] we have described how these compound critiques are identified (using the Apriori data mining algorithm), ranked and selected. In this section we will review this critique generation algorithm. In addition, we will discuss a number of shortcomings of this standard approach to dynamic critiquing that have led to the development of a new variant called incremental critiquing. In the next section we will detail the latest version of incremental critiquing; an earlier version has been presented in [13].

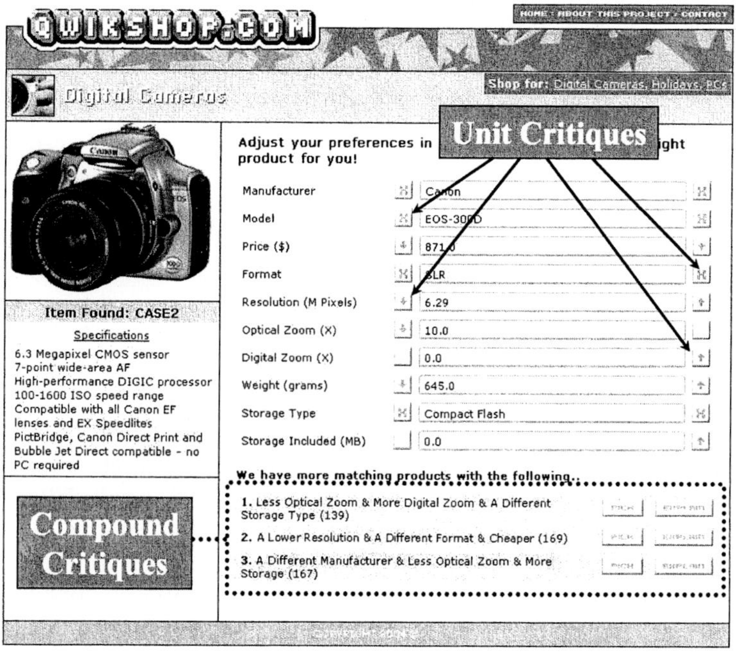

Fig. 1. A digital camera recommender system that implements unit and compound critiquing

2.1 The Standard Dynamic Critiquing Approach

The standard approach to dynamic critiquing has been previously described by [6,12]. The basic idea is that during every recommendation cycle, in addition to selecting a new case to recommend to the user, the system should also present a set of compound critiques that describe the feature relationships that exist between the remaining cases. For example, in Figure 1 we see an example of a compound critique leading to 169 cases with *less resolution* and a *different format* for a *cheaper* price. Generating these compound critiques involves 3 steps:

STEP 1 - Generating Critique Patterns: For a given recommendation cycle each of the remaining cases is redescribed by a *critique pattern* which captures the relationship between each case and the current recommended case. For example, Figure 2 shows an example from the Digital Camera domain. The resulting critique pattern reflects how a case *c* differs from the current case in terms of individual directional feature critiques. For example, the critique pattern shown includes a "<" critique for Resolution— we will refer to this as [*Resolution* <]—because the comparison case has a less pixels than the current recommendation.

STEP 2 - Mining Compound Critiques: This step involves identifying recurring patterns of unit critiques within the current set of critique patterns.

	Current Case	Case c from CB	Critique Pattern
Manufacturer	Canon	Sony	!=
Model	Powershot S500	DSC-V1	!=
Format	Ultra Compact	Ultra Compact	=
Resolution (M Pixels)	5.1	5.0	<
Optical Zoom (X)	3	4	>
Digital Zoom (X)	4.1	4	<
Weight (grams)	215	298	>
Storage Type	Compact Flash	Memory Stick	!=
Storage Included (MB)	32	16	<
Price (Euro)	443.00	455.00	>

Fig. 2. Generating a critique pattern

This is similar to the market-basket analysis task where the well-known Apriori algorithm [1] has been used to characterize recurring itemsets as association rules of the form $A \rightarrow B$. During this stage, Apriori is applied during each cycle to the remaining product cases in order to identify groups of recurring unit critiques; we might expect to find the co-occurrence of unit critiques like $[Resolution >]$ infers $[Price >]$. Apriori returns lists of compound critiques of the form $\{[Resolution >], [Price >]\}$ along with their *support* values (the percentage of critique patterns for which the compound critique holds).

STEP 3 - Grading Compound Critiques: It is not practical to present large numbers of different compound critiques as user-feedback options in each cycle due to interface restrictions. A filtering strategy is used to select the k most useful critiques for presentation purposes based on their support values; compound critiques with low support values have the ability to eliminate many product cases from consideration if chosen. The work of [12] has looked at a number of ways to filter critiques, concluding that preferring critiques with low support values has the potential to offer the best recommendation efficiency benefits.

2.2 Consistency and Continuity

Regardless of the type of critiquing used (unit or compound, or a mixture of both), or the manner in which the critiques have been generated (fixed versus dynamic), there are a number of important issues that need to be kept in mind from an application deployment perspective. This is especially important when it comes to anticipating how users are likely to interact with the recommender system. In particular, users cannot be relied upon to provide consistent feedback over the course of a recommendation session. In fact this is almost inevitable since many users are unlikely to have a clear understanding of their requirements at the beginning of a recommendation session. Indeed in our experience many users rely on the recommender as a means to educate themselves about the features of a product-space. As a result users may select apparently incompatible critiques during a session as they explore different areas of the product space in order to build up a clearer picture of what is available. For example, in one cycle we may find a prospective digital camera owner looking for a camera that is *cheaper* than the current 500 euro recommendation, but later on she may ask for a camera that is *more expensive* than another 500 euro recommendation. There are a number of reasons for this inconsistent feedback: perhaps she has made a mistake; perhaps she is just interested in seeing what is available at the higher price; or perhaps her preferences have changed from the start of the session as she recognises the compromises that are associated with lower priced cameras [9].

For the most part, recommender systems that employ critiquing tend not to consider the implications of such inconsistency or changes in user behaviour. Most focus on the current critique and the current case only, without considering the critiques that have been applied in the past. This, we argue, can lead to serious problems, depending on whether critiques are implemented as hard or soft constraints. For instance, if the recommender uses each critique to permanently filter-out incompatible product-cases (a hard constraint), then a user may find that there are no remaining cases when they come to change their mind. For example, having indicated a preference for sub-500 euro cameras early-on, the user will find the recommender unable to make recommendations for more expensive cameras in future recommendations.

As a result of problems like this, such a strict filtering policy is usually not employed by conversational recommender systems in practice. Instead of permanently filtering-out incompatible cases, irrelevant cases for a particular cycle tend to be temporarily removed from consideration, but may come to be reconsidered during future cycles as appropriate. Of course this strategy introduces the related problem of how past critiques should influence future recommendations, especially if they conflict or strengthen the current critique.

Current implementations of critiquing tend to ignore these issues in the blind hope that users will either behave themselves — that they will responsibly select a sequence of compatible critiques in pursuit of their target product — or that they will have the patience to backtrack over their past critiques in order to try alternatives. In our experience this approach is unlikely to prove successful. In real user trials common complaints have included the lack of consistency between successive recommendation cycles that arise because of these issues.

3 Incremental Critiquing

Incremental critiquing is a direct response to the issues outlined above [13]. It is designed to give due consideration to past critiques during future recommendation cycles by maintaining a record of the critiques that have been applied (compound and unit) by the user in the current recommendation session (See Figure 3). This record serves as a type of in-session critiquing-based user model, $U = \{U_1, ..., U_n\}$ (where U_i is a single unit critique), and it is used during recommendation to influence the choice of a new product case, along with the current critique; see also the work of [5,14] for related ideas. The key idea is that the critiques that a user has applied so far are a reflection of their evolving understanding of the product space and subsequent preference requirements. At the end of each cycle, after the user has selected a new critique, we add this critique to the user model.

3.1 Modelling the User

To maintain an accurate user model, however, is not quite as simple as storing a list of previously selected critiques. As we have mentioned above, some critiques may be *inconsistent* with earlier critiques. For example, in the case of a camera recommender, a user selecting a critique for *higher resolution*, beyond the *5M Pixels* of the recommended case, during one cycle may later *contradict* themselves by indicating a preference for *lower resolution* than the *2M Pixels* offered by a subsequent case. In addition, a user may *refine* their requirements over time. They might start, for example, by indicating a preference for more than *128MB* of memory (with a *more memory* critique on a current case that offers *128MB*). Later they might indicate a preference for more than *256MB* of memory with a *more memory* critique on a case that offers *256MB*.

```
CB: casebase, U: user-model, q: query, t: chosen critique, r: recommended item

1.  define Incremental-Critiquing(q, CB)
2.  U = {}
3.  t = {}
4.  repeat
5.     r ← ItemRecommend(q, CB, t, U)
6.     t ← UserReview(r, CB)
7.     q ← QueryRevise(q, r)
8.     U ← UpdateModel(U, t, r)
9.  until UserAccepts(r)

10. define UserReview(r, CB)
11.    t ← user critique for some feature ∈ r
12.    CB ← CB - {r}
13. return c

14. define QueryRevise(q, r)
15.    q ← r
16. return q

17. define UpdateModel(U, t, r)
18.    If IsCompound(t) then
19.       t-set ← UnitCritiques(t)
20.    else
21.       t-set ← {t}
22.    Endif
23.    For each t ∈ t-set
24.    do
25.       U ← U - contradict(U, t, r)
26.       U ← U - refine(U, t, r)
27.       U ← U + {<t, r>}
28.    EndFor
29. return U

30. define ItemRecommend(q, CB, t, U)
31.    CB' ← {i ∈ CB | Satisfies(i,t)}
32.    CB'' ← sort CB' by decreasing Quality
33.    r ← top item in CB''
34. return r
```

Fig. 3. The Incremental Critiquing algorithm

Our incremental critiquing strategy [13] deals with inconsistencies such as the above by updating the user model with the most recent critique only after pruning previous critiques, which conflict with it, (see lines 23-26 in Figure 3). Thus, prior to adding a new critique all existing critiques that are inconsistent with it are removed from the user model. Similarly, if the new critique is a refinement of existing critiques then it is assumed to override these earlier critiques and they are deleted from the model. To keep things simple, we deal with compound critiques by splitting them up into their constituent unit critiques so that the update procedure then involves making a set of unit directional preference updates.

3.2 Biasing Recommendation

The basic idea behind the user model is that it should be used to *bias* (i.e., more effectively control) the recommendation process, prioritising those product cases that are compatible with the majority of the recorded critiques. This can be thought of as a generalisation of the standard approach to critiquing-based recommendation, in which the current recommendation cycle is constrained by the current critique only as part of a two-step process. First, the remaining cases are filtered by eliminating all of those that fail to satisfy the current critique. Next, these filtered cases are rank ordered according to their similarity to the current recommendation.

We modify this procedure in an important way. Instead of ordering the filtered cases on the basis of their similarity to the recommended case alone, we also compute a compatibility score for each candidate case, which is essentially the percentage of critiques in the user model that this case satisfies (see Equation 1 and note that $satisfies(U_i, c')$ returns a score of 1 when the critique, $U_{i.}$ satisfies the filtered case, c, and returns 0 otherwise). Thus a case that satisfies 3 out of the 5 critiques in a user model obtains a compatibility score of 0.6.

$$Compatibility(c', U) = \frac{\sum_{\forall i} satisfies(U_i, c')}{|U|} \quad (1)$$

$$Quality(c', c, U) = \alpha * Compatibility(c', U) + (1 - \alpha) * Similarity(c', c) \quad (2)$$

This compatibility score is then combined with the candidate's (c') similarity to the recommended case, c, in order to obtain an overall quality score (see Equation 2). This quality score is used to rank order the filtered cases prior to the next recommendation cycle. The case with the highest quality is then chosen as the new recommendation (see lines 30-34 in Figure 3).

Importantly, in this updated version of incremental critiquing, a weighting function has been introduced. The α parameter can be used to adjust the relative weight that is given over to previous critiques during the current recommendation cycle. In our experiments we have set this parameter to 0.75 so that more weight is placed on compatibility with past critiques than current-case similarity. This setting was found to work best in our digital camera domain through off-line evaluation but should not be viewed as a judgement on the optimal value for this parameter. It is likely that different recommendation scenarios will lead to different values for α. Indeed, an interesting avenue for future research is to consider how this parameter may be learned automatically. It is also likely, for example, that different users may benefit from different α setting; a user with a clear understanding of their requirements will probably provide more consistent feedback, thus obviating the need for a high α value. In certain cases it may even be useful to consider varying α as a session proceeds. However, such considerations are beyond the scope of this paper.

The essential point is that the above formulation allows us to prioritise those candidate cases that: (1) satisfy the current critique; (2) are similar to the previous recommended case; and (3) satisfy many previous critiques. In so doing we are implicitly treating the past critiques in the user model as *soft constraints* for future recommendation cycles; it is not essential for future recommendations to satisfy all of the previous critiques, but the more they satisfy, the better they are regarded as recommendation candidates. Moreover, given two candidates that are equally similar to the previously recommended case, our algorithm will prefer the one that satisfies the greater number of recently applied critiques. Furthermore, there are many ways that we could have combined compatibility and similarity, and alternatives are left for future work.

4 Evaluation

Previously we have reported on a number of evaluations of dynamic critiquing [6,12]. However, these studies have always used artificial user data, and as such can only serve as a guide when it comes to truly understanding the benefits of dynamic critiquing. In this section we describe the results of a large-scale live-user trial. We are especially interested in understanding how users interact with the compound critiques that are produced according to the standard and incremental dynamic critiquing approaches by the different critiquing strategies. We pay particular attention to aspects of recommendation efficiency, comparing standard dynamic critiquing to incremental critiquing.

4.1 Setup

Users for our trial were made up of both undergraduate and postgraduate students from the department of Computer Science at University College Dublin. Trial participants were invited to use our Digital Camera Recommender (see Figure 1) from December 13 to December 20, 2004. The trial consisted of two parts. In the first part, each trialist was asked to participate in a so-called *training* session so that they could become acquainted with the critiquing mode of interaction. Here they were presented with a specific camera case as a starting point and then asked to *shop* from this case to locate their ideal camera. In the second part, they were presented with a fixed *start* case and *target* case. The users were then asked to locate the target case by using critiques (unit or compound) of their choice. There were 25 different start–target pairs and these were randomly assigned at the beginning of every session. Trialists were permitted to use the system as often as they liked. This setup ensured that any learning effect was minimised as it is unlikely that users started at the same point more than once.

Here we report on results from part 2 of the trial, which generated 1092 user sessions from 76 unique users. The trialists were made up of 53% undergraduate and 47% postgraduate students with 61 male and 15 female participants. The standard dynamic critiquing approach (*Standard*) and the new incremental critiquing approach (*Incremental*) were used on different days of the trial (unbeknownst to the users) and a variety of session details were logged for each user session.

4.2 Recommendation Efficiency

Recommendation efficiency is always an important consideration when it comes to evaluating conversational recommender systems [8,11]. Users are notoriously intolerant of protracted recommendation dialogs that require a lot of feedback, so the ability of a recommender system to guide the user efficiently to their target product will have an important bearing on its deployment success.

Previously we have shown how the use of compound critiques can lead to short recommendation sessions than the use of unit critiques on their own. For now we are primarily interested in the relative efficiency of the *Standard* and *Incremental* strategies, although we will return to the issue of compound versus unit critiques in a moment. In Figure 4 we present the overall average session length and compound critique application frequency for the different versions of our recommender system.

The results show a clear benefit accruing to the *Incremental* strategy. On the days when this strategy was used, the average session length was only 7.5 cycles as compared to 11.44 cycles for the sessions produced when *Standard* dynamic critiquing was used; in other words, the standard sessions are, on average, almost 50% longer than the incremental critiquing sessions. Remember both critiquing strategies generate compound critiques in the same way, but their recommendation processes differ, with *Incremental* allowing past critiques to influence the current recommendation. This advantage due to *Incremental* suggests it is better able to use the compound critiques in order to focus the search in on the target product. We also see that these critiques are used slightly more frequently, than those produced by the standard dynamic critiquing method.

It is also important to consider the value of compound critiques relative to unit critiques. To do this we divide the sessions produced using *Standard* and *Incremental* into two groups each by splitting them by the median compound

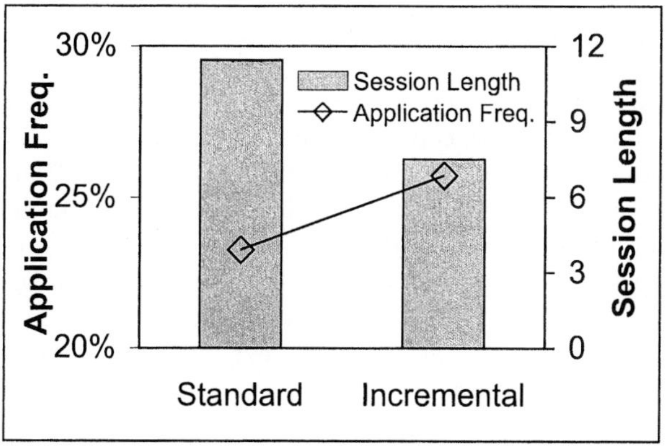

Fig. 4. Average session length and compound critique application frequency for *Standard* and *Incremental* dynamic critiquing strategies

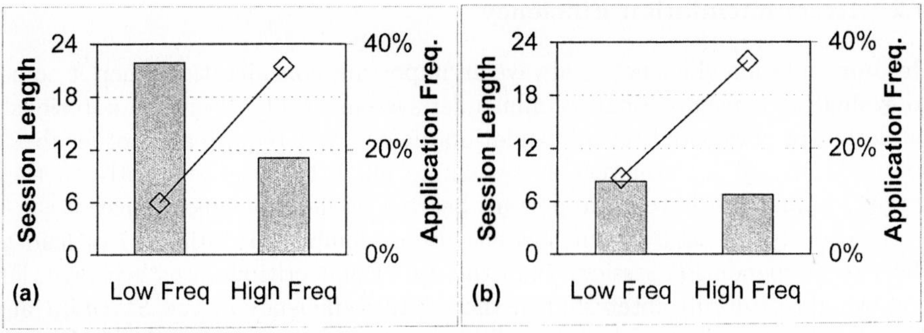

Fig. 5. The average session length for low frequency and high frequency sessions for the (a) *Standard* and (b)*Incremental* dynamic critiquing strategies. Note that the average application frequency for each group of sessions is also shown

critique application frequency for each strategy. This allows us to compare the sessions produced when relatively few compound critiques are used (the *low frequency* sessions) to the sessions when compound critiques are used more often (the *high frequency* sessions). The results are presented in Figure 5. In each chart (for *Standard* and *Incremental*) we see that the average session length for the low frequency sessions is longer than the average session length for the high frequency sessions. For example, in the case of the *Standard* approach, we see that the low frequency sessions are almost twice the length of the high frequency sessions and for the *Incremental* approach the low frequency sessions are more than 20% longer than the high frequency sessions. While there is a greater relative benefit (between low and high frequency sessions) for the *Standard* approach than the *Incremental* approach, we must remember that the *Incremental* sessions are significantly shorter than the *Standard* sessions to begin with.

4.3 Target Analysis

The results of the previous section show that there is a significant advantage for users who frequently use compound critiques. Moreover, the *Incremental* strategy is capable of delivering more efficient recommendation sessions than the *Standard* strategy. Of course these results reflect recommendation efficiency across all target product-cases and users and as such it is not clear if they are biased towards certain targets of users. For example, it might be that the benefits observed are due to large improvements for a relatively small number of targets of users. In this section, and the next, we will answer such questions by examining recommendation efficiency on a target-by-target and user-by-user basis. For reasons of space we will focus on the *Incremental* version of dynamic critiquing only; as our best performing strategy this takes priority over *Standard.*

Figure 6 presents the results for each of the 25 target product cases used in the trial. It is worth noting here that in dividing the sessions into low frequency and high frequency sessions we used the median application frequency observed

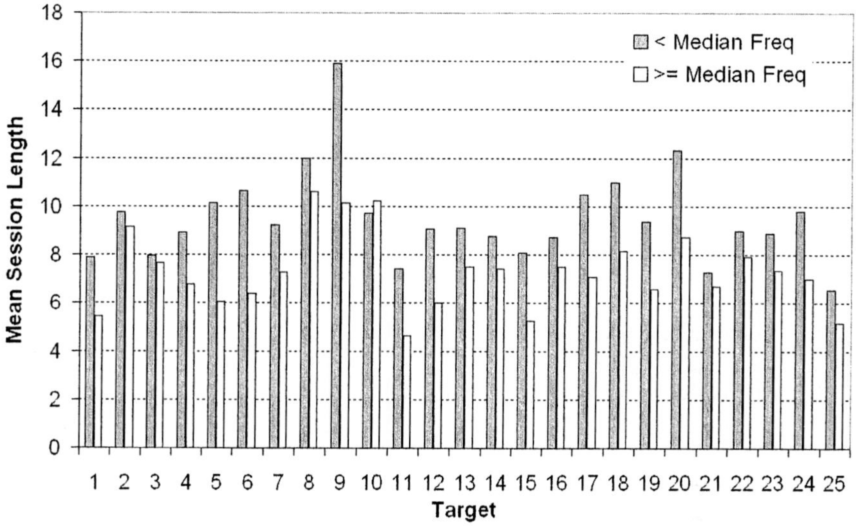

Fig. 6. The average session lengths for low frequency and high frequency incremental critiquing sessions on a target-by-target basis

for the sessions associated with each target product case. The results indicate a clear benefit for the high frequency sessions for nearly every target product case. The average improvement in session length, for the high frequency sessions, is just under 25% and in a number of cases it is above 35%. These benefits are all significant at the 99% significance level. The only exception is noted for target case number 10, where there is a 4% increase in session length due to the high frequency sessions, but in this instance this difference is not statistically significant.

4.4 User Analysis

We adopt a similar methodology to compare the low and high frequency sessions for *Incremental* on a user-by-user basis, although this time we select the top 13 users who had take part in the most individual sessions. This allowed us to ensure that all of these users had participated in recommendation sessions involving all 25 of the target product cases.

The results are presented in Figure 7, once again as the average session length observed for the low frequency and high frequency sessions for each user. Note also that the low and high frequency sessions are separated according to the median application frequency for each individual user. The results clearly show a significant advantage for each user: there is a 25% average reduction in session length for the high frequency sessions across all users. The benefit that is due to the more frequent use of compound critiques appears to be closely related with baseline (low frequency) session length for each user. In particular, the correlation between the low frequency session lengths and the relative session length reduction observed for the corresponding high frequency sessions is 0.83.

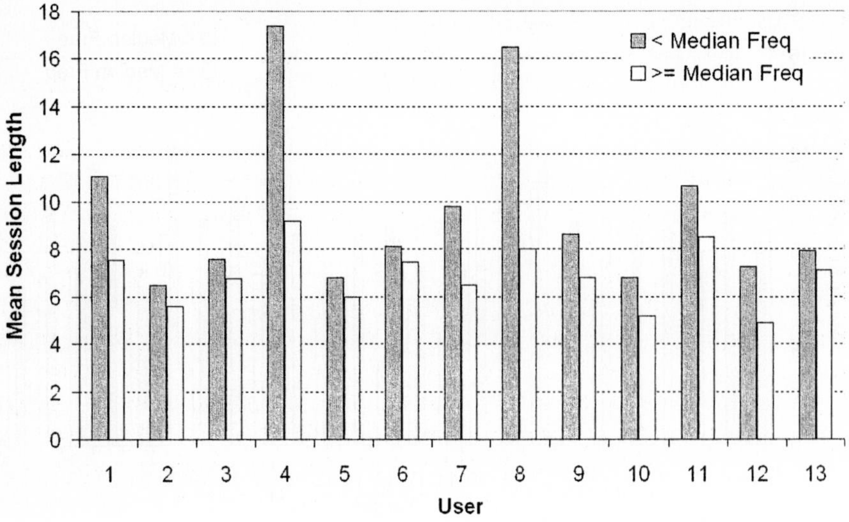

Fig. 7. The average session lengths for low frequency and high frequency incremental critiquing sessions on a user-by-user basis

5 Discussion

In related work (see [7]) we have examined different aspects of how users interact with compound critiques during recommendation sessions. In particular, we were especially interested in how the usage of compound critiques tends to change during the course of a cycle. We found that compound critique usage is most prevalent during the early stages of a recommendation session and users have a tendency to use unit critiques in the later cycles. This make sense because compound critiques allow the user to take large jumps through the product-space. This is useful early on as the user tries to focus in on a particular region of a product-space. However, once the user is in the correct region then the finer-grained unit critiques are more useful in order to locate a precise target product.

One of the issues that remains to be investigated concerns the cognitive load associated with the interpretation of compound critiques. Most of the compound critiques generated by our algorithms are made up of 3 separate unit critiques — although this could be limited to 2 if required — and it is interesting to consider whether this means it will take a user 3 times as long to interpret a compound critique than a unit critique. In addition, while the above results indicate that sessions are shorter, in terms of their number of cycles, with frequent compound critique use, this does not mean that they are shorter in total elapsed time. Given the additional complexity of compound critiques it is possible that the high frequency sessions will take longer than the low frequency sessions, in which case their value will very much depend on how users perceive the trade-off between the number of cycles in a session (and the degree of feedback associated with these cycles) and session time. Users may be willing to accept longer sessions, in terms of their time, if they require less feedback. We are currently investigating these issues.

Related to this cognitive load issue is that of critique labelling. Currently, each compound critique is made up of the concatenation of unit critiques, but a more efficient labelling may be possible since oftentimes compound critiques can be translated into more efficient representations. For example, consider the compound critique, $\{[Price >], [Resolution >], [Format =]\}$ in relation to a *$1000, 5M pixel, SLR* camera. This compound critique suggests that the user is looking for some *more professional* camera and so it should be possible to label it as such without greatly affecting its interpretability. The advantage of this is that most users will understand that a more professional camera is likely to come at a higher price and with a better resolution; they may all not realise the importance of the SLR format, but this should not be a significant problem. We intend to investigate if relabelling compound critiques in this way makes them easier (and faster) to interpret.

6 Conclusions

Critiquing is an important form of feedback for conversational recommender systems. Dynamic critiquing is a recent critique-generation strategy that automatically creates compound (multi-feature) critiques during each recommendation cycle. Both standard and incremental approaches generate their compound critiques in the same way, but incremental critiquing improves on dynamic critiquing by allowing the past critique-selections of a user to influence future recommendations.

In this paper we have compared standard dynamic critiquing and incremental critiquing using live-user data from a prototype digital camera recommender system. The results are consistent with previously reported artificial-user trials. They show that dynamic and incremental critiquing are capable of delivering significant reductions in session length. They also show that incremental critiquing enjoys a significant session length advantage over standard dynamic critiquing.

References

1. R. Agrawal, H. Mannila, R. Srikant, H. Toivonen, and A. Inkeri Verkamo. Fast Discovery of Association Rules in Large Databases. *Advances in Knowledge Discovery and Data Mining*, pages 307–328, 1996.
2. R. Burke, K. Hammond, and B. Young. Knowledge-based Navigation of Complex Information Spaces. In *Proceedings of the Thirteenth National Conference on Artificial Intelligence*, pages 462–468. AAAI Press/MIT Press, 1996. Portland, OR.
3. R. Burke, K. Hammond, and B.C. Young. The FindMe Approach to Assisted Browsing. *Journal of IEEE Expert*, 12(4):32–40, 1997.

4. B. Faltings, P. Pu, M. Torrens, and P. Viappiani. Design Example-Critiquing Interaction. In *Proceedings of the International Conference on Intelligent User Interface(IUI-2004)*, pages 22–29. ACM Press, 2004. Funchal, Madeira, Portugal.
5. G. Linden, S. Hanks, and N. Lesh. Interactive Assessment of User Preference Models: The Automated Travel Assistant. In C. Paris A. Jameson and C. Tasso, editors, *User Modeling: Proceedings of the Sixth International Conference*, pages 67–78. Springer Wien, 1997.
6. K. McCarthy, J. Reilly, L. McGinty, and B. Smyth. On the Dynamic Generation of Compound Critiques in Conversational Recommender Systems. In P. De Bra, editor, *Proceedings of the Third International Conference on Adaptive Hypermedia and Web-Based Systems (AH-04)*, pages 176–184. Springer, 2004. Eindhoven, The Netherlands.
7. K. McCarthy, J. Reilly, L. McGinty, and B. Smyth. On the Evaluation of Dynamic Critiquing: A Large-Scale User Study. *Submitted to the Twentieth National Conference on Artificial Intelligence (AAAI-05)*, 2005. Pittsburgh, Pennsylvania, USA.
8. D. McSherry. Minimizing Dialog Length in Interactive Case-Based Reasoning. In Bernhard Nebel, editor, *Proceedings of the Seventeenth International Joint Conference on Artificial Intelligence (IJCAI-01)*, pages 993–998. Morgan Kaufmann, 2001. Seattle, Washington.
9. D. McSherry. Similarity and Compromise. In D. Bridge and K. Ashley, editors, *Proceedings of the Fifth International Conference on Case-Based Reasoning (ICCBR-03)*, pages 291–305. Springer-Verlag, 2003. Trondheim, Norway.
10. Q.N. Nguyen, F. Ricci, and D. Cavada. User Preferences Initialization and Integration in Critique-Based Mobile Recommender Systems. In *Proceedings of Artificial Intelligence in Mobile Systems 2004, in conjunction with UbiComp 2004*, pages 71–78. Iniversitat des Saarlandes Press., 2004. Nottingham, UK.
11. P. Pu and P. Kumar. Evaluating Example-based Search Tools. In *Proceedings of the ACM Conference on Electronic Commerce (EC 2004)*, pages 208–217. ACM Press, 2004. New York, USA.
12. J. Reilly, K. McCarthy, L. McGinty, and B. Smyth. Dynamic Critiquing. In P.A. Gonzalez Calero and P. Funk, editors, *Proceedings of the European Conference on Case-Based Reasoning (ECCBR-04).*, pages 763–777. Springer, 2004. Madrid, Spain.
13. J. Reilly, K. McCarthy, L. McGinty, and B. Smyth. Incremental Critiquing. In M. Bramer, F. Coenen, and T. Allen, editors, *Research and Development in Intelligent Systems XXI. Proceedings of AI-2004*, pages 101–114. Springer, 2004. Cambridge, UK.
14. S. Sherin and H. Lieberman. Intelligent Profiling by Example. In *Proceedings of the International Conference on Intelligent User Interfaces (IUI 2001)*, pages 145–152. ACM Press, 2001. Santa Fe, NM,.

Case Based Representation and Retrieval with Time Dependent Features

Stefania Montani and Luigi Portinale

Dipartimento di Informatica, Università del Piemonte Orientale,
Alessandria, Italy

Abstract. The temporal dimension of the knowledge embedded in cases has often been neglected or oversimplified in Case Based Reasoning systems. However, in several real world problems a case should capture the evolution of the observed phenomenon over time. To this end, we propose to represent temporal information at two levels: (1) at the *case level*, if some features describe parameters varying within a period of time (which corresponds to the case duration), and are therefore collected in the form of time series; (2) at the *history level*, if the evolution of the system can be reconstructed by retrieving temporally related cases.

In this paper, we describe a framework for case representation and retrieval able to take into account the temporal dimension, and meant to be used in any time dependent domain. In particular, to support case retrieval, we provide an analysis of similarity-based time series retrieval techniques; to support history retrieval, we introduce possible ways to summarize the case content, together with the corresponding strategies for identifying similar instances in the knowledge base. A concrete application of our framework is represented by the system RHENE, which is briefly sketched here, and extensively described in [20].

1 Introduction

The Case Based Reasoning (CBR) methodology [1] is particularly appealing in those domains where acquiring and formalizing knowledge would be a significantly hard and time consuming task.

As a matter of fact, CBR allows one to build a knowledge base of past situations (*cases*), which represent an operative form of knowledge, that can be reused in present problems, possibly after an adaptation step. Representing a real-world situation as a case is often straighforward: given a set of meaningful features for the application domain, it is sufficient to identify the value they assume in the situation at hand; sometimes a case also stores information about the solution applied and the outcome obtained. Due to this quick procedure, in many applications the knowledge acquisition bottleneck can be extremely reduced with respect to the exploitation of other reasoning methodologies.

The relative simplicity of defining cases has often led researchers to neglect or oversimplify a very important aspect of the knowledge embedded in past situations: the *temporal dimension*. On the other hand, in several (especially medical)

H. Muñoz-Avila and F. Ricci (Eds.): ICCBR 2005, LNAI 3620, pp. 353–367, 2005.

applications, the need of accounting for time is widely recognized. Actually, in many domains cases cannot be interpreted merely as snapshots of the world at a given time instant: in a lot of real problems a case should capture the evolution of the observed phenomenon over time. In medical practice, for example, before prescribing a therapy (i.e. the case solution) the physician needs to keep in mind the clinical history that led the patient to the current situation; actually, the pattern of the patient's changes is often more important than the final state [18]. Similarly, forecasting tasks often require an analysis of temporal sequences of observations or of interactions between involved agents [25]. The definition of a case as a set of feature/value pairs needs therefore to be refined.

In particular, we envision the possibility of addressing the temporal dimension at two levels:

1. at the *case level*, if some features describe parameters varying within a period of time (which corresponds to the case duration), and are therefore collected in the form of time series;
2. at the *history level*, if the evolution of the system can be reconstructed by retrieving temporally related cases (e.g. in a medical domain, cases concerning consecutive visits of a given patient).

As an example, in hemodialysis treatment it is possible to define a case as a dialysis session, which includes time series features, that justify the need of accounting for temporal information at the case level. Moreover, in clinical practice physicians use to judge the patient's behaviour in the latest two weeks (i.e. they deal with a history of a few consecutive cases); only in particularly critical situations, they enter the detail of single sessions. Both levels are therefore needed in this context.

If we want to guarantee consistent results, we have to take into account the fact that the temporal dimension complicates not only the knowledge representation task, but the retrieval process as well. In particular, similarity-based time series retrieval has to be addressed on the one hand, while strategies for matching patterns made by "consecutive" cases needs to be defined.

In this paper, we describe a framework for case-based representation and retrieval meant to be used in any time dependent domain. In particular, in section 2 we describe related works; in section 3, we deal with knowledge representation and retrieval at the *case level*, while in section 4 we extend our discussion to the *history level*. Section 5 describes how our theoretical work is being applied in the system RHENE [20], a tool for managing patients in a hemodyalisis regimen. Finally, section 6 is devoted to conclusions and future work.

2 Related Work

Despite the need of accounting for the temporal dimension in a CBR system may appear important, rather interestingly the representation of time-dependent information and its impact on the CBR cycle [1] have been scarcely inspected in the literature.

Actually, just a few works in this sense exist. Most of them afford the problem of representing and retrieving cases with time-extended features (i.e. time series), and each work is substantially limited to fit a single application domain: robot control [24], process forecast [21,26], process supervision [10], prediction of faulty situations [14] and time course prognoses for medical problems [27]. Almost all of these contributions adopt a representation of temporal knowledge requiring that absolute time *points* are associated with the temporal objects being modelled. This hypothesis may be unrealistic in many applications, where only relative, and often qualitative, temporal knowledge is available; a more suitable *interval*-based model [3] has been chosen only in [14] (see section 3.1 for details on these knowledge representation concepts). Moreover, all works share two main limitations: (1) in most cases, since they have been thought to support a specific application, their generalizability is limited or not discussed at all; (2) they address the temporal dimension only at the *case level*. With respect to issue 1, actually a more general framework for case representation and retrieval with time-dependent features has been proposed in [13]; this paper deals with the problem of time series similarity and proposes a complex retrieval strategy; nevertheless, it is still limited to the *case level* temporal dimension.

On the other hand, a recent contribution [29] deals with temporal information at the *history level*, in the respiratory sinus arrhythmia domain. More interestingly, [19] presents an application independent logic formalism addressing history representation. From the temporal model point of view, this work is particularly interesting because it accommodates both points and intervals as primitive time elements. Nevertheless, how to deal with retrieval is not described; the authors only claim that graph similarity algorithms could be adopted. Moreover, they still do not address the temporal dimension in CBR as a whole, because features in the form of time series are not taken into account.

Finally, temporal knowledge representation for CBR is discussed in [8]. In this work, both points and intervals are exploited as well. However, here a clear distinction between cases and histories is not provided. In particular, a single case captures the overall evolution of the system under observation (i.e. the patient, since the work is applied to a medical domain), but snapshots of the feature values, limited to specific time intervals, are used for retrieval. Thus, to our knowledge, our work represent a meaningful effort towards a more comprehensive treatment of the two levels of the temporal dimension, as introduced in section 1.

3 The Temporal Dimension in Case-Based Retrieval: The Case Level

3.1 Case Representation

In our framework, we adopt a model for representing temporal information based on both the *point* and the *interval* primitives, in order to deal with as much real world situations as possible (see also [19]). In particular:

- a *point* is identified by an absolute (i.e. numeric) or relative (i.e. qualitative) temporal coordinate, expressed with respect to the reference system and the granularity of the application domain;
- an *interval* is identified by an ordered pair of points, which represent its starting point and its ending point respectively.

Given these premises, we have to detail what we mean for *case*, and how temporal information at the case level can be formalized.

As previously observed, in some real world applications, it may be limiting to conceive a case as an instantaneous situation, where all feature values are singletons and remain unchanged. In our framework, therefore, some features can take the form of (typically discretized) uni-dimensional time series. In addition, we associate to each case an *interval* - Case Interval (CI) henceforth - meant to represent the period of time in which all the feature values were measured.

With respect to the CI, features must satisfy these requirements:

1. each feature in the form of a single value has to be measured at a time point which is included between the starting and the ending point of the CI;
2. for a feature in the form of a time series, each value has to respect requirement (1) above.

3.2 Case Retrieval

Case retrieval needs to cope with the different types of features that can be defined in a case: time stamped single valued data points, and time series (we make the hypothesis that all features values at the case level are raw data).

Although it is not necessary, the different nature of features could suggest to treat them in different ways in the retrieval process. Without the expectation of providing an exhaustive panorama of alternatives, we would like to propose a modular architecture, that appears relatively general, in the sense that its elements can be skipped or differently combined, in order to obtain new solutions.

The proposed retrieval process (see figure 1) can be sketched as follows (at a very high level):

- use (some) single valued features for a *classification/grouping step*, to reduce the search space for retrieval itself;
- perform a *multi-step retrieval* in the output class:
  1. select some particularly relevant time series features;
  2. search for a set of cases similar to the query one in the direction of one of the selected features at a time;
  3. provide some kind of *combination* of the sets of locally similar cases identified above;
  4. order the results on the basis of all features, including also time stamped data points.

As regards the *combination* of locally similar cases, to be merged into a unique set, different alternatives may be devised. A possible combination function is

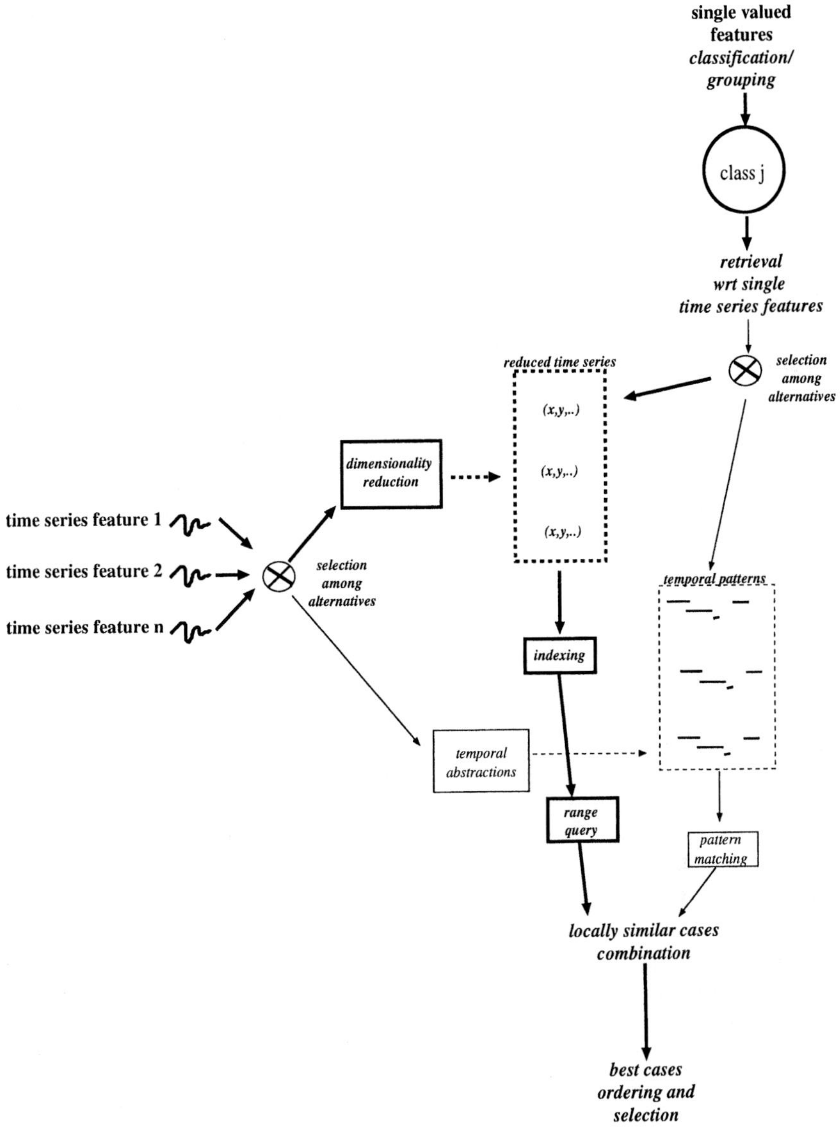

Fig. 1. A general architecture for case retrieval with time varying features. A classification/grouping step may be used to reduce the search space. Retrieval then takes place, in the direction of a single time series feature at a time. To optimize similarity-based time series retrieval, it is possible to select one out of two alternatives: (1) reduce dimensionality (e.g. by applying DFT) and then exploit spatial indexing techniques; (2) summarize the raw data by applying Temporal Abstractions (TA) and then exploit pattern matching techniques. Locally similar cases are then properly combined to produce the final output. The modules of the general architecture that have been implemented in the system RHENE (namely: classification, dimensionality reduction, indexing, range query and combination - see section 5) are highlighted in bold. Notice that, even if not shown in the figure, the process involves a query represented by raw time series data that are reduced or abstracted depending on the retrieval technique that is used (i.e. range query on an index structure or pattern matching over TA)

intersection. Suppose that locally similar cases were extracted through a set of range queries, one in each feature's direction; intersection extracts the cases that satisfy the request of being within all the specified ranges of similarity contemporaneously. Clearly this is quite a strong requirement. A less strict result may be obtained by using union as a combination function. In this hypothesis, a case will be globally accepted if it belongs at least to one range of similarity. Clearly, other combination operators may be introduced as well.

As a concrete example of multistep retrieval, section 5 describes the architecture of the system RHENE [20], developed by the authors in collaboration with the University of Pavia in Italy. RHENE's architecture instantiates a subset of the modules of figure 1, highlighted in bold.

While the retrieval of cases with single valued features is a classical topic of CBR, we can spend a few words on the retrieval of cases with time series features. For the sake of clarity, we will concentrate on the search of cases similar to the input one in the direction of one particular parameter, which is in the form of a discretized time series.

A wide literature exists about how to optimize similarity-based retrieval of time series. Before entering the details, we propose to distinguish between two main directions:

- apply a dimensionality reduction technique;
- summarize the raw data by means of a technique able to derive higher level information from them, such as Temporal Abstractions [6].

Blocks applying these methods in the general retrieval architecture can be recognized in figure 1. The following subsections provide a deeper insight of these two alternative procedures.

Dimensionality Reduction. In the literature, most of the approaches to similarity-based time series retrieval are founded on the common premise of dimensionality reduction (see the survey in [12]).

As a matter of fact, a discretized time series can always be seen as vector in an n-dimensional space (with n typically extremely large). Simple algorithms for retrieving similar time series take polynomial time in n. Multidimensional spatial indexing (e.g. resorting to R-trees [11]) can even lead to sub-linear retrieval; nevertheless, these tree structures are not adequate for indexing high-dimensional data sets [7].

One obvious solution is thus to reduce the time series dimensionality, by means of a transform that preserves the distance between two time series, or underestimates it: in this case a post-processing step will be required, to filter out the so-called "false alarms"; the requirement is never to overestimate the distance, so that no "false dismissals" can exist [12]. Widely used transforms are the Discrete Fourier Transform (DFT) [2], and the Discrete Wavelet Transform (DWT) [9].

DFT maps time series to the frequency domain. DFT application for dimensionality reduction stems from the observation that, for the majority of real-world time series, the first (1-3) Fourier coefficients carry the most meaningful information, and the remaining ones can be safely discarded. Moreover, Parseval's theorem [22] guarantees that the distance in the frequency domain is the same as in the time domain, when resorting to any similarity measure that can be expressed as the Euclidean distance between feature vectors in the feature space. In particular, resorting only to the first Fourier coefficients can underestimate the real distance, but never overestimates it.

On the other hand, wavelets are basis functions used to represent other functions. The wavelet transform can be repeatedly applied to the data, obtaining that each application brings out a higher resolution of the data, while at the same time it smoothes the remaining data. The output of the DWT consists of the remaining smooth components and of all the accumulated detail components. DWT, like any orthonormal transform, preserves the Euclidean distance as the DFT does. The number of wavelet coefficients to be kept, although lower than the original data dimensionality, is often higher than in the case of DFT application.

Retrieval of series transformed either by DFT or by wavelets can then benefit from the use of spatial index structures, such as the R-tree [11], the X-tree [7], and the TV-tree [31], whose features are widely discussed in the database literature, or from other specific indexing techniques (see e.g. [23]).

A different approach to dimensionality reduction is Piecewise Constant Approximation (PCA) (see e.g. [16,17]): it consists in dividing a time series into k segments, and in using their average values as a k-dimensional feature vector (where obviously $k << n$, the original data dimensionality). The best value of k can also be estimated.

The choice of the most cost-effective transformation to apply should be done on the basis of the application at hand.

Temporal Abstractions. While dimensionality reduction is a widely accepted technique for optimizing similarity-based retrieval of time series, the use of Temporal Abstractions (TA) [28,6] in this field is not often reported. Nevertheless, we believe it represents a valuable alternative to dimensionality reduction itself, in particular when:

- a more *qualitative* abstraction of the time series values is sufficient;
- a clear mapping between raw and transformed data has to be made available;
- the mapping itself needs to be easily interpretable by end users as well.

TA is an Artificial Intelligence methodology able to solve a *data interpretation task* [28], whose goal is the one of deriving high level concepts from time stamped data. Through TA, huge amounts of temporal information, like the one embedded in a time series, can be effectively mapped to a compact representation, that not only summarizes the original longitudinal data, but also abstracts meaningful behaviours in the data themselves.

Operatively, the basic principle of TA methods is to move from a *point-based* to an *interval-based* representation of the data [6], where: (i) the input

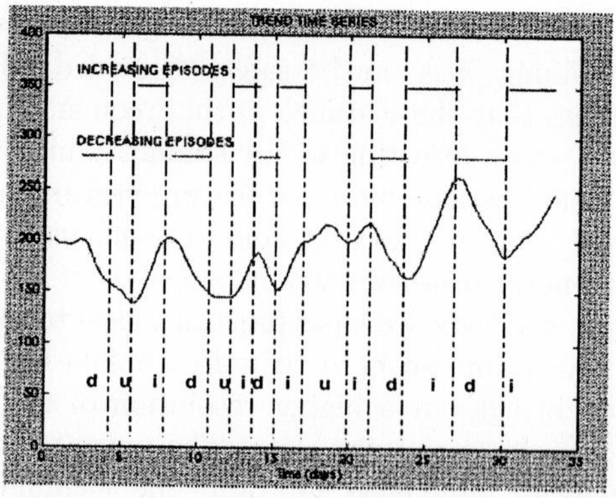

Fig. 2. An example of trend TA, applied to a blood glucose level time series [5]. The abstraction produces a pattern where symbols d, i, u stand for *decreasing*, *increasing* and *undecided* respectively

points (*events* henceforth) are the elements of the discretized time series; (ii) the output intervals (*episodes* henceforth) aggregate adjacent events sharing a common behaviour, persistent over time. More precisely, the method described above should be referred to as *basic* TA [6].

Basic abstractions can be further subdivided into *state* TA and *trend* TA. *State* TA are used to extract episodes associated to *qualitative levels* of the monitored feature, e.g. low, normal, high values; *trend* TA are exploited to detect specific *patterns*, such as increase, decrease or stationarity, from the time series. The output results of a basic TA depend on the value assigned to specific parameters, such as the granularity (the maximum temporal gap between two events allowed for aggregating them into the same episode) and the minimum extent (the minimum time extent for considering an episode relevant) for state TA, and the slope (the minimum allowed rate of change in an episode) for trend TA.

Complex TA [6] can be defined as well: instead of aggregating events into episodes, complex TA aggregate two series of episodes into a set of episodes of higher level (i.e., they abstract output intervals over precalculated input intervals). In particular, complex abstractions search for specific *temporal* relationships between episodes which can be generated from a basic abstraction or from other complex abstractions. The relation between intervals can be any of the temporal relations defined by Allen [3]. This kind of TA can be exploited to extract patterns that depend on the course of several features, or to detect patterns of complex shapes in a single feature.

If the time series has been pre-processed through TA, similarity based retrieval can benefit of the use of pattern matching techniques. Sequence matching can in fact be performed by a number of well-established methods [30] like dynamic programming based on edit distance approach [32], suffix tree-based approaches [33] or general formal transformations of patterns [15]. For example the framework in [15] defines similarity between a pattern A and a pattern B

(in a formal pattern language P) as a function of the transformations (defined on a transformation language T) needed to reduce B to A (or vice versa). The approach allows one to answer also queries such as "find all patterns similar to some pattern A, but not similar to pattern B". Figure 2 shows an example of a trend TA producing a pattern (over a granularity based on days) where symbols d, i, u stand for *decreasing*, *increasing* and *undecided* respectively.

Finally, we can notice that the use of TA can be limited to query the case library, if we do not want to explicitly abstract raw time series data, but we still want to maintain the capability of using the language of TA at the query level. For example, [34] introduces an algorithm where a symbolic query (in the form of sequence of symbols like those produced by a TA) can be answered over a database of raw time series data, by producing those subsequences that best match the query itself, following specific abstraction rules (like for instance those that may be used to define a TA).

4 The Temporal Dimension in Case-Based Retrieval: The History Level

By history we mean a set of temporally related or time consecutive cases, which refer to the same "object" or "entity" (e.g. the same patient in a medical domain, or the same class of devices in a fault diagnosis domain). Histories could be of various length; actually the number of cases that compose a history is a typical application dependent parameter. Histories themselves could be built "on the fly", when instances similar to the input one have to be retrieved; alternatively, they may be precompiled, and stored in a memory in which history search will then take place. In the case of precompilation, supposing that the history length is a known parameter[1], all possible histories could be built from the library of cases, or just a subset of them. The system could then precalculate all the histories for the given patient (or for all the patients in the case base), within the given time window. Of course, a trade-off exists between the cost of precompilation (and history storage) and the complexity of retrieval if histories have to be built just at retrieval time.

History retrieval can be the only goal of the retrieval system or it can be exploited as a search space reduction step (alternative to classification/grouping, see section 3.2), to be followed by case retrieval itself, which will then be focused only on the cases composing the retrieved histories. Figure 3 presents an architecture where history retrieval provides the first results, at a high level of abstraction; if the user is interested in more details, case retrieval (on a search

[1] This is not necessarily an unrealistic assumption. Actually, in some (e.g. medical) applications, the temporal window to take into account (i.e. the history length) could be well identified on the basis of the domain knowledge, and could also be explicitly provided by a guideline. For example, in hemodialysis treatment, the temporal window is normally made of two weeks, which correspond to a sequence of 6 consecutive cases.

space shrinked as described above), will refine the output, concentrating e.g. on more specific features values (at the case level).

4.1 History Representation

It is worth noting that history retrieval requires less detailed information with respect to case retrieval: the modelled object behaviour is being observed from a higher level perspective; therefore, for each case composing the history, the case content has to be somehow summarized.

To this hand, we envision different possibilities:

- first, a single value, "valid" in all the CI, can be assigned to each feature (see also [19]). This is trivially the case if the feature is a single data point. Dealing with time series, on the other hand, the value could correspond e.g. to the mean, or to the most frequent value in the feature measurements; more interestingly, it could be obtained as a *pattern approximately stable over the CI*, typically extracted through TA techniques, applied to the original data;
- as a second possibility, summarization can be obtained through a *granularity change*: a history can be interpreted as a "macro-case", whose features derive from the corresponding features in the cases composing the history. For time series, the macro-case features would be time series (inter-case data) of multidimensional time series (intra-case data). This information needs to be synthesized, for example through some sufficient statistics indexes, such as the median and the 10th and 90th percentiles of each variable. The macro-case features would then become the series of the medians and of the percentiles (or simply the series of the values for single valued features) over all the cases reported in the history. In the resulting macro-case, all features will then be in the form of time series. This second possibility seems more easily applicable if cases don't overlap in time.

In the next section, we discuss proper retrieval strategies for both the summarization alternatives.

4.2 History Retrieval

When each case has been mapped to a *pattern stable over an interval*, TA and pattern matching techniques immediately appear as good candidates for retrieval.

In particular, when intervals are the input to the TA process, complex TA (see section 3.2) can be applied to extract temporal patterns in the history, that correspond to significant behaviours in the process being observed. For example, a peak in a case feature f defined by two consecutive cases can be identified by a complex TA of the form "an increasing trend in f *meets* a decreasing trend in f", where *meets* is an operator of Allen's interval algebra [3]. The mechanism can still be applied if the cases are (partially) overlapping. Once meaningful patterns have been identified in the query history, similar histories can be extracted relying upon pattern matching techniques. As for the case level, various retrieval architectures could be designed; typically, some features could be more relevant than others in history retrieval, and could be used for the selection of very relevant histories, to be then ordered on the basis of all feature values (see section 3.2 and figure 3).

On the other hand, if a *granularity change* has been applied, the problem is basically reduced to case retrieval, and the considerations of section 3.2 hold. In this situation, all case features are in the form of time series, that require a preprocessing for optimizing retrieval itself. Since in history retrieval the goal is the one of abstracting higher level concepts from raw data, the use of TA appears particularly appealing in this case as well. Pattern matching techniques will then help for a similarity-based search in the case memory (see figure 3). In particular, some ground cases features are now mapped to more than one history features (e.g. median and percentiles, or mean and standard deviation). The different meaning of these features could correspond to a different role in the retrieval process. For example, a preprocessing step could filter out histories in which standard deviation values are too high. Alternatively, if a weight defines the importance of each feature (at the case level), the weight of a case feature that has been mapped to a mean and a standard deviation at the history level could be decomposed in two numbers, to be assigned as the weights of the mean and of the standard deviation respectively. A combination (e.g. the product) of the two numbers (at the history level) would provide the weight of the original feature at the case level.

5 The Framework in Practice: The RHENE System

RHENE (**R**etrieval of **HE**modialysis in **NE**phrological disorders) is a multi-step case retrieval system applied to the domain of patients affected by nephropatologies and treated with hemodialysis [20]. Defining a dialysis session as a case, retrieval (at the case level) has to operate both on single valued and time series features.

RHENE implements a subpart of the modules of the general architecture in figure 1 (highlighted in bold).

In particular, a preliminary classification/grouping step, based on single-valued features, reduces the retrieval search space. Intra-class retrieval then takes place by considering time series features, and is articulated as follows: (1) locally similar cases (considering one feature at a time) are extracted and the *intersection* of the retrieved sets is computed; (2) global similarity is computed, as a *weighted average* of local distances, and the best cases are listed. For similarity-based time series retrieval (step (1)), we rely on dimensionality reduction, and in particular on DFT. Thanks to specific index structures (i.e. k-d trees and TV trees) range queries can be efficiently performed on our case base. Both ranges and weights are tunable parameters; this choice provides the tool with great flexibility.

The current prototype has been positively tested on a case base of more than 6500 cases, belonging to 48 real patients.

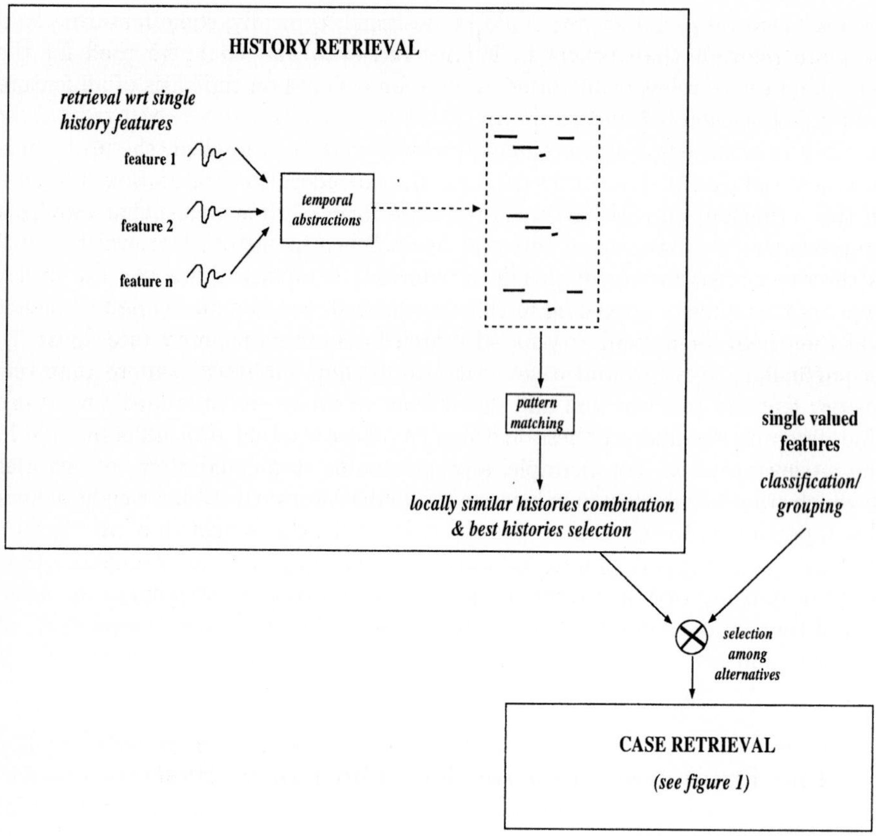

Fig. 3. A general retrieval architecture, in which history retrieval can be used, in alternative to classification/grouping, to reduce the search space for case retrieval. Case retrieval can then be exploited to obtain more detailed results, concentrating on more specific features values. History retrieval is sped up by the use of TA and of pattern matching techniques. For the case retrieval block, please refer to figure 1. As in case of figure 1, we omit here to explicitly show the query

In the future, we plan to work at the history level as well, by redefining a case as a longer monitoring period (see section 4), typically made by all the dialysis sessions of a patient within two weeks. As a matter of fact, as observed in the introduction, this enlarged granularity is closer to the viewpont from which physicians use to evaluate the dialysis data and to judge the patient's evolution over time. A tool (called EMOSTAT) able to summarize the raw data along these lines, and to provide an off-line monitoring facility to nephrologists, has already been implemented at the University of Pavia [4]. In particular, in EMOSTAT time series data are synthesized through the median and the 10th and 90th percentiles of each monitoring variable.

This tool is going to be integrated with RHENE[2], in order to implement history retrieval. On the history features, we want to look for particular patterns (e.g. episodes of increasing values, peaks, etc.), that we will highlight by preprocessing the data through TA, and by applying approximate string matching techniques. As a second step, the physician will be allowed to enter the detail of the cases composing the retrieved histories, and formulate stricter queries, on the basis of feature values of particular interest. History retrieval will therefore be available as an autonomous facility, or as a preprocessing step for case retrieval, as described in figure 3. The overall architecture resulting from the integration of the two systems will provide a support for patient examination and therapy evaluation, but could also be adopted as a means for assessing the quality of the hemodialysis service, producing a useful input from the knowledge management perspective. Technically speaking, quality assessment requires to fulfil two tasks: (1) discover relationships between the time patterns of the process data and the performance outcomes; (2) retrieve similar critical patterns within the process data, in order to assess their frequency. While EMOSTAT is able to address task (1), the role of RHENE is the one of implementing task (2), thus providing a comprehensive approach towards the realization of an auditing procedure, able to summarize the dialysis sessions from a clinical quality viewpoint.

6 Conclusions and Future Works

In this paper, we have presented a domain-independent framework for dealing with the temporal dimension in case representation and retrieval. In particular, we have proposed a multi-step retrieval architecture whose modules can be differently instantiated and combined, in order to cover the various needs of the possible application domains. An example of implementation is represented by the system RHENE, described in section 5. RHENE currently implements a subpart of the overall architecture, limited to the case level. In the future, we plan to deal with knowledge representation and retrieval at the history level as well, in order to provide physicians with a more flexible tool, that will enable them to inspect patients' data by referring to different time granularities. This work, which will be supported by a grant of the Italian Ministry of Education, will be limited to a specific application domain. Nevertheless, it will represent a first step towards a better understanding of the advantages possibly provided by the methodology proposed in this paper, and will allow us to inspect its usability in practice.

References

1. A. Aamodt and E. Plaza. Case-based reasoning: foundational issues, methodological variations and systems approaches. *AI Communications*, 7:39–59, 1994.

[2] This work will be supported by the grant PRIN 2004 number 2004094558, funded by the Italian Ministry of Education.

2. R. Agrawal, C. Faloutsos, and A.N. Swami. Efficient similarity search in sequence databases. In D. Lomet, editor, *Proc. 4th Int. Conf. of Foundations of Data Organization and Algorithms*, pages 69–84. Springer-Verlag, Berlin, 1993.
3. J.F. Allen. Towards a general theory of action and time. *Artificial Intelligence*, 23:123–154, 1984.
4. R. Bellazzi, C. Larizza, P. Magni, and R. Bellazzi. Temporal data mining for the quality assessment of a hemodialysis service. *Artificial Intelligence in Medicine (in press)*.
5. R. Bellazzi, C. Larizza, P. Magni, S. Montani, and M. Stefanelli. Intelligent analysis of clinical time series: an application in the diabetes mellitus domain. *Artificial Intelligence in Medicine*, 20:37–57, 2000.
6. R. Bellazzi, C. Larizza, and A. Riva. Temporal abstractions for interpreting diabetic patients monitoring data. *Intelligent Data Analysis*, 2:97–122, 1998.
7. S. Berchtold, D.A. Keim, and H.P. Kriegel. The x-tree: an index structure for high-dimensional data. In *Proc. VLDB 96*, pages 28–39. Morgan Kaufman, San Mateo, CA, 1996.
8. I. Bichindaritz and E. Conlon. Temporal knowledge representation and organization for case-based reasoning. In *Proc. TIME-96*, pages 152–159. IEEE Computer Society Press, Washington, DC, 1996.
9. K.P. Chan and A.W.C. Fu. Efficient time series matching by wavelets. In *Proc. ICDE 99*, pages 126–133. IEEE Computer Society Press, Washington, DC, 1999.
10. B. Fuch, A. Mille, and B. Chiron. Operator decision aiding by adaptation of supervision strategies. In *Case-Based Reasoning Research and Development, LNAI*, pages 23–32. Springer-Verlag, Berlin, 1995.
11. A. Guttman. R-trees: a dynamic index structure for spatial searching. In *Proc. ACM SIGMOD*, pages 47–57. ACM Press, New York, NY, 1984.
12. M.L. Hetland. A survey of recent methods for efficient retrieval of similar time sequences. In H. Bunke M. Last, A. Kandel, editor, *Data Mining in Time Series Databases*. World Scientific, London, 2003.
13. M. Jaczynski. A framework for the management of past experiences with time-extended situations. In *Proc. ACM conference on Information and Knowledge Management (CIKM) 1997*, pages 32–38. ACM Press, New York, NY, 1997.
14. M.D. Jaere, A. Aamodt, and P. Skalle. Representing temporal knowledge for case-based prediction. In S. Craw and A. Preece, editors, *Proc. European Conference on Case Based Reasoning (ECCBR) 2002, in: Lecture Notes in Artificial Intelligence 2416*, pages 174–188. Springer-Verlag, Berlin, 2002.
15. H.V. Jagadish, A.O. Mendelzon, and T. Milo. Similarity based queries. In *Proc. 14th ACM Symp. on Principles of Database Systems*, San Jose, CA, 1995.
16. E. Keogh. Fast similarity search in the presence of longitudinal scaling in time series databases. In *Proc. Int. Conf. on Tools with Artificial Intelligence*, pages 578–584. IEEE Computer Society Press, Washington, DC, 1997.
17. E. Keogh, K. Chakrabarti, M. Pazzani, and S. Mehrotra. Dimensionality reduction for fast similarity search in large time series databases. *Knowledge and Information Systems*, 3(3):263–286, 2000.
18. E.T. Keravnou. Modeling medical concepts as time objects. In *Proceedings AIME 1995, LNAI 934*, pages 67–90. Springer-Verlag, Berlin, 1995.
19. J. Ma and B. Knight. A framework for historical case-based reasoning. In K.D. Ashley and D.G. Bridge, editors, *Proc. International Conference on Case Based Reasoning (ICCBR) 2003, in: Lecture Notes in Artificial Intelligence 2689*, pages 246–260. Springer-Verlag, Berlin, 2003.

20. S. Montani, L. Portinale, R. Bellazzi, and G. Leonardi. Rhene: a case retrieval system for hemodialysis cases with dynamically monitored parameters. In P. Funk and P.A. Gonzales Calero, editors, *Proc. European Conference on Case Based Reasoning (ECCBR) 2004, in: Lecture Notes in Artificial Intelligence 3155*, pages 659–672. Springer-Verlag Berlin, 2004.
21. G. Nakhaeizadeh. Learning prediction from time series: a theoretical and empirical comparison of cbr with some other approaches. In *Topics in Case-Based Reasoning, LNAI 837*, pages 65–76. Springer-Verlag, Berlin, 1994.
22. A.V. Oppenheim and R.W. Shafer. *Digital signal processing.* Prentice Hall, London, 1975.
23. D. Patterson, M. Galushka, and N. Rooney. An effective indexing and retrieval approach for temporal cases. In *Proc. 17th FLAIRS 2004, AAAI Press, Miami*, 2004.
24. A. Ram and J.C. Santamaria. Continuous case-based reasoning. In *Proc. AAAI Case-Based Reasoning Workshop*, pages 86–93, 1993.
25. F.E. Ritter and J.H. Larkin. Developing process models as summaris of hci action sequences. *Human Computer Interaction*, 9:345–383, 1994.
26. S. Rougegrez. Similarity evaluation between observed behaviours for the prediction of processes. In *Topics in Case-Based Reasoning, LNAI 837*, pages 155–166. Springer-Verlag, Berlin, 1994.
27. R. Schmidt, B. Heindl, B. Pollwein, and L. Gierl. Abstraction of data and time for multiparametric time course prognoses. In *Advances of Case-Based Reasoning, LNAI 1168*, pages 377–391. Springer-Verlag, Berlin, 1996.
28. Y. Shahar. A framework for knowledge-based temporal abstractions. *Artificial Intelligence*, 90:79–133, 1997.
29. M. Sollenborn and M. Nilsson. Building a case-base for stress diagnosis: an analysis of classified respiratory sinus arrhythmia sequences. In *Proc. Case-Based Reasoning in the Health Sciences Workshop, European Conference on Case Based Reasoning (ECCBR) 2004.*
30. G.A. Stephen. String searching algorithms. In *Lecture Notes Series in Computing*, volume 3. World Scientific, 1994.
31. V.S. Subrahmanian. *Principles of Multimedia Database Systems.* Morgan Kaufmann, San Mateo, CA, 1998.
32. E. Ukkonen. Algorithms for approximate string matching. *Information Control*, 64:100–118, 1985.
33. E. Ukkonen. Approximate matching over suffix trees. In *Lecture Notes in Computer Science*, volume 684, pages 228–242. Springer Verlag, 1993.
34. B.B. Xia. Similarity search in time series data sets. Technical report, School of Computer Science, Simon Fraser University, 1997.

The Best Way to Instil Confidence Is by Being Right

An Evaluation of the Effectiveness of Case-Based Explanations in Instilling User Confidence

Conor Nugent, Pádraig Cunningham, and Dónal Doyle

Department of Computer Science, Trinity College Dublin
{Conor.Nugent, Padraig.Cunningham, Donal.Doyle}@cs.tcd.ie

Abstract. Instilling confidence in the abilities of machine learning systems in end-users is seen as critical to their success in real world problems. One way in which this can be achieved is by providing users with interpretable explanations of the system's predictions. CBR systems have long been understood to have an inherent transparency that has particular advantages for explanations compared with other machine learning techniques. However simply supplying the most similar case is often not enough. In this paper we present a framework for providing interpretable explanations of CBR systems which includes dynamically created discursive texts explaining the feature-value relationships and a measure of confidence of the CBR system's prediction being correct. We also present a means by which the trade-off between being overly confident or overly cautious can be evaluated and different methods compared. We have carried out a preliminary user evaluation of the framework and present our findings. It is clear from this evaluation that being right is important. It appears that caveats and notes of caution when the system is uncertain damage user confidence.

1 Introduction

CBR systems have long been understood to have an inherent transparency that has particular advantages for explanations compared with other machine learning techniques [1]. The realisation that there is a need to make machine learning systems more interpretable and user friendly has brought this fact back into focus in recent years. Research by Cunningham et al. found that CBR explanations where the user is simply supplied with the most similar case are more convincing than rule-based explanations in some domains [2].

Recently researchers have begun to look at ways in which this method can be improved upon. The issue with case-based explanations lies in the perceived appropriateness of the presented cases to the validity of the prediction. This is an issue that has received a lot of attention in the CBR community. In CBR explanations, the ability of the user to make meaningful comparisons between the query and the retrieved explanation case is of critical importance to the success of

H. Muñoz-Avila and F. Ricci (Eds.): ICCBR 2005, LNAI 3620, pp. 368–381, 2005.

the explanation [3]. CBR systems are not wholly transparent and much domain knowledge can be contained within the similarity metrics used in the system. It is implicitly assumed in simple CBR explanations systems that the user has this same domain knowledge and so the appropriateness of the explanation case is clear. However, this may not be the case and the relevance of the retrieved case may be lost on novice users. This is an issue that McSherry has addressed in his ProCon System [4]. McSherry has focused on making the relationship between the feature values within a case and its predicted value explicit. Similarly we address this issue in our case-based explanation system for black-box systems [5]. However in our approach we used localised information to ensure that our system captured any non-linear feature interactions that occurred in the feature space.

In other work, Doyle et al. have focused on the observation that the nearest retrieved case in a CBR system may not be the best case to present as an explanation [6]. They use these cases to form *a fortiori* arguments in favour of the CBR systems prediction. They argue that in classification tasks, cases that are between the query case and the decision boundary provide more convincing explanations. That is, cases that are more marginal on the important criteria are more convincing. With such cases the user is better able to assess whether the classification of the target case is justified.

The primary motivation in providing users of CBR systems with interpretable explanations is to increase their confidence in the system. However, as is pointed out by Cheetham and Price, people can quickly lose confidence in a system if it makes predictions which then turn out to be incorrect [7]. To address this issue Cheetham and Price propose using confidence measures to alert the user when a system may be making a mistake.

We have developed an explanation framework for CBR systems which attempts to address the issue of providing user confidence by providing interpretable explanations coupled with a measure of confidence of the systems prediction. We have performed preliminary evaluations on the explanation framework and the results are presented.

The paper is structured as follows. Section 2 outlines how the framework works. Section 3 outlines a methodology for investigating the trade-offs in generating estimates of system confidence. Section 4 describes the evaluation we have carried out and presents the results of those evaluations. Finally we end with the conclusions in Section 5.

2 Explanation Framework

We have developed a framework for providing interpretable explanations in CBR systems. The explanations produced by the framework contain a number of elements;

- Cases that form *a fortiori* arguments,
- Discursive text describing the effects of differences in feature-values between the Query Case and the Explanation Case,
- A measure of confidence in the system's prediction.

The framework expands on earlier work in which we used localised models to help explain the feature-value relationships in regression tasks [5]. The two key aspects of our localised approach are; the generation of a local case-base and the use of a local model. The local model is used to help describe the feature-value relationships and to inform the search for an explanation case. In this paper we describe an implemenation for use in binary classification problems. To build a local case-base in such problems we simply use a Nearest Neighbour algorithm to create a subset case-base of the original case-base. First we find the Query Case's nearest neighbours and include them in our new subset case-base until we have at least K cases of each of the two classes. This ensures that our local case-base traverses the decision boundary in the area of our Query case. Once we have our localised case-base we then build our local model on it. As a model to use to capture the local information stored in the casebase we have selected to use logistic regression models. Logistic regression models are quite simple yet powerful and allow us to realise all the elements of our explanation framework listed above. In the coming sections we discuss the logistic regression model and how it is used in the generation of explanations.

2.1 Logistic Regression

Logistic regression, like linear regression, produces a set of coefficients from which the relationship of an input variable to the target class variable can be deduced. However unlike linear regression, logistic regression coefficients don't directly correspond to slope values in the same way. Logistic regression models are restricted to binary tasks and the two possible class values are coded as being either 0 or 1. Because the value predicted by the model, the conditional mean, is no longer an unbounded value as in linear regression but a value between 0 and 1, the data is fitted to a distribution that ensures the outputted value always meets this bounding criteria.To do this the logistic distribution is applied as can be seen below (1).

$$Y(x) = \frac{e^{\beta_0+\beta_1 x}}{1+e^{\beta_0+\beta_1 x}} \tag{1}$$

Here $Y(x)$ is the conditional mean for a particular value of x while β_0 and β_1 are the model parameters. The distribution produces the conditional mean, a value between 0 and 1, for any given inputted value of x. Importantly, for binary problems the conditional mean is in fact the probability of class 1 given x. This allows us, in a very direct way, to determine the level of belief of an input x belonging to a particular class. Using such measures of belief we can inform users of our confidence in a particular solution. Exactly how this is done is discussed in greater detail in Sections 2.2 and 3.

At first glance this model looks quite intimidating and seems to offer no hope of offering an insight into the relationship between x and our class variable. However, the logistic distribution is chosen because it can be easily transformed into another form which has many of the desirable properties of a linear regression model. By applying the logit transform, Equation 2, we end up with a simple and interpretable model, the logit (3).

$$g(x) = \ln \frac{Y(x)}{1 - Y(x)} \tag{2}$$

$$g(x) = \beta_0 + \beta_1 x \tag{3}$$

The parameters of the logit model can easily be converted into odds ratios. The odds ratio of an event is the odds of that event occurring over the odds of it not happening. For instance if someone were to state the odds ratio of smokers to non-smokers getting cancer is 2 then this would mean smokers are twice as likely to develop cancer as non-smokers. Alternatively, if we looked at the relationship the other way round, non-smokers to smokers, we would get an odds ratio of 0.5. This means that non-smokers are half as likely to get cancer. In general an odds ratio greater then one for possibility A over possibility B means A makes the event more likely than the alternative while an odds ratio of less then one means it makes it less likely. The logistic regression model makes the calculation of odds ratios quite easy and this is extremely useful and informative. It is this simple relationship between the model coefficients and the odds ratio and their natural interpretation that has made logistic regression such a popular tool. We will discuss in a very general sense how this is done as it will be of use in Section 2.3 where we use the logistic regression model to explain the differences in feature-values between the query case and the explanation case.

In order to extract the odds ratio, two steps are taken. First the logit difference is found. Imagine we are interested in the odds ratio of two different events, $x = c$ and $x = d$. the logit difference can be calculated as in Equation 4. The logit difference, ld, is simply the difference in the logit function for the two values of x we are interested in. Once this value has been obtained it can then be converted into an odds ratio, see Equation 5.

$$\textit{Logit Difference}(x = c, x = d) = g(c) - g(d) = ld \tag{4}$$

$$\textit{Odds Ratio}(x = c, x = d) = e^{ld} \tag{5}$$

One of the major reasons for the popularity of the logistic regression model is that in many cases it is not necessary to calculate the logit difference. If the model variables have been properly coded then the desired information usually can be obtained by inspecting the model coefficients directly (chapter 4, [8]). However for our purposes since we are interested in specific cases and not general trends we can simply find the odds ratio for specific values using Equation 5. Once we have the odds ratio the relationship between input variable and the class variable is clear. We have focused most of our discussion on examples with only a single input variable for simplicity sake but the above observations are also true in multi-variable problems. In the next section we discus how exactly information derived from the logistic regression model can be used to provide convincing explanations.

2.2 Finding a Fortiori Cases and a Measure of Confidence

Using the local logistic regression model we can generate *a fortiori* arguments dynamically and without any prior domain knowledge. As discussed in Section

Table 1. Explanation Case Retrieval Process

Features	Query Case	Nearest Neighbour 1	Nearest Neighbour 2	Nearest Neighbour 3
Weight	88	82	79	76
Duration	120	120	120	120
Gender	Male	Male	Male	Male
Meal	Full	Full	Full	Full
Units	5.2	5.0	7.2	4.6
BAC	Under	Under	Under	Under
Probability	0.98	0.97	0.89	0.96

2.1 Logistic Regression models allow us to generate a probability for a given set of inputs. In the explanation case retrieval process we can then use this to find an explanation case that is nearer the decision boundary and so a more convincing argument. We consider each of the cases in our localised case-base as a candidate case for inclusion in the explanation. By passing each of our candidate explanation cases through our local logistic model using Equation 1 we can generate a probability for each. A case that is nearer the decision boundary and of the same class as our CBR system has predicted will have a more marginal probability and so this should be the case we select.

To make this process a little clearer we will discus it in relation to the Blood Alcohol Content (BAC) domain [2,6]. The task involves using information such as peoples weight, gender, number of units of alcohol consumed to predict whether someone's blood alcohol content (BAC) exceeds the drink driving limit. We built a simple Nearest Neighbour algorithm on the data set and applied our framework to providing explanations of it's predictions. After the Query Case has been classified we can then build our logistic model on our local data. In Table 1 we can see the Query Case, its predicted classification and three candidate explanation cases which are in fact the Nearest Neighbours used to classify it. In order to select a case to use in our explanation we first run each of the cases including the Query Case through our local logistic regression model. This gives us the set of probabilities that can also be seen in Table 1. We can see that Nearest Neighbour 2 has the lowest probability and so is the case nearest the decision boundary. This is an alternative to the explanation utility framework described by [6] for selecting the cases to present to the user which make more convincing arguments than the nearest neighbours. Although Nearest Neighbour 2 had consumed more units of alcohol and weighed less, they were under the limit so it seems reasonable that our Query Case should be too.

We can make this argument more explicit to the end user by explaining the effects of the feature differences between the Query Case and Explanation Case. In the next section we will outline how this can be done using the local logistic regression model. As Cheetham and Price point out, being able to provide a measure of prediction confidence is an extremely useful asset in maintaining end-users confidence in a system [7]. By substituting the Query Case values into Equation 1 we can derive a probability of the Query Case being a certain class. If this probability is below a certain threshold we can inform the user that confidence is low. How this threshold might be decided upon is discussed in Section 3. When the confidence in a decision is low we should consider presenting the user with extra information to help them in making their decision. One way in which this can done is by presenting the user with counter examples, cases that are similar but have a different classification. We will discus the selection of counter examples in Section 2.4.

2.3 Explaining Feature-Value Relationships

The logistic regression model can be used to determine the effects of differences in cases. Using Equations 4 and 5 from Section 2.1 we can substitute each of the feature differences into the equations individually and get an odds ratio for each. Using the odds ratio we can then determine the effect of the change. As discussed in section 2.1 an odds ratio greater than 1 means that a feature difference makes an event more likely and vice versa. Looking at each feature difference in turn we can then make lists of features differences that make the classification more likely and those that have the opposite effect. Canned texts are then used to describe the feature differences appropriately. As an example of how this process is carried out consider the Weight feature in the Sample Explanation in Table 2. Using the logistic regression models we find that the odds ratio is less than one when the Explanation and Query Case values, 79 and 57 kilograms respectively, are

Table 2. Sample Explanation

	Query Case	**Explanation Case**
Weight (kgs)	57.0	79.0
Duration (mins)	240.0	240.0
Gender	Male	Male
Meal	Full	Full
Amount (Units)	12.6	9.6
BAC		Over

The prediction for the individual in the Quey Case is: **Over the limit**

The confidence that this prediction is correct is: **high**

Discursive Text:

In support of this prediction we have the person presented by the Explanation Case who was also Over the limit. `Weight` being lighter and `Amount` being bigger have the effect of making the Query individual more likely to be Over the limit than the Explanation individual.

Table 3. Sample Explanation with Counter Example

	Explanation Case	**Query Case**	**Counter Example**
Weight (kgs)	52.0	53.0	73.0
Duration (mins)	270.0	330.0	210.0
Gender	Male	Female	Male
Meal	Lunch	Lunch	Lunch
Amount (Units)	9.1	10.4	9.0
BAC	Over		Under

The prediction for the individual in the Query Case is: **Over the limit**

The confidence that this prediction is correct is: **low**

Discursive Text:

In support of this prediction we have the person represented by the Explanation Case who was also Over the limit. `Gender` being `Female` and `Amount` being bigger have the effect of making the Query individual more likely to be Over the limit than the Explanation individual. However, `Weight` being heavier and `Duration` being longer have the effect of making the Query individual less likely to be Over the limit than the Explanation individual

As there is low confidence in the prediction we also have a counter example of someone who is similar but Under the limit for you to inspect

`Duration` being longer has the effect of making the Query individual more likely to be Under the limit than the counter example. However, `Weight` being lighter, `Gender` being `Female` and `Amount` being bigger have the effect of making the Query individual less likely to be Under the limit than the counter example

substituted into Equation 4 and the odds ratio determined using Equation 5. This then means that the Query Cases' value for this feature, 57, contributes to making the Query Case more likely to be Over the limit than the Explanation Case. By simple inspection of the feature values we can determine that Query Case value is less than the Explanation value and the term *lighter* is retrieved from a stored set of relationship terms specific to describe this relationship. This process is carried out for each of the features differences and the discursive text built up as can be seen in Table 2. It is worth noting that if the case-base used to build the local model doesn't adequately represent the problem, counter intuitive explanations can be produced. For instance we found that if too few cases were used `duration` could be heavily correlated with `units` and so a larger `duration` value could be seen as evidence in favour of being over the limit.

2.4 Presenting Counter Examples

By presenting the user with similar cases that lie either side of the decision boundary we can help them make a more informed decision. This kind of approach has previously been introduced by Leake et al. [9] who used *bracketing cases* to help delineate the limits of the problem being considered. When confidence is low we can adopt a similar approach: presenting the user with cases from either side of the decision boundary and using discursive texts to explain how the feature values affected the different classifications. Again using the logistic regression model in the same way that it was used to find *a fortiori* arguments it is possible to find the nearest case on the opposite side of the decision boundary.

In Table 3 we can see the type of counter example explanation produced. The user is presented with both explanation cases either side of the Query Case and a discursive text describing the effects of differences between each of the cases and the Query Case. It is hoped that this will help the user in deciding whether to accept the prediction or reject it.

3 Investigating Confidence Measures

The key issue in providing any confidence measure is ensuring that when it is confident it is correct without bringing too many correct predictions into question. Constantly supplying users with predictions that we are unsure about is bound to damage their confidence in the system. There often is a trade-off between the two and a tolerance level where the level of confidence versus pessimism is acceptable must be chosen. This can make comparing different schemes less than straightforward as one scheme may be better at one level of tolerance and another at a different level. The characteristics of this problem led us to investigate adapting ROC curves to the task [10]. We can characterize our wish for accurate confidence as being our Confident Correct Rate (CCR) as defined in Equation 6. Likewise we can encapsulate our need to minimise pessimism in the Not Confident Correct Rate ($NCCR$) as defined in Equation 7.

$$CCR = \frac{CC}{CC + CI} \tag{6}$$

$$NCCR = \frac{NCC}{NCC + NCI} \tag{7}$$

Where CC is the number of times the measure is confident and the system is correct and CI is the number of times measure is confident and the system is incorrect. Likewise NCC is the number of times the measure is not confident and the system is correct and NCI is the number of times the system is not confident and is right to be so. To make the definition of these parameters a little clearer we have displayed them in the form of a truth table in Table 4. Our scheme for confidence requires one parameter K, the number of cases of each class that is required in order to stop the local case-base building process. As an example of how the methodology we described can be used to investigate the

Table 4. A Truth Table Defining the Equation Parameters

	Incorrect	Correct
Confident	CI	CC
Not Confident	NCI	NCC

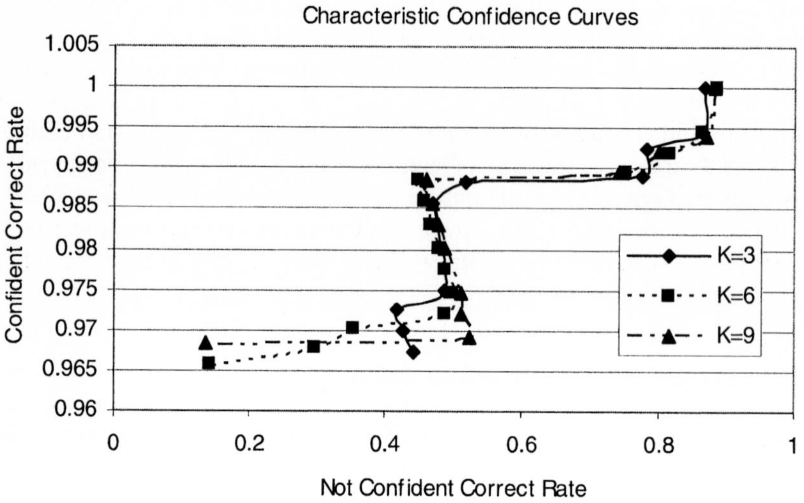

Fig. 1. The Characteristic Confidence Curves for the UCI Spam Data set for a Range of K Values

confidence measure trade-off we have applied it two data sets; the BAC set and a Spam data set from the UCI repository. In our confidence scheme we must chose a level of probability that we must have in a prediction in order to be confident in it. We performed leave-one-out cross-validations on both data sets recording the required statistics while varying both K and the confidence threshold. We then plotted the results of the evaluation on Characteristic Confidence Curves which are very similar to ROC curves as can be seen in Figures 1 and 2. For each scheme there is a separate curve and the points on those curves represent different threshold levels for those schemes. Like in ROC curves our ideal solution would lie in the top left hand corner and the solution which is nearest this point optimises the trade-off. However different applications may have restrictions about how often the system can be confident and incorrect. It is quite easy using the characteristic curves to find the scheme that best meets these requirements. It is also possible eliminate certain schemes as being definitely worse than another (like in ROC curves) if the curve of one scheme lies entirely inside another then it is worse than that scheme.

In Figure 1 we can see that the three different schemes are all quite closely aligned but that generally the scheme for k=6 out performs the others although at certain points k=3 is slightly more favourable. Likewise in Figure 2 we can see

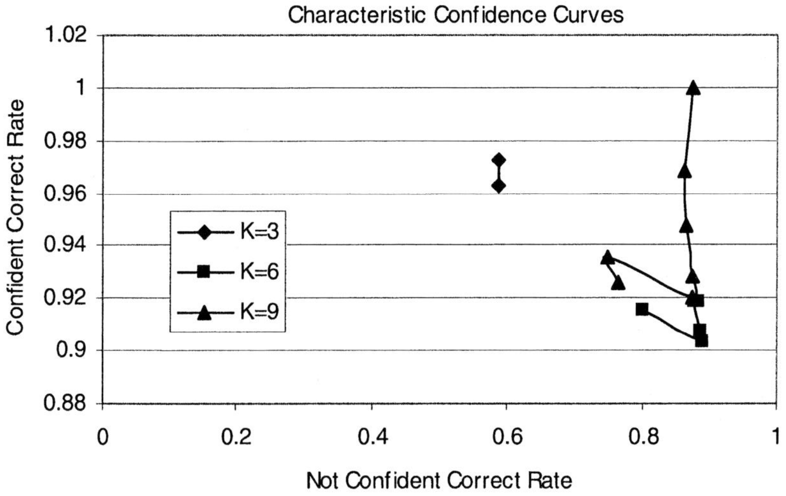

Fig. 2. The Characteristic Confidence Curves for the BAC Data set for a Range of K Values

Table 5. The Confidence Measures Results

	Spam		BAC	
	Incorrect	Correct	Incorrect	Correct
Confident	13	366	3	78
Not Confident	18	3	7	10

that our best solution is clearly when k=3 as the two points on its curve lie far closer to the upper left hand corner than any others. There are only two points on the k=3 curve because it very quickly goes from being entirely not confident to reaching the minimum possible threshold value. The minimum threshold value is the probability of 0.5 as any belief below this actually represents a belief in the other class in binary problems. As an example of how accurately we can predict confidence we chose the two points on both graphs that maximised the trade-off. These can be see in Table 5.

In the case of the Spam data set we are Confident and Correct 91.5% of the time while being Confident and Incorrect just 3.25% of the time. Importantly we are not confident when correct less than 1% of the time. In the alcohol data set Confident and Correct 79% of the time while Confident and Incorrect 3% of the time.

4 Evaluation

In this section we examine the results of a preliminary investigation into the effectiveness of the explanation framework. In order to assess the usefulness of the framework's explanations we performed a user trial. We will now outline the structure of the user trial and discuss our findings.

4.1 User Trials

In designing the user trial there were three principle questions we wished to address; do people find the explanations understandable and useful, do the explanations increase users' confidence in the case-based system and finally can the explanations alert users to when the system might be in error. The case-base on which the trial was carried out was again the Blood Alcohol Content case-base [2,6]. We built a simple Nearest Neighbour algorithm on the data set and applied our framework to providing explanations of its predictions.

In the trial, subjects were given a questionnaire in which they were shown three different forms of explanation;

- **The Full Framework Explanation:** This is an explantion that includes the selected *a fortiori* explantion case, a discursive text and a measure of confidence as seen in Table 2.
- **Case-based Explanation:** In this form of explanation the subject is just shown the selected *a fortiori* case as evidence in favour of the prediction.
- **No Explanation:** The user is just presented with the feature-values of the query and the systems prediction.

The trial subjects were shown four examples of each type of explanation and asked two questions after each example shown;

- **Question One:** Do you think the prediction is correct?
- **Question Two:** How would you rate this Explanation?

Below each question the trial subject had five options to select from. In question one the options were; No, Maybe No, Don't Know, Maybe Yes and Yes. In question two the options were; Poor; Fair; Okay, Good and Very Good.

To assess the use of explanations in terms of alerting users to when the system might be in error one of the four examples shown of each explanation type was a mis-classification. Twelve people from a number of different academic backgrounds took part in the evaluation and the results are discussed in the next section.

User Trial Results: In question one we looked at the frequencies with which users chose each of the five options when the prediction made by the system was correct. These can be see in Figure 3. It is clear that the explanations given by the framework give the users far greater confidence in the system than either of the other two schemes. The trial subjects answered *Yes* 88% for the time with just four answers being anything other than yes. Three people answered *Maybe Yes*, one *Don't Know* and there were no negative answers. We also examined the users responses when the system had made an incorrect classification and the results can be seen in Figure 4. The graph of frequencies reveals a very

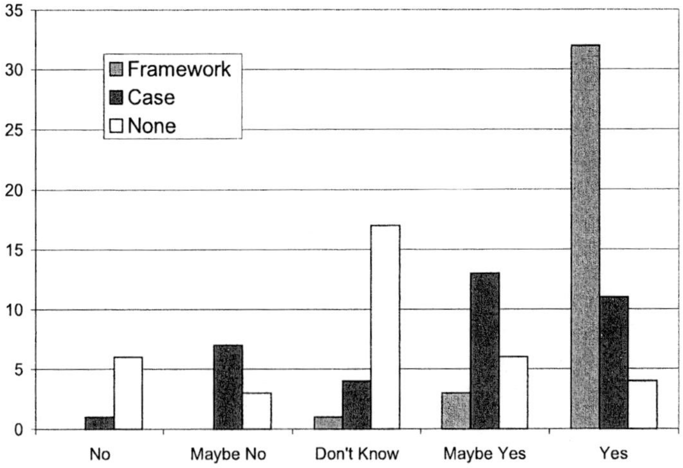

Fig. 3. The distribution of user responses when the system predictions were correct

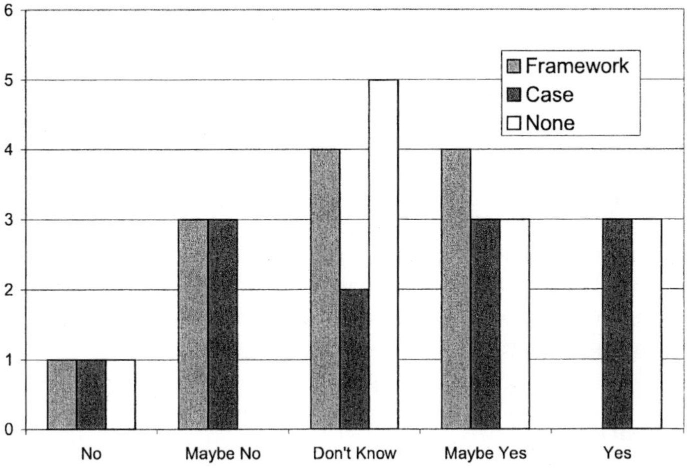

Fig. 4. The distribution of user responses when the system predictions were wrong

different user response pattern. Although no one responded *Yes* in the case of the explanations produced by the framework there is far less certainty in the users' responses.

In question two we were trying to determine how satisfactory people found the explanations. We coded the trial subjects responses as being a number between one and five. One being *Poor* and five being *Very Good.* We then looked at the average value given to each explanation for each scheme. The results are shown

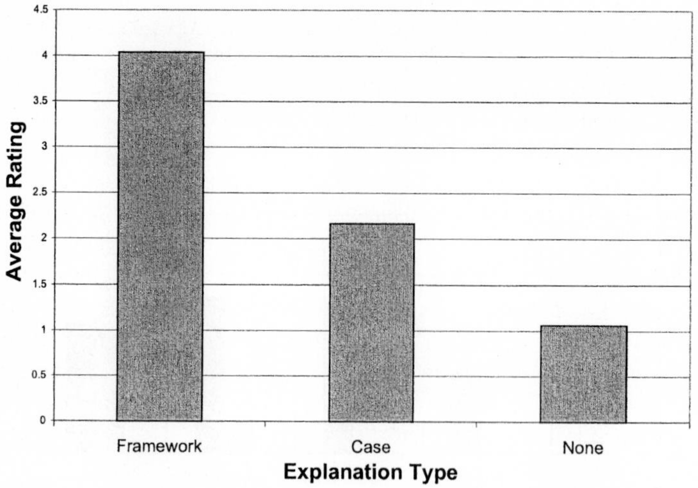

Fig. 5. The Average Rating Scores for Question Two of the Explanations Produced by Each Different Scheme

in Figure 5. Clearly people found the framework explanations to be far more satisfying then the other two schemes and generally the rating for the framework explanation was quite high.

It is worth noting that although the ratings were still high there was a noticeable dip in the average ratings for explanations when confidence is low and the user was presented with counter examples. From comments returned by test subjects the addition of a counter example at times of uncertainty led to confusing explanations. Such confusion may damage user confidence in the system. We would like to do a further survey to investigate the use of counter examples in greater detail. However it is clear that generally the framework explanations added to users confidence in the system's predictions however user confidence was damaged when the system made errors.

5 Conclusions

In this paper we have addressed the issue of instilling confidence in the ability of machine learning systems in their users. We have developed an explanation framework which supplies users with interpretable explanations of the systems predictions along with a measure of confidence in that prediction. We have also presented a means by which the trade-off between being overly confident or overly pessimistic can be inspected and different methods compared.

We carried out a preliminary evaluation on the explanation framework and have found that the use of interpretable explanations does indeed increase confidence in the system as can be seen in Figure 3. The addition of discursive text explaining the relationship between the presented explanation and the query cases clearly had an effect in instilling this confidence as can be seen in the satisfaction ratings shown in Figure 5. However, when the system fails this confidence can be damaged. This can be clearly seen in Figure 4 as the users display far less certainty about the system prediction compared with when the system is correct. This could be a result of the extra cognitive load associated with the explanations produced when the level of confidence is low. However users were still unable to reliably perceive that the system was making an error and so their confidence in the system could be lost when the resulting error becomes evident. It seems that notifying the user of uncertainty in the recommendation from the system creates an element of doubt and confidence could be damaged.

This a matter that has only been touched on in our preliminary investigation and it is one which we would like to address further in a more comprehensive study. In the future we would also like to investigate localised logistic regression as a CBR classification technique as well as find improved means by which we can generate local case-bases.

References

1. Leake, D.: Case-Based Reasoning: Experiences, Lessons and Future Directions. AAAI/MIT Press (1996)
2. Cunningham, P., Doyle, D., Loughrey, J.: An evaluation of the usefulness of case-based explanation. In Ashley, K.D., Bridge, D.G., eds.: Case-Based Reasoning Research and Development, 5th International Conference on Case-Based Reasoning (ICCBR 2003). Volume 2689 of Lecture Notes in Computer Science., Springer (2003) 122–130
3. Nugent, C., Cunningham, P.: A case-based explantion system for black box systems. Artificial Intelligence Review (2005) To Appear.
4. McSherry, D.: Explanation in case-based reasoning: an evidential approach. In: 8th UK Workshop on Case-Based Reasoning. (2003) 47–55
5. Sørmo, F., Cassens, J., Aamodt, A.: Explanation in case-based reasoning: Perspectives and goals. Artificial Intelligence Review (2005) To Appear.
6. Doyle, D., Cunningham, P., Bridge, D., Rahman, Y.: Explanation oriented retrieval. In Funk, P., Calero, P.A.G., eds.: Advances in Case-Based Reasoning, 7th. European Conference on Case-Based Reasoning (ECCBR 2004). Volume 3155 of Lecture Notes in Computer Science., Springer (2004) 157–168
7. Cheetham, W., Price, J.: Measures of solution accuracy in case-based reasoning systems. In Funk, P., Calero, P.A.G., eds.: Advances in Case-Based Reasoning, 7th. European Conference on Case-Based Reasoning (ECCBR 2004). Volume 3155 of Lecture Notes in Computer Science., Springer (2004) 106–118
8. Hosmer, D., Lemeshow, S.: Applied Logistic Regression. 2nd edn. Wiley (2000)
9. Leake, D., Birnbaum, L., Hammond, K., Marlow, C., Yang, H.: An integrated interface for proactive, experience-based design support. In: Proceedings of the 2001 International Conference on Intelligent User Interfaces. (2001) 101–108
10. Flach, P., Blockeel, H., Ferri, C., Hernandez-Orallo, J., Struyf, J. In: Decision support for data mining: introduction to ROC analysis and its application. Kluwer Academic Publishers (2003) 81–90

Cooperative Reuse for Compositional Cases in Multi-agent Systems

Enric Plaza

IIIA - Artificial Intelligence Research Institute,
CSIC - Spanish Council for Scientific Research,
Campus UAB, 08193 Bellaterra, Catalonia (KoS)
Vox: +34-93-5809570, Fax: +34-93-5809661
enric@iiia.csic.es
http://www.iiia.csic.es

Abstract. We present a form of case-based reuse conducive to the cooperation of multiple CBR agents in problem solving. First, we present a form of constructive adaptation for configuration tasks with compositional cases. We then introduce CoopCA, a multi-agent constructive adaptation technique for case reuse. The agents suggest possible components to be added to the ongoing configuration problem, allowing an open, distributed process where components used in cases of different agents are pooled together in a principled way. Moreover, the agents can use their case base to inform about a similarity-based likelihood that the suggested component will be adequate for the current problem. We illustrate CoopCA by applying it to the task of agent team formation[1].

1 Introduction

We present a form of case-based reuse conducive to the cooperation of multiple CBR agents in problem solving. First, we present a form of constructive adaptation for configuration tasks with compositional cases. Constructive adaptation is composed of the Hypotheses Generation and the Hypotheses Ordering processes. Then we introduce CoopCA, a multi-agent constructive adaptation technique for case reuse, showing how Hypotheses Generation can be extended to a multi-agent system. The agents suggest possible components to be added to the ongoing configuration problem, allowing an open, distributed process where components used in cases of different agents are pooled together in a principled way. Moreover, the agents can use their case base to inform about a similarity-based likelihood that the suggested component will be adequate for the current problem. This information is used by the Hypotheses Ordering process that thus

[1] Thanks to David Aha who during ECCBR-2004 in Madrid observed that distributed and multi-agent approached to CBR focused on the Retrieve process and wondered aloud why Reuse process had not been extended to cover distributed and multi-agent scenarios. This work has been partially supported by the CBR-ProMusic project (IC2003-07776-C02-02) and the SAMAP project (TIC2002-04146-C05-01).

H. Muñoz-Avila and F. Ricci (Eds.): ICCBR 2005, LNAI 3620, pp. 382–396, 2005.

explores the configuration space guided by the cases of all the involved agents. We illustrate CoopCA proposal by applying this technique to the task of agent team formation.

1.1 Generative Reuse with Constructive Adaptation

The Reuse process in case-based reasoning when the solution is a complex structure, like a plan or a design, can be performed in two ways: transformational reuse and generative reuse [1]. *Transformational Reuse* takes the solution structure of one (or several) retrieved case(s) and *transforms* that structure using some specific algorithm or search process until a new solution structure is found that is adequate for the new problem [6, 7]. *Generative Reuse*, on the other hand, generates the new solution *by construction*; the generative process uses past cases (and their similarity to the new case) to construct the solution structure of the new case. The canonical technique in CBR literature for planning tasks is derivational analogy [9].

Constructive adaptation (CA), as presented in [8], is a general technique for generative reuse based on two basic notions: a) that building a solution for a new case is a search process, and b) that the search process is guided by a similarity measure over the precedent cases stored in a case base. The third basic idea of CA is that there are two related but distinct tiers of representation, namely case representation (useful to compute similarities) and state representations (useful to perform search process). Therefore, CA proposes a two-tiered process for constructive adaptation, as shown in Fig. 1. Notice that CA fulfills the requirements for being a form of *compositional adaptation* [11, 10] since CA is a reuse technique where solution parts coming from multiple cases are reused and combined together.

This paper presents a more specific version of the Constructive Adaptation approach adequate for design and configuration tasks. Although less general than [8],

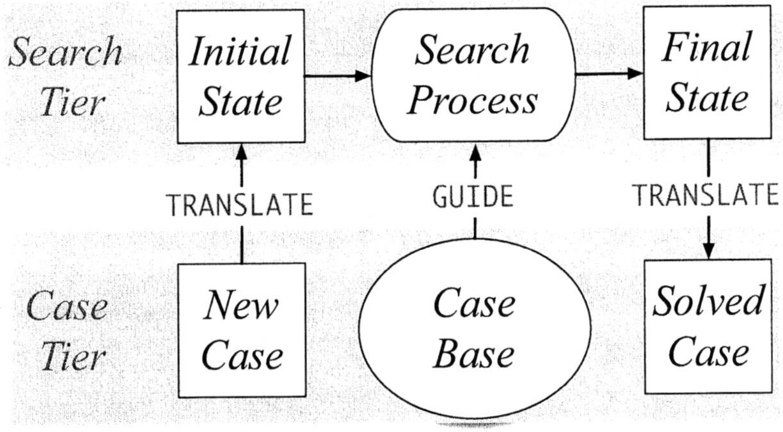

Fig. 1. The two-tiered process of constructive adaptation

this specialization allows us to define CA in a more detailed and formal manner. The contribution of this paper is three fold. First, we present an abstract and formal specification of *Compositional Cases*, a case description formalism that is adequate for CBR systems dealing with design and configuration tasks. The second contribution is a detailed description of Constructive Adaptation for design and configuration tasks using Compositional Cases. Finally, we present CoopCA, a distributed form of CA applied to team formation in multiagent systems.

2 Constructive Adaptation for Compositional Cases

Configuration tasks are amenable to be supported in CBR systems using compositional cases— i.e. cases that express the relation between a *component* and the *role* it plays in the object being configured. For instance, in the task of configuring a PC, *HardDrive* is a role and *ATA/IBM-DJSA-210* is a component that can fulfill that role.

Constructive adaptation is composed of the *Hypotheses Generation* (HG) and the *Hypotheses Ordering* (HO) processes. Both HG and HO work upon states (see Fig. 1) representing a partial configuration being considered by the system. Concerning compositional cases, HG takes a state and generates new states with refined partial configurations; specifically it takes a open role R_i and generates a new state for each particular component C_j that can fulfill role R_i. Components C_j are obtained by retrieval of the configurations in case-base with a role R_i.

Concerning Hypotheses Ordering, HO orders open states assessing the similarity of the state's partial configuration with respect to the case base of configurations. Specifically, let C_j in role R_i be the last component added to a state; HO will give the state a rank value that is the highest similarity of a case with C_j in role R_i with respect to the current problem. Notice that we are assessing similarity comparing the problem specification and not the solutions (the configuration of the cases and the partial configuration of the state).

The only requirement to use CoopCA in a configuration task is that the CBR system has to be able to describe the characteristics that specify the possible components that may fill a role. We will call this description as a *task specification* (or simply a *task*) of a role[2]. As we will see, task specification is the means used to inform other agents about the current focus of interest in the reuse process. Then, the agents receiving a task specification can use it as a query to their case base —and from which the components satisfying it are retrieved.

2.1 A Framework for Compositional Cases

This section develops a domain-independent description framework for case-based compositional design (or configuration, in the following we will use both terms synonymously).

[2] The simplest task specification is just a role name R_i; however, often some constraints on the type and/or properties of components that can legally fill the role are expressed in the task specification.

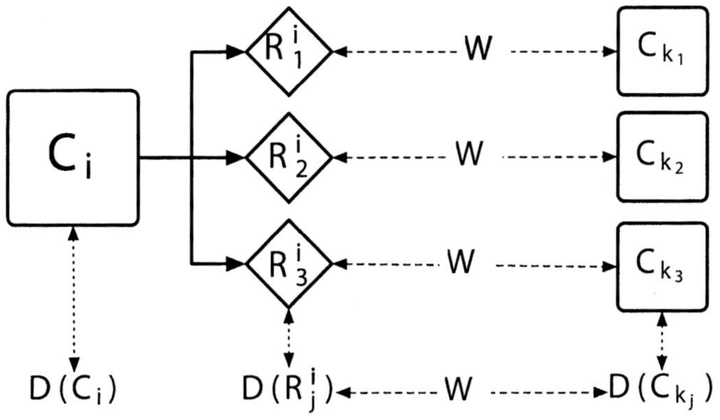

Fig. 2. Compositional cases consist of a complex component C_i that specifies the roles for the required subcomponents (R^i_j) and the bindings (W) of those roles with further components (C_{k_j}). Compositional cases and roles have descriptions (D) used to establish valid matchings in the application domain

First, we will define a language $\mathbb{L} = \langle \mathcal{R}, \mathcal{T}, \mathcal{C}, \mathbb{O} \rangle$ for compositional design, where $\mathcal{R}$ is the set of roles, $\mathcal{T}$ is the set of *tasks*, $\mathcal{C}$ is the set of components, and $\mathbb{O}$ is an object language with a subsumption $(\sqsubseteq)$ relation[3] used to describe tasks and components. Moreover, a task $T_j \in \mathcal{T}$ is a triple $T_j = \langle R, C, D \rangle$ where R is a role in component C and D is a description $D(R)$ of the characteristics that specify the possible components that may fill role R. We will use the dot notation to refer to an element of a tuple, e.g. $T_j.R$ denotes the role of task T_j.

We will distinguish two types of components $(\mathcal{C} = \mathcal{C}_E \cup \mathcal{C}_X)$, namely elementary and complex components. As shown in Fig. 2, a complex component $C_i \in \mathcal{C}_X$ is a pair $\langle D, T \rangle$ where the D is a description of the component $D(C_i)$ in the object language $\mathbb{O}$ and T is the collection tasks $\{T_j\}_{j=1...n}$, where a task is a triple $\langle R^i_j, C_i, D(R^i_j) \rangle$ describing a role R^i_j of C_i. An elementary component is simply one that has no tasks.

Component matching $(T_j \preceq C_k)$ is a relation that establishes whether a component C_k is suitable for task T_j. This fact is determined by checking if the descriptions of the component satisfies the description of the task's role: $D(R^i_j) \preceq_{\mathbb{O}} D(C_k)$. Since both descriptions, $D(R^i_j)$ and $D(C_k)$, are expressed in the object language $\mathbb{O}$ the relation $\preceq_{\mathbb{O}}$ also depends on the object language.

Definition 1. ***(Binding)*** *A* binding $W = (T_j \doteq C_k)$ *is the assignment of a specific component* C_k *to a particular role* $T_j.R$ *of a component* $T_j.C$.

We note $\mathcal{W}$ as the set of all possible bindings in a language $\mathbb{L}$ and $W.T$ (resp. $W.C$) the task (resp. component) of a binding W. A binding $W = (T_j \doteq C_k)$ is *legal* when their elements satisfy the component matching relation $T_j \preceq C_k$.

[3] Subsumption is the inverse relation to satisfaction: given two formulae $\psi, \psi' \in \mathbb{O}$ that ψ *subsumes* ψ' $(\psi \sqsubseteq \psi')$ if all that is true for ψ is also true for ψ' (or that ψ' satisfies ψ).

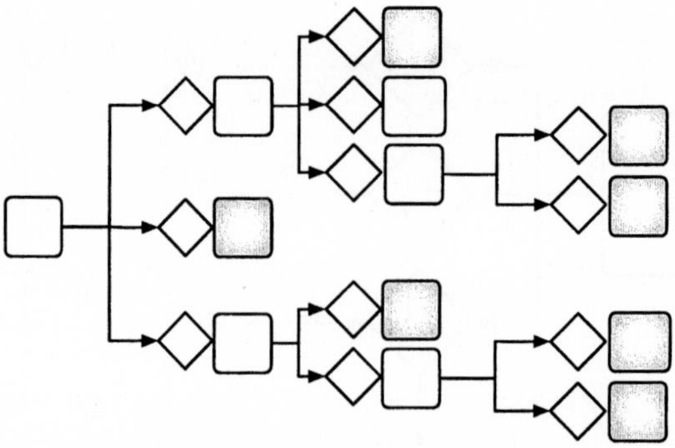

Fig. 3. Compositional cases represent a configuration that is complete and valid; this figure shows a configuration with 12 roles that is complete (since all roles are bound). Elementary components are shown as gray boxes

Definition 2. ***(Configuration)*** *A* configuration $K \in \mathcal{K}$ *is a collection of bindings* $K = \{W_i = (T_j \doteq C_k)\}_{i=1...m}$. *If all bindings are* legal *we say the configuration* K *is* valid.

A configuration may be partial or complete: intuitively a configuration is complete when every task introduced by a complex component is bound to some other component, and otherwise it's partial. We can now define a *composite case*, and for that purpose we will assume that a problem specification (or *query*) Q is a special type of task $Q = \langle -, -, D(Q) \rangle$, namely one that has no role or component but only a description $D(Q)$ in the object language $\mathbb{O}$ specifying the requirements that a solution to the problem has to satisfy.

Definition 3. ***(Composite Case)*** *A composite case is a pair* (Q, K) *where* $(Q \doteq C_i) \in K$ *and* K *is both valid and complete.*

Notice that the above definitions of a complete and valid configuration K does not imply that is satisfies the requirements put forward by Q. In fact, this is the information provided by a (correct) case base; that is to say, a case (Q_r, K_t) states that it is known that K_t is an adequate solution for Q_r. As we will see in the following sections, this is the information source that will be used by the process of constructive adaptation.

2.2 Compositional Design Specialized Descriptions

In order to specialize the general description of constructive adaptation (CA) to the task of compositional design we will make a further assumption concerning the descriptions of tasks and components. We will assume from now on that tasks and components are described as pairs (B, A) — where B are the *Before-formulae* (or *preconditions*) and A are the *After-formulae* (or *goals*) that characterize what they assume to be true in the world *before* and *after* they are used inside a configuration.

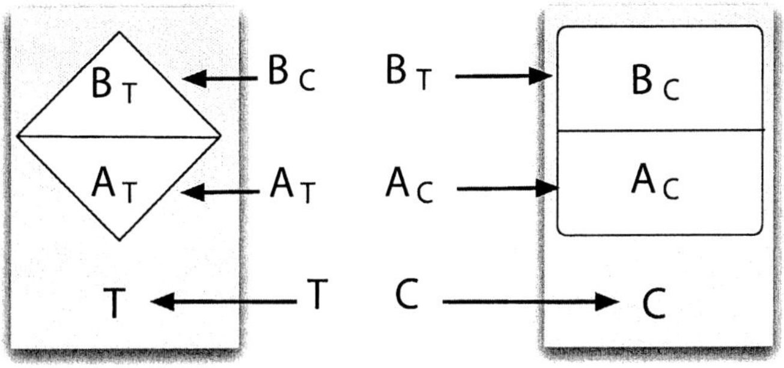

Fig. 4. Matching $T \preceq C$ between a task (role or user query) T and a component C is valid when their *Before-formulae* and *After-formulae* satisfy the plug-in matching criteria

Concerning a component C with $D(C) = (B_C, A_C)$, A_C is a collection of formulae in language $\mathbb{O}$ that express what is true after a component is used for some role with a legal binding, while B_C express what C assumes to be true in the designed configuration (and should be provided by some other component in the configuration in order to insure that C fulfills its role).

Concerning a task $T = \langle R, C, D(R) \rangle$ with $D(R) = (B_T, A_T)$, A_T is a collection of formulae in language $\mathbb{O}$ that express what needs to be true after whatever component has been chosen to fulfill role R in C, while B_T express that which any component fulfilling role R of C can assume to be true.

Now, since a problem query Q is also a task, it will be a tuple $(Q = \langle -, -, (B_Q, A_Q) \rangle)$, where $Q.D$ is a pair of B- and A-formulae. Notice that the interpretation of the task induced by a query is the following: A_Q are the goals that the configured design has to satisfy and B_Q specifies the statements that can be assumed to be true by the configured design.

Component matching may now also be specialized to this description framework. Since the matching $T_j \preceq C_k$ is defined as $D(R^i_j) \preceq_{\mathbb{O}} D(C_k)$, now we have that the matching can be defined over B-formulae and A-formulae. Adopting the usual notion of matching from software components literature (often called *plug-in matching*) we have that $T_j \preceq C_k$ is

$$(B_T \sqsupseteq B_C) \wedge (A_T \sqsubseteq A_C) \tag{1}$$

that is to say, $(A_T \sqsubseteq A_C)$ the component's A-formulae satisfy all task's A-formulae (all of task's goals are achieved by the component) and $(B_T \sqsupseteq B_C)$ the task's preconditions satisfy all component's preconditions (i.e. a component can achieve the same goals with equal or less stringent preconditions).

2.3 Compositional Design Constructive Adaptation

We will present now the search process of constructive adaptation for compositional design. For this purpose, we will define what a state is, how states are generated (Hypotheses Generation) and how to select the state to be expanded (Hypotheses Ordering).

Definition 4. *(State) A state Z given a query Q is a tuple* $Z(Q) = \langle B^{\perp}, A^{\perp}, B^{\top}, A^{\top}, W^{\perp}, W^{\top}, W^{H}\rangle$, *where*

1. *$B^{\perp}$ and $A^{\perp}$ are open B- and A-formulae, i.e. those not satisfied in Z*
2. *$B^{\top}$ and $A^{\top}$ are closed B- and A-formulae, i.e. those satisfied in Z*
3. *$W^{\perp}$ is the set of open bindings (those tasks that are not bound to any component in Z), $W^{\top}$ is the set of closed bindings (those tasks already bound to a component in Z), and W^{H} is the last binding (that introduced in the predecessor state of Z)*

A state Z is valid *when all bindings in $Z.W^{\top}$ are valid.*

As we have seen, constructive adaptation is a two-tiered process where case-based problem solving works both at the case representation tier and the state representation tier. Therefore, we will need some mapping functions that both tiers. The first function *initial state* ($\mathtt{IS} : \mathcal{Q} \rightarrow \mathcal{Z}$) that transforms a query Q into an (initial) state $Z_0(Q)$, as follows

$$\mathtt{IS}(Q) = \langle \emptyset, Q.D.A, Q.D.B, \emptyset, Q, \emptyset, \emptyset\rangle$$

that is to say, a state where the Q's B-formulae become *closed preconditions*, A-formulae become *open goals*, there are no closed bindings, and the only open binding the query itself (recall that the query is a special task).

Hypothesis Generation. The *Hypothesis Generation* function ($\mathtt{HG} : \mathcal{Z} \rightarrow 2^{\mathcal{Z}}$) generates the successor states of a state Z_i in three steps: 1) an open task is selected, 2) the components that match that task are gathered, and 3) a successor state is generated for each of the components that can be bound to the task. Specifically:

1. (**Open Task Selection**). HG selects a task $T^{j}_{Z_i}$ from the state's open bindings $Z_i.W^{\perp}$. This selection is random since there is no reason to order the open tasks.
2. (**Component Gathering**). HG gathers the set of components that match this task: $C(T^{j}_{Z_i}) = \{C | T^{j}_{Z_i} \preceq C\}$. There are two ways of gathering components:
   (a) (*Catalog Component Gathering*) If all components descriptions are placed in a repository then we only have to check for those components $C(T^{j}_{Z_i})$ in the catalog that satisfactorily match the task description . This approach is adequate when all information on components (a Catalog) is directly available.
   (b) (*Case-based Component Gathering*) If the component descriptions available are those used in previous configurations stored as cases then a CBR system with a retrieval technique supporting subsumption ($\sqsubseteq$) can infer which components will match the selected task —since we have already defined $\preceq$ in terms of $\sqsubseteq$ in (1).

3. **(Successor States).** HG generates a new *successor state* for each component $C^k \in C(T^j_{Z_i})$, were a successor state is defined as follows

$$succ(Z_i, T^j_{Z_i}, C^k) = \langle B^\perp, A^\perp, B^\top, A^\top, W^\perp, W^\top, W^H \rangle$$

where $T^j_{Z_i}$ is no longer an open task in $W^\perp$ and a new binding $T^j_{Z_i} \doteq C^k$ has been added to $W^\top$. Essentially the new component C^k achieves some new goals not yet achieved in Z_i and therefore $A^\top$ and $A^\perp$ are updated accordingly. Moreover, if C^k has subtasks they are added to $W^\perp$ and since each subtask introduces A-formulae and B-formulae again $A^\top$ and $A^\perp$ need to be updated accordingly.

Hypothesis Ordering. The essential notion of constructive adaptation is to use cases similar to the current problem to guide the search process. Since in compositional design a problem query $Q = (B_Q, A_Q)$ is a specification of the properties desired for the solution (A_Q) plus the assumptions of what can be assumed to be true (B_Q), we need a similarity relation S between Q and the problem specification part of composite cases (Q_i, K_i). Thus, for a case base $\Sigma = \{(Q_i, K_i)\}_{i=1\ldots N}$, the relation S provides a ranking $\mathbf{S}$ of the cases based on the value $S(Q, Q_i)$, as follows

$$\mathbf{S}(Q, \Sigma) = \{\langle (Q_i, K_i), S(Q, Q_i) \rangle\}_{i=1\ldots N}$$

Next, we have to transform this case ranking into a ranking of the open states $\mathcal{Z}^{open}_t(Q) \subset \mathcal{Z}$ at a step t in the CA process.

For this purpose, consider the latest hypothesis to which the CA process is committed to in an open state, namely the last component added to the configuration and stored in $Z.W^H$. Since CA will pick the highest ranking state in $\mathcal{Z}^{open}_t(Q)$ to expand (generating successor states) we are interested into assessing how likely that the partial configuration of an open state Z is to lead to a correct solution. Since comparing the whole structure of the of the partial configuration with the case base would be excessively time consuming, CA will assess this likelihood by considering only the latest hypothesis $Z.W^H$ of each open state. Notice that the the other hypothesis were considered in previous steps of the search process.

Let us note $Z.W^H.C$ the component C_j bound by the latest hypothesis $Z.W^H = (T_i, C_j)$ in state Z and let be $\Sigma|_{(T_i \doteq C_j)} \subset \Sigma$ the subset of cases in the case base where the component C_j fills role T_i. Since the similarity relation S induces also a ranking $\mathbf{S}(Q, \Sigma|_{(T_i, C_j)})$ on the cases in this subset, we can now define the function M that yields the similarity degree of highest ranking case in $\Sigma|_{(T_i, C_j)}$, namely

$$M(\Sigma, T_i, C_j) = max(\{S(Q, Q_k) | (Q_k, K_k) \in \Sigma|_{(T_i, C_j)}\}) \quad (2)$$

The ranking relation $\mathbf{R}$ induces a ranking over the open states by computing a heuristic value r_i for each open state $Z_i \in \mathcal{Z}^{open}_t(Q)$:

$$\mathbf{R}(\mathcal{Z}^{open}_t(Q)) = \{\langle Z_i, r_i \rangle\}_{Z_i \in \mathcal{Z}^{open}_t(Q)\rangle} \;;\; r_i = M(\Sigma, Z_i.W^H.T, Z_i.W^H.C)$$

that is to say, each open node Z_i is ranked according to the degree of similarity of the highest ranking case that has current hypothesis component $Z_i.W^H.C$ fulfilling the current hypothesis role $Z_i.W^H.T$.

Goal Test. The last element of constructive adaptation is the *Goal Test* function GT: $\mathcal{Z} \rightarrow \{True, False\}$. Goal Test checks whether a state Z is solution, i.e. whether the state corresponds to a valid solution that satisfies the problem query Q:

$$\texttt{GT}(Z,Q) = Valid(Z) \wedge Satisfies(Z,Q) = (Z.W^{\perp} = \emptyset) \wedge (Z.A^{\perp} = \emptyset) \wedge (Z.B^{\perp} = \emptyset)$$

namely, there are no open bindings left ($Z.W^{\perp} = \emptyset$), all $Q.A$ goals are satisfied ($Z.A^{\perp} = \emptyset$), and there is no B-formula required by a configured component that is not satisfied ($Z.B^{\perp} = \emptyset$).

Notice that in CA the similarity relation S is left open and may vary across different application domains and representation languages used to specify the problem query Q. In our agent team formation application we have used SHAUD, a similarity relation for feature terms [3], but other similarity relations can be used — e.g. edit distance [2] for musical applications using feature terms, or RIBL-2 for Horn clause representation[4].

3 Multi-agent Cooperative Constructive Adaptation

In this section we will present a distributed framework for case reuse using constructive adaptation. For this purpose we will focus on a particular application that is essentially distributed: team formation of cooperative agents. Team formation is the process by which, given a task to be achieved specified by a user or an agent, such that no single agent is capable of achieving it, a selection of agents with the required capabilities is made and then organized as a multi-agent team with the required interactions protocols to coordinate those agents.

The reason we focus of team formation is that a distributed form of the case reuse process only makes sense if the *knowledge* used for reuse is itself *distributed.* Multi-agent systems can be characterized precisely by this fact: there is no central repository containing the required knowledge. In other words, each agent has a local view of the problem solving episodes in which it has been involved, and each agent has its specific capabilities (and its individual knowledge).

We will now present the cooperative constructive adaptation (CoopCA) technique in the framework of agent team formation. CoopCA assumes that the agents are willing to cooperate in forming a team and sharing the necessary information. The next subsections will first express the concept of team as a compositional case and later will present the distributed reuse technique of CoopCA.

3.1 Teams as Compositional Cases

Agent teams can be modeled as compositional cases; in fact, the ORCAS framework [5] represents agent teams as compositional cases and uses case-base reasoning to form teams adequate for specific tasks. Recall the general schema of

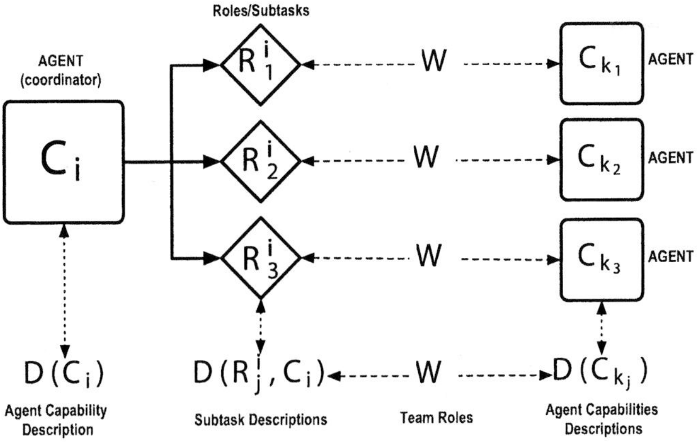

Fig. 5. Team as a compositional case

compositional cases in Fig. 2: an agent team fills this schema if we interpret components C_i as agents, roles R^i_j as subtasks, component descriptions $D(C_i)$ as descriptions of *agent capabilities*, and role descriptions $D(R^i_j)$ as descriptions of agents subtasks as shown in Fig. 5. A team is formed when the bindings W are established associating to each role/subtask an agent with a capability suitable to achieving that task. We say an agent that an agent C_i acts as *coordinator* of the agents that play the roles/subtasks $\{R^i_j\}_{j=1\ldots n}$ defined by C_i. Moreover, an agent C_k plays role R^i_j in a team when a binding $W = (T_j \doteq C_k)$ exists, and agent C_k can either solve role/subtask R^i_j either alone or defines further subtasks $\{R^k_j\}_{j=1\ldots m}$ that will be achieved by a subteam of which C_k is the coordinator.

We will view the process of team formation as a *compositional design* task. Let us assume there is a user that poses a query Q to a *broker*, i.e. an agent that will be in charge of designing the team structure, then negotiate the specific agents that will fulfill the team roles, and finally setting up the interaction protocols for the agent team. In this paper we will deal mainly with the first stage, namely designing the team structure, although some issues on selecting agents will be briefly discussed. Concerning the second and third stages, no CBR is used there, but see [5] for details. Now, the current approach in multi-agent systems (MAS) is to assume there is one or several "yellow pages" services where agents register their capabilities.

Our model, however, will be to use an experience-based approach. Specifically, we assume that the broker agent that uses CBR on a case base composed of previous teams; the broker will try to use CoopCA to form new teams by reusing old teams in its case base. In fact, these two approaches to find adequate agents as team components are called in Section 2.3 *Catalog Component Gathering* (since yellow pages is a catalog of agent capabilities) and *Case-based Component Gathering* (since the new team will have capabilities used in past teams stored in the case base). Moreover, these two approaches are not incompatible: the broker may resort to use the yellow pages catalog if need be.

Finally, notice that what we call *broker agent* is in fact a role; that is to say, there is no such a thing as *the* broker, but a number of agents that have played the *broker role* in forming new teams. Therefore, there is no unique and centralized repository of cases describing teams; instead, we have that agents playing the role of brokers have individual case bases storing their experience in team formation. We can now see that the knowledge for team formation is essentially distributed and thus the *reuse process* that CoopCA embodies should be such that makes use to this distributed knowledge as far as possible. In what follows, we will call a description of a team stored as a case in the case base of an individual agent a *team-case.*

3.2 Cooperative Constructive Adaptation

The assumptions made by CoopCA for any given broker agent a_b are the following: 1) there is a collection of agents $\mathcal{B}^l(a_b)$ that played the role broker and store their team designs on an individual case base; and 2) there is an *acquaintance relation* $\mathbb{A}(a_b, a_k)$ among the agents in $\mathcal{B}^l(a_b)$ such that for an agent a_b then $\forall a_k \in \mathcal{B}^l(a_b) : \mathbb{A}^l(a_b, a_k)$; i.e. either $\mathbb{A}(a_b, a_k)$ (a_k is an acquaintance of a_b) or there is a chain of acquaintances of length not larger that l that links a_b and a_k. When an agent a_b receives a query Q that requires a team a_b will use CoopCA to design such a team using the collective experience on past teams of the agents in $\mathcal{B}^l(a_b)$. Moreover, notice that in a MAS framework there are several agents that can possess the same capability and, thus, the same *team design* can be realized by different collections of agents. We assume in the following that the capabilities are the *components* of CoopCA for team design.

CoopCA follows basically the CA search process described in section 2.3 and summarized in Fig. 6 with a few modifications. The broker a_b that receives the query Q will perform the CA search process (i.e. it will generate new states and maintain the open and closed states) but it will need the help of other agents to generate the hypothesis and to rank them. In other words, *Hypothesis Generation* and *Hypothesis Ordering* will require the broker to communicate with other agents and use the acquired information to generate and order the hypothesis during search. Let us first consider Hypothesis Generation and later we will turn to Hypothesis Ordering.

Cooperative Hypothesis Generation. The cooperative hypothesis generation function will generate the successor states with the help of other agents in $\mathcal{B}^l(a_b)$. For this purpose we need to modify the second step (*Component Gathering*) —while steps *Open Task Selection* and *Successor States* are not modified. We will use a distributed form of *Case-based Component Gathering* such that a_b will send a message (containing a task description) to its acquaintance agents $\mathbb{A}(a_b, a_k)$; in turn they will send this message to their acquaintance agents up to l times. Those agents in $\mathcal{B}^l(a_b)$ that receive the message and find a component in their case bases that satisfy that task description will answer to the broker a_b with a message containing a component and a degree of similarity.

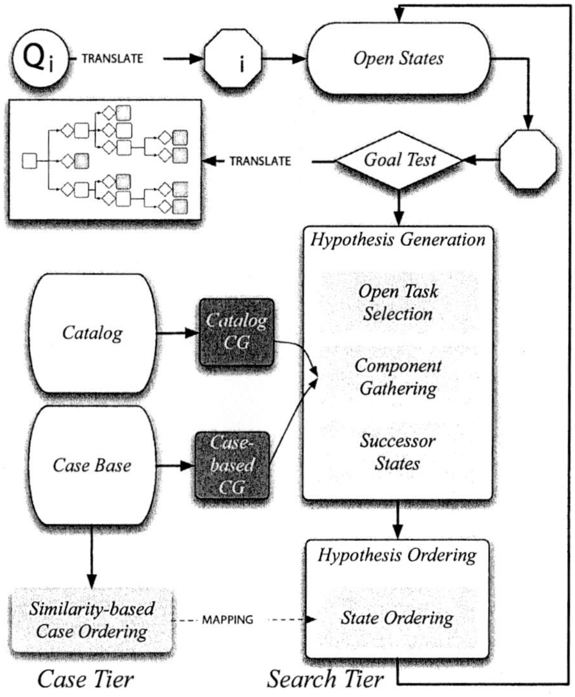

Fig. 6. Constructive adaptation two-tiered process

More formally, the broker agent interacts with its acquaintance agents to obtain the information concerning a specific task in the following steps:

(1) Start Cooperation: First the broker agent a_b informs its acquaintance agents of the task to be performed and sends a message m_1 containing the query $Q = (B_Q, A_Q)$. This information is forwarded by a_b's acquaintances to their respective acquaintances until all agents in $\mathcal{B}^l(a_b)$ receive this information. Notice that Q will be used by the agents to compute the similarity using equation (2). The agents are of course free to decline to cooperate, so only those that send back an acceptance message before a time τ_{m_1} will be considered in the following steps as members of the multi-agent system $\mathcal{A}$.

(2) Current Task: Let T^j be the current task given by *Open Task Selection*. The broker agent broadcasts a message m_2 containing the task description T^j to the agents in $\mathcal{A}$ and waits for their answers before time τ_{m_2}. Figure 7 shows a snapshot of the visualization tool of the ORCAS platform with the current state of a CBR broker agent using constructive adaptation; notice the goals on the left (the first 6 achieved and the last 3 still open) and the task/capability bindings of the current sate on the right (tasks in light color and components in darker color).

(3) Available Capabilities: Every agent $a_k \in \mathcal{A}$ will receive message m_2 and execute the *Case-based Component Gathering* process over their case base

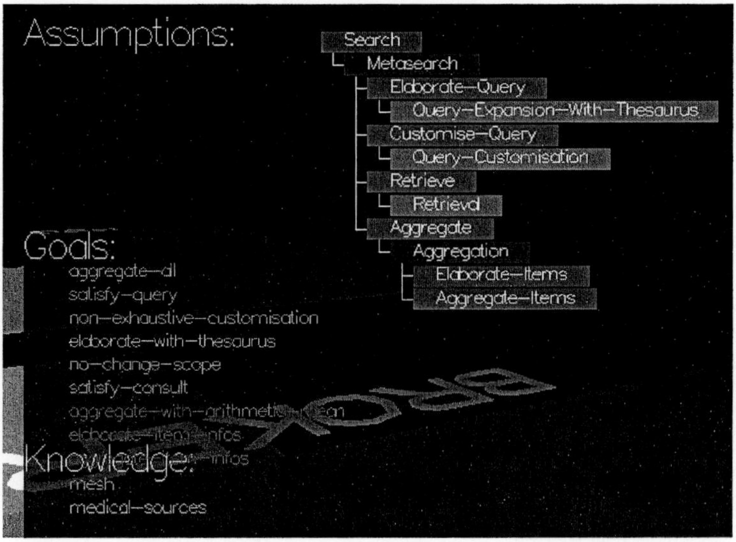

Fig. 7. Image capture of the CBR broker in ORCAS

retrieving a set of components $C^k(T^j)$ that match the task description T^j. Notice that a retrieved "component" is in fact a specific agent that uses a capability in some role in some team-case, and what interests the broker a_b are the available capabilities matching the current task T^j. For each component $C_i \in C^k(T^j)$ agent a_k will send a message m_3 with a tuple $\langle T, C, A, M \rangle$ containing:

$$\langle T^j, C_i, \mathcal{A}_k(C_i), M_k(C_i) \rangle$$

where C_i is a capability adequate for task T^j, $\mathcal{A}_k(C_i)$ is the set of agents known to a_k that possess capability C_i, and $M_k(C_i)$ is the maximum degree of similarity—defined in *Hypothesis Ordering* in equation (2).

(4) Hypothesis Generation: After the broker a_b has received a set of messages $\mathcal{M}_3$ of type m_3 the set of available capabilities $C^k(T^j) = \bigcup_{m \in \mathcal{M}_3} m.C$ is known. Next, a new successor state is generated for each capability $C_i \in C^k(T^j)$, and this ends the Hypothesis Generation precess. Moreover a_b also builds a list of available agents $\mathcal{A}(C_i) = \bigcup_{m \in \mathcal{M}_3(C_i)} m.A$ for each capability $C_i \in C^k(T^j)$ from the relevant messages $\mathcal{M}_3(C_i) = \{m \in \mathcal{M}_3 | C_i = m.C\}$.

(5) Hypothesis Ordering: Since $\mathcal{M}_3$ also contains the similarity information needed for Hypothesis Ordering, the broker simply has to aggregate the values coming from different agents for each capability $C_i \in C^k(T^j)$. For our purposes, the maximum similarity value is a good option so a capability C_i will have as similarity value $M(\mathcal{A}, T^j, C_i) = max_{m \in \mathcal{M}_3(C_i)} m.M$. This value allows the broker to use the ranking relation $\mathbf{R}$ to order the open states in the constructive adaptation process. Once *Hypothesis Ordering* finishes, then either the search is terminated by the *Goal Test* and the next step is (6), or it moves to step (2).

(6) Agent Selection and Instruction: When the team design is finished the broker a_b has a complete specification of the hierarchical team structure. This last step consists of selecting for each particular task/capability ($T^j \doteq C_i$) binding an agent with capability C_i, i.e. one of the set $\mathcal{A}(C_i)$ built in step (3). We will not go into the details of this process (explained in [5]), suffice to say the broker has to negotiate with the candidate agents and select a crew to fully staff the team and then provide the selected agents with the instructions on how to coordinate to achieve the global task.

We have seen that CoopCA is a straightforward extension of constructive adaptation for compositional cases for multi-agent scenarios. CoopCA is in fact applicable to scenarios where the knowledge exploited in the Reuse process is in some way distributed over a collection of entities, e.g. web services.

4 Conclusion

This paper discusses three different but related issues relevant to case-based reasoning. First, the definition of compositional cases as a useful abstraction for a wide variety of CBR applications in design and configuration tasks; compositional cases are however limited to tasks where the designed structure is hierarchical. Second, constructive adaptation (CA) for compositional cases specializes the basic ideas of CA [8] in a generic reuse algorithm that is valid for any CBR system that espouses compositional cases for a task; CA for compositional cases leaves open which representation language $\mathbb{O}$ is used for B-formulae and A-formulae. The language $\mathbb{O}$ can be anyone (from Horn clauses to description logics to simple concept taxonomies) such that has defined both a) an operation of subsumption (or satisfaction), and b) a similarity measure for relational cases (e.g. SHAUD [3] in ORCAS, edit distance [2] in musical CBR applications, or RIBL-2 [4] for Horn clauses).

Third, we have shown that CA can be extended in a natural way to a distributed design task, and we have focused on applying CoopCA to the task of agent team formation. CoopCA shows the power of applying CBR to multi-agent systems tasks such as team formation. Often in MAS agents are supposed to be capable of reasoning and learning but they rarely are on practice. Let's think about the *yellow pages* approach to team formation: agents are assumed to go to the yellow pages every time a new team is to be formed: this is just because agents are assumed not to learn. We have shown that learning team-cases a broker agent will not need to repeat needles work for every team it forms. Once a broker a_b has formed a team for task T^i and a new task T^j similar to T^i arrives, a_b already knows most of the components (agents and their capabilities) that most likely will be in the new team. Thus learning cases decreases not only search costs but also communication costs among agents. In fact, since in a given environment most tasks tend to be repetitive, CoopCA shows that the CBR approach offers a straightforward way to form teams efficiently.

Currently CoopCA is simply using a best-first search regime with similarity-based heuristic; as future work we want to use more powerful (satisficing) search regimes that would allow also to minimize solution costs.

References

1. Agnar Aamodt and Enric Plaza. Case-based reasoning: Foundational issues, methodological variations, and system approaches. *Artificial Intelligence Communications*, 7(1):39–59, 1994.
2. J. Ll. Arcos, M. Grachten, and R. López de Mántaras. Extracting performer's behaviors to annotate cases in a CBR system for musical tempo transformations. In Kevin D. Ashley and Derek G. Bridge, editors, *Proceedings of the Fifth International Conference on Case-Based Reasoning (ICCBR-03)*, number 2689 in Lecture Notes in Artificial Intelligence, pages 20–34. Springer-Verlag, 2003.
3. Eva Armengol and Enric Plaza. Relational case-based reasoning for carcinogenic activity prediction. *Artificial Intelligence Review*, 20:121–141, 2003.
4. W. Emde and D. Wettschereck. Relational instance-based learning. In Lorenza Saitta, editor, *Machine Learning - Proc. 13th Int. Conf. Machine Learning*, pages 122 – 130. Morgan Kaufmann, 1996.
5. Mario Gómez and Enric Plaza. ORCAS: Open, reusable and configurable multi-agent systems. In *Proc. Third International Joint Conference in Autonomous Agents and Multiagent Systems*, pages 144–152. ACM Press, 2004.
6. K. J. Hammond. *Case-based Planning.* Academic Press, 1989.
7. T. Heinrich and J. L. Kolodner. The roles of adaptation in case-based design. In *Proc. AAAI Worksop on Case-based Reasoning.* AAAI, 1991.
8. Enric Plaza and Josep-Lluís Arcos. Constructive adaptation. In *Advances in Case-Based Reasoning*, volume 2416 of *Lecture Notes in Artificial Intelligence*, pages 306–320. Springer Verlag, 2002.
9. Manuela M. Veloso and Jaime G. Carbonell. Derivational analogy in PRODIGY. *Machine Learning*, 10(3):249–278, 1993.
10. W. Wilke and R. Bergmann. Techniques and knowledge used for adaptation during case-based problem solving. In *IEA/AIE (Vol. 2)*, pages 497–506, 1998.
11. W. Wilke, B. Smyth, and P. Cunningham. Using configuration techniques for adaptation. In *Case-based Reasoning Technology*, volume 1400 of *Lecture Notes in Artificial Intelligence*, pages 139–168. Springer Verlag, 1998.

Evaluating the Effectiveness of Exploration and Accumulated Experience in Automatic Case Elicitation

Jay H. Powell[1], Brandon M. Hauff[2], and John D. Hastings[1]

[1] University of Nebraska at Kearney,
Dept. of Computer Science & Information Systems,
Kearney NE 68849, U.S.A
hueljh@hotmail.com, hastingsjd@unk.edu
[2] University of Nebraska at Lincoln,
Dept. of Computer Science & Engineering,
Lincoln NE 68588, U.S.A
brandon@genxian.com

Abstract. Non-learning problem solvers have been applied to many interesting and complex domains. Experience-based learning techniques have been developed to augment the capabilities of certain non-learning problem solvers in order to improve overall performance. An alternative approach to enhancing pre-existing systems is automatic case elicitation, a learning technique in which a case-based reasoning system with no prior domain knowledge acquires knowledge automatically through real-time exploration and interaction with its environment. In empirical testing in the domain of checkers, results suggest not only that experience can substitute for the inclusion of pre-coded model-based knowledge, but also that the ability to explore is crucial to the performance of automatic case elicitation.

1 Introduction

Non-learning problem-solving algorithms are commonly used to solve problems in a variety of complex and challenging domains including the application of alpha-beta search to checkers [1] and the use of the null-move heuristic in chess [2]. Such non-learning, non-adaptable algorithms are sufficient for domains that are either simple, static, or deterministic, but are incapable of adapting to changing environments. For domains that are sufficiently complex or dynamic, it has been argued that a system capable of learning and adapting to its environment is needed [3]. DeJong and Schultz [4] describe a technique for designing and implementing architectures for extending the capabilities of non-learning systems by automatically extending the knowledge bases of static problem solvers. Unfortunately, the process of enhancing a pre-existing problem solver is complicated by the fact that interfacing with the underlying problem solver can be difficult, and by the fact that overall problem-solving abilities can be hampered by the abilities of the underlying problem solver.

An alternative approach to augmenting a non-learning problem solver is for a system to acquire knowledge automatically without the need for predefined domain knowledge. One existing technique for the automatic capture of knowledge without a reliance

H. Muñoz-Avila and F. Ricci (Eds.): ICCBR 2005, LNAI 3620, pp. 397–407, 2005.

upon prior domain knowledge is automatic case elicitation [5]. Automatic case elicitation is a case-based reasoning (CBR) technique that relies on the system's ability to explore its domain in real time through trial and error in order to acquire knowledge from scratch. Due to its exploratory capabilities and case-based knowledge acquisition techniques, automatic case elicitation is particularly well suited to learning in domains with observable outcomes (e.g. robot navigation or game playing).

This paper extends initial research on automatic case elicitation detailed in Powell et al. [5]. In contrast to this previous research, the methodologies described in this paper make use of a probabilistic approach to case selection to ascertain the value of exploration in an unknown environment in the context of automatic case elicitation. This paper compares automatic case elicitation against non-exploring experience based learning techniques to further determine the merit of free exploration within an automatic case elicitation system.

We detail automatic case elicitation in Section 2, and follow in Section 3 with a brief overview of extending non-learning systems through experience-based learning. We compare the two approaches in Section 4. Section 5 sets forth an empirical evaluation that demonstrates that experience can substitute for predefined knowledge, and that exploration is crucial to the performance of automatic case elicitation. We close with a discussion of related work in Section 6.

2 Automatic Case Elicitation

Automatic case elicitation (ACE) is a learning technique whereby a CBR system automatically acquires knowledge (in the form of cases) from scratch during real-time trial and error interaction with its environment without reliance on pre-coded domain knowledge (e.g. rules or cases). A probabilistic reinforcement learning approach is utilized to evaluate the effectiveness of each case (acquired or stored) after an interaction is complete, providing a means for an ACE system to learn and improve from experience. The use of reinforcement learning [6] allows an automatic case elicitation system to be used in environments which are capable of being explored as well as allow for the system to learn from its experiences (e.g. autonomous robot navigation or game playing). For implementation purposes, a case contains the following:

1. an observation or snapshot of the environment,
2. the action taken in response to the observation, and
3. a rating of the success of the applied action in meeting a goal.

Figure 1 illustrates the procedure *Ace*, the primary reasoning module within a system using automatic case elicitation. *Ace* operates on the sequence of observations (O_1 through O_n) made during interaction with the environment and completes at the point at which the effectiveness of the interaction can be determined (e.g. in chess, the effectiveness of an interaction will be determined at the completion of a game). For each observation of the environment (O_i), the system selects and applies actions (A) suggested by its case library until a change in the environment is observed. The process of selecting and applying an action is as follows. First, the system finds and loads the set

```
Procedure Ace( )
    C := case base
    AC := φ              ; applied cases
    While success of interaction unknown Do
        O_i := ObserveEnvironment( )
        M := MatchingCases(C, O_i)
        Repeat
            A := Decision(M)
            ApplyAction(A)
            O_j := ObserveEnvironment( )
        Until O_i ≠ O_j
        AC := AC ∪ Case(O_i, A)
    End While
    AC := Evaluate(AC)
    Store(C, AC)
End Ace
```

Fig. 1. ACE Algorithm for Interacting within an Environment

```
Function Decision(var M : matching cases) : Action
    If M = φ
        A := NewAction( )
    Else If Rating(M_0) ≥ Random(0..1)
        A := ExtractAction(M_0)
    Else
        M = M - M_0
        A := Decision(M)
    End If
    Return A             ; action to take
End Decision
```

Fig. 2. ACE Algorithm for Determining the Appropriate Action

of all cases whose observation closely[1] matches the current observation. If the current situation is novel or sufficiently distant from prior experience, the set of matching cases returned will be empty. If the current scenario has previously been encountered, the system makes use of an indexing scheme which counts the distinct elements in the case to quickly retrieve all cases which most closely correspond.

Once an ACE system has determined the set of matching cases (possibly empty), it calls the function *Decision*, illustrated in Figure 2. *Decision* selects and returns an action to apply. *Decision* may need to be invoked multiple times in order for the agent to formulate a legal action. In automatic case elicitation, the legality of an action is not determined by the system itself, but by the environment in which the system is interfacing (e.g. a chess engine). In other words, an ACE system attempts an action and observes whether changes to the environment occur in response. If so, the system

[1] The current implementation of ACE handles only exact matches, but will in the future support "close" matches in a domain-independent fashion.

has entered a new situation, and will react accordingly. Otherwise, it would attempt a different action.[2]

The action returned by *Decision* depends on M, the set of matching cases given by *Ace*. When M is empty (i.e., the system has encountered a novel situation), *Decision* generates a new random action. When applying random actions to a new situation, *Ace* repeatedly calls *Decision* until a valid random action (i.e., one which affects the environment) is found. This technique for the generation of new actions through random exploration is utilized because an ACE system does not rely on any pre-coded domain knowledge. Without the dependence on pre-coded knowledge or exterior problem solving techniques, random exploration is necessary for the acquisition of the minimum knowledge to operate in a given domain.

If cases are found in the case-base which correspond to the current state of a system's environment, the *Decision* module determines which of the returned cases to apply, if any. A case from the set M (arranged from M_0 to M_n in descending order based upon case ranking) is chosen on a pseudo-random basis to encourage exploration. The probability $P(M_0)$ of the most successful case in the set, M_0, being selected is equal to the case's rating, the derivation of which will be discussed later. The probability of the system iterating deeper through the list of matching cases is $1-P(M_0)$. The probability of case M_i being selected is

$$P(M_i) = (1 - P(M_0)) \times (1 - P(M_1)) \times ... \times (1 - P(M_{i-1})). \quad (1)$$

If the highest-rated case M_0 is not selected for reuse, then it is removed from the set M and *Decision* is called again. If the entire set of matching cases is searched and no case has been chosen for reuse, a new random action is created using the process described above. This approach differs from previous implementations of automatic case elicitation which made use of a win/loss ratio, as compared to the current use of probability to select cases for reuse. The motivation for implementing this new case selection algorithm was to encourage exploration and the subsequent growth of the system's knowledge base.

Once an ACE system has created an action, it applies the action and observes the resulting consequences. If changes in the environment are observed, the ACE system remembers the action (along with the observation of the environment). For new situation/action pairs, a new case is created. Reused cases are simply remembered so that their success rating can be updated.

Upon the completion of the interaction, *Evaluate* is called to update the ratings of each applied case. Each case is rated according to its success in attaining a goal at the completion of the interaction using the formula

$$r_n = \begin{cases} \frac{1}{2}s_0 & \text{if n} = 0, \\ \frac{1}{2}s_n + \frac{1}{2}r_{n-1} = (\frac{1}{2})^1 s_n + (\frac{1}{2})^2 s_{n-1} + ... + (\frac{1}{2})^{n+1} s_0 & \text{if n} > 0 \end{cases} \quad (2)$$

[2] Disregarding actions which do not immediately result in an observable change in the environment is less than desirable for domains in which a combination of actions are needed to affect a single change in the environment. For such domains, a case structure that encapsulates a sequence of actions is likely required.

In (2), r_i represents the rating (between 0.0 and 1.0 inclusive) and s_i represents the outcome (1 for success, 0 for failure) of the ith application of a case within the environment. The purpose of this formula is to provide a decaying memory representation of each case, where the consequences of applying a case early in the system's life (when cases are applied with little thought) are quickly forgotten. In contrast to work on forgetting complete cases [7,8], only the older applications of a case, not the cases themselves, are forgotten by mathematically diminishing their affect on the case rating. The rating of each case initially tends to fluctuate near 0.5 early in the system's life, while success or failure is equally probable and the system is simply attempting to learn valid domain behavior. As the system gains experience, the case's ranking can tend towards either 1 (highly successful) or 0 (completely ineffectual). Upon completion of *Evaluate*, the ratings for each of the applied cases, *AC*, have been updated and any new cases are committed to the case library using the procedure *Store*.

3 Extending Non-learning Systems Through Experience-Based Learning

DeJong and Schultz [4] describe the use of experience-based learning in improving the capabilities of non-learning systems by automatically extending the knowledge bases of static problem solvers. In their approach, actions in the knowledge base are initially suggested by the underlying problem solver. Over time, their system applies only those experiences proven to produce the best results. They illustrate that proper application of experience-based learning algorithms in combination with an underlying static problem solver can lead to the development of a system capable of quickly recalling and applying actions from the knowledge base.

To demonstrate their approach, they made use of the system GINA, an experience-based learning Othello game-playing agent. GINA relied upon a static minimax lookahead agent as the foundation of the system's experience base. When GINA encountered a scenario which did not exist in its knowledge base, it was able to consult its underlying problem solver for advice and commit the given advice to memory. At the conclusion of each game, a minimax algorithm was used to apportion credit to every move used during the game that could be found in the agent's experience base. In their paper, the authors suggested that their approach could be applied to other domains with success similar to theirs.

4 Comparison of Methodologies

The primary purpose of this paper is to compare and contrast automatic case elicitation against the technique by DeJong and Schultz [4] in order to demonstrate the power of exploration. For the purposes of testing, the performance of the two approaches is compared in the domain of checkers. A DeJong agent was created which can play checkers. Automatic case elicitation is demonstrated in the system CHEBR (CHeckers case-Based Reasoner), a system in which CBR agents utilize automatic case elicitation to learn and test their expertise in the game of checkers.

Several key differences exist between the DeJong approach and automatic case elicitation in the knowledge acquisition process. A DeJong system relies upon an underlying problem-solver and thus begins its life with pre-existing domain knowledge. When a situation is encountered that is novel or sufficiently distant from prior experience, such a system can query its problem-solver for pre-programmed guidance. When a scenario is encountered that is similar to previous experience, a system can refer back to its knowledge base for advice. At the end of each game played, a minimax algorithm is used to distribute credit to each individual move, based on how the move affected the rest of the game.

A CHEBR agent begins its life with no prior domain knowledge. Domain knowledge is acquired through a process of trial and error interaction with the checkers environment, rather than relying upon pre-programmed decision-making capabilities. In its infancy, a CHEBR agent will perform many incorrect actions until valid behavior is encountered, as dictated by the environment. Valid actions taken by the agent (in this case specific checkers moves) are stored as cases and committed to the agent's case-base, along with a rating which is used as a predictive measure of the case's future worth. In CHEBR, all experiences are stored as cases, instead of generalizations of experiences or environment states. When a CHEBR agent assigns credit to an action, it assigns credit based on the final outcome of the interaction with the environment, rather than apportioning credit based on how the move affected the rest of the game. As a CHEBR agent gains experience, the need to rely upon arbitrary move generation is greatly reduced as the requisite behavior for survival is stored in the agent's case-base.

The power and flexibility of a CHEBR agent is tied in part to its ability to acquire knowledge from scratch. With no pre-programmed domain rules, a CHEBR agent is given free reign to explore its environment. This is contrasted by the limited abilities of an agent designed around a pre-existing problem solver. Static underlying problem solvers can be inherently inflexible, due to the fact that their capabilities are hard-coded. Relying upon the decision-making skills of agents with limited flexibility in novel situations can hinder the ability of an agent to derive unique or "creative" solutions to new situations. An agent given the power to explore freely has the potential to generate inventive solutions to previously un-encountered situations.

5 Results

Automatic case elicitation (through the system CHEBR) was tested in repeated two hour training sessions against a static lookahead agent without any experience-based learning augmentations, as well as the DeJong agent with experience-based learning capabilities.

Figure 3 illustrates the winning percentages of CHEBR in competition with a standard four-ply lookahead agent utilizing a minimax algorithm and alpha beta pruning. Figure 4 illustrates the winning percentages of CHEBR in competition with a DeJong agent that makes use of the same four-ply lookahead agent as its core. The results shown were duplicated through repeated training sessions with a slight variability in results due to the use of random move generation on the part of CHEBR. As the lookahead and DeJong agent's shown made use of predefined domain knowledge, they were able

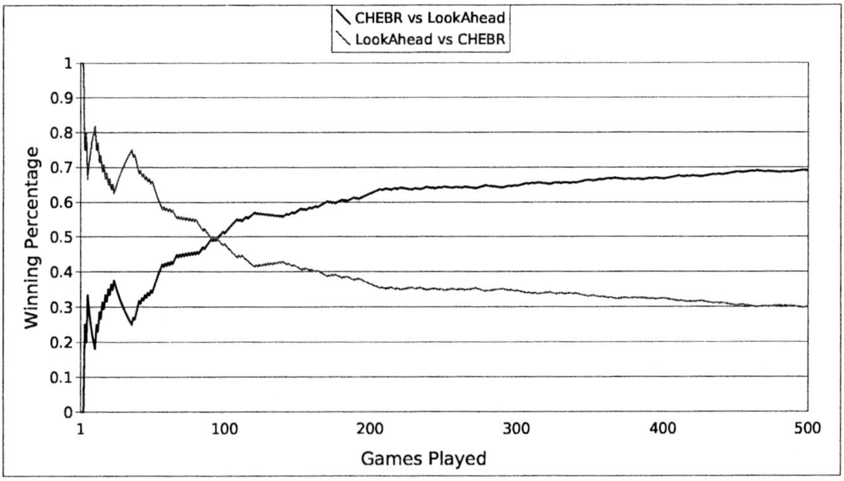

Fig. 3. Agent Win/Loss Ratio for CHEBR vs. Lookahead

to defeat CHEBR a significant portion of the time during the initial stages of game play while CHEBR was learning and exploring its environment. However, after approximately one hundred to two hundred games (about one-tenth of each training session), the winning rates of CHEBR and its opposition converged. For the remainder of each training session, CHEBR's acquired knowledge, through exploration, was sufficient to clearly defeat its opponents a majority of the time. The eventual slow growth rate of CHEBR's win ratio could be caused by overtraining against each particular opponent.[3]

As illustrated by Figures 3 and 4, it was slightly more difficult for CHEBR to adapt to the DeJong agent and defeat it as compared to the lookahead agent, helping to confirm the results of DeJong and Schultz, which state that augmenting an pre-existing problem solver using experience-based learning can create a more capable reasoner than the underlying system alone.

We believe that CHEBR's ability to defeat the DeJong approach lies in its ability to explore. To support this argument, a non-exploring version of CHEBR (Non-Explore CHEBR) was created. In Non-Explore CHEBR, the abilities to explore by applying random move selection as well as random move generation were removed and replaced with a four-ply lookahead. Figure 5 illustrates the winning percentages of CHEBR in competition with Non-Explore CHEBR. The results tentatively confirm that automatic case elicitation in CHEBR depends heavily on the ability to explore.

Although CHEBR began its life with no prior domain knowledge (cases), it proved capable of acquiring knowledge about its environment through repeated exploration and interaction with its environment. As CHEBR gained experience and acquired knowledge, it was able to learn the behavior required to succeed. Further training allowed CHEBR to refine its case-base sufficiently to defeat each of its opponents a majority of

[3] CHEBR is generally quick to adapt to new opponents. However, the speed with which CHEBR is able to conquer new opponents is diminished as the size of the case library becomes extremely large.

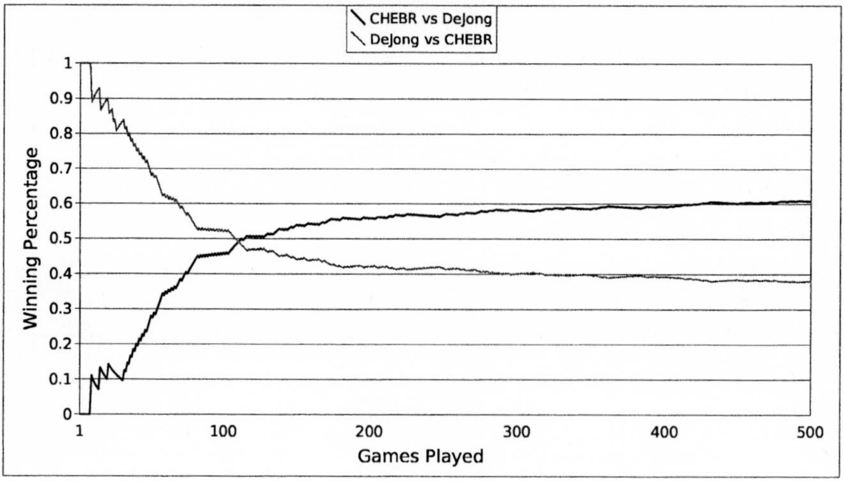

Fig. 4. Agent Win/Loss Ratio for CHEBR vs. DeJong

the time. CHEBR's ability to explore allowed it to locate and exploit the weaknesses of its opponents, and as a result created a challenging and adaptable game player. The inability of the lookahead and DeJong agents to explore due to a fundamental reliance on a static rule-based system prevented them from responding to new situations created by CHEBR. The results suggest that experience can substitute for the inclusion of pre-coded model-based knowledge as seen in the success of CHEBR against the DeJong agents (which use model-based knowledge). The results further suggest that the ability to explore is crucial to the performance of automatic case elicitation which relies primarily on its ability to acquire new experiences.

6 Related Work

Previous work has investigated the automatic generation of cases from predefined expert knowledge. For example, the planning system SHOP/CCBR [9] automatically acquires cases from manually entered project plans. A related approach has been seen in chess games [10,11] which use CBR for chess play by automatically generating case libraries from sets of pre-existing grandmaster games. Shih [12] integrates CBR and the idea of sequential dependency to learn bridge play from a set of existing games. In contrast, automatic case elicitation does not compile cases from manually entered or existing data, but instead acquires knowledge automatically through the experiences of the agents who learn completely from scratch.

CBR has also seen use in a real-time games. For example, Fagan and Cunningham [13] describe the use of case-based plan recognition to predict a player's actions in real time interaction with the game Space Invaders. Construction of the plan library is delayed until after the player has played the game three times, although it would seem possible that the system would not require such a delay. The authors suggest that their

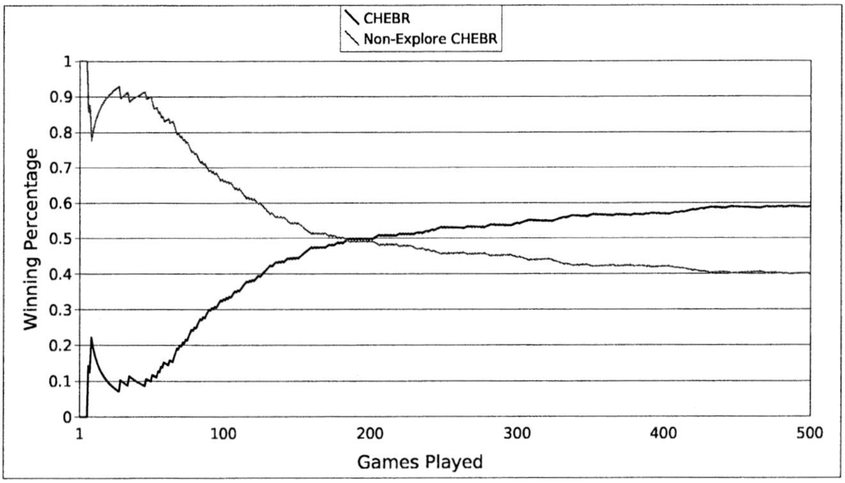

Fig. 5. Agent Win/Loss Ratio for CHEBR vs. Non-Exploring CHEBR

approach could be extended to adjust the behavior of non-player characters, although such an action selection mechanism is not present.

Wendler and Lenz [14] employ CBR in a real-time setting to appropriately position soccer agents based on previously collected cases. Their agents learn during the game and adapt their behavior accordingly. In contrast to our approach, Wendler and Lenz do not use CBR as their sole reasoning technique.

MAYOR [15] is a player of the simulation game SimCity and is based on a pre-defined understanding of an incomplete world model. A case-based planner complements the world by using a library of plans manually built prior to game play. In automatic case elicitation, cases are gathered in real time and are used as the sole reasoning mechanism.

Goodman [16,17] describes the use of off-line built decision-tree induction projectors to predict the outcome of various actions during game play in Bilestoad. Automatic case elicitation differs in that agents learn in real time and projection is not coded as a separate step but is instead encapsulated within individual case ratings.

Samuel [18,19] describes the use of rote-learning and argues that a program can learn to play a domain better than the creator. A lookahead of two or three plays is used to find moves to be scored for a checker game. Samuel's approach requires that the game must have at least one intermediate goal. Automatic case elicitation differs in that it does not require intermediate goals, instead utilizing only the final success rating of the interaction with its environment. In addition, automatic case elicitation does not use a pre-existing reasoner such as that described by Samuel.

Likhachev et al. [20] use CBR to tune the parameters used to guide a robot through obstacles. The cases provide a mapping from mathematical sensor input to sensor parameters that guide a robot. Over time, the results of applying a case are used to further fine tune the contained parameters. Similar to our approach, Likhachev et al. use randomness to encourage exploration. In an extension to this work, Kira and Arkin [21] describe the use of forgetting as a means to compensate for a limited case library size when moving the robot to different environments. Our approach in a sense makes use of a forgetting mechanism inherent to the case rating. The approach described by Likhachev et al. and Kira and Arkin is relatively domain specific. In contrast, we feel our approach is generally applicable in a wide variety of domains.

7 Conclusion

For domains that are sufficiently complex or dynamic, a system capable of learning and adapting to its environment is needed. One approach is to extend the capabilities of a non-learning system with a mechanism that automatically records and evaluates experiences. An alternative known as automatic case elicitation supports the automatic capture of knowledge from scratch in real time without a reliance upon prior domain knowledge. In testing in the domain of checkers, an agent using automatic case elicitation (CHEBR) was shown to successfully defeat opponents using a standard lookahead agent, and an agent using experience-based learning with an underlying lookahead agent. In addition, CHEBR minus the ability to explore was shown to perform at a lower level than when using full automatic case elicitation. The results suggest not only that experience can substitute for the inclusion of pre-coded model-based knowledge, but also that the ability to explore is crucial to the performance of automatic case elicitation.

References

1. Schaeffer, J.: One Jump Ahead: Challenging Human Supremacy in Checkers. Springer Verlag (1997)
2. Beal, D.F.: A generalised quiescence search algorithm. Artificial Intelligence **43** (1990) 85–98
3. Grefenstette, J.J., Ramsey, C.L.: An approach to anytime learning. In: Proceedings of the Ninth International Machine Learning Workshop, San Mateo, CA, Morgan Kaufmann (1992) 189–195
4. DeJong, K.A., Shultz, A.C.: Using experience-based learning in game-playing. In: Proceedings of the Fifth International Conference on Machine Learning, San Mateo, California, Morgan Kaufmann (1988) 284–290
5. Powell, J.H., Hauff, B.M., Hastings, J.D.: Utilizing case-based reasoning and automatic case elicitation to develop a self-taught knowledgeable agent. In Fu, D., Orkin, J., eds.: Challenges in Game Artificial Intelligence: Papers from the AAAI Workshop (Technical Report WS-04-04), AAAI Press (2004) 77–81
6. Kaelbling, L.P., Littman, M.L., Moore, A.P.: Reinforcement learning: A survey. Journal of Artificial Intelligence Research **4** (1996) 237–285
7. Smyth, B., Keane, M.T.: Remembering to forget: A competence-preserving case deletion policy for case-based reasoning systems. In: Proceedings of the 14th International Conference on Artificial Intelligence (IJCAI-95), Montreal, Canada (1995) 377–382
8. Watanabe, H., Okuda, K., Fukiwara, S.: A strategy for forgetting cases by restricting memory. IEICE Transactions on Information and Systems (1995) 1324–1326

9. Mukkamalla, S., Muñoz-Avila, H.: Case acquisition in a project planning environment. In: Proceedings of the Sixth European Conference on Case-based Reasoning (ECCBR-02), LNAI 2416, Springer-Verlag (2002) 264–277
10. Flinter, S., Keane, M.T.: On the automatic generation of case libraries by chunking chess games. In: Proceedings of the First International Conference on Case Based Reasoning (ICCBR-95), LNAI 1010, Springer Verlag (1995) 421–430
11. Sinclair, D.: Using example-based reasoning for selective move generation in two player adversarial games. In: Proceedings of the Fourth European Workshop on Case-Based Reasoning (EWCBR-98), LNAI 1488, Springer-Verlag (1998) 126–135
12. Shih, J.: Sequential instance-based learning for planning in the context of an imperfect information game. In: Proceedings of the Fourth International Conference on Case-Based Reasoning (ICCBR-01), LNAI 2080, Springer-Verlag (2001) 483–501
13. Fagan, M., Cunningham, P.: Case-based plan recognition in computer games. In: Proceedings of the Fifth International Conference on Case-Based Reasoning (ICCBR-03), LNAI 2689, Springer Verlag (2003) 161–170
14. Wendler, J., Lenz, M.: CBR for dynamic situation assessment in an agent-oriented setting. In Aha, D.W., Daniels, J.J., eds.: Case-Based Reasoning Integrations: Papers from the AAAI Workshop (Technical Report WS-98-15), Madison, WI, AAAI Press (1998)
15. Fasciano, M.J.: Real-time case-based reasoning in a complex world. Technical Report TR-96-05, Computer Science Department, University of Chicago (1996)
16. Goodman, M.: Projective visualization: Acting from experience. In: Proceedings of the Eleventh National Conference on Artificial Intelligence (AAAI-93), Menlo Park, Calif., AAAI Press (1993) 54–59
17. Goodman, M.: Results on controlling action with projective visualization. In: Proceedings of the Twelfth National Conference on Artificial Intelligence (AAAI-94), Menlo Park, Calif., AAAI Press (1994) 1245–1250
18. Samuel, A.L.: Some studies in machine learning using the game of checkers. IBM Journal on Reseach and Developement **3** (1959) 211–229
19. Samuel, A.L.: Some studies in machine learning using the game of checkers, ii – recent progress. IBM Journal on Reseach and Developement **11** (1967) 601–617
20. Likhachev, M., Kaess, M., Arkin, R.C.: Learning behavioral parameterization using spatio-temporal case-based reasoning. In: Proceedings of the 2002 IEEE International Conference on Robotics and Automation. Volume 2. (2002) 1282–1289
21. Kira, Z., Arkin, R.C.: Forgetting bad behavior: Memory management for case-based navigation. In: Proceedings of the 2004 IEEE/RSJ International Conference on Intelligent Robots and Systems (IROS). (2004) 3145–3152

HYREC: A Hybrid Recommendation System for E-Commerce*

Bhanu Prasad

Department of Computer and Information Sciences, Florida A&M University, Tallahassee, FL 32307, USA
bhanu.prasad@famu.edu

Abstract. Product recommendation is very important in business to customer (B2C) e-commerce. Automated Collaborative Filtering (ACF) is an important approach for product recommendation. However, a major drawback with this approach is that it can't avoid the "sequence recognition problem", explained in this paper. Here we present a system that addresses the sequence recognition problem by recording and utilizing the users' purchase patterns and ratings. The proposed system is a fruitful combination of ACF and Case-Based Reasoning Plan Recognition (CBRPR) methods. The evaluation studies prove that the hybrid system provides better performance when compared to ACF and CBRPR methods used individually.

1 Introduction

The internet has been transforming the commercial activities such as shopping, negotiation, and auctions into e-commerce activities such as e-shopping, e-negotiation, and e-auctions since the end of the last century. There are two types of e-commerce applications. The first one focuses on importing existing products and selling them online and the second one focuses on the intelligent techniques. The first one is a natural mapping from the traditional commerce and the latter is considered as an intelligent transformation from the traditional commerce to intelligent e-commerce. CBR plays a major role in the development of this latter category of e-commerce.

In recommendation systems, a set of products that best matches the user's profile and/or specifications is retrieved and recommended to the user. If the user likes one or more of the retrieved products then he selects those products. In some systems, it is possible for the user to refine the specifications, and the recommendation process continues until he is satisfied or until he exits the process.

* This research was partly supported by the National Science Foundation under the Grant Award CNS-0424556. The views and conclusions contained in this document are those of the author and should not be interpreted as representing official policies, either expressed or implied, of the US government or any of the sponsoring organizations.

H. Muñoz-Avila and F. Ricci (Eds.): ICCBR 2005, LNAI 3620, pp. 408 – 420, 2005.

1.1 Automated Collaborative Filtering

Automated collaborative filtering is used to automate word-of-mouth recommendations [29, 32, 34]. If a person *A* matches strongly with another person *B* in rating a set of given products then it is possible to predict the rating of a new product by *A*, if *B*'s rating for that product is available. In other words, let us assume that three users *X*, *Y*, and *Z* have a common interest in the products *P1*, *P2*, and *P3*. The users *X* and *Y* bought the products *P4* and *P5* and rated them high. The ACF system will thereby recommend the products *P4* and *P5* to user Z. A common way of implementing the ACF systems is by using the *mean squared difference formula* [13].

There are two types of ACF approaches namely non-invasive and invasive, based on the type of data available or based on how the users' preferences are recorded [20, 35]. An invasive approach requires explicit user feedback. In this approach, users' preferences are floating numbers between 0 and 1. A non-invasive approach observes the user's behavior, requiring no more input than the user's normal interaction with the system. In this approach, the preferences are Boolean values. An example is provided to explain these two types. Let us assume the following scenario. There are five products *P1*, *P2, P3*, *P4,* and *P5* available in an online shop. User *X* bought the products *P1*, *P2*, and *P5* and rated them. In an invasive approach, the ratings could be 0.4, 0.9, 0, 0, and 0.8. The same ratings will become 1, 1, 0, 0, and 1 in a non-invasive approach. The values 0 indicate that the user has not rated the products. A problem with the non-invasive approach is that the user's rating for a product is considered as 1 even if the user rated it very low. As a result, the non-invasive approaches need feedbacks from more users than the invasive approaches.

The Grouplens system [25, 31] is aimed to provide pseudonymous collaboration filtering solutions for movies and Usenet news. Video Recommender [21] and Ringo [34] are used for web-based and email systems that provide recommendations on movies and music respectively.

In ACF systems, a user doesn't need to enter all his recommendations at the same time. The ratings can (and normally will) be entered incrementally. There are two immediate consequences of this. The first is that the recommendations will improve as more ratings are accumulated in the system. Secondly, the time lag in the recommendations means that the recommendation set will not be completely self consistent (if the data were complete, there would be no need for ACF to predict the missing patterns/sequences).

1.2 Case-Based Reasoning in B2C E-Commerce

CBR has been widely used in e-commerce. It is used to create automated sales assistants and automated reasoning agents for online technical support [18, 39]. In addition, CBR has been successfully applied for product retrieval, product selection, product recommendation, product negotiation, and related activities of e-commerce [6, 14, 16, 24, 26, 30, 36, 38, 41]. A widely used formula for CBR in identifying and recommending similar products is *nearest neighbor retrieval*, which is based on *weighted Euclidean distance* [40].

Learning the similarity and/or the utility of the retrieved cases is another important problem addressed by some CBR approaches [5]. These approaches focused on: (1)

Learning similarity measures between cases, without a need for pre-classified cases [36] and (2) Acquiring the preferences of users from the return sets of products [7, 30].

There are some hybrid approaches for product retrieval and recommendation. The approach presented by Burke [9] is predominantly knowledge-based, as ACF is used only during the post processing stage. Some systems check whether there are a sufficient number of feedbacks from previous users [37]. If the number is less than a threshold then CBR is used, otherwise ACF is used. The system presented by Hayes et al. [20] uses case retrieval nets to relate different users' feedbacks to form the cases. Some systems use CBR to perform ACF [17]. Hayes and Cunningham [19] present an approach for improving the ACF by leveraging a content-based technique that captures the context of the users. The approach consists of a two stage retrieval process where ACF recommendations are ranked according to the users' current interests. The recommendation system presented by Balabanovic and Shoham [3] combines the content-based and ACF approaches, although the system is not intended for recommending products. Cotter and Smyth [12] presents a system that is used as a personalized TV (PTV) program recommendation guide. This system is based on nearest neighbor and ACF methods.

1.3 Plan Recognition

Plan Recognition (PR) is the process of observing the current actions/behavior of an agent to predict its future actions. AI approaches are extensively used for PR. For example, Kautz [22] is based on deduction; Ferguson and Allen [15] is based on abduction; Charniak and Goldman [10] is based on probabilistic methods; Bui [8] is based on Markov decision processes; and the methods presented by Kerkez and Cox [23] and Hayes et al. [20] are based on CBR. The work presented by Yang et al. [42] combines data mining and CBR, allowing cases (i.e., plans) to be mined efficiently.

There are two types of PR methods, namely intended and keyhole [11, 22]. In the first approach, the observed system conveys its findings to the observer, and this kind of setup is useful in interactive systems [2, 22] as the aim of these systems is to help the observer. If there is no interactive communication between the observer and the observed system then it is called keyhole [1, 11]. The keyhole approaches are used in competitive environments such as games, in which the observed system does not cooperate with the observer. PR systems use a library of previous plans in predicting the actions of the agents. For real world problems, the library construction is automated using some AI techniques [4, 23, 27].

2 System Details

Here we discuss the details of the proposed system. In the first section we present the "sequence recognition problem". The later sections present more details of the system.

2.1 Sequence Recognition Problem

Let us assume the following situation. Some users bought the books Mathematics-1, Mathemathics-2, Mathematics-3, Mathematics-4, and Mathematics-5 from an ACF system. Note that the users have bought these products on different dates, but the order of the purchase is as above. The users highly rated these products. A new user bought Mathematics-3 and later Mathematics-4, is now looking for recommendations from the system. Obviously the recommendation includes Mathematics-1 and Mathematics-2. But the recommendation is of no use because the users who bought Mathematics-3 and Mathematics-4 never bought Mathematics-1 or Mathematics-2 in the past. As another example, assume that some users bought manual lawn mowers and used them well for some time and later bought power lawn mowers to best meet their purpose. But ACF systems recommend manual lawn mowers to those who just bought the power lawn mowers. These kinds of recommendations are very common with ACF because it simply records the set of products and their ratings but does not recognize the sequence/order (i.e., temporal dependencies) of the purchases. As a result, the recommendations may not be of much use. This problem is named the sequence recognition problem in this paper. The paper presents a system to overcome this drawback by combining the ACF and CBRPR approaches. The system is named HYREC.

2.2 Plan Representation and Utilization

Capture, organization, and utilization of the users' purchase sequences (i.e., patterns) and their feedback is an important issue. The plan-base (i.e., library of plans) is created automatically by observing and recording the users' purchase sequences and the feedbacks. In this system, the users' purchase sequences and feedbacks are represented as a collection of plans. There is exactly one plan that corresponds to each user of the system. A plan consists of an ordered sequence of states. Each state contains a product bought by the user, the identity of the user, the feedback he supplied, and the time of purchase. A state *S1* precedes another state *S2* in a plan if the purchase time of the product in *S1* is earlier than that of *S2*. The user feedbacks are of invasive type. Note that a plan is also divided and organized as sub-plans, as explained in Section 2.3.

The plan recognition process is of intended type and it works on $(i+1)$ steps to recommend the product(s) to the user. Here i represents the number of products that are most recently purchased by the user. Generally i is set to 2. The process is explained.

A conflict set of sub-plans is determined, based on the products purchased by the user. The set consists of sub-plans having the following properties: (i). The length of each sub-plan $\geq (i + 1)$ and (ii). The products in the first i adjacent (i.e., consecutive) states respectively match with the i most recent products purchased by the user. Now there are two cases, namely Case 1 and Case 2.

Case 1: If the conflict set is non-empty then the product having the following three characteristics is recommended to the user. (i). The product is well-rated in the majority of the sub-plans in the conflict set (ii). The product is in the $(i + 1)^{th}$ or the above state (iii). The product is in the nearest state, while traversing each of the sub-plans from left to right.

In case there is more than one product that fulfills these conditions then the product that is most recently purchased is recommended. If there is more than one product that is most recently purchased (note: these products are named "competing products at level i") then i is incremented by 1 and the entire process is repeated.

Case 2: If the conflict set is empty then the sub-plans, in each of which the following two conditions are satisfied, are added to the conflict set. (i). The products that are purchased by the target user are in the same sequence but not necessarily adjacent. (ii) The products that are well-rated by other users, but are not purchased by the target user, are not presenting in between the products that are purchased by the target user.

Now there are four cases and these cases are executed in the specified order.

Case 2.1: If the conflict set is non-empty then recommend a product, as explained in Case 1.

Case 2.2: If the conflict set is empty and $i > 2$ then the competing products at level (i - 1) are recommended as various options to the user. Note that there are at least two competing products at level (i – 1) because the process initially started with $i = 2$ and the current situation $i > 2$ implies that there were competing products at all the levels starting from 2 to (i - 1).

Case 2.3: If the conflict set is empty and $i = 2$ then the entire process is performed by reducing the value of i by 1, provided the process is not already performed for this reduced value of i. If the process is already performed for this reduced value then the competing products at level 1 are recommended as various options to the user.

Case 2.4: If the conflict set is empty and $i = 1$ then no product is recommended. This case is true if and only if the product that is most recently bought by the target user is bought by no other user in the past.

The algorithm is formally presented below. In this, we consider that K is the total number of products the user ever purchased from the system. The algorithm starts with $i := 2$ if $K \geq 2$. If $K = 1$ then the algorithm starts with $i := 1$. It is assumed that the value of K is at least one. Otherwise, the algorithm doesn't work. In this discussion, ":=" represents the assignment operator.

Algorithm(i)

/* INTIALIZATION */

1. Conflict set S := Empty.
   Pi, ..., P1 are respectively the i most recent products purchased by the user. Here, *P1* is the most recent and *Pi* is the least recent among all.
   SSP1 := The set of all existing sub-plans that start with *Pi*.
   SSP2 := An empty set.
   COMPETING-PRODUCTS-AT-LEVELi := Empty.

/* DETERMINE THE CONFLICT SET BASED ON THE PURCHASE SEQUENCE OF THE PRODUCTS */

2. Repeat the following operations in the specified order until *SSP1* is empty. Randomly select a sub-plan *SP* from *SSP1*. Remove *SP* from *SSP1*. Add *SP* to *SSP2*. Add *SP* to S if and only if all the products in the first (i + 1) adjacent states of *SP* are rated and also the products in the first i adjacent states respectively match with *Pi,..., P1*.

/* CHECK THE CONFLICT SET */

3. If S is empty then go to Step 4 else go to Step 6.

/* DETERMINE THE CONFLICT SET BASED ON THE WELL-RATED PRODUCTS, BUT RELAXING THE "ADJACENT" CONDITION */

4. Repeat the following operations in the specified order until *SSP2* is empty. Randomly select a sub-plan *SP* from *SSP2*. Remove *SP* from *SSP2*. Add it to *S* if and only if it fulfills all the following conditions: (i). *Pn* is well-rated in *SP* for $1 \leq n \leq i$ (ii). If $i > 1$ then *Pn* follows (not necessarily adjacent) *P(n +* 1) for $1 \leq n < i$, in *SP* (iii). If $i > 1$ then there is no well-rated product in between *P(n* + 1) and *Pn* for $1 \leq n < i$, in *SP*.

/* CHECK THE EMPTYNESS OF THE CONFLICT SET AGAIN AND PERFORM THE OPERATIONS*/

5. Check the following conditions and perform the corresponding operations in the specified order: (i). If *S* is non-empty then go to Step 6. (ii). If *S* is empty and $i > 2$ then all the products from *COMPETING-PRODUCTS-AT-LEVEL* (*i* - 1) are recommended as various options. Go to Step 8. (iii). If *S* is empty and $i = 2$ then $i := 1$ and then *Algorithm*(1), provided *Algorithm*(1) is not already executed in the past. If it is already executed in the past then all the products from *COMPETING-PRODUCTS-AT-LEVEL*(1) are recommended as various options. (iv). If *S* is empty and $i = 1$ then go to Step 7.

/* DETERMINE THE NEXT PRODUCT BASED ON THE RATINGS, MAJORITY AND SEQUENCE */

6. A product *P* from *S* is selected for recommendation if it fulfills the following condition. *P* is well-rated in the majority of the sub-plans in S and there is no other well-rated product between *P1* and *P*, while traversing each of these sub-plans from *P1* towards the end of the sub-plan.

   If more than one product that fulfills the above condition then do the following in the specified order: (i). If there is a single product that is most recently bought then recommend that product and then go to Step 8. (ii). If more than one recent product exists then do the following in the specified order.

   (a). Add all these competing products to *COMPETING-PRODUCTS-AT-LEVELi*. (b). If $i < K$ then $i = i + 1$ and then *Algorithm(i)* (c). If $i = K$ then all the products from *COMPETING-PRODUCTS-AT-LEVELi* are recommended as various options.

/* CONFLICT SET IS STILL EMPTY */

7. No recommendation.

/* REPEAT OR QUIT THE PROCESS */

8. If the user purchases a product then $K := K + 1$.
   $i := 2$ if $K \geq 2$.
   $i := 1$ if $K = 1$.
   If the user purchases a product and he is looking for another product then go to Step 1. Else exit the process.

In the above algorithm, any product for which the recommendation rating is 0.5 or more is considered as well-rated. Two examples are provided in the next section.

2.3 Storage and Recommendation of Sub-plans

Plan retrieval is an important issue because it is performed continuously while the users buy new products. Each product is represented using a unique integer. The plan library is implemented as a hash-table and the sub-plans are stored in bins. The bins are indexed by a common product number. This approach is borrowed from Kerkez and Cox [23]. It is observed that a plan of length *pl* has (*pl* - (*sl* - 1)) sub-plans of length *sl*. The retrieval process is explained using two examples. The timings and the users' identities are not shown in these examples.

Example 1:

Consider the following sample conflict set.
1/0.6 → 2/0.2 → 6/0.4 → 3/0.7 → 4/0.8 → 9/0.1
1/0.7 → 2/0.3 → 15/0.2 → 7/0.6 → 8/0.4
1/0.2 → 2/0.7 → 6/0.3 → 3/0.4
1/0.8 → 2/0.6 → 4/0.2 → 7/0.8 → 12/0.9
1/0.1 → 2/0.4 → 5/0.1 → 6/0.9
1/0.5 → 2/0.4 → 23/0.4 → 3/0.1

Assume that a user, who already bought the products 1 and 2 respectively, is looking for recommendation. In this example, there are 6 sub-plans in the conflict set. The first sub-plan conveys the fact that a user bought the products 1, 2, 6, 3, 4, and 9 and the ratings for these products are 0.6, 0.2, 0.4, 0.7, 0.8, and 0.1 respectively. Other sub-plans have similar meanings. Product 7 is recommended to the user, based on the algorithm in Section 2.2. Steps 4 and 5 of the algorithm are not executed for this example.

Example 2: Consider the following sample conflict set.
1/0.6 → 2/0.2 → 4/0.8 → 3/0.7 → 4/0.8 → 9/0.1
1/0.7 → 2/0.3 → 15/0.2 → 7/0.6 → 8/0.4
1/0.2 → 2/0.7 → 6/0.3 → 3/0.4
1/0.8 → 2/0.3 → 4/0.7 → 7/0.8 → 12/0.9
1/0.1 → 2/0.4 → 5/0.1 → 6/0.9
1/0.5 → 2/0.4 → 4/0.6 → 3/0.8

Assume that a user, who already bought the products 1 and 4 respectively, is looking for recommendations. Product 3 is recommended to the user, based on the algorithm in Section 2.2. The value of *S* is found to be empty at Step 3 of the algorithm. Steps 4 and 5 of this algorithm are executed. The condition (i) of Step 5 is found to be true. In addition, the condition, "If more than one product that fulfills..." of Step 6 of this algorithm is not true for this example.

Users' purchase trends may change over time. This notion is explained in the next section.

2.4 The Change of Trend: Detection and Adjustment

The change of trend can be explained by using a simple example. Users who bought a TV may prefer to buy a digital video recorder rather than a VHS recorder, due to the convenience with digital recorders. In other words, the users' purchase trend is changed from TV→ VHS-recorder to TV→ Digital-recorder.

In general, if a user does not buy the recommended product but instead selects another product, then it should not be treated as a change of trend. This is because there may not be many qualified products/plans in the system or the user might have already purchased the recommended product elsewhere. But if the acceptance rate of the recommendations starts decreasing and falls below a threshold value then the situation is treated as a change of trend. In this system, if the acceptance rate of the recommended products starts decreasing monotonically and falls below 50% then it is considered as a change of trend. Once it is detected, the system changes its recommendation process as follows. The sub-plans that are recorded on or after the date on which the acceptance rate initially started decreasing monotonically will only be considered for recommendation. This restriction aims to prevent the older sub-plans, which are now found to be less effective in the recommendation process, from influencing the future recommendation decisions of HYREC. Evaluation details are presented in the next section.

3 Evaluation

In this section we discuss the effectiveness of the proposed approach by conducting some experiments. The evaluation is conducted on an experimental server located at www.technologyai.com. 25,000 different users and 950 different products were involved in the evaluation process.

In this discussion, the following conventions are followed. If HYREC is unable to provide any recommendation or if it provides a recommendation and the user doesn't buy any product then it is considered as a recommendation failure. If the user purchases a different product that is not in the list of recommendations then HYREC gets the user's feedback on whether the list of recommendations stimulated him to purchase the different product. If the answer is "no" then the recommendation is considered as a failure. If the answer is "yes" then it is considered as a success. This is

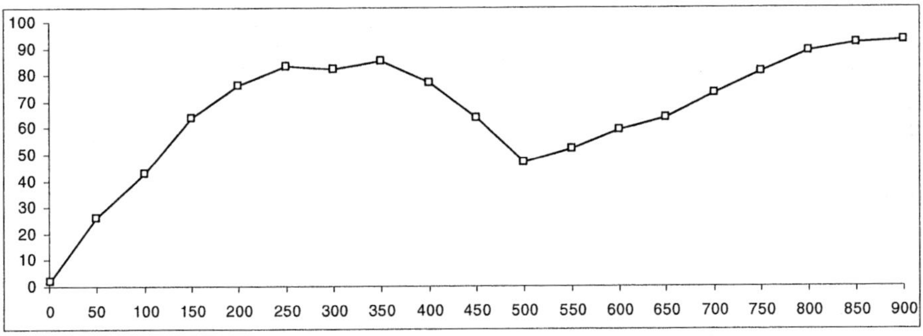

Fig. 1. Number of plans on the X-axis vs. product acceptance rate on the Y-axis. The arc corresponds to HYREC

because HYREC fulfilled the goal of increasing the purchases. Any other situation, which is not discussed above, is also treated as a successful recommendation. The details of the experiments are presented.

3.1 Experiment 1

The relation between the number of plans and the effectiveness of the recommendations is studied in this experiment. Fig. 1 corresponds to HYREC. The X-axis represents the number of plans and the Y-axis represents the acceptance rate of the recommendations. After the first 350 plans, the acceptance rate started decreasing monotonically and it eventually fell below the threshold value (50%) at around the 500th plan. As a result, only the sub-plans that are recorded on or after Nov 22nd 2004 (corresponding to the location (350, 85) in the graph) are considered for the recommendation purposes. Note that the date is not shown in the graph due to simplicity reasons. After the adjustment in the recommendation process, the acceptance rate has quickly increased. We further investigated the relationship between the number of plans and the product acceptance rate by modifying the definition of the change of trend for which the acceptance rates were 30% and 80% respectively. In case of 30%, we observed that more plans are required (i.e., it takes more time) to reach higher acceptance rates, once the change of trend is detected. As a result, the users may loose trust in HYREC if the threshold value is too low. In case of 80%, we observed that the system triggered the change of trend, although sometimes there was no change of trend detected in the real world.

3.2 Experiment 2

In this experiment, HYREC is compared with ACF approach and two different kinds of CBRPR approaches. The ACF approach and the CBRPR approaches used in this experiment are explained.

The ACF approach considers 2 common products in order to provide a recommendation. The recommendation process is explained using an example. Assume that $X1,\ldots, Xn$ ($n \geq 2$) are the users of the system. $P1$ and $P2$ are the products that are

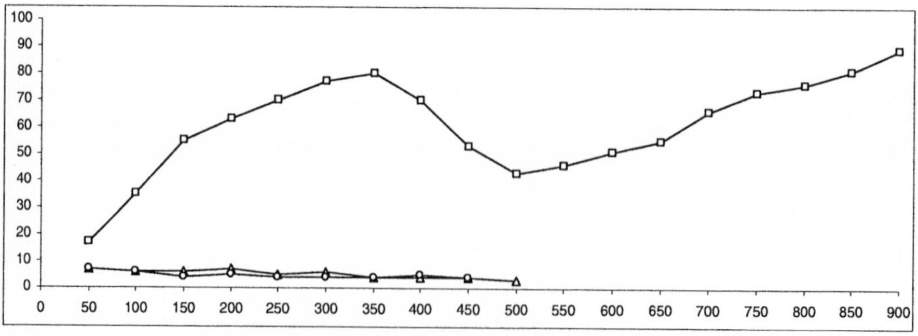

Fig. 2. Number of products on the X-axis vs. product acceptance rate on the Y-axis. The arcs connecting the squares, triangles, and circles correspond to HYREC, ACF and 1st kind of CBRPR respectively

most recently purchased by *X1* and subsequently received high ratings from him. Assume also that the users *X2,..., Xn* purchased the products (not necessarily in the given order) *P1, P2, P3,..., Pm* ($m \geq 3$) and rated them high. Then the ACF system recommends *P3,..., Pm* to *X1*. In this example, *P1* and *P2* are the "2 common products" mentioned above. The ACF approach is implemented by using the mean squared difference formula.

The CBRPR approaches work on 3 steps, without considering the users' ratings for the products. A conflict set of plans is determined, based on the products purchased by the user. In the 1st kind of CBRPR approach, all the products those immediately follow the sequence (in the sub-plans of the conflict set) are recommended as various options to the user. In the 2nd kind of CBRPR approach, the product that immediately follows the sequence (in the sub-plans of the conflict set) and is present in the majority of these sub-plans is recommended. If more than one such product exists then the one that is most recently purchased is recommended. Still if there is more than one such product exists then all these competing products are recommended as different options.

In Fig. 2, the arcs connecting the squares, triangles, and circles correspond to HYREC, ACF, and the 1st kind of CBRPR respectively. The X-axis represents the number of products in the system and the Y-axis represents the acceptance rate of the recommendations. From this graph, we can observe that the acceptance rate of HYREC increased with the number of products. But the rate started decreasing monotonically and it eventually fell below the threshold value (50%). Later the rate started increasing, once the sub-plans that were recorded after a particular date were only considered, as explained for Fig 1. But in case of the ACF approach and also in case of the 1st kind of CBRPR approach, the acceptance rates were very low because they were recommending too many products to the users, introducing confusion. The acceptance rate for the 2nd kind of CBRPR, which is not shown in this figure, is almost similar to that of the 1st kind of CBRPR. This is because the products, which were not considered by HYREC due to their low ratings, played a vital role in the recommendation process of the 2nd kind of CBRPR.

4 Conclusions

In this paper we presented a hybrid approach for product recommendation. We observed that the results will slightly vary based on the interface issues such as how many products are displayed and recommended at a time.

In HYREC, there is no provision for the users to correct their purchasing mistakes, which they have noticed at a later stage. For example, if a user bought a product *P1* before *P2* and later noticed that he would have bought *P2* before *P1* (i.e., he noticed that *P2* is a prerequisite to properly use *P1*) then it is a purchasing mistake. We are investigating the mechanisms on how to rectify this.

In this system, the plans are considered to be linear. HYREC has no mechanism to handle non-linear plans. We are also working on other heuristics to identify the change of trend.

In this work, we assumed that a user purchases a product only once. But in some cases, the same product or the same sequence of products may be purchased more than once. We are investigating the mechanisms on how to handle this kind of knowledge. We are also investigating the mechanisms to identify the temporal dependencies among the products that are purchased by a user at the same time.

The ACF systems have to deal with extremely sparse data. By considering the sequence of products (rather than the "set" of products used in ACF), HYREC is only considering a part of the available data. Hence, the sparse data issue is more important for HYREC, when compared to the traditional ACF systems. We are investigating some solutions, including those provided by Sarwar et al. [33], to address this issue.

In some cases, the sequence of purchases doesn't matter. For example, buying the music CDs produced by two different artists. We are working on improving HYREC so that, in these cases, the performance is at least equal to that of an ACF system.

As mentioned by Pazzani [28], the current recommendation systems have little or no commonsense in identifying the users' goals. A lot of work needs to be done to address this issue.

References

1. Albrecht, D. W., Zukerman, I., Nicholson, A., Bud, A.: Towards a Bayesian Model for Keyhole Plan Recognition in Large Domains. Proceedings of the 6th International Conference on User Modelling (1997) 365-376.
2. Allen, J. F., Perrault, C. R.: Analyzing Intention in Dialogues. Artificial Intelligence, Vol. 15, No. 3 (1980) 143-178.
3. Balabanovic, M., Shoham, Y.: Fab: Content-based, Collaborative Recommendation. Communications of the ACM, 40(3) March (1997).
4. Bauer, M.: Acquisition of User Preferences for Plan Recognition. Proceedings of the 5th International Conference on User Modelling (1998) 936-941.
5. Bergmann, R., Richter, M.M., Schmitt, S., Stahl, A., Vollrath, I.: Utilityoriented Matching: A New Research Direction for Case-Based Reasoning. Professionelles Wissensmanagement: Erfahrungen und Visionen, Proceedings of the 1st Conference on Professional Knowledge Management, Shaker (2001).
6. Bergmann, R., Schmitt, S., Stahl, A.: Intelligent Customer Support for Product Selection with Case-based Reasoning, E-commerce and Intelligent Methods. Physica-Verlag, (2002) 322-341.
7. Branting, K.L.: Learning Feature Weights from Customer Return-Set Selections, Journal of Knowledge and Information Systems, 6(2) (2004).
8. Bui H.H.: Efficient Approximate Inference for Online Probabilistic Plan Recognition. Technical Report 1/2002, School of Computing, Curtin University of Technology, Perth, WA, Australia (2002).
9. Burke, R.: Integrating Knowledge-Based and Collaborative-Filtering Recommender Systems. Proceedings of the AAAI-99 Workshop on AI for Electronic Commerce (1998).
10. Charniak, E., Goldman, R.: A Bayesian Model of Plan Recognition. Artificial Intelligence Journal, Vol. 64 (1993) 53-79.
11. Cohen, R., Song, F., Spencer, B., van Beek, P.: Exploiting Temporal and Novel Information from the User in Plan Recognition. User Modelling and User-Adapted Interaction, Vol. 1, No. 2 (1981) 125-148.
12. Cotter, P., Smyth, B.: PTV: Intelligent Personalised TV Guides. Proceedings of the 12th Innovative Applications of Artificial Intelligence (IAAI-2000) Conference, AAAI Press (2000).

13. Cunningham, P.: Intelligent Support for E-commerce. Keynote speech slides presented at the International Conference on Case-Based Reasoning (ICCBR 1999). Also available at: http://www.cs.tcd.ie/Padraig.Cunningham/iccbr99-ec.pdf (1999), Accessed on December 26 2004.
14. Cunningham, P., Bergmann, R., Schmitt, S., Breen, S., Smyth, B, Traphoener, R.: Intelligent Support for Online Sales: The Websell Experience. http://www.aic.nrl.navy.mil/ papers/2001/AIC-01-003/ws3/ws3toc6.pdf (2001) Accessed on December 26 2004.
15. Ferguson, G., Allen, J.F.: Events and Actions in the Interval Temporal Logic. Journal of Logic and Computation, Special Issue on Actions and Processes, Vol. 4, No. 5 (1994) 531-579.
16. Gronau, N., Kreymborg, C., Laskowski, F.: Improving Information Retrieval in Knowledge Management Systems using CBR - The Multi Reuse Approach of the Project TO_KNOW. Proceedings of the 1st Indian International Conference on Artificial Intelligence, Hyderabad, India (2003) 779-788.
17. Hammond, K., Schmitt, K.: A Case-Based Approach to Knowledge Navigation. Proceedings of the AAAI Workshop on Indexing and Reuse in Multimedia Systems, AAAI Press (1994).
18. Hayes, C., Cunningham, P.: Shaping a CBR view with XML. Proceedings of the 3rd International Conference on Case-based Reasoning (2000) 468-481.
19. Hayes, C., Cunningham, P.: Context Boosting Collaborative Recommendations. Knowledge-Based Systems, Vol. 17, No. 2-4 (2003) 131-138.
20. Hayes, C., Cunningham, P., Smyth, B.: A Case-based Reasoning View of Automated Collaborative Filtering. Proceedings of 4th International Conference on Case-Based Reasoning. LNAI 2080 (2001) 234-248.
21. Hill, W., Stead, L., Rosenstein, M., Furnas, G.: Recommending and Evaluating Choices in a Virtual Community of Use. Proceedings of Conference on Human Factors in Computing Systems (1995)
22. Kautz., H.: A Formal Theory of Plan Recognition and its Implementation. In Allen, J., Pelavin, R., Tenenberg, J. (eds.): Reasoning About Plans. Morgan Kaufmann, San Mateo, California, USA (1991) 69-125.
23. Kerkez, B., Cox, M.: Incremental Case-Based Plan Recognition Using State Indices. Proceedings of 4th International Conference on Case-Based Reasoning (2001) 291-305.
24. Kohlmaier, A., Schmitt, S., Bergmann, R.: A Similarity-based Approach to Attribute Selection in User Adaptive Sales Dialogs. Proceedings of the 4th International Conference on Case-Based Reasoning, Lecture Notes in Artificial Intelligence 2080, Springer (2001) 306–320.
25. Konstan, J., Miller, B., Maltz, D., Herlocker, J., Gordon, L., Riedl, J.: GroupLens: Applying Collaborative Filtering to Usenet News. Communications of the ACM, 40(3) (1997) 77-87.
26. Kowalczyk, R., Pham, A., Rahwan, D.: Intelligent Agents for One-to-Many Automated E-Commerce Negotiation. Proceedings of the Australasian Computer Science Conference, Australia (2002).
27. Lesh, N., Rich, C., Sidner, C.: Using Plan Recognition in Human-Computer Collaboration. Proceedings of the 7th International Conference on User Modelling (1999) 23-32.
28. Pazzani, M.J.: Beyond Idiot Savants: Recommendations and Common Sense. Beyond Personalization 2005: A Workshop on the Next Stage of Recommender Systems Research, held in conjunction with the 2005 International Conference on Intelligent User Interfaces (IUI 2005), San Diego, California, USA (2005). The paper is also available at: http://www.grouplens.org/beyond2005/position/pazzani.pdf. Accessed on March 18 2005.

29. Perry, P.: Resources on Collaborative Filtering, http://www.paulperry.net/notes/cf.asp. Accessed on December 26 2004.
30. Prasad, B.: Learning the Users' Preferences in E-Commerce: A Weight-adjustment Approach. International Journal of Knowledge-Based and Intelligent Engineering Systems, Vol. 8, No. 4 (2004) 205-211.
31. Resnick, P., Iacovou, N., Suchak, M., Bergstrom, P., Riedl, J.: GroupLens: An Open Architecture for Collaborative Filtering of Netnews. Proceedings of the ACM 1994 Conference on Computer Supported Cooperative Work (CSCW '94), Chapel Hill, NC, USA, 1994.
32. Resnick, P., Varian, H.R.: Recommender Systems. Special issue of Communications of the ACM 40(3) (1997).
33. Sarwar, B.M., Karypis, G., Konstan, J.A., Riedl, J.: Item-based Collaborative Filtering Recommendation Algorithms. Proceedings of the 10th International World Wide Web Conference (WWW10), Hong Kong (2001).
34. Shardanand, U., Maes, P.: Social Information Filtering: Algorithms for Automating "Word of Mouth". Conference on Human Factors in Computing Systems (1995).
35. Sollenborn, M., Funk, P.: Category-Based Filtering and User Stereotype Cases to Reduce the Latency Problem in Recommender Systems. 6th European Conference on Case Based Reasoning, ECCBR2002, Springer Lecture Notes, Aberdeen, Scotland (2002) 395-405.
36. Stahl, A.: Learning Feature Weights from Case Order Feedback. Proceedings of the 4th International Conference on Case-Based Reasoning, Lecture Notes in Artificial Intelligence, Springer 2080 (2001) 502–516.
37. Tran, T., Cohen, R.: Hybrid Recommender Systems for Electronic Commerce. Proceedings of the AAAI-00 Workshop on Knowledge-Based Electronic Markets, USA, (1999).
38. Vollrath, I., Wilke, W., Bergmann, R.: Case-Based Reasoning Support for Online Catalog Sales. IEEE Internet Computing, 2(4) (1998) 45-54.
39. Watson, I.: Applying Case-Based Reasoning: Techniques for Enterprise Systems. San Francisco, California, USA: Morgan Kaufmann Publishers (1997).
40. Wettschereck, D., Aha, D.W.: Weighting Features. Proceedings of the 1st International Conference on Case-Based Reasoning, Springer, New York, USA (1995).
41. Wilke, W.: Knowledge Management for Intelligent Sales Support in Electronic Commerce. Ph.D. Dissertation, University of Kaiserslautern, Germany (1999).
42. Yang, Q., Li, I.T.Y., Zhang, H.H.: Mining High-Quality Cases for Hypertext Prediction and Prefetching. Proceedings of the 4th International Conference on Case-Based Reasoning (ICCBR 2001), Springer-Verlag (2001).

Extending jCOLIBRI for Textual CBR*

Juan A. Recio[1], Belén Díaz-Agudo[1], Marco A. Gómez-Martín[1], and Nirmalie Wiratunga[2]

[1] Dep. Sistemas Informáticos y Programación, Universidad Complutense de Madrid, Spain
jareciog@fdi.ucm.es, {belend, marcoa}@sip.ucm.es
[2] School of Computing, The Robert Gordon University, Aberdeen AB25 1HG, Scotland, UK
nw@comp.rgu.ac.uk

Abstract. This paper summarises our work in textual Case-Based Reasoning within jCOLIBRI. We use Information Extraction techniques to annotate web pages to facilitate semantic retrieval over the web. Similarity matching techniques from CBR are applied to retrieve from these annotated pages. We demonstrate the applicability of these extensions by annotating and retrieving documents on the web.

1 Introduction

jCOLIBRI is an object-oriented framework for developing Case Based Reasoning (CBR) applications[2][1]. It provides most of the code needed to represent structured cases, methods and similarity functions used in these systems. jCOLIBRI includes facilities to work with different case representations, namely, first order logics, data based records or XML files. In CBR past experiences are generally available in structured form. However in domains where past experiences are documents, there is a need to map these in to structure/semi-structured cases to enable informed comparison and retrieval. Textual CBR involves reasoning with past experiences that are stored in text form. We believe that jCOLIBRI needs to be extended to support Textual CBR if it is to achieve its aim of of providing a general CBR framework.

Textual CBR (TCBR) analyses texts of a given domain and typically builds semi-structured cases with which new text can be meaningfully compared. Domain-specific ontologies that are acquired manually are often employed for this purpose. TCBR systems in the literature have been developed for specific domains. Consequently it is hard to establish a common architecture that can cover needs of the TCBR community. Although a general framework may not cater to domain-specific requirements, we hope that textual extensions to jCOLIBRI will provide system developers with sufficient functionality to create a workable initial system solution. However the general framework of jCOLIBRI is particularly suited for content retrieval over the web. Semantic Web is based on the

* Supported by the Spanish Committee of Science & Technology (TIC2002-01961).
[1] http://sourceforge.net/projects/jcolibri-cbr/

H. Muñoz-Avila and F. Ricci (Eds.): ICCBR 2005, LNAI 3620, pp. 421–435, 2005.

availability of meta-data describing web content. The difficulty is that relevant documents on the WWW must first be manually annotated before semantic retrieval is possible. Therefore an obvious application of jCOLIBRI will be to apply its textual extensions to help with this annotation task.

This paper summarises our work in extending jCOLIBRI to operate over experiences that are recorded in text form. Key decisions concerning mapping of text into cases and functionality provided by jCOLIBRI to achieve this mapping and retrieval will be discussed. We demonstrate the usability of these extensions with retrieval over documents obtained from the web.

2 Case Structure

One of the main challenges is to establish structures with which text can be represented as cases. Many textual CBR systems work with cases that operate over plain text but typically we need representations that can combine both text (unstructured) and structured data. This is discussed in [16] with the example of a help-desk application. Here the operator assigns values to attributes concerning product details and also writes textual annotations in a separate text attribute. Here a mixed representation is required to facilitate effective reuse.

As jCOLIBRI uses the composite pattern, it allows us to represent these semi-structured cases easily. A case is composed by several individuals that can also be composed by other individuals. So we need only define an individual subclass that represents texts and is composed of other attributes within the case. This mixed representation can be very useful when the developer needs to extract information from texts whereby it can be stored as a text attribute within the case. This structure is shown in Figure 1.

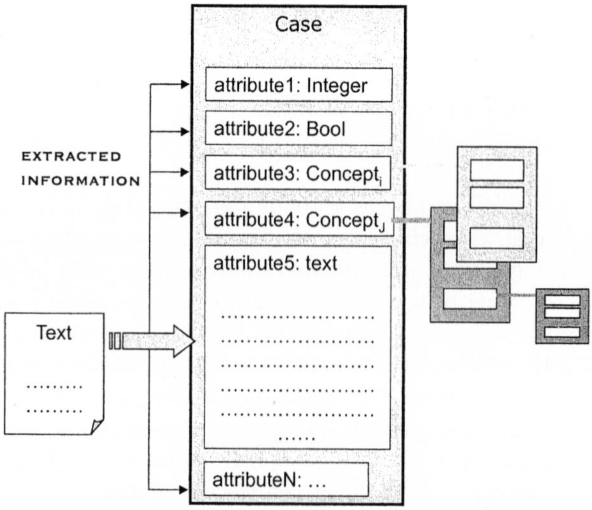

Fig. 1. jCOLIBRI semi-structure case representation

3 Generic Framework for TCBR

Once the case structure is defined the next issue is to identify the different forms of functionality that can be offered by a general framework. It should be flexible enough to facilitate knowledge artifacts that are commonly needed for TCBR but without having to rely on domain-specific details. There does not appear to be a standard or consensus about the structure of a textual CBR system. This is mainly due to the different knowledge requirements in application domains. For classification applications typically only a basic stemmer algorithm and a cosine similarity function is needed, while with other applications more intense Natural Language Processing (NLP) derived structures are employed (see [3] and [5]).

Although a common functionality for TCBR systems is difficult to establish, several researchers have attempted to define the different knowledge requirements for TCBR([7], [15]). We have chosen the Lenz layered model [9] as a reference architecture because it is one of the most generic architectures and its flexibility allows for different combinations and/or additions of new text processing mechanisms. We also believe that any TCBR framework should be developed with two views in mind:

Involved Technologies: Using texts as a source of information implies a Natural Text Processing to prepare the data for being extracted using Information Retrieval (IR) algorithms.

Domain Relation: These technologies can use domain specific or independent information during the data processing. This is a key idea behind the development of the framework as it should provide efficient domain-independent functionalities but also general and extensible domain-dependent ones.

jCOLIBRI should implement all these features but also allow developers to skip some of them when required (for instance due to high computational costs associated with an algorithm).

4 Theoretic Model

Lenz [9] proposes a layer division for textual cases processing:

Keyword Layer. This layer separates texts into terms, removes stop-words, stem terms and calculates statistics about frequency of terms. It also proposes a part-of-speech tagger in this layer that could be useful by the following ones. This layer is domain-independent, so it can be shared between applications.

Phrase Layer. Recognises domain-specific phrases using a dictionary. Here, the problems are that some parts of the phrase can be separated and that the dictionary must be built manually.

Thesaurus Layer. This layer identifies synonyms and related terms. Methods implemented in this layer must be reusable in the query stage of the CBR cycle. WordNet can be used as an english thesaurus. This phase is domain-independent.

Glossary Layer. Is the domain-specific version of the thesaurus layer. So it is desirable to define a common interface for both layers. The main difficulty with this layer resides in the glossary acquisition.

Feature Value Layer. With semi-structured cases, this layer extracts features about the case and stores it as ⟨attribute, value⟩ pairs in the case representation. It is also domain-specific.

Domain Structure Layer. Uses the previous layer to classify documents in a high level. It assigns "topic" features to the cases that can be useful in the indexing process.

Information Extraction Layer. Some parts of the texts can be better represented with a structured approximation. This layer accomplish this task. (note that this functionality can overlap with the two previous layers).

These layers can be grouped into Case Representation and Information Retrieval layers. Keyword, Phrase and Feature value layers are applied in the case representation using natural language processing, whereas Thesaurus, Glossary, Domain Structure and Information Extraction (IE) layers are related to Information Retrieval (IR).

5 Natural Language Processing Using Maximum Entropy

Most of the algorithms outlined here are very common in IR and NLP and there are standard implementations than can be applied in the domain-independent layers. This is very important in the NLP layers because there are several algorithms that can be applied. In these layers jCOLIBRI uses the Maximum Entropy method that is one of the most powerful and extensible algorithms. Before describing the implementation of the NLP layers within the jCOLIBRI architecture, we will first outline the main ideas behind it.

A simple definition of maximum entropy could be: model all that is known and assume nothing about that which is unknown. In other words, given a collection of facts, choose a model consistent with all the facts, but otherwise as uniform as possible (see [10] and [12]).

On the engineering level, using Maximum Entropy is an excellent way of creating programs which perform very difficult classification tasks very well. This is proved in Adwait Ratnaparkhi's dissertation [13], where the author shows that this technique can achieve state-of-the-art performance in NLP. The main reason is that with NLP problems it is impossible to find a complete set of training examples. This is due to the variability of the language, so it is not correct to add "information" constraints from the examples.

To illustrate this idea, consider this Ratnaparkhi's example. Suppose the task is to estimate a joint probability distribution p defined over $\{x, y\} * \{0, 1\}$. Furthermore suppose that the only facts known about p are that $p(x, 0) + p(y, 0) = 0.6$ and that $p(x, 0) + p(y, 0) + p(x, 1) + p(y, 1) = 1.0$. This problem consists of learning the values marked with a "?" in Table 1(a). There are many consistent ways to fill in its the cells; Table 1(b) shows one of them. The Principle of Maximum Entropy recommends the assignment in Table 1(c), which is the most non-committal assignment of probabilities that meets the constraints on p.

Table 1. Maximum Entropy Examples

p(a,b)	0	1	
x	?	?	
y	?	?	
total	0.6		1.0

(a) Unknown distribution

p(a,b)	0	1	
x	0.5	0.1	
y	0.1	0.1	
total	0.6		1.0

(b) One possible distribution

p(a,b)	0	1	
x	0.3	0.2	
y	0.3	0.2	
total	0.6		1.0

(c) Maximum Entropy inferred distribution

The Maximum Entropy model has been implemented and applied to Natural Language tasks in the *OpenNLP* package[2]. It is divided into independent layers that can be used separately, providing a stop-word remover, sentence detector, part-of-speech tagger, grammar layer and, in the future, an interface to WordNet. The main advantage of this implementation is that it can be extended easily, training the algorithm with new data to adapt it to new situations (for example, languages other than English).

6 jCOLIBRI Extended Architecture

jCOLIBRI is built around a task/method ontology, a knowledge level description [11] that guides the framework design, determines possible extensions and supports the framework instantiation process. Tasks and methods are described in terms of domain-independent CBR terminology which is mapped into the classes of the framework.

Although various authors have applied knowledge level analysis to CBR systems, the most relevant work is the CBR task structure developed in [1]. At the highest level of generality, they describe the general CBR cycle in terms of four tasks (4 Rs): *Retrieve* the most similar case/s, *Reuse* its/their knowledge to solve the problem, *Revise* the proposed solution and *Retain* the experience. Each one of the four CBR tasks involves a number of more specific sub-tasks. There are methods to solve tasks either by decomposing it into subtasks or by solving it directly. The task structure identifies a number of alternative methods for a task, and each method sets up further subtasks in turn. This form of task-method-subtask analysis is carried on to a level of detail whereby tasks are decomposed into primitives with respect to the available knowledge. Importantly it is the decomposed primitive that can then be associated with a resolution method.

jCOLIBRI standard version provides a task ontology and a library of methods that resolve the tasks (usually named as Problem Solving Methods PSMs). This task ontology is shown in Figure 2. The framework is designed to support the construction of CBR systems taking advantage of the task/method division paradigm described previously. Building a CBR system is a configuration process where the system developer selects the tasks the system must fulfill (one or

[2] http://opennlp.sourceforge.net

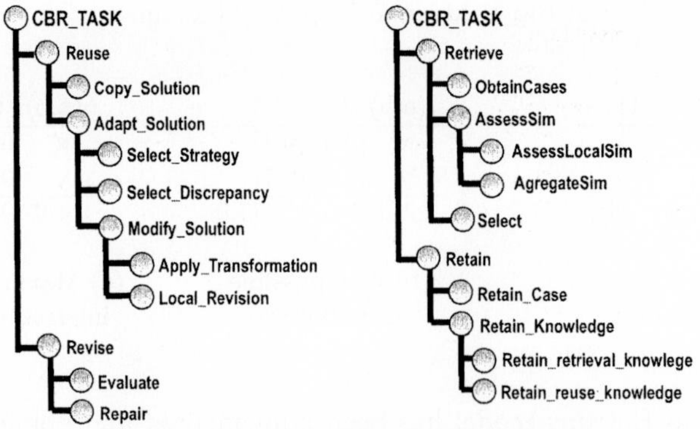

Fig. 2. CBROnto Task Structure

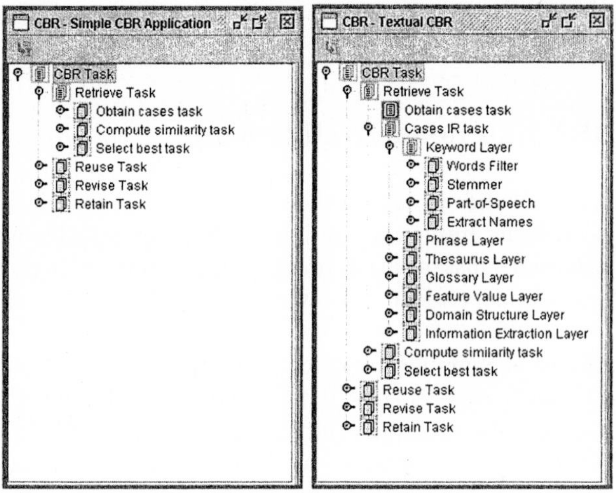

Fig. 3. Task decomposition and tasks related with textual CBR

more) and, for every task, the system developer assigns the method that will do the job. In order to alleviate framework instantiation effort, jCOLIBRI provides a number of GUI tools [14] that support the management of tasks and methods as well as the construction of the particular combination of tasks/methods that defines a CBR system. A simple CBR application configured using the GUI is shown in Figure 3. Once the CBR system configuration is specified, jCOLIBRI will generate a code template with most of the code needed to run the specified CBR system. The textual extension provides new text related tasks with associated methods for resolution. In this manner, a new textual CBR application can also be developed using the jCOLIBRI GUI tools by configuring the system as depicted in Figure 3.

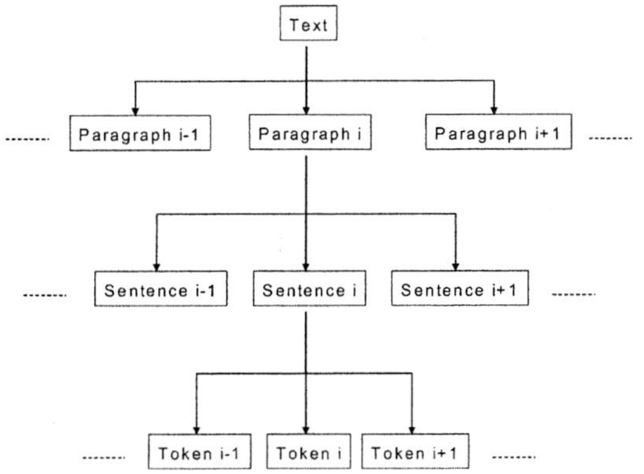

Fig. 4. Text Structure

6.1 Textual Cases

We mentioned before that textual cases are implemented as jCOLIBRI individuals (i.e. a part of a case) to allow the representation of semi-structured cases. Such a representation will consist of Texts decomposed into Paragraphs, then into Sentences, and finally Tokens (see Figure 4). Tokens store information belonging to a word, such as:

- CompleteWord: The original string.
- StemmedWord: Stemmed string, output of StemmerMethod.
- PosTag: POS tag, output of PartofSpeechMethod.
- TokenIndex: Token position within the paragraph.
- WordPosition: Word position within the paragraph raw data.
- RelatedTokens: Collection of WeightedRelation objects that relate similar tokens.
- IsName: Boolean value to indicate if the token is a name, output of ExtractNamesMethod.
- IsNotStopWord: Boolean value to indicate if the token is not a stop word, output of WordsFilterMethod.

Sentences and paragraphs are used to structure the data and as information containers. Text is the final container and the object directly stored inside jCOLIBRI individuals.

6.2 Textual Methods

The new library of methods contain implementations of the Lenz layers. These methods are configured using the GUI to define CBR applications. Available methods are:

Words Filter. Filters and tokenizes the text removing stop-words and special characters.

Part-of-Speech Tagging. This method uses a Maximum Entropy tagger (implemented by *OpenNLP*) to assign Part-of-Speech tags.

Stemmer Algorithms. This method can perform several stemmer algorithms for different languages. It uses the *Snowball*[3] external package that also defines a stemmer language to allow parsing other languages.

Name Extraction. Selects the main names of the text using a Maximum Entropy algorithm.

Phrase Identification. Extracts Phrases using Regular Expressions. Developers can define phrase using a configuration file like:

```
#Rules Format:
# [FeatureName]FeatureRegularExpresion
# Examples:
[Compaq Presario 2100](Compaq|HP|Hewlett-Packard)? Presario 2100
```

This example rule finds the same concept (a computer model) which can be written using different words. The concrete syntax to specify each rule is described in the configuration file.

Glossary. Relates query words to cases words using a domain specific glossary. It also uses a configuration file where developers can define the similarity between words:

```
# Glossary Format:
# [Part-of-Speech Tag]{Similarity} word1 word2 ... wordn
#Examples (TCBR domain)
[NOUN]{2} case instance
[NOUN]{3} cbr nbr
[NOUN]{1} word term speech
```

Here the developer must specify the part-of-speech tag, because the same word can have different meanings if it is used as a verb, noun, adjective, etc. These rules also allow the definition of three levels of similarity between words.

Thesaurus (WordNet). Relates query words to case words using WordNet. This method takes advantage of the same idea as in the FAQ Finder System [6], which is to improve query and case matching by taking into account relationships between words. It has been implemented using an external package called *JWordNetLibrary* (*JWNL*) that defines a simple API to WordNet.

Feature Extraction. Extracts features using Regular Expressions and stores it as attribute-value pairs:

```
#Rules Format:
#[FeatureName]{FeaturePosition}FeatureRegularExpresion
#FeatureName is used to store the extracted information
#Examples:
[Person]{2}(Mr.|Mss.) ((\p{Lu}(\w+|\.)\s)+)
[University]{1}((\p{Lu}\w+\s)+)University
[Company]{1}((\p{Lu}\w+\s)+)(Inc\.|Corporation|Associates|Bank)
```

[3] Snowball (http://snowball.tartarus.org) supports English, French, Spanish, Portuguese, Italian, German, Dutch, Swedish, Norwegian, Danish, Russian and Finnish.

These examples extract features by identifying typical structures: a person name is often preceeded by Mr or Ms, a company name is followed by Inc, Corporation, Associates, etc.

Topic Classification. Associates a Topic using extracted Features and Phrases as conditions. This layer defines a top level description of the text that can be very useful for indexing purposes. It uses a configuration file as:

```
# Rules Format:
# [Topic] <FeatureName,value> <FeatureName,value>... <Phrase> <Phrase>
# Topic: Topic classification
# FeatureName: FeatureName defined in the features extraction Layer
# value: FeatureName value. It also can be '?', meaning any value.
# Phrase: You can use the phrases detected in the phrase Layer
# Example
[MyProyect]<University,Complutense de Madrid><Person,Juan Antonio>
         <Company,?> <Compaq Presario 2100>
```

This example shows a description of a topic. A text about a project should have features about a university, a person and the PC of that person.

Basic Information Extraction. Extracts texts information and stores it in case individuals (if defined). This is the idea behind Figure 1. If the textual processing finds a feature with a label and there is an individual within the case with this label then the method will copy the content of the feature to the individual.

Finally, notice that jCOLIBRI only provides the option of using these methods. It is not mandatory to use them in every applications. It provides the system with the option of choosing all or a subset of available methods (ignoring the rest). Table 2 summarizes the implementations that are provided with each layer.

Table 2. Layers Architecture

Layer	Domain Specific	Functionality	ExternalPackages
Keyword Layer	No	Terms identification, stemming and part-of-speech tagging	*OpenNLP*, *SnowBall*
Phrases Layer	Yes	Domain-specific phrases identification	*OpenNLP*
Thesaurus Layer	No	Synonymous and related words identification	*JWNL*
Glossary Layer	Yes	Relates application-specific terms	*OpenNLP*
Features Value Layer	Yes	Extracts relevant attributes	-
Domain Structure Layer	Yes	Extracts global features	-
Information Extraction Layer	Yes	High Level Structure representation of some text parts	-

```
ALEJO'S PRESTO TRATTORIA
4002 Lincoln Blvd., Marina del Rey
(310) 822-0095
While cooking in some of the finest (and most expensive) restaurants
in L.A., chef Alejo had an idea. Why not open a small, intimate eatery
that serves the same gourmet food at lower prices? Alejo's now has two
restaurants serving delectable, homemade Italian specialties like pasta
primavera ($6.95), linguine pescatore (shrimp, squid and clams, $9.95)
and chopped salad (\$4.95). Try the authentic paella ($10.95) on Friday
and Saturday nights, and don't forget Alejo's famous classic, spaghetti
and meatballs ($6.95). Lunch Mon.-Fri., dinner seven nights. Beer and
wine (Westchester); takeout. AE, DIS, MC, V.
```

Fig. 5. Restaurant example

6.3 Textual Similarity Functions

Usually, TCBR extracts information from the plain text and creates structured cases that are compared later. Even so, it can be useful to provide similarity functions that work directly with the text. jCOLIBRI provides these textual similarity functions, which are based on the vector space representation and are applicable to token relations created with the Wordnet layer:

- Cosine Coefficient: $|(o_1 \cap o_2)|/(\sqrt{|o_1|} * \sqrt{|o_2|})$
- Dice Coefficient: $2 * |(o_1 \cap o_2)|/(|o_1| + |o_2|)$
- Jaccard Coefficient: $|(o_1 \cap o_2)|/(|o_1| \cup |o_2|)$
- Overlap Coefficient: $|(o_1 \cap o_2)|/\min(|o_1|, |o_2|)$

As example, these functions could be applied to compare attribute 5 in Figure 1.

7 Experimental Results

To illustrate jCOLIBRI's Textual extensions, we have developed a restaurant adviser system. The entire case base contains roughly 100 different restaurants extracted from a traditional web page[4]. These pages contain texts with descriptions of restaurants, that have been also used in the Ariadne project [8]. Once the visualisation information has being removed and HTML tags are dropped, the information of each restaurant includes name, address and a description about its offer, as it is shown in Figure 5.

We identified 13 common attributes (location, food type, prices, time tables, dishes, etc.), and then developed an ontology to categorise the extracted information into 15 location types, 20 food concepts, 13 timetable categories and 100 categories of dishes. Then domain dependent knowledge (in the form of rules and regular expressions) for each layer was created for the restaurant application:

[4] Available in http://www.laweekly.com/food/listsearch.php

Phrases: To detect restaurant food types:
`[FISH DISHES]fish|seafood|shrimp|swordfish`
`[MEAT DISHES]meat|chicken|beef`
`[PASTA DISHES]pasta|spaghetti`

Features: The regular expression extracts the name of the chefs. It should appear with the word "chef" followed by another words that begin with a capital letter:
`[CHEF]{2}(chef) ((\p{Lu}\w+\s)+)`

Glossary: The glossary contains synonyms in the restaurants/food context:
`[NOUN]{1} burger hamburger`

Domain Structure. This layer is used to assign topics or identifiers to the restaurants by means of rules. For example, if the texts contains *"Alejo"* in the *CHEF* feature and contains the *PASTA* phrase, then this text depicts the *"Alejo's Restaurant"*
`[Alejo's Restaurant]<CHEF,Alejo><PASTA>`

In order to illustrate the advantages of jCOLIBRI's algorithms for retrieving text represented using the structuring provided by different layers, we have perform queries using three different approaches:

- Using Information Retrieval (IR) techniques with textual queries.
- Using Information Retrieval and Information Extraction (IE) with textual queries:
- Using Information Retrieval and Information Extraction with structured queries (the user has to choose several values for an attribute in a structured form).

The test set consisted of 30 manually categorised texts with the correct values.

As regard the similarity calculation, in the IR experiment we used the cosine coefficient ($|(o_1 \cap o_2)|/(\sqrt{|o_1|} * \sqrt{|o_2|})$) without any structured calculated by Java code external to jCOLIBRI. On the other hand, the similarity in the other two experiments is computed using both the query and the cases. We calculate local similarity using the ontologies described above. These ontologies store attributes similarity: location, food type, timetable and dish. We also use simple numeric calculations for the remaining attributes. Once the local similarity is ascertained, the system computes the global similarity using the following formula:

$$\begin{aligned} GlobalSimliarity = {} & 0.2 * LocationSim + 0.3 * FoodTypeSim + \\ & 0.1 * PriceSim + 0.1 * TimeTableSim + \\ & 0.2 * DishesSim + 0.1 * OthersSim \end{aligned} \tag{1}$$

Where *TimeTableSim* is the average of the *breakfast, lunch* and *dinner* similarities, while *OthersSim* is the average of the *Alcohol, Takeout, Delivery* and *Cathering* similarities.

An example of IE with textual query is *"italian pasta restaurant"*. With this query, the application retrieve the "ALEJO'S PRESTO TRATTORIA" restaurant (case `87e704`) showed in Figure 5. The log reported by the system is:

Table 3. Example of query using IR+IE with structured query

	Location	FoodType	Price	BreakFast	Lunch	Dinner	Dishes	Alcohol	Takeout	Delivery	Catering	Parking
Q	Beverly Hills	Japanese	7	never	never	Sat	beef	true	true	false	true	true
C	Torrance	Japanese	9.95	never	7d	7d	..,beef,...	true	true	false	false	true
LS	0.5	1	0.8525	1	1	1	1	1	1	1	0	1

```
Query: jcolibri.cbrcase.CBRCaseRecord@4a5c78 --> Attribute:
text_relation Value: Paragraph 0: italian pasta restaurant
   Sentence 0. Position: 0 Data: italian pasta restaurant
      Token:
         POSTag: NNP                CompleteWord: italian
         is name: false             StemmedWord: italian
         Word Position: 0           Token Index: 0
         IsNotStopWord: true

Retrieved Case: jcolibri.cbrcase.CBRCaseRecord@87e704 -->
Attribute: text_relation Value: Paragraph 0: While cooking in some
of the finest (and most expensive) ...
   Sentence 0. Position: -1 Data: While cooking in some of the finest ...
      Token:
         POSTag: IN                 CompleteWord: While
         is name: false             StemmedWord: while
         Word Position: 0           Token Index: 0
         IsNotStopWord: false
      Token:
         POSTag: NN                 CompleteWord: cooking
         is name: false             StemmedWord: cook
         Word Position: 6           Token Index: 1
         IsNotStopWord: true
```

Finally, Table 3 shows an example of use of IE + IR with structured query. The first row (row Q) shows the values of each attribute established by the user. For example, the user has specified that she does not mind if the restaurant is open at lunch time, because she will *never* go at that time. One of the cases retrieved by the system is shown in row C, and the similarity between each attribute in the query and the case is shown in row LS. For example the local similarity in the attribute *Lunch* is calculated using an specific ontology, and report that the similarity is 1, because the user does not mind if it is open at that time. With these local similarities, the Global Similarity is calculated using (1).

In order to be able to compare the results of each approach, we define:

$$Precision = RETREL/RET$$
$$Recall = RETREL/REL$$

Where RET is the set of all pages the system has retrieved for a specific query, and REL is the set of relevant pages for the query. $RETREL = RET \cap REL$ i.e. set of the retrieved relevant pages.

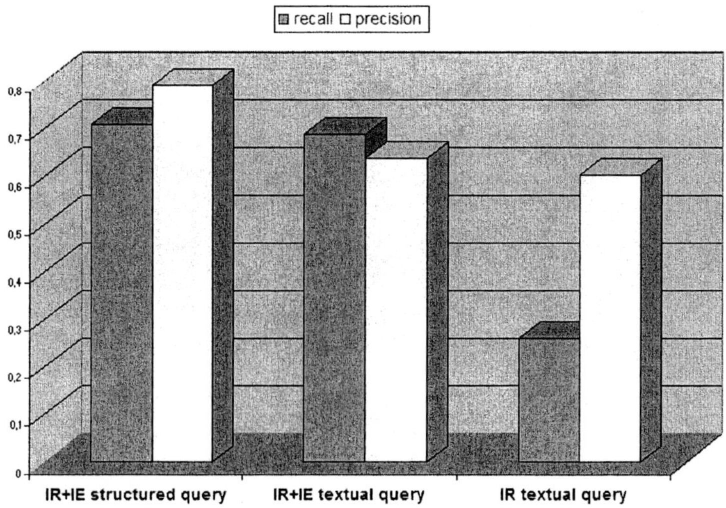

Fig. 6. Experimental Test

After launching several queries in the system we obtained the results showed in Figure 6. The experiment shows a better result with the structured query, obviously caused by the loss of information when extracting the attributes from the textual query. The computed similarity with the most significant case using IR+IE was usually higher than 0.75 while the higher similarity value in the pure IR approach was 0.35. That is the reason of the low recall obtained using this approach.

8 Related Work

Textual CBR systems with knowledge requirements at the token level, borrow retrieval mechanisms from information retrieval ([6], [16]). jCOLIBRI is able to facilitate case representations that are keyword based and provides case matching functionality using coefficient similarity functions.

In domains such as law and education there is a need to analyse text from a semantic instead of a token level. We believe that jCOLIBRI is able to assist developers because it enables part-of-speech tagging and provides functionality to incorporate feature extraction rules. Its ability to operate with regular expressions is particularly useful to specify indexing vocabulary consisting of keyword combinations as in the SMILE system [4] or as logical combinations extracted for text routing and filtering tasks [17].

Information extraction techniques are often employed to represent text data in template form, where extraction rules are used to fill slots of the template [15]. Description of template slots and rules for filling these slots can also be facilitated by jCOLIBRI by use of regular expressions and rules. However unlike state-of-the-art information extraction tools (e.g. AUTOSLOG) jCOLIBRI does not automatically learn extraction from annotated sentences [5].

9 Conclusions

This paper summarizes our work in extending the jCOLIBRI framework for textual CBR. The utility of this extension was demonstrated by developing a TCBR system for restaurant recommendation over the web. We have enhanced jCOLIBRI's library of PSMs to facilitate common techniques in the areas of textual CBR. For this purpose we have incorporated techniques from Information Retrieval and provided basic Information Extraction functionality. This is important in itself because it widens jCOLIBRI's applicability and importantly gives coverage to a very important type of CBR.

We have shown an experiment where CBR similarity computation techniques were applied to retrieve annotated pages from the Web. We have pointed out an emerging application area to use CBR techniques in general, and Textual CBR in particular. Tagging an HTML page for the semantic Web is a manual process. We propose the use of automatic techniques based on Textual CBR and Information Extraction.

References

1. A. Aamodt and E. Plaza. Case-based reasoning: Foundational issues, methodological variations, and system approaches. *AI Communications*, 7(i), 1994.
2. J. J. Bello-Tomás, P. A. González-Calero, and B. Díaz-Agudo. jCOLIBRI: An object-oriented framework for building cbr systems. In *Proceedings of Advances in Case-Based Reasoning, 7th European Conference, ECCBR-04, Madrid, Spain*, pages 32–46, 2004.
3. M. Brown, C. Förtsch, and D. Wissmann. Feature extraction - the bridge from case-based reasoning to information retrieval.
4. S. Brüninghaus and K. D. Ashley. Bootstrapping case base development with annotated case summaries. In *Proceedings of Case-Based Reasoning and Development, Third International Conference, ICCBR-99, Seeon Monastery, Germany*, volume 1650 of *Lecture Notes in Computer Science*. Springer, July 1999.
5. S. Brüninghaus and K. D. Ashley. The role of information extraction for textual CBR. In *Proceedings of the 4th International Conference on Case-Based Reasoning, ICCBR '01*, pages 74–89. Springer-Verlag, 2001.
6. R. D. Burke, K. J. Hammond, V. A. Kulyukin, S. L. Lytinen, N. Tomuro, and S. Schoenberg. Question-answering from FAQs files: Experiences with the FAQ-finder system. *AI Magazine*, 18:57–66, 1997.
7. K. M. Gupta and D. W. Aha. Towards acquiring case indexing taxonomies from text. In *Proceedings of the Seventeenth International FLAIRS Conference*, pages 307–315, Miami Beach, FL, 2004. AAAI Press.
8. C. K. Ion Muslea, Steve Minton. Wrapper induction for semistructured, web-based information sources. In *Proceedings of the Conference on Automatic Learning and Discovery CONALD-98*, 1998.
9. M. Lenz. Defining knowledge layers for textual case-based reasoning. In *Proceedings of the 4th European Workshop on Advances in Case-Based Reasoning, EWCBR-98*, pages 298–309. Springer-Verlag, 1998.
10. C. D. Manning and H. Schütze. *Foundations of Statistical Natural Language Processing*. The MIT Press, Cambridge, Massachusetts, 1999.

11. A. Newel. The knowledge level. *Artificial Intelligence*, 18:87–127, 1982.
12. K. Nigam, J. Lafferty, and A. McCallum. Using maximum entropy for text classification, 1999.
13. A. Ratnaparkhi. Maximum entropy models for natural language ambiguity resolution, 1998.
14. J. A. Recio-García and B. Díaz-Agudo. An introductory user guide to jCOLIBRI 0.3. Technical Report 144/2004, Dep. Sistemas Informáticos y Programación, Universidad Complutense de Madrid, Spain, November 2004.
15. R. Weber, D. W. Aha, N. Sandhu, and H. Munoz-Avila. A textual case-based reasoning framework for knowledge management applications. In *Proceedings of the 9th German Workshop on Case-Based Reasoning. Shaker Verlag.*, 2001.
16. D. Wilson and S. Bradshaw. Cbr textuality. In *In Proceedings of the Fourth UK Case-Based Reasoning Workshop.*, 1999.
17. N. Wiratunga, I. Koychev, and S. Massie. Feature selection and generalisation for textual retrieval. In *Proceedings of the Seventh European Conference on Case-Based Reasoning, ECCBR-04*, pages 806–820, Madrid, Spain, 2004. Springer.

Critiquing with Confidence

James Reilly, Barry Smyth, Lorraine McGinty, and Kevin McCarthy

Adaptive Information Cluster*, Smart Media Institute,
Department of Computer Science, University College Dublin (UCD), Ireland
{james.d.reilly, barry.smyth, lorraine.mcginty, kevin.mccarthy}@ucd.ie

Abstract. The ability of a CBR system to evaluate its own confidence in a proposed solution is likely to have an important impact on its problem solving and reasoning ability; if nothing else it allows a system to respond with *"I don't know"* instead of suggesting poor solutions. This ability is especially important in interactive CBR recommender systems because to be successful these systems must build trust with their users. This often means helping users to understand the reasons behind a particular recommendation, and presenting them with explanations, and confidence information is an important way to achieve this. In this paper we propose an explicit model of confidence for conversational recommendation systems. We explain how confidence can be evaluated at the feature-level, during each cycle of a recommendation session, and how this can be effectively communicated to the user. In turn, we also show how case-level confidence can be usefully incorporated into the recommendation logic to guide the recommender in the direction of more confident suggestions.

1 Introduction

Conversational recommender systems help users navigate through complex information spaces, such as product-spaces in an e-commerce setting [1,2,3,4,12,29,30,31]. Typically users are guided through a sequence of recommendation cycles. In each cycle a new product is suggested and the user can provide feedback in order to guide the next cycle. This process continues until the user is satisfied with a new recommendation or until they abandon their search. A significant degree of research has been devoted to various aspects of such recommender systems. One important theme has been on the different forms of feedback (e.g., value elicitation, ratings-based, critiquing, preference-based) that might be used during each cycle, with a particular emphasis on how different approaches impact recommendation efficiency and quality [18,24,25,31].

Critiquing, in particular, has emerged as an important form of feedback that is well-suited to many complex product domains where users have only a partial understanding of a feature-space. A critique is a constraint over the value-space of a specific feature (*unit critique* [4,5,11,22]) or a group of features (*compound critique* [4]). For example, when shopping for a digital camera a user might

* This material is based on works supported by Science Foundation Ireland under Grant No. 03/IN.3/I361.

H. Muñoz-Avila and F. Ricci (Eds.): ICCBR 2005, LNAI 3620, pp. 436–450, 2005.

look for one with high resolution, without having a precise resolution in mind. When presented with a 2M pixel camera he might select a *'greater resolution'* critique in order to constrain the next recommendation cycle to those cameras with a higher resolution. Recently a number of researchers have begun to build on the original critiquing work of Burke & Hammond [5], in order to improve the performance of critique-based recommenders [11,24,27,28].

A second important theme concerns the interactive nature of conversational recommender systems. The ability of a recommender system to *explain* or *justify* its recommendations is now seen as a vital step in the development of systems that are capable of fully engaging with the user [21,23,30]. An important part of such explanation components includes the ability of a recommender system to evaluate its own confidence in the recommendations it makes. Thus, recommender systems need *confidence models* and the availability of an accurate model of confidence can allow the recommender to respond more effectively to a user's needs. For example, by communicating its confidence along with its recommendations, a recommender system can help the user to better understand the reliability of these recommendations. Alternatively, a confidence model can help the recommender decide whether it is even appropriate to make a recommendation at a given point in time; there is probably little point in making any recommendations if all of the best options have a very low associated confidence.

We investigate the use of a feature-based confidence model in a critique-based conversational recommender system. This model develops an estimate of confidence in relation to each case feature during the course of a recommendation session. High confidence indicates that the recommender is confident that the value of a feature in the current recommended case is likely to be correct with respect to the user's needs. Low confidence means that the recommender system is not sure about the current feature-value. We describe how these confidence values can be presented to the user during recommendation. Users can help to improve the recommender systems confidence level for features with low confidence scores by providing feedback in relation to these features. We show that in this way users can benefit from significantly shorter recommendation sessions when compared to a standard critique-based recommender.

2 Related Work

The notion of confidence is relatively new to case-based reasoning and the first introduction appears to be the work of Cheetham [6,7]. This work highlights how CBR systems can estimate their own confidence in the solutions they propose and how this can be used during reasoning. Cheetham [7] argues that in the past CBR systems have often relayed confidence in an implicit manner. For example, case similarity scores are often presented to users and interpreted as a form of confidence or reliability information. Other systems have attempted to *simulate* solutions to convince the user of their bona fides (e.g., CHEF's recipe simulator [13]) and the work of Massie et al. [16] has argued that confidence can be conveyed through visualisation techniques by helping users to understand the relationship between retrieved cases and through exposing deficiencies in the reasoning process.

Recent work in the area of case-based explanation is also closely related to the confidence concept, with explanations and justifications often used to encode a form of confidence. For example, Nugent and Cunningham [23] propose that providing explanatory feedback gives a user confidence in prediction tasks (such as blood alcohol levels); that is, by alerting the user to when the system is not confident of a prediction, it is more likely the system will be trusted in the long term. In related work [21], McSherry shows that increased transparency through explanation can prevent users from incorrectly inferring the relationship between feature-values and the prediction. Instead McSherry's ProCon system provides the user with additional relational information, and ProCon informs them as to whether a particular feature is a supporter or opposer of a given prediction. Shimazu's ExpertClerk [30] is an example of a CBR recommender that uses explanation as a means of securing user confidence. ExpertClerk can explain why it is proposing two contrasting product options, allowing the user to provide feedback in different ways. The idea is that the explanations help the user provide feedback which in turn helps the system make more confident suggestions in the next cycle.

In general, it is probably more useful to think of explanation and confidence as complementary concepts. Returning to the seminal work of Cheetham [6,7], we see the development of the first explicit model of confidence in a CBR system. This model is based on a set of *confidence indicators* and a method for converting these indicators into a confidence value. Here case similarity (i.e., the similarity between a retrieved case and a target problem) is seen as the fundamental indicator of confidence alongside measures such as the typicality of the target problem with respect to the case-base, the deviations in the solutions suggested by the retrieved cases and the percentage of cases retrieved that suggest a specific solution. These indicators act as the raw confidence data and they must be mapped on to a specific scale by the confidence model. Cheetham [7] describes how this can be achieved using nonlinear regression techniques in order to fit confidence indicators to solution errors. This provides a piecewise linear function that allows confidence to be calculated from indicators such as similarity, typicality and solution deviation. The resulting confidence measures can be usefully applied in a variety of ways. For example, [7,8] describes how confidence is used in the colour-matching application developed by GE to evaluate whether the colour match suggested by the CBR system should be accepted or if the more labour-intensive manual colour matching process should be started.

More recent work has seen Cheetham et al. [9] extend this original confidence model by including up to 14 secondary confidence indicators derived from different measures of case and solution similarity. These secondary indicators include such things as: the sum of the similarities for retrieved cases with the best solution; the number of cases retrieved with the best solution etc. The point is that there is an inferred relationship between the values of these indicators and the confidence of a system in a given solution. This time they expose this relationship by adopting a machine learning approach. C4.5 [26] is used in a leave-one-out test to determine which indicators are most predictive of confidence; those indicators that are the best determiners of solution correctness. The resulting decision tree can be used as the basis for a confidence calculation based on acceptable error rates. This approach can lead to the production of a symbolic or numeric estimate of confidence and this confidence model can be optimised as cases are added and deleted from the case-base over time [9]. This approach has been trialled in a number of applications (including residential real estate valuation, diagnostic applications etc.) with some success; simply put, using confidence as a way to evaluate when a CBR system should say "I don't know" in response to a target problem has been shown to improve overall system performance; see also the work of McLaren [19] for related work.

3 Confidence-Based Critiquing

In this paper we are especially interested in the notion of confidence and the idea that, by maintaining a model of confidence, a recommender system may be able to provide a more effective platform for interactive recommendation. In particular, we see such a model as a way to improve a recommender system in two important ways. First, by presenting confidence values to the user we can help him to better understand the recommendations that are made. For example, if a system can provide a reliable estimate of its confidence then a user may be better able to appreciate the likelihood that the recommendation will be a good one. Indeed, more fine-grained confidence estimates, at the level of individual features, may help the user to better appreciate gaps in the recommender's current understanding of his needs.

The second way that a confidence model can improve a recommender system is by allowing confidence to influence the next recommendation cycle. For example, when selecting a new case for the next cycle we can focus not only its similarity to the current query but also on its confidence. In this way, we can bias recommendation in the direction of cases that are similar to the current case (in a manner that satisfies the current critique) *and* that the system is confident about. Thus, all other things being equal, more confident cases are preferred over less confident ones and, a less similar case may be preferred over a more similar case if the system has a higher degree of confidence in it. In this section we describe a model of confidence that is designed with conversational recommendation systems in mind, specifically those that employ critiquing as their primary source of feedback. This model is unique in that it is based on modelling confidence at the individual feature-level and we show how this can be used to generate a case-level model that can guide the recommendation process.

3.1 A Model of Confidence

In this section we discuss how a confidence model can be constructed from user feedback during a recommendation session, relative to the feature values of the cases that remain at a given recommendation cycle. During each new recommendation cycle, the confidence of individual features is updated based on the user's recent feedback (in this case, their recent critique). We will describe how confidence is computed differently for ordinal and nominal features and how feature-level confidence can be combined to produce case-level confidence.

Modelling the Confidence of Ordinal Features. Consider a particular recommendation cycle where the recommended item is a camera with *Price=$500.* How confident might the recommender system be that the user is looking for a camera with this price? Our idea is to look at the past critiques that the user has provided over the *Price* feature. Suppose that the user has applied the following sequence of critiques *[Price < 1000],[Price < 750],[Price > 400].* All of these critiques satisfy the price of the current suggestion and so we might be relatively confident about this price compared to a situation where the user's past critique sequence was say *[Price < 1000],[Price < 400],[Price > 200].* In the latter only 66% of the critiques satisfy the current price. We can use this idea to calculate confidence over ordinal features by simply calculating the percentage of past critiques that a given feature value satisfies. In this way the confidence model, m_f for each each ordinal feature f is associated with a set of past critiques, $\{c_1, ..., c_n\}$ (see Equation 1) and the confidence value for a particular value, v of f is given by Equation 2.

$$m_f = \{c_1, ..., c_n\} \tag{1}$$

$$Confidence(f, v) = \frac{\sum_{\forall c_i \epsilon m_f} satisfies(c_i, v)}{|m_f|} \tag{2}$$

Modelling the Confidence of Nominal Features. The semantics of critiques differ when applied to nominal features compared to ordinal features. In the latter, in our implementation, we only offer a *not equal to* critique, so that the user can indicate *[Manufacturer <> Sony]* when they do not want a Sony camera. Because of this it is not appropriate to use the confidence model developed above for ordinal features; in experiments we found that the confidence values did not develop in a useful manner, especially in relation to ordinal features with large value spaces.

$$m_f = \{w_1, ..., w_k\} \tag{3}$$

$$Confidence(f, v) = \frac{w_v}{\sum_{\forall w \epsilon m_f} w} \tag{4}$$

As a result, we took the opportunity to develop a different confidence model for ordinal features, one in which we maintain a set of confidence weights for each feature value; thus m_f is made up of a set of feature weights as shown in Equation 3. These weights are all initialised to 1 and during the course of the recommendation session, based on the critiques that are applied for f, they are updated using a variation of the Monte-Carlo method for reinforcement learning [14]. Simply put, if a user uses the critique *[Manufacturer <> Sony]* then the weight associated with the *Sony* value for the $Manufacturer$ feature is decremented while the weights associated with all other feature values that the user may be interested in are incremented. Computing an overall confidence value for a given value of some nominal feature f is then a matter of computing the weight of this value relative to the other values of this feature as shown in Equation 4; note w_v refers to the weight in m_f that corresponds to the value v for f.

Modelling the Confidence of a Case. In their own right the individual feature-level confidence values can be used to provide the user with direct feedback about how confident the recommender system is about specific feature values in the current recommended case; see Section 3.3. These confidence values can also be combined to produce an overall value of case-level confidence. The most straightforward way to do this is by simply computing the average of the feature-level confidence values as shown in Equation 5. In the next section we will describe how these case-level confidence estimates can be used to guide the recommendation process itself.

$$Confidence(C) = \frac{\sum_{\forall(f,v)\epsilon C} Confidence(f,v)}{|C|} \tag{5}$$

3.2 Confidence-Based Recommendation

Our recommendation algorithm is a version of comparison-based recommendation [17]. In each cycle a case is suggested based on the system's view of the user's query. During each cycle the user is offered an opportunity to provide feedback (in this case in the form of a critique—see lines 10-13 in Figure 1) and the system's view of the user is updated; in the current work the critiqued case becomes the new query as per lines 14-16 in Figure 1. Usually the new query and the critique are used as the basis for selecting the next case to recommend to the user, by selecting a case, from those that satisfy the current critique, which is maximally similar to the current query. However, in this work we change the algorithm to take account of confidence during recommendation.

The first change sees the inclusion of a *model update* routine (see line 8 and lines 17-22 of Figure 1) to update the current confidence model during each cycle. This involves updating the feature-level models, m_f, for each ordinal and nominal feature as described above. The second change occurs in line 31 of Figure 1. Instead of simply selecting a new recommended case based on similarity to the current query (q), the new case or item (i) is selected based on its *quality*, where quality is a function of query similarity and its case-level confidence as shown in Equation 6. Notice that the relative importance of confidence and query similarity can be manipulated through the α parameter in the obvious way and we will investigate different setting of this parameter in our evaluation.

$$Quality(q,i) = \alpha \bullet Confidence(i) + (1-\alpha) \bullet Similarity(q,i) \tag{6}$$

```
CB: case-base, M: confidence model, q: query, c: chosen critique, r: recommendation

define Confidence-Critiquing(q, CB)
M = {m1,m2,..., mn} where n = # features
c = {}
do
    r ← ItemRecommend(q, CB, c, M)
    c ← UserReview(r, CB)
    q ← QueryRevise(q, r)
    M ← UpdateModel(M, c, r)
until UserAccepts(r)

define UserReview(r, CB)
  c ← user critique for some f ∈ r
  CB ← CB - {r}
return c

define QueryRevise(q, r)
  q ← r
return q

define UpdateModel(M, c, r)
  For each mi ∈ M
  do
    mi ← UpdateFeatureModel(mi, c, r)
  EndFor
Return M

define UpdateFeatureModel(m, c, r)
  if IsOrdinal(m) then
    m ← UpdateOrdinal(m, c, r)
  else IsNominal(m) then
    m ← UpdateNominal(m, c, r)
Return m

define ItemRecommend(q, CB, c, M)
  CB' ← {i ∈ CB | Satisfies(i,c)}
  CB'' ← sort CB' by decreasing Quality
  R ← top item in CB''
return R
```

Fig. 1. High-level algorithm for confidence-influenced critiquing

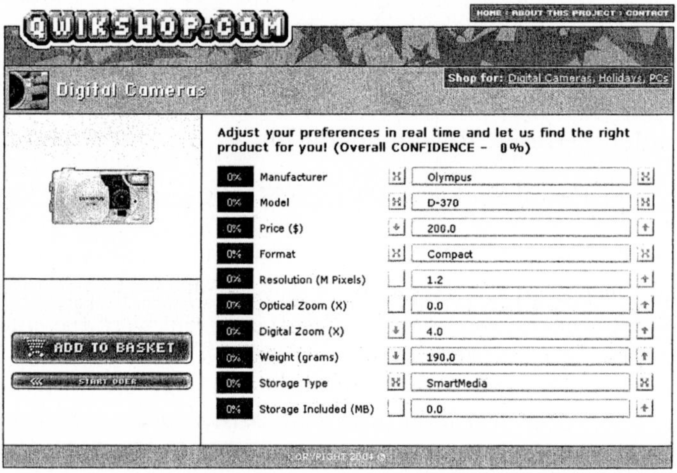

Fig. 2. At the start of a session the system has low confidence in its recommendations

3.3 An Example Session

In this section we will look at an example walk-through of confidence-based recommendation at work. We have incorporated the nominal and ordinal feature confidence values and the overall confidence score into a prototype Digital Camera recommender system. There are many different ways in which we could have achieved this, some more effective than others. For example, [15] describes a live-user evaluation of a number of different explanation visual techniques for a collaborative filtering movie recommender. From that evaluation, it was found that presenting explanation information graphically was an effective way of conveying sometimes complex information, in a way that could be quickly understood by the users.

Accordingly, our system presents the confidences values as percentage scores and colour-codes them. Figures 2-4 illustrate how we have added the case-level and feature-level scores to our standard recommendation interface; obviously these interface changes are in the early stages of development and we expect further refinements in due course. One of the advantages of placing the confidence scores on the interface is that it allows users to understand which features the system is confident about and which features it is uncertain about. We hope that by providing feedback on these uncertain features users can help the recommender system to improve the quality of its recommendations during each cycle and so reduce average session length. Figures 2-4 help to explain how individual feature confidence and overall confidence values evolve during the course of a session. In Figure 2, at the start of a recommendation session, the user is presented with a low-end compact camera for 200 Euro. The feature confidence values appear to the left of the individual features and are colour-coded to represent low (0-33% as red), medium (33%-66% as amber) and high (66% - 100% as green) levels of confidence. Initially all feature confidence values are at 0% and overall confidence in this recommendation is also 0%.

Figure 3 corresponds to a mid-session cycle. The user has made a series of critiques and is presented with a Casio camera for 485 Euro. Up until now the user has been concentrating on critiquing the *Price*, *Format* and *Resolution* features, and the system's confidence in these features has increased. The overall confidence of the system is now 36%. In Figure 4, the user is recommended a camera they are happy to purchase; a high-end Canon with an overall confidence

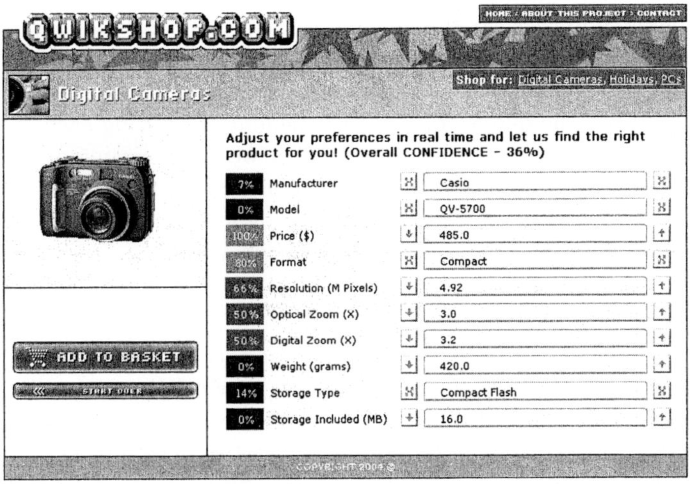

Fig. 3. Towards the middle of a session we find the recommender able to make suggestions with increasing levels of confidence; many of the feature confidence values have now increased and the overall confidence is now at 36%

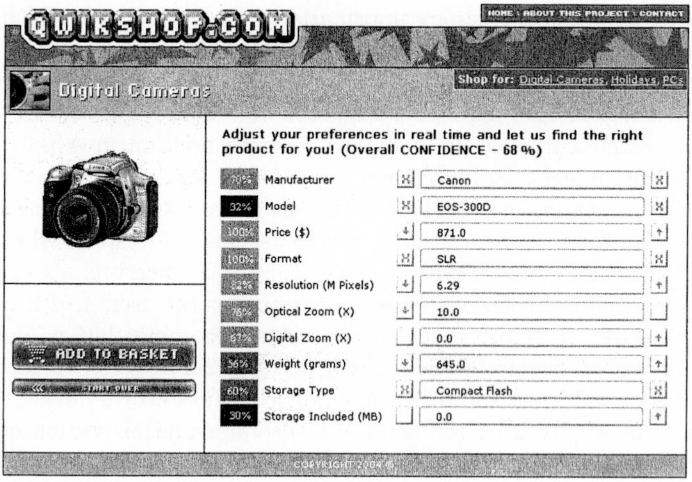

Fig. 4. At the end of the session the user has selected their camera. At this point system confidence is relatively high (68%)

of 68%. The system is now confident about 6 of the 10 features in the current case and is uncertain about only two features (*Model* and *Storage*).

4 Evaluation

In the previous section we have described our confidence model and how its confidence values might be usefully communicated to the user. One of the advantages of this approach is that it allows users to understand which features the system is confident about and which features it is uncertain about. By providing feedback about these uncertain features users can help the recommender system to improve the quality of its recommendations during each cycle and so reduce average session length. In this section we test this hypothesis using a well-known recommender dataset. In particular, we look at a range of factors including how confidence changes over time during a typical recommender session and its potential impact recommendation efficiency.

4.1 Setup

We follow the evaluation methodology as described in [17,18] to run a series of test recommendation sessions over the well-known PC dataset. This dataset consists of 120 PC cases each described in terms of 8 features including *type, manufacturer, processor, memory* etc. We test two recommender systems. A standard critiquing-based recommender (STD) serves as a baseline. Using this recommender we assume that, during each cycle, our 'users' (see below) will select a random critique from among those that are compatible with their target case. As an alternative, our confidence-based recommender system (CONF) develops a confidence model and we assume that users will critique those features that present with low confidence values (with ties broken by random choice). By default we set α to 0.75 unless otherwise stated.

As in [17,18], each case (*base*) in the case-base is temporarily removed and used in two ways. First it serves as the basis for a set of queries constructed by taking random subsets of its features. We focus on subsets of 1, 3 and 5 features to allow us to distinguish between hard, moderate and easy queries, respectively. Second, we select the case that is most similar to the original base. These cases serve as the recommendation *targets* for the experiments. Thus, the base represents the ideal query for a 'user', the generated query is the initial query that the 'user' provides to the recommender, and the target is the best available case for the 'user', based on their ideal; this best case may not contain the initial features themselves. Each generated query is a test problem for the recommender, and in each recommendation cycle the 'user' picks a critique that is compatible with the known target case; that is, a critique that, when applied to the remaining cases, results in the target case being left in the filtered set of cases. As mentioned above, the STD recommender sees users choosing among the compatible critiques essentially at random, while CONF users critique low confidence features. Each leave-one-out pass through the case-base is repeated 50 times and recommendation sessions terminate when the target case is returned.

4.2 The Evolution of Confidence

Our model is composed of a set of confidence scores for each feature of a recommendation. Each score indicates how confident the recommender is that the value of a feature is correct for the user in question. In this section we consider how confidence evolves during the course of a typical session.

We begin by looking at how these feature-level confidence scores tend to change over time. We divide confidence into 3 value ranges—*low*, *medium* and *high*—as discussed in Section 3. We measure the feature-level confidence values during each cycle and count the average number of low, medium and high confidence features. The results (averaged over all cycles for queries containing a single initial feature) are presented in Figure 5(a) as the average number of features in each confidence category across a range of cycles, from the start of a session up to cycle 14. During the first cycle most features, except the initial feature, have low confidence but as the sessions progresses there is a gradual increase in the number of features with medium and high levels of confidence. For example, by the 7th cycle the recommender is highly confident about the values of nearly half of the features. By the 14th cycle there are typically very few (< 2) features falling in to the low confidence category.

Ideally we would like to see case-level confidence improve as sessions progress—the feature-level results suggest that this is likely—and the case-level results presented in Figure 5(b) confirm this. Once again these results are based on single-feature initial queries and this time we present average case-level confidence values over the first 14 cycles. Case-level confidence is seen to grow rapidly for the first 8 cycles, up to just over 50%, and then levels off after this at about 60%. These results indicate that case similarity and confidence are combining

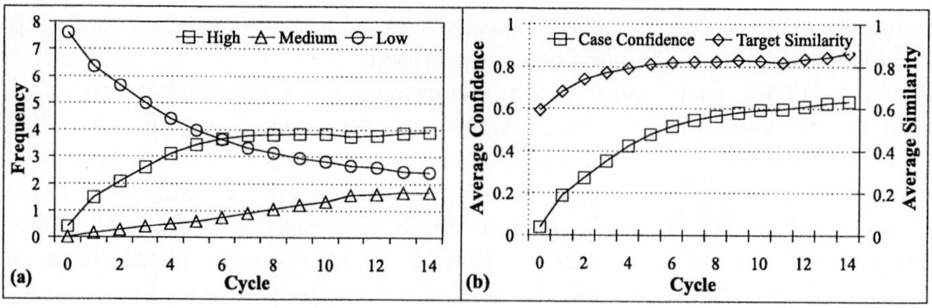

Fig. 5. (a) Feature confidence levels vs cycle number; and (b) Case confidence and target similarity vs cycle number

effectively during recommendation to drive the recommender towards more confident cases. The graph also show how similarity to the target case grows in line with confidence; the correlation between confidence and target similarity is 0.89.

4.3 Recommendation Efficiency

One of the key measures of success for conversational recommenders is recommendation efficiency or session length. Recommenders that present users with good recommendations are likely to produce shorter and more successful cycles [10,20]. Our basic assumption is that by conveying feature-level confidence values to the user, the system can encourage the user to provide more effective feedback by highlighting the features that the system is not sure about. If the user provides feedback on these features then our confidence-based approach should converge on the target product more efficiently. In this section and the next we explore different aspects of recommendation efficiency by comparing our confidence-based approach to the standard critiquing approach. We measure recommendation efficiency in terms of session length—that is, the number of cycles its takes for the user to find their target case—running the leave-one-out test for the PC dataset for the STD and CONF variations. In fact we run 4 different variations of CONF for different settings of α (0.25,...,1) in order to vary the influence that the confidence model has on each cycle.

Summary Efficiency Results. Summary results are presented in Figure 6 as the average session lengths, over all query types, for the different system variations. We can see that confidence-based recommendation has a clear and significant advantage over standard critiquing, with all 4 CONF variations outperforming the standard system; the best session length reduction (36%) is found for CONF with $\alpha = 0.75$. In general, allowing confidence to have a greater influence over each recommendation cycle tends to improve session lengths, but only up to a point. Beyond $\alpha = 0.75$ we find that session lengths tend to increase again, although it is significant that even with $\alpha = 1$ session lengths remain shorter than STD; remember at $\alpha = 1$ each recommendation cycle is influenced by the applied critique and the confidence model only. So while confidence is

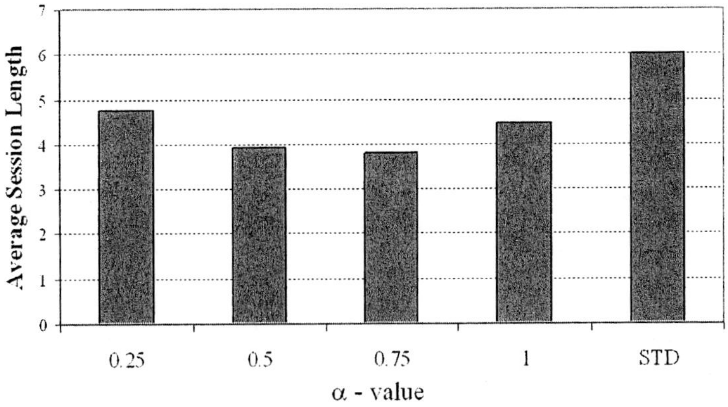

Fig. 6. Session lengths of a confidence-based recommender vs a standard critiquing-based recommendation

important during recommendation selection it is not optimal and case similarity still has a role to play.

Query Difficulty. Earlier we mentioned how our initial queries could be divided into different classes by their expected difficulty levels, in terms of the number of initial features (1, 3 or 5) they contain. In Figure 7(a) we present the average session length results for each of the 5 recommender system variations, grouped according to different levels of query difficulty. Once again, the results point to a significant advantage due to confidence-based critiquing. In all cases the confidence-based systems present with shorter sessions than STD, but the scale of the reduction is influenced by query difficulty. In particular we see the greatest difference in session length for the most difficult queries. For example, for these queries the average session length for STD is about 10, compared to 5.4 (for CONF with $\alpha = 0.75$), a reduction of 46%. This reduction falls to about 40% for moderate queries (containing 3 initial features) and to just over 20% for the simplest queries with 5 fully specified features. A similar trend is seen for other values of α. This dependency on query difficulty is perhaps to be expected perhaps since easier queries naturally result in shorter sessions and thus there are fewer opportunities for low-confidence features to be critiqued and hence fewer opportunities for their benefit to be felt.

4.4 Preference Tolerance

The previous evaluations assume the user is looking for a very particular product and that the recommendation session terminates only when they have found this product. In reality, it is likely that users will be more flexible with their requirements and that they may be satisfied with close matches to their ideal product. The question then becomes whether this greater tolerance of partial target matches has any significant impact on the performance of the confidence-based approach relative to the standard critiquing approach. To evaluate this

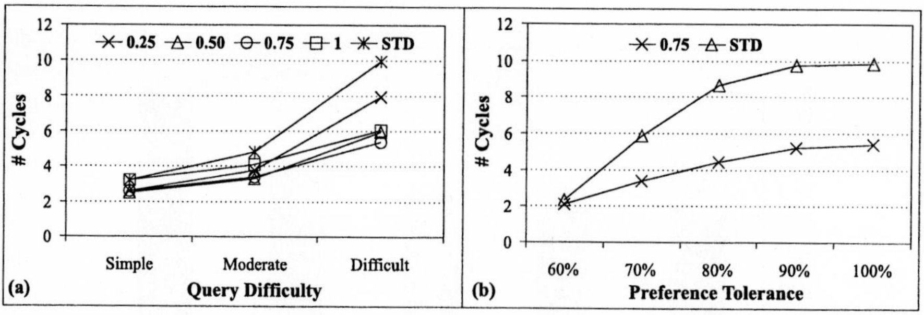

Fig. 7. Average session lengths for (a) varying query difficulty and, (b) varying preference tolerance

idea, we relaxed the termination condition—so that a session could terminate once a case was recommended that was within a set similarity threshold of the ideal target—and we repeated the above efficiency test.

The results are presented above in Figure 7(b) for α=0.75. As expected, relaxing the terminating condition results in shorter recommendation for both the standard critiquing-based approach and the confidence-based approach. For example, at the 100% similarity threshold level—this corresponds to the previous setup where the user is looking for an exact target match—sessions take on average almost 10 cycles for standard critiquing, but fall to about 6 cycles if the user is willing to accept a 70% match. Once again, the confidence-based system out-performs the STD system for all levels of preference tolerance. At the lowest similarity threshold level (60%), the confidence-influenced system reduces session lengths by 10.2%, relative to STD, but this then rises to above 45% for similarity thresholds of 80% and above.

5 Conclusions

Explanations and confidence have an important role to play in recommender systems both as a way of engendering user trust and as a means by which the system can judge how best to respond to users. We have presented a confidence model that is designed for conversational recommender systems, in general, and critiquing-based approaches in particular. We have described how this model can be developed, through user feedback, by estimating confidence at the feature-level and at the case-level. In turn, we have proposed how this model can be used at recommendation time in order to inform users about the recommender's current confidence, in the hope that users will focus their feedback in a way that helps to improve overall confidence. We have also described how case-level confidence can be used to good effect during recommendation, by supplementing traditional case similarity, in order to guide the recommender towards more confident suggestions. Finally, we have demonstrated how this confidence-based recommendation strategy helps to improve recommendation efficiency, leading to reductions of up to 50% in average session length.

References

1. David W. Aha, Leonard A. Breslow, and Héctor Muñoz-Avila. Conversational Case-based Reasoning. *Applied Intelligence*, 14(1):9–32, 2001.
2. J. Allen, G. Ferguson, and A. Stent. An Architecture for More Realistic Conversational Systems. In *Proceedings of Intelligent User Interfaces 2001 (IUI-01)*, pages 1–8, 2001. Santa Fe, NM.
3. D. Bridge. Product Recommendation Systems: A New Direction. In D. Aha and I. Watson, editors, *Workshop on CBR in Electronic Commerce at The International Conference on Case-Based Reasoning (ICCBR-01)*, 2001. Vancouver, Canada.
4. R. Burke. Interactive Critiquing for Catalog Navigation in E-Commerce. *Artificial Intelligence Review*, 18(3-4):245–267, 2002.
5. R. Burke, K. Hammond, and B.C. Young. The FindMe Approach to Assisted Browsing. *Journal of IEEE Expert*, 12(4):32–40, 1997.
6. W. Cheetham. *Case-Based Reasoning with Confidence.* Ph.D. Thesis, Rensselaer Polytechnic Institute, 1996.
7. W. Cheetham. Case-Based Reasoning with Confidence. In E. Blanzieri and L. Portinale, editors, *Proceedings of the Fifth European Conference on Case-Based Reasoning, EWCBR '00*, pages 15–25. Springer, 2000. Trento, Italy.
8. W. Cheetham. Benefits of Case-Based Reasoning in Color Matching. In D. Aha and I. Watson, editors, *Proceedings of the International Conference on Case-Based Reasoning (ICCBR-01)*, pages 589–596. Springer-Verlag, 2001. Vancouver, Canada.
9. W. Cheetham and J. Price. Measures of Solution Accuracy in Case-Based Reasoning Systems. In P. A. González Calero and P. Funk, editors, *Proceedings of the European Conference on Case-Based Reasoning (ECCBR-04)*, pages 106–118. Springer, 2004. Madrid, Spain.
10. M. Doyle and P. Cunningham. A Dynamic Approach to Reducing Dialog in On-Line Decision Guides. In E. Blanzieri and L. Portinale, editors, *Proceedings of the Fifth European Workshop on Case-Based Reasoning, (EWCBR-00)*, pages 49–60. Springer, 2000. Trento, Italy.
11. B. Faltings, P. Pu, M. Torrens, and P. Viappiani. Designing Example-Critiquing Interaction. In *Proceedings of the International Conference on Intelligent User Interface(IUI-2004)*, pages 22–29. ACM Press, 2004. Funchal, Madeira, Portugal.
12. M. Göker and C. Thompson. Personalized Conversational Case-based Recommendation. In E. Blanzieri and L. Portinale, editors, *Proceedings of the 5th European Workshop on Case-based Reasoning, (EWCBR-00)*, pages 99–111. Springer, 2000.
13. K.J. Hammond. CHEF: A Model of Case-Based Blanning. In *Proceedings of AAAI-86.* AAAI Press/MIT Press, 1986. Cambridge, MA.
14. M.E. Harmon. *Reinforcement Learning: A Tutorial.* 1996.
15. Jonathan L. Herlocker, Joseph A. Konstan, and John Riedl. Explaining Collaborative Filtering Recommendations. In *Proceedings of the 2000 ACM Conference on Computer Supported Cooperative Work*, pages 241–250, 2000. ACM Press.
16. S. Massie, S. Craw, and N. Wiratunga. Visualisation of Case-Based Reasoning for Explanation. In *Proceedings of the the Explanation Workshop of the Seventh European Conference on Case-Based Reasoning (ECCBR-04)*, pages 135–144, 2004. Madrid, Spain.
17. L. McGinty and B. Smyth. Comparison-Based Recommendation. In Susan Craw, editor, *Proceedings of the Sixth European Conference on Case-Based Reasoning (ECCBR-02)*, pages 575–589. Springer, 2002. Aberdeen, Scotland.

18. L. McGinty and B. Smyth. Tweaking Critiquing. In *Proceedings of the Workshop on Personalization and Web Techniques at the International Joint Conference on Artificial Intelligence (IJCAI-03)*. Morgan-Kaufmann, 2003. Acapulco, Mexico.
19. B. McLaren and K. Ashley. Helping a CBR Program Know What It Knows. In D. Aha and I. Watson, editors, *Proceedings of the International Conference on Case-Based Reasoning (ICCBR-01)*, pages 377–391. Springer-Verlag, 2001. Vancouver, Canada.
20. D. McSherry. Minimizing Dialog Length in Interactive Case-based Reasoning. In Bernhard Nebel, editor, *Proceedings of the Seventeenth International Joint Conference on Artificial Intelligence (IJCAI-01)*, pages 993–998. Morgan Kaufmann, 2001. Seattle, Washington.
21. D. McSherry. Explanation in Case-based Reasoning: An Evidential Approach. In B. Lees, editor, *Proceedings of the Eighth UK Workshop on Case-Based Reasoning (UKCBR-03)*, page 4755, 2003.
22. Q.N. Nguyen, F. Ricci, and D. Cavada. User Preferences Initialization and Integration in Critique-Based Mobile Recommender Systems. In *Proceedings of Artificial Intelligence in Mobile Systems 2004, in conjunction with UbiComp 2004*, pages 71–78. Iniversitat des Saarlandes Press., 2004. Nottingham, UK.
23. C. Nugent and P. Cunningham. A Case-Based Explanation System for 'Black-Box' Systems. In *Proceedings of the Explanation Workshop of the 7th European Conference on Case-Based Reasoning (ECCBR-04)*, pages 155–164, 2004. Madrid, Spain.
24. P. Pu and B. Faltings. Decision Tradeoff Using Example Critiquing and Constraint Programming. *Special Issue on User-Interaction in Constraint Satisfaction. CONSTRAINTS: an International Journal.*, 9(4), 2004.
25. P. Pu, B. Faltings, and M. Torrens. User-Involved Preference Elicitation. In *Proceedings of the Workshop on Configuration at the Eighteenth International Joint Conference on Artificial Intelligence (IJCAI 2003)*, 2003. Acapulco, Mexico.
26. J.R. Quinlan. *C4.5: Programs for Machine Learning.* Morgan Kaufmann, 1993.
27. J. Reilly, K. McCarthy, L. McGinty, and B. Smyth. Dynamic Critiquing. In P. A. González Calero and P. Funk, editors, *Proceedings of the European Conference on Case-Based Reasoning (ECCBR-04)*, pages 763–776. Springer, 2004. Madrid, Spain.
28. J. Reilly, K. McCarthy, L. McGinty, and B. Smyth. Incremental Critiquing. In M. Bramer, F. Coenen and T. Allen, editors, *Research and Development in Intelligent Systems XXI. Proceedings of AI-2004*, pages 101–114. Springer, 2004. Cambridge, UK.
29. J. Ben Schafer, Joseph A. Konstan, and John Riedl. E-Commerce Recommendation Applications. *Data Mining and Knowledge Discovery*, 5(1/2):115–153, 2001.
30. H. Shimazu, A. Shibata, and K. Nihei. ExpertGuide: A Conversational Case-based Reasoning Tool for Developing Mentors in Knowledge Spaces. *Applied Intelligence*, 14(1):33–48, 2002.
31. B. Smyth and L. McGinty. An Analysis of Feedback Strategies in Conversational Recommender Systems. In P. Cunningham, editor, *Proceedings of the Fourteenth National Conference on Artificial Intelligence and Cognitive Science (AICS-2003)*, 2003. Dublin, Ireland.

Mapping Goals and Kinds of Explanations to the Knowledge Containers of Case-Based Reasoning Systems

Thomas R. Roth-Berghofer[1,2] and Jörg Cassens[3]

[1] Knowledge-Based Systems Group, Department of Computer Science,
University of Kaiserslautern, P.O. Box 3049, 67653 Kaiserslautern
[2] Knowledge Management Department,
German Research Center for Artificial Intelligence DFKI GmbH,
Erwin-Schrödinger-Straße 57, 67663 Kaiserslautern, Germany
thomas.roth-berghofer@dfki.uni-kl.de
[3] Norwegian University of Science and Technology (NTNU),
Department of Computer and Information Science (IDI),
7491 Trondheim, Norway
jorg.cassens@idi.ntnu.no

Abstract. Research on explanation in Case-Based Reasoning (CBR) is a topic that gains momentum. In this context, fundamental issues on what are and to which end do we use explanations have to be reconsidered. This article presents a prelimenary outline of the combination of two recently proposed classifications of explanations based on the type of the explanation itself and user goals which should be fulfilled. Further on, the contribution of the different knowledge containers for modeling the necessary knowledge is examined.

1 Why Bother to Explain?

In everyday human-human interactions explanations are an important vehicle to convey information in order to understand one another. Explanations enhance the knowledge of the communication partners in such a way that they accept certain statements. They understand more, allowing them to make informed decisions. According to Schank [1] explanations are the most common method used by humans to support their decision making.

This is supported by Spieker's investigation into natural language explanations in expert systems [2]. We identify some typical reactions of humans as soon as we cannot follow a conversation:

- we ask our conversation partner about concepts that we did not understand,
- we request justifications for some fact or we ask for the cause of an event,
- we want to know about functions of concepts,
- we want to know about purposes of concepts, and
- we ask questions about his or her behavior and how he or she reached a conclusion.

H. Muñoz-Avila and F. Ricci (Eds.): ICCBR 2005, LNCS 3620, pp. 451–464, 2005.

All those questions and answers are used to understand what has been said and meant during a simple conversation. An important effect of explanations is that the process of explaining certainly has some effect on one's trust in the competence of a person or machine: We keep our trust, we increase or decrease it. At least, providing explanations makes decisions more transparent, and motivates the use to further use the system.

The need for explanations provided by knowledge-based systems is well-known and was addressed by such fields as expert systems. For knowledge-based systems, explanations and knowledge acquisition are the only two communications channels with which they interact with their environment.

The adequacy of explanations as well as of justifications is dependent on pragmatically given background knowledge. What counts as a good explanation in a certain situation is determined by context-dependent criteria [3,4].

The more complex knowledge-based systems get, the more explanation capabilities the users expect when using such systems. This requirement was recognized early on in expert systems research and development [5,6,7]. Considerable results were produced, but research activity decreased together with the general decline of expert systems research in the 1990s. The major problems in connection with classical expert systems seemed to be solved.

At the same time there was an increasing interest on this topic in Case-Based Reasoning (CBR) [8,9]. At the turn of the century, we find the issue discussed again in the context of knowledge-based systems [10,11]. Recently, we can see a renewed focus in CBR on this track of research. ECCBR 2004 featured, for example, a workshop on Explanation in Case-Based Reasoning as well as a couple of papers on explanation at the main conference [12,13].

Research on explanation is of interest today because it can be argued that the whole scenario on research on knowledge-based systems has changed [14]: knowledge-based systems are no longer considered as boxes that provide a full solution to a problem. Problem solving is seen as an interactive process (a socio-technical process). Problem description as well as the special input can be incomplete and changing. As a consequence, there has to be communication between human and software agents. Communication requires mutual understanding that can be essentially supported by explanations. Such explanations can improve the problem solving process to a large degree.

It is important to note here that the term explanation can be interpreted in two different ways. One interpretation deals with explanations as part of the reasoning process itself. The other interpretation deals with usage aspects: making the reasoning process, its results, or the usage of the result transparent to the user. In this paper, we will focus on the second interpretation.

The remainder of this paper is organized as follows: In the next section, we describe the setting for explanation-aware CBR systems as being a component of socio-technical systems. In section 3, we present two perspectives on explanation that can help understand and organize what to explain and when. The subsequent section focusses on knowledge containers and their contribution to the explanation capabilities of CBR systems. In Section 5, we propose a system design process achitecture. We explore further on the relations of explanation goals, explanation kinds, and knowledge containers in a simplified example. We conclude our paper with an outlook on further research.

2 Explanation in Socio-Technical Systems

Whenever one talks about a 'system' one has to clarify what is meant by that term. In decision- support scenarios, the human and the computer are the decision system. Such socio-technical systems can for example be modelled with the help of the Actor Network Theory, ANT ([15,16]). The basic idea here is fairly simple: whenever you do something, many influences on *how* you do it exist. For instance, if you visit a conference, it is likely that you stay at a hotel. How you behave at the hotel is influenced by your own previous experience with hotels, regulations for check-in and check-out, the capabilities the hotel offers you (breakfast room, elevators).

So, you are not performing from scratch, but are influenced by a wide range of factors. The aim of the ANT is to provide a unified view on these factors and your own acting. An actor network in this notion is *the act linked together with all of its influencing factors (which again are linked), producing a network* (see [16, p. 4]).

In this network, you find both technical and non-technical elements. In the ANT, technological artifacts can stand for human goals and praxis. Hotel keys, for example, are often not very handy, because the hotel owner has *inscribed* his intention (that the keys do not leave the hotel) into metal tags (which is why the guests *subscribe* to the owners intention: they do not want to carry this weight). A software system for workflow management is a representation of organizational standards in the company where it is used (and makes human users follow these standards).

One advantage of the ANT in the setting of intelligent systems is that it already comprises technical artifacts and humans in the same model. Humans and artifacts are to a certain degree exchangeable and can play the same role in the network. But in contrast to traditional artifacts, which are merely passive (black boxes in which human interests are subscribed) or which active role is restricted to translating intentions of the designer into changes of the praxis of the user, AI systems play a more active role. It has also been argued that intelligent systems have to show certain capabilities usually ascribed to humans in order to interact with the user in a meaningful way [17], and we would include the ability to give good explanations.

Moreover, the issue of 'trust' is generally important for socio-technical systems. 'Trust' can be defined in different ways, for the purpose of this paper it is sufficient to describe the problem as to whether and to which degree a human is willing to accept proposals from technical components, and to which degree he is willing to give up control. For a detailed survey on different definitions of trust in the context of automation systems, see e.g. [18]. In the context of expert systems, it has been shown that explanation capabilities have a large effect on the user's acceptance of advices given by the system [19].

To summarize, the ability of an IT system to give good explanations is important for the functioning of a socio-technical system. Good explanations depend on the context, it would therefore be helpful to be able to include an analysis into the system design process.

3 Views on Explanations

In this section, we outline two perspectives on explanation: The *Explanation Goals* focus on user needs and expectations towards explanations and help to understand *what* the system has to be able to explain and *when* to explain something. The *Kinds of Explanations* focus on different *types* of explanations, their *usefulness* for the user, and how they can be represented in the different *knowledge-containers* [20].

Any kind of interactivity implies that one has some kind of user model that provides answers based on what the user knows and what he or she does not know [21]. The user (probably) knows about the used vocabulary, about general strategies, policies, or procedures to follow, and about (most of) the standard situations in the given problem domain. But he or she may not know all the details and data, about rare cases and exceptions, and about consequences of combinatorial number of interactions of different alternatives. Then, a basic approach to explanation would be to not comment on routine measures (without being asked), to emphasize on exceptional cases (e.g., exceptions from defaults and standards, exceptions from plausible hypotheses), and to allow for further questions.

It is hard to anticipate user needs due to two main reasons [21]: First, not all of the needs must be met, but those important to the user. Second, all deficits and their estimated importance depend on the specific user. Thus, personalization is a basic requirement, not only some added value.

3.1 Explanation Goals

Sørmo et al. [22,23] suggest several explanation goals for Case-Based Reasoning systems (which are valid for knowledge-based systems, in general). They also argue that those goals are indeed reachable because case-based reasoners are mostly made to perform limited tasks for a limited audience, thus allowing to make reasonable assumptions about the user's goals and the explanation context. The identified explanation goals are:

Transparency: Explain how the system reached the answer
"I had the same problem with my car yesterday, and charging the battery fixed it."

The goal of an explanation of this kind is to impart an understanding of how the system found an answer. This allows the users to check the system by examining the way it reasons and allows them to look for explanations for why the system has reached a surprising or anomalous result. If transparency is the primary goal, the system should not try to oversell a conclusion it is uncertain of. In other words, fidelity is the primary criterion, even though such explanations may place a heavy cognitive load on the user. The original *how* and *why* explanations of the MYCIN system [24] would be good examples.

This goal is most important with knowledge engineers seeking to debug the system and possibly domain experts seeking to verify the reasoning process [10]. It is also reasonable to think that in domains with a high cost of failure it can be expected that the user wishes to examine the reasoning process more thoroughly.

Justification: Explain why the answer is a good answer
"You should eat more fish - your heart needs it!"
"My predictions have been 80% correct up until now."

This is the goal of increasing the confidence in the advice or solution offered by the system by giving some kind of support for the conclusion suggested by the system. This goal allows for a simplification of the explanation compared to the actual process the system goes through to find a solution. Potentially, this kind of explanation can be completely decoupled from the reasoning process, but it may also be achieved by using additional background knowledge or reformulation and simplification of knowledge that is used in the reasoning process.

Empirical research suggests that this goal is most prevalent in systems with novice users [25], in domains where the cost of failure is relatively low, and in domains where the system represents a party that has an interest in the user accepting the solution.

Relevance: Explain why a question asked is relevant
"I ask about the more common failures first, and many users do forget to connect the power cable."

An explanation of this type would have to justify the strategy pursued by the system. This is in contrast to the previous two goals that focus on the solution. The reasoning trace type of explanations may display the strategy of the system implicitly, but it does not argue why it is a good strategy. In conversational systems, the user may wish to know why a question asked by the system is relevant to the task at hand. It can also be relevant in other kinds of systems where a user would like to verify that the approach used by the system is valid. In expert systems, this kind of explanations was introduced by NEOMYCIN [24].

Conceptualization: Clarify the Meaning of Concepts
"By 'conceptualization' we mean the process of forming concepts and relations between concepts."

One of the lessons learned after the first wave of expert systems had been analyzed was that the users did not always understand the terms used by a system. This may be because the user is a novice in the domain, but also because different people can use terms differently or organize the knowledge in different ways. It may not be clear, even to an expert, what the system means when using a specific term, and he may want to get an explanation of what the system means when using it. This requirement for providing explanations for the vocabulary was first identified by Swartout and Smoliar ([7]).

Learning: Teach the user about the domain
"When the headlights won't work, the battery may be flat as it is supposed to deliver power to the lights."

All the previous explanation goals involve learning – about the problem domain, about the system, about the reasoning process or the vocabulary of the system. Educational systems, however, have learning as the primary goal of the whole system. In these systems, we cannot assume that the user will understand even definitions of terms, and may need to provide explanations at different levels of expertise. The goal of the system is typically not only to find a good solution to a problem, but to explain the solution process to the user in a way that will increase his understanding of the domain. The goal can be to teach more general domain theory or to train the user in solving problems similar to those solved by the system. In other words, the explanation is often more important than the answer itself. Systems that fulfill the relevance and transparency goals may have some capabilities in this area, but a true tutoring system must take into account how humans solve problems. It cannot attempt to teach the user a problem solving strategy that works well in a computer but that is very hard to reproduce for people.

For the remainder of this paper we will not focus on the learning goal since it is specifically targeted towards educational systems.

3.2 Kinds of Explanations

Roth-Berghofer [26] looks at explanations from a knowledge-container perspective. He addresses the issue of what can naturally be explained by the four containers (see Section 4).

One starting point is the work of Spieker [2] on the usefulness of explanations. According to Spieker, there are five useful kinds of explanations he discusses in the context of expert systems:

Conceptual Explanations: They are of the form 'What is ... ?' or 'What is the meaning of ... ?'. The goal of conceptual explanations is to build links between unknown and known concepts. Conceptual explanations can take different forms:

- Definition: "What is a bicycle?" "A bicycle is a land vehicle with two wheels in line. Pedal cycles are powered by a seated human rider. A bicycle is a form of human powered vehicle."
- Theoretical proposition: "What is force?" "Force is Mass times Acceleration."
- Prototypical example: "What is a bicycle?" "The thing, the man there crashed with."
- Functional description: "What is a bicycle?" "A bicycle serves as a means of transport."

Conceptual explanations are answers to extensional or descriptional questions.

Why-explanations: Why-explanations provide causes or justifications for facts or the occurrence of events. Whereas the first concept is causal in nature and not symmetrical, the latter only provides evidence for what has been asked for. For example:

- Justification: "Why is it believed that the universe expands?" "Because we can observe a red shift of the light emitted by other galaxies."
- Cause: "Why is it believed that the universe expands?" "Because, according to the Big Bang theory, the whole matter was concentrated at one point of the universe and the whole matter moves away from each other."

Why-explanations explain single events or general laws and can consist of single causes/justifications (among others) or a complete list of causes/justifications.

How-explanations: How-explanations are a special case of why-explanations, describing processes that lead to an event by providing a causal chain. They are similar to action explanations (see below) that answer how-questions. How-questions ask for an explanation of the function of a device, for example:

- "How does a combustion engine work?" "A combustion engine is an engine that operates by burning its fuel."

Purpose-explanations: The goal of *Purpose-explanations* is to describe the purpose of a fact or object. Typical questions are of the form 'What is ... for?' or 'What is the purpose of ...?', for example:

- "What is a valve for?" "The valve is used to seal the intake and exhaust ports."

Cognitive Explanations: Cognitive Explanations explain or predict the behavior of 'intelligent systems' on the basis of known goals, beliefs, constraints, and rationality assumptions. There are action and negative explanations:

- Action explanation: "Why was this seat post selected?" "For the given price, only one other seat post for this bicycle is currently available. But that seat post is too short."
- Negative explanation: "Why was no carrier chosen?" "A carrier is only available for touring bikes. The user did not choose a touring bike."

4 Knowledge Containers

Knowledge containers, according to Richter [27,28], contain and structure the knowledge of a knowledge-based system. A knowledge container is a collection of knowledge that is relevant to many tasks. For rule-based systems, for instance, one can easily identify facts and rules as important knowledge containers. For CBR systems, Richter describes four knowledge containers: *vocabulary*, *similarity measures*, *adaptation knowledge*, and *case base*. They are depicted in Fig. 1.

The *vocabulary* defines attributes, predicates, and the structure of the domain schema. Thus the vocabulary forms the basis for all of the other three containers. Hierarchies, if available, can be used to order domain concepts.In object-oriented

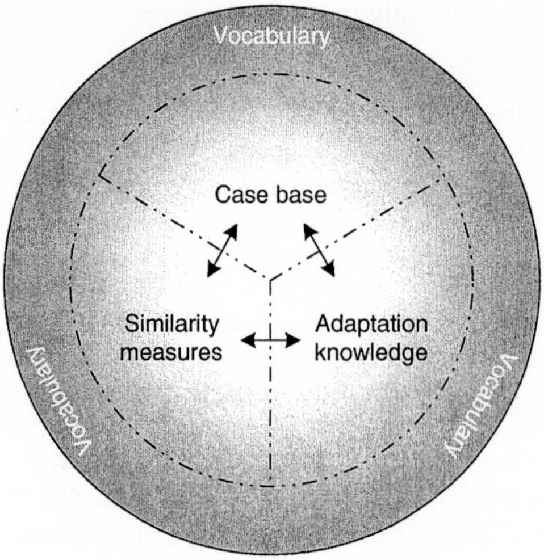

Fig. 1. The four knowledge containers of a CBR system

models, inheritance (*is-a*) and decomposition (*part-of*) induce hierarchical orderings quite naturally. Additional ontological relations can further add hierarchical information. Those hierarchies can be exploited for conceptual and (partly) for purpose explanations (because the ordering often is inferred from specialization/generalization). Other easily available information is information on the kind of attribute. *Input attributes* may be used to infer information for *retrieval attributes* as well as for filling *output attributes* of a query or a case. For example, imagine a CBR system for PC configuration in an electronic commerce scenario. The request for a multimedia PC triggers completion rules for filling such retrieval attributes as `processor` and `graphic card` accordingly. Not specified attributes of the query automatically become output attributes. The CBR system now could use the information for cognitive explanations based on why it filled the retrieval attributes etc.

The knowledge that determines how the most useful case is retrieved and by what means the similarity is calculated, is held by the *similarity measures* container, which can be further divided into the sub-containers for local similarity measures and amalgamation functions. Each local measure compares values of one attribute of a case. It contains domain knowledge, e.g., about different processor speeds or graphic cards. Amalgamation functions are task oriented and contain utility knowledge (relevances for the task, e.g., the importance of the graphic card vs. the importance of the processor speed when selecting a multimedia PC). The already mentioned completion rules provide knowledge about dependencies between attributes.

The *adaptation knowledge* container covers the knowledge for translating a prior solution to fit a given query and the *case base* stores the experience of the CBR system, i.e., the cases. Knowledge about the types of cases used by

Table 1. Knowledge containers and their contribution to explanations [26]

Knowledge container	contributes to
Vocabulary	conceptual explanations, why-explanations, how-explanations, and purpose explanations
Similarity measures	why-explanations, how-explanations, purpose explanations, and cognitive explanations
Adaptation knowledge	why-explanations, how-explanations, and cognitive explanations
Case base	why-explanations, how-explanations, and context

the case-based reasoner, such as *homogeneous* vs. *heterogeneous* and *episodic* vs. *prototypical* cases [29] as well as cases of *rule* vs. *constraint* type [30], structures this knowledge container further.

Table 1 shows an overview of which knowledge container contributes to which kind of explanation (see [26] for details).

5 Exploring the Relations of Goals and Kinds

As we have outlined before, there is a need to take the context of explanations as well as different goals with and types of explanation into account. A methodology for the development of explanation-aware CBR systems should therefore comprise components for the workplace analysis (like ANT described in section 2 or activity theory [31]) as well as methods to translate the analytical findings into system synthesis. Further on, this process has to be integrated with methods for the continuous maintenance of the CBR system [32]. We propose therefore a overall process architecture as depicted in figure 2.

During the remainder of this article, we will propose a 3-step process to identify which explanations a CBR system should be able to give and to understand how to make the necessary knowledge accessible in the different knowledge containers (see the grey box in figure 2):

1. Use the *Explanation Goals* perspective to identify user needs for explanations from a user model and system view which takes the usage situation into account.
2. Use the *Explanation Kinds* view to find useful prototypical explanations and assess the requirements for contents that have to be modeled into the system.
3. Use the different *Knowledge Containers* to store the necessary knowledge to support the different kinds of explanation identified.

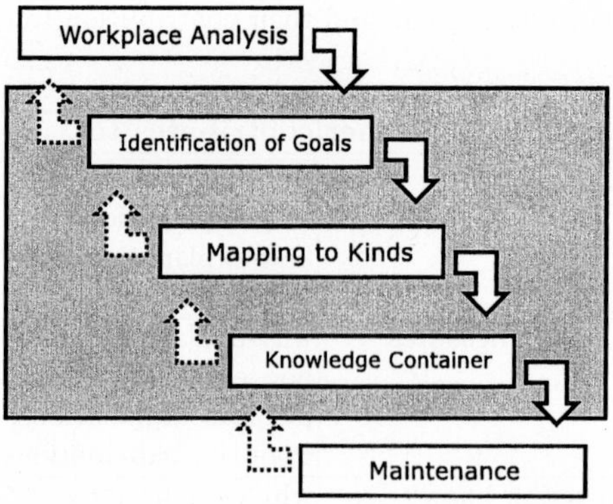

Fig. 2. The overall process architecture

The mapping of goals to kinds and kinds to containers, respectively, is not necessarily a one to one relation which can be followed mechanically. The mapping proposed in this paper gives rather hints for the modeling task by focusing the work of the system designer on probable solutions.

As a simplified example, we look at a case-based diagnostic system for engine failures. We have a mixed initiative dialogue system where the system can ask questions about the engine status and the user can voluntarily provide information he deems important.[1] The system can give detailed explanations on possible causes for the problems as well as advice on how to avoid future occurrences. It is supportive, e.g., the user should be enabled to understand similar situations in the future without having to rely on the system.

There is no adaptation of cases since we are purely interested in the possible cause of a failure and not a solution to solve this problem. Further on, we assume the system to be capable of generating plausible and justified explanations itself without going into details about the underlying mechanism.

Conceptualization goal fullfilled by a conceptual explanation (definition): During the symptom assessment, the system asks the user to fill in the specific gravity of the fuel. The user is not familiar with the term specific gravity so he asks the system to explain this. The system gives this explanation in the form of a *conceptual explanation*, in our example as a *definition*:
User: "What is the specific gravity?"
System: "It is a measure of the density of a liquid relative to the density of water, with water having a specific gravity of 1.0."

Following our argument on the contribution of different Knowledge Containers to explanation kinds, the necessary knowledge for this kind of answers would come from the *vocabulary* of the system. Undoubtedly, conceptual explanations

[1] Please, keep in mind that there are other possible human computer interfaces than natural language dialogue systems as depicted here for exemplary reasons. For example, one possibility is to provide the user with pre-formulated queries from which he or she can choose the most appropriate one.

need much more knowledge than provided in most CBR systems, even in knowledge rich systems such as CREEK [33,34], where general (domain-dependent) knowledge is represented as semantic network.[2]

Relevance goal fullfilled by a causal why-explanation: The user can further on ask to know why the system asked this specific question. The system should give explanations which set the question asked into context with the symptoms already known. This can be described in terms of a *causal why-explanation:*
User: "Why is the density of the fuel interesting?"
System: "Air/Fuel ratio is based on pounds of AIR to pounds of FUEL. Changing the specific gravity of your fuel can have a profound affect on the A/F ratio of your engine since carburetors are metered by volume."

Again, the necessary knowledge to answer this question can be found in the *vocabulary*. This causal why-explanation will typically rely on the domain knowledge modelled in the vocabulary of the system.

Justification goal fullfilled by a theoretical conceptual explanation: The system finally presents a solution to the user which requires him to change the spark lead time. In this situation, the user might want to know why this is a solution. This goal can be satisfied by presenting a *theoretical conceptual explanation*:
User: "How is this adjustment related to the problem of too much CO_2 in the exhaust gases?"
System: "Different fuels and engine setups require different spark lead times. When using a wrong timing, the combustion process is suboptimal, and this will lead to high CO_2 values."

Also here, the necessary knowledge can best be stored in the *vocabulary* container. In order to answer this question we need some explicitly modeled domain knowledge. A knowledge poor CBR system could only point to cases and its own similarity measure and leave it to the user to find the explanation himself.

Transparency goal fullfilled by a cognitive explanation: The user might not be fully satisfied and tries to understand how the system came up with this answer. The system can explain the reasoning process using a *how explanation*:
User: "How did you come up with this answer?"
System: "Looking at my case base we can see that the most relevant cases had problems with the spark lead time as well, with only the exception of those cases where the problem can be explained by the wrong type of fuel."

The explanatory knowledge for this question can be found in the *similarity measure* of the system. The system needs to be able to explain why it delivered a certain case in terms of its similarity assessment. The *case base* container provides the context for the explanation by restricting the problem space to the

---

[2] In CREEK, explanations are generated to explain reasoning steps or to justify conclusions to the user, but mainly for the internal use of the reasoner.

available cases. Please note that a knowledge rich CBR system might be able to explain the absence of certain features in the solution case by referring to its domain knowledge, stored in the *vocabulary*.

6 Conclusions and Future Research Directions

We have outlined a unified view on explanations in Case-Based Reasoning, which takes both the goals of the user and the type of an explanation into account. Both perspectives are to a certain degree independent from each other.

The next step in our fellow work is to integrate an explanation goals view with methods for the analysis of workplace situations like ANT and activity theory (as proposed, e.g., by Cassens [31]) and integrate the explanation kind perspective with existing design and maintenance methodologies (such as INRECA [35] and SIAM [32]).

We want to develop further our structural view on explanations and supporting knowledge available in CBR systems, with the ultimate goal of providing a methodology on how to develop explanation-aware CBR systems in the future.

References

1. Schank, R.C.: Explanation Patterns: Understanding Mechanically and Creatively. Lawrence Erlbaum Associates, Hillsdale, NJ (1986)
2. Spieker, P.: Natürlichsprachliche Erklärungen in technischen Expertensystemen. Dissertation, University of Kaiserslautern (1991)
3. Cohnitz, D.: Explanations are like salted peanuts. In Beckermann, A., Nimtz, C., eds.: Proceedings of the Fourth International Congress of the Society for Analytic Philosophy. (2000) `http://www.gap-im-netz.de/gap4Konf/` Proceedings4/titel.htm [Last access: 2004-08-11].
4. Leake, D.B.: Goal-Based Explanation Evaluation. In: Goal-Driven Learning. MIT Press, Cambridge (1995) 251–285
5. Swartout, W.: What Kind of Expert Should a System be? XPLAIN: A System for Creating and Explaining Expert Consulting Programs. Artificial Intelligence **21** (1983) 285–325
6. Buchanan, B.G., Shortliffe, E.H.: Rule-Based Expert Systems: The MYCIN Experiments of the Stanford Heuristic Programming Project. Addison Wesley, Reading (1984)
7. Swartout, W., Smoliar, S.: On Making Expert Systems More Like Experts. Expert Systems **4** (1987) 196–207
8. Leake, D.B., ed.: Case-Based Reasoning: Experiences, Lessons, & Future Directions. AAAI Press/MIT Press, Menlo Park (1996)
9. Schank, R.C., Kass, A., Riesbeck, C.K., eds.: Inside Case-Based Explanation. Lawrence Erlbaum Associates, Hillsdale, New Jersey (1994)
10. Gregor, S., Benbasat, I.: Explanations From Intelligent Systems: Theoretical Foundations and Implications for Practice. MIS Quarterly **23** (1999) 497–530
11. Swartout, W.R., Moore, J.D.: Explanation in second generation expert systems. In David, J., Krivine, J., Simmons, R., eds.: Second Generation Expert Systems. Springer Verlag, Berlin (1993) 543–585

12. Gervás, P., Gupta, K.M., eds.: Proceedings of the ECCBR 2004 Workshops. Number 142-04 in Technical Report, Madrid, Departamento de Sistemas Informáticos y Programación, Universidad Complutense Madrid (2004)
13. Funk, P., Calero, P.A.G., eds.: Advances in Case-Based Reasoning: Proceedings ECCBR 2004. Number 3155 in LNAI, Berlin, Springer (2004)
14. Richter, M.M.: Remarks on current explanation research in artificial intelligence (2005) Personal notes.
15. Latour, B.: Technology is Society made Durable. In Law, J., ed.: A Sociology of Monsters. Routledge (1991) 103–131
16. Monteiro, E.: Actor-Network Theory. In Ciborra, C., ed.: From Control to Drift. Oxford University Press (2000) 71–83
17. Pieters, W.: Free Will and Intelligent Machines. Project Report, NTNU Trondheim (2001)
18. Lee, J.D., See, K.A.: Trust in Automation: Designing for Appropriate Reliance. Human Factors **46** (2004) 50–80
19. Ye, L.R., Johnson, P.E.: The impact of explanation facilities on user acceptance of expert systems advice. MIS Q. **19** (1995) 157–172
20. Richter, M.M.: The knowledge contained in similarity measures. Invited Talk at the First International Conference on Case-Based Reasoning, ICCBR'95, Sesimbra, Portugal (1995)
21. Richter, M.M.: Prinzipien der Künstlichen Intelligenz. 2. edn. B. G. Teubner, Stuttgart (1992)
22. Sørmo, F., Cassens, J.: Explanation goals in case-based reasoning. [12] 165–174
23. Sørmo, F., Cassens, J., Aamodt, A.: Explanation in Case-Based Reasoning – Perspectives and Goals. To be publisehd (2005)
24. Clancey, W.J.: The epistemology of a rule-based expert system: A framework for explanation. Artificial Intelligence **20** (1983) 215–251
25. Mao, J.Y., Benbasat, I.: The Use of Explanations in Knowledge-Based System: Cognitive Perspectives and a Process-Tracing Analysis. Journal of Managment Information Systems **17** (2000) 153–179
26. Roth-Berghofer, T.R.: Explanations and case-based reasoning: Foundational issues. In Funk, P., Calero, P.A.G., eds.: Advances in Case-Based Reasoning, Springer-Verlag (2004) 389–403
27. Richter, M.M.: The knowledge contained in similarity measures. Invited Talk at the First International Conference on Case-Based Reasoning, ICCBR'95, Sesimbra, Portugal (1995) http://wwwagr.informatik.uni-kl.de/~ lsa/CBR/Richtericcbr95remarks.html [Last access: 2002-10-18].
28. Lenz, M., Bartsch-Spörl, B., Burkhard, H.D., Wess, S., eds.: Case-Based Reasoning Technology: From Foundations to Applications. Volume LNAI 1400 of Lecture Notes in Artificial Intelligence. Springer-Verlag, Berlin (1998)
29. Watson, I.: Survey of CBR application areas (1999) Invited Talk at the 3rd International Conference on Case-Based Reasoning ICCBR.
30. Richter, M.M.: Generalized planning and information retrieval. Technical report, University of Kaiserslautern, Artificial Intelligence – Knowledge-based Systems Group (1997)
31. Cassens, J.: Knowing what to explain and when. [12] 97–104
32. Roth-Berghofer, T.R.: Knowledge Maintenance of Case-Based Reasoning Systems – The SIAM Methodology. Volume 262 of Dissertationen zur Künstlichen Intelligenz. Akademische Verlagsgesellschaft Aka GmbH / IOS Press, Berlin, Germany (2003)

33. Aamodt, A.: Explanation-driven case-based reasoning. In Stefan Wess, K.D.A., Richter, M., eds.: Topics in Case-Based Reasoning, Berlin, Springer-Verlag (1994)
34. Aamodt, A.: Knowledge-Intensive Case-Based Reasoning in CREEK. [13] 1–15
35. Bergmann, R., Althoff, K.D., Breen, S., Göker, M., Manago, M., Traphöner, R., Wess, S.: Developing Industrial Case-Based Resoning Applications: The INRECA Methodology. Second edn. LNAI 1612. Springer-Verlag, Berlin (2003)

An Approach for Temporal Case-Based Reasoning: Episode-Based Reasoning*

Miquel Sánchez-Marré[1], Ulises Cortés[1], Montse Martínez[2], Joaquim Comas[2], and Ignasi Rodríguez-Roda[2]

[1] Technical University of Catalonia, Knowledge Engineering & Machine Learning Group, Campus Nord-Edifici Omega, Jordi Girona 1-3, 08034 Barcelona, Catalonia University of Girona
{miquel, ia}@lsi.upc.edu

[2] Chemical & Environmental Engineering Laboratory, Campus de Montilivi s/n, 17071 Girona, Catalonia
{montse, quim, ignasi}@lequia.udg.es

Abstract. In recent years, several researchers have studied the suitability of CBR to cope with dynamic or continuous or temporal domains. In these domains, the current state depends on the past temporal states. This feature really makes difficult to cope with these domains. This means that classical individual case retrieval is not very accurate, as the dynamic domain is structured in a temporally related stream of cases rather than in single cases. The CBR system solutions should also be dynamic and continuous, and temporal dependencies among cases should be taken into account. This paper proposes a new approach and a new framework to develop temporal CBR systems: Episode-Based Reasoning. It is based on the abstraction of temporal sequences of cases, which are named as *episodes*. Our preliminary evaluation in the wastewater treatment plants domain shows that Episode-Based Reasoning seems to outperform classical CBR systems.

1 Introduction

Continuous or dynamic or temporal domains commonly involve a set of features, which make them really difficult to work with, such as: (1) a large amount of new valuable experiences are continuously generated, (2) the current state or situation of the domain depends on previous temporal states or situations of the domain, and (3) states have multiple diagnoses.

This means that classical individual case retrieval is not very accurate, as the dynamic domain is structured as a temporally related stream of cases rather than in single cases. The CBR system solutions should be also dynamic and continuous, and temporal dependencies among cases should be taken into account.

* The partial support of TIN2004-01368 and DPI2003-09392-C02-01 Spanish projects and IST-2004-002307 European project are acknowledged.

H. Muñoz-Avila and F. Ricci (Eds.): ICCBR 2005, LNCS 3620, pp. 465 – 476, 2005.

Some typical examples are the monitoring and on-line control of dynamic processes such as power stations control, wastewater treatment plants control, and jet plane control. Some applications in the medical domain are the monitoring of patients in an intensive care unit, or the diagnosis and/or the prognosis and cure of some medical diseases. Also, the forecasting of some meteorological or seismic phenomena and autonomous robot navigation are instances of such temporal domain.

Our approach proposes a new framework for the development of temporal CBR systems: *Episode-Based Reasoning*. It is based on the abstraction of temporal sequences of cases, which are named as *episodes*. In this kind of domains, it is really important to detect similar temporal episodes of cases, rather than similar isolated cases. Thus, a more accurate diagnosis and problem solving of the dynamic domain could be done taking into account such temporal episodes of cases rather than only analysing the current isolated case.

Working with episodes instead of single cases is useful in temporal domains, but also raise some difficult tasks to be solved, such as:

- How to determine the length of an episode,
- How to represent the episodes, taking into account that they could be overlapping,
- How to represent the isolated cases,
- How to relate them to form episodes,
- How to undertake the episode retrieval,
- How to evaluate the similarity between temporal episodes of cases,
- How to continually learn and solve new episodes.

The paper answers almost all of these questions, and proposes a new approach and a new framework to model temporal dependencies by means of the episode concept. The Episode-Based Reasoning framework can be used as a basis for the development of temporal CBR systems. The new framework provides mechanisms to represent temporal episodes, to retrieve episodes, and to learn new episodes. Episode adaptation is not discussed, as it is highly domain-dependant, and will be studied in the near future.

An experimental evaluation is presented in the paper as an example of the new framework for temporal domains.

1.1 Related Work

From a logical point of view, temporal features in automated reasoning have been widely studied within the field of Artificial Intelligence. For instance, the logic of time work by van Benthem [1]; the work by Allen [2, 3, 4] about the temporal interval logic; or the work of temporal logic by Ma and Knight [5, 6] and by Shoham [7]; or the circumpscriptive event calculus by Shanahan [8]. All these approaches model reasoning processes under temporal constraints, which can modify the truth of logic assertions.

In CBR systems, this temporal reasoning in continuous or dynamical domains was not studied until recently. Ma & Knight [9] propose a theoretical framework to support historical CBR, based on relative temporal knowledge model. Similarity evaluation is based on two components: non-temporal similarity, based on elemental cases, and temporal similarity, based on graphical representations of temporal references.

Most related publications, such as those of [10, 11] use temporal models with absolute references. [12] use a qualitative model derived from the temporal interval logic from Allen. In [13, 14, 15], several approaches are proposed in the field of mobile robots, emphasising the problem of the continuity of data stream in these domains. However, none of these do not give an answer for temporal episodes. In addition, they focused more on the predicting numerical values, which can be described as time series, rather than on using the correlation among cases forming an episode. In [16], we proposed a method for sustainable learning in continuous domains, based on a relevance measure.

Anyway, we are not aware of any approach proposing a mechanism for explicit representation for both temporal episodes and isolated cases, and addressing the problem of overlapping temporal episodes. Also the feature dependency among isolated cases forming an episode are not addressed by main known approaches, and rather they provide temporal logic reasoning mechanisms, which cannot solve all related problems.

1.2 Overview

This paper is organised as follows. In Section 1, the scope of the problem and some related work are discussed. Section 2 defines the basic terminology of the approach. Section 3 defines the EBR memory model. In Section 4, the episode retrieval step is described. Section 5 details the similarity evaluation between episodes. Section 6 describes a case study where the approach has been used. Conclusions and some future work are outlined in Section 7.

2 Basic Terminology for Episode-Based Reasoning Model

Definition 1. An *isolated case*, or simply *a case* describing several features of a temporal domain at a given moment *t*, is defined as a structure formed by the following components:

(:case-identifier	CI
:temporal-identifier	*t*
:case-situation-description	CD
:case-diagnostics-list	CDL
:case-solution-plan	CS
:case-solution-evaluation	CE
)	

An isolated case will have an associated identifier (CI), as well as a temporal identifier (*t*). This time stamp could be measured in any unit of time, depending on the temporal domain at issue. Thus, it could be the month, the day, the hour, the minute, the second or any other unit. The description of the domain situation at a given moment (CD), is a snapshot of the state of the domain, which will consist of the values (V_i) of the different attributes (A_i) characterising the system:

$$CD = ((A_1 \;\; V_1)\;(A_2 \;\; V_2)\;...\;(A_N \;\; V_N)) \tag{1}$$

In the temporal domains being addressed by our proposal, the basic data stream describing the domain can be structured as a feature vector. This hypothesis is not a great constraint, since most of real temporal systems use this formalism, and also because other structured representations can be transformed into a vector representation. Notwithstanding, some information loss can occur with this transformation process.

Formally, an isolated case at a given time *t* is:

$$C_t = <CI, t, CD, CDL, CS, CE> \quad (2)$$

For instance, an isolated case in the domain of volcanic and seismic prediction domain, could be as follows:

(	:case-identifier	CASE-134
	:temporal-identifier	27/11/2004
	:case-situation-description	((SEISMIC-ACT Invaluable) (DEFORMATIONS mean-value) (GEOCHEMICAL-EVOL normal) (ELECT-PHEN level-1))
	:case-diagnostics-list	(No-eruption, Seismic-pre-Alert)
	:case-solution-plan	(Alert-Emergency-Services)
	:case-solution-evaluation	correct
	)	

Definition 2. A *temporal episode* of cases of length *l*, which is a sequence of *l* consecutive cases in time, is a structure formed by the following components:

(	:episode-identifier	EI
	:initial-time	t
	:episode-length	l
	:episode-description	ED
	:episode-diagnosis	d
	:episode-solution-plan	ES
	:episode-solution-evaluation	EE
	:initial-case	C_t
	:final-case	C_{t+l-1}
	)	

Formally, an *episode* with diagnostic *d*, length *l*, which starts at a given instant time *t* is:

$$E^{d}_{t,l} = <EI, t, l, ED, d, ES, EE, C_t, C_{t+l-1}> \quad (3)$$

From a temporal point of view, an *episode* with diagnostic *d*, length *l*, which starts at initial time *t* can be described as the sequence of *l* temporal consecutive cases:

$$E^{d}_{t,l} = [C_t, C_{t+1}, C_{t+2}, \ldots, C_{t+l-1}] \quad (4)$$

3 Episode-Based Reasoning Memory Model

There are several choices to organise and to structure the memory of our Episode-Based Reasoning (EBR) system. Some previous models in the literature had not taken into account some key points. Main outstanding features to be considered are the following. (1) The same *case* could belong to different *episodes*. (2) The description, or state depicted by a *case* could correspond to several situations or problems (multiple diagnostics) at the same time, and not only one, as it is assumed by most CBR system models. (3) Episodes could overlap among them, and this fact should not imply a case base representation redundancy of the common cases overlapped by the episodes. (4) Episode retrieval, and the case retrieval for each case belonging to an episode, should be as efficient as possible.

Taking into account these facts, our memory proposal will integrate hierarchical formalisms to represent the episodes, and flat representations for the cases. Thus, both episode and case retrieval will be fast enough. This representation model will set an abstraction process that allows splitting the temporal episode concept and the real case of the domain. Discrimination trees for the episodes (Episode Base or EpB), and a flat structure for cases (Case Base or CsB) are proposed.

The discrimination tree enables to search which episodes should be retrieved, according to the feature values of the current episode description. Episodes have the appropriate information to retrieve all cases belonging to them.

This structure of the experience base or memory of the EBR system allows one case to belong to more than one episode. In addition, it allows the overlapping of episodes, and even though the extreme scenario, which is very common in complex temporal real domains, where the exactly same cases form several different episodes.

This integration of the hierarchical Episode Base and the flat Case Base is depicted in Figure 1. The nodes are labelled with the predictive features or attributes (A_i) and branches are labelled with the discrete values (Low, Normal or High for instance) of attributes.

To increase even more the efficiency and accuracy of the retrieval step, the use of the mechanism of *episode* abstraction by means of *episode prototypes* or *meta-episodes* is proposed. This technique was originally proposed in [17] for a case base. Here it is used for *episode* categorisation instead.

The *meta-episodes* and induced *episode bases* are semantic patterns containing aspects considered as relevant. These relevant aspects (features and feature ordering) constitute the basis for the biased search in the *general episode base*. The use of these relevant aspects is in fact equivalent to using declarative bias during the *identification phase*, prior to searching cases within the case base. This new step adds the use of domain knowledge-intensive methods to understand and bias the new problem within its context.

The setting of several *meta-episodes* induces the splitting of the *general episode base* into several *episode bases* with different hierarchical structures. Each *episode base* will store similar episodes that can be characterised with the same set and order of predictive features.

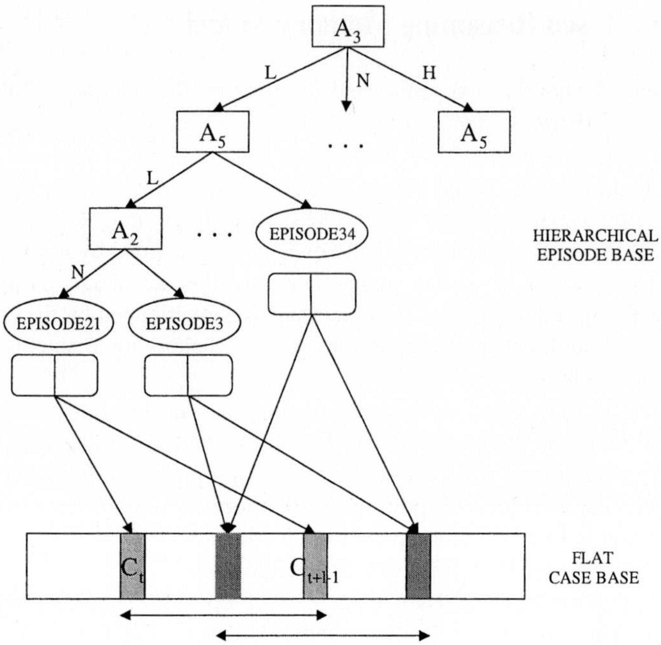

Fig. 1. Mixed memory model using both episodes and cases

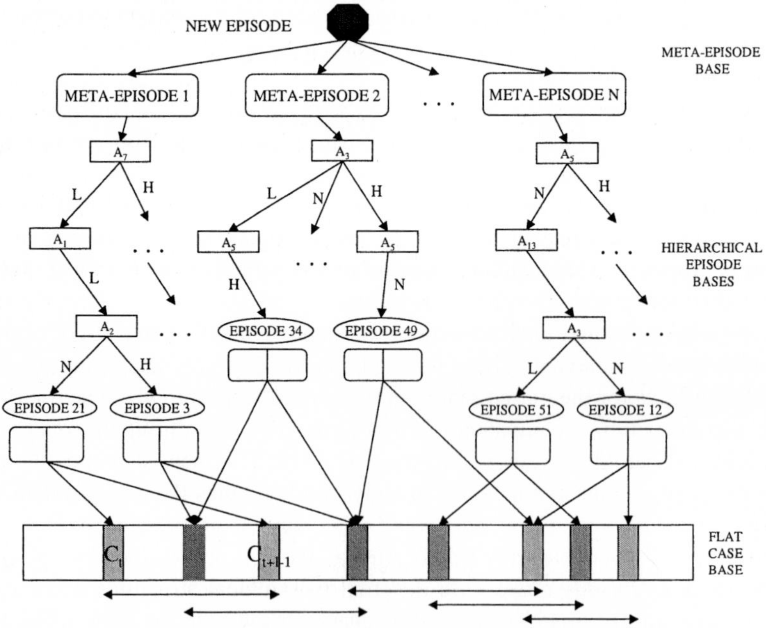

Fig. 2. Hierarchical three-layered memory structure

In the retrieval step, first, the EBR system will search within the previously established classification to identify which kind of *episode* it is coping with. For each established class (*meta-episode*) there will be a possible different set of specific discriminating features and a different *episode base*. Then, the retrieval will continue in the *episode base/s* induced by the *meta-episode/s* best matching the current episode.

The memory model of the approach is composed by a set of meta-episodes, which will constitute the Meta-Episode Base (MEpB). For each meta-episode there exists a hierarchical Episode Base (EpB). Cases are organised within a flat case base (CsB).Also there exists a Meta-Case Base (MCsB) for the diagnostic list computation of a case. This *hierarchical three-layered structure* will allow a more accurate and faster retrieval of similar episodes to the current episode/s. Figure 2 shows this memory structure.

4 Episode Retrieval

Retrieval task of episodes is activated each time the EBR system receives a new *current case* (C_{ct}) with data gathered from the domain, at the current time (*ct*). First step is *getting the possible diagnostics of the current case.*

This label list can be obtained by different ways. For example, using a *set of inference rules*, which can diagnose the state or situation of the domain from the relevant features. These classification rules could be directly collected from domain experts or could be induced from real data. Another way is using the *meta-cases* technique, and to evaluate the similarity between the current case (C_{ct}) and the meta-cases. The current case is labelled with the diagnostic labels of most similar meta-cases. Meta-cases can be obtained, in the same way as the rules: from experts or from an inductive clustering process. In our proposal, meta-cases technique is used.

Next step is the *generation of possible episodes* arising from the current case. This means to check whether some episodes are continuing from prior cases to the current case, and/or to build new episodes, which are starting from the current case. At this time, finished episodes are detected, and the EBR system can learn new episodes, which will be added to the EBR system memory. Figure 3 depicts several alternative episode formation and episode ending from current case.
For each *possible current episode*, most similar episodes must be retrieved. Retrieval task proceeds with the *hierarchical three-layered memory structure* as explained before in section 3.

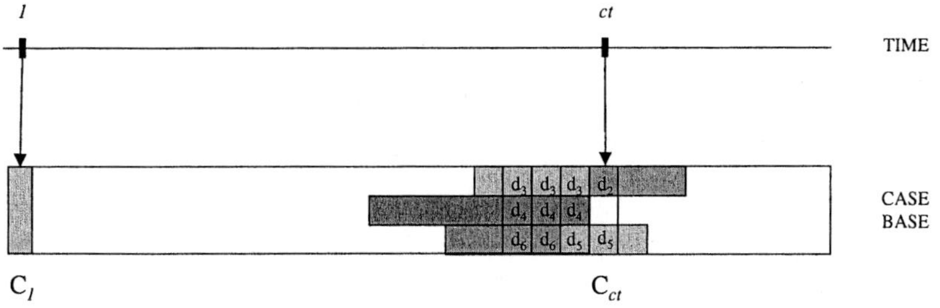

Fig. 3. New and/or continued episodes arising from the current case

For each one of the *retrieved episodes* and the corresponding current episode, a degree of similarity is computed. This value is computed through an episode similarity measure, which will be described in next section. Each retrieved episode is added to a sorted list of episodes by decreasing degree of similarity. Thus, at the end of the process, the *first episode* of the list is the episode with a higher similarity value to a possible current episode. The EBR system will use this episode to solve the domain problem, but other policies, such as user-dependent choice, are envisioned. Similar episode retrieval task can be described as follows:

Input: C_{ct}, EpB, MEpB, CsB, MCsB
Sorted_Ep_L ← ∅
CDL_{ct} ← Get_Diagnostics_Current_Case (C_{ct}, MCsB)
for each d ∈ CDL_{ct} do
if ($ct = 1$) or (d ∉ CDL_{ct-1}) then {new episodes}
Retr_Ep ← Retr_Sim_Episodes ($E^{d}_{ct,1}$, MEpB, EpB)
Eval_Ep ← Eval_Sim_Episodes ($E^{d}_{ct,1}$, Retr_Ep)
Sorted_Ep_L ← Sorted_Add (Eval_Ep, Sorted_Ep_L)
else {continued episodes}
l ← Comp_Ep_Length (ct, d, CsB)
Retr_Ep ← Retr_Sim_Episodes ($E^{d}_{ct-l,l+1}$, MepB, EpB)
Eval_Ep ← Eval_Sim_Episodes ($E^{d}_{ct-l,l+1}$, Retr_Ep)
Sorted_Ep_L ← Sorted_Add (Eval_Ep, Sorted_Ep_L)
endif
endfor
if $ct \neq 1$ then
for each (d ∈ CDL_{ct-1}) and (d ∉ CDL_{ct}) do {ended episodes}
l ← Comp_Ep_Length (ct, d, CsB)
EpB ← EpB + Learn_New_Episode ($E^{d}_{ct-l,l}$) {add a new Ep}
endfor
endif

Returns: Sorted_Ep_L {First Ep is the most similar}
where the computation of episode length can be done as follows:

Input: ct, d, CsB
$t \leftarrow ct - 2$; $l \leftarrow 1$
if $t \neq 0$ then
CDL_t ← Get_Diagnostics_Case (C_t, CsB)
while d ∈ CDL_t do
$l \leftarrow l + 1$
$t \leftarrow t - 1$
endwhile
endif

Returns: l

5 Episode Similarity

Episodic similarity evaluation is based on the computation of a similarity value within the float interval [0,1], between a possible current episode (Ep_ct) and each one of the retrieved episodes (Retr_Ep). This function could be described as follows:

Input: Ep_ct, Retr_Ep
Eval_Ep $\leftarrow \varnothing$
for each Ep $\in$ Retr_Ep do
  Sim_Degree_Ep $\leftarrow$ Episodic_Sim (Ep, Ep_ct)
  Eval_Ep $\leftarrow$ Eval_Ep $\cup$ Build_Pair (Sim_Degree_Ep, Ep)
endfor

Returns: Eval_Ep
Episodic similarity between two episodes is computed based on the aggregation of the similarity values among cases belonging to each episode. Episodes are compared based on a left alignment of cases. There are two different scenarios. For equal length episodes, episodic similarity is computed as an equally weighted mean value among the similarity values between each pair of corresponding cases. For different length episodes, only similarity values for cases until reaching the minimum length of both episodes are considered. The computed value is normalised into the interval [0,1]. This episodic similarity measure can be formalised as:

$$Sim_{Ep}(E^{d}_{t1,l1}, E^{d}_{t2,l2}) = \begin{cases} \frac{1}{l}\sum_{i=1}^{l} Sim_C(C_{t1+i-1}, C_{t2+i-1}) & if \quad l1 = l2 = l \\ \frac{1}{max(l1,l2)} \sum_{i=1}^{\min(l1,l2)} Sim_C(C_{t1+i-1}, C_{t2+i-1}) & if \quad l1 \neq l2 \end{cases} \tag{5}$$

where Sim_C can be computed with any case similarity measure. In this approach, *L'Eixample* measure [18] is proposed, because some performance tests done showed it as one of the best measures.

6 An Experimental Evaluation

Biological wastewater treatment is a complex process that involves chemical and biological reactions, kinetics, catalysis, transport phenomena, separations, and so on. The quality of the treated water must be always maintained in a good condition to minimise any environmental impact. Nevertheless, some features such as the inflow changes, both in quantity and in quality, and the population variation of the microorganisms over time, both in quantity and in the relative number of species, makes the process very complex. In addition, the process generates a huge amount of data from different sources (sensors, laboratory analyses and operator's observations), but these data are often uncertain, subjective or vague.

In the wastewater treatment plant (WWTP) operation, problems frequently appearing such as solids separation problems, biological foam in the bioreactors or underloading derived from storms and heavy rains. Some of them affect the process for long periods of time. Due to the lack of a well-defined model capable of simulating the process under the influence of these problems, classical control has been ruled out as suitable single control technique. However, operators have to make decisions to manage the process in their day-to-day operation, even when it is affected by multiple problem episodes at the same time. They learn a valuable knowledge that optimally managed can be decisive when facing similar problems in the future.

Classical CBR has been successfully applied to manage the biological process of wastewater treatment plants [19, 20, 21], especially to control single non-biological situations with fast dynamics such as mechanical, physical or electrical problems. However, CBR showed limitations to face up complex problems with slow dynamics. A prototype of EBR is currently being validated at the Girona wastewater treatment plant [22] since September, 2004. The tool has been developed to manage solids separation problems in the process. A three-layered architecture has been proposed, and 21 different variables are used to compare and retrieve the episodes (six variables provided on-line from sensors and meters, nine gathered from the laboratory, and the remaining six variables correspond to microscopic observations of the biomass). Preliminary results show that EBR improves the support of the decision-making process when facing problematic situations with temporal dependency of data with respect to conventional CBR systems. Specifically, this initial experimental evaluation enables to state that the EBR approach provides more precise diagnosis of new episodes arising in the process as well as that solution plans of past episodes retrieved (the more similar ones) are more useful than with the conventional CBR approach.

The efficiency of EBR in diagnosing new cases was evaluated by using historical cases of the year 2004, which include the situation description (by means of the 21 variables), the diagnosis lists (obtained from real diagnosis of the process) and the solution plan. Through 2004, 28 different episodes of solids separation problems, with episode length varying from 2 days up to 73 days and some of them overlapped, were detected, representing the 69% of the whole year. The results obtained using EBR and CBR approaches were compared with the real diagnosis of the labelled cases of 2004. The conventional CBR approach gave already a high precision of about 91% when diagnosing the current problem [23]. However, an efficiency of 97% in determining the correct diagnosis of episodes was obtained when using the EBR system, including correct diagnosis of isolated cases and correct identification of episodes (determination of initial and final cases).

Concerning the usefulness of the solution plans provided by the most similar case/episode retrieved, the use of EBR also contributes to obtain more useful control plans to solve the complex problems arising in the process. The solution plan and solution evaluation retrieved from the most similar episodes helped plant operators to determine a long-term control strategy. An episode control plan, containing all the control actions applied during a whole episode and the evaluation of its application, was more useful for plant operators to solve a slow dynamic problem than the solution plan provided by the isolated case retrieved by the CBR approach. Therefore, during these problematic situations, the retrieval of similar past episodes helped the system to define new control plans to restore the process, proving that EBR can easily manage multiple diagnosis of the process status, giving real support to the operators. The results with the EBR system showed even higher efficiency than when CBR was applied in the same domain of WWTPs but for solving general problems, where around 80% of efficiency was obtained [24].

7 Conclusions and Future Work

In this paper, most of the questions raised in section 1 have been answered. A new framework and a new approach, based on the *episode* concept have been presented. Episode-Based Reasoning is a promising model to manage the temporal component of many real world domains, with continuous data flow. This approach supports the temporal dependency of data on past cases to solve a new case, improving the accuracy of basic CBR systems. Also, multiple diagnostics of a state or situation of the domain can be managed. Basic model terminology about *episodes* and *isolated cases* has been given. The *three-layered architecture memory model* for the EBR has been proposed, and the *retrieval procedure* has been detailed. Furthermore, the *similarity evaluation* step has been explained too, and the *learning of new episodes* has been outlined within the retrieval algorithm.

There are some outstanding features in the proposal. The abstraction procedure from real data, structured in cases, towards temporal episodes is one of them. Multiple diagnostics of real cases are identified and managed by the model. The distinction between episodes and cases allows episode overlapping over the same real data without data redundancy. The hierarchical three-layered structure of the EBR memory, composed by Meta-Episodes, Episode Bases, and the Case Base enables a fast access to similar past episodes to current episodes.

This model has been partially tested in a real domain, as explained in section 6. Supervision of WWTP is a hard real problem, which is a very good benchmark for the new EBR approach. Results from the experimentation have shown a very good potential of the EBR model, and an improved performance output has been obtained.

One concern to be solved in the future is the uncontrolled increase of the Case Base and the Episode Bases. New Episodes can be learnt only if they are relevant enough, but new cases management is not so easy. A splitting of the Case Base by some time unit: year, month, or so, could be a first approach. There are other features to be taken into account in the near future. The extension of the EBR approach to formalise the adaptation step, and the solution evaluation task should be precisely stated into the main EBR cycle.

Of course, some tuning of the approach can be made at several points. Finally, the validation of the whole EBR model should be extended to other real domains to check the usefulness, the consistency, the efficiency and the generalisation of our approach.

References

1. J. van Benthem. *The Logic of Time*, Kluwer Academic, Dordrecht, 1983.
2. J. Allen and G. Ferguson. Actions and Events in Interval Temporal Logic. *The Journal of Logic and Computation*, 4(5):531-579, 1994.
3. J. Allen. Towards a General Theory of Action and Time. *Artificial Intelligence*, 23:123-154, 1984.
4. J. Allen. Maintaining knowledge about temporal intervals. *Communications of the ACM*, 26(11):832-843, 1983.
5. J. Ma and B. Knight. Reified Temporal logic: An Overview. *Artificial Intelligence Review*, 15:189-217, 2001.

6. J. Ma and B. Knight. A General Temporal Theory. *The Computer Journal*, 37(2):114-123, 1994.
7. Y. Shoham. Temporal Logics in AI: Semantical and Ontological Considerations, *Artificial Intelligence*, 33: 89-104, 1987.
8. M.A. Shanahan. Circumscriptive Calculus of Events, *Artificial Intelligence*, 77(2):249-384, 1995.
9. J. Ma and B. Knight. A Framework for Historical Case-Based Reasoning. In *Procc. of 5th Int. Conference on Case-Based Reasoning (ICCBR'2003)*, pages 246-260, LNCS2689, 2003.
10. M. Jaczynski. A Framework for the Management of Past Experiences with Time-Extended Situations. In *Proc. of the 6th Int. Conference on Information and Knowledge Management (CIKM'97)*, pages 32-39, Las Vegas, Nevada, USA, November 1997.
11. G. Nakhaeizadeh. Learning Prediction of Time Series: A Theoretical and Empirical Comparison of CBR with Some Other Approaches. In *Proceedings of the Workshop on Case-Based Reasoning*, pages 67-71, AAAI-94. Seattle, Washington, 1994.
12. M. Jaere, A. Aamodt, and P. Shalle. Representing Temporal Knowledge for Case-Based Reasoning. In *Proc. of the 6th European Conference, ECCBR 2002*, pages 174-188, Aberdeen, Scotland, UK, September 2002.
13. M. Likhachev, M. Kaess and R. C. Arkin. Learning Behavioral Parameterization Using Spatio-Temporal Case-Based Reasoning. *Procc. of IEEE Int. Conference on Robotics and Automation (ICRA 2002)*, 2002.
14. M. T. Rosenstein and P. R. Cohen. Continuous Categories for a Mobile Robot. IJCAI-99 Workshop on Sequence Learning, pages 47-53, 1999.
15. A. Ram and J. C. Santamaría. Continuous Case-Based Reasoning. *Artificial Intelligence*, 90:25-77, 1997.
16. M. Sànchez-Marrè, U. Cortés, I. R.-Roda and M. Poch, Sustainable case learning for continuous domains. *Environmental Modelling & Software* 14:349-357, 1999.
17. M. Sànchez-Marrè, U. Cortés, I. R.-Roda and M. Poch. Using Meta-cases to Improve Accuracy in Hierarchical Case Retrieval. *Computación y Sistemas* 4(1):53-63, 2000.
18. H. Núñez, M. Sànchez-Marrè and U. Cortés. Improving Similarity Assessment with Entropy-Based Local Weighting. In *Procc. of 5th Int. Conference on Case-Based Reasoning (ICCBR'2003)*, pages 377-391, LNAI-2689, Trondheim, Norway. June 2003.
19. J. Wiese, A. Stahl and J. Hansen. Possible Applications for Case-Based Reasoning in the Field of Wastewater Treatment. In Procc. of 4th ECAI Workshop on Binding Environmental Sciences and Artificial Intelligence (BESAI'04), pages 10-1:10-10, 2004.
20. R.-Roda, I., Sànchez-Marrè, M., Comas, J., Cortés, U. and Poch, M. Development of a case-based system for the supervision of an activated sludge process. *Environmental Technology*, 22(4): 477-486, 2001.
21. Kraslawski A., Koiranen T. and Nystrom L. Case-Based Reasoning System for Mixing Equipment Selection, *Computers & Chemical Engineering*, 19:821-826, 1995.
22. M. Martínez, M. Sànchez-Marrè, J. Comas and I. Rodríguez-Roda. Case-Based Reasoning, a promising tool to face solids separation problems in the activated sludge process. *Water Science & Technology*, in press, 2005.
23. M. Martínez, C. Mérida-Campos, M.Sànchez-Marrè, J. Comas and I. Rodríguez-Roda. Improving the efficiency of Case-Based Reasoning to deal with activated sludge solids separation problems. Submitted to *Environmental Technology* (2005)
24. I. Rodríguez-Roda, M. Sànchez-Marrè, J. Comas, J. Baeza,, J. Colprim, J. ,Lafuente, U. Cortés, and M. Poch. A Hybrid Supervisory System to Support Wastewater Treatment Plant Operation, *Water Science & Technology* 45(4-5), 289, 2002.

How to Combine CBR and RBR for Diagnosing Multiple Medical Disorder Cases

Wenqi Shi and John A. Barnden

School of Computer Science, The University of Birmingham,
Edgbaston, Birmingham, B15 2TT, UK
W.Shi@cs.bham.ac.uk

Abstract. Multiple disorders are a daily problem in medical diagnosis and treatment, but most expert systems make an implicit assumption that only single disorder occurs in a single patient. We show the need for performing multiple disorder diagnosing, then inspired by the common idea of combining CBR with Rule-based Reasoning, we present a hybrid approach for diagnosing multiple faults. We applied our hybrid reasoning approach to two medical casebases taken from real world applications demonstrating the promise of the approach. The method could also be applied to other multiple fault domains, e.g. car failure diagnosis.

1 Introduction

The Medical Diagnosis problem has absorbed lots of the attention of AI researchers, since the medical domain is not well understood in some ways by human beings and AI has the potential to help diagnosis. Multiple disorders are a daily problem in medical diagnosis and treatment. However, due to a common diagnosis assumption (single-fault assumption) in diagnostic problem-solving domain, only one single disorder or fault is assumed to cover all the observed findings [12].

Many medical expert systems for diagnosis and treatment have been investigated since the middle of the 1970s. The MYCIN System of the Stanford Heuristic Programming Project [6] was possibly one of the first expert systems which attempted to use the concepts of AI, i.e. production rules to help diagnosis and treatment advice in the domain of bacteremias (then expanded to include meningitis). But the need to generate of rules and the static knowledge structure highlight the knowledge acquisition problem which most expert systems suffered from. In contrast to this, the case-based reasoning methodology uses previous experience for current problem solving, thus reducing the costs of knowledge acquisition and maintenance, and has therefore become popular in experience rich domains, e.g., medical domain.

However, using naive case-based reasoning to handle multiple disorders faces a major challenge. For instance, for a single disorder casebase dealing with 100 disorders, the chance of reusing a case is roughly one in a hundred. But owing to the combinatorial situation, the chance of reusing a case with even 3 independent

H. Muñoz-Avila and F. Ricci (Eds.): ICCBR 2005, LNAI 3620, pp. 477–491, 2005.

diagnoses from 100 alternatives is roughly just one in a million. In one of our real world applications, the casebase contains about 7 disorders per case on average, and has 221 disorders in total, thus the chance of reusing an entire previous case is quite small. Atzmueller and Baumeister proved the naive case-based method was only able to solve about 3% of the cases on their real world dataset [2].

In this paper, we present a hybrid approach which uses case-based reasoning and rule-based reasoning to target multiple disorder problems. This hybrid reasoning approach has been evaluated on two medical casebases taken from real world applications and demonstrated to be promising.

The rest of the paper is organised as follows: In section 2, we will explain the need for performing multiple disorder diagnosis, give some notations concerning the multiple disorder problem, and review previous work on multiple disorders. In the following section, we describe how we generate rules from inductive learning, define the similarity measure we are using, and explain in detail how to combine case-based reasoning and rule-based reasoning. In section 4, we evaluate our method by applying it to two real world medical casebases, and compare it with other methods. We conclude the paper with some points worth noting, and pointers to some promising directions for the future.

2 Multiple Disorder Problem

2.1 The Need for Performing Multiple Disorder Diagnosis

Most previous medical expert systems follow a single disorder assumption, which stems from the fact that finding minimal sets of disorders that cover all symptoms for a given patient is generally computationally intractable (NP-hard) [23]. But in spite of the difficulty for expert system implementation, reality needs to be faced in the real world application.

As medical documentations become more and more structured, it is not rare to see more than one disease in a patient record. This is especially true for old people and those with many chronic diseases (e.g. diabetes, high brood pressure) or a syndrome (e.g. Aids). One of the casebases we got from the real world contains an overall number of 221 diagnoses and 556 symptoms, with a mean $M_D = 6.71 \pm 04.4$ of diagnoses per case and a mean $M_F = 48.93 \pm 17.9$ of relevant findings per case. Disorders in this casebase include diseases such as Fat liver/Liver greasing (K76.0), Illness of the Thyroid (E07.9), Kidney illness (N28.9), Nephrolithiasis (N20.0), Struma (E04.9) etc. Moreover, multiple disorders occur in psychiatric cases as well, approximately 63.3% of incarcerated adolescents had 2 or more psychiatric disorders [22].

In this context, the observed set of the symptoms for a given patient may be better explained by more than one disorder.

2.2 Multiple Disorder Notation

We define necessary notions concerning our knowledge representation schema as follows: Let Ω_D be the set of all possible diagnoses, and $d \in \Omega_D$ be a disease patient may have. Let Ω_A the set of all attributes. To each attribute $a \in \Omega_A$ a range $dom(a)$ of values is assigned. Further we assume Ω_F to be the (universal) set of findings, and a finding $f \in \Omega_F$ is $(a = v)$, where $a \in \Omega_A$ is an attribute and $v \in dom(a)$ is an assignable value to attribute a.

Let CB be the case base containing all available cases that have been solved previously. A case $c \in CB$ is defined as a tuple as follows

$$c = (\mathcal{F}_c, \mathcal{D}_c, I_c) \tag{1}$$

$\mathcal{F}_c \subseteq \Omega_F$ is the set of findings observed in the case c. The set $\mathcal{D}_c \subseteq \Omega_D$ is the set of diagnoses for this case. I_c contains additional information, like therapy advices or prognostic hints. In CBR-problems the findings are commonly called *the problem description*, while the diagnoses are described as the *solution* of the case.

2.3 Previous Work on MD Problem

INTERNIST matches symptoms and diseases in general internal medicine based on forward and backward conditional probabilities [17]. It generates multiple disorders with likelihood, but it does not deal with the interacting disorders properly because if the findings can be explained by a disorder, then these findings will be deleted immediately, no matter how these findings could also lead to diagnosis of another disorder.

HYDI decomposes knowledge from the causal models into diagnosis units to prevent re-computation for similar problem to improve efficiency [12]. It can produce multiple disorder output about heart diseases, but the diagnosis units in HYDI largely rely on the causal models built in Heart Failure Program (HF) on heart disease. Only when all the causal models for other disorders are available could HYDI's method be applied to diagnose other disorders.

HEPAR$\prod$ [19] extends the structure of Bayesian network and [8] uses belief networks to diagnose multiple disorders, but they are both based on the medical literature and conversations with medical domain experts, which highlights the knowledge acquisition problem.

Set-covering theory [20] has been combined with CBR, and partition class method was used in SONOCONSULT to solve multiple disorder problem [4]. Since these two methods are recent work and they are using CBR as well, we will focus on analysing and comparing our method with them in the evaluation section.

3 Combining CBR and RBR for Multiple Disorders

Case-based Reasoning (CBR) employs existing experience to support problem solving without necessarily understanding the underlying principles of application domain. It has been demonstrated to be suitable for weak theory domains, especially for medical domain [9].

However, case-based diagnosis handling multiple disorders is still a challenging task. Majority of the work done so far is using CBR to diagnose single disorder, little work has been concentrated on multiple disorder [9]. In this paper, we combine CBR and RBR to handle this problem.

In this section, we describe how we generate rules from inductive learning, define the similarity measure we are using, and explain how compositional case-based reasoning works, and how we combine case-based reasoning and rule-based reasoning to compensate for the weakness of naive case-based reasoning on multiple disorder problem.

3.1 Inductive Learning of Diagnostic Rule

Diagnostic rule is one of wide spread formalisms for medical decision-making. But for most of expert systems, the rules are difficult to get, because the generation of diagnostic rules has the knowledge acquisition problem and how to maintain the rules. In our method, to reduce the knowledge elicitation costs, we propose an inductive learning method to generate diagnostic rules. It can be refined by applying different types of background knowledge.

Inspired by [3], we apply the χ^2 *test for independence* [26]to identify dependencies between findings f and diagnoses d. For small sample sizes, the Yates' correction has been applied for a more accurate result. In general, all possible combinations between diagnoses $d \in \Omega_D$ and findings $f \in \Omega_F$ have to be taken into account. However, to reduce the search space, we only consider the set of findings f which co-occur with disorder d.

$$\chi^2(f,d) = \frac{(m+n+p+q)(mq-np)^2}{(m+n)(p+q)(m+p)(n+q)} \tag{2}$$

where m is the number of cases when finding f and disorder d co-occur, n is the number of cases when finding f happens but disorder d does not appear, p is the number of cases when finding f does not appear but disorder d happens, and q is the number of cases when neither of f nor d happens.

For those tuples $<f,d>$ with $\chi^2(f,d) > th1$ ($th1 = 3.84$ when $p = .05$, $df = 1$), we measure the quality of the dependency by using the ϕ coefficient

$$\phi(f,d) = \frac{mq-np}{\sqrt{(m+n)(p+q)(m+p)(n+q)}} \tag{3}$$

According to Cohan's guidelines for effect size, we consider the pairs $< f,d >$ with $\phi_{fd} > 0.25$ as strong relation effect; those pairs $< f,d >$ with $\phi_{fd} > 0.09$ as medium relation effect; those pairs $< f,d >$ with $\phi_{fd} > 0.01$ as weak relation effect. We then define the diagnostic rule on those tuples $< f,d >$ with strong relation effect, which means the finding f is significantly important for diagnosing disorder d.

Definition 1 (Diagnostic Rule). *A diagnostic rule R is defined as follows:*

$$R : f \xrightarrow{\phi_{fd}} d \tag{4}$$

where $f \in \Omega_F$ and $d \in \Omega_D$. For each rule, the coefficient ϕ_{fd} (defined in equation 3) is marked as the effect of the dependency ($\phi_{fd} > 0.25$). Finding f is called significant finding for disorder d.

We outline the inductive learning process as follows:

1. Construct all the finding-disorder pairs $< f, d >$ for those f and d occur in cases of the casebase CB.
2. For each finding-disorder pair, compute χ^2_{fd}=$\chi^2(f, d)$.
3. If χ^2_{fd} is greater than $th1$, then define f as significant finding for diagnose d.
4. For each significant finding f of each diagnose d, compute the correlation $\phi_{fd} = \phi(f, d)$.
5. For those tuples $< f, d >$ with $\phi_{fd} > 0.25$, define corresponding Diagnostic Rules.

After finishing inductive learning of diagnostic rules, we figure out which findings are significant for some disorders, which will help in our future reasoning procedure.

3.2 Overall vs. Partial Similarity Measure

To compare the similarity of a query case c with another case c', we measure two similarities. One is based on all the findings observed in both retrieved case and query case, called *Overall Similarity*. Another one is based on those *significant* findings, to measure how the retrieved case is similar on these features, with the query case. We call the similarity measure on significant features as *Partial Similarity*. We use both overall similarity measure and partial similarity measure in our retrieval to get better suitable cases.

For both of these two similarities, we apply Manhattan distance for continuous or scaled parameters,

$$\mathrm{md}(x_i, y_i) = |\frac{x - y}{a_{max} - a_{min}}| \tag{5}$$

and Value Difference Metric (VDM) for discrete parameters[25].

$$\mathrm{vdm}(x_i, y_i) = \frac{1}{|\Omega_D|} \cdot \sum_{d \in \Omega_D} |\frac{N(a = x_i|d)}{N(a = x_i)} - \frac{N(a = y_i|d)}{N(a = y_i)}| \tag{6}$$

where x and y are values of parameter a in case c and c' respectively.

The final similarity is measured as follows:

$$\mathrm{Similarity}(c, c') = \frac{1}{m} \sum_{i=1}^{m} \omega_i md(x_i, y_i) + \frac{1}{n} \sum_{j=1}^{n} \varpi_j vdm(x_j, y_j) \tag{7}$$

where m is the number of continuous or scaled findings, n is the number of discrete findings for overall similarity measure. When measuring partial similarity, m is the number of continuous or scaled *significant* findings, n is the number of discrete *significant* findings.

One difference of overall similarity and partial similarity is that the findings taken into account vary. Another difference is that the weights, which have been set for respective findings, are different.

3.3 Compositional Case-Based Reasoning

Compositional Case-based Reasoning is inspired from the concept of compositional adaptation, which was originally developed for configuration tasks. Compositional Adaptation decomposes problems into sub-problems and retrieves those sub-problems in the casebase, and then combines different parts of the solutions of similar cases [24].

In our multiple disorder situations, decomposition can't be performed without the help of experts. This is because the findings cannot automatically be separated into different subsets which will be diagnosed to corresponding diseases in final solution. Thus in our application, we discard the concept of decomposition which need to divide observed findings into groups, but accept the concept of composition which combine different parts of the solutions of similar cases, and we developed our compositional CBR [1].

When we apply compositional CBR on multiple disorder problem, we assume that in the multiple disorder situations, not all the diagnoses in the solutions of the k most similar cases will be suggested as the final diagnoses. Only the diagnoses with a high occurrence among the k most similar cases have a high probability to appear in the final solution of the query case. At the same time, we assume that the more similar the retrieved case is to the query case, the higher the probability that the diagnoses in this retrieved case will appear in the final solution. Thus, we add weights to the frequency of diagnoses in the set of retrieved cases.

Definition 2 (Similarity-Weighted Frequency). *The similarity-weighted frequency of a diagnosis d is the weighted frequency of d within the k most similar cases.*

$$\mathrm{Fqc}(d) = \frac{\sum_{i=1}^{k} W_i \cdot \delta(C_i, d)}{\sum_{i=1}^{k} W_i}, \tag{8}$$

where $d \in \Omega_D$ is a diagnosis; $C_i \in CB$ is the ith *most similar case to the query case; $\delta(C_i, d)$ is 1 if d occurs in C_i, and 0 otherwise. W_i represents the associated weight, where we used the squared relative similarity between C_i and the query case C_q.*

CompositionalCBR (C_q, CB, $SimilaritySet$, k)
{ $KMostSimiCase$ = **Retrieve_MostSimi** (C_q, CB, $SimilaritySet$, k);
for each disorder d in casebase CB
{ $Fqc(d)$ = **Calculate_Fqc**(d, $KMostSimiCase$);}
return Fqc;}

In Compositional CBR, we retrieve the most k similar cases, and calculate the frequency for each disorder.

Not all the disorders will be suggested as final diagnosis, only those diagnoses with high similarity-weighted frequency will be included into the candidate solution. We introduce a candidate solution defined as follows:

Definition 3 (Candidate Solution). *A candidate solution*

$$CS = \{D \in \Omega_D : Fqc(D) \geq \epsilon\}, \tag{9}$$

is the set of diagnoses with a similarity-weighted frequency above a dynamic threshold $\epsilon = \alpha * \max_{D \in \Omega_D} Fqc(D)$*. where* α *is a coefficient.*

3.4 Combining CBR with RBR

We combine CBR with RBR in two ways: firstly we use the diagnostic rules to figure out those significant findings, and help retrieval procedure in Compositional CBR. Secondly, we use the rule-based reasoning to generate the candidate diagnoses and adapt the solutions from CBR.

When we refine compositional CBR with the diagnostic rules, we first construct diagnostic rules ($R : f \xrightarrow{\phi_{fd}} d$), and then look through the query case to *Match* the given findings with the antecedents of the diagnostic rules to find out those significant findings *PartialSimSet*. We retrieve cases from the casebase by measuring the partial similarity on *PartialSimSet*, and get the $k1$ most similar cases. We retrieve cases from the casebase again but using the overall similarity measure on *OverallSimSet*, and get the $k2$ most similar cases. The disorder frequency for each disorder is calculated for both $k1$ and $k2$ most similar case sets. Then we take a weighted sum of the disorder frequencies from the two retrievals to compose the final solution (W_p, W_o present the weights for disorder frequency in the retrieval based on partial similarity and overall similarity).

We summarise it as follows:

Hybrid CBR&RBR algorithm
{ Given a query case C_q and casebase CB,
  $DiagnosticRules$ = **ConstructRules**(CB);
  $PartialSimSet$ = **Match**(C_q, $DiagnosticRules$);
  $OverallSimSet$ = **AllFinding**(C_q);
  $Fqc_{partial}$ = **CompositionalCBR**($C_q, CB, PartialSimSet, k1$);
  $Fqc_{overall}$ = **CompositionalCBR**($C_q, CB, OverallSimSet, k2$);
  $PhiSet$ = **RuleBasedReasoning**(C_q));
  for each disorder d in casebase CB
  { $Fqc(d) = W_p * Fqc_{partial}(d) + W_o * Fqc_{overall}(d)$
    if $((Fqc(d) >= \epsilon) \,||\, (PhiSet(d) > \phi))$
    { **Add_Solution** (d, *solution*); }}
  return *solution*;}

When we perform rule-based reasoning, we use our diagnostic rules to match observed findings, and calculate the possibilities of each disorder occurrence ($PhiSet(d)$). The higher the $PhiSet(d)$ is, the more confidently d should be included into final solution, according to rule-based reasoning. The disorders, either Compositional CBR recommends ($Fqc(d) >= \epsilon$) or rule-based reasoning recommends ($PhiSet(d) > \phi$), will be suggested to the doctors as the final diagnoses. Here we set ϕ be a high threshold, thus only those disorders which rule-based reasoning very much recommends will be considered.

4 Evaluation

This section presents the evaluation of our approach. We applied two casebases from the knowledge-based documentation and consultation system for sonography SonoConsult, an advanced and isolated part of HepatoConsult [11].

4.1 Experimental Setup

Casebase 1 consists of 1370 cases, among which are 31 single disorder cases and 1339 multiple disorder cases. Originally *Casebase 1* has 3506 attributes, consisting of 1911 symptom attributes (findings) and 1595 disorder attributes.

In the procession of analysing the *Casebase 1*, we detect that not all these 3605 attributes are meaningful to us. Lots of attributes do not even have a value in all those 1370 cases, they are all presented by '?'. Thus we preprocess *Casebase 1*, after preprocessing, *Casebase 1* contains an overall number of 137 diagnoses and 286 symptoms, with a mean $M_d = 7.60 \pm 4.12$ of diagnoses per case and a mean $M_f = 52.99 \pm 15.89$ of relevant findings per case and a mean $M_{d/f} = 8.80 \pm 5.65$ of findings per diagnose per case.

The second evaluation casebase (we call *Casebase 2*) consists of 744 cases, among which there are 65 single disorder cases and 679 multiple disorder cases. The casebase contains an overall number of 221 diagnoses and 556 symptoms, with a mean $M_D = 6.72 \pm 04.40$ of diagnoses per case and a mean $M_F = 71.13 \pm 23.11$ of relevant findings per case and a mean $M_{d/f} = 15.46 \pm 12.52$ of findings per diagnose per case.

4.2 Evaluation Metrics

In the usual task of assigning an example to a single category, the accuracy is just the percentage of cases which are correctly classified. But to quantitatively measure the accuracy of multiple disorder diagnosis, the simple accuracy measurement does not fit.

We adopt the Intersection Accuracy [7], as a measure for multiple disorder problems. Intersection accuracy is derived by the two standard measures: *sensitivity* and *Specificity.*

Definition 4 (Intersection Accuracy). *The Intersection Accuracy $\mathcal{IA}(c,c')$ is defined as*

$$\mathcal{IA}(c,c') = \frac{1}{2} \cdot \left(\frac{|\mathcal{D}_c \cap \mathcal{D}_{c'}|}{|\mathcal{D}_c|} + \frac{|\mathcal{D}_c \cap \mathcal{D}_{c'}|}{|\mathcal{D}_{c'}|} \right) \tag{10}$$

where $\mathcal{D}_c \subseteq \Omega_D$ is the set of correct diagnoses, and $\mathcal{D}_{c'} \subseteq \Omega_D$ is the set of diagnoses generated by the system.

Besides Intersection Accuracy, we also measure *Standard Accuracy* which is defined as $(T^+ + T^-)/N$, where T^+(True Positives) is the number of disorders in the correct diagnosis that are also in the system diagnosis ($|\mathcal{D}_c \cap \mathcal{D}_{c'}|$), T^-(True Negatives) is the number of disorders which are neither in the correct diagnosis nor in the system diagnosis, and N is the total number of disorders.

Moreover, sensitivity is defined by (T^+/C^+), where T^+ is True Positives, C^+ is the number of disorders in the correct diagnosis. Sensitivity measure accuracy over the disorders actually present. Specificity is defined as (T^-/C^-), where T^- is True Negatives and C^- is the number of disorders not in the correct diagnosis. Specificity measures the accuracy over disorders which are not present.

When our system diagnoses for patients, it will estimate the confidence level for the results it generates. To those cases with low confidence level, the system will mark these cases as unsolved cases and seek for doctor's help. Thus, another measure is the percentage of the solved cases. We define the mean intersection accuracy to be the average intersection accuracy of all solved cases.

4.3 Refine Compositional CBR with RBR

The objective of this evaluation was to examine at a detailed level the performance of the system with Compositional CBR refined with RBR on both *Casebase 1* and *Casebase 2*.

We used 10 fold cross-validation. The test cases are from one fold of the casebase, while the remaining 9 fold of the casebase will be used to construct diagnostic rules and help case retrieval. The detailed results on *Casecase 1* are presented in Fig. 1. In order to illustrate the performance improvements offered by refining compositional CBR with RBR, Fig. 1. also includes the results of using compositional CBR only. Finally, for comparison purposes, Fig. 1. includes the results of applying naive case-based reasoning on *casebase 1* and the results of only using Rule-based Reasoning on the casebase. (Naive CBR retrieve the most similar case from the casebase and propose the solution of this similar case as final solution for the query case; Rule-based Reasoning uses diagnostic rules to match observed findings for diagnosing)

The graphs in Fig 1 illustrate a number of things:

- Naive Case-based reasoning can not cope with multiple disorder problem efficiently: percentage of solved case stays below 20% for most of the 10 folds, overall percentage of solved case is 16.13%.
- Rule-based reasoning could solve more cases than Naive CBR, but significant decrease in intersection accuracy and standard accuracy have been noticed.
- Compositional CBR significantly improved the performance than naive CBR and Rule-based Reasoning, in both 10 fold measure and the overall results, which demonstrates the relevance of this method in the multiple disorder situation
- After refining compositional CBR with RBR, Intersection Accuracy improved for each fold, although the percentage of solved case slightly drops on some folds. The overall result for solved percentage is 76.64%, where that for compositional CBR is 77.81%. Both Sensitivity and Specificity increase after the refinement.

Fig. 2. presents the detailed results on *Casebase 2* which illustrates the following results:

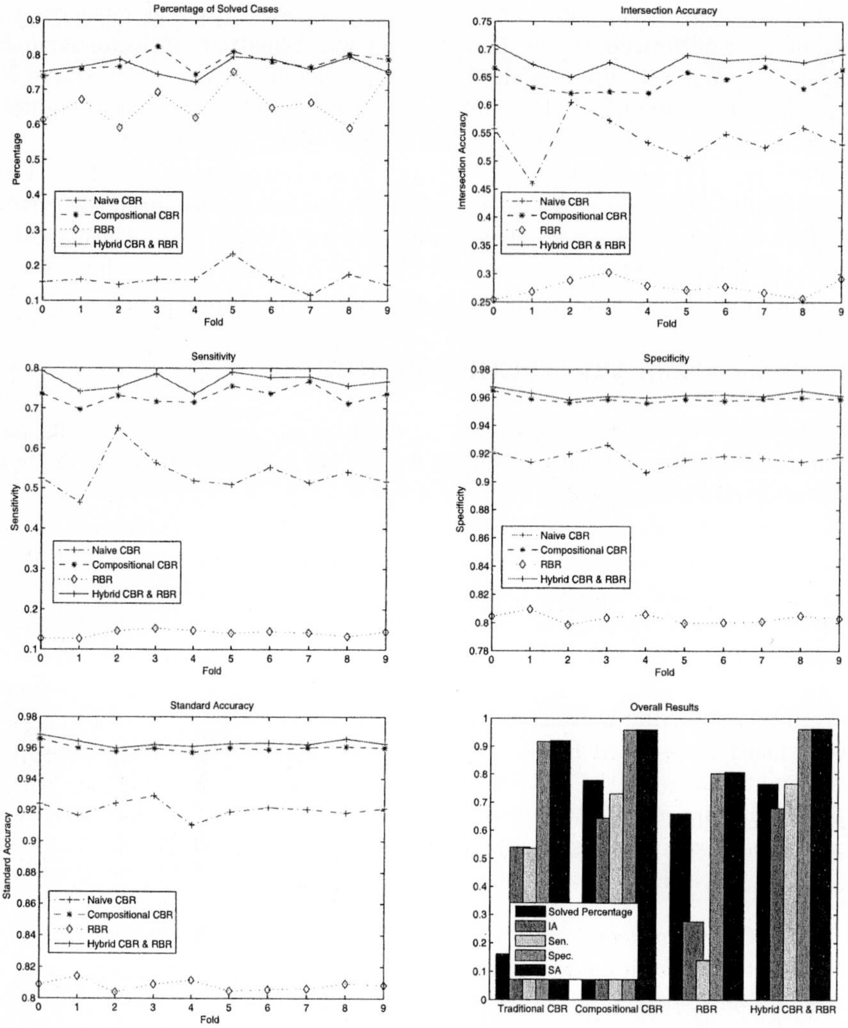

Fig. 1. Results of Casebase 1: 1370 cases

- Naive Case-based reasoning solves less than 10% for each of 10 folds. Intersection Accuracy varies greatly from each fold, which may be due to the size of casebase and Naive CBR fails to find the most similar case with similar diagnostic solution.
- The performance of Compositional CBR and Rule-based Reasoning on *Casebase 2* is similar to that on *Casebase 1*.
- Hybrid CBR and RBR method improved both percentage of solved cases and Intersection Accuracy, compared to Compositional CBR. This is possibly because not only RBR is used to generate candidate diagnose, not also inductive diagnostic rules are helping improve the performance of composi-

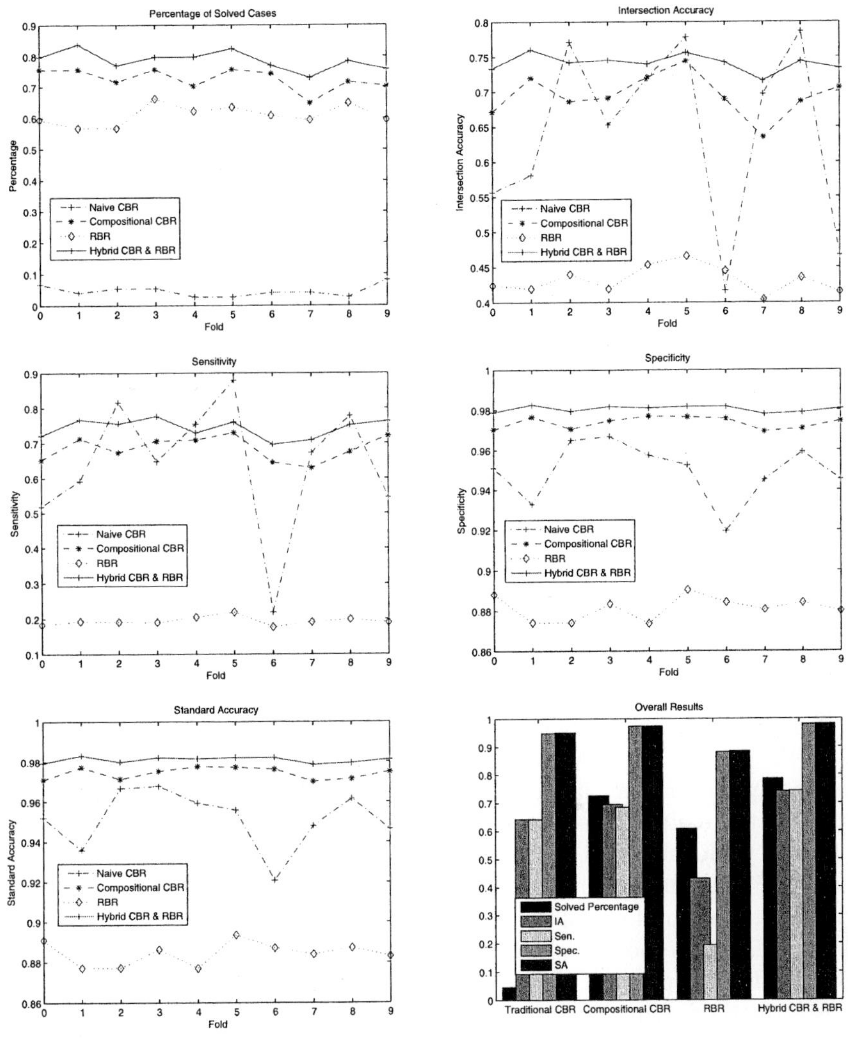

Fig. 2. Results of Casebase 2: 744 cases

tional CBR here by retrieving the cases from the casebase based on partial similarity.

We also notice that Intersection Accuracy is more suitable for evaluating multiple disorder problems than Standard Accuracy. Since the number of potential disorders is much larger than the number of disorders actually present ($T^- >> T^+$), Standard Accuracy stays high for all these four methods compared above. We even can get perfect specificity by assuming that all cases have no disorder and get perfect sensitivity by assuming that all cases have got all disorders. Thus Intersection accuracy is a better measure which avoids such extremes.

4.4 Ours vs. Set-Covering Strategy

In another experiment, we compared our method with Naive CBR, Set-Covering method [4] and Partition Class method [2] on *Casebase 2*. These four methods were implemented and evaluated using the same casebase. The set-covering approach combined case-based reasoning and set-covering models for diagnosis. The partition class method uses partitioning knowledge provided by the expert to split cases into several parts. Decomposed cases are retrieved and combined to get the candidate solution. The evaluation results are shown in the following table.

Table 1. Comparison of the approaches, using 744 cases

744 Cases from the SonoConsult Case Base		
Approach	*solved cases (percentage)*	*mean IA*
Naive CBR	20 (3%)	0.66
Set-Covering	502 (67%)	0.70
Hybrid CBR and RBR	582 (78%)	0.74
Partition Class	624 (84%)	0.73

The results in the first line show, that the Naive CBR method performs poorly with cases having multiple disorders. Naive CBR utilising no adaptation and no additional background knowledge can only solve 3% of the cases in the case base, which is obviously insufficient. Hybrid CBR and RBR solves 582, i.e., 78% of the cases in the case base, with a mean accuracy of 0.74, which performs significantly better than naive CBR. This demonstrates the relevance of this method in the multiple disorder situation.

Hybrid CBR and RBR is performed better than the set-covering approach. This is probably due to: The set-covering approach returns candidate cases with all their solutions and no sophisticated adaptation step is applied, while Hybrid CBR and RBR method compose the final diagnosis in its adaptation process, by only selecting parts of the solutions of the similar cases. The knowledge-intensive method using partition class knowledge performs best. However the multiple CBR method and the set-covering approach do not need background knowledge, and so can be applied in arbitrary situations when the partitioning knowledge is not available, while the partition class strategy needs additional background knowledge.

5 Related Research

Most of CBR/RBR hybrids have taken either of two approaches to integratation. The first approach is to have two separate systems, both CBR and RBR systems can solve the problem independently. If the problem can't be solved by finding a matched case, rule-based reasoning will be called [15]. Or RBR is applied first, when it fails to provide an acceptable solution, CBR will be utilised to retrieve similar cases to generate possible solutions [21]. The second approach is that take either RBR or CBR as the essential system, and the alternative provides some overall functionality. A LA CARTE [18] tunes the rules by using cases which store evaluations and hypothetical alternatives to the rules. Anapron [10] supplements the rule-based reasoning by using cases to fill in small pockets of exceptions in the rules. DIAL [14] combines general rules and previous adaptation cases to learn case adaptation knowledge. CAMPER [16] contributes an initial menu that meets multiple numeric constraints and RBR allows "what if" analysis of alternatives in the domain of nutritional menu planning.

There is some work combining CBR with Model-based reasoning (MBR). The classic system CASEY which diagnoses heart failures [13], integrated case-based reasoning with an early MBR System. When CASEY could not find a close enough case to match a new case, the early MBR system was recalled. CARMA incorporates numeric models developed by entomologists with specific cases of past infestations. The integration of CBR and MBR improves the accuracy, since neither CBR nor MBR alone could produce accurate predictions because of incomplete models and few cases [5].

Our system differs from previous approaches to combination. First of all, our approach generates diagnostic rules by inductive learning, which reduces the knowledge acquisition bottleneck, compared to acquiring rules or models from domain experts. Secondly, CBR is intrinsically enhanced by the RBR module. Case retrieval is enhanced by measuring the partial similarity based on the significant findings derived from rules. Thirdly, when constructing final diagnosis, we combine the results from CBR and RBR by including a given disorder in the final solution of its strongly recommended by either CBR or RBR. Therefore the final solution can be a mixture of CBR recommendations and RBR recommendations.

6 Conclusion and Future Work

In this paper, we introduce a hybrid approach to deal with multiple disorder problems. We combine compositional case-based reasoning and Rule-based Reasoning to construct diagnostic solution from a multiple disorder casebase. Using real medical data, this method has been demonstrated to be promising.

There are several points worth noting about our approach. Firstly, the case-based reasoning method itself corresponds to the diagnosing process that physicians use when they recall former similar diagnostic case for diagnosis. Secondly our method is different from other CBR and RBR hybrids. It generates diagnostic rules by inductive learning, and CBR is intrinsically enhanced by RBR, and it construct final diagnosis by considering both CBR and RBR recommendations. Thirdly, our system deals with the problem of multiple disorder, which hasn't been identified by most knowledge-based diagnostic systems [9]. Fourthly, our approach uses flexible knowledge, and allows the automatic generation of the knowledge base from an existing database, which not only makes the system easy to integrate into existing clinical information systems, but also reduces the knowledge acquisition problem.

There are also many opportunities for future work. Firstly, we believe that employing learning methodology to explore interactions between disorders will help to filter the candidate disorders or to add potential disorders during case adaption. Secondly, experiments in other domains are desirable. Our work has the potential to be used to diagnose multiple faults in other diagnostic problem areas, such as diagnosis problems concerning machine faults.

References

1. M Atzmueller, W Shi, J Baumeister, F Puppe, and J A Barnden. Case-based approaches for diagnosing multiple disorders. In *Proceedings of the 17th International Florida Artificial Intelligence Research Society Conference 2004 (FLAIRS-2004)*, pages 154–159, USA, 2004. AAAI Press.
2. Martin Atzmueller, Joachim Baumeister, and Frank Puppe. Evaluation of two strategies for case-based diagnosis handling multiple faults. In *Proceedings of the 2nd German Workshop on Experience Management(GWEM 2003)*, Luzern, Switzerland, 2003.
3. Martin Atzmueller, Joachim Baumeister, and Frank Puppe. Quality measures for semi-automatic learning of simple diagnostic rule bases. In *Proceedings of the 15th International Conference on Applications of Declarative Programming and Knowledge Management (INAP 2004)*, Potsdam, Germany, 2004.
4. Joachim Baumeister, Martin Atzmueller, and Frank Puppe. Inductive learning for case-based diagnosis with multiple faults. In S.Craw and A.Preece, editors, *Advances in Case-based Reasoning (ECCBR2002)*, pages 28–42. Springer Verlag, 2002. Proceedings of the 6th European Conference on Case-based Reasoning.
5. L. Karl Branting. Integrating cases and models through approximate-model-based adaptation. In *Multimodal Reasoning: Papers from the 1998 AAAI Spring Symposium*, pages 1–5, Menlo Park, CA, 1998. AAAI Press.
6. Bruce G. Buchanan and Edward H. shortliffe, editors. *Rule-Based Expert Systems The MYCIN Experiments of the Stanford Heuristic Programming Project.* Addison-Wesley Publishing Company, 1984.
7. Thompson Cynthia A and Raymond J. Mooney. Inductive learning for abductive diagnosis. In *Proc. of the AAAI-94*, volume 1, pages 664–669, 1994.
8. Linda Gaag and Maria Wessels. Efficient multiple-disorder diagnosis by strategic focusing. In A Gammerman, editor, *Probabilistic Reasoning and Bayesian Belief Networks*, pages 187–204, London, 1995. UCL Press.
9. Lothar Gierl, Mathias Bull, and Rainer Schmidt. Cbr in medicine. In Mario Lenz etc., editor, *Case-based Reasoning Technology:From Foundations to Applications*, pages 273–297. Springer-Verlag, 1998. ISBN 3-540-64572-1.
10. Andrew R. Golding and Paul S. Rosenbloom. Improving rule-based systems through case-based reasoning. In *Proceedings of the National Conference on Artificial Intelligence*, pages 22–27, Anaheim, 1991. MIT Press.
11. Matthias Huettig, Georg Buscher, Thomas Menzel, Wolfgang Scheppach, Frank Puppe, and Hans-Peter Buscher. A Diagnostic Expert System for Structured Reports, Quality Assessment, and Training of Residents in Sonography. *Medizinische Klinik*, 99(3):117–122, 2004.
12. Yeona Jang. *HYDI: A Hybrid System with Feedback for Diagnosing Multiple Disorders.* PhD thesis, Massachusetts Institute of Technology, 1993.

13. Phyllis Koton. *Using Experience in Learning and Problem solving.* PhD thesis, Massachusetts Institute of Technology, 1988.
14. David B. Leake. Combining rules and cases to learn case adaptation. In *Proceedings of the Seventeenth Annual Conference of the Cognitive Science Society*, pages 84–89. Cognitive Science Society, 1995.
15. M. R. Lee, W. Y. Wong, and D. M. Zhang. A knowledge-based framework for clinical incident management. *Expert Systems with Application*, 17:315–325, 1999.
16. C.R. Marling, G.J. Petot, and L.S. Sterling. Integrating case-based and rule-based reasoning to meet multiple design constraints. *Computational Intelligence*, 15(3):308–332, 1999.
17. R. A. Miller, H. E. Pople, and J. D. Myers. Internist-1:an experimental computer-based diagnostic consultant for general internal medicine. *New england Journal of Medicin*, 8(307):468–476, 1982.
18. Yoshio Nakatani. Tuning rules by cases. In Stefan Wess, Klaus-Dieter Althoff, and Michael M. Richter, editors, *Topics in Case-based Reasoning: First European Workshop, EWCBR-93*, pages 313–324, Berlin Heidelberg New York, 1993. Springer-Verlag.
19. Agnieszka Onisko, Marek J. Druzdzel, and Hanna Wasyluk. Extension of the heparii model to multiple-disorder diagnosis. In M. Klopotek etc., editor, *Intelligent Information Systems*, pages 303–313. Physica-Verlag, 2000.
20. Yun Peng and James A. Reggia. *Abductive Inference Models for Diagnostic Problem-Solving.* Springer-Verlag, 1990.
21. J. Surma and K. Vanhoff. Integrating rules and cases for the classification task. In *Lecture Notes in Artificial Intelligence 1010, Proceeding of 1st ICCBR*, pages 325–334. Springer Verlag, 1995.
22. Thaddeus PM Ulzen and Hayley Hamiton. The nature and characteristics of psychiatric comorbidity in incarcerated adolescents. *Original Research*, 43(1), 1998.
23. Staal Vinterbo and Lucila O. Machado. A genetic algorighm approach to multi-disorder diagnosis. *Artificial Intelligence in Medicine*, 18(2):117–132, 2000.
24. Wolfgang Wilke and Ralph Bergmann. Techniques and knowledge used for adaptation during case-based problem solving. In *IEA/AIE (Vol. 2)*, pages 497–506, 1998.
25. D. Randall Wilson and Tony R. Martinez. Improved heterogeneous distance functions. *Journal of Artificial Intelligence Research*, 1997.
26. Robert S. Witte and John S. Witte. *Statistics.* John Wiley & Sons, Inc, 2004.

Case-Based Student Modeling Using Concept Maps

Frode Sørmo

NTNU, Department of Computer Science, Division of Intelligent Systems,
Sem Sælands vei 7-9, NO-7491 Trondheim, Norway
frodeso@idi.ntnu.no

Abstract. Intelligent Tutoring Systems require student models to tailor tutoring to the individual student. This paper presents CREEK-Tutor, an exercise-oriented tutoring system that uses a student modeling technique based on case-based reasoning to find students of similar competence. We describe a similarity measure for concept maps in student modeling is described, and present an initial evaluation of the approach.

1 Introduction

In tutoring and educational support systems, it is important to have a model of the student's competence that is as accurate as possible. This student model can be created in a number of ways, such as asking the student questions before the tutoring session starts, or tracking behavior during the session. Early intelligent tutoring systems using the first method matched the student to prototypical student profiles and used these to customize the tutoring [1]. Using case-based reasoning, the natural choice is to use real student profiles instead of prototypical profiles and using the concrete experience from these students to tailor the new session such as is done for instance in [2,3].

In this paper we present a case-based approach to student modeling that use *concept maps* as a central mechanism for the student himself to represent what he knows about a domain. A concept map is an informal knowledge representation that allows a student to relate concepts in a domain in a way visually similar to what is done in semantic networks. Our hypothesis is that using the student's own representation of what he or she knows in the form of a concept map will help us to predict the student's competence on practical exercises. We test this using an early version of the CREEK-Tutor system, which is an intelligent tutoring system focused on assisting students in solving exercises in areas such as mathematics, computer programming and medical diagnosis, where exercises are usually an important part of the learning process. In order to tie these exercises to the textbook knowledge and help the system in developing an accurate student model, CREEK-Tutor asks the student to draw concept maps.

In Section 2, we will give a brief background of the concept map techniques and introduce a similarity measure for comparing concept maps in the context of student modeling. In Section 3, we present the CREEK-Tutor system where we use case-based reasoning with cases containing concept maps in order to predict student com-

H. Muñoz-Avila and F. Ricci (Eds.): ICCBR 2005, LNAI 3620, pp. 492 – 506, 2005.

petence. Section 4 contains a description of the evaluation of data we collected in an experiment with 48 students using our system to solve Java programming exercises.

2 Concept Maps

Concept maps (sometimes called topic maps) were originally designed as an education aid to assist students in organizing the concepts in a limited domain by connecting them with labeled links [4]. They have since been widely used on many levels of education from elementary school to university studies as an aid to help people conceptualize and organize their knowledge. The concept maps looks similar to semantic networks (see Figure 1 for an example), but while the goal of a knowledge representation in the AI sense is to establish a common representation between human and computer, the concept map is primarily meant as an aid in human learning, organization and communication. Even when concept maps are represented through a computer tool, the computer is not typically expected to understand the contents any more than a word processor would understand this paper. It may provide helpful tips (such as on spell checking in a word processor), but it is not expected to reason over the contents.

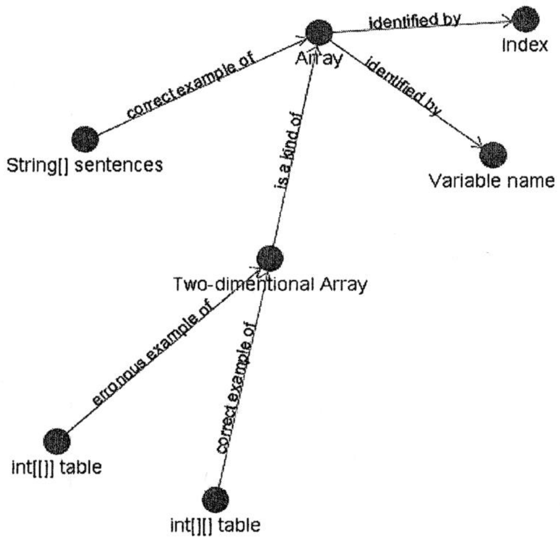

Fig. 1. A simple concept map: "Arrays in Java"

Various styles of concept maps have been used and evaluated in a wide variety of educational settings to present, organize and assess information. The technique has also been used to support performance in business and government, for instance in assisting knowledge management. In this paper, we will focus on using concept maps as evaluation tools, but we recommend [7] for an in-depth survey.

2.1 Concept Maps as Tools of Assessment

Concept maps were introduced by Novak as a way for students to organize their knowledge about a particular topic in a free-form way [4]. Although some simple rules were presented to limit their complexity and to help the student in structuring the concepts, the student was essentially free to form any concepts and links. Because a student's concept map is an expression of the student's knowledge, Novak also suggested that the maps could be used to assess the student's knowledge about a domain. The original proposal from Novak was based on an expert (teacher) examining the concept map and awarding points based on structure, inclusion of relevant concepts, relations and examples. This and later point-based scoring techniques provide guidelines, but they depend to some degree on the judgment of the evaluator and are hard to automate. Completely free-form approaches may also lead the student to (at best) different conceptualizations of the domain and (at worst) to model something quite different from what we wish to evaluate.

In order to guide the students towards modeling the intended topic, it is normal for concept map based assessment tools to use a less free-form approach to mapping. This may range from concept maps that are almost complete where the student's task is to fill in missing links, link names or concept names, to simply providing hints about the central concepts in the domain. Ruiz-Primo[8] identifies a scale from low to high directedness in the approach to concept mapping (Figure 2).

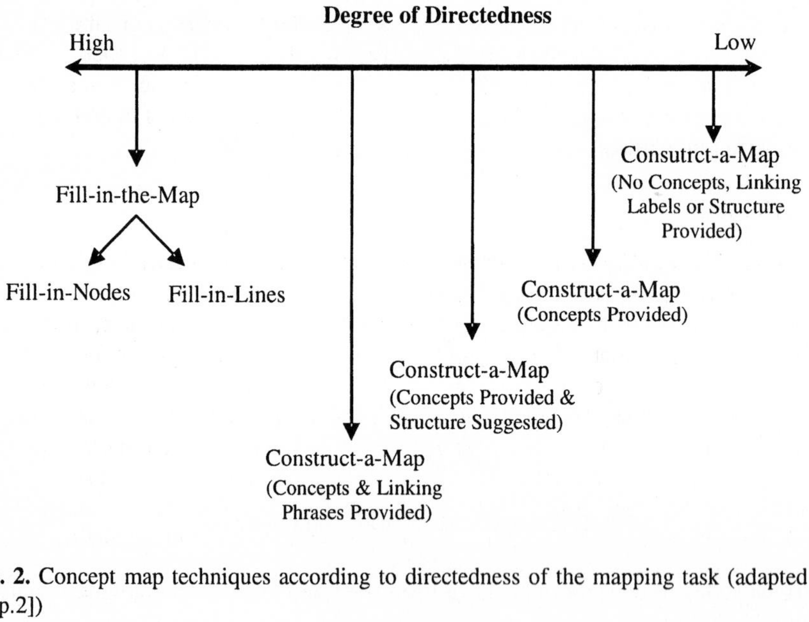

Fig. 2. Concept map techniques according to directedness of the mapping task (adapted from [8, p.2])

The computational approaches to assessing concept maps tend to gravitate towards the high directedness end of this scale. The most obvious reason for this is that because the concept maps are not easily understood by a computer, it is hard to automate the assessment. While constrained maps do not necessarily make it possible to understand the maps, it makes it easier to compare concept maps. This allows a computer system to compare concept maps created by students to a teacher or expert map and thus grade it on the similarity to this map. Researchers from CRESST (Center for

Research on Evaluation, Standards and Student Testing) have investigated computerized techniques using this approach [9]. In their approach, the teacher will first draw a concept map for a topic, and then the concepts and linking names are extracted from this map. The students are then asked to form a map using the same concepts and link-names, which greatly simplifies computational scoring. This method corresponds to the Construct-a-Map (Concepts & Linking Phrases Provided) on the middle of the degree-of-directedness scale in Figure 2.

In our research, we have used a similar approach to what is done in the CRESST research, where the student is presented with a pre-made list of concepts and link labels. This is primarily motivated by pragmatic concerns in allowing the comparisons of maps to be automated, but we also wish to ensure that the maps produced by students are constrained within the topic decided by the teacher, while also allowing the student some degree of freedom of expression. Our approach is different from the CRESST approach in that our goal is not to score the student's concept map by its similarity to the teacher's map, but to use it to find students that are similar in ability.

Leake and Canas et.al. [5,6] have developed a case-based approach to use concept maps in knowledge management, but their goal is not primarily to assess the similarity of different people modeling the same topic. Their goal is to assist domain experts in the process of knowledge modeling. The experts should be treated as equals, and as such they cannot constrain the expression of the modeler to concepts or labels that are used by others. Neither is such information easily available since the experts typically model domains and topics not already known by the system. Because of this, they are faced with the harder task of finding mappings between the elements of concept maps made by different experts.

2.2 Definitions

Concept maps follow the basic syntactical structure of labeled graphs. While there are typically also other considerations when creating concept maps, these are usually not absolute rules and harder to encode explicitly in the syntax. For instance, many mapping methods require that the map should be hierarchical with general concepts generally positioned higher on the surface used to draw the map. This means that when storing conceptual maps, it is important to store the position of nodes on the surface in order to be able to reproduce them exactly as drawn. However, when multiple persons are asked to draw the same map, the positions of the nodes can vary much between different maps even if the graph are the same. Because of this we do not currently use the node's position when computationally comparing concept maps and below we use definitions that do not include positional information.

We will use the definitions of Champin and Solnon [10] to facilitate comparing our approach for the similarity of concept maps to their more general approach for comparing labeled graphs. Given a set of vertex labels L_V and edge labels L_E, Champin and Solnon defines a labeled graphs as a triplet $G = \langle V, r_V, r_E \rangle$ where

- V is a finite set of vertices
- $r_V \subseteq V \times L_V$ defines a relation that associates vertices with labels.
- $r_E \subseteq V \times V \times L_E$ defines a relation that defines the edges between vertices and associates a label with each edge.

Using this definition, r_V and r_E completely describe the graph as they contain both the vertex labels and edge labels.

As an example, the concept map pictured in Figure 1 can be represented formally using the above definition as:

L_V = *{Array, Index, Variable name, String[] sentences, Two-dimensional Array, int[[]] table, int[][] table},*
L_E = *{identified by, is a kind of, correct example of, erroneous example of}*
V = *{a, b, c, d, e, f, g},*
r_V = *{(a, Array) (b, Index) ,(c, Variable name), (d, String[] sentences), (e, Two-dimensional Array), (f, int[[]] table), (g, int[][] table)},*
r_E= *{(a, b, identified by), (a, c, identified by), (d, a, correct example of), (e, a, is a kind of), (f, e, erroneous example of), (g, e, correct example of)}.*

2.3 Similarity of Concept Maps

In order to measure the similarity of two graphs with different sets of vertices, it is necessary to create a mapping function between the sets of vertices and then measure the similarity between each different possible mapping. Unfortunately, the problem of searching this space for the maximum similarity of the two graphs is combinatorial - as Champin and Solnon points out, the problem is more general than the isomorph graph problem that is known to be NP complete. If the task is to compare the similarity of any two concept maps, a greedy approach such as that proposed by Champin and Solnon may be required.

Fortunately, the constraints we have introduced on the concept maps makes comparing the maps much less complex. Although we allow the teacher to first model the domain freely by creating any labeled graph, the student may use only the concepts (vertex labels) and edge labels used in the teacher's map. The student is free to use any of the vertex labels, but may not create more than one vertex using the same label. He may then draw any edge between any of the vertices using edge labels defined in the teacher's map, and these edge labels may be used on as many edges as the student wants. In order to separate the free-form maps created by teachers from the constrained maps formed by students, we will call the former *teacher maps* and the latter *student maps* in the discussion below.

This means that given a teacher map $G_t = <V_t, r_{Vt}, r_{Et}>$, we can compare two student maps represented by two labeled graphs $G_1 =<V_1, r_{V1}, r_{E1}>$ and $G_2 =<V_2, r_{V2}, r_{E2}>$ where $V_1, V_2 \subseteq V_t$. Because both V_1 and V_2 are subsets of V_t, the r_{V1}, r_{V2}, r_{E1} and r_{E2} relations are all defined over the same set of vertices V_t. In essence, the teacher creates the mapping ahead of time, and guarantees a one-to-one correspondence between vertices used in the student maps. Because the vertex labels L_V and edge labels L_E are also the same, the degree of overlap between the graphs can be measured by doing intersection operations on the vertices and edges. Because the major computational complexity associated with comparing graphs is finding this mapping, this makes computing the similarity of this kind of concept maps trivial. We use a similarity measure that is an adaptation of the Jaccard Coefficient also used by Champin and Solnon, which measure the difference between the union and intersection of the two graphs.

Through testing we have found that some students like to place all the available concepts on the drawing surface before drawing relations between them. This may leave them with several concepts that are not connected to the graph, and if they are included in the similarity measure they may introduce inaccuracies when compared to another student that places concepts on the drawing surface on demand. The presence or non-presence of concepts in the graphs are thus not really indicative of similarity. Because of this, we only use the relations to measure the similarity (see Figure 3).

$$\mathrm{sim}(G_1,G_2) = \frac{|r_{E1} \cap r_{E2}|}{|r_{E1} \cup r_{E2}|}$$

Fig. 3. Similarity measure for comparing student maps

Another interesting property of the pre-defined set of vertices and edge labels is that it imposes a finite number of degrees of freedom on the student when creating the concept map. There is $|V|^2 * |L^E|$ possible relations that can be included in a student map formed from any given teacher map. In theory, this allows us to represent the student maps as bit vectors, where each dimension in the vector represents the presence or non-presence of one of the possible relations. Although this would allow standard instance-based similarity measures to be used, it is a space-inefficient representation of the map since very few of the possible relations will be present in any one map.

3 The CREEK-Tutor System

The goal of the CREEK-Tutor system is to use case-based reasoning (CBR) techniques to assist students in solving exercises. We look primarily at domains such as mathematics, computer programming and medical diagnosis where the student typically combines text-book learning with some form of learning through exercises. In particular we would like to address three major issues in these domains:

- Helping the student to find exercises appropriate to his skill level.
- Relating the textbook learning to the exercises.
- Assisting the student in solving the exercises.

In order for the system to assist the student in this, it needs to know the capabilities of the student. To capture this, most intelligent tutoring systems (ITS) have student models that contain an overview of what the student knows about the domain, and this knowledge can then be applied to tailoring the tutoring to the student. Typically, a student model consists of an overlay of an expert model that records whether the student knows about each piece of knowledge in the expert model [1]. In addition, many systems contain a library of common misconceptions in the domain (bug libraries) and attempts to identify if the student is likely to subscribe to any of the known misconceptions. Case-based reasoning has been used in the past to assist in student-modeling (see e.g. [2,3]). Given a student model, an ITS system should find learning tasks for the student that will challenge his skills without being too difficult for the student to solve. This task could be a specific learning goal, or an exercise designed to train some operational skill as in [11] where exercises are formed to train Air Traffic Control operators.

In the previous section, we briefly reviewed how concept maps can be used to help students organize their knowledge and suggested that concept maps might be used to assess a student's knowledge. However, concept maps primarily measure declarative knowledge of the type gained from lectures and textbooks rather than the internalized skill gained from exercises. On the other hand, cases may serve well as examples and potential exercises, but do not serve equally well in associating these concrete examples with generalized knowledge gained, for instance, through reading textbooks.

The CREEK-Tutor system is an approach to exercise tutoring that combines concept maps and case-based reasoning and their relative strengths in episodic and generalized knowledge. The method of the system can be summarized as:

- Exercise Selection:
  1. Ask student to draw a concept map of a particular topic.
  2. Find similar concept maps drawn by other (previous or prototypical) students.
  3. Predict the difficulty of exercises based on performance of students found to have similar concept maps.
  4. Suggest an exercise of appropriate difficulty level.
  5. Justify exercise selection by showing which part of the concept map it addresses.
- Exercise Solution Support:
  1. If student asks for help, look at current state of problem solving.
  2. Match current state of problem solving to reasoning traces performed by previous or prototypical students solving the same exercise
  3. Suggest next step in reasoning trace
  4. Justify reasoning step by displaying the part of matched student's concept map relevant for this reasoning step.

In the work presented in this paper, we will focus on the exercise selection part of the system. Of particular interest is if it is possible to use concept maps in a case-based reasoning technique to assess how difficult a set of exercises will be for a particular student. Will, for instance, two students with similar concept maps be at the same skill level? Will they find the same exercises easy and will they have problems with the same exercises? This is by no means assured – even though concept maps may reflect the level of declarative knowledge, this kind of knowledge does not necessarily correlate with the ability to solve more practical exercises.

In order to test if concept maps may be used in this manner, we have developed an environment for exercise solving for use in beginner courses in Java programming. This domain was chosen for several reasons. First and foremost, it has the combination of textbook and practical knowledge, and exercises are central to teaching programming. Second, the nature of programming makes it easy for computers to evaluate the students' exercises – one obvious test is for instance if the program compiles. Other automated tests may also be designed in a similar fashion to how unit tests are created in normal software development. Finally, as a computer department, we have good access to the students in programming courses, and it is a subject matter we are ourselves fairly well versed in. Our first trials using CREEK-Tutor has not focused on real-time exercise selection for the students, but has served as an environment where student combine concept map creation with solving traditional programming exercises. The results was recorded and used as an offline dataset that contains for each student a concept map and various measures of how the student performed on each programming task. This dataset allows us to analyze various case-based reasoning strategies for predicting a student's competence based on his concept map.

3.1 Representation

For the representation of both cases and concept maps formed by teachers and students, we used the CREEK system. In CREEK, cases and general knowledge are stored in a densely coupled semantic network [12] and this fits will with the graph-based concept maps. The major representation features in CREEK are, as in concept maps, labeled concepts and relations. The concepts in CREEK correspond to the nodes and the relations to the edges the graph-based formalism presented in Section 2.

This means that the teacher may model his expert maps directly in CREEK using a graphical user interface we have developed. This tool is similar in style to the concept map editor from CREEK-Tutor (described in Section 3.2 and shown in Figure 3), but here the teacher is given complete freedom to model his concept map, including the ability to create new labeled concepts, relation labels and relations between concepts.

As described in Section 2, we only allow the students to describe their concept maps using the concepts and relation labels defined by the teacher. They may, however, create any set of relations over these concepts. In order to represent these student maps, we require the capability to represent disparate graphs in the same semantic network and associate them with student cases. This is solved by a recent addition to the representational language of CREEK that makes it possible to store *submodels* containing a subset of the relations and concepts in a given model. These submodels may be associated with a concept in the semantic network, for instance the concept representing a student's case. When a student adds a concept to his concept map by dragging it to the drawing surface, this is represented in CREEK as adding this concept to the submodel associated with the student. Similarly, when the student draws a relation, this relation is added to his submodel.

The case representation we use in this paper only use the concept map in the matching process. In addition to this, retained cases have stored information about which exercises the student managed to solve and which remained unsolved.

3.2 Exercise Environment

The CREEK-Tutor exercise environment is a general environment for solving exercises and may be extended for particular subjects. Typically, the exercise starts with a text page explaining the background for the exercise. Following this, the student is asked to assemble a concept map on the topic of the exercise before he is presented

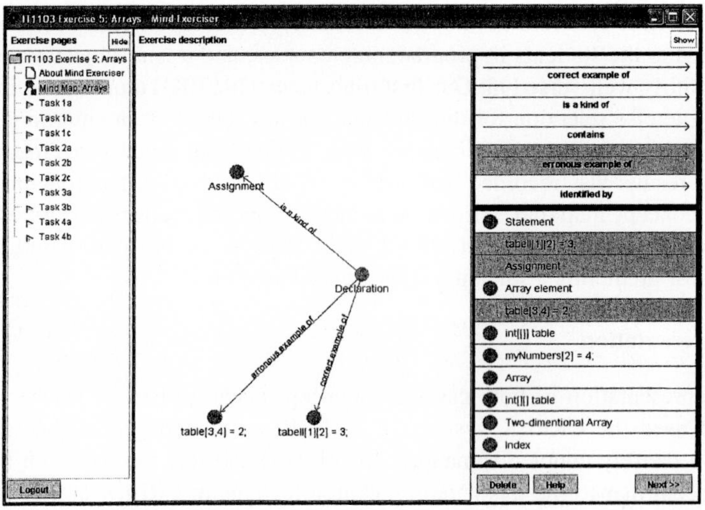

Fig. 4. The CREEK-Tutor page for assembling concept maps. Concepts are dragged-and-dropped using the mouse from the bottom list on the right hand side to the drawing area in the middle. Relation labels are chosen from the top list on the right hand side and are drawn using the mouse. Concepts may only be used once

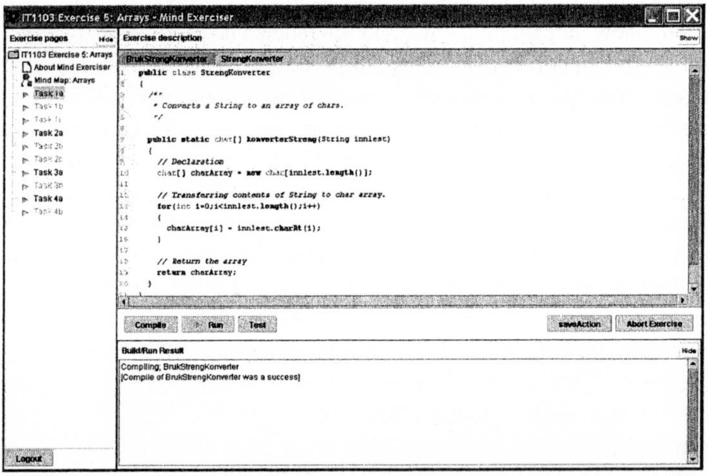

Fig. 5. The programming task environment in CREEK-Tutor. The right bottom pane contains the output from compiling or running the program, while the larger top pane contains an editor where the student may create or change the program code

with a set of tasks to accomplish. In this paper we describe a use of CREEK-Tutor in assisting a Java programming course, and as such these tasks are typically programming problems. The exercise author is also allowed to define a path through the tasks, specifying that one must be solved before another will be accessible.

The first task presented to the user in is assembling a concept map for the topic of the exercise (Figure 4). In designing the exercise for the experiment, we chose to force the students to complete the concept map before they are allowed to start the programming tasks, and they were not allowed to update the concept map once the programming tasks are started. This is done to provide us with a dataset where we know that the concept maps are created before the exercises are solved.

After the student has finished the concept map, the "Next" button takes him to the next task. The tasks are also listed on the left-hand side.

The programming task page is a simple development environment that consists of a short textual description of the task, a text editor (possibly containing a pre-made program that must be modified) and buttons to compile and run the program (Figure 5). In addition the user has a "Test" button that will use automated tests on the program output and source code to determine if the goal of the task has been accomplished.

4 Evaluation

We have performed an initial evaluation of CREEK-Tutor by using the exercise environment described in Section 3.2 to gather data from students performing exercise in an entry level Java programming course. Our first goal is to use this data to test our hypothesis that the concept maps formed by students may be used to predict competence on the programming exercise task. As we have mentioned, this is not necessarily the case since the skill involved in creating actual Java programs are different from the theoretical knowledge about programming. In an attempt to bridge this gap between the theoretical knowledge and practical skill, we included a lot of examples of program code snippets, such as "int[] integerArray" in the concept maps. These statements should be identified as correct or erroneous examples of higher level concepts in the map. For instance, "int[] integerArray" could be connected to "Declaration" by a "correct example of" relation.

The second goal of our experiment was to gather more qualitative information about how student model using concept maps in this domain, with an eye to how we can better integrate the theoretical and practical aspects.

In all, 48 out of approximately 130 students attending the basic programming class volunteered to participate in the experiment. Participation in the experiment gave the same credit as delivering a required exercise in the course, as long as students either finished all the tasks or were present working on them during two three-hour sessions. Only two of the students were able to complete all the tasks in the six-hour period, and these students finished late in the six hour period. This means that the resulting dataset contains a fairly accurate snapshot of what tasks the students were able to solve in the six hours of exercise work.

The students participating in the project could receive help from a teaching assistant during the exercise, but they would not be given the solution of any tasks outright. The students were also allowed to ask each other and discuss the solutions.

Based on the dataset gathered from the CREEK-Tutor environment, we have evaluated our first attempt at creating a case-based reasoner to assess the difficulty of the various programming tasks based on the concept maps of the students. From the dataset, we formed one case for each student. Each case contains the concept map created by the student as well as an entry for each programming task. So far, this entry only contains information about if the student managed to solve this task or not. We have gathered additional information, but this is not used in the quantitative evaluation so far.

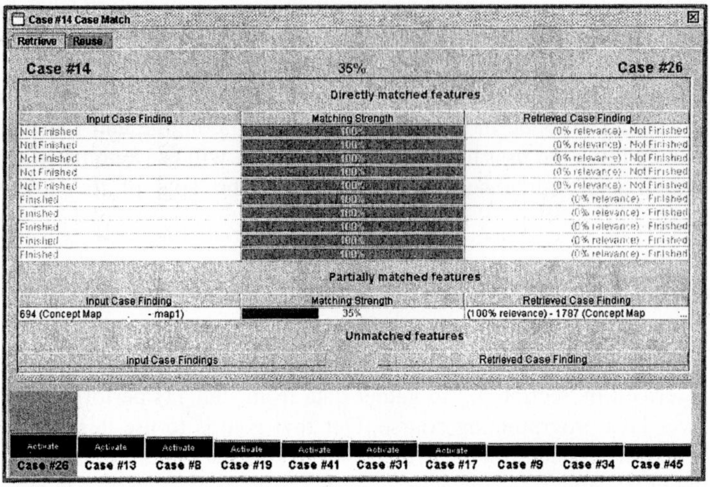

Fig. 6. The result of a case matching in CREEK-Tutor. "Case #14" represents a student, and the only feature used in the case matching is the partially matched concept map that is found to be 35% similar to the concept map of Case #26 (the other features that are 100% matches above are all part of the solution and thus not used for matching). This proved to be a very good solution, as the student represented by Case #26 managed to solve exactly the same exercises as the student represented by Case #14 although their concept maps only overlapped by 35%

The task of the case based reasoner is to predict what exercises a student will be able to solve based on this student's concept map. This is similar to classic machine-learning classification tasks, except that the data we use as the basis for classification is in the format of a labeled graph.

In the retrieval phase of the case-based reasoning, CREEK-Tutor attempts to match the concept map of the input case to all the concept maps of the students in the case base using the similarity measure provided in Section 2.3. Figure 6 contains a sample output of a classification of a case using this method.

In evaluating the performance of the case-based reasoner on our dataset, we did a standard leave-one-out cross validation where we removed one case at a time from the case base and used the remaining cases to classify the removed case. The goal of the classification was to predict how the student performed on the ten programming tasks included in the exercise. Initially, we used only the nearest case, and thus the classifications consisted of copying the solution profile from this case. When more than one case were used, the k nearest neighbors voted on each task.

We compared this with a baseline where for each task the majority class was chosen as the prediction. Although almost all students were able to solve the easy tasks, very few solved the most difficult tasks. This caused the frequency of the majority class to vary widely from one task to the next. In particular the very easy and very hard tasks had a very high frequency for the majority class, but the middle difficulty tasks discriminated better between the students, giving a baseline close to 50% (see Figure 7).

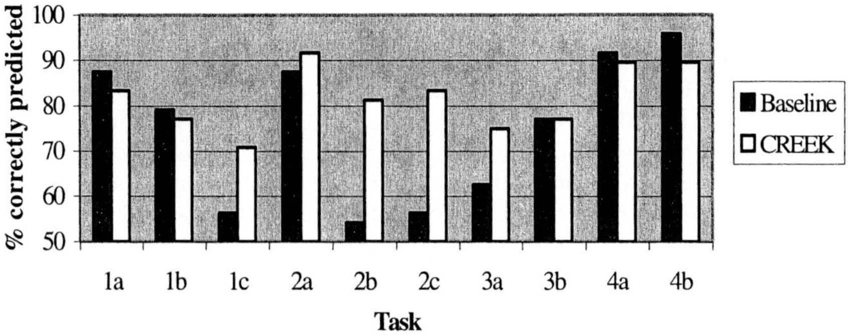

Fig. 7. Breakdown of the performance of the CREEK-Tutor classifier compared to the baseline for each programming task given to the student. While the baseline for the very easy tasks (1a,1b and 2a) and very hard tasks (3b, 4a and 4b) are high and hard to beat, Creek show a very large improvement over the baseline in the more discriminate tasks (1c, 2b, 2c and 3a)

The results of testing showed that CREEK-Tutor were able to predict correctly how the student fared on an average of 8.42 out of the 10 tasks, or 84%. This compares to the baseline based on the majority class that guessed on average 7.65 correct out of the 10 tasks, or 77%. The CREEK-Tutor prediction is significantly ($p < 0.05$ on a standard paired T-Test) better than the baseline. When we break down the predictions to the individual tasks, it becomes clearer what is the source of this increase – CREEK-Tutor is seemingly able to accurately predict what students will be able to solve the tasks of middle difficulty, although there is far less room for improvement over the baseline on the less discriminating tasks.

We did find, however, that some of the concept maps overlapped very little with any other maps. If only the cases where the best matched case were over 20% similar on the concept map was included, we were left with 28 cases. Repeating our test with these 28, we found that the accuracy increased to 91% (significant to $p < 0.01$).

When we first found these results, we were a bit surprised by how well the case-based reasoner predicted exercise competence from the concepts maps. Because the concept maps focus more on the theoretical side of the programming, we did not expect the correlation to be quite as strong. Further investigations revealed that there is an alternative reason that may explain these results – student cooperation. In our data collection, we attempted to stay as close to real-life exercise solving as possible, which allowed students to cooperate and discuss the solutions. While we informally observed that many students worked alone, quite a few students discussed the tasks in pairs (although groups bigger than pairs were not observed). This means that while the students separately solved the task through the systems, it is likely that they were influenced by their cooperation partner. If this is the case, it is likely that not only would their concept maps be similar, but it is also more likely that they were able to solve the same exercises. Since we in our leave-one-out cross validation technique only remove one of the student cases at a time, any cooperating partner will be left in the case base, and it is likely to be the most similar case.

We have yet to conclude the degree to which the case based reasoner predicts cooperation or competence based on the concept maps. We have, however, done some further analysis in order to come closer to an answer. We repeated the evaluation using k=3 so that the result is averaged over the three most similar cases. As we have mentioned, we did not observe significant cooperation in groups over two, so this should diminish the influence of eventual cooperation partners. This method did indeed show a drop in the accuracy to 78%, which is not a significant increase over the baseline. However, this includes very many matches where the concept maps matched very poorly. If we again limit ourselves to the cases that were classified with an average of at least 20% similarity, we find that 26 cases fulfill this criterion, and the prediction accuracy increases to 87% compared to a baseline for this set of cases of 77% (significant to $p < 0.05$).

In our last experiment we purposely ignore the most similar case when doing retrieval and use only the second most similar case. This is an unusual approach to case-based reasoning, but in our situation it should eliminate eventual cooperation partners, if we assume that they are represented by the most similar case. However, it also ignores the most similar case for those students that did not cooperate or where the cooperation partner was not very similar. At the very least, it ought to give us a lower bound, given that there is no cooperation in groups of more than two. The test on the full case base showed that the accuracy decreased dramatically when using this approach – the classifier achieved only 76% accuracy, which is a slight decrease in accuracy compared to the baseline, although this is not a significant difference.

5 Conclusion

We have demonstrated that although concept maps may seem like complex structures, they are not very computationally expensive to match in a case-based reasoning process as long as they relate to a common teacher map that defines the concepts and relation labels.

Unfortunately, our evaluation leaves us unable to conclude at this time if concept maps will be useful in predicting how students that are not cooperating perform on exercises. It is likely that additional experiments are required for conclusive evidence on this. Our qualitative analysis of the concept maps suggests that the students produce surprisingly different maps even with the restrictions imposed. Although many of these differences result from confusion about the domain, others are just different from the teacher's conceptualization but not necessarily wrong. This suggests that there may be something to be gained from using case-based reasoning to match a student's concept map to other students' maps instead of comparing it to the teacher map, although the approach used so far may be too unconstrained to get good matches because students with low knowledge of the topic tend to create maps that have large parts that do not match any other student (or teacher) maps. For this reason, we would like to explore if partial concept maps may be indicative of particular misconceptions so that these can be identified even in a "noisy" map.

We would also like to investigate further how the declarative nature of concept maps may be brought closer to the practical nature of exercises. Our first attempts at bridging this gap included using program statements as concrete examples in the concept maps, but further analysis is required to see if this approach is enough to make the concept maps relevant for the exercises.

The concept maps may also serve as knowledge sources for explanation. For instance, partial concept maps can be associated with each exercise, and exercises can be matched with student's concept maps with the goal of identifying those maps that require relatively small changes in the student's current map, along with an illustration of what changes – additions or modifications – the system suggests will be illustrative for the exercise. In this way, the CBR system helps the student associate declarative and practical knowledge.

References

1. Wenger, E.: Artificial Intelligence and Tutoring Systems: Computational and Cognitive Approaches to the Communication of Knowledge. Morgan Kaufmann, Los Altos, CA (1987)
2. Seitz A.: A case-based methodology for planning individualized case oriented tutoring. Case Based Reasoning Research and Development Third International Conference on Case Based Reasoning, ICCBR 99 Proceedings (Lecture Notes in Artificial Intelligence Vol 1650). Springer Verlag, Berlin, Germany (1999) 318-28
3. Shiri A., Aimeur E., Frasson C.: SARA: a case-based student modeling system. Advances in Case Based Reasoning 4th European Workshop, EWCBR 98 Proceedings. Springer Verlag, Berlin, Germany (1998) 394-403
4. Novak, J.D: and Gowin, D.B: Learning How to Learn. Cornell University Press, Ithaca, NY (1984)
5. Canas, A.,Leake., D.B., Maguitman, A.: Combining Concept Mapping with CBR: Towards Experience-Based Support for Knowledge Modeling. Proceedings of the Fourteenth International Florida Artificial Intelligence Research Society Conference. AAAI Press, Menlo Park (2001) 286-290.
6. Leake, D.B., Maguitman, A. and Canas, A.: Assessing Conceptual Similarity to Support Concept Mapping. Proceedings of the Fifteenth International Florida Artifical Intelligence Research Socity Conference. AAAI Press, Menlo Park (2001) 186-172
7. Canas, A.: A Summary of Literature Pertaining to the Use of Concept Mapping Techniques and Technologies for Education and Performance Support, http://www.ihmc.us/users/acanas/Publications/ConceptMapLitReview/IHMC%20Literature%20Review%20on%20Concept%20Mapping.pdf (last access 06.02.05) (2003)
8. Ruiz-Primo, M.A.: Examining Concept Maps as an Assessment Tool. Proc. Of the First Int. Conference on Concept Mapping. Pamplona, Spain, http://cmc.ihmc.us/papers/cmc2004-036.pdf (last access 13.04.05) (2004).
9. O'Neil, H.F., Klein D.C.D.: Feasibility of Machine Scoring of Concept Maps. CSE Technical Report 460. CRESST (1997)
10. Champin, P.A. and Solnon, C.: Measuring the Similarity of Labeled Graphs. Case-Based Reasoning Research and Development: Proc. Of ICCBR 2003. Springer, Trondheim, Norway (2003) 80-95

11. Dong Mei Zhang, Alem L.: Using case-based reasoning for exercise design in simulation-based training. Intelligent Tutoring Systems Third International Conference, ITS '96 Proceedings. Springer Verlag, Berlin, Germany (1996) 560-568
12. Aamodt A.: A Knowledge-Intensive Integrated Approach to Problem Solving and Sustained Learning. PhD. Dissertation. University of Trondheim, Department of Electrical Engineering and Computer Science, Trondheim (1991)

Learning Similarity Measures: A Formal View Based on a Generalized CBR Model

Armin Stahl

German Research Center for Artificial Intelligence DFKI GmbH,
Research Group Image Understanding and Pattern Recognition (IUPR),
Erwin-Schrödinger-Str. 57, 67663 Kaiserslautern, Germany
Armin.Stahl@dfki.de

Abstract. Although similarity measures play a crucial role in CBR applications, clear methodologies for defining them have not been developed yet. One approach to simplify the definition of similarity measures involves the use of machine learning techniques. In this paper we investigate important aspects of these approaches in order to support a more goal-directed choice and application of existing approaches and to initiate the development of new techniques. This investigation is based on a novel formal generalization of the classic CBR cycle, which allows a more suitable analysis of the requirements, goals, assumptions and restrictions that are relevant for learning similarity measures.

1 Introduction

The concept of similarity is certainly one of the most important and characteristic aspects of Case-Based Reasoning (CBR). In spite of the importance of similarity measures, clear methodologies for defining them efficiently and accurately are still missing. Instead, similarity measures are often defined in an ad hoc manner or one simply applies quite general distance metrics. When defining more complex measures that take account of domain knowledge, this is often done in an unstructured and not in a goal-directed fashion and often only experienced and skilled knowledge engineers are able to produce satisfactory results. Therefore, different machine learning approaches have been developed in order to facilitate the definition of similarity measures. However, the choice and application of an accurate learning approach is also a difficult task since one often is not aware of the actual requirements, goals, assumptions and restrictions of the application domain, the employed CBR system and the available learning techniques. Hence, learning is often performed in a trial-and-error fashion. Basically, when considering the application of learning techniques, some important questions have to be answered first, for example:

- What is the desired semantics of the similarity measure?
- What kind of training data is suitable and how can it be acquired?
- Which learning techniques are suitable to achieve best results?

H. Muñoz-Avila and F. Ricci (Eds.): ICCBR 2005, LNAI 3620, pp. 507–521, 2005.

Until now little or no work to clarify these questions and to provide a categorization of current learning approaches has been done. Only for learning feature weights in classification tasks such a categorization has been provided [19]. One problem when trying to answer the questions above is, that this requires a deeper understanding of the relationships between CBR functionality, application requirements, training data and available learning algorithms. In order to be able to analyze these relationships, a unified terminology and a certain degree of formality is mandatory. Unfortunately, the common CBR model [2] seems not to be suited to represent a good foundation because it is described rather informally and does not accurately model all important aspects.

Therefore, the goal of this paper is to provide a formal foundation and terminology for analyzing and categorizing approaches to learning similarity measures. Therefore, first a generalization and formalization of the classic CBR cycle is introduced in Section 2. An overview and first categorization of existing learning techniques is presented in Section 3. Finally, in Section 4 we examine some important issues for future research towards improved approaches for learning similarity measures.

2 A Formal Generalized Model for CBR

The classical CBR cycle introduced by Aamodt and Plaza [2], consisting of the four basic steps *retrieve*, *reuse*, *revise* and *retain*, is certainly the most established and accepted model for CBR. The success of this model may be explained by its simplicity and clarity, in particular for CBR novices. However, for describing and analyzing certain current research issues and popular application scenarios we argue, this classical model has some crucial limitations.

2.1 Limitations of the Classical CBR Cycle

In the following, we want to discuss some of the deficiencies of the classical CBR cycle in order to motivate the introduction of a more generalized model capturing also some of the current developments in CBR research.

CBR-Scenarios: Problem-Solving vs. Utility-Oriented Matching. One motivation of CBR was to imitate problem solving strategies of humans in order to enable computers to solve problems more efficiently. Hence, the traditional CBR cycle assumes a typical problem solving situation, i.e. the input—also called *query*—is expected to describe a problem and the output is expected to describe a corresponding solution suggestion. Typical application tasks that fit this assumption are classic problems of artificial intelligence such as classification, diagnosis, configuration or planning.

This assumption was the decisive factor for the structure of today's CBR systems, the underlying concepts, and the central paradigm of CBR: *"Similar problems have similar solutions"*. One quite important consequence of the problem solving scenario is the traditionally used structure to described case knowledge. Here, a case is supposed to consist of the following two distinct parts:

Problem part: The problem part describes a particular problem situation of the past, e.g. in a diagnosis situation a set of symptoms and other relevant information about the entity under consideration.

Solution part: The solution part describes a corresponding solution successfully applied to solve the past problem, e.g. a correct diagnosis and a corresponding therapy. Although cases are usually supposed to contain only 'good' solutions, the solution part may contain any further information that might be useful when trying to reuse the solution, e.g information about the quality of the solution, justifications, explanations, etc.

In classical CBR applications, one is often interested only in the information contained in the solution part, whereas the problem part is used as an index to find useful solution information. However, in recent years CBR techniques have been applied very successfully to other application tasks that actually do not match this problem solving scenario. One important characteristic of such scenarios is a different case structure, where a clear distinction between a problem and a solution part is impossible. A typical example of such applications is product recommendation[8]. Here, queries represent requirements and wishes of customers with respect to desired products. Cases contain descriptions of available products and the task of the CBR system is to identify particular products that are most suitable to fulfill the given customer demands.

In principle this task could be solved in the traditional case-based manner. Therefore, one would have to store customer queries of the past—representing the problems—together with the description of successfully sold products—representing the solutions. Here, it would be sufficient to store only a product-ID to describe products uniquely. New customer queries then could be compared with customer queries of the past using similarity measures in order to select products that probably will also be bought by current customers.

However, most case-based product recommendation systems follow a different approach. Here, a case typically consists of a detailed description of an available product solely. In order to select suitable products, a customer query is compared with these product descriptions by applying an accurate similarity measure.

The product description can be interpreted as the solution part of traditional cases but the traditional problem part (here this would be a past customer query) is missing completely. Hence, such systems compare problems, namely current customer queries, directly with solutions, namely product descriptions. This procedure does not really comply with the traditional idea of CBR. Instead, it may be characterized as *utility-oriented matching* [3] because one tries to estimate the utility of a solution for a given problem more or less directly. Similar situations also occur in other applications scenarios, for example, in the area of Knowledge Management. Most of those scenarios have in common that they may be seen more as intelligent information retrieval than actual problem solving.

Advanced CBR Techniques. Another limitation of the traditional CBR cycle is that it does not consider some crucial aspects and issues of current CBR systems sufficiently which have come into the focus of research just recently. Some quite important of those issues are for example:

Dialog Strategies: The traditional CBR cycle assumes a formalized query given as input prior to the actual reasoning process without considering how this query can be obtained. However, the efficient acquisition of an accurate query is a crucial issue in diagnosis tasks and has also come into focus of research in the area of product recommendation systems recently [14].

Explanation: A popular topic of current CBR research is explanation [1]. However, the traditional CBR cycle does not explicitly consider the generation of explanations about presented solutions or the underlying reasoning process.

Feedback: An important characteristic of the traditional CBR cycle is the possibility to learn new cases during the retain phase. Although Aamodt and Plaza have mentioned the possibility to learn not only cases but also general knowledge (e.g. refining indexes), the traditional CBR cycle does not explicitly introduce a feedback loop which is required to realize advanced learning approaches.

2.2 A Formal Generalization of the Classical CBR Cycle

In this section we introduce a more general and more formal model for CBR. This model aims to avoid some of the deficiencies of the classical CBR cycle. Although it does not capture all aspects of current CBR research, at least it represents a foundation for analyzing certain CBR functionality in more detail. Our main goal is to introduce a formalism that can be used to examine important aspects to be considered when developing approaches for learning similarity measures. In the future the model may be extended to describe other, still disregarded CBR aspects. An illustration of the model is shown in Fig. 1.

The starting point is a given informal *situation* s in the application environment which triggers some more or less abstract information need. The task of a

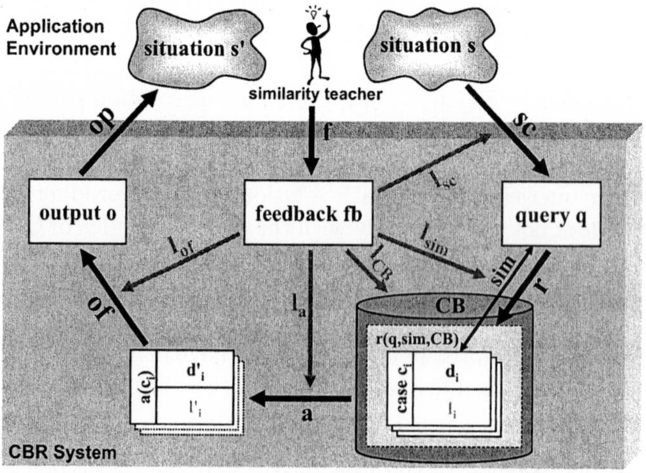

Fig. 1. A Formal Model for CBR

CBR system is to provide the necessary information by generating a corresponding output o. For example, in the traditional problem solving scenario, s is an unsolved problem for which a solution is required and o may be the description of suitable solution or a solution method, respectively. In a first step the situation s has to be described formally in order to obtain a query q that can be processed by the CBR system:

Definition 1 (Situation-Characterization, Query). *A situation characterization $sc : \mathcal{S} \rightarrow \mathcal{Q}$ where $\mathcal{S}$ is the situations space and $\mathcal{Q}$ is the query space, characterizes the informal situation s formally through query $q = sc(s)$. The set of all situation characterizations is denoted by $\mathcal{SC}$.*

In practice, sc implements certain transactions between the application environment and the CBR system. In the simplest case it might import query data from some data source but usually the query will be acquired from the user, for example, by providing a query form or by performing an elaborate dialog [14].

In the next step, q has to be compared with cases in the case base in order to select cases that are expected to contain information that is useful for satisfying the information need of s.

Definition 2 (Case, Case Characterization, Case Lesson, Case Space). *A case c is a tuple $(d, l) \in \mathcal{D} \times (\mathcal{L} \cup \emptyset)$ where d is called a case characterization and l is called a case lesson. $\mathcal{D}$ and $\mathcal{L}$ are the corresponding spaces of case characterizations and case lessons. $\mathcal{C} = \mathcal{D} \times \mathcal{L}$ is called the case space and the set of available cases $CB = \{c_1, \ldots, c_m \mid c_i \in \mathcal{C}\}$ is called the case base.*

In our model we explicitly allow empty lesson parts, i.e. a case may consist of a characterization only. It is important to note, that case characterizations have not necessarily to represent problem descriptions but any information that is useful to estimate the utility of cases. This means, that cases may also be characterized by using solution information.

Definition 3 (Similarity Measure). *A similarity measure is a function $sim : \mathcal{Q} \times \mathcal{D} \rightarrow [0, 1]$. To simplify the notation we write $sim(q, c)$ instead of $sim(q, d)$ for representing the similarity between a query q and a case $c = (d, l)$. The set of all similarity measures is denoted by $\mathcal{SIM}$.*

Definition 4 (Retrieval Function). *A retrieval function $r : \mathcal{Q} \times \mathcal{SIM} \times \mathcal{P}(CB) \rightarrow \mathcal{P}(CB)$ returns a subset of the case-base CB for a given query q according to a given similarity measure $sim \in \mathcal{SIM}$. The returned cases $c_r \in r(q, sim, CB)$ are assumed to be ordered w.r.t. to their corresponding similarity values $sim(q, c_r)$.*

We do not make any assumptions about the realization of r, e.g. it might simply return the most similar case, i.e. $r(q, sim, CB) = \arg\max_{c_i \in CB} sim(q, c_i)$. After having retrieved a set of cases, the information contained in the retrieved cases may be adapted in order to construct a new, more accurate case:

Definition 5 (Adaptation Function). *An adaptation function $a : \mathcal{Q} \times \mathcal{P}(CB) \rightarrow \mathcal{C}^k$ generates a set of new cases $\{c_{a_1}, \ldots, c_{a_k}\}$ given a set of input cases*

$\{c_1, \ldots, c_n\}$ with $c_i \in CB$, $n, k \geq 1$ and a query q. The set of all adaptation functions is denoted by $\mathcal{A}$.

Typically it holds $k \leq n$. If a single adapted case c_{a_i} is constructed from several input cases, this is called *compositional adaptation*. A simple example are voting policies like those applied in k-nearest-neighbor classification. In systems without adaptation, a is considered to be the identity function with respect to the input cases. The result of the adaptation process is used as source information for generating the final output of the CBR system:

Definition 6 (Output Function, Output Space). *Given a query q and set of cases $\{c_1, \ldots, c_n\}$, the output function $of : \mathcal{Q} \times \mathcal{P}(C) \rightarrow \mathcal{O}$ generates an output $o = of(q, c_1, \ldots, c_n)$ where $\mathcal{O}$ is the space of outputs. $\mathcal{OF}$ denotes the set of all output functions.*

In principle one might put a lot of 'intelligence' into the output function, but in practice the output function typically is used

- to select appropriate cases to be returned to the application environment, e.g. to ensure the right degree of diversity,
- to extract the required information from the given cases, e.g. class labels,
- to generate additional explanations in order to explain the result of the CBR system to the users.

The resulting output then is returned to the application environment in order to satisfy the information need of the initial situation s:

Definition 7 (Output Processing Function). *The output processing function $op : \mathcal{S} \times \mathcal{O} \rightarrow \mathcal{S}$ generates a new situation $s' = op(s, o)$ by applying the output o to situation s within the application environment.*

In practice, the output processing function typically is an informal process which is executed within the application environment with little or no support from the CBR system. For example, a suggested therapy in a medical diagnosis situation will be applied by a doctor where the new situation s' will be a modified state of health of the patient. If s' is still associated with an unsatisfied information need, it might be used as a new initial situation for executing the cycle again.

For enabling a CBR system to improve its performance by applying learning strategies it must receive feedback from the application domain about the actual usefulness of its output:

Definition 8 (Feedback Function). *The feedback function $f : \mathcal{S} \times \mathcal{O} \rightarrow \mathcal{F}$ evaluates the usefulness of output o for situation s and returns some feedback $fb = f(s, o)$, where $\mathcal{F}$ is called the feedback space.*

Here, we do not assume a particular form of feedback but in Section 3.2 we will discuss this issue with respect to learning similarity measures in more detail. Feedback may be used by the CBR system to improve its functionality by modifying one or several of its knowledge containers [13]:

Definition 9 (Learning Functions). *The following functions allow to modify the case base CB, the similarity measure sim, and the adaptation function a w.r.t. given feedback:*

$$l_{CB} : \mathcal{Q} \times \mathcal{O} \times \mathcal{F} \times \mathcal{P}(C) \to \mathcal{P}(C)$$

$$l_{sim} : \mathcal{F} \times \mathcal{SIM} \to \mathcal{SIM}$$

$$l_a : \mathcal{F} \times \mathcal{A} \to \mathcal{A}$$

The function l_{CB} realizes the traditional idea of learning in CBR systems, namely a modification of the case base, e.g. by storing new or deleting obsolete cases. While l_{sim} and l_a allow to learn general knowledge already considered in the classical CBR cycle, one might also introduce similar learning functions, e.g. l_{sc} for improving dialog strategies [14] or l_{of} for improving the generation of explanations.

2.3 Advantages of the Generalized CBR Model

In principle, our general model can be divided into the same phases as the classical CBR cycle: The functions sc and r implement the retrieval phase, the functions a and of implement the reuse phase, the functions op and f represent the revise phase and the learning functions l_x implement the retain phase.

However, by abstracting from the traditional problem solving scenario, the model is more suitable to describe popular 'modern' application scenarios such as product recommendation. For example, we do not assume that a case consists of a problem and a solution part. Instead, cases may only consist of case characterizations that may describe arbitrary information. This also means that queries and case characterizations do not necessarily have the same semantics, for example, they do not both represent problem descriptions. We will discuss this issue again in Section 4.

By introducing additional processes in the form of the situation characterization and the output function, our model can also be used to describe new research directions such as dialog strategies and explanations more accurately than possible with the classical CBR cycle. Moreover, by introducing the feedback function and a set of learning functions, it enables a better description of advanced learning approaches beyond storing of new cases.

However, the model in its current version is not intended to capture all aspects of any CBR application. For example, more complex dialog strategies that involve case retrieval cannot be described exclusively with sc but require a repeated execution of the entire cycle. Nevertheless, the model may represent a good foundation to be extended for explaining other functionality of CBR systems.

2.4 The Goal of a CBR System

Before we use the introduced model to analyze the task of learning similarity measures, first we will discuss some important general consequences of it.

A CBR system's goal is to generate an output o that is maximally useful for satisfying the information need of a given situation s, i.e. it should help to reach a new, improved situation s' by exploiting the information contained in o. In a formal view, an optimal CBR system should realize the following goal function:

Definition 10 (Goal Function, Utility Function). *The goal function* $g : \mathcal{S} \rightarrow \mathcal{O}$ *generates an output* o *that is maximally useful for a given situation* s*, i.e.* $g(s) := \arg\max_{o \in \mathcal{O}} u(s, o)$*, where* $u : \mathcal{S} \times \mathcal{O} \rightarrow \mathbb{R}$ *is the domain specific utility function.*

In practice u is usually only implicitly and informally defined within the application environment. However, during the lifetime of a CBR system certain information about u may be provided by the feedback function f. Depending on the application scenario, u may be influenced in many ways, e.g., by

- the correctness of suggested solutions,
- the outputs' degree of applicability or reusability,
- the satisfaction of the user (e.g. a customer) or
- the output's information gain for the user.

The basic idea of a CBR system is to acquire and encode knowledge about u by using different knowledge containers [13], namely the *vocabulary*, the *case base*, the *similarity measure* and the *adaptation knowledge*[1]. The vocabulary defines the important aspects required to describe situations, cases, outputs and feedback, i.e. it determines $\mathcal{Q}$, $\mathcal{C}$, $\mathcal{O}$ and $\mathcal{F}$. Traditionally, the cases represent known points of u corresponding to a maximal or at least high utility and adaptation knowledge defines knowledge about additional points or certain subspaces of u. Finally, the similarity measure should encode knowledge about the relationships between different points of the input space of u. However, due to the difficulty of acquiring this knowledge, the employed similarity measures often only represent quite simple heuristics about the typically expected shape and smoothness of u.

In order to facilitate the acquisition of similarity knowledge and the definition of more accurate similarity measures, several learning approaches have been developed, e.g. see [19,16]. In the following we investigate important general issues of such learning approaches in more detail on the basis of the previously introduced formal CBR model.

3 Learning Similarity Measures: A Formal Analysis

CBR systems often generate output that is composed of a set of independent output alternatives. This functionality is typically desired when presenting the output to human users, e.g. alternative products to customers. Here, we assume that only single retrieved cases $c_r \in r(q, sim, CB)$ are adapted and used to generate a single output alternative o_r. This means, first we do not consider

[1] In our formal model represented through the adaptation function a.

compositional adaptation. The entire output then is an ordered collection of alternative outputs $o = (o_1, o_2, \ldots, o_k)$, where the order is based on the computed similarities, i.e. it holds $\forall\ 1 \leq i < j \leq k\ sim(q, c_i) \geq sim(q, c_j)$. We assume that the utility of o only depends on the sum of the o_r's utilities and their ranking[2]. According to our formal CBR model the utility of an output alternative o_r is defined as

$$u(s, o_r) = u(s, of(q, a(q, c_r))) = u(s, of(sc(s), a(sc(s), c_r)))$$

Moreover, we assume that $u(s, o_r)$ can be expressed by numbers of the interval $[0, 1]$, i.e. it holds $u : S \times O \to [0, 1]$ where a value of 1 represents the maximal possible and 0 represents the minimal possible utility. From now on, we assume that a and of are static, i.e. that the adaptation and output function are not modified during the lifetime of the CBR system.

3.1 Semantic of Similarity Measures

In general, the basic task of a similarity measure is to estimate the a-posteriori utility of a given case c_r, i.e. in the best case $sim(q, c_r)$ should approximate the a-priori unknown utility $u(s, of(q, a(q, c_r)))$ as closely as possible. This would obviously require that sim is completely informed about the remaining parts of the CBR system, namely the functions a and of as well as about the external utility function u. In practice this ideal property of sim usually cannot be achieved, and hence sim represents a more or less well informed heuristic only.

Retrieval Requirements. Before defining a similarity measure for a particular CBR application one should be aware of the application specific requirements on the expected output. Basically, a similarity measure should help to realize the goal function g, i.e. to maximize the utility of the output $u(s, o)$. According to our assumptions on o we can deduce different criteria that an optimal similarity measure sim_o should fulfill, namely:

Determining the Most Useful Case: In certain application scenarios, in particular when processing the output within the application environment automatically, only a single output alternative is of interest, i.e. $o = \{o_1\}$. Then it should hold:

$$\arg\max_{c_r \in CB} sim_o(q, c_r) = \arg\max_{c_r \in CB} u(s, o_r)$$

Separating Useful and Useless Cases: Often the utility of output alternatives is of a binary nature, i.e. an o_r may be useful or completely useless. In some application scenarios binary output utility can be achieved by introducing artificial utility thresholds, e.g. in information retrieval, the retrieved documents are simply treated as 'relevant' or 'irrelevant'. In such situations we

[2] This assumption does not hold in some application scenarios, e.g. if a certain diversity of the output alternatives is desired.

may demand the following from sim_o: Let $CB^+ = \{c_i \in CB \mid u(s, o_i) \geq \theta\}$ be the set of useful and $CB^- = \{c_i \in CB \mid u(s, o_i) < \theta\}$ be the set of useless cases, then

$$\forall c_i \in CB^+, c_j \in CB^- : sim_o(q, c_i) > sim_o(q, c_j)$$

Ranking the Most Useful Cases: Let $CB^u = \{c_i \in CB \mid u(s, o_i) \geq \sigma\}$ be the set of most useful cases. One may demand that sim_o ranks these cases correctly:

$$\forall c_i, c_j \in CB^u, \forall c \in CB \setminus CB^u : \begin{array}{l} sim_o(q, c_i) > sim_o(q, c_j) \Leftrightarrow u(s, o_i) > u(s, o_j) \\ \wedge\ sim_o(q, c_i) > sim_o(q, c) \end{array}$$

Approximating the Utility of the Most Useful Cases: Although in most present CBR applications a good approximation of the cases' absolute utility is not the main goal when defining *sim*, such a requirement would help the user to judge the reliability of each presented o_r:

$$\forall c_r \in CB^u : sim_o(q, c_r) \simeq u(s, o_r)$$

The first three criteria only demand that the similarity measure partially reproduces the preference relation induced by the utility function, i.e. one is only interested in an estimate of the cases' *relative utility* with respect to other cases. The last requirement is stronger since it requires an approximation of the cases' *absolute utility.*

Probabilistic Similarity Measures. Up to now we have implicitly assumed, that it is possible, at least in principle, to compute the utility $u(s, o_r)$ given only q and c_r. However, in practice this often does not apply because one is confronted with incomplete and/or noisy data or non-deterministic domains and hence with uncertainty. For example, queries as well as case characterizations often do not contain all information required to describe the underlying situations and cases sufficiently. In such situations a probabilistic interpretation of similarity values seems to be more accurate, i.e. the value $sim(q, c_r)$ then may be interpreted as the probability that the resulting output o_r is maximally useful given q and c_r, i.e. $sim(q, c_r) := P(u(s, o_r) = 1 \mid q, c_r)$. Nevertheless, this interpretation is consistent with the previously discussed demands on sim_o as well.

3.2 Training Data

When thinking about developing or applying an approach for learning similarity measures, one of the most crucial issues is the quality and the amount of available training data. When being confronted with little and noisy training data, many learning techniques tend to overfit the training data resulting in poor generalization performance.

In principle, the training data must contain some implicit or explicit knowledge about the a-posteriori utility of certain cases. This means for a case c_r and a given query q certain information about $u(s, o_r)$ is required. According to our formal CBR model we assume that such information can be obtained via the feedback function f either *offline* during a particular training phase or *online* during the application of the CBR system. In the following we discuss different types of such *utility feedback*.

Utility Feedback. Basically, information about the a-posteriori utility $u(s, o_r)$ of a case c_r given a query q may be provided in different ways:

Absolute Case Utility Feedback (ACUF): One possibility is to provide information about the absolute value of $u(s, o_r)$. Here, the feedback space F is defined as $(Q \times C \times [0, 1])^n$. This means feedback fb consists of a collection of *training examples* $fb = (te_{11}, \ldots, te_{lk})$ where a single training example $te_{ij} = (q_i, c_j, u(s, o_j))$ represents utility feedback for a particular case c_j w.r.t. a given query q_i.

Absolute Utility Feedback (AUF): When allowing compositional adaptation, i.e. $o = of(q, a(q, c_1, \ldots, c_n))$, a special kind of absolute utility feedback can be acquired. In this situation, the utility of o cannot simply be traced back onto the utility of individual cases. Then F is defined as $\mathcal{Q} \times \mathcal{O} \times [0, 1]$ where corresponding training examples $te = (q, o, u(s, o))$ represent information about the performance of the entire CBR system for a given query q.

Relative Case Utility Feedback (RCUF): Another possibility is to provide information about $u(s, o_r)$ only in a relative manner with respect to other output alternatives. By defining F as $(\mathcal{Q} \times \mathcal{C} \times \mathcal{C} \times \mathcal{UR})^n$ where $\mathcal{UR}$ represents a set of relation symbols (e.g. $\mathcal{UR} = \{<, \leq, =, \geq, >, \neq\}$) a training example can be represented as a tuple $te = (q, c_i, c_j, R)$ where $u(s, o_i) R u(s, o_j)$ for some $R \in \mathcal{UR}$.

Absolute feedback (ACUF/AUF) is mandatory for learning similarity measures that are intended to approximate absolute utility values. When only focusing on a reproduction of the induced preference relation, RCUF feedback is sufficient. However, depending on the desired semantic one should acquire feedback for different cases.

Acquisition of Training Data. Now we describe how the introduced kinds of feedback can be acquired in practice, i.e. how to implement the feedback function f. Basically, two different approaches are possible.

The first approach is *self-optimization*. In traditional problem solving scenarios, i.e. if case characterizations d_i describe past (problem) situations s_i and case lessons l_i represent corresponding outputs (typically solutions) with high utility, a CBR system is able to extract training data from its case base CB. On the one hand, cases themselves can be interpreted as ACUF where each case c_i represents a training example $te = (d_i, c_i, u(s_i, o_i))$. Information about $u(s_i, o_i)$ may be contained in case lessons or $u(s_i, o_i) = 1$ is assumed.

On the other hand, additional feedback can be obtained by performing a *leave-one-out-crossvalidation*, i.e. single cases c_i are temporarily removed from CB and d_i is used as query q_i. The resulting output o (or o_r) then has to be compared with an output l_i known to have high utility (mostly $u(s_i, l_i) = 1$ is assumed). Depending on the implementation of a the corresponding feedback is typically of the kind ACUF or AUF.

Self optimization is applied by most existing approaches for learning similarity measures, typically for feature weight learning in classification scenarios (see Section 3.3). Here, training examples are simply defined as $te_{ACUF} = (d_i, c_r, u(s_i, o_r))$ or $te_{AUF} = (d_i, o, u(s_i, o))$, respectively, where $u(s_i, o_{(r)}) = 1 \Leftrightarrow o_{(r)} = l_i$ (i.e. if the classification is correct) and $u(s_i, o_{(r)}) = 0$ otherwise. In [18] we have proposed a generalization of this approach where we set $u(s_i, o_{(r)}) = sim_S(o_{(r)}, l_i)$, i.e. we employ a domain specific *solution similarity measure* $sim_S : \mathcal{O} \times \mathcal{L} \rightarrow [0, 1]$ in order to estimate the utility of the generated output in non-classification domains or when misclassification costs [20] have to be considered.

An approach to utilizing self optimization in the utility-oriented matching scenario by generating RCUF is described in [17,16]. Here, the influence of the adaptation function a on the target similarity measure sim_T is estimated by evaluating the utility of adapted cases with a given utility measure represented by an additional similarity measure sim_U that can be defined more easily than sim_T.

The second approach for acquiring training data is to *ask some similarity teacher*. In the utility-oriented matching scenario an extraction of training data from the case base is usually impossible because here the cases do not contain information about u. For example, pure descriptions of technical products contain no explicit knowledge about their suitability for particular customer demands[3]. Therefore, utility feedback has to be provided by an external *similarity teacher* who possesses certain knowledge about u. In principle, the previously mentioned measures sim_S and sim_U as well as external simulation procedures might be interpreted as artificial similarity teachers. However, often only human domain experts or the system's users are able to provide the required feedback, but only a few learning approaches consider human similarity teachers [6,9,21].

3.3 Learning Techniques

In this section we give an overview on techniques that have been applied for learning similarity measures in CBR. The following aspects may be used to categorize the techniques:

- the desired semantic of the target similarity measure (cf. Section 3.1)
- the type of the training data and the corresponding approach to acquisition (cf. Section 3.2)
- the representation of the similarity measure to be learned
- the applied learning algorithm
- whether background knowledge is used to improve the learning process

[3] In current CBR applications this knowledge is often inferred by applying simple distance metrics.

Basically, the representations used to model similarity measures determine the hypothesis space $\mathcal{SIM}$. Here, we can distinguish the following commonly applied approaches:

Feature Weights: Because in many CBR systems only simple weighted distance metrics are employed, modifying the weights assigned to features in feature-value based case representations is often the only possibility to influence the similarity measure [19]. Here, one also distinguishes between global and local (e.g. case specific) weighting methods.

Local Similarity Measures: Most commercial CBR tools allow us to define local similarity measures for each feature in order to be able to incorporate more domain specific knowledge. Suitable learning techniques must be able to learn the particular parameters used to describe such local similarity measures [16,17].

Probabilistic Similarity Models (PSM): Another possibility to represent similarity measures are probabilistic models. Here, the similarity function is encoded using probability distributions which have to be determined by using appropriate techniques (e.g. frequency counts, kernel estimation techniques, neural networks, etc.) [7,4].

For characterizing learning techniques, Wettschereck and Aha [19] have introduced the following categorization:

Incremental Hill-climbers: Here, single training examples (typically based on ACUF or AUF) trigger the modification of the similarity measure after each pass through the CBR cycle. Existing approaches [5] increase or decrease feature weights in classification scenarios, where success driven $(te = (q, c_r, 1))$ and failure driven $(te = (q, c_r, 0))$ policies can be distinguished.

Continuous Optimizers: The idea of continuous optimizers is to collect a sufficiently large training data set first and to apply optimization approaches afterwards in order to generate a similarity measure that shows optimal results on this training data.
Typically, this is realized by minimizing a particular error function which compares generated outputs with corresponding utility feedback contained in the training data. For learning feature weights, gradient descent approaches have shown good results [15,19,20]. While most existing approaches apply ACUF or AUF, we have proposed an approach that utilizes RCUF in order to enable learning in the utility-oriented matching scenario [16]. For more complex local similarity measures we have developed a corresponding evolutionary algorithm [17,16].
PSM are usually also learnt by applying continuous optimizers which either optimize probabilistic error functions [12] or estimate underlying probability distributions by applying statistical and Bayesian methods [7].

Ignorant Methods: These methods do not exploit explicit feedback, but only perform a statistical analysis of the ACUF contained in CB, for example, to determine accurate feature weights based on class distributions [4].

Concerning the incorporation of background knowledge into the learning process, few approaches have been developed so far. Approaches that use background knowledge in order to improve the performance of an evolutionary algorithm have been presented in [11,10].

4 Conclusions and Future Work

In the first part of this paper we have presented a novel formal generalization of the classical CBR cycle. The advantages of this model are its generality, allowing us to describe recent developments in CBR research more accurately, and its formality, allowing more detailed analyses of important research issues. In the second part we have used the novel model to analyze crucial questions concerning the development of approaches for learning similarity measures. On the one hand, this analysis allows us to categorize existing learning techniques in order to simplify the choice of accurate techniques in particular applications. On the other hand, it represent a good foundation for future research.

While traditional approaches towards learning similarity measures in CBR mainly focus on learning of feature weights by employing ACUF/AUF, recently developed approaches also allow to employ RCUF which can be acquired in non-classification scenarios more easily than ACUF/AUF. Moreover, these approaches also enable learning of complex local similarity measures.

For future research we intend to develop new approaches towards the application of PSM. In our view, PSM have some advantages compared with explicit models (e.g. feature weights, local similarity measures). On the one hand, they may allow to weaken the hard attribute independence assumptions underlying common representations. Moreover, they would allow the definition of similarity measures in utility-oriented matching scenarios where it might hold: $\mathcal{Q} \neq \mathcal{D}$. For example, this would allow to compute 'similarities' between abstract queries (e.g. "I want a PC suited for video processing") and precise product descriptions (e.g. HD-Size = 200GB). However, existing learning approaches for PSM are only applicable in classification scenarios. To employ PSM in other scenarios we plan to develop techniques to learn PSM from RCUF. Moreover, we want to investigate how to incorporate background knowledge efficiently. Last but not least we want to develop new techniques that aim to learn similarity measures that approximate the absolute utility values as closely as possible. This would allow to build more dependable CBR systems because the user would get information about the reliability of the presented output.

References

1. Proceedings of the ECCBR-2004 Workshop on Explanation, 2004.
2. Aamodt, A., Plaza, E. Case-based Reasoning: Foundational Issues, Methodological Variations, and System Approaches. *AI Communications*, 7(1):39–59, 1994.
3. Bergmann, R., Richter, M.M., Schmitt, S., Stahl, A., Vollrath, I. Utility-Oriented Matching: A New Research Direction for Case-Based Reasoning. In *Proceedings of the 1st Conference on Professional Knowledge Management.* Shaker, 2001.

4. Blanzieri, E., Ricci, F. Probability Based Metrics for Nearest Neighbor Classification and Case-Based Reasoning. In *Proceedings of the 3rd International Conference on Case-Based Reasoning.* Springer, 1999.
5. Bonzano, A., Cunningham, P., Smyth, B. Using Introspective Learning to Improve Retrieval in CBR: A Case Study in Air Traffic Control. In *Proceedings of the 2nd International Conference on Case-Based Reasoning.* Springer, 1997.
6. Branting, K. Acquiring Customer Preferences from Return-Set Selections. In *Proceedings of the 4th International Conference on CBR.* Springer, 2001.
7. Breuel, T. Character Recognition by Adaptive Statistical Similarity. In *Proceedings of the 7th Int. Conf. on Document Analysis and Recognition.* Springer, 2003.
8. Burke, R. The Wasabi Personal Shopper: A Case-Based Recommender System. In *Proceedings of the 11th International Conference on Innovative Applications of Artificial Intelligence*, 1999.
9. Coyle, L., Cunningham, P. Exploiting Re-ranking Information in a Case-Based Personal Travel Assistent. In *Workshop on Mixed-Initiative Case-Based Reasoning at the 5th International Conference on Case-Based Reasoning.* Springer, 2003.
10. Gabel, T. On the Use of Vocabulary Knowledge for Learning Similarity Measures. In *Proceedings of the 3rd German Workshop on Experience Management.* Springer, 2005.
11. Gabel, T., Stahl, A. Exploiting Background Knowledge when Learning Similarity Measures. In *Proceedings of the 7th European Conference on Case-Based Reasoning.* Springer, 2004.
12. Lowe, D. Similarity Metric Learning for a Variable-Kernel Classifier. *Neural Computation*, 7, 1993.
13. Richter, M. M. The Knowledge Contained in Similarity Measures. Invited Talk at ICCBR'95, 1995.
14. Schmitt, S. *Dialog Tailoring for Similarity-Based Electronic Commerce Systems.* dissertation.de, 2003.
15. Stahl, A. Learning Feature Weights from Case Order Feedback. In *Proceedings of the 4th International Conference on Case-Based Reasoning.* Springer, 2001.
16. Stahl, A. *Learning of Knowledge-Intensive Similarity Measures in Case-Based Reasoning*, volume 986. dissertation.de, 2004.
17. Stahl, A., Gabel, T. Using Evolution Programs to Learn Local Similarity Measures. In *Proceedings of the 5th International Conference on CBR.* Springer, 2003.
18. Stahl, A., Schmitt, S. Optimizing Retrieval in CBR by Introducing Solution Similarity. In *Proceedings of the Int. Conf. on AI.* CSREA Press, 2002.
19. Wettschereck, D., Aha, D. W. Weighting Features. In *Proceeding of the 1st International Conference on Case-Based Reasoning.* Springer, 1995.
20. Wilke, W., Bergmann, R. Considering Decision Cost During Learning of Feature Weights. In *Proceedings of the 3rd European Workshop on CBR.* Springer, 1996.
21. Zhang, Z., Yang, Q. Dynamic Refinement of Feature Weights Using Quantitative Introspective Learning. In *Proceedings of the 16th International Joint Conference on Artificial Intelligence*, 1999.

Knowledge-Rich Similarity-Based Classification

Timo Steffens

Institute of Cognitive Science, Osnabrueck, Germany
timosteffens@gmx.de
http://www.cogsci.uos.de/~tsteffen

Abstract. This paper proposes to enhance similarity-based classification with different types of imperfect domain knowledge. We introduce a hierarchy of knowledge types and show how the types can be incorporated into similarity measures. Furthermore, we analyze how properties of the domain theory, such as partialness and vagueness, influence classification accuracy. Experiments in a simple domain suggest that partial knowledge is more useful than vague knowledge. However, for data sets from the UCI Machine Learning Repository, we show that even vague domain knowledge that in isolation performs at chance level can substantially increase classification accuracy when being incorporated into similarity-based classification.

1 Introduction

Case-Based Reasoning (CBR) is mainly considered a knowledge-light approach that is suited for domains in which no perfect domain knowledge exists. However, there is increasing research in the subbranch of knowledge-intensive CBR on how to incorporate domain knowledge. The focus is on acquiring knowledge for case adaptation (e. g. [30,14]), the vocabulary [10], and case-specific knowledge [14]. The retrieval component is often enhanced by explanation-based knowledge [1,4]. In this paper we focus on similarity measures for classification and show how different types of domain knowledge can be exploited in order to improve classification accuracy.

One contribution of this paper is to show that domain knowledge can be useful even if it is imperfect (e. g. partial or vague). This will alleviate the knowledge acquisition bottleneck, as it reduces the requisites of obtaining expert knowledge. The other main contribution is to propose a hierarchy of knowledge types which were previously seen as unconnected.

Although similarity-based classification is only used in domains where no perfect domain theories exist, often there exists imperfect domain knowledge and isolated chunks of knowledge [1,4,7,19]. For example, in [1] open and weak domain theories were integrated into a CBR system. Similarly, matching knowledge was used to improve the performance of the well-known PROTOS system [19]. Furthermore, it was shown that the combination of CBR and a domain theory outperforms both CBR and the theory itself [7]. In contrast to weak theories, strong domain theories were used to filter irrelevant features [4].

H. Muñoz-Avila and F. Ricci (Eds.): ICCBR 2005, LNAI 3620, pp. 522–536, 2005.

We present a new approach that exploits imperfect domain knowledge in similarity-based classification mainly by inferring abstract features. Furthermore, we analyze the impact of the knowledge's vagueness and partialness.

The next section introduces a hierarchy of knowledge types. Section 3 discusses properties of imperfect domain theories. Section 4 gives an overview over how knowledge types can be exploited in similarity measures and how they improve classification accuracy. Section 5 reports experiments with two domains from the UCI Machine Learning Repository [5]. Finally, the last section concludes and outlines future work.

2 Types of Domain Knowledge

This section discusses which types of knowledge are useful for similarity-based classification. Previous works incorporated isolated knowledge types (e. g., matching knowledge [19] or contextual knowledge [28]). A systematic analysis of which knowledge types are useful will provide insights into which information should be learned from the instances if the knowledge is not explicitly given. For each knowledge type we will refer to CBR systems that employ such knowledge.

It should be noted that we do not start from the knowledge types as proposed by knowledge representation work, such as frames, scripts, and semantical networks. Rather, we group the types from the perspective of how they can be used and incorporated into similarity measures.

For the examples, we use the following notation: $C_1, C_2, C_3 \in \mathbb{R}$ are continuous attributes. $D_1, D_2 \in \mathbb{Z}$ are discrete attributes. $P(x)$ is a binary concept applicable to instance x. $C_i(x)$ or $D_i(x)$ denote the value of instance x for attribute C_i or D_i. $w \in \mathbb{R}$ is a weight.

We categorize the relevant types of knowledge into a hierarchy (see figure 1), stating that methods that can be used for a knowledge type can also be used for its subtypes. At the most general level, we distinguish *virtual attributes* [20] (or *derived attributes*) from *distributional knowledge*. The latter includes knowledge about the range and distribution of attributes and their values. Knowledge about the range of an attribute is commonly used to normalize the attribute similarity

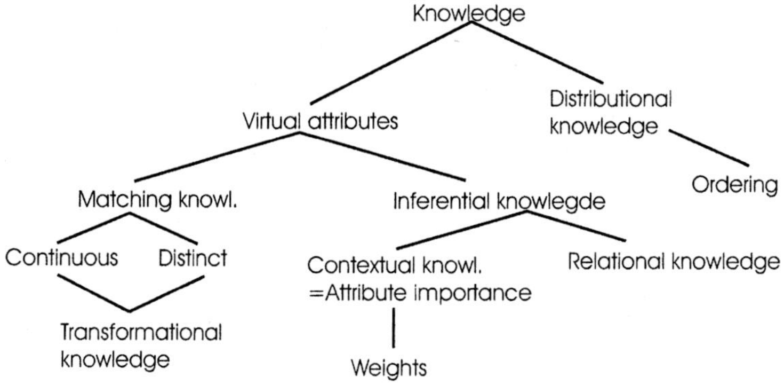

Fig. 1. Hierarchy of knowledge types

to [0,1]. Since this type of knowledge is widely used in CBR, we focus on the less researched type of knowledge that can be formalized as virtual attributes.

Virtual attributes are attributes that are not directly represented in the cases but can be inferred from other attributes [20]. They are common in database research. In CBR, virtual attributes are useful if the monotonicity-principle is violated. If $sim(A,B) > sim(A,C)$ is necessary to reflect class membership, then there must at least be one pair of local similarities, so that $sim(A_i,B_i) > sim(A_i,C_i)$. If such a pair does not exist, the similarity measure must make use of interdependencies between attributes. For example, the similarity may not depend on two attributes A_1, A_2 themselves, but on their difference $A_1 - A_2$. Virtual attributes can express such interdependencies (e. g., $deposit(A) = income(A) - spending(A)$) and can also encapsulate non-linear relations.

We further distinguish between *matching knowledge* and *inferential knowledge*. Discrete matching knowledge states that two values of an attribute are equivalent. The PROTOS system made extensive use of this type of knowledge [19]. Also taxonomies are instantiations of matching knowledge and were used in CBR [3]. Continuous matching knowledge defines regions in the instance space. Examples: $C_1(x) > 30 \;\wedge\; C_1(x) < 50$ (continuous) and $D_1(x) \equiv D_1(y)$ (discrete). This can be formulated as virtual attribute, stating that an attribute is a member of the interval or is identical to one of the equivalent values.

Matching knowledge can be used to match syntactically different attributes that are semantically equivalent. Note that for binary virtual attributes, matching knowledge is hardly different from inferential knowledge (apart from the label/predicate name). Only if the virtual attribute has more than two possible values, matching knowledge is different from inferential knowledge.

Transformational knowledge is a special form of matching knowledge where usually some arithmetic or operations are involved in order to map a point in the instance-space to another point. For example, transformational knowledge has been used to establish identity despite geometric rotation (e. g. [22]). Example: $C_1(x) = rotate(C_1(y), 30)$ The similarity of two attributes is maximal if they can be transformed into each other or if they are identical.

Inferential knowledge specifies the value of an attribute that is inferrable from some other attributes' values. This type of knowledge has been used in explanation-based CBR (e. g. [1]). Example: $P(x) \leftarrow C_1(x) > 30 \wedge C_1(x) < 50$ Note that the condition part makes use of matching knowledge.

Contextual knowledge is a special form of inferential knowledge. It states that some feature is important given some other features. For an overview over contextual features, refer to [28]. Example: $important(P(x)) \leftarrow C_1(x) > 30 \wedge C_1(x) < 50$.

In our hierarchy, *weights* are a special form of contextual knowledge. They express the importance of a feature on a continuous scale. Thus, we can express feature weights in a global way ($important(P(x), w) \leftarrow TRUE$), or in a local way ($important(P(x), w) \leftarrow C_1(x) > 30 \wedge C_1(x) < 50$). The virtual attribute perspective is usually lost for global weights, since the $TRUE$ condition is not stated explicitly. Contextual knowledge and weights can be called "attribute importance" knowledge.

Relations are special forms of inferential knowledge, since whether a relation holds or not is inferred from attributes. The condition part uses at least two different attributes. Relational knowledge for similarity is prominent in computational modelling of human categorization [16]. Example: $P(x) \leftarrow C_1(x) > C_2(x)$. Note that relations usually make use of matching knowledge in the condition part, as they define regions in which the relation holds.

Ordering of nominal feature values is a subtype of distribution knowledge. It establishes a dimension in the instance space. In [26] it was shown that knowledge of the ordering of discrete feature values can increase classification accuracy.

In previous work [23] we used goal-dependency networks (GDNs) as proposed in [25]. In this framework, GDNs are a combination of relational knowledge about the subgoal-relation and contextual knowledge (a property is important if a certain subgoal is active).

3 Properties of Domain Theories

Domains in which CBR is applied usually lack a perfect domain theory. Hence, the domain theories that we work with have at least one of the following properties (cf. Figure 2). In this paper, we focus on partial and vague domain theories.

- **Partialness:** This is the case if some parts of the domain are not modelled, for example a) if conditions are used but not defined, or b) the relation of intermediates or directly represented case attributes ("observables") to the classification goal is not known, or c) the classification goal does not exist in the rulebase at all. Note that these situations correspond to gaps at the "top" or "bottom" of the domain theory [17].
- **Vagueness:** Values can only be given within a certain confidence interval. If a value is selected from the interval, it is likely to be incorrect.
- **Inconsistency:** There are two or more rules (or even alternative theories) that make different classifications and it is not known which one is correct. CBR is often used to overcome this problem, because the cases provide knowledge on which classification is correct for certain cases.

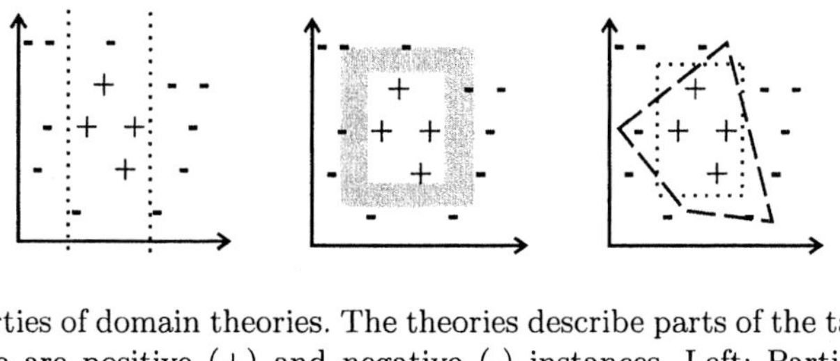

Fig. 2. Properties of domain theories. The theories describe parts of the target concept, of which there are positive (+) and negative (-) instances. Left: Partial knowledge, only parts of the concept boundaries are known. Middle: Vague knowledge, concept boundaries are believed to be somewhere within the shaded areas. Right: Inconsistent knowledge, different rules make differing predictions

4 Effects of Incorporating Knowledge Types

In this section we show how to incorporate different knowledge types, show their effects on the classification accuracy, and also report on experiments about partial and vague knowledge. Due to space limitations we focus on the general method of virtual attributes (which can be used for all of its subtypes) and on a special method for matching knowledge.

4.1 Virtual Attributes

Every virtual attribute forms an additional dimension of the instance space (see Figure 3 (right)). This is most intuitive for numerical attributes. An example is the concept $expectedWealthTillRetirement(C) = (65 - age(C)) * income(C)$ Unfortunately, these dimensions can change assumptions about instance distributions and are most likely not orthogonal to the other dimensions, since they are inferrable from other attributes.

In this paper we focus on binary virtual attributes. Although formally they are additional dimensions, they can be visualized as separating lines within the original instance space (see Figure 3 (left)). They divide the instance space into two regions. For example, $taxFree(C) \leftarrow income(C) < 330$ may divide some instance space into salaries that are or are not subject to paying taxes in Germany. We will show that virtual attributes that describe target concept boundaries are especially useful.

Since virtual attributes are defined by other attributes, a hierarchy of attributes can be formed. At the bottom level are attributes that are directly represented in the cases (observables), at the top level are attributes that correspond to the classification goals. In between are intermediate attribuets [17]. Intermediate attributes that are fully defined (i. e., that do not have gaps at the bottom of the domain theory) can be computed from the values of observables and other intermediates. We propose to use intermediates as virtual attributes. This can be accomplished by adding them to the local similarities of the similarity measure, that is, $s_i = 1$, iff both instances satisfy the intermediate concept or both do not satisfy it, and $s_i = 0$ otherwise. In the following, additional attributes are assumed to be discrete.

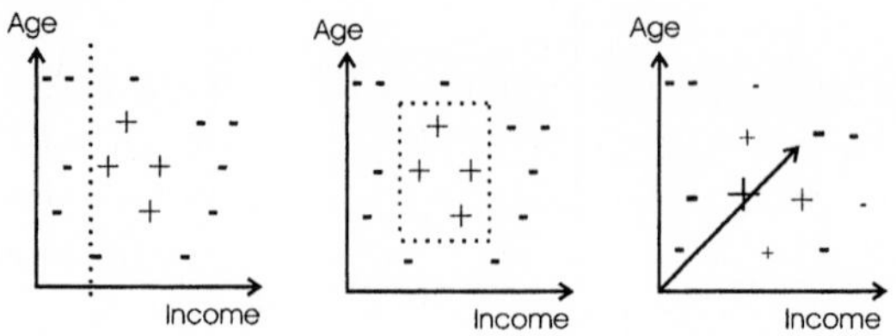

Fig. 3. Types of virtual attributes. Left: A binary virtual attribute divides the instance space into instances satisfying or not satisfying it. Middle: A conjunction of binary attributes. Right: The most general type of virtual attributes is to add a dimension to the instance space

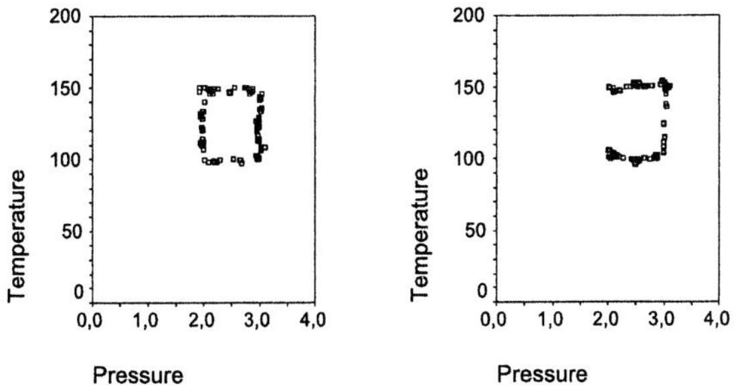

Fig. 4. Distribution of classification errors for the target concept $hardened(C) \leftarrow temp(C) > 100 \wedge temp(C) < 150 \wedge press(C) > 2 \wedge press(C) < 3$ without virtual attributes (left) and with the virtual attribute $V(C) \leftarrow press(C) <= 2$ (right)

Let us look at how binary virtual attributes influence classification. Assume for sake of illustration that the instance space is formed by the attributes *temp* and *press* denoting the temperature and pressure of a manufacturing oven. Let us assume furthermore that the (to be approximated) target concept is $hardened(C) \leftarrow temp(C) > 100 \wedge temp(C) < 150 \wedge press(C) > 2 \wedge press(C) < 3$. The error distribution of an unweighted kNN-classifier for the target concept is depicted in Figure 4 (left). Not surprisingly, the misclassifications occur at the boundaries of the target concept.

Now let us analyze the effect of different amounts and different qualities of domain knowledge on the classification. In order to control the independent variables like partialness and vagueness of the domain knowledge, we created a simple test domain. There were two continuous attributes X and Y, uniformly distributed over the interval [0,100]. The target concept was $T(C) \leftarrow X(C) > 30 \wedge X(C) < 70 \wedge Y(C) > 30 \wedge Y(C) < 70$. There were 100 randomly generated cases in the case-base and 200 test cases were used. Each experiment was repeated 1000 times with random cases in the case-base and random test cases. We used a square centered in the instance space as target concept, because it is one of the few concepts for which the optimal weight setting for kNN-classification can be calculated analytically. The optimal weight setting for the target concept is to use equal weights [15]. Thus, the accuracy of 1-NN with equal weights is the optimal accuracy that can be achieved without adding additional attributes.

Partialness of the domain theory: In this experiment, we operationalize the partialness of the domain knowledge as number of known target concept boundaries. The more boundaries are known, the less partial it is.

Adding virtual attributes that correctly specify a boundary of the target concept makes the misclassifications at those boundaries disappear (see Figure 4 (right)). Thus, by adding virtual attributes that describe a boundary correctly, the classification accuracy is increased (see Figure 5).

Obviously, even partial knowledge (e. g. adding only one virtual attribute) can improve classification accuracy. A formal treatment will be published elsewhere due to space constraints. In short, classification errors can be approximated as

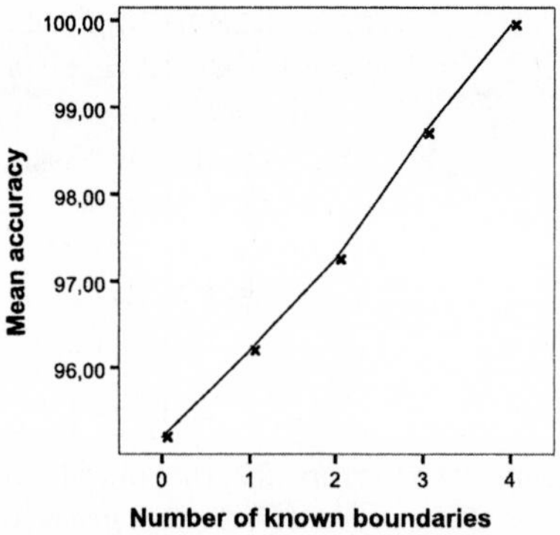

Fig. 5. Percentage of correctly classified cases with different numbers of target concept boundaries described by virtual attributes

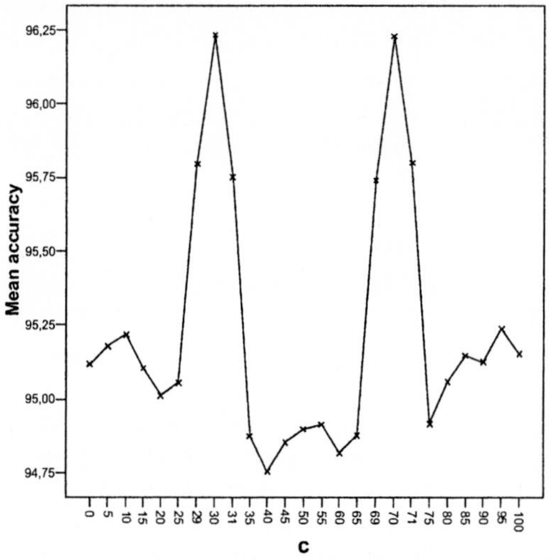

Fig. 6. Accuracy of similarity measures using a virtual attribute of the form $V(c) \leftarrow X(C) < c$, where c is plotted on the horizontal axis. c-axis is stretched at the position of the concept boundaries

sum of the errors on concept boundaries [15]. The classification error is reduced by each concept boundary that is specified.

In this experiment we assumed that the virtual attributes were correct. In the next experiment we analyzed the influence of the correctness of virtual attributes.

Correctness: Vague knowledge can be informally described as knowing that an attribute should be more or less at a certain value. The higher the vagueness, the higher is the probability for high incorrectness. We operationalize correctness of a virtual attribute as its distance from the correct value. We created virtual attributes of the form $V(C) \leftarrow X(C) < c$, where c was varied from 0 to 100 at steps of 5. Remember that the correct X-value (which was used in the domain theory to generate the cases) was 30. The accuracy of classification when adding these virtual attributes is depicted in Figure 6.

The results are somewhat disappointing. The accuracy drops rapidly if the virtual attribute is inaccurate. Fortunately, the accuracy with inaccurate virtual attributes is not much lower than using no virtual intermediates (the accuracy of a similarity measure with no virtual attribute is equivalent to setting c=0 or c=100). The second peak at $X = 70$ which is the other boundary on the X-attribute is due to the fact that similarity-based classification is direction-less: only the position of the concept boundary has to be known, the side on which positive and negative instances are located is encoded in the cases.

These experiments with a simple domain suggest that partial knowledge is more useful than vague knowledge. Adding partial knowledge is likely to increase the classification accuracy, whereas vague knowledge is only useful if there is good evidence that the knowledge is correct.

4.2 Matching Knowledge

Matching knowledge is a specialization of virtual attributes. Thus, matching knowledge can be used to define an additional attribute as described in section 4.1. Additionally, it can be used to specify that values in a certain subregion should be viewed as equivalent (i. e., set their similarity to the maximal value). In comparison to using matching knowledge as virtual attribute, using it to specify equivalence does not require setting or learning weights. In this section we empirically compare the equivalence method and the virtual attribute method.

Defining equivalence within intervals is for example done in discretizing continuous attributes. In contrast, here we do not discretize the whole range of an attribute, but only an interval. As a further difference, matching knowledge usually specifies subregions using several dimensions, not just one dimension.

For simplicity, here we only cope with matching knowledge which specifies an interval on one dimension. Informally, such knowledge corresponds to the information that certain values behave identically, e. g. "the machine behaves identically within the interval from 2.6 to 3.2 bar pressure".

In the experiments, we assume that there are two continuous variables X and Y, both in the range [0,100]. The target concept is again (like in the experiments with virtual attributes) $T(C) \leftarrow X(C) > 30 \wedge X(C) < 70 \wedge Y(C) > 30 \wedge Y(C) < 70$. There were 100 random cases in the case-base, 200 random test cases were used, and this setting was repeated 3000 times. All attribute (including the additional one) weights were equal in both methods.

In the equivalence method, the local similarity for attribute X is defined as:

$$s(x_1, x_2) = \begin{cases} 1 & : \ if\ x_1 = x_2 \vee (l \leq x_1 \leq r \ \wedge \ l \leq x_2 \leq r) \\ 1 - |x_1 - x_2|/100 & : \ else \end{cases}$$

This is the same local similarity as used in the other experiments, except that the similarity is also 1 if both values are within the interval [l,r]. This corresponds to matching knowledge which states that differences between cases in this interval

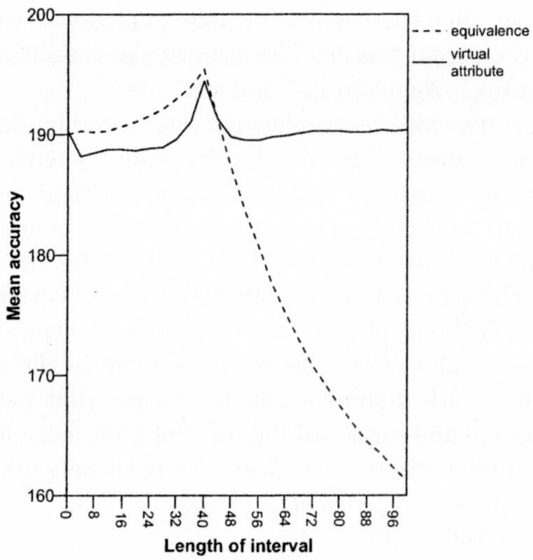

Fig. 7. Accuracy of a similarity measure using matching knowledge as virtual attribute and as equivalence within an interval

are due only to their difference on the other dimension. To simulate the effects of vague knowledge, the interval-length was varied from 0 to 100 for a centered interval at $X = (r + l)/2 = 50$. Thus, perfect matching knowledge would state the interval-length to be 40, and $l = 30, r = 70$.

In the virtual attribute method, a predicate is defined as follows: $V(C) \leftarrow X(C) \geq l \wedge X(C) \leq r$ The local similarity for this additional attribute is 1 iff both cases satisfy the predicate, and 0 else.

The accuracy of the similarity measure for the different intervals is plotted in Figure 7. The baseline (i. e., using no matching knowledge) is equivalent to setting the interval length to zero. Apparently, both ways of using matching knowledge can improve classification accuracy dramatically. While the baseline classifies 190.0 cases correctly on average, both knowledge-rich methods correctly classify more than 195.0 cases if the matching knowledge is perfect. However, the equivalence method is more robust concerning vague knowledge that estimates the interval too small, as the shallow slope suggests. In contrast, the virtual attribute method degrades faster if the knowledge estimates the interval as too big. On the other hand, it does not degrade as dramatically as the equivalence method for very inaccurate knowledge.

5 Experiments in Real Domains

5.1 The Domains

The domain of the previous sections allowed us to vary the incorrectness and partialness of the domain theory and to create pure forms of knowledge types. However, since the domain was handcrafted and simple, we ran additional experiments with two data sets from the UCI Machine Learning Repository. We used only data sets that provided imperfect domain theories. Note that some data sets in the repository come along with perfect domain models, as the instances were created by those models. But we used only data sets whose domain theories were imperfect. Contextual, matching and inferential knowledge is present in these domain theories, but in a mixed manner. Thus, we used the most general method of virtual attributes to incorporate the knowledge.

- Japanese Credit Screening (JCS): This domain comes with a domain theory that was created by interviewing domain experts. Accordingly, the theory is imperfect and classifies only 81% of the cases correctly.
- Promoter gene sequences (PGS): Its domain theory reflects the knowledge of experts in the field of promoter genes. It is highly inaccurate and performs at chance level when used in isolation [27]. We included this domain to serve as a worst case scenario, since the domain knowledge is most inaccurate.

5.2 The Virtual Attributes

The domain theories of JCS and PGS have been created by domain experts for real world applications. Hence, they do not separate positive from negative instances in a perfect way. The accuracy of the JCS domain theory is 81%, the accuracy of the PGS domain theory is only 50%. The structure of both theories is depicted in Figure 8.

Most of the intermediate concepts contain several knowledge types. For example, *rejected_age_unstable_work* defines regions and an additional attribute and states that in this context *age* and *number_years* are important:

```
rejected_age_unstable_work(S) :-
    age_test(S, N1),
    59 < N1,
    number_years_test(S, N2),
    N2 < 3.
```

Although the concepts are highly imperfect, our experiments show that these concepts can improve classification accuracy when used as virtual attributes in similarity measures. Not all intermediate concepts will increase classification accuracy when used as virtual attributes [24]. Hence, mechanisms to select or weight virtual attributes are necessary. We apply several existing weighting approaches which will be described in the next section.

5.3 Weighting Methods

According to the classification of weighting methods as proposed in [29], we selected four methods with performance bias, and six with preset bias (i. e., statistical and information-theoretic methods).

- Performance bias: Weighting methods with a performance bias classify instances in a hill-climbing fashion. They update weights based on the outcome of the classification process. The performance bias is known to perform well

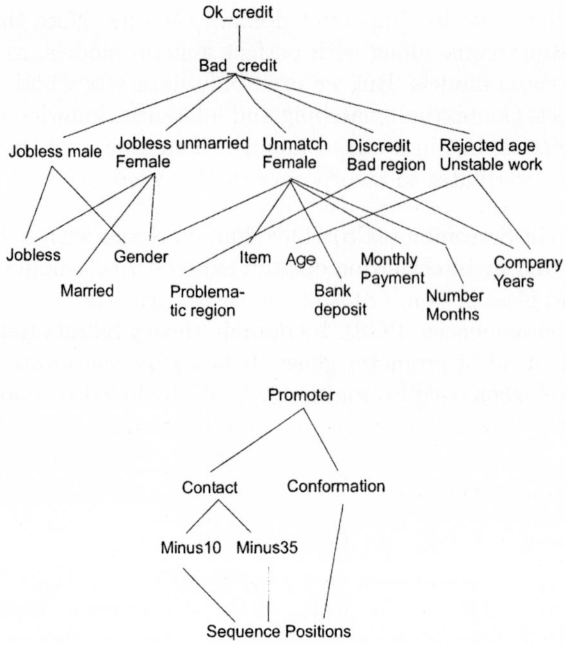

Fig. 8. The domain theory of the JCS domain (top) and of the PGS domain (bottom)

if there are many irrelevant features [29]. Since the intermediate concepts of the domain theories can be assumed to be relevant, we expected performance bias methods to perform badly.

1. EACH [21] increases the weight of matching features and decreases the weight of mismatching features by a hand-coded value.
2. IB4 [2] is a parameter-free extension of EACH. It makes use of the concept distribution and is sensitive to skewed concept distributions. It assume that the values of irrelevant features are uniformly distributed.
3. RELIEF [12] is a feature selection- rather than feature weighting-algorithm. It calculates weights based on the instance's most similar neighbors of each class and then filters attributes whose weights are below a hand-coded threshold. We used extensions for non-binary target classes and kNN with $k > 1$ as proposed in [13].
4. ISAC [6] increases weights of matching attributes and decreases weights of mismatching attributes by a value that is calculated from the ratio of the prior use of the instance. The more often the instance was retrieved for correct classifications, the higher the update value.

– Preset bias: The bias of the following weighting methods is based on probabilistic or information-theoretic concepts. They process each training instance exactly once.

1. CCF [8] binarizes attributes and weights them according to the classes' probability given a feature.
2. PCF [8] is an extension of CCF which takes the distribution of the feature's values over classes into account. It calculates different weights for different classes.
3. MI [9] calculates the reduction of entropy in the class distribution by attributes and uses it as the attribute weight.
4. CD [18] creates a correlation matrix of the discretized attributes and the classes. The weight of an attribute increases with the accuracy of the prediction from attribute value to class.
5. VD [18] extends CD in that it considers both the best prediction for a class and the predictions of all attributes.
6. CVD [18] combines CD and VD.

5.4 Results

For brevity, we will refer to the similarity measure which uses only observables as the *non-extended* measure. The similarity measure which uses virtual attributes will be called *extended.* For evaluation we used the leave-one-out method.

Table 1. Classification accuracies of the non-extended similarity measures and the extended measures. The columns report the accuracies for the unweighted classification and for several weighting methods

Domain	unw.	EACH	RELIEF	IB4	ISAC	CCF	PCF	MI	CD	VD	CVD
JCS (w/o)	74.19	74.19	78.23	74.19	72.58	72.58	72.58	74.19	74.19	72.58	71.77
JCS (w/)	74.19	72.58	<u>79.03</u>	72.58	<u>79.03</u>	<u>73.39</u>	<u>75.0</u>	<u>75.0</u>	<u>77.42</u>	<u>75.0</u>	<u>75.0</u>
PGS (w/o)	86.79	89.62	96.23	88.68	50.0	85.85	87.74	68.87	88.68	77.36	83.02
PGS (w/)	85.85	<u>93.40</u>	96.23	<u>90.57</u>	<u>96.23</u>	<u>91.51</u>	86.79	<u>98.11</u>	88.68	<u>97.17</u>	<u>87.74</u>

For most of the weighting methods, the extended similarity measure performs better than the non-extended one. In table 1 we underline the accuracy of the extended similarity measure if it outperformed the non-extended similarity measure when using the same weighting method. In the PGS domain, seven of ten weighting methods perform better if the similarity measure is extended with virtual attributes. Even more so, in the JCS domain the accuracies of eight of ten weighting methods were improved by using virtual attributes.

In its optimal setting, with an accuracy of 98.11% our approach performs also better than the results from the literature reported for the PGS domain. The accuracy of KBANN in [27] is 96.23%, which to our knowledge was the highest accuracy reported so far and also used the leave-one-out evaluation. We found no classification accuracy results for JCS in the literature[1].

[1] The domain often referred to as 'credit screening' with 690 instances is actually the credit card application domain.

Obviously, these improvements are not restricted to a certain class of weighting methods. Methods with performance bias (most notably ISAC), information-theoretic bias (i. e. MI), and with a statistical correlation bias (e. g. VD) benefit from processing virtual attributes.

Even in the PGS domain, the improvements are substantial. This is surprising, since the domain knowledge is the worst possible and classifies at chance level when used for rule-based classification. This is a promising result as it shows that adding intermediate concepts may increase accuracy even if the domain theory is very inaccurate. We hypothesize that this is due the fact that even vague rules-of-thumb provide some structure in the instance space which will be exploited by the similarity measure.

6 Conclusion and Future Work

The main contribution of this paper is to show that several types of imperfect domain knowledge from domain theories can enhance similarity-based classification. We showed in the domains from the Machine Learning Repository that even highly inaccurate (i. e., in our sense, vague) domain knowledge can be exploited to drastically improve classification accuracy. This facilitates knowledge elicitation from domain experts as it removes the requirements of completeness and accurateness. Furthermore, we proposed a hierarchy of knowledge types that were previously researched in isolation and showed that they can be incorporated as virtual attributes. The benefit of such a hierarchy is to guide CBR designers which types of knowledge should be acquired from domain experts or should be extracted from the instances by statistical or machine learning methods. Future work includes experiments in further domains and transforming intermediate attributes by feature generation [11].

References

1. Agnar Aamodt. Explanation-driven case-based reasoning. In Stefan Wess, Klaus-Dieter Althoff, and Michael M. Richter, editors, *Topics in Case-Based Reasoning*, pages 274–288. Springer, 1994.
2. David W. Aha. Tolerating noisy, irrelevant and novel attributes in instance-based learning algorithms. *International Journal of Man-Machine Studies*, 36(2):267–287, 1992.
3. Ralph Bergmann. On the use of taxonomies for representing case features and local similarity measures. In Lothar Gierl and Mario Lenz, editors, *Proceedings of the Sixth German Workshop on CBR*, pages 23–32, 1998.
4. Ralph Bergmann, Gerhard Pews, and Wolfgang Wilke. Explanation-based similarity: A unifying approach for integrating domain knowledge into case-based reasoning. In Stefan Wess, Klaus-Dieter Althoff, and Michael M. Richter, editors, *Topics in Case-Based Reasoning*, pages 182–196. Springer, 1994.
5. C. L. Blake and C. J. Merz. UCI repository of machine learning databases, 1998.

6. Andrea Bonzano, Pdraig Cunningham, and Barry Smyth. Using introspective learning to improve retrieval in cbr: A case study in air traffic control. In David Leake and Enric Plaza, editors, *Proceedings of the second ICCBR conference*, pages 291–302, Berlin, 1997. Springer.
7. Timothy Cain, Michael J. Pazzani, and Glenn Silverstein. Using domain knowledge to influence similarity judgements. In *Proceedings of the Case-Based Reasoning Workshop*, pages 191–198, Washington D.C., U.S.A., 1991.
8. Robert H. Creecy, Brij M. Masand, Stephen J. Smith, and David L. Waltz. Trading mips and memory for knowledge engineering. *Communications of the ACM*, 35(8):48–64, 1992.
9. Walter Daelemans and Antal van den Bosch. Generalization performance of backpropagation learning on a syllabification task. In *Proceedings of the Third Twente Workshop on Language Technology: Connectionism and Natural Language Processing*, pages 27–37, Enschede, The Netherlands, 1992. Unpublished.
10. Belen Diaz-Agudo and Pedro A. Gonzalez-Calero. Knowledge intensive cbr made affordable. In Agnar Aamodt, David Patterson, and Barry Smyth, editors, *Proceedings of the Workshop Program at the Fourth International Conference on Case-Based Reasoning*, 2001.
11. Tom Elliott Fawcett and Paul E. Utgoff. Automatic feature generation for problem solving systems. In Derek H. Sleeman and Peter Edwards, editors, *Proceedings of the 9th International Conference on Machine Learning*, pages 144–153. Morgan Kaufmann, 1992.
12. Kenji Kira and Larry A. Rendell. A practical approach to feature selection. In Derek H. Sleeman and Peter Edwards, editors, *Proceedings of the Ninth International Workshop on Machine Learning*, pages 249–256. Morgan Kaufmann Publishers Inc., 1992.
13. Igor Kononenko. Estimating attributes: Analysis and extensions of RELIEF. In F. Bergadano and L. de Raedt, editors, *Proceedings of the European Conference on Machine Learning*, pages 171–182, Berlin, 1994. Springer.
14. David B. Leake and David C. Wilson. Combining CBR with interactive knowledge acquisition, manipulation and reuse. In Klaus-Dieter Althoff, Ralph Bergmann, and Karl Branting, editors, *Proceedings of the Third International Conference on Case-Based Reasoning*, pages 203–217, Berlin, 1999. Springer-Verlag.
15. Charles X. Ling and Hangdong Wang. Computing optimal attribute weight settings for nearest neighbour algorithms. *Artificial Intelligence Review*, 11:255–272, 1997.
16. Douglas L. Medin, Robert L. Goldstone, and Dedre Gentner. Respects for similarity. *Psychological Review*, 100(2):254–278, 1993.
17. Raymond J. Mooney and Dirk Ourston. Constructive induction in theory refinement. In Lawrence Birnbaum and Gregg Collins, editors, *Proceedings of the Eighth International Machine Learning Workshop*, pages 178–182, San Mateo, CA, 1991. Morgan Kaufmann.
18. H. Nunez, M. Sanchez-Marre, U. Cortes, J. Comas, I. Rodriguez-Roda, and M. Poch. Feature weighting techniques for prediction tasks in environmental processes. In *Proceedings of the 3rd Workshop on Binding Environmental Sciences and Artificial Intelligence (BESAI 2002)*, 2002.
19. Bruce W. Porter, Ray Bareiss, and Robert C. Holte. Concept learning and heuristic classification in weak-theory domains. *Artificial Intelligence*, 45(1-2):229–263, 1990.
20. Michael M. Richter. Fallbasiertes Schliessen. *Informatik Spektrum*, 3(26):180–190, 2003.
21. Steven Salzberg. A nearest hyperrectangle learning method. *Machine Learning*, 6(3):251–276, 1991.

22. Joerg W. Schaaf. Detecting gestalts in CAD-plans to be used as indices. In Angi Voss, editor, *FABEL - Similarity concepts and retrieval methods*, pages 73–84. GMD, Sankt Augustin, 1994.
23. Timo Steffens. Adapting similarity-measures to agent-types in opponent-modelling. In Mathias Bauer, Piotr Gmytrasiewicz, Gal A. Kaminka, and David V. Pynadath, editors, *Workshop on Modeling Other Agents from Observations at AAMAS 2004*, pages 125–128, 2004.
24. Timo Steffens. Similarity-measures based on imperfect domain-theories. In Steffen Staab and Eva Onaindа, editors, *Proceedings of STAIRS 2004*, pages 193–198. IOS Press, Frontiers in Artificial Intelligence and Applications, 2004.
25. Robert E. Stepp and Ryszard S. Michalski. Conceptual clustering: Inventing goal-oriented classifications of structured objects. In Ryszard S. Michalski, Jaime G. Carbonell, and Tom M. Mitchell, editors, *Machine Learning: An Artificial Intelligence Approach*, volume II. Morgan Kaufman Publishers, Inc., Los Altos, CA, 1986.
26. Jerzy Surma. Enhancing similarity measure with domain specific knowledge. In *Proceedings of the Second European Conference on Case-Based Reasoning*, pages 365–371, Paris, 1994. AcknoSoft Press.
27. Geofrey G. Towell, Jude W. Shavlik, and Michael O. Noordenier. Refinement of approximate domain theories by knowledge based neural network. In *Proceedings of the Eighth National Conference on AI*, volume 2, pages 861–866, 1990.
28. Peter Turney. The management of context-sensitive features: A review of strategies. In *Proceedings of the Workshop on Leaning in Context-sensitive Domains at the 13th International Conference on Machine Learning*, pages 60–65, 1996.
29. Dietrich Wettschereck, David W. Aha, and Takao Mohri. A review and empirical evaluation of feature weighting methods for a class of lazy learning algorithms. *Artificial Intelligence Review*, 11:273–314, 1997.
30. Wolfgang Wilke and Ralph Bergmann. Techniques and knowledge used for adaptation during case-based problem solving. In *Proceedings of the 11th International Conference on Industrial and Engineering Applications of Artificial Intelligence and Expert Systems*, volume 2, pages 497–506, Berlin, 1998. Springer.

Autonomous Creation of New Situation Cases in Structured Continuous Domains

Haris Supic[1] and Slobodan Ribaric[2]

[1] Faculty of Electrical Engineering, University of Sarajevo, Skenderija 70, 71000 Sarajevo, Bosnia and Herzegovina
haris.s@bih.net.ba

[2] Faculty of Electrical Engineering and Computing, University of Zagreb, Unska 3, 10 000 Zagreb, Croatia
slobodan.ribaric@fer.hr

Abstract. A case-based reasoning (CBR) system that continuously interacts with an environment must be able to autonomously create new situation cases based on its perception of the local environment in order to select the appropriate steps to achieve the current mission goal. Although many continuous problem domains seem appropriate for case-based reasoning, a general formal framework is still missing. This paper presents a step in the direction of developing such a formal model of autonomous creation of new situation cases. The model is based on the notion of the step for attentional shift. This notion allows us to define the representation scheme for situation cases. We have introduced two types of situation cases: contextual cases and action cases. The solution component of contextual cases, also called a contextual behavior routine, is used as a resource to direct the attention of the CBR system to the relevant aspects of the local environment. The solution component of action cases, also called an action behavior routine, is used to guide selection of manipulative steps. There are two key roles of steps for attentional shift in our model. The first one is that steps for attentional shift represent a description structure of situation cases. The second role is that steps for attentional shift represent an abstract representation of actions by which the CBR system moves the attention to the relevant aspects of a local environment.

1 Introduction

Case-based reasoning systems have traditionally been used to perform high-level reasoning in problem domains that can be adequately described using discrete, symbolic representations. In general, a case consists of a problem, its solution and an outcome [1, 2]. Although many continuous situations seem appropriate for case-based reasoning, a general formal framework is still missing. Several issues need to be addressed. Consider, for example, a robot navigation problem [3]. What is the scope of a single case? What are the cases in an autonomous navigation domain? Is the entire mission a case, or some part of it? Which parts? How can we identify them? In continuous environments, it is not so obvious where the cases start or end. Examples

H. Muñoz-Avila and F. Ricci (Eds.): ICCBR 2005, LNAI 3620, pp. 537 – 551, 2005.

of CBR systems that use case-based methods in continuous environment are given in [3, 4, 5, 6]. Olivia et al. [7] describe a framework that integrates CBR capabilities in a BDI (belief, desire, intention) architecture. The relationships between autonomous systems and CBR systems constitute the research reported in [8, 9]. Situations in which case boundaries are not obvious are often situations in which planning and acting are interleaved. In this paper we develop an approach to continuous *CBR system-environment* interaction that we called *stepwise case-based reasoning* (SCBR). The SCBR approach uses *plan cases* to support the planning process and *situation cases* to support the acting of an SCBR system. This paper does not focus on plan cases, but only notions which refer to plan cases that are relevant for better understanding of situation cases will be defined in this work.

Most continuous environments contain structures that remain static during the lifetime of a system. These static structures represent local environments and each local environment represents a particular context. An SCBR system that performs stepwise case-based reasoning is adequate for the environments that contain identifiable configurations (structures) of the local environment. In this paper, types of identifiable local environments are called *contextual classes*. Furthermore, concrete examples of local environments are called *contextual instances*. This means that such structured environments can be described as a set of contextual instances. To help in understanding the term contextual class used throughout the paper, we show an example of autonomous navigation in an indoor environment. Figure 1 shows the graphical representation of the contextual classes for autonomous navigation tasks in indoor environments. Each contextual class is characterized by its specific configuration of relevant perceivable objects in the local environment.

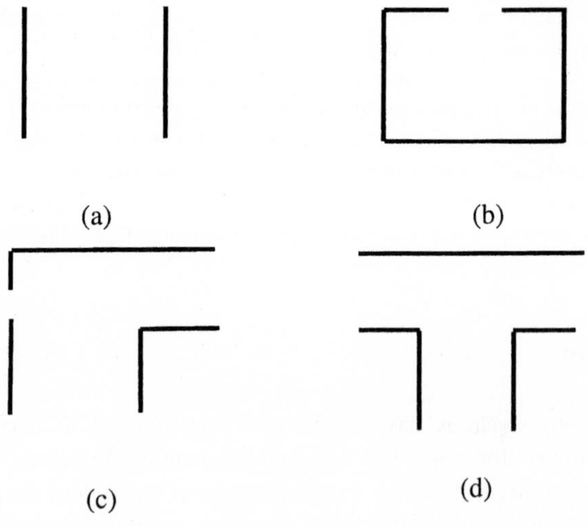

Fig. 1. Examples of contextual classes for autonomous navigation tasks in indoor environments. The figure shows contextual classes as follows: (a) Hallway, (b) Room, (c) L-shaped junction, (d) T-shaped junction. Each contextual class is characterized by its specific configuration of relevant perceivable objects in the local environment

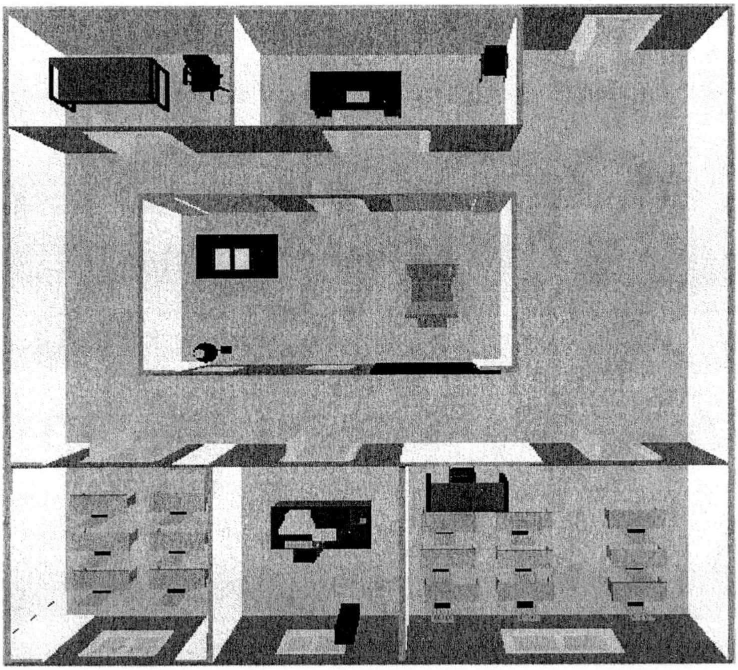

Fig. 2. Example of an indoor environment that contains instances of contextual classes that are illustrated in Figure 1

Figure 2 shows an indoor environment. This indoor environment is created using the set of contextual classes shown in Figure 1.

The rest of this paper is organized as follows. In the next section we describe the model of the SCBR system-environment interaction. In Section 3 we give the basic definitions associated with the representational scheme of the situation cases. This scheme is described in Section 4. In Section 5 we outline the stepwise case-based reasoning cycle. An illustration for autonomous navigation in indoor environments is given in Section 6. Section 7 draws conclusions and discusses the future work.

2 Model of the SCBR System-Environment Interaction

An SCBR system is an entity that can perceive and affect its environment. We first introduce the three basic terms: *environment, perception stimulus and step.*

Definition 1 (Environment). *An environment is defined as everything that surrounds an SCBR system. Formally, an environment E is defined as the four-tuple* $E=(E_m, E_c, PI, US)$*, where*

- E_m *is a part of the environment that is manipulated by the SCBR system,*
- E_c *is a part of the environment that cannot be manipulated, but represents contextual constraints,*

- *PI is a perception interface, and*
- *US is a user of the SCBR system.*

We do not make any assumptions about the representational structure of the elements E_m and E_c. Notice that the SCBR system does not have a complete influence over its environment, it just has a partial influence. According to our interaction model, we assume that the environment also contains a *perception interface* that generates perception stimuli. A user of an SCBR system defines new missions. Also, a user can give directions to the SCBR system when the SCBR system is unable to select an appropriate step.

Definition 2 (Perception stimulus). *A perception stimulus is a sensory information about the environment used as an input to the SCBR system.*

Definition 3 (Step). *A step is any action selected by the SCBR system. According to our interaction model, there are three types of steps as follows:*

- *the act of shifting the attention is called a step for attentional shift,*
- *the act of changing some part of the world external to the SCBR system is called an action step, and*
- *the act of asking for help is called a step for help.*

Now, we will briefly describe *the SCBR system-environment* interaction. The SCBR system and environment interact at each of a sequence of interaction loops. Each interaction loop includes the following phases:

1. perceive the environment,
2. select a step, and
3. step execution.

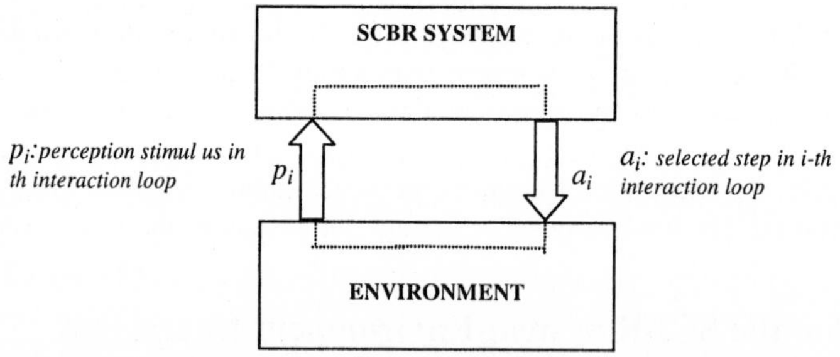

Fig. 3. The SCBR system-environment interaction loop. Each interaction loop includes the following phases: 1. perceive the environment, 2. select a step, and 3. execute the selected step

Throughout each interaction loop, the SCBR system receives a perception stimulus, $p_i \in P$, where P is a set of all possible perception stimuli, and on that basis selects a step $a \in A$, where A is the set of all possible steps. One interaction loop later, as a consequence of its step, the SCBR system finds itself in a new situation. Figure 3 shows the SCBR system-environment interaction. The SCBR system does not use case-based reasoning in each step selection phase of an interaction loop. Instead, throughout certain interaction loops, the SCBR system routinely selects steps without reasoning processes. Throughout these interaction loops the SCBR system uses behavior routines that are selected by case-based reasoning from a certain previous interaction loop. We define behavior routine in Section 3, and describe stepwise case-based reasoning cycles in Section 5.

3 Basic Definitions

In this section we introduce the formal definitions associated with the representational scheme of the situation cases that are described in Section 4. First, we will introduce the notion of intention. An intention refers to what the SCBR system intends to do or achieve. Intentions direct an SCBR system's attention to the relevant aspects of the local environment. A relationship between intentions and steps for attentional shift is formally defined in Section 5. Definition 4 introduces the classification of intentions in our model.

Definition 4 (Intentions). *Let I denote a set of all intentions that can be selected by the SCBR system,*

$$I=\{i_1, i_2, \ldots, i_j, \ldots i_{|I|}\},\ 1 \le j \le |I|. \quad (1)$$

This set can be partitioned into two disjoint sets I_p *and* I_c *such that* $I = I_p \cup I_c$, *and* $I_p \cap I_c = \varnothing$, *where*

- I_p *is a set of all plan intentions, and*
- I_c *is a set of all contextual intentions.*

Each intention starts a selection of a step for attentional shift. Plan intentions and contextual intentions are in hierarchical relationships. A plan intention represents an SCBR system's desire to move from one contextual instance to another contextual instance. A contextual intention represents an SCBR system's desire that is the most appropriate for the given contextual conditions. A contextual intention tends to promote the fulfillment of a plan intention. The selection of contextual intention depends on the current contextual conditions, but plan intentions can be planned at the beginning of the current mission. Plan intentions are planned in advance at the beginning of the current mission due to the fact that the environment contains certain static structures that do not change over time. This is an opposite of the contextual intentions. Contextual intentions will have to be left unspecified until the situation in which they are required arises and relevant perception attributes of the local environment can be determined by selecting an appropriate step for attentional shift. For example, a plan intention for autonomous navigation tasks is "*exit-from-room*". Following are some examples to illustrate contextual intentions: "*move-right-to-avoid-obstacle*", "*left-wall-following*" etc.

Definition 5 (Perception attribute). *A perception attribute is a relevant feature of the environment that is important to the SCBR system's next step selection.*

To act in a continuously changing environment, an SCBR system must be able to react appropriately to changes and unexpected events in the environment. To overcome this problem, we have introduced the notion of the step for attentional shift. An attention can be seen as a filter that decides which aspects of the local environment are relevant to the current situation [10]. However, the step for attentional shift represents the act of shifting the attention to the currently relevant attributes of the local environment. By applying this step, an SCBR system can autonomously create new situation cases that reflect changes in the local environment.

Definition 6 (Step for attentional shift). *Let UA denote a set of all perception attributes,* $UA=\{A_1, A_2, \ldots A_i, \ldots A_{|UA|}\}$, $i=1,2,\ldots|UA|$. *A step for attentional shift f is an n-tuple* $f=(A_1, A_2, \ldots A_n)$ *where*

- A_i *is a perception attribute,* $i=1,2,\ldots n$.

Each perception attribute A_i *corresponds to exactly one domain* D_i, $i=1, 2, \ldots n$. *A domain is a set of values from which one or more perception attributes draw their actual values.*

Therefore, the task of a step for attentional shift is to extract the appropriate aspects of the local environment in the current situation. This step is an abstract representation of the SCBR system's perceptual action. We have used the formalization in Section 4 for describing the representational scheme of situation cases.

We now introduce the classification of steps for attentional shift. Let F denote a set of all steps for attentional shift that can be selected by the SCBR system. This set can be partitioned into three disjoint sets F_c , F_a and $\{f_{qc}, f_{qa}, f_r\}$ where

- F_c is the set of all contextual steps for attentional shift,
- F_a is the set of all action steps for attentional shift, and
- $\{f_{qc}, f_{qa}, f_r\}$ is the predefined set containing three elements where

  f_{qc} denotes a step for attentional shift to the outcome of a contextual behavior routine, f_{qa} denotes a step for attentional shift to the outcome of an action behavior routine, and f_r denotes a step for attentional shift for revision of a currently selected behavior routine. The role of these steps in stepwise case-based reasoning cycles is described in Section 5.

Section 6 of this paper illustrates the basic notions of the stepwise case-based reasoning approach: plan intentions, contextual intentions, contextual steps for attentional shift and action steps for attentional shift. Also, this section describes relationships among these notions in the SCBR system's reasoning cycles. As mentioned earlier, we assume that the environment contains a perception interface that is capable to interpret selected steps for attentional shift and generate a perception stimulus according to the selected step *f*.

Definition 7 (Synthetic perception stimulus). *Let f denote a step for attentional shift* $f=(A_1, A_2,\ldots, A_n)$ *and let* D_i, $i=1,2,\ldots n$, *denote a domain of a perception attribute* A_i. *A Synthetic perception stimulus over a step for attentional shift* sp_f *is an n-tuple* $sp_f=(v_1, v_2 \ldots, v_n)$, $v_i \in D_i$, $i=1,2,\ldots n$.

Notice that a synthetic perception stimulus is a special kind of perception stimuli. An SCBR system receives a synthetic perception stimulus from a perception interface as a consequence of a previously selected step for attentional shift.

Definition 8 (Action step). *An action step m is an n-tuple* $m=(v_1, v_2, \ldots v_p) \in \boldsymbol{R}^p$ *that represents manipulative actions selected by the SCBR system that change some part of the world external to the SCBR system.*

In the rest of this paper we will use M to denote a set of all manipulative actions that can be selected by an SCBR system,

$$M=\{m_1, m_2, \ldots, m_j, \ldots m_{|M|}\},\ 1 \leq j \leq |M| \qquad (2)$$

3.1 Behavior Routines

As mentioned earlier in this paper, the SCBR system does not use case-based reasoning throughout each interaction loop. Instead, throughout certain interaction loops, the SCBR system routinely selects steps based on behavior routines that are generated by case-based reasoning throughout certain previous interaction loop. We will now introduce the three types of behavior routines: *plan behavior routines, contextual behavior routines, and action behavior routines.*

Definition 9 (Plan behavior routines). *Let* I_p *denote a set of all plan intentions. A plan behavior routine* b_p *is an n-tuple* $b_p=(i_1, i_2, \ldots i_j, \ldots i_n)$ *where*

– $i_j \in I_p$, $j=1,2,\ldots n$.

In this paper we concentrate on the situation cases, and on certain notions which refer to plan cases and are relevant for understanding the description of situation cases. An example of such notion is a plan behavior routine. As described in Section 5, a behavior routine directs the selection of contextual steps for attentional shift.

Definition 10 (Contextual behavior routines). *Let* I_c *denote a set of all contextual intentions. A contextual behavior routine* b_c *is an n-tuple* $b_c=(i_1, i_2, \ldots i_j, \ldots i_m)$ *where*

– $i_j \in I_c$, $j=1,2,\ldots m$.

As described in Section 4, a contextual behavior routine represents the solution component of a contextual situation case.

Definition 11 (Action behavior routines). *Let M denote a set of all action steps. An action behavior routine* b_a *is an n-tuple* $b_a=(m_1, m_2, \ldots m_j, \ldots m_p)$ *where*

– $m_j \in M$, $j=1,2,\ldots p$.

An action behavior routine represents the solution component of an action case. Different types of behavior routines represent a behavior of an SCBR system at various levels of abstraction. Plan behavior routines and contextual behavior routines direct the attention to the relevant aspects of the local environment. Action behavior routines provide a selection of the appropriate manipulative steps.

4 The Representation Scheme for Situation Cases

The definitions presented in Section 3 allow for a formal description of the notion of a situation case in terms of its components. First, we introduce the description component of a situation case.

4.1 Description Component of Situation Cases

Definition 12 (Description component of situation cases). *A description component of situation cases d is a two-tuple* $d=(f, sp_f)$ *where*

- f *is a step for attentional shift, and*
- sp_f *is a synthetic perception stimulus over the step for attentional shift f.*

An Alternative Interpretation of a Description Component. A description component of a situation case could be alternatively interpreted as follows. In general, each n-tuple $t=(v_1, v_2, \ldots v_i, \ldots v_n)$ can be interpreted as a function,

$$t: \{1,2, \ldots n\} \rightarrow \{v_1, v_2, \ldots v_n\},$$

where

- $t(i)=v_i$, $i=1,2,\ldots n$.

In this way, elements f and sp_f could also be represented as functions. Since the sp_f function operates on $f^{-1}(A_i)$, we can write the composition as $sp_f(f^{-1}(A_i))$. Let's call the new function $d(A_i) = sp_f(f^{-1}(A_i))$, $i=1,2,\ldots n$. Figure 4 shows a graphical representation of the function $d=sp_f \circ f$ where $\circ$ denotes the composition of functions.

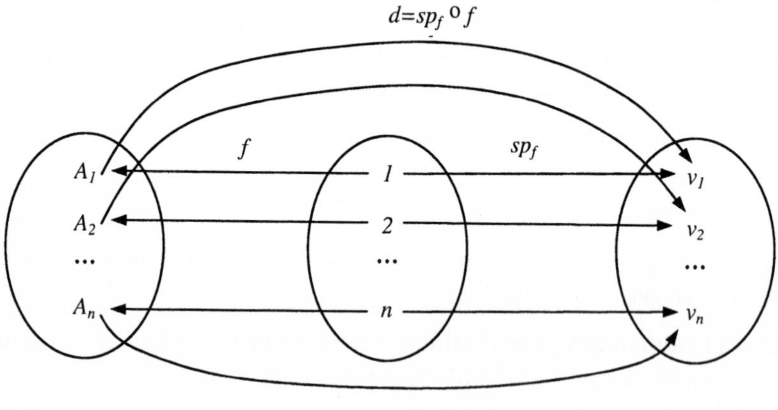

Fig. 4. The graphical representation of a description component as a composition function $d=sp_f \circ f$

4.2 An Example

Let $f=(A_1, A_2, A_3)$ represent the step for attentional shift and let sp_f be a synthetic perception stimulus over f. The step f can be represented in another way as the function f:

$$f: \{1, 2, 3\} \rightarrow \{A_1, A_2, A_3\},$$

where

- $f(1)=A_1, f(2)=A_2, f(3)=A_3$.

Furthermore, let $sp_f=(0.5,\ 1.8,\ 3.5)$ represent the synthetic perception stimulus over the step for attentional shift f. The synthetic perception stimulus sp_f can be represented in another way as the function sp_f:

$$sp_f : \{\ 1,\ 2,\ 3\ \} \rightarrow \{\ 0.5,\ 1.8,\ 3.5\ \},$$

where

- $sp_f(1)=0.5,\ sp_f(2)=1.8,\ sp_f(3)=3.5$.

The inverse of the function f is the f^{-1} where

- $f^{-1}(A_1)=1, f^{-1}(A_2)=2, f^{-1}(A_3)=3$.

The composite function $d=sp_f(f^{-1}(A_i)),\ i\in\{1,2,3\}$, represents the description component of a situation case where

- $d(A_i)=0.5,\ d(A_i)=1.8,\ d(A_3)=3.5$.

The composite function d could be represented in another way as:

$$d=\{(A_1,\ 0.5),\ (A_2,\ 1.8),\ (A_3,\ 3.5)\}\ . \tag{3}$$

4.3 Outcome Component of Situation Cases

As stated earlier in this paper, F denotes a set of all possible steps for attentional shift. This set contains elements denoted by f_{qc} and f_{qa} , where

- f_{qc} is a step for attentional shift to the outcome of contextual behavior routines, and
- f_{qa} is a step for attentional shift to the outcome of action behavior routines.

Therefore, when an SCBR system wants to complete a current situation case, it must select a step that shifts the attention to the perception attributes that describe an outcome of execution of behavior routines. In other words, the SCBR system must select one of the steps: f_{qc} or f_{qa}. A selection of one of the two steps will cause the perception interface to generate a perception stimulus that represents the outcome component of a situation case. The following definitions describe the outcome component of a contextual case and the outcome component of an action case.

Definition 13 (Outcome component of a contextual case). *Let $f_{qc}=(A_{c1},\ A_{c2},\ ...A_{cn})$ denote a step for attentional shift to an outcome of contextual behavior routines. An outcome component of a contextual case is a perception stimulus $sp_f=(v_1,v_2,...v_i...v_n)$, $v_i\in D_{ci}$, $i=1,2,...n$, where D_{ci} is a domain of a perception attribute A_{ci}.*

Definition 14 (Outcome component of an action case). *Let $f_{qa}=(A_{a1},\ A_{a2},\ ...A_{am})$ denote a step for attentional shift to an outcome of action behavior routines. An outcome component of an action case is a perception stimulus $sp_f=(v_1,v_2,...v_i,...v_m)$, $v_i\in D_{ai}$, $i=1,2,...m$, where D_{ai} is a domain of a perception attribute A_{ai}.*

4.4 Definitions of Situation Cases

The definitions presented in Section 3 and subsections 4.1 and 4.3 allow for a formal definition of the two types of situation cases called *contextual cases* and *action cases.*

Definition 15 (Contextual case). *Let F_c denote a set of all contextual steps for attentional shift. A contextual case is a three-tuple $c_c=(d_c, b_c, q_c)$ where*

- *d_c is a description component of a situation case $d=(f, sp_f)$, where f is a contextual step for attentional shift, $f\in F_c$, and sp_f is a perception stimulus over the step f,*
- *b_c is a contextual behavior routine, and*
- *q_c is an outcome component of a contextual case.*

Notice that a contextual behavior routine represents a solution component of a contextual case. This component describes how to choose the appropriate contextual intentions in situation described by a description component d_c.

Definition 16 (Action case). *Let F_a denote a set of all action steps for attentional shift An action case is a three-tuple $c_a=(d_a, b_a, q_a)$ where*

- *d_a is a description component of a situation case, $d_a=(f, sp_f)$, where f is an action step for attentional shift, $f\in F_a$, and sp_f is a perception stimulus over the step f.*
- *b_a is an action behavior routine, and*
- *q_a is an outcome component of an action case.*

Notice that an action behavior routine represents a solution component of an action case. This component describes how to choose the appropriate manipulative action steps in situation described by a description component d_a. The relationship between contextual cases and action cases throughout stepwise case-based reasoning cycles is presented in Section 6.

Contextual cases include not only a description of the relevant aspects of the local environment, but also information about how to select the appropriate contextual intentions in this situation. On the other side, action cases include not only a description of the relevant aspects of a local environment for next action step selection, but also information on how to select the appropriate action steps to manipulate a part of the environment E_m.

4.5 Examples of Situation Cases

Here we show the two situation cases: the contextual case c_c and the action case c_a. We use the following perception attributes: distance from obstacle to the left wall *(L)*, distance from obstacle to right wall *(R)*, distance from obstacle *(D)*, angle to front-right corner of obstacle (θ) and distance from current position to right wall *(W)*. All perception attributes are illustrated in Figure 5. Let the set I_c as a part of the dictionary of the SCBR system, among others contains elements: *mrao (moving-right-to-avoid-obstacle)* and *md (moving-to-door)*. Furthermore, let action steps be represented as a three-tuple $m=(\Delta x, \Delta y, \Delta\theta)$ where Δx denotes the shift of the robot in *X* direction, Δy denotes the shift of the robot in *Y* direction and $\Delta\theta$ denotes the shift of the robot orientation. Table 1 gives the formal specifications for the contextual case $c_c=(d_c,b_c,q_c)$. Table 2 gives the formal specifications for the action case $c_a=(d_a,b_a,q_a)$.

The meaning of the outcome components is determined by the steps for attentional shift to the outcome of behavior routines. We will assume the following steps:

- $f_{qc}=(\Delta S, \Delta T)$, *and*
- $f_{qa}=(\Delta T)$,

where ΔS denotes the perception attribute that represents a distance, and ΔT denotes the perception attribute that represents a time interval.

Table 1. An example of a contextual case for autonomous navigation in structured domains

description, d_c	$d_c = (f, sp_f),\ f = (L, R),\ sp_f = (1, 2)$
solution, b_c	$b_c = (mrao, md)$
outcome, q_c	$q_c = (5, 1)$

Table 2. An example of an action case for autonomous navigation in structured domains

description, d_a	$d_a = (f, sp_f), f = (D, \theta, W), sp_f = (1, 1.5, 3)$
solution, b_a	$b_a = (a_1, a_2),\ a_1 = (1, 2,1.2),\ a_2 = (3, 0, 0)$
outcome, q_a	$q_a = (4.5)$

The outcome component $q_c=(5, 1)$ of the contextual case c_c indicates the traveled distance $\Delta S=5$ by applying behavior routine b_c, and time interval $\Delta T=1$ it takes the robot to travel the distance ΔS. The outcome component $q_a=(4.5)$ of the action case c_a indicates the time interval $\Delta T=4.5$ that robot took to execute the behavior routine b_a. Therefore, the meaning of outcome components of situation cases is determined by the meanings of the perception attributes that constitute steps for attentional shift to the outcome of behavior routines.

5 Outline of Stepwise Case-Based Reasoning Cycles

We now introduce a connectivity function *cf* that is used throughout stepwise case-based reasoning cycles. This function connects intentions and steps for attentional shift.

Definition 17 (Connectivity function): *A connectivity function cf defines the mapping from a set of all intentions* $I = I_p \cup I_c$ *to a set of all steps for attentional shift* $F = F_c \cup F_a$, $cf: I_p \cup I_c \rightarrow F_c \cup F_a$, *with the following properties:*

- $cf(i) \in F_c$ *if* $i \in I_p$, *and*
- $cf(i) \in F_a$ *if* $i \in I_c$.

The phases of stepwise case-based reasoning while the SCBR system is situated in a certain contextual instance are now outlined.

<Create new contextual case>: From a plan behavior routine the SCBR system selects a current plan intention i_p. Using a connectivity function, a contextual step for attentional shift is selected, $f=cf(i_p)$, and a perception interface sends a synthetic perception sp_f to the SCBR system. In this way, the description component of the new contextual case is created, $d_c=(f, sp_f)$.

<Retrieve contextual case>: The contextual case similar to the new contextual case is retrieved from the casebase. Contextual behavior routines $b_c=(i_{c1}, i_{c2}, ...i_{cn})$ is obtained from the retrieved case. The behavior routine is adapted to the new conditions.

<Create new action case>: Using a connectivity function *cf* an action step for attentional shift *f* is selected and a perception interface sends a synthetic perception sp_f to the SCBR system. Thus, the description component of the new action case is created, $d_a=(f, sp_f)$.

<Retrieve action case>: An action case similar to the new action case is retrieved from the casebase. Action behavior routine $b_a=(m_1, m_2, ...m_n)$ is obtained from the retrieved case. The behavior routine is adapted to the new conditions. An action behavior routine b_a is an ordered sequence of action steps m_i, $i=1,2,...n$.

<Reuse of action case>: In this phase, the action behavior routine $b_a=(m_1,m_2,....m_n)$ is used by a step by step approach. In this phase, after each selected action step m_i, the action behavior routine b_a is evaluated. It must be checked if the behavior routine as a plan to achieve a current contextual intention is adequate. When all action steps are selected and executed, the step for attentional shift to the outcome of the action behavior routine is selected. The SCBR system receives a perception stimulus that represents the outcome component of the new action case.

<Retain action case>: The new action case is stored in the casebase.

<Revise contextual behavior routine>: In this phase, before selection of a new contextual intention i_c from the contextual behavior routine b_c, this routine is revised and eventually adapted. If the contextual behavior routine $b_c=(i_{c1}, i_{c2}, ...i_{cn})$ contains unrealized contextual intentions, then the reasoning goes to the phase *<Create new action case>*, else the SCBR system selects a step for attentional shift to the outcome of the current contextual routine. As a result of the selected step, the SCBR system receives a perception stimulus that represents the outcome component of the new contextual case. The SCBR system's reasoning cycles continue with the phase denoted as *<Retain contextual case>*.

<Retain contextual case>: The new contextual case is stored in the casebase. The SCBR system selects a next plan intention from the current plan behavior routine b_p, and reasoning cycles continue with the phase denoted *as <Create new contextual case>*.

6 An Illustration

To help in understanding how stepwise case-based reasoning model works, we show one situation from autonomous navigation domain. The SCBR system's planning module generates a current plan intention, based on plan cases. The solution component of plan cases is an ordered sequence of plan intentions. An SCBR system selects a current plan intention i_p. Assume that the current plan intention is "*exit-from-room*". This intention directs the SCBR system's attention to the relevant perception attributes: distance from obstacle to the left wall (*L*) and distance from obstacle to the right wall (*R*) (see Figure 5). Formally, the SCBR system selects the contextual step for attentional shift $f=(L, R)$. A perception interface generates the synthetic perception stimulus $sp_f=(1, 2)$. Thus, the new contextual case is created $c_c=(d_p, ?, ?)$, $d_p=(f, sp_f)$, where ? denotes temporarily undefined components. Then, the most similar contextual case is retrieved from the casebase $rc_c=(d_c, b_c, q_c)$, and the solution component b_c is adapted to the new conditions. The adapted solution component of the retrieved case is an ordered sequence of contextual intentions. Assume, that this component is $b_c=(mrao, md)$ where

- *mrao* denotes the contextual intention "*move-right-to-avoid-obstacle*", and
- *md* denotes the contextual intention "*move- to-door*".

The SCBR system selects the intention *mrao* that directs the attention to the relevant perception attributes: distance from obstacle *(D)*, angle to front-right obstacle's corner *(θ)*, and distance from right wall *(W)* (see Figure 5). Formally, the SCBR system selects the action step for attentional shift $f=(D, \theta, W)$. Then, the perception interface

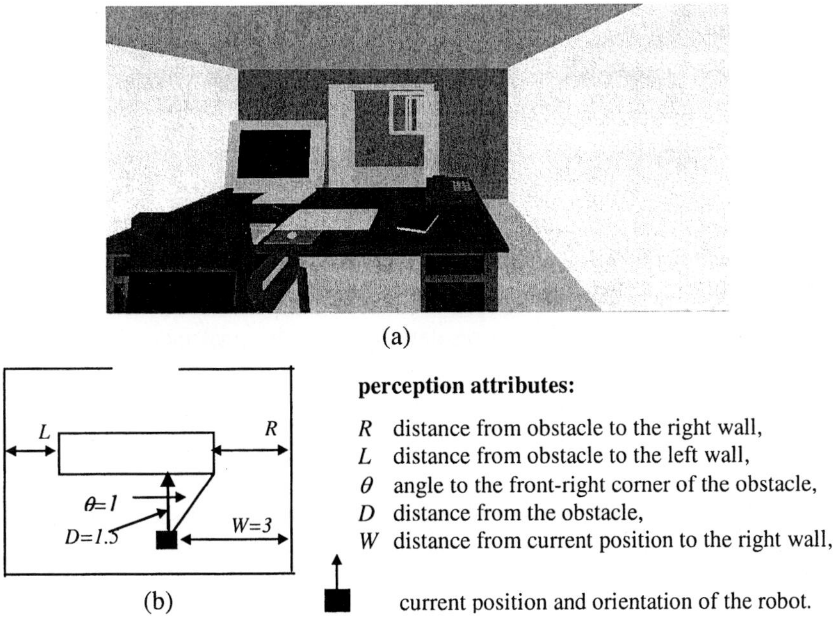
(a)
L
R
θ=1
D=1.5
W=3
(b)
perception attributes:
R distance from obstacle to the right wall,
L distance from obstacle to the left wall,
θ angle to the front-right corner of the obstacle,
D distance from the obstacle,
W distance from current position to the right wall,
current position and orientation of the robot.

Fig. 5. An illustration of the perception attributes for autonomous navigation in indoor environments. (a) A simulated vision from the current position of the robot (b) 2D representation of the relevant perception attributes for the current situation

generates the synthetic perception stimulus $sp_f=(1.5, 1, 3)$ over the step for attentional shift f. The step for attentional shift f and the synthetic perception sp_f are elements of the new action case's description component, $d_a=(f, sp_f)$. Then, the most similar action case is retrieved, $c_a=(d_a, b_a, q_a)$ and the solution component b_a is adapted to the new conditions. The adapted solution component b_a is an ordered sequence of action steps. The SCBR system selects the action steps from b_a and controls the path of a moving robot.

When all action steps are selected and executed, the step for attentional shift to the outcome of the action behavior routine is selected. As a result of the selected step, the SCBR system receives a perception stimulus that represents the outcome component of the new action case. The new action case is stored in the casebase. Before selection of the intention *md* (*"moving-to-door"*) from the contextual behavior routine b_c, this routine is revised and eventually adapted. When all contextual intentions from the contextual behavior routine b_c are achieved, the SCBR system selects the step for attentional shift to the outcome of the current contextual behavior routine. As a result of the selected step, the SCBR system receives a perception stimulus that represents the outcome component of the new contextual case. The new contextual case is stored in the casebase. Furthermore, the SCBR system selects a next plan intention i_p from the plan behavior routine b_p, and stepwise case-based reasoning cycles are repeated throughout the new contextual instance similarly as previously described for achieving the plan intention "*exit-from-room*".

7 Conclusions

We have presented an approach to autonomous creation of new situation cases. The central notion of this approach is the step for attentional shift. There are two key roles of the step for attentional shift in our formal model. The first one is that steps for attentional shift represent description structures of situation cases. The second role is that steps for attentional shift represent an abstract representation of actions by which the SCBR system moves the SCBR system's attention to the relevant aspects of a local environment. We believe that the SCBR approach may have a more general application than autonomous navigation in indoor environments. The next step in this line of research should concentrate on developing an original indexing scheme for efficient situation case retrieval.

References

1. Aamodt, A., Plaza, E.: Case-Based Reasoning: Foundational Issues, Methodological Variations and System Approaches, in *AICOM* (1994), vol 7(1), 39-59
2. Kolodner, J.L.: *Case–Based Reasoning*. Morgan Kaufmann Publishers, Inc., San Mateo, CA, (1993)
3. Ram, A., Arkin, R.C.: Case-Based Reactive Navigation: A Case-Based Method for On-line Selection and Adaptation of Reactive Control Parameters in Autonomous Systems. Tech. Rep. GIT-CC-92/57,College of Computing, Georgia Institute of Technology, Atlanta,USA, (1992)

4. Kruusmaa, M.: Global Navigation in Dynamic Environments Using Case-Based Reasoning, in Autonomous Robots, Kluwer, Vol 14, No. 1, Jan. 2003, pp. 71 – 91. (2003)
5. Corchado J. M. i Laza R.: Creation of Deliberative Agents Using a CBR Model. Computing and Information Systems Journal. Vol 8, No 2, pp 33-39, ISBN: 1352-9404. (2001)
6. Urdiales, C., Perez, E.J., Vázquez-Salceda, J., Sandoval, F.: A Hybrid Architecture for Autonomous Navigation Using a CBR Reactive Layer. Proceedings of the 2003 IEEE/WIC International Conference on Intelligent Agent Technology (IAT 2003), Halifax, Canada, pp 225-232. IEEE Computer Society 2003. ISBN 0-7695-1931-8. (2003)
7. Olivia, C., Chang, C.F., Enguis, C.F., Ghose ,A.K.: Case-Based BDI Agents: An Effective Approach for Intelligent Search on the World Wide Web, AAAI Spring Symposium on Intelligent Agents in Cyberspace, CA: AAAI Press, pp 20-27 (1999).
8. Martin, F. J., Plaza, E., Arcos J.L.: Knowledge and Experience Reuse through Communications among Components (peer) Agents. International Journal of Software Engineering and Knowledge Engineering, Vol. 9, No. 3, pp. 319-341, (1999).
9. Wendler, J. and Lenz, M. : CBR for Dynamic Situation Assesment in an Agent-Oriented Setting. Proc. AAAI-98 Workshop on CBR Integrations, Madison ,USA, (1998).
10. Balkenius, C. and Hulth, N.: Attention as selection-for-action: a scheme for active perception. In Schweitzer, G., Burgard, W., Nehmzow, U., and Vestli, S. J. (Eds.), *Proceedings of EUROBOT '99* (pp. 113-119). IEEE. (1999)

Retrieval and Configuration of Life Insurance Policies

Alexander Tartakovski[1], Martin Schaaf[2], and Ralph Bergmann[1]

[1] University of Trier, Department of Business Information Systems II, 54286 Trier, Germany
{Alexander.Tartakovski, bergmann}@wi2.uni-trier.de
[2] University of Hildesheim, Institute for Mathematics and Applied Computer Science, Data and Knowledge Management Group, 31113 Hildesheim, Germany
schaaf@dwm.uni-hildesheim.de

Abstract. When searching for the right life insurance product, one can either confide in her/his insurance broker or fill out lengthy questionnaires at Internet Portal sites before gathering a large amount of knowledge for interpreting the results. While the first alternative is risky, the second is cumbersome. In this paper, we present an approach that overcomes these drawbacks. It makes use of Structural Case-Based-Reasoning (SCBR) extended by the concept of generalized cases. Here, each insurance product is represented as a generalized case and therefore similarity assessment and indexing of case bases consisting of generalized cases is one of the topics of this paper.

1 Introduction

In this paper, we present an approach for selecting life insurance policies that makes use of the *Structural Case-Based-Reasoning* (SCBR) extended by the concept of *generalized cases* [3]. It is developed to overcome several drawbacks by searching for a suitable policy by a prospective customer.

Nowadays, trading life insurance products is usually done in cooperation with an insurance broker who can offer several products from a limited amount of insurance companies. Life insurances are configurable and the decision about their suitability requires the broker to perceive the personal and financial situation of the client, to consider the desired degree of protection and, of course, to keep in mind his own acquisition commission. However, even the best insurance broker can offer only a small fraction of insurance products available on the market. As a consequence, clients are required to obtain additional information like independent comparisons of insurance products. Meanwhile, some dedicated portal sites on the Internet provide interactive assistance for finding suitable insurance products based on questionnaires. However, such questionnaires either cover only a small amount of important facts or are cumbersome to fill out. In addition, they do not allow the client to emphasize personal preferences and other aspects important to him, e.g. she/he may be flexible for the insurance premium but fixed to a particular insurance sum. The ranking of the insurance products is usually done only according to one specific attribute that is

H. Muñoz-Avila and F. Ricci (Eds.): ICCBR 2005, LNAI 3620, pp. 552–565, 2005.

functionally dependant on the others. Neither the functions behind nor the rationales how the attributes of a particular insurance product depend on each other are disclosed and, in fact, will be rarely understood by a potential client. This, again, requires confidence, but this time in the programmer and his abilities.

Following the approach, presented in this paper, each insurance product is represented as a generalized case. Thereby, the products can be retrieved and configured according to customer requirements. The potential customer is free to provide as much information about his desired degree of protection, financial, and personal situation as she/he wants. Furthermore, it is possible for her/him to emphasize specific requirements to the insurance by providing weights.

Section 2 introduces the concept and details to temporary life insurance products. Section 3 provides an approach for similarity assessment between a customer query and a life insurance product and furthermore, an approach for indexing of product databases. The methodology presented in this section is generic and can be used for other domains where items to be retrieved can be represented as generalized cases. Section 4 provides an evaluation of approaches presented in this paper. Since nonlinear optimization solvers are employed for the purpose of similarity assessment, efficiency and quality of retrieval are important criteria regarded in this section.

2 Temporary Life Insurance

There are several different types of insurance products on the market. Among them the well-known cash value life insurance, temporary life insurance, property-linked life insurance and so on. Furthermore, products of the same type offered by diverse insurance companies often differ in their price structure and benefits.

We demonstrate our approach on an example of the classical temporary life insurance described in [1, 6]. Of course, it can be applied to temporary life insurance products of different companies and also to the other types of life insurance products.

We start this section with a brief introduction to the general temporary life insurance. Then we continue with a classical example and go hereby especially into the corresponding insurance formula and its parameters.

2.1 Concept of Temporary Life Insurance and Search for Right Policy

A temporary life insurance is a special form of life insurance. It is a contract where the insurer pays the insurance sum if the death of the assured person occurs within a specific period [1]. During this period the assured person pays the insurance premium e.g. on an annual base. The aim of a temporary life insurance is first of all the financial security of the assured person's affiliates.

To pick the right policy, the customer should provide some personal data and requirements to the insurer or insurance broker. Important personal data is e.g. the age, the sex, the health status, and some lifestyle information e.g. smoker/ no smoker, sports and so on. The requirements can contain the favored insurance duration, insurance sum, and insurance premium. They have not to be completely specified, e.g. providing insurance duration and insurance sum could be sufficient for insurance broker to choose some offers. Furthermore, the broker is usually not strictly bound to fulfill all requirements exactly. For instance he may propose to slightly reduce the insurance sum or duration if this results in a favorable premium.

2.2 Parameters and Formula of Temporary Life Insurance

A single insurance product is, to a certain degree, parameterized and therefore configurable. The personal data reflects data that cannot be changed within a short period of time. Therefore, from the customer perspective, they are constant values. Contrary, the requirements to the contract are parameters that can be affected directly by the customer.

For simplicity but without loss of generality, the insurance formula (1) [1, 6] regarded in this work is limited to healthy males with a normal lifestyle. The parameters used in the formula are:

- age - x,
- period of insurance – n,
- insurance sum – C,
- insurance premium p.a. - Π.

The formula defines the dependencies between the parameters and therefore all their valid assignments:

$$\Pi = C\frac{f(x,n)+\alpha(1-g(x,n))+\gamma h(x,n)}{(1-\beta)h(x,n)} \tag{1}$$

It is based on the principle of equivalence between expected benefit of the insured person and expected benefit of an insurance company. Both expected values are calculated using mortality tables. Furthermore, this formula includes different fees reflecting the costs of the insurance company: α-, β- and γ-costs:

- α-costs are acquisition costs. A customer pays them only once when signing the contract. This kind of costs covers expenditure for advertisement, for medical examination, broker's acquisition commission, and so on.
- β-costs are collection costs. This kind of costs covers all activities concerning the collection of fees.
- γ-costs are administration costs. This kind of costs covers all internal costs except acquisition costs.

The functions $f(x,n)$, $g(x,n)$, *and* $h(x,n)$[1] are the standard functions for the insurance mathematics and therefore, they can be found in product-formulas of different insurance companies. Their values depend on customer age x, period of insurance n, but also on the mortality table and the assumed interest. The exact explanation of these terms goes beyond the scope of this paper. The interested reader may refer to the books [1, 6].

---

[1] Insurance mathematicians often use other names for the functions $f(x,n)$, $g(x,n)$, *and* $h(x,n)$, namely: $A^1_{x\overline{n}|}, A_{x\overline{n}|}^{\;\;1}, \ddot{a}_{x\overline{n}|}$.

3 Configuration and Retrieval of Temporary Life Insurance Policies

This section provides a new method for solving the task of configuring and selecting life insurance policies. It will be demonstrated using an example of the classical temporary life insurance described in [1, 6].

The approach is applicable for systems supporting customers as well as insurance brokers and is based on structural CBR extended by the concept of *generalized cases*. The section begins with an introduction of its general idea and carries on with a detailed description of its realization.

3.1 General Idea of Configuration and Retrieval

Before the beginning of configuration and retrieval process the customer provides her/his personal data and requirements to a wanted contract. The requirements shouldn't be complete and exact, e.g. the customer provides a wanted period of insurance and an insurance sum, but doesn't provide an exact insurance premium, since the wanted contract price is unknown to her/him. In this case the customer might communicate if she/he is interested on chip policies with a possibility of not satisfying other requirements or if the other requirements have greater priority than the price. Since every contract could be a trade-off between requirements the customer might provide their priorities e.g. through weights. This approach is more flexible than questionnaires, since on the one hand, it allows the customer to provide incomplete information and on the other hand, it allows a providing of priorities.

After receipt of information from a customer most suitable products should be presented according to their best configuration. Hereby, every retrieved product is configured according to the customer requirements and their priorities. To get the most suitable products a retriever component ranks the products according to a satisfaction grade of requirements. In contrast to a broker, such a computer-aided system can offer much more products of different companies.

Since this idea can be realized using the concepts of generalized cases and structural CBR, the next section begins with a brief introduction of the both concepts.

3.2 Extension of Structural CBR Approach Through Generalized Cases

The structural CBR (SCBR) approach has been proven useful when modeling and searching for products within e-commerce scenarios. Its extension by the new concept of generalized cases allows the representation of complex and configurable products, for instance, parameterized insurance products. SCBR with generalized cases has been successfully applied and tested for management of reusable electronic design components [2, 4, 10]. Following the structural CBR approach, each case is described by a finite set of attribute-value pairs that characterize the problem and the solution. In contrast to a traditional case, a generalized case doesn't cover only a point of the case space *CS* but a whole subspace of it [3]. Therefore, the simple formalization for a generalized case *GC* is:

$$GC \subseteq CS \qquad (2)$$

The usual way for representing generalized cases defined over numerical domains is applying constraints for the definition of a subspace like (real domain, here):

$$GC = \{x \in IR^n \mid c_1(x) \geq 0 \wedge \ldots \wedge c_k(x) \geq 0 \wedge c_{k+1}(x) = 0 \wedge \ldots \wedge c_l(x) = 0\} \quad (3)$$

The concept of generalized cases implies the extension of similarity measures. In [3, 10] the similarity between a query and a generalized case has been defined as the similarity between the query and the most similar point-case contained in the generalized case:

$$sim^*(q, GC) := \max\{sim(q,c) \mid c \in GC\} \quad (4)$$

According to this definition, the value of the extended similarity function $sim^*(q,GC)$ is equal to the similarity $sim(q,c)$ between a query q and the most similar point case c contained in the generalized case.

The similarity assessment problem can be viewed as a specific optimization problem [7], which is maximizing or minimizing an objective function under restrictions given through constraints. By defining the objective function as $f(x):=sim(q,x)$ and the feasible set $F:=GC$ the similarity assessment problem is transformed to a specific optimization problem.

3.3 Modeling of Temporary Life Insurance Products

A single temporary life insurance product can be viewed as a generalized case with parameterized attributes: age - x, period of insurance – n, insurance sum – C, and insurance premium - Π. The first step is the definition of the description space that is a Cartesian product spanned by attribute domains. The domains regarded in this work are summarized in the following table:

Table 1. Domains of the description space

Attribute	Domain	Integer/Real
x	{18, 19, … , 64}	integer
n	{1, 2, … ,47}	integer
C	[100, 1000000]	real
Π	[10, 5000]	real

Then, particular insurance products can be entered as a single constraint and stored as described in [2]. Some insurance companies use different mortality tables with the consequence that the functions $f(x,n)$, $g(x,n)$, *and* $h(x,n)$ differ. In order to get the right values, none standard tables should be saved together with product constrains.

3.4 Modeling Similarity Measures

Since the definition of a similarity measure for generalized cases is based on traditional similarity measures, the first step is to define the local similarities for each attribute. The local similarities for *n*, *C*, and Π shouldn't be symmetric. For example, the customer is satisfied when getting a cheaper product or a product with a greater period of insurance as required.

The aggregation function is usually the weighted sum, with weights provided by a user in the query. By specifying the weights the customer emphasizes attributes that are important for him. For example the insurance sum is a very important criterion for some customer and he chooses a great weight for this attribute.

The similarity measure for generalized cases defined in [3] is adequate for insurance products retrieval. This measure defines the similarity between a query and a product as a similarity between the query and the most similar configuration of the product. It means that each product is qualified according to its best configuration.

3.5 Similarity Assessment and Configuration

In this work we use the methods of mathematical optimization for solving the similarity assessment and configuration problem for generalized cases [2]. As mentioned before, the similarity assessment can be viewed as a specific optimization problem. When making use of optimization software, it should be transferred to the adequate standard class of optimization problems. Since, the formula types regarded in this work have numerical parameters – real and integer, the adequate class is *Mixed Integer Nonlinear Problem (MINLP)* [5,8]. The standard problem of this class has the following formulation:

$$\begin{aligned} &\min_{x,y} f(x,y) \\ &s.t.\ c_1(x,y) \geq 0, \\ &\qquad \dots \\ &\qquad c_k(x,y) \geq 0, \\ &\qquad c_{k+1}(x,y) = 0, \\ &\qquad \dots \\ &\qquad c_l(x,y) = 0, \\ &\qquad x \in IR^m,\ y \in Z^n \end{aligned} \tag{5}$$

Table 2. Values of *f(x,n), g(x,n), and h(x,n)*

n	f(x,n)	g(x,n)	h(x,n)
24	0.17	0.36	16.24
25	0.18	0.34	16.6
26	0.19	0.32	16.94

The transformation should map the insurance formula to a single or several constraints and the similarity function to the objective function *f*. Such a mapping introduces a difficulty with the functions *f(x,n), g(x,n), and h(x,n)*, which values are depending on integer age and period of insurance. The following table provides values of insurance terms for a 40 years old male using mortality table: 1960/62 males, Germany [6].

The generalized case and hereby the configuration space according to these values is represented in figure 1.

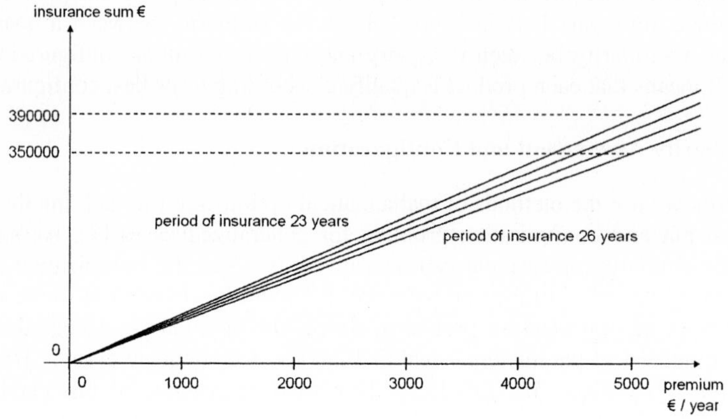

Fig. 1. Temporary life insurance as a generalized case

In [2] a first approach is presented, which transforms the similarity assessment problem for generalized cases defined over mixed, continuous and discrete, domains into a MINLP problem. Using this approach, the insurance formula can be transformed into constraints used by MINLP taking the discrete character of insurance values into account. The transformation will be explained on the concrete temporary life insurance product, which is derived from formula (1) by using the values of $f(x,n)$, $g(x,n)$, and $h(x,n)$ according to the table 2 and by assuming the interval $n \in \{24,\dots,26\}$, and costs $\alpha=0.025$, $\beta=0.01$, $\gamma=0.002$.

By applying *if-then* conditions the instantiated formula can be understood as the following one:

$$\begin{aligned} &if\ n = 24\ then\ \Pi = C\frac{0.17+0.025(1-0.36)+0.002\cdot 16.24}{(1-0.01)\cdot 16.24}, \\ &if\ n = 25\ then\ \Pi = C\frac{0.18+0.025(1-0.34)+0.002\cdot 16.6}{(1-0.01)\cdot 16.6}, \\ &if\ n = 26\ then\ \Pi = C\frac{0.19+0.025(1-0.32)+0.002\cdot 16.94}{(1-0.01)\cdot 16.94}. \end{aligned} \tag{6}$$

In order to get MINLP compatible constraints, the following steps are necessary: Instead of the variable n, three new binary variables must be introduced: n_{24}, n_{25}, $n_{26} \in \{0,1\}$. These correspond to the variable n as follows: $n=i$ iff $n_i=1$. To avoid that several variables get the value 1 a new constraint must be introduced: $n_{24} + n_{25} + n_{26} = 1$. Consequently, the formulas (3) can be transferred to standard MINLP constraints as follows:

$$n_{24}\left(C\frac{0.17+0.025(1-0.36)+0.002\cdot 16.24}{(1-0.01)\cdot 16.24}-\Pi\right)=0,$$
$$n_{25}\left(C\frac{0.18+0.025(1-0.34)+0.002\cdot 16.6}{(1-0.01)\cdot 16.6}-\Pi\right)=0,$$
$$n_{26}\left(C\frac{0.19+0.025(1-0.32)+0.002\cdot 16.94}{(1-0.01)\cdot 16.94}-\Pi\right)=0,$$
$$n_{24}+n_{25}+n_{26}=1,$$
$$C,\Pi\in IR,\quad n_{24},n_{25},n_{26}\in IB \tag{7}$$

Because of the substitution the corresponding local similarity must be changed to:

$$sim_{period}(q_{period},n)\Rightarrow sim'_{period}(q_{period},n_{24},n_{25},n_{26})=$$
$$n_{24}\cdot sim_{period}(q_{period},24)+n_{25}\cdot sim_{period}(q_{period},25)+n_{26}\cdot sim_{period}(q_{period},26) \tag{8}$$

The objective function of the MINLP is then the following one:

$$\max_{n_{24},n_{25},n_{26},C,\Pi} w_1 sim'_{period}(q_{period},n_{24},n_{25},n_{26})+w_2 sim(q_{sum},C)+w_3 sim(q_{premium},\Pi) \tag{9}$$

The objective function (9) together with the constraints (7) is the wanted MINLP.

The majority of available optimization software tools calculate not only an optimal value of an objective function, but additionally a feasible variable assignment corresponding to the optimal value. This assignment is the desired configuration of temporary life insurance products for the scenario regarded in this work.

Furthermore, it is possible to control the accuracy of the optimization software. Increasing the accuracy leads to a better configuration, but a poorer performance. Respectively, decreasing the accuracy decrease the configuration quality, but improves the performance.

3.6 Index Based Retrieval Methods

This section includes an overview of indexing methods presented in [2] and an approach to apply them to case bases consisting of insurance.

Similarity Based Index Method

This method presented for the first time in [2] consists of two parts: an index-builder and a retriever.

Because of the high complexity of the similarity assessment problem for generalized cases the index-builder uses a fix similarity measure for generating an index structure. It partitions the case space into hyperrectangles with faces parallel to the coordinate planes. Every subspace is a potential place holder for a query. Regarding some subspace and some generalized case one can estimate the upper and the lower similarity bounds between the query belonging to an arbitrary point in the subspace, and the case. Doing this not for one case, but for a whole case base, the partial order in terms of similarity can be estimated. The cases having many predecessors, e.g. 10, can be directly excluded, since the customer usually doesn't like to get a large result set. The index-builder stores the remaining cases in conjunction with the partition.

When a customer provides the query, the retriever determines the subspace the query belongs to. Furthermore the retriever load the cases stored together with the subspace and performs the sequential retrieval.

Kd-Tree Based Retrieval Method

The second method presented in [2] adopts the idea of kd-trees [9]. In contrast to the first method it doesn't use the similarity measure, but only the case base for building an index-structure. It consists also of two parts: an indexer, building the adopted kd-tree, and a retriever searching in the tree using a backtracking strategy.

The adopted kd-tree differs from the standard one in the way of storing cases. The original structure is, among other things, the partition of a description space with cases allocated to subspaces including them. Every common point case is allocated to exactly one subspace. Since the generalized cases are sets of possibly infinitely number point cases it is allowed in the adopted variant to allocate cases to subspaces having a not empty intersection with them. Therefore, one generalized case can be allocated to several subspaces.

Indexing Insurance Products

As noticed in section 2, a single insurance product is configurable with respect to personal data of a customer and his requirements to the contract. Since a customer is usually not interested in products that don't match his personal data, e.g. his age, it makes sense to take this fact in account by building of index structures.

The main idea to achieve the improvement of a retrieval performance is to construct, as far as possible, a separate index structure for each individual configuration of personal data.

The personal data in case of the regarded formula for temporary life insurance products is reflected through the age parameter. Therefore index structure can be constructed for every age-value using insurance products restricted to the selected age. After a customer provides his age and his requirements the corresponding index structure is chosen and the products are configured with respect to the customer's requirements.

3.7 Characteristics of Insurance Products of Different Types and Companies

As mentioned before, in previous sections we regarded a special case of the temporary life insurance. The specialty of this insurance is the linear dependence between the premium and the insurance sum by the fixed value of the period of insurance. There are companies having other price structure where the linearity between these parameters doesn't hold [1]. Therefore, the single constraints are not linear in contrast to the regarded case.

Furthermore, different types of life insurances have partly different parameters. For instance, cash value life insurance has additionally a second insurance sum for the case a customer survives the period of insurance.

There are companies mixing life insurance with disability insurance to one product, with a consequence that the number of flexible parameters increases.

4 Empirical Evaluation of Similarity Assessment and Retrieval

This section provides an empirical evaluation of the similarity assessment and index-based retrieval methods for the domain of life insurance products. The first part of the evaluation determines the average computation time for a single similarity assessment depending on chosen characteristics of the products. The second one determines the speedup of the performance by using index-based methods.

4.1 Testing the Similarity Assessment

According to the section 3.5, life insurance products differ on the number of flexible attributes, on the type of constraints (linear / nonlinear) and, furthermore, on the domains of attributes (discrete / continuous). Adding the accuracy of the optimization software, i.e. the allowed absolute error, to these characteristics, completes the set of test-criteria.

General Test Setup

- The optimization software used in the evaluation is GAMS[2] (General Algebraic Modeling System). It encapsulates several solvers which are developed for different classes of optimization problems. For similarity estimation by mixed, discrete and continuous domains, such as the insurance products domain, the MINLP solver GAMS/BARON is chosen. It requires two further solvers, an LP solver GAMS/CPLEX and an NLP solver GAMS/MINOS.
- The computer used by the evaluation is a Pentium 4, 3.0 GHz, with 3 GB RAM, and the platform is MS-Windows 2000.
- The case bases are constructed with a case generator, which is developed especially for this evaluation. It allows generating case bases according to all variations of the chosen criteria.
- Similarity functions used in all test cases are constructed by the weighted average as an amalgamation function and nonlinear local similarities. Therefore all similarity assessment problems regarded here are reduced to NLPs (nonlinear optimization problems) or MINLPs (mixed integer nonlinear optimization problems).

Test Cases

a. Test Setup: The case generator produces 3 case bases, each with 200 cases. The domain models of the case bases include respectively 2, 4 and 8 flexible attributes. All attributes are defined over the same continuous domain. Furthermore, each generalized case in each case base is defined over 8 linear constraints. In this case similarity assessment problems are reduced to optimization problems by introducing of variables in place of attributes and by taking all constraints over. The aim of the test is the calculation of the average duration of a single similarity assessment depending on the number of variables in the corresponding optimization problem and

[2] Produced through GAMS Development Corporation.

accuracy. The accuracy hereby is a maximal allowed absolute error, which is a stopping condition for the solver.

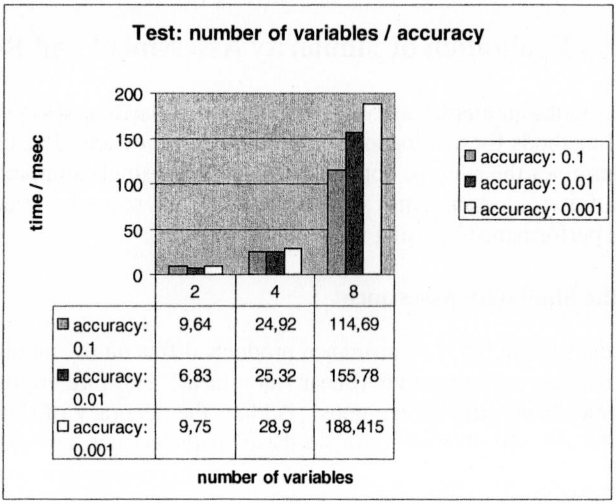

Results: According to the chart, the average computation time for a single similarity assessment is strongly (exponential) depending on the number of flexible attributes. Consequently, only similarity assessment problems can be solved quickly that are reducible to an optimization problem with a few variables. The solver accuracy plays a role in terms of the similarity assessment performance by 8 or more variables and is rather irrelevant by fewer variables.

b. Test Setup: This test differs from the first one through one criterion. Instead of solver accuracy this test case regards the percentage of discrete attributes among all attributes.

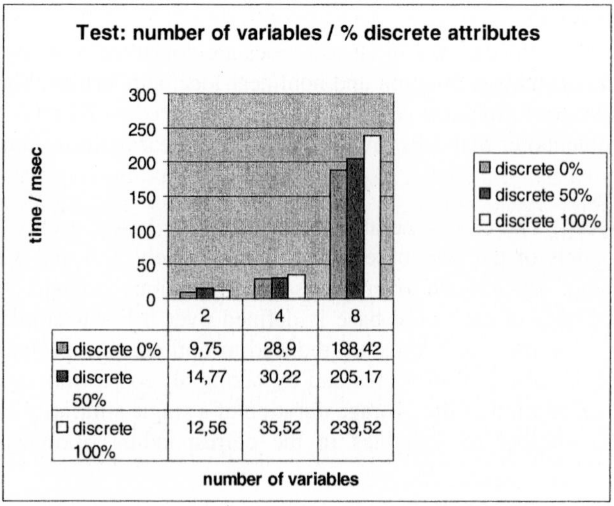

Results: According to the evaluation, the average duration of a single similarity computation increases by increasing the number of discrete attributes. However, the number of variables seems to be the most significant criterion affecting the performance.

4.2 Evaluation of Retrieval Methods

The evaluation of the similarity assessment presented in the previous section shows that the performance decreases already by a small amount of variables. Therefore, the application of index-based retrieval methods is very important for the domain of life insurances. This section includes a general evaluation of the effectiveness of these index structures.

Test Setup:

- Both retrieval methods partition the case space by building an index-tree. The recursive construction is:

  1. selection of some attribute
  2. selection of a separation point for the attribute
  3. creation of two subspaces separated by the separation point
  4. stop or recursive partition the subspaces

  The attributes are selected in a fix order and the separation points are on the medians of the types of attributes. Furthermore, the maximal tree depth is restricted to 5 and to 10. By achieving this depth the both algorithms stop to partition the subspaces in current branch.

- The size of case base is 200 generalized cases.
- Case bases are constructed with 2, 4 and 8 continuous attributes.
- Every generalized case is described through 8 linear constraints.
- The chosen size of a retrieval set is 10 cases.

Results: According to the table 3, both index-based methods improve the retrieval step significantly, when comparing with the sequential retrieval. The required tree-depth by both methods is strongly dependant on the number of variables. Larger number of variables leads to larger tree-depth and therefore to larger index structure. E.g. the tree depth of 10 is insufficient for 8 variables (see table 3). In this case the much greater index structure is required. Based on these facts, further improvements of both index-based methods are necessary. Currently, by the recursive partitioning of the case space the attributes are selected in the fix order and the separation points are on the medians of the types of attributes. It is planed to develop two heuristics for each method improving the required median tree-depth. The first one should determine the attribute to be used for partitioning the case base in the current brunch. The second one should determine the exact value used for splitting the case base.

Surprisingly, at the depth 10 the kd-tree based method provides nearly the same number of similarity evaluations as the similarity based index method. It is remarkable, that the similarity based index method becomes much more information for the indexing, namely the similarity function, and doesn't outperform the other one.

Table 3. Evaluation of Retrieval Methods

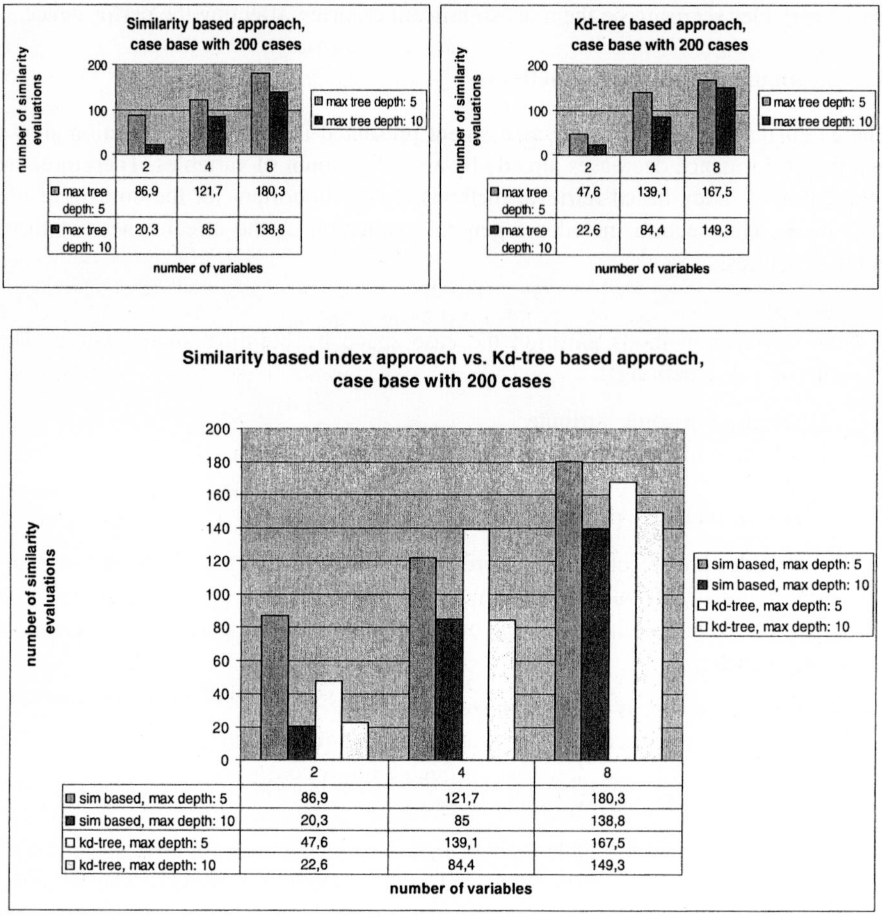

5 Conclusion and Future Work

In this paper we showed an approach for the retrieval and selection of temporal life insurance policies based on Structural CBR that makes use of generalized cases, a concept that allows the representation of configurable products as cases. In contrast to the widespread questionnaires, which currently provide some kind of assistance for assessing insurance products, this facilitates to emphasize personal preferences and works even in the case when the user provides only incomplete information about his personal and financial situation. For the next months it is planned, to launch an experiment with three different student groups. Each group has to select insurance products for a set of imaginary clients respective their personal and financial situation. One group has to use only the Internet; another will work in cooperation with professional insurance brokers; the third group uses the approach developed so far.

Furthermore, we provide an empirical evaluation of sequential and two index based retrieval methods. We show that on the one hand the index based methods improve the retrieval significantly. On the other hand we show that the similarity assessment for cases with more as eight flexible parameters has poor performance and leads to great index-structures in order to compensate the drawback. Therefore, it is planned to improve both index-based methods through heuristics saving retrieval time, indexing time and memory by clever partitioning the description space.

References

1. Gerber, H.U.: Life Insurance Mathematics. Springer-Verlag, Berlin Heidelberg (2001)
2. Tartakovski, A., Schaaf, M., Maximini, R., and Bergmann, R.: MINLP Based Retrieval of Generalized Cases, Proceedings of 7th European Conference, ECCBR 2004. In Peter Funk, and Pedro A. González Calero, editors, Advances in Case-Based Reasoning, LNAI3155, pages 404-418, Madrid, Spain, Springer Verlag, Berlin Heidelberg New York (2004)
3. Bergmann, R.: Experience management. Springer-Verlag Berlin Heidelberg New York (2002)
4. Maximini, R. and Tartakovski, A.: Approximative Retrieval of Attribute Dependent Generalized Cases. In Workshop on Knowledge and Experience Management (FGWM 2003), Karlsruhe Germany (2003)
5. Leyffer, S.: Deterministic methods for mixed integer nonlinear programming. PhD Thesis, Department of Mathematics and Computer Science, University of Dundee (1993)
6. Isenbart, F., and Münzner H.: Lebensversicherungsmathematik für Praxis und Studium. Dr. Th. Gabler Verlag (1994)
7. Mougouie, B., and Bergmann, R.: Similarity Assessment for Generalized Cases by Optimization Methods. In S. Craw, and A. Preece, editors, European Conference on Case-Based Reasoning (ECCBR'02), volume 2416 of LNAI, Springer (2002)
8. Tawarmalani, M., Sahinidis, N.: Convexification and global optimization in continuous and mixed-integer nonlinear programming: Theory, algorithms, software, and applications. Kluwer Academic Publishers, Boston MA (2002)
9. Wess, S., Althoff, K.D., Derwand, G.: Using k-d trees to improve the retrieval step in case-based reasoning. University of Kaiserslautern (1993)
10. Bergmann, R., Vollrath, I., and Wahlmann, T.: Generalized cases and their application to electronic designs. In E. Melis, editor, *7th* German Workshop on Case-Based Reasoning, 1999.

Analogical and Case-Based Reasoning for Predicting Satellite Task Schedulability

Pete Tinker[1], Jason Fox[1], Collin Green[3],
David Rome[4], Karen Casey[4], and Chris Furmanski[2]

[1] HRL Laboratories, LLC, 3011 Malibu Canyon Road, Malibu, CA 90265, USA
[2] Formerly HRL Laboratories, LLC
[3] NASA Ames Research Center
[4] Raytheon Company
patinker@hrl.com, jrfox@hrl.com,
cgreen@mail.arc.nasa.gov, drrome@raytheon.com,
klcasey@raytheon.com, chris@furmanski.net

Abstract. Satellites represent scarce resources that must be carefully scheduled to maximize their value to service consumers. Near-optimal satellite task scheduling is so computationally difficult that it typically takes several hours to schedule one day's activities for a set of satellites and tasks. Thus, often a requestor will not know if a task will be scheduled until it is too late to accommodate scheduling failures. This paper presents our experiences creating a fast Analogical Reasoning (AR) system and an even faster Case-Based Reasoner (CBR) that can predict, in less than a millisecond, whether a hypothetical task will be scheduled successfully. Requestors can use the system to refine tasks for maximum schedulability. We report on three increasingly narrow approaches that use domain knowledge to constrain the problem space. We show results that indicate the method can achieve >80% accuracy on the given problem.

1 Introduction

This paper examines the adaptation and application of Analogical Reasoning (AR) techniques to a pressing real-world problem: task scheduling for satellite resources. The problem is important because during times of crisis many organizations must compete for scarce satellite resources. Because task scheduling can take many hours, users submit requests in advance with no assurance their requests will be included in a near-term schedule. Schedules are then produced in batch mode for the current set of requested tasks. Given a set of satellite resources, can we predict, quickly and accurately whether a specific new task will be scheduled?

The remainder of the paper is organized as follows. We first discuss the problem of interest, then present prior relevant work in Analogical Reasoning and the use of CBR in general for schedulability prediction. We present descriptions of three solution implementations. For the most promising implementation, we supply experimental results, including performance data. A short conclusion expands on the utility of our method.

H. Muñoz-Avila and F. Ricci (Eds.): ICCBR 2005, LNAI 3620, pp. 566 – 578, 2005.

1.1 Satellite Task Scheduling

This section describes the problem we attempted to solve and the parameters associated with it. We chose to consider a scenario that closely matched real-world conditions, using realistic satellite task data and parameters. Under typical operating conditions the scheduling situation remains consistent over time, especially in terms of the number of tasks requested and the distribution of task priorities. However, world events can trigger a surge in demand for satellite resources. As more resources are needed, the number of requests increases, as does the average request priority.

Because the parameters of competing tasks are unknown, a requester generally does not know if a task is schedulable until the complete schedule is produced. A schedule typically takes several hours to compute. As a result, requestors cannot make decisions that depend on knowing if the scheduler will fulfill their request. Their tasks may not be scheduled because other requestors parameterized tasks differently "squeezed out" their request. Fig. 1 illustrates the current situation with the "legacy" scheduler currently used; later we will introduce a proxy "HRL" scheduler that mimics the proprietary scheduler as closely as possible.

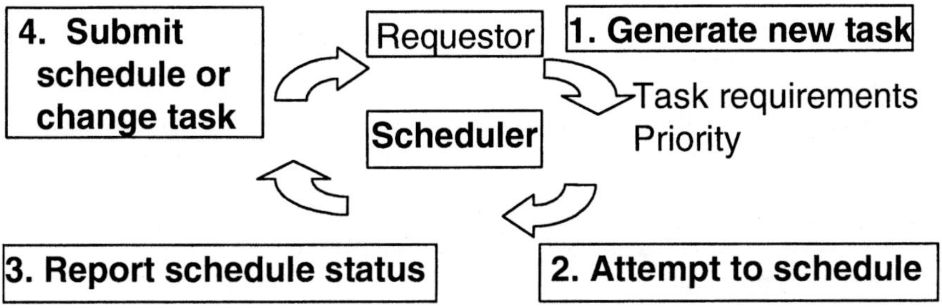

Fig. 1. Current satellite task scheduling relies on experience-based trial and error

This problem motivated us to determine if an AR engine could predict the likelihood that a given task would be scheduled, based on the previous performance of the legacy scheduler. We also explored the effects of changes in demand (and other parameters) on the speed and accuracy of AR and CBR performance. Additionally, we evaluated the ability of the CBR engine to suggest how requests might be altered to improve the probability of being scheduled. Fig. 2 shows our proposed scheduling system with prediction.

We based our experiments on the best available data regarding current satellite task loads. Our sponsoring organization, Raytheon Intelligence and Information Systems (IIS) in Aurora, Colorado, characterized the data.

Our work incorporates these assumptions:

- All tasks are independent (due to a limitation in the legacy scheduler).
- Each task occupies a single time window (tasks cannot be split).

- There are 50 to 60 satellite sensors that can be tasked.
- There are 10 to 60 task types, which describe the task's sensor and time requirements. A task type may be able to use more than one satellite to satisfy its requirements.

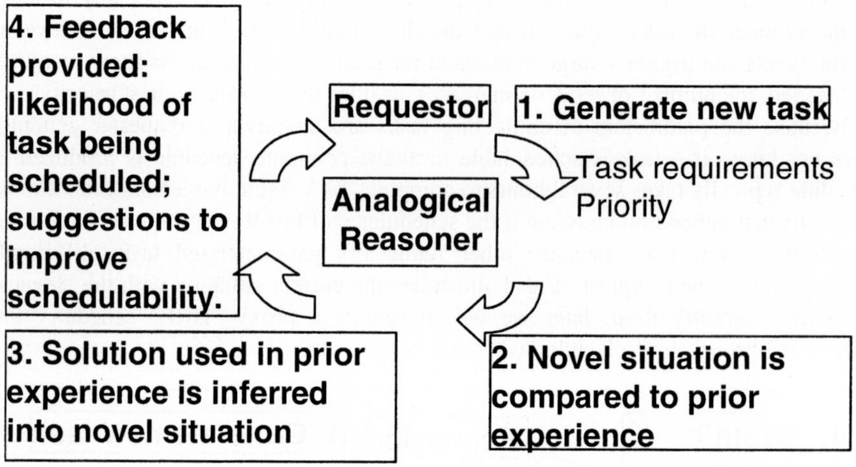

Fig. 2. Analogical Reasoning eliminates the need for a costly complete schedule

- The scheduler coordinates multiple satellites, targets, and sensors.
- 4800 to 12500 tasks are submitted for scheduling per day.
- Tasks are assigned one of five task priorities (lower is more important).
- Each task requires from five to 120 minutes to complete.
- The number of tasks and sensors implies a typical 2:1 – 4:1 resource oversubscription.
- The Knowledge Base (KB) from which analogies can be made includes data from 30 to 365 days.

Each task is described by a vector of feature values that include task type, start and end execution times (in minutes from the start of the day), and priority. A task's type determines the satellites it may use, the duration of the task (time, in minutes, for the task to execute), and the length in minutes of the time window during which the task may be scheduled. We derive two additional features from these base features. *Flexibility* is defined as the ratio of a task's duration to its windows; *subscription* is defined as the ratio of the total time requested by all tasks of this type, during a predetermined range of dates for which data have been collected, to the total time available to perform this task type by all satellites during the same period. For historical data used to construct a KB, we also include whether or not the HRL scheduler actually scheduled each task.

2 Prior Work

2.1 Analogical Reasoning

HRL Laboratories, LLC has constructed a performance-optimized general Analogical Reasoner called SAGE (Self-Aware Generalization Engine)[1]. SAGE's network structure is adapted from the LISA model [1]. LISA (Learning and Inference with Schemas and Analogies) is a symbolic-connectionist model of structure mapping that employs distributed representations of objects and predicates (e.g. the entity "John" might be represented by a collection of units that describe features like "adult", "human", "male", etc.), and local symbolic representations to manipulate the distributed elements (e.g., there is a single unit called "John" that is connected to the collection of distributed units).

SAGE and LISA are distinct from traditional symbolic models of analogy in that they use both local and distributed representations of objects and predicates. The distributed representations are implemented across a pool of semantic units that represent generic concepts. These semantic units are shared among all objects and predicates, and SAGE, like LISA, calculates the similarity of two objects or predicates as similar as a function of their overlap in the semantic space (instead of relying on string comparisons or externally-provided pairwise similarity scores). These semantic units are the basis of the correspondences SAGE finds between conceptually similar entities.

At the same time, SAGE avoids many pitfalls of non-symbolic (purely connectionist) systems by implementing localist tokens for each instance of an object or predicate. The localist tokens allow SAGE to track multiple instances of a single type of object or predicate, and to represent objects and predicates independently. That is, an object or predicate's representation is invariant across the statements or propositions into which it enters.

The combination of distributed and localist representations renders SAGE a symbolic system, and at the same time captures the flexibility of connectionist networks. As such, SAGE is an excellent architecture for simulating analogical reasoning, which depends on the ability to encode the (fuzzy) similarity of objects and predicates, but also requires an appreciation of the abstract structure of information.

Like LISA, SAGE's goal is to discover analogical correspondences between a familiar situation (a source) and a novel situation (a target). These correspondences may stem from relational symmetries, object similarities, or a combination of the two. SAGE finds correspondences by activating nodes in the network representing the source (Fig. 3), and allowing activation to pass into the network representing the target (Fig. 4) through shared semantics (Fig. 5). The spread of activation in SAGE's network is carefully controlled so that information about the structure of the source network is accurately represented by the pattern of activation on the shared semantic units. Consequently, activation vectors are established in the target network that reflect the structure of the source network. The arrows in Fig. 3-5 represent the direc-

[1] A paper detailing SAGE is in preparation for AAAI 2005. If accepted, an appropriate reference will be "Furmanski, C., Green, C., & Fox, J. Efficient dynamic binding in a neural network for analogical reasoning. In M.Veloso & S. Kambhampati (Eds.): Proceedings of the 20th National Conference on Artificial Intelligence (AAAI 2005), (xxx-xxx). Menlo Park, CA: AAAI Press.

tion of activation passing. Note that in Fig. 5 there are no arrows between the target task and the semantic layer. This figure represents a hypothetical situation in which activation values are suppressed to allow us to make a distinction between relational and superficial similarity and are therefore not propagated further.

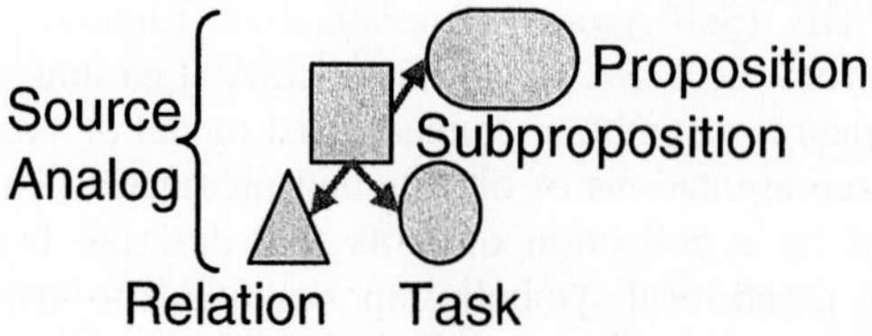

Fig. 3. SAGE source analogs are represented by a set of nodes describing propositional relations between entities

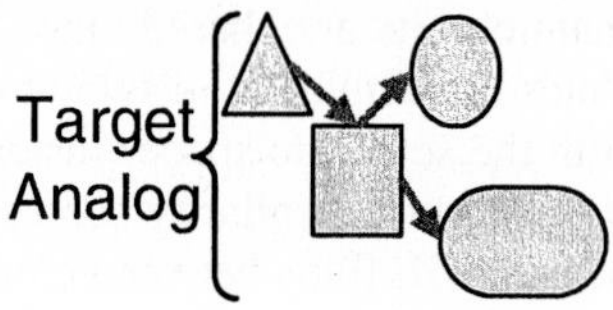

Fig. 4. SAGE target analogs are represented by similar sets of nodes

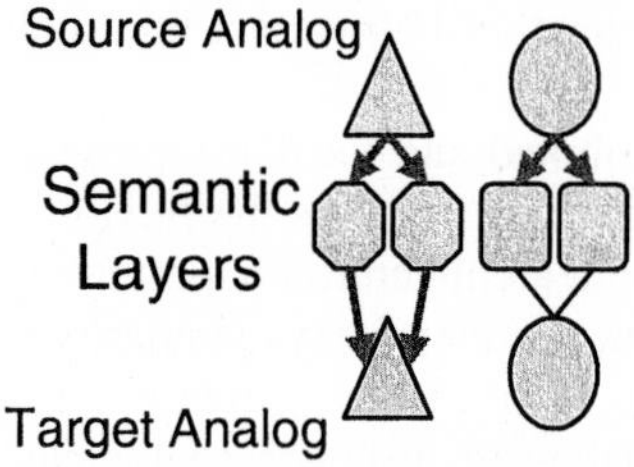

Fig. 5. Source and target analogs are related through semantic layers

Once activation vectors have been established in the target network, SAGE begins calculating correspondences. Each unit in the source is restricted to correspond with units in the target of the same type. Disambiguating which specific target unit best corresponds requires a comparison of the evidence for various mappings. By competitively normalizing the strengths of alternative mappings, SAGE finds the best overall mapping of the source and target networks.

2.2 Schedulability Prediction

Most prior work on schedulability has focused on scheduling real-time processes, especially computing processes [2,3]. The approaches taken generally attempt to provide a functional determination of schedulability using either rate-monotonic algorithms (RMA) or a small set of exemplars [4]. The first approach does not accommodate using a large number of task features in considering schedulability. The second approach can use many features extracted from the exemplar set; however, the exemplar set must be shown to be representative of all possible tasks, and this has not been accomplished.

3 Three AR/CBR-Based Prediction Algorithms

We implemented and evaluated three different prediction algorithms, summarized in Table 1. We derived each later algorithm from earlier ones, incorporating new insights about the impact of domain knowledge. We first considered using SAGE as described above; based on knowledge of our goals, however, we progressed to increasingly narrow, but more efficient mechanisms. Algorithms 1 and 2 used networks similar to SAGE, but removed some node types, simplifying the activation passing. Algorithm 3's structure and execution were very different: it removed the network structure completely, eliminated activation passing, and used simple hashing to find good source analogs for each target. Algorithm 3 was, in effect, a CBR derived from an AR.

We generated source analog tasks on a per-day basis; that is, we constructed a full day's worth of tasks before attempting to schedule them, and one day's task set and schedule did not affect subsequent days' tasks or schedules. We generated "ground truth" schedules using an HRL-constructed one-pass deterministic scheduler that assigned a metric to each task. We sorted the tasks according to the metric and assigned one at a time to the first available resource across all satellites. We collected extensive data on the tasks, resources, and schedules to establish adequate criteria for forming the KB and target analogs.

Table 1. Summary of algorithm properties

	Task Structure Source to Target	Task Structure Target to Source	Discrete Feature Matching
Knowledge Base	task specialized network	task specialized network	feature hashing
Matching Strategy	activation passing	activation passing	Feature matching
Theoretic Time Complexity	$O(kn^2)$	$O(kn)$	$O(kn)$
Magnitude of k	small constant	large constant	small constant
Measured Time Complexity	$t = 0.03n^{1.6}$	$t = 0.08n$	$t = 0.03n$
Ease of use	Knowledge base is straightforward	Knowledge base is straightforward	Must define feature metrics

We tested each algorithm on synthetic data modeled closely on actual situational and task data derived from Raytheon Company sources as described earlier. We represented source and target analogs by task feature vectors of the form

[Duration Priority Flexibility Subscription Scheduled]

We used the feature **scheduled** only for source analogs to indicate, for a source/target pair, whether the target could be predicted to be scheduled or not. For target analogs, this value provides a "ground truth" to determine the accuracy of our predictions.

After building the KB from the source analogs, we submitted target analogs one at a time to the algorithm under consideration. For each target, we found the single analog with the highest activation, and determined if it would have been scheduled. We then compared this schedulability with the actual schedulability of the target analog as provided by the HRL scheduler.

3.1 Task Structure with Activation Passing from Source to Target

Our analysis of SAGE indicated that much of its execution time would be spent in activation passing that did not contribute to the identification of matches. This "wasted" work results from including knowledge of relationships between individual tasks that we could assume were independent. Since we were interested only the schedulability of one specific target task, we did not need to know the relationships between tasks to predict the schedule outcome of any given target task. We therefore eliminated all parts of the network that described inter-task relationships: proposition, subproposition, relation, and relation semantic nodes.

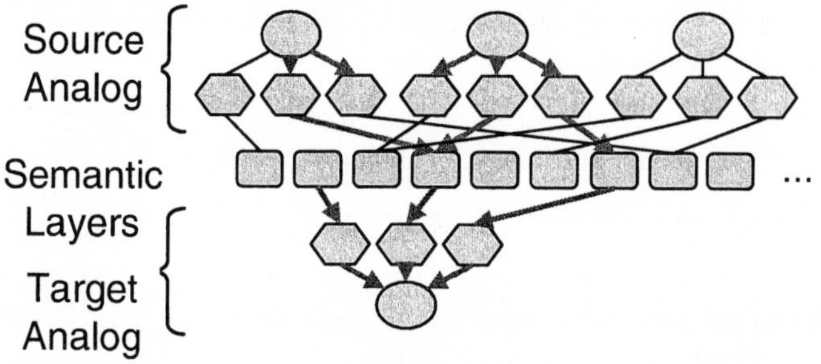

Fig. 6. Algorithms 1 and 2 operated without certain types of SAGE nodes and did not use direct activation propagation. This figure shows activation spreading from source to target

To accommodate relative contributions of each feature type, we added task features to the network. With task features, we could modify the weight (importance) of different task features, e.g., priority versus duration. Fig. 6 shows the reduced network. We refer to Algorithm 1 as "source to target" because we began activation at the subproposition (source task) level. Algorithm 1 is similar to using SAGE in operation, but with the revised network structure. Algorithm 1 manifested very large activation vectors, since there were a great many (> 10,000) source analogs.

3.2 Structure with Activation Passing from Target to Source

Noting the very large activation vectors of Algorithm 1, we modified the process to produce "target-to-source" activation. Algorithm 1 began activation at the highly-populated source task level; in this algorithm we began the activation at the (single) target task. Each task had relatively few (< 5) features, so the size of activation vectors grew more slowly. Furthermore, we could add features without significantly impacting the memory or computational requirements for accumulating the large activation vectors.

Algorithm 2's performance is superior to Algorithm 1's because it explores a much smaller fraction of network nodes. The reduction arises because Algorithm 2 only visits nodes that are directly connected to the (single) target task rather than the (many) source tasks. Overall efficiency improves as the combinatorial explosion of activations decreases.

3.3 Discrete Feature Matching

In the same manner as Algorithm 1 followed from the full SAGE approach by pruning unnecessary node types, Algorithm 3 followed from Algorithm 2. We noted that we could consider the problem starting from the target task rather than the source tasks, and that we could consider only features of the tasks rather than the tasks themselves. These conditions meant that we could remove activation passing entirely,

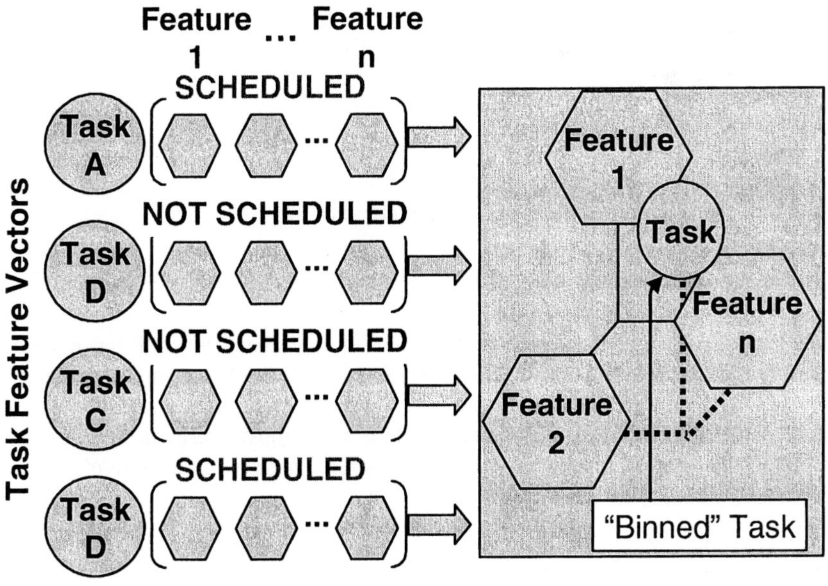

Fig. 7. Algorithm 3 eliminates the network, resulting in very fast execution

relying instead on a simpler feature matching. Algorithm 3 could not reasonably be called an AR algorithm, but rather a CBR algorithm. Fig. 7 illustrates the process used for Algorithm 3.

In Algorithm 3, we collected identical discretized source analog (task) feature vectors using a very fast binning approach based on hashing of feature values. When we had collected all source analogs, we identified the bin corresponding to the target analog's feature vector. This bin contained source analogs whose n-dimensional (n = number of task features selected for matching) feature vectors matched that of the target analog. Potentially there were as many bins as the cardinality of the power set of feature values. In practice, the number of bins produced was usually much smaller: our sample data sets had only 10% to 30% of the potential bins occupied with at least one source task. The small fraction of populated bins followed from using fewer features, each with a small number of possible discrete values, and from the algorithmic behavior of the scheduler producing sets of tasks.

Fig. 8 illustrates the effect of reducing the number of network nodes considered and the direction of activation flow. While Algorithms 1, 2, and 3 all exhibit linear time behavior, the rate of increase is much smaller for Algorithms 2 and 3.

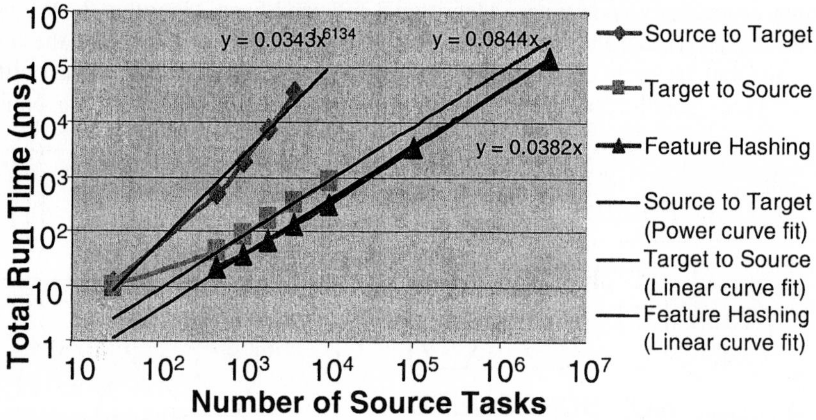

Fig. 8. Algorithms 2 and 3 perform faster than Algorithm 1; Algorithm 3 is fastest

The size of a bin's population was important in appraising the confidence we could put in any source/target matching. Bins with few source analogs produce lower confidence in the matching results than bins with a many because the probabilistic sampling is poorer. Bins with more source analogs were most useful in identifying discriminators (feature combinations that had a strong positive or negative correlation with actual schedulability).

4 Experimental Results

Algorithm 3 proved to be the fastest of the three implemented solutions, and this section supplies detailed results of its speed and accuracy. Fig. 9 illustrates our experimental setup. A parameterized scheduler ("HRL Scheduler") acted as a proxy for the legacy Raytheon scheduler. For a given set of parameters, it created a set of tasks and scheduled them to the best of its capabilities. The scheduler produced $n+1$ sets of tasks and accompanying schedules. We used the first n sets of tasks to construct the Analogical Reasoning KB (source analogs). We used the final task set as a set of target analogs for which the AR/CBR engine would predict schedulability. Each set was completely independent of all other sets.

After we created the KB for a series of task sets, the AR/CBR engine received each of the tasks in the last run as a target analog. The reasoner then produced a prediction of whether the target task would have been scheduled, suggested task parameter changes to improve the likelihood of being scheduled, timing results, and reported the accuracy of the prediction by comparing it to the result of actually scheduling the task in the context of the final run of the set. Table 2 summarizes these results.

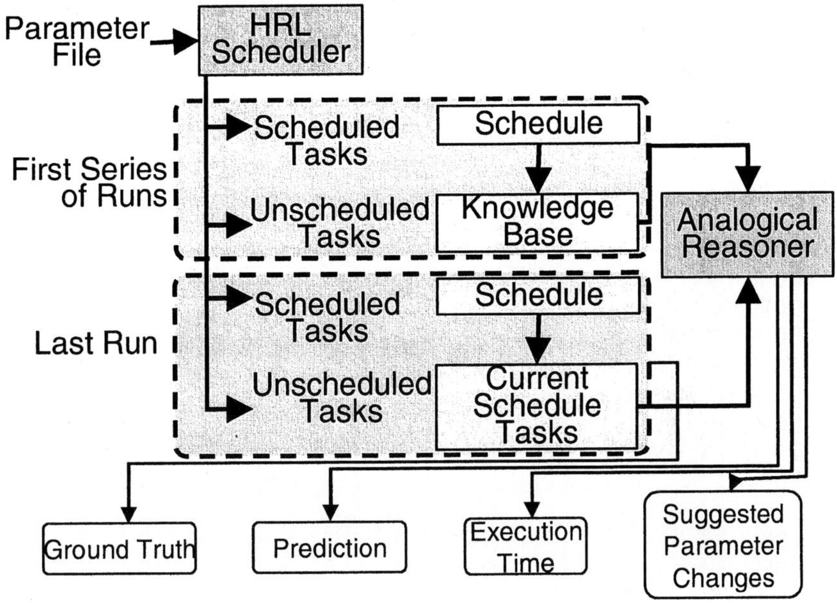

Fig. 9. We used this general architecture for detailed analysis of Algorithm 3

Table 2. Algorithm 3 performance summary

Tasks in KB	6192485	Build Knowledge Base	37.6 microseconds
Predictions	89810	Precompute KB	.001 microseconds
Accuracy	87.83%	Prediction	37.2 microseconds

Table 3 lists the "standard" parameters we used to determine prediction accuracy. Fig. 10 shows the prediction accuracy achieved by Algorithm 3 on the standard parameters and variations from those parameters. The dotted line (and second bar) indicates the accuracy using the standard parameters. The bars represent the accuracy when we made specific changes to the standard task parameters. It was our intent to determine the resilience of the prediction mechanism to sudden changes in task characteristics. These changes can occur, for example, when world conditions change suddenly, resulting in rapid changes in the user community and the characteristics of the tasks users submit for scheduling. It is worth noting that 100% accuracy is theoretically impossible; the scheduling algorithms whose behavior we are trying to predict are non-deterministic. Two runs on the same data will rarely produce the same result, limiting our ability to predict any single task outcome.

Table 3. Standard Parameters

Number of days represented in knowledge base	30
Number of satellites	60
Number of tasks (source analogs) per day	7,500 to 12,500
Task priority mean	3
Task priority standard deviation	1.2
Task duration mean (minutes)	8
Task duration standard deviation	10

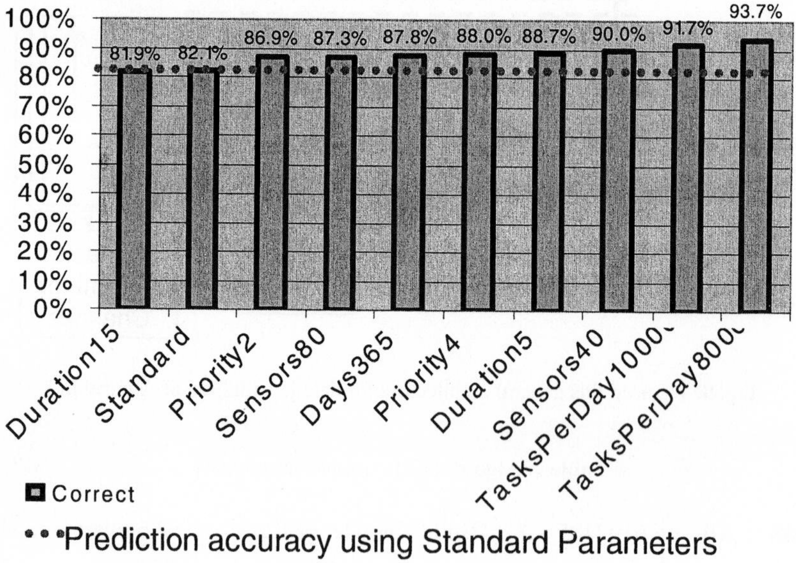

Fig. 10. Prediction accuracy for Standard Parameters and variations

One of the salient extensions we implemented for Algorithm 3 is the ability to suggest how the request could be altered to improve the likelihood of being fulfilled by the legacy scheduler. It does this by creating hypothetical target analogs that are slight variants of the original target. If the hypothetical target produces a higher probability of being scheduled, the altered feature value is suggested to the user. The user can then decide if the change satisfies his requirements, and, if so, can submit it with a greater confidence that it will be scheduled.

The effect of changing task parameters varies greatly from parameter to parameter, as illustrated in Figs. 11 through 14. Fig. 11 shows the number of tasks per priority level as well as the number of tasks scheduled with those priorities. Fig. 12 shows the relationship between priority value and schedulability (on a scale from 0.0 to 1.0). The generally high values in Fig. 12 mean that priority is, overall, a good discriminator. (However, a priority value near the mean is not a good discriminator due to the dip in Fig. 12's group) Figs. 13 and 14 show similar data for task duration. The graph in Fig 14 is overall much lower than that of Fig. 12, meaning that there is less correlation between duration and schedulability. A task's duration is not a good predictor of its schedulability.

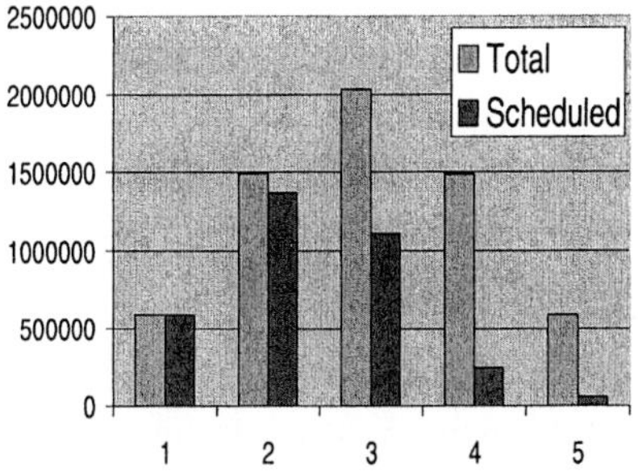

Fig. 11. Task priority vs. number of tasks scheduled and unscheduled

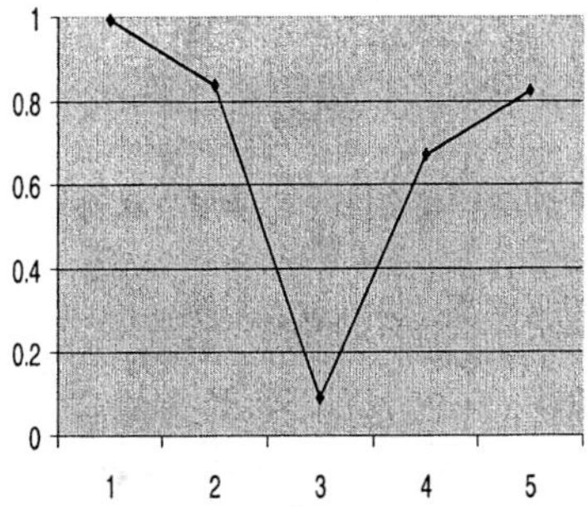

Fig. 12. Task priority vs. schedulability probability over all tasks

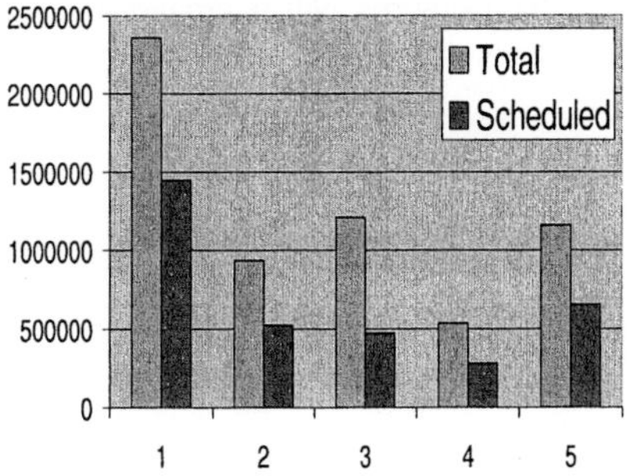

Fig. 13. Task duration vs. number of tasks scheduled and unscheduled

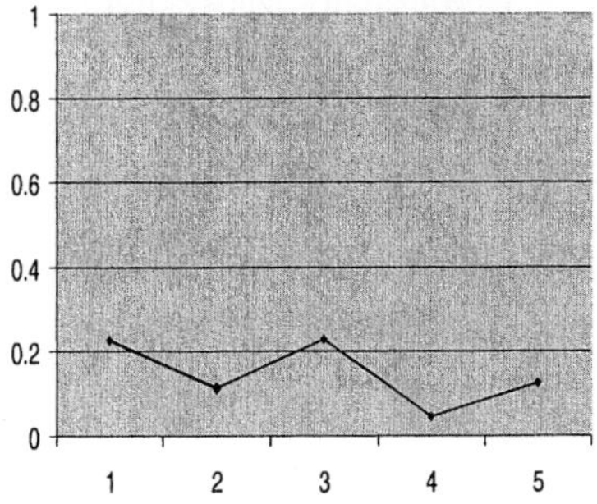

Fig. 14. Task duration vs. schedulability pro-bability over all tasks

5 Conclusion

The work reported here demonstrates the utility of Analogical and Case-Based Reasoning for a problem of great practical significance. Through a series of optimizations to our initial Analogical Reasoning algorithm, we achieved a capability to predict, with accuracies typically > 80%, whether a given satellite task would be scheduled. The time to make the prediction was so small that a great many such predictions could be made, enabling users to customize their requests for maximum probability of successful scheduling. This level of fast and accurate predictability has not been available in the past, and can eliminate many lost opportunities for efficient satellite usage. Fast and accurate schedulability prediction gives decision makers the ability to take action (such as changing parameters) rather than wait for the results of time consuming batch scheduling. The results have the potential to change the way people use and think about scheduling.

The prediction process requires no significant cost or change to the existing scheduling infrastructure. It can be used with Raytheon's legacy scheduler, augmenting its utility without affecting its performance. The legacy scheduler needs to collect and record information about tasks it attempts to schedule, in order to build the prediction KB. Otherwise, no changes are necessary.

References

[1] Hummel, J.E., and Holyoak, K.J. A symbolic-connectionist theory of relational inference and generalization. Psychological Reviews, 2003 Apr; 110(2):220-64

[2] Sweeney, John, and Li, Huan Li, and Grupen, Rod and Ramamritham, Krithi. Scalability and Schedulability in Large, Coordinated, Distributed Robot Systems. International Conference on Robotics and Automation, Sept 2003.

[3] Heidmann, Paul S. A Statistical Model for Designers of Rate Monotonic Systems. Proceedings of the Second Annual Rate Monotonic User's Forum (hosted by the SEI), November, 1993.

[4] Martí-Campoy, Antonio and Sáez, Sergio and Perles, Angel and Busquets, Jose Vicente. Schedulability analisys in EDF scheduler with cache memories. 9th International Conference on Real-Time and Embedded Computing Systems and Applications, 2003.

Case Adaptation by Segment Replanning for Case-Based Planning Systems*

Flavio Tonidandel and Marcio Rillo

Centro Universitário da FEI – UniFEI,
Av. Humberto de A. Castelo Branco, 3972
09850-901 - São Bernardo do Campo – SP - Brazil
{flaviot, rillo}@fei.edu.br

Abstract. An adaptation phase is crucial for a good and reasonable Case-Based Planning (CBP) system. The adaptation phase is responsible for finding a solution in order to solve a new problem. If the phase is not well designed, the CBP system may not solve the desirable range of problems or the solutions will not have appropriate quality. In this paper, a method called CASER – Case Adaptation by Segment Replanning – is presented as an adaptation rule for case-based planning system. The method has two phases: the first one completes a retrieved case as an easy-to-generate solution method. The second phase improves the quality of the solution by using a generic heuristic in a recursive algorithm to determine segments of the plan to be replanned. The CASER method does not use any additional knowledge, and it can find as good solutions as those found by the best generative planners.

1 Introduction

The adaptation phase of a CBR (Case-Based Reasoning) system is responsible for finding a solution from a retrieved case. Specifically for Case-Based Planning systems, the adaptation phase is important for finding good quality plans, where the quality refers to the solution plan length and the rational use of resources and time.

However, a high quality solution is not easy to find. In fact, searching for an optimal solution is *NP-Hard* [12] even for generative planning or case-based planning systems. Actually, many solutions usually obtained by case-based planning systems [14] are longer than necessary. Although there is no advantage for adapting plans over a complete regeneration of a new solution in the worst case, as shown by Nebel and Koehler [12], the adaptation of plans can be the best choice in most situations [6] and it has great potential to be better than planning from scratch [2].

Gerevini and Serina [6] propose the ADJUST-PLAN algorithm that adapts an existing plan in order to find a solution to a new problem. Their algorithm, although not designed for Case-Based Planning (CBP) systems, adapts an existing plan instead of finding an entire plan when the problem is modified. The main problem of the

* This work was partially supported by FAPESP under contract number 98/15835-9.

H. Muñoz-Avila and F. Ricci (Eds.): ICCBR 2005, LNAI 3620, pp. 579 – 594, 2005.

algorithm is that its technique requires constructing an entire planning graph, which can be computationally expensive for complex domains [6].

Another approach is the Planning by Rewriting paradigm [1]. It addresses the problem of adapting a solution plan through rewriting rules in order to find a better quality plan. However, rewriting rules are domain-dependent rules that can be determined by hand or by a learning process [1], which requires some extra knowledge about the domain.

In contrast of the previous approaches, this paper presents an domain-independent adaptation process. This method, called CASER (*Case Adaptation by Segment Replanning),* has two phases. First it finds a low quality solution by a simple completion of the retrieved case, and then the second phase uses the FF-heuristic [9] to detect sub-plans (or segments) in the solution plan that can be replanned in order to improve the quality of the solution.

This paper focuses in a STRIPS-like version of the CASER method, where just the number of steps can define a solution plan's quality. Its improving to deal with metrical and temporal domains is discussed in the discussion section.

2 Solution Quality and Plan Adaptation

The challenge of most plan adaptation processes is to determine which part of a plan must be adapted in order to achieve a correct solution, guaranteeing its high quality.

In a case-based planning domain, a case is a plan and the improvement of the case quality in the STRIPS-version is the reduction of the number of actions that guides the plan from the initial state to the final state. The purpose of an adaptation process applied to a Case-Based planning system is to change, add or even delete appropriate actions of the case in order to find a better solution.

There are in the literature dedicated efforts on adaptation processes. One adaptation process is the ADJUST-PLAN method [6], which refines a plan until it becomes a new solution. In fact, it tries to find a complete solution from a given plan by refining sub-plans on the graph created by the Graphplan system [4]. It is well specified to work in a domain where problems are partially modified and, consequently, some sub-graphs used to solve previous problems can be re-used to find and refine a solution to a new problem. However, in general, when a case is retrieved from a case base, the case does not contain any previous planning graph, forcing the ADJUST-PLAN method to create the entire graph. The process to create an entire graph can be computationally expensive and the method can be unable to be used efficiently in case-based systems. Similar to ADJUST-PLAN is the replanning process called SHERPA [10]. Although not designed to improve solution quality, it finds replanned solutions whose qualities are as good as those achieved from scratch [10].

The adaptation of a plan can also be useful for generative planning systems. A new planning paradigm, called Planning by Rewriting (PbR), uses an adaptation phase, called rewriting, that turns a low quality plan into a high quality plan by using some domain dependent rules. PbR is a planning process that finds an easy-to-generate solution plan and then adapts it to yield a better solution by some domain-dependent rules. These rules can be designed by hand or through an automated learning process

[1]. In both cases, PbR needs additional domain specific knowledge and a complete specification of the rules or some training instances for the learning process.

In fact, there is no adaptation method which finds and improves the solution quality from a retrieved case without any additional knowledge besides standard planning knowledge, such as an operator's specification and initial and goal states.

This paper introduces a domain-independent and anytime behavior adaptation process, called CASER (*Case Adaptation by Segment Replanning*), that finds an easy-to-generate solution with low quality and adapts this solution to improve it. It follows the same idea as PbR. However, this method does not require any additional domain knowledge apart from an operator's specification, an initial state and a goal state. As we discuss later, the CASER method is very useful for case-based planners that uses Action Distance-Guided (ADG) similarity [13] to retrieve cases, as used in the FAR-OFF system [14], or even for those CBP systems where the solutions are usually longer than necessary.

3 The CASER Method

The CASER method has two main phases, namely:

1. The completion of a retrieved case in order to find a new solution (easy-to-generate solution); It uses a modified version of the FF planning system [9] to complete the case.
2. A recursive algorithm that replans solution segments in order to improve the final solution quality by using a modified version of the FF-heuristic and of the FF planning system [9].

The two processes do not use any additional knowledge and use a generative planning system, which is a modified version of the original FF planning system [9] in this STRIPS-like version, described below.

3.1 A Modified Version of the FF Planner

The original FF planning system, as presented in [9], is designed to plan in a fast way by extracting an useful heuristic, called FF-heuristic, from a relaxed graph similar to GraphPlan [4] graph but without considering delete lists of actions. The FF-heuristic is the number of actions of the relaxed plan extracted from the relaxed graph. The FF planner uses the FF-heuristic to guide the Enforced Hill-climbing search to the goal.

In order to improve the efficiency of the FF planner, Hoffmann and Nebel [9] introduces some additional heuristics that prunes states, such as the *added-goal deletion* heuristic. In this modified version of the FF planner, the FF-heuristic is used in its regular form with a small modification: it permits that the relaxed graph expands further until a fixpoint is reached.

As defined by Hoffmann and Nebel [9], the relaxed graph is created by ignoring the delete list of the actions. It is constituted by layers that comprise alternative facts and actions. The first fact layer is the initial state (*initst*). The first action layer contains all actions whose preconditions are satisfied in *initst*. Then, the add lists of these actions are inserted in the next fact layer together with all facts from the previous fact layer, which leads to the next action layer, and so on. The regular specification of the FF-heuristic is that the relaxed graph is expanded until all goals are in the last fact layer. With the modification discussed above, the relaxed graph must be created until a fixpoint is found, i.e., when there are no more fact layers that are different from the previous ones.

With the relaxed graph created until the fixpoint, a relaxed solution can be found for any state that can be reached from *initst*. The process of determining the relaxed solution, following Hoffmann and Nebel [9], is performed from the last layer to the first layer, finding and selecting actions in layer *i-1* if it is the case that their add-list contains one or more of goals initialized in layer *i*. After that, the preconditions of the selected actions are initialized as new goals in their previous and corresponding layer. The process stops when all unsatisfied goals are in the first layer, which is exactly the initial state. The relaxed solution is the selected actions in the graph and the estimate distance is the number of actions in this relaxed solution.

The FF-heuristic returns, therefore, the number of estimated actions between *initst* and any possible state reached from *initst*. We will use this heuristic in the modified version of the FF planner.

However, the modification of the FF-heuristic to expand the graph until fixpoint is not enough for the modified version of the FF planner. In fact, we must also change the *added-goal deletion* heuristic. In its regular specification, the *added-goal deletion* heuristic does not consider a state on which a goal that has been just reached can be deleted by the next steps of the plan in the search tree. The heuristic analyzes the delete lists of all actions in the relaxed solution provided by the FF-heuristic. If a reached goal is in the delete list of any action in the relaxed solution, the FF planner does not consider this state in the search tree.

The heuristic works fine when the goal contains no predicates that are easy to change, like *handempty* in the Blocks World domain or the *at(airplane,airport)* in the logistic domain. If one of these easy-to-change predicates is in the goal, the FF planner can not find a solution.

For example, consider that the initial state of a planning problem in Blocks World domain is *on(A,B), clear(A), ontable(B)* and *holding(C)*; and the goal is *on(A,C)* and *handempty*. The regular solution plan must have many actions that delete the *handempty* predicate. The FF planning system, therefore, is unable to find a solution because the *added-goal deletion* will try to avoid that the *handempty* be deleted and, consequently, it will prune the next states.

Since the CASER method will consider complete and consistent states as goals, called *extended goals*, it would experience some problems by using the original FF planning system to find an alternative plan. Therefore, in order to avoid this problem, we implemented a modified version of the FF planning system. In this version, a *relaxed added-goal deletion* heuristic is implemented.

The *relaxed added-goal deletion* heuristic does not prune a state if the predicate goal reached has one of the following conditions:

1. It is presented in the add-list of more than one action;
2. It is the unique predicate in a precondition of at least one action.

The first condition excludes predicates like *holding(_)* and *handempty* in the Blocks World domain. The second condition allows that a specific action with a unique predicate in preconditions can be used.

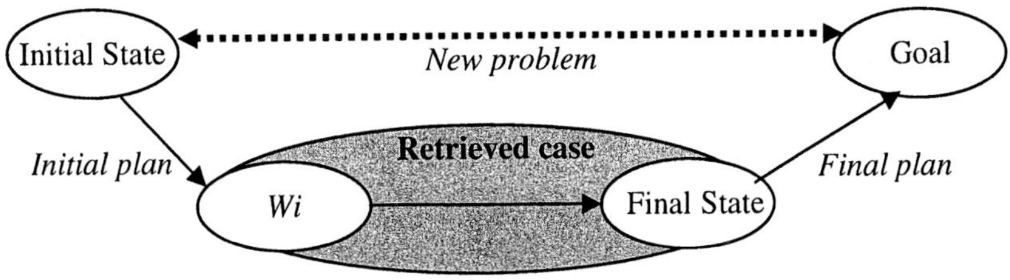

Fig. 1. The Completion Process – it shows the retrieved case and its *Wi* and Final State. Given a new problem, the retrieved case becomes a sub-plan of the solution composed by the Initial Plan + Retrieved Case + Final Plan

Besides the *relaxed added-goal deletion* heuristic, the modified version of the FF planner has also the following features:

- It does not switch to the complete Best First Search if a solution was not found by using Enforced Hill-Climbing search;
- It avoids an specific action as the first action in the solution plan;
- It allows to specify the maximal length of a solution;
- It allows to specify an upper-time limit time to find a solution.

The first constraint described above is imposed because it is not important to find a solution at any time cost; the remaining three items are imposed to permit the CASER method to focus the FF planning to its purpose.

The aim of these modifications is not to improve the FF planning system capacity, but only adapts the system to be used in the CASER method. Since these modifications relax some FF planner features, there is also a great probability that the original system outperforms this modified version.

3.2 The Completion Process – The First Phase

The easy-to-generate solution may be obtained by completing a retrieved case. Each retrieved case must be a plan (a complete solution of an old problem) and it must have its correct sequence of actions.

In fact, the CASER method in this first phase receives an initial state, a goal state and a totally ordered plan from the retrieved case that does not match on either of two states necessarily. In other words, the retrieved case is a sub-plan of the solution.

The completion of the case must extract the precondition of the retrieved case. This precondition is called *Wi* [13]. Informally, *Wi* is a set of those literals that are deleted by the plan and that must be in the initial state necessarily. It is equal to the result of the foot printing method used by PRODIGY/ANALOGY system [17].

The completion phase of the CASER process finds a simple way to transform the retrieved case into a solution. It just tries to expand the retrieved case backward in order to match the initial state and expand it forward in order to satisfy the goal.

The backward expansion is a plan, called *initial plan,* that bridges the initial state and the retrieved case. This plan is found by a generative planner applied from the initial state to *Wi* of the case, where *Wi* is the goal to be achieved. Since the *Wi* may be an extended goal, the CASER method uses the modified version of FF planning system as its generative planner. Figure 1 shows the completion process.

```
procedure CASER_completion(retrieved_case, initst, goalst)
Wi ← find_Wi (retrieved_case);
FS ← find_final_state(retrieved_case);
Initial_plan ← modified_FF(initst, Wi);
Final_plan ← modified_FF(Final_state, goalst);
return Initial_plan + retrieved_case + Final_plan;
end;
```

Fig. 2. The completion algorithm. The initst is the initial state of a problem and goalst is the goal state. The modified_FF finds a plan from its first argument to its second argument

The forward expansion is similar to the backward expansion, but it finds a plan, called *final plan*, that fits the final state of the case and the goal of the new problem. The final state of the case can be easily found by executing the actions effects of the new adapted case (*initial plan* joined with the retrieved case) from the initial state.

The final state of the case becomes a new initial state for the modified FF-planner that finds the *final plan* from this final state direct to the new goal.

At this stage of the CASER method, a complete solution of the new problem is stated by the joint of *initial plan*, retrieved case and *final plan*. Figure 2 summarizes the algorithm of this first phase.

However, as stated before, the solution obtained by the completion phase is just an easy-to-generate plan and it may not have appropriate quality since it can have more actions than necessary. The second phase of the CASER method is designed to reduce the length of the plan and, consequently, increases its quality.

3.3 The Recursive Replanning Process – The Second Phase

The planning search tree is usually a network (e.g. a graph) of actions composed of all states and all actions in a specific domain. For total-order planners, a solution plan is necessarily a sequence of actions, and it can be represented as a path in a directed graph where each node is a consistent state and each edge is an action.

Considering a distance function, h^d, it is possible to estimate the number of actions between two planning states. If this function is applied to estimate the distance from an initial state to all other states in a directed graph, it is possible to determine the costs of reaching each state from the initial state in number of actions.

However, there is no accurate distance function to determine optimal costs for each state without domain specific rules or that takes reasonable time to do it. An approximation of these optimal costs can be obtained by using a heuristic function used by the heuristic search planners, such as FF-heuristic [9] and HSP-heuristic [5]. Considering the recent results of the FF system, the FF-heuristic is one of the best choices to be used in this cost estimation. It was also successfully used in other methods, such as the ADG similarity [13] and the FAR-OFF system [14].

The CASER method uses the FF-heuristic in its second phase in order to calculate the cost of each state and to determine the segments for replanning. This second phase was first published in [15] as the SQUIRE method (Solution Quality Improvement by Replanning) for refining solution plans from generative planning system. This paper improves this method and uses it to adapt plan reused from cases.

```
procedure det_costs(plan, initst)
fixpoint ← create_relaxed_graph(initst)
S0 ← initst;
v0 ← 0;
i ← from_state;
while i < number of actions of the plan do
      i ← i+1;
      Si ← execute_action (Ai of the plan on the Si-1 state)
      vi ← determine_relaxed_solution(Si);
      endwhile
return array of values <v0,v1,v2,v3..,vn>
end;
```

Fig. 3. Algorithm of a function that determines the distances of each intermediate state from the initial state `initst` of a `plan`. The `from_state` variable is the number of the first state that must be considered in the `plan`

The second phase has two steps. The first step determines the cost of each intermediate state of a solution plan provided by the completion phase. The algorithm in Figure 3 calculates, given an initial state and a solution plan, the estimated distance of each intermediate state from the initial state by using the FF-heuristic.

In order to determine the final and the intermediate state, the algorithm executes each action of the plan from the initial state (function *execute_action* in Figure 3).

The functions *create_relaxed_graph* and *determine_ relaxed_solution* in Figure 3 are algorithms extracted from the FF-heuristic [9]. The function *create_relaxed_ graph* is modified to expand the graph until a fixpoint is found.

The algorithm of Figure 3 returns an array of costs that contains the distance estimation value of each intermediate state from the initial state. In an optimal or optimized plan, these values must increase constantly from the beginning to the end. Any value that is less than the value before it can indicate a hot point of replanning, because it indicates a possible return in the directed graph of search. This value and its respective state are called ***returned***.

The main idea of the CASER method is to find a misplaced sub-plan by detecting three kind of potential states: a Returned State (***Sr***) which is a potential state of a misplaced sub-plan, a Back State (***Sb***) that would be the final part of the misplaced sub-plan; and a State with Misplaced action (***Sm***) that would be the initial part of the sub-plan. Therefore, the misplaced sub-plan would be formed by the actions between ***Sm*** and ***Sb*** states. Figure 4 summarizes the main idea of the CASER method.

Definition 1: (Returned State) For a plan with **<S_0,S_1,S_2,S_3,...,Sn>** intermediate states, a **Sr** is an intermediary state where its value, obtained by a heuristic function, h^d, is less than the value of S_{i-1}.

This ***returned*** value indicates that its respective intermediate state is nearer to the initial state than the intermediate state immediately before it. The ***returned*** state and its ***returned*** value are indicated as S_r and v_r respectively. The CASER method detects the first occurrence of a ***returned*** state in the solution plan. The algorithm that determines the ***Sr*** and ***vr*** is presented in Figure 5. The symbol ***Sr*** just indicates that this point can be a part of a misplaced segment.

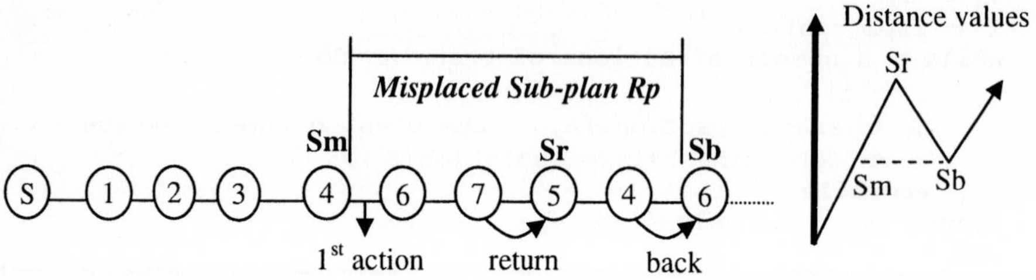

Fig. 4. A solution plan with the intermediate state represented as circles with their respective values and a misplaced sub-plan

```
function determine_Sr (<v0,v1,v2,v3..,vn>, from_state)
retv ← 0;
i ← from_state;
while (retv=0) and (i<n) do
        i ← i+1;
        if vi<vi-1 then retv ← i;
        endwhile
return retv;
end;
```

Fig. 5. Algorithm to detect the first occurrence of ***Sr*** and ***vr*** in a plan from the State `from_state`. The variable retv stores the position of the Sr state in the solution plan

After detecting a ***Sr***, the CASER method tries to detect the next intermediate state that continues to pursue the goal. This intermediate state, called ***Sb***, and its respective value ***vb***, indicate for the CASER method the point where the plan back to converge directly to the goal after the ***Sr*** state.The back State (***Sb***) an its value (***vb***) is determined as follows:

Definition 2: (Back State) Given a plan with **<S_0,S_1,S_2,S_3,...,Sn>** intermediate states, and a state ***Sr,*** a ***Sb*** state is a state S_i , with i>r, where its value ***vb***, obtained by a heuristic function, h^d, is more than or equal to the S_{i-1} value.

The idea of the CASER method is to create an alternative plan that bridges the correct segments of the solution with the segment of the plan after the state ***Sb***. This alternative plan will substitute a misplaced sub-plan, called ***Rp***, which the last state is the ***Sb*** State. Figure 6 presents the algorithm that detects the Back State and its value.

In order to determine the beginning of the misplaced sub-plan ***Rp***, the CASER method finds a state with the highest value among all states before ***Sr*** but less than the ***vb*** value. This state, called ***Sm***, becomes the initial state of a possible misplaced sub-plan, and its value is indicated as ***vm***. Formally, ***Sm*** can be defined as follows:

Definition 3: (State with misplaced action) Given a plan with **$<S_0,S_1,S_2,S_3,...,Sn>$** intermediate states, and a state ***Sr*** and the ***vb*** value, a ***Sm*** state is a state S_i, with $i<r$, where its value ***vm*** is the highest value among all other intermediate states $<S_0,S_1,S_2,S_3,...,S_{r-1}>$ and less than ***vb*** value.

```
function determine_Sb (<v0,v1,v2,v3..,vn>, r)
backv ← 0;
i ← r;
while (backv=0) and (i<n) do
        i ← i+1;
        if vi>=vi-1 then backv ← i;
        endwhile
return backv;
end;
```

Fig. 6. Algorithm to detect the first occurrence of ***Sb*** and ***vb*** in a plan from the position ***r***. The variable backv stores the position of the ***Sb*** state in the solution plan

```
function determine_Sm(<v0,v1,v2,v3..,vn>, r, b)
misv, i ← 0;
for i ← 0 to r-1 do
        if (vi>misv) and (vi<vb) then misv ← vi;
        endfor;
return misv;
end;
```

Fig. 7. Algorithm to detect the first occurrence of ***Sm*** and ***vm*** in a plan from the first state to the position ***r***-1. The ***Sm*** is that state that has the highest value less than ***vb*** value. The variable misv stores the position of the ***Sm*** state in the solution plan

The algorithm that determines the position of ***Sm*** and ***vm*** in the solution plan is given in Figure 7. In fact, the CASER method considers the ***Sm*** as a state immediately before a possible sub-plan with misplaced actions and that must be replanned.

The ***Rp*** sub-plan, then, is formed by the actions between ***Sm*** and ***Sb***. The ***Sm*** can be considered the initial state and the state **Sb** as the final state of the ***Rp*** sub-plan.

```
function CASER_replan(plan, initst, from_state, maxtime, maxbktk)
<v0,v1,..,vn> ← det_costs(plan,initst);
r ← determine_Sr(<v0,v1,..,vn>,from_state);
if r<>0 then
  b ← determine_Sb(<v0,v1,v2,..,vn>,r);
  m ← determine_Sm(<v0,v1,v2,..,vn>,r,b);
  Rp ← the sub-plan between Sm and Sb;
  bktk ← 0;  // controls the number of backtrackings
  i ← m;
  isRp ← false;
  while (time<maxtime) and (i>0) and (bktk<maxbktk) and not(isRp) do
          <vp0,vp1..,vpn> ← det_costs(Rp,Si);
          if determine_Sr(<vp0,vp1,vp2,..,vpn>,0)= 0 then
              isRp ← true;
              else
              i ← i-1;
              Rp ← plan between Si and Sb;
              endif;
         endwhile
  if isRp then Rp ← call modified_FF (Si,Sb) with
              - changing the 1st action of Rp;
              - maximal_length ← b-i-1;
              - time < maxtime;
  if Rp = null then isRp ← false;
  endif;
if not(isRp) then
       from_state ← b;
       else
       substitute Rp in plan between Si and Sb;
       endif
if time<maxtime then  plan ← CASER_replan(plan,initst,from_state);
return plan;
end;
```

Fig. 8. The complete CASER second phase algorithm. It needs a solution plan, an initial state (`initst`) and the first position of the plan that will be considered (`from_state`). It also needs the maximal time and the maximal number of backtracking (maxbktk)

However, the actions of the sub-plan ***Rp*** can not be misplaced by themselves, and the ***returned*** value can be caused by any other action before ***Sm***. To determine if the ***Rp*** sub-plan really contains misplaced actions, the algorithm *det_costs*, presented in Figure 3, is applied for the ***Rp*** sub-plan. If there is any returned value in the ***Rp*** sub-

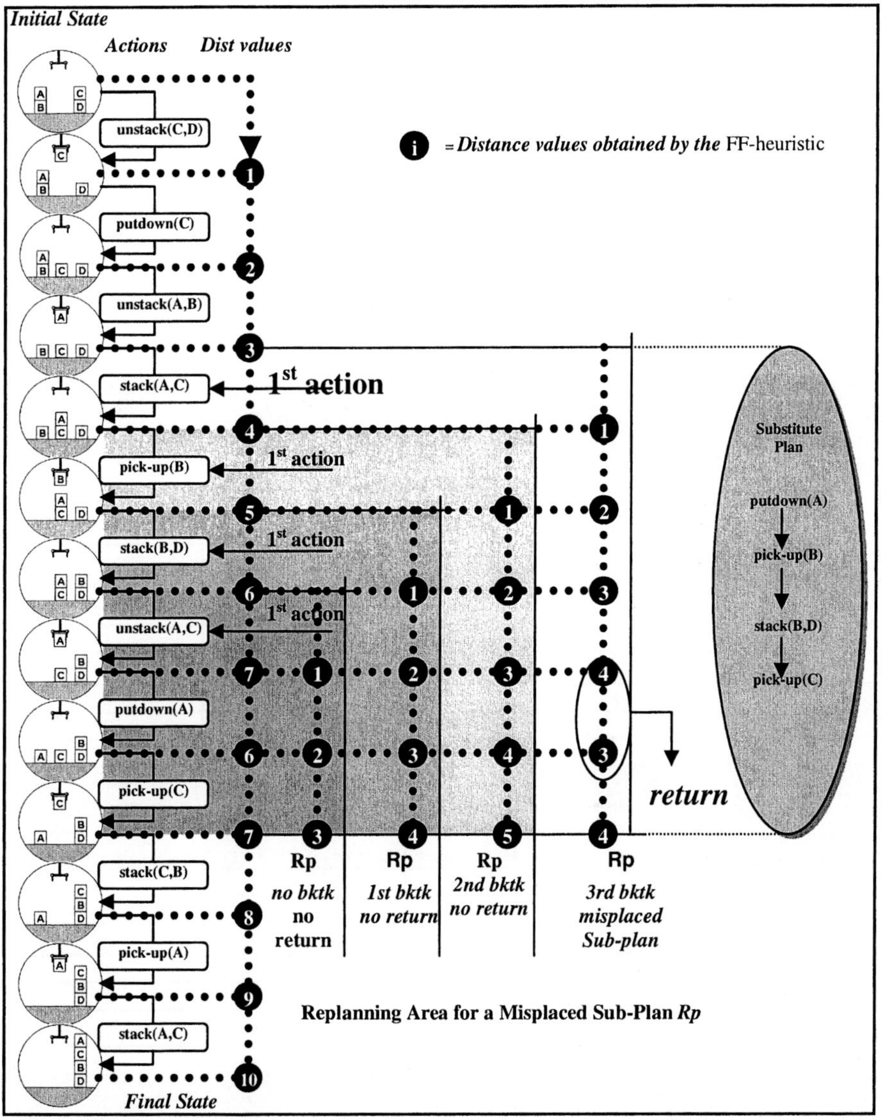

Fig. 9. Example of the 2nd phase of the CASER applied in a plan of the Blocks World domain

plan, it becomes a potential misplaced sub-plan that must be replaced. If the ***Rp*** does not contain any returned value by itself, then the initial state of the ***Rp*** sub-plan is *backtracked*. The new initial state becomes the state immediately before the state ***Sm***. The algorithm *det_costs* is applied to this new ***Rp*** sub-plan in order to determine if it contains a returned state or not. The state backtracking continues until the initial state is reached or a misplaced sub-plan is detected.

When a misplaced sub-plan ***Rp*** is determined, the CASER method starts the replanning process by calling the modified version of the FF planning system to create an alternative plan to the ***Rp*** sub-plan. This alternative plan cannot have the same first action and must have fewer actions than the ***Rp*** sub-plan. The objective of changing the first action is to force the planning system to find an alternative solution. If no other alternative plan is found, the CASER backtracks the initial state of the ***Rp*** sub-plan and tries again. The backtracking continues until the initial state of the plan is found or until a specific number, ***maxbktk***, of backtrackings are performed.

If there is no backtracking and no alternative solution is found, the CASER method continues to detect points of replanning after the ***Sb*** State.

Table 1. Results of the CASER method applied to some STRIPS domains. The time is in milliseconds and #act means number of the actions in the plan solution

DriverLog Dmain Problems IPC´02	CASER METHOD					LPG system reference results in quality track
	1st phase		2nd phase	Final results		
	time	#act	time	time	#act	#act
dlog-01	12	11	70	82	9	7
dlog-02	24	19	65	89	19	20
dlog-03	13	33	231	244	20	12
dlog-04	27	31	119	146	28	16
dlog-05	31	22	105	136	21	18
dlog-06	300	22	1835	2135	16	17
dlog-07	4846	30	125	4971	26	13
dlog-08	340	32	776	1116	30	22
dlog-09	21	31	120	141	31	23
dlog-10	10978	28	90	11068	23	17

Logistic domain problems IPC´00	CASER METHOD					FF system reference results
	1st phase		2nd phase	Final Results		
	time	#act	time	time	#act	#act
LOGISTICS-04-0	14	26	68	82	26	49
LOGISTICS-05-0	23	45	175	198	41	49
LOGISTICS-06-0	19	33	70	89	33	25
LOGISTICS-07-0	45	63	851	896	53	36
LOGISTICS-08-0	66	52	170	236	43	31
LOGISTICS-09-0	65	56	205	270	49	36
LOGISTICS-10-0	200	86	425	625	74	46

Blocks World Domain Problems IPC´00	CASER METHOD					Reference Results	
	1st phase		2nd phase	Final Results		FF	HSP
	time	#act	time	Time	#act	#act	#act
BLOCKS-04-0	11	6	70	81	6	6	6
BLOCKS-05-0	2	12	105	107	12	12	12
BLOCKS-06-0	19	26	255	274	12	16	12
BLOCKS-07-0	22	40	1640	1662	22	20	26
BLOCKS-08-0	52	26	1665	1717	26	18	18
BLOCKS-09-0	30	42	1511	1541	30	30	40
BLOCKS-10-0	22	34	9285	9307	34	34	98
BLOCKS-11-0	44	38	3296	3340	34	32	44
BLOCKS-12-0	35	42	5600	5635	42	36	36

On the other hand, if an alternative plan is found, it substitutes the ***Rp*** sub-plan and the CASER method continues to detect points of replanning after the ***Sb*** state until the final state is reached. The complete CASER algorithm is presented in Figure 8. Figure 9 shows the behavior of the backtracking for an example in the Blocks World domain. The replanning process can be fast due to two factors. One is the use of a modified FF planning that permits the system to work with a complete state as goal. The other is that the modified FF must find a plan with a limited length what can reduce the time to find long solutions. However, the numbers of backtrackings and the complexity of a solution plan can turn the CASER method into a time consuming process.

Because of this time consuming risk, the CASER method allows the user to define the maximal time that the method can try to improve the solution quality and also the maximal number of backtrackings that the process can do.

4 Empirical Tests

The complete CASER method was tested in some STRIPS-model domains for some retrieved cases obtained by the FAR-OFF Case-Based Planning system [14]. The cases retrieved by the FAR-OFF system are from a case base with random cases generated by a case base seeder [15].

The STRIPS domains used in the tests are retrieved from the IPC'00 (International Planning Competition) [3] and IPC'02 [11]. The problems considered in the tests are the first one proposed in those competitions for each domain.

The tests, in Table 1, show the performance and results of the CASER method when applied to a retrieved case in Blocks World, Logistic and DriverLog domains.

The solutions of the LPG [7], FF [9] and HSP [5] planning systems in IPC'02 [11] and IPC'00 [3] planning competitions are used as a comparative result of the quality of the solution. They had one of the best results in such domains and provide a good validation for CASER results.

The tests were performed in a Windows® environment on a Pentium® III 450 MHz computer with 512 Mbytes of RAM memory and considering a number of backtrackings limited to 15. As stated by Tonidandel and Rillo [15], in a general frame, the use of unlimited backtracking is not relevant for the quality solutions, and it still spends much more time than when a limited of 15 backtracking is imposed. In addition, there is no imposition of time limit, even though the CASER method allows that the user specifies a maximal time that can be used to improve the solution. The definition of a limited time for replanning does not affect the planning problem solution; it only reduces the time for the improvement of the solution quality.

The second phase of the CASER method reduces the easy-to-generate solution in most of the situations and for some of them it reduces up to the optimal plan length. There is some quality improvement from the easy-to-generate solution in the tests, as can be seen in BLOCKS 6.0 and BLOCKS 7.0 problems where the replanning phase reduces the easy-to-generate solution in about 50%.

The tests results show that the CASER method is effective for a case-based planning system (e.g. the FAR-OFF system) in all domains considered in the tests. Considering the solution quality provided by the generative planning systems, the CASER returns the best solution in about 35% of the results. These results do not empirically prove that the CASER is better than generative planners; they just show that the CASER method works suitably. The CASER method is just a part of an entire case-based planning system and, therefore, it can not be compared with an entire generative planner in terms of solution quality and time performance.

The time spent by the second phase of the CASER method depends on the number of returned values and misplaced sub-plans. Since the more actions a plan have, the higher is the possible number of returned values and misplaced sub-plans. Therefore, the CASER method takes more time to adapt a solution plan with more actions.

5 Discussion

Considering the conditions of the tests, the CASER method is a very promising tool of case adaptation. The tests were performed in hard conditions. The cases retrieved by the FAR-OFF system are not very similar to the possible solution because they are retrieved from a case base constituted by random cases, from where retrieved cases are not necessarily good similar cases. A random case is created by a Case-Based Seeding process that finds random initial and goal states and applies a generative planning system to find a plan between the states [16].

In fact, even with a retrieved case from a case base filled of random cases and with the same knowledge used by generative planners, the CASER can return some best solutions, about 35% of the solutions in the tests. The results only show that the CASER method can work well with the same knowledge provided to a generative planner.

However, there are some efficiency bottlenecks that must be solved. One of these bottlenecks is the behavior of the CASER method that tries to replace an optimal sub-plan in some situations (e.g. BLOCKS-5.0 test). It is caused by the FF-heuristic, which is not appropriate to detect whether a plan is optimal or not. Because of this, the time of replanning applications is higher than necessary occasionally. Other heuristics or some new verification methods will be considered in the future.

The CASER method does not guarantee to find an optimal solution of a specific problem because it only analyses the intermediate states and the final state that were provided by the solution plan. The method is restricted to reduce the plan found by an easy-to-generate phase. For instance, if an optimal solution of a specific problem is to consider another final state than that provided by the easy-to-generate plan, the CASER method is unable to find this optimal solution. This limitation of the CASER method is responsible for the difficulty that this method presented in the DriverLog domain. This limitation will be analyzed in our future research.

This version of CASER method is designed to improve the solution quality by decreasing the number of steps of the solution plan. However, this method is not restricted to the solution length, but it can also be extended to deal with complex domains with resources and time.

In order to work in domains with numerical variables, a heuristic function that estimates the cost of a state by taking in consideration these numerical values must be available. The metric-FF planner system [8] provides a metric-heuristic that can be used to extend the CASER method to numerical domains. However, it will be left for further studies.

6 Conclusion

The CASER method, presented in this paper, is an domain-independent method to adapt retrieved cases. The method uses the FF-heuristic and a modified version of the FF planning system to determine and find a solution from a retrieved case by a recursive quality improvement algorithm with anytime behavior.

The first phase of the CASER method just finds an easy-to-generate solution whereas its second phase modifies some misplaced sub-plans and bad segments of the entire solution in order to improve the solution quality.

The empirical tests show that the CASER method is a promising adaptation process that can find good quality solutions for case-based planning systems. The most important feature of the CASER method is that it does not require any additional knowledge neither any other process like invariants extractions or learning algorithms. In fact, the CASER is a method that can be applied to any planning domain without any specification of adaptation rules or extra domain dependent information.

The method proposed in this paper focuses on the plan length and does not consider time or resources. This method will be extended in the future to support domains with such features.

References

1. Ambite, J. L.; Knoblock C. A..Planning by Rewriting. In: *Journal of Artificial Intelligence Research*, 15, (2001), 207-261.
2. Au, T.; Muñoz-Avila, H.; Nau, D. S. On the Complexity of Plan Adaptation by Derivational Analogy in a Universal Classical Planning Framework. In: *Craw, S.; Preece, A. (Eds.)Procedings of the 6th European Conference on Case-Based Reasoning - ECCBR-2002*. Lecture Notes in Artificial Inteligence. Vol 2416. Springer-Verlag. (2002) 13-27.
3. Bacchus, F. AIPS-2000 Planning Competition Results. Available in: http://www.cs.toronto.edu/aips2000/. (2000)
4. Blum, A.; Furst M. Fast Planning through Planning Graphs Analysis, Artificial Intelligence, 90, (1997) 281-300.
5. Bonet, B; Geffner, H. Planning as Heuristic Search. *Artificial Intelligence.* 129 (2001) 5-33.
6. Gerevini A.; Serina, I. Fast Adaptation through Planning Graphs: Local and Systematic Search Techniques. In: *Proceedings of the 5th International Conference on Artificial Intelligence Planning and Scheduling AIPS´00.* AAAI Press. (2000).112-121.
7. Gerevini A.; Serina, I.. LPG: A Planner Based on Local Search for Planning Graphs with Actions Costs. In: *Preprints of the 6th International Conference on Artificial Intelligence Planning and Scheduling AIPS´02.* AAAI Press. (2002) 281-290.
8. Hoffmann J. Extending FF to Numerical State Variables, in: *Proceedings of the 15th European Conference on Artificial Intelligence*, Lyon, France (2002)
9. Hoffmann, J.; Nebel, B. 2001. The FF Planning System: Fast Plan Generation Through Heuristic Search. *Journal of Artificial Intelligence Research.* 14 (2001) 253 – 302.
10. Koenig,S. , Furcy, D., Bauer, C. Heuristic Search-Based Replanning. In: *6th Proceedings of the International Conference on Artificial Intelligence on Planning and Scheduling (AIPS-2002).* Toulouse. (2002).

11. Long, D.; Fox, M. The 3rd International Planning Competition - IPC'2002. Available in http://www.dur.ac.uk/d.p.long/competition.html. (2002).
12. Nebel,B. ; Koehler, J. Plan reuse versus plan generation: A theoretical and empirical analysis. *Artificial Intelligence*, n. 76, p.427-454,. Special Issue on Planning and Scheduling (1995).
13. Tonidandel, F.; Rillo, M. An Accurate Adaptation-Guided Similarity Metric for Case-Based Planning In: *Aha, D., Watson, I. (Eds.) Proceedings of 4th International Conference on Case-Based Reasoning (ICCBR-2001).* Lecture Notes in Artificial Intelligence. vol 2080. Springer-Verlag. (2001) 531-545.
14. Tonidandel, F.; Rillo, M. 2002. The FAR-OFF system: A Heuristic Search Case-Based Planning. In: *Proceedings of 6th International Conference on Artificial Intelligence on Planning and Scheduling (AIPS-2002).* Toulouse. (2002).
15. Tonidandel, F.; Rillo, M. Improving the Planning Solution Quality by Replanning. In: *Anais do VI Simpósio Brasileiro de Automação Inteligente.* Bauru São Paulo (2003).
16. Tonidandel, F.; Rillo, M. A Case base Seeding for Case-Based Planning Systems. In: *Lemaitre, C., Reyes, C., Gonzales, J (Eds.) Proceedings of 9th Ibero-American Conference on AI (IBERAMIA-2004).* Lecture Notes in Artificial Intelligence. vol 3315. Springer-Verlag. (2004) 104-113.
17. Veloso, M. Planning and Learning by Analogical Reasoning. Lecture Notes in Artificial Intelligence, Vol 886. Springer-Verlag. (1994).

Selecting the Best Units in a Fleet: Performance Prediction from Equipment Peers

Anil Varma, Kareem S. Aggour, and Piero P. Bonissone

GE Global Research, One Research Circle,
Niskayuna, NY 12309
{varma, aggour, bonissone}@research.ge.com

Abstract. We focus on the problem of selecting the few vehicles in a fleet that are expected to last the longest without failure. The prediction of each vehicle's remaining life is based on the aggregation of estimates from 'peer' units, i.e. units with similar design, maintenance, and utilization characteristics. Peers are analogous to neighbors in Case-Based Reasoning, except that the states of the peer units are constantly changing with time and usage. We use an evolutionary learning framework to update the similarity criteria for peer identification. Results indicate that learning from peers is a robust and promising approach for the usually data-poor domain of equipment prognostics. The results also highlight the need for model maintenance to keep such a reasoning system vital over time.

1 Introduction

The problem of selecting the best units from a fleet of equipment occurs in many military and commercial applications. For example, given a specific mission profile, a commander may have to decide which five armored vehicles to deploy in order to minimize the chance of a breakdown. In the commercial world, rail operators often need to make decisions on which locomotives to use in a train traveling from coast to coast with time sensitive shipments. Asset selection for complex electromechanical equipment is often driven by heuristics and/or expert opinions. Some 'obvious' strategies include picking the newest, the most recently serviced, or the latest model equipment.

Long-term data that allows reliability and MTBF (mean time between failure) computations at the fleet and individual unit level can also drive such decisions. However, this work was motivated by the special needs of military equipment on new platforms. In the case of a new aircraft, tank, or ship, there is simply no long-term data to assess reliability across the vast range of potential missions. Second, the usage pattern of military equipment can be described as a sequence of 'pulses'—long periods of inactivity followed by relatively short periods of intense usage. Given the possibility of very sparse deployment history on any individual unit, how can we best assess its feasibility for a new mission in a new environment and terrain?

We present an approach where the time-to-failure prediction for each individual unit is computed by aggregating its own track record with that of a number of 'peer' units—units with similarities along three key dimensions: system design, patterns of

H. Muñoz-Avila and F. Ricci (Eds.): ICCBR 2005, LNAI 3620, pp. 595 – 609, 2005.

utilization, and maintenance history. The notion of a 'peer' is close to that of a 'neighbor' in CBR, except that the states of the peers are constantly changing. Odometer-type variables like mileage and age increase, and discrete events like major maintenance or upgrades occur. It is reasonable to assume that after every significant mission, the peers of a target unit may change based upon changes in both the unit itself, and the fleet at large. This is in contrast to a conventional diagnostic system such as the locomotive CBR system described by Varma and Roddy (1999), where, once stored in the case base, the case description remains static.

Our results suggest that estimating unit performance from peers is a practical, robust and promising approach. Two types of experiments were conducted—retrospective estimation and prognostic estimation. In the first experiment, we explore how well the median time-to-failure for any unit can be estimated from the equivalent median of its peers. In the second experiment, for a given instant in time, we predict the time to the next failure for each unit using the history of the peers.

Because we use estimates composed from peers, constructing an effective similarity criterion for peer selection is critical (as it is for any case-based reasoning system). However, because the elements in the case base are changing with time, systematically evaluating and updating the similarity criterion for peer selection is necessary. We use an evolutionary algorithm to tune the similarity criterion, and show than an evolutionary learning framework contributes significantly to keeping the reasoning process vital.

Section 2 provides an overview of the motivation for this work, the data sources, and the experimental setup. Section 3 reviews related work and approaches. Sections 4 and 5 focus on the system design, parameter optimization, and model maintenance using the evolutionary learning framework. Section 6 presents the results, and Section 7 contains our conclusions.

2 Problem Framework

2.1 Motivation

In military deployments, commanders often have to select a subset of available units from a fleet to last the duration of a mission in a self-sustained manner. Data from the National Training Center in Fort Irwin, California indicate that M1A1 tanks and Bradley vehicles have a non-mission-capable rate of 27% → 46% over a 7-day mission duration ('pulse') for half and full tempo operations respectively. The US Defense Advanced Research Projects Agency (DARPA) approached GE Global Research to explore learning and reasoning methodologies to address this unit selection problem, characterized by sparse data over a wide variety of performance environments, making direct application of standard statistical techniques difficult. We seek to predict mission reliability by using a *collective* of equipment *peers* for a given unit, each with limited performance data.

The specific application domain is an extension of the locomotive diagnostics system described by Varma and Roddy (1999). GE Rail remotely monitors about 4000 locomotives, and uses a case base of fault logs to diagnose if any proactive maintenance is needed. The case base is populated with successful diagnoses verified by actual repair, represented as about a 3-day fault log supplying the input variables and the maintenance action code as the output variable. The cases are episodic, have definite beginning and ending times, and do not change once entered into the case base. The system has been operational for about 6 years.

In working with DARPA's steering committee, we determined that the extensive remote monitoring and diagnostics data accumulated by GE Rail could prove an excellent surrogate for conducting experiments for the selection phase of mission support.

	Data Category	Source
1.	Design & Configuration Information	GE Rail
2.	Maintenance Information	
	- Fault Codes	EOA Service
	- Recommendations	GE Rail
	- Repairs	GE Rail / Railroads
3.	Utilization Information	Railroads

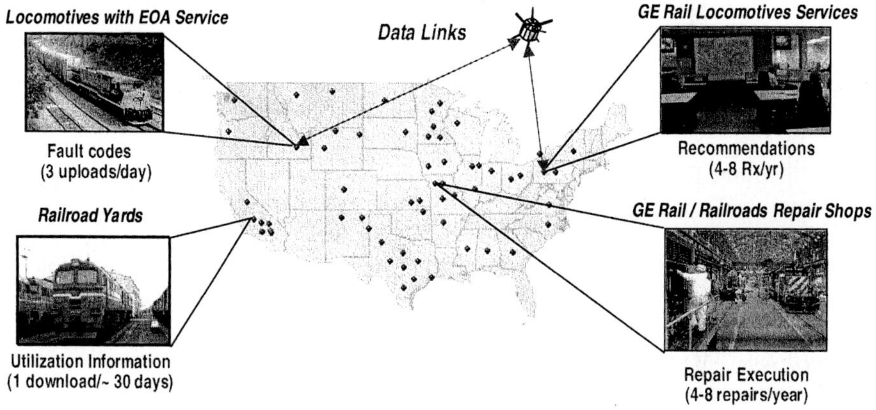

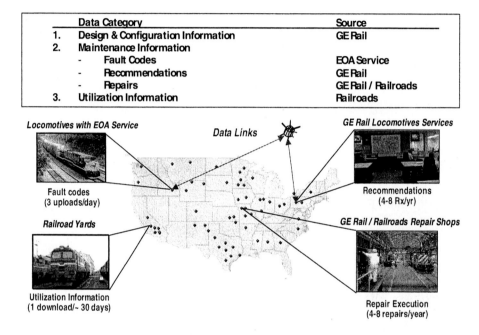

Fig. 1. Locomotive Design, Maintenance, and Utilization Data Sources

2.2 Data Sources

As shown in Figure 1, three distinct types of data are available for each locomotive:

1. **Design and Configuration:** This data was obtained from GE Rail as the original equipment manufacturer. This includes information about the locomotive model, in-service date, upgrades, options and configuration items.
2. **Maintenance:** This information was obtained from the GE Expert on Alert™ (EOA) center in Erie, Pennsylvania. Data from each locomotive is uploaded to the center three times a day. The EOA diagnostic tools analyze this data and if a problem is identified, a workflow case is created for review by a monitoring engineer. The expert can then issue a Red, Yellow or White recommendation (Rx) to the railroad, or choose to wait. A Red recommendation implies serious problems that need to be addressed in the next 3-5 days. A Yellow

recommendation should be addressed in the next 7-14 days, and a White recommendation is usually informational with no impending failure expected.

Once a Red or Yellow recommendation is delivered, the actual repair is carried out soon afterwards. The measure of 'time to failure' from any given point in time is the time until the next repair.

Table 1 shows a sequence of Red recommendations issued on a particular unit. The Rx Close Date indicates the date of repair. Each entry in column 5 (days from previous Red or Yellow repair) indicates the length of time that the unit operated without a failure.

Table 1. Maintenance Recommendation Information

SERIAL NO	RECOMMENDATION DELIVERY DATE	URGENCY	RX CLOSE DATE	DAYS from previous RED or YELLOW repair
1001	7/28/2002 18:14	R	7/29/2002 21:39	12.72
1001	7/16/2002 23:03	R	7/17/2002 4:20	14.01
1001	7/2/2002 7:47	R	7/3/2002 4:01	15.78
1001	6/13/2002 9:25	R	6/14/2002 20:38	6.94

3. **Utilization:** Each locomotive records parameters on-board that are cumulative in nature, and consequently monotonic. Examples of these include, age, mileage, total megawatt hours developed, total hours moving, and total hours idle. About every 30 days, these are downloaded by the railroad and stored. Additional parameters can be computed from these values. Table 2 shows columns indicating the cumulative hours spent by a unit in any one of 8 'notches' or gear positions. These, divided by total operating time, provide what percentage of time the unit spends in lower vs. higher gear positions—an approximation to an operating profile.

Table 2. Utilization Information

DOWNLOAD DATE	CUM N1 HS	CUM N2 HRS	CUM N3 HRS	CUM N4 HRS	CUM N5 HRS	CUM N6 HRS	CUM N7 HRS	CUM N8 HRS	CUM BRAKE HRS	CUM ENGINE HRS MOVING	DELTA ENGINE HRS MOVING
5-Apr-03	361.4	148.6	136.5	102.5	91.2	72.6	46.6	254.0	274.8	1,488.13	31.8
2-Apr-03	351.6	142.6	130.8	100.4	89.5	71.3	46.1	253.5	270.5	1,456.30	43.4
28-Mar-03	340.5	138.4	127.0	97.4	86.5	68.8	44.3	247.4	262.6	1,412.90	116.5
	...									...	
28-Jul-01	259.0	113.1	97.7	79.5	72.1	55.9	36.4	176.0	196.4	1,086.24	0.0

We consolidated and scrubbed the data from GE Rail and utilization data from Union Pacific to generate a case base with 1,178 locomotives. A single data vector was associated with each unit, containing raw data such as age, mileage, and number of repairs/year as well as compound variables generated from the raw data (number of repairs per 100,000 miles, for example).

2.3 Experiment Description and Metrics

The data collected for the experiment spanned approximately two years. To simulate the military scenario of a sequence of missions, we selected three instances in time approximately six months apart, as indicated in Figure 2. We refer to these as time slices. The first time slice was on 22 May 2002. Treating this date as the present time, the case base had data on 262 units. By Slice 2, about six months later on 01 Nov 2002, the case base had data on 634 units, as several locomotives entered service or had at least two failure events to provide a time-to-failure computation. Slice 3 was set at 01 May 2003, and by this time data was available on 845 units. Once we imposed the requirement that each unit have at least two failures recorded, the number of usable units declined from 1178 to 965.

After consulting with domain experts, we restated the objective as: At the beginning of each time slice, select the best 20% of the locomotives, measured by their ability to operate the longest without requiring repair (starting at the beginning of the time slice). With this definition, the performance metric was easily computed. At Slice 1, with a fleet of 262 locomotives, a given algorithm would pick 52 locomotives that it determined to be the best. Because this was historical data, the locomotives could be ranked by how they actually performed, producing the top 52 "golden units" based on actual time to failure. The success rate was defined as the number of golden units selected by the algorithm divided by the total number of golden units. If a given algorithm, after picking 52 units, had 20 golden units in its pool, its performance would be 20/52 = 38%. Once the mission was over, the case base would be updated with any new fleet data, and the selection process would be repeated for the next mission.

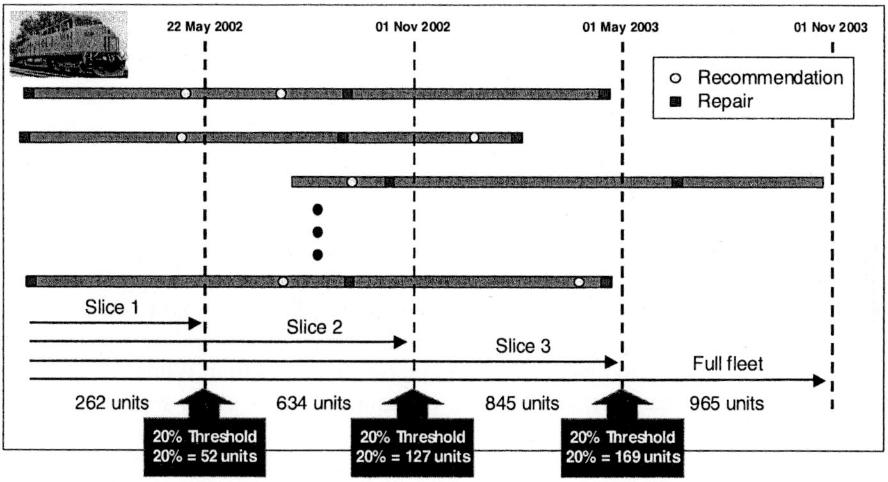

Fig. 2. Experiment Time Slices and Unit Counts

For our experiment, the performance metric was computed once for each slice. With chronological data, Slice 2 had the benefit of seeing the aging of the Slice 1 units, the addition of some new units, as well as information on the performance of the algorithm on Slice 1. Similarly, Slice 3 benefits from both Slice 1 and 2. We expected that with increasing information, the selection performance would improve.

3 Background

Three main concepts are embedded in this work. The first is the notion of estimating electromechanical equipment readiness from the performance of other similarly used and maintained units. This is especially applicable to military domains where any single unit may not get enough usage to build a long individual track record to estimate its fitness for a given mission. We address this through incremental learning from experience fragments drawn from fleet peers. This application is probably most relevant to the maintenance community, and we will not discuss it in detail in this paper.

The second concept of interest is the idea of viewing an equipment fleet as a case base whose cases evolve with time, with extended time histories describing their state. The notion of a 'case' in a case-based system is often episodic in nature. A case traditionally captures a set of attributes that define an episode of interest at a particular instant in time—whether a customer call, meal plan, or a failure requiring diagnosis, with an associated outcome. The episode, once captured as a case, is itself not expected to change (though its relevance calculation may be weighed by the age of the case).

We believe the notion of peers and peer-based-reasoning is a useful specialization of the general CBR approach when dealing with a case base of complex equipment. Representing and reasoning with time-extended cases has been discussed by a variety of authors in different domains. The notion that the state of each case in a case base can be a function of time was referred to as 'Continuous Case-Based Reasoning' and identified as distinct from discrete, symbolic representations by Ram and Santamaria (1997). They describe Continuous CBR in the context of a driving task, where problem solving is incremental due to limited prior knowledge, and continuous adaptation and learning is essential to incorporate new experiences. An important issue raised by the authors is case representation—whether the entire experience to date is a single case, or if there should be a criterion that defines the scope of a single case. In our application, a major maintenance or overhaul could define such a splitting criterion. Jaczynski (1997) focuses on the retrieval aspects of cases that reflect time-extended situations. He distinguishes between sampled numeric series and event-based time series. In our application, each unit is associated with a sequence of maintenance events, and to that extent meets the second definition. While we have not made an attempt to characterize the series of maintenance events in a richer context, this is a logical extension of our work.

Schlaefer, Schröter, et al. (2001) and Fritsche, Schlaefer, et al. (2002) describe using CBR on a series of medical tests for kidney transplant recipients. Their data is described as a "series of infrequent measurements at irregular intervals." They utilize dynamic time warping (Berndt and Clifford 1996) to normalize multiple series for similarity computation and retrieval. In our application, events in a locomotive's history are not represented as a time series to be used for similarity matching. We use the 'odometer' approach, where the entire history is summarized in a state vector. We feel that this is a limitation, since the type and sequence of maintenance events, upgrades, and missions are likely to have a significant impact on readiness.

The third concept of interest is the importance of model maintenance, including both adaptation and optimization, and its special importance in peer-based reasoning. As time passes, the attributes of the object under consideration change, and so do its peers. This is in addition to the expected turnover in the case base as units are decommissioned and new units enter service. The learning task here is to update the 'similarity metric' or the criterion for peer selection.

Research in the CBR community has focused extensively on case based maintenance. Leake and Wilson (1998), in their review of CBR maintenance dimensions, point out that the indexing scheme is an integral part of the case base along with the cases themselves. Smyth (1998) describes a strategy for case deletion with minimal impact on performance—a pruning approach. Zhang and Yang (1998) also stress index maintenance to keep a CBR system current. They propose an iterative approach to weight refinement. An evolutionary algorithm handles the corresponding function in our application. Leake and Wilson (1999) explicitly address the situation when changing tasks and environment could render part of the case base obsolete or invalid. They identify problem-solution regularity as a basic premise of CBR and advocate monitoring performance over time to spot a decline in this measure. In our application, unit to peer *irregularity* over time is almost a given, and the analogous issue becomes how often to update the 'peer selection' or similarity metric to maintain performance while incorporating new knowledge. In our experiments, similarity metric updates occur at each of the three time slices. Results presented later highlight the need for continual adaptation and parameter optimization.

4 System Implementation

Each case in the case base represents a distinct locomotive with a number of features associated, including age, mileage, and parameters related to maintenance and repair history. Neighbor retrieval is based on these features, resulting in peers that are of similar design and usage. Each locomotive record also contains a record of its own pulse durations between repairs, i.e., how long the train was in a useful state. These pulses represent the availability durations of the locomotives, and so the peer's pulses are used to predict the remaining availability of the probe.

The CBR system was implemented using SOFT-CBR: a Self-Optimizing Fuzzy Tool for Case-Based Reasoning (Aggour, Pavese, et al. 2003). SOFT-CBR is an extensible, component-based tool with a number of pre-existing modules to implement a CBR system in Java. SOFT-CBR significantly reduced the implementation and testing cycles for these experiments, as it provided large portions of the functionality pre-built and pre-tested.

SOFT-CBR is configured using an eXtensible Mark-up Language (XML) file. Changing the parameters in the file can change the attributes used to define cases, the method by which similarities are calculated, and determine what types of outputs are valid. Optimizing the engine requires the optimization of a set (or subset) of the parameters in this configuration file. The SOFT-CBR modules used are described below.

4.1 Retrieve

An Oracle database contains the complete case base, with individual cases occurring as single rows in a table. In SOFT-CBR, neighbors are first retrieved, and then a similarity score is calculated between the probe and each neighbor. The probe refers to the unit for which we are trying to predict the remaining life.

Neighbor Retrieval
A SOFT-CBR case base component is responsible for constructing an SQL database query to retrieve peers of the probe case. Each case in the case base is represented by an array of *N* distinct features, creating an *N*-dimensional feature space. To retrieve neighbors, a range query is constructed around each numerical feature, defining an *N*-dimensional hyperrectangle in the feature space. A single support value s_i is defined for each dimension *i*. Neighbors are retrieved if and only if each of their features x_i fall within the support of the probe's features p_i, such that $p_i - s_i \le x_i \le p_i + s_i \ \forall$ $i=1,\ldots,N$. The case base component returns all cases that appear similar to the probe (fall within this hyperrectangle), and then the engine uses a similarity calculation component to rank them.

Similarity Calculation
A Truncated Generalized Bell Function (TGBF) (Jang 1993) along each dimension is a fuzzy membership function that produces a score representing the degree of similarity of that feature. For each dimension *i*, a separate $TGBF_i(x_i;a_i,b_i,p_i)$ function exists centered at the feature values of the probe p_i, as shown in Equation 1. Here, ε is a truncation parameter, e.g. $\varepsilon = 10^{-5}$.

$$TGBF_i(x_i;a_i,b_i,p_i) = \begin{cases} \left[1+\left|\dfrac{x_i-p_i}{a_i}\right|^{2b_i}\right]^{-1} & if \quad (x_i-p_i) > \varepsilon \\ 0 & otherwise \end{cases} \tag{1}$$

Feature value x_i is determined from the peer and value p_i is from the probe, so each $TGBF_i$ has only two free parameters, a_i and b_i. This function was selected because it affords these two degrees of freedom, enabling the control of both the spread and curvature of the fuzzy membership function.

The most similar peers should be the closest to the probe along all *N* dimensions, so a similarity measure defined as the intersection of the individual $TGBF_i$ values is used. Further, to represent the different relevance that each criterion should have in the evaluation of similarity, a weight w_i is attached to each feature. The similarity measure *S(p,x)* between probe *p* and neighbor *x* becomes a weighted minimum operator, as shown in Equation 2, where weights $w_i \in [0,1]$.

$$S(p,x) = \min_{i=1}^{N}\{\max[(1-w_i), TGBF_i(x_i;a_i,b_i,p_i)]\} \tag{2}$$

The set of values for the supports s_i, weights w_i, and parameters a_i and b_i are design choices that impact the proper selection and ranking of peers. Each value is initially chosen by hand and then optimized using an evolutionary algorithm.

4.2 Reuse

Once identified, the peers are used to make a prediction of the remaining operational availability of the probe locomotive. Each pulse begins with the return of a locomotive to service, and ends with an event that renders the locomotive temporarily unavailable (a breakdown or scheduled or unscheduled maintenance). The SOFT-CBR reuse component uses the peer's historical pulses to first estimate the next pulse of each peer. These estimates are then aggregated to predict the remaining availability of the probe. If no neighbors are retrieved, then a default value specified in the configuration file is used. This default value represents "no decision" from the engine.

Each neighbor x has m_x historical pulses, which can be represented in a vector $H_x = [P_{1,x}, P_{2,x}, \ldots, P_{m,x}]$. For each neighbor, the goal is to determine the duration of the next pulse $P_{m+1,x}$. There was not enough historical data to generate reliable local regressions, so simpler models were experimented with, such as averages and medians. It was found that the most reliable way of generating the next pulse $P_{m+1,x}$ from the pulse vector H_x was to use an exponential average that gives more relevance to the most recent information. The exponential average function can be found in Equation 3, where weight $\alpha \in [0.5,1]$. Also critical to the performance of the model is the choice of the value of α.

$$\begin{aligned} P_{m+1,x} &= \overline{P}_{m,x} = \alpha P_{m,x} + (1-\alpha)\overline{P}_{m-1,x} \\ &= \alpha \sum_{i=2}^{m} (1-\alpha)^{m-i} P_{i,x} + (1-\alpha)^{m-1} P_{1,x} \end{aligned} \tag{3}$$

These individual predictions $P_{m+1,x}$ are aggregated to make a prediction $P_{m+1,p}$ of the remaining availability of the peer. A weighted average of the individual neighbor predictions is calculated, using the similarities of the peers as weights. Equation 4 shows the specific weighted average calculation.

$$P_{m+1,p} = \frac{\sum_{x=1}^{n} S(p,x) \times P_{m+1,x}}{\sum_{x=1}^{n} S(p,x)} \tag{4}$$

5 Optimization

The CBR had a number of parameters that required tuning to identify an optimal combination of values. Using the Evolutionary Algorithm (EA) already implemented in SOFT-CBR greatly simplified the task of optimizing the CBR's parameters. EA's (Goldberg 1989; Holland 1992) define an optimization paradigm based on the theory of evolution and natural selection.

An EA is composed of a population of individuals ("chromosomes"), each of which contains a vector of elements that represent distinct tunable parameters within the CBR configuration. For our system, given N dimensions in the universe of features, the chromosome vector c can be found in Equation 5.

$$
\begin{aligned}
c = [s_1, s_2, \dots, s_N; w_1, w_2, \dots, w_N; (a_1, b_1), (a_2, b_2), \dots, (a_N, b_N); \alpha] \\
\textit{where} \quad s_i = \text{retrieval support parameters} \\
w_i \in [0,1] = \text{feature weights} \\
(a_i, b_i) = TGBF_i \text{ parameters} \\
\alpha = \text{exponential average weight}
\end{aligned}
\tag{5}
$$

Figure 3 visualizes how the EA and CBR interact in SOFT-CBR. A chromosome defines a complete configuration of the CBR, so an instance of the CBR can be initialized for each chromosome, as shown in Figure 3. On the left-hand side there is a population $P(t)$ of chromosomes c_i, each of which go through a decoder to allow them to initialize a CBR on the right. The CBR then goes through a round of leave-one-out testing.

The EA maintains a population of 30 individuals evolved over 200 generations. Two types of mutation (randomly permuting parameters of a single chromosome) are used to produce new individuals in the population pool: Gaussian and uniform. The more fit chromosomes in generation t will be more likely to be selected for mutation and pass their genetic material to the next generation $t+1$. Similarly, the less fit solutions will be culled from the population. At the conclusion of the EA's execution, the single best chromosome is written to the SOFT-CBR configuration file as the new CBR configuration.

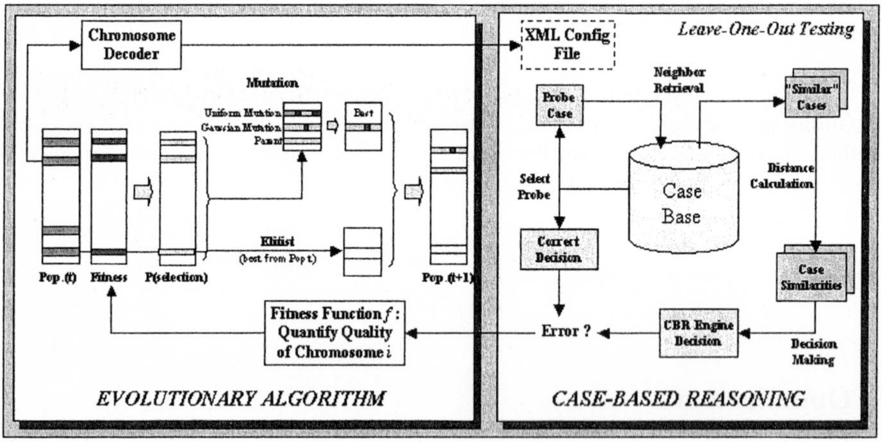

Fig. 3. EA and CBR Interaction

The quality of the CBR instance (the "fitness" of the chromosome) is determined by analyzing the results of the leave-one-out testing. A fitness function f is used to give a quantitative representation of the quality of the output. The objective of the experiment is to identify the top 20% of the locomotive population based on remaining availability, so the fitness function is defined by ordering each test case in descending order by the prediction $P_{m+1,p}$ of their remaining pulses. The top 20% are then selected, and this predicted top 20% is compared to the actual top 20%—the golden units. Equation 6 is then used to give a final fitness score *f(c)* to the chromosome. A True Positive is simply a locomotive predicted to be in the top 20% that was in the actual top 20%. A False Positive is a locomotive falsely predicted to be in the top 20%.

$$f(c) = \frac{TP}{TP + FP} \quad \text{where} \quad TP = \text{count of True Positives}, \quad FP = \text{count of False Positives} \tag{6}$$

6 Results and Analysis

Earlier we mentioned some simple heuristics that might be used for unit selection. We tested these by selecting the best 20% of the fleet sorted on the dimensions in Table 3. Through random selection, a sample should have 20% of its population composed of the verified golden units. It is interesting to note that the newest units by age, or those with the lowest mileage produced selections that were no better than the random selection. Having a low frequency of maintenance appeared to provide the best performance.

Table 3. Single Heuristic Classification Results

Single Heuristic	% of Correctly Classified Units
Lowest Mileage	17%
Newest Units	18%
Random	20%
Highest Energy (MWHRS) Generated	24%
Highest Miles / Hours Moving	26%
Highest Percentage Hours Moving	29%
Lowest Percentage of: Subsystem 10 Failures	38%
Lowest Ratio: Recommendations / Age [Rx/yr]	49%

We next used Weka (Witten and Frank 2000), a freely available data-mining software suite, to perform k-Nearest Neighbor retrieval over each time slice with leave-one-out testing. Some parameters like the aggregation function and number of neighbors to retrieve were manually tuned through trial and error. As the prediction variable, we used the median time to failure for each unit, and the best 20% were defined as those with the best medians. This was a first step to see how well peers can approximate an individual units' retrospective performance. The average performance achieved on a 10-fold cross-validation run was reported. The results are shown in Figure 4.

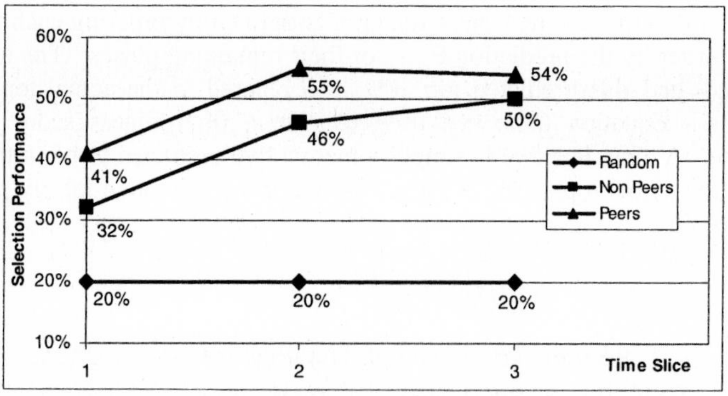

Fig. 4. Results of 1st Set of Experiments (Manual Tuning)

Using peers consistently outperformed the best available non peer-based single heuristic at each time slice. Another aspect of interest was that the number of peers required for the best estimates appeared to stabilize at ~1% of the total fleet size. These promising results led us to develop a CBR system with the ability to evolve the best parameter settings for peer retrieval and aggregation. This produced varying gains in performance, as shown in Table 4, in the column 'Evolved Peers'.

Table 4. Results with Evolutionary Tuning of Peer Selection Parameters

	Selection Performance			
Slice	Evolved Peers	Peers	Non-Peer	Random
1	48.1%	41%	32%	20%
2	55.6%	55%	46%	20%
3	60.4%	54%	50%	20%

After these experiments we approached our final objective—predicting the best units for the next mission. The retrospective median used earlier was replaced by the time-to-failure for each unit immediately after each slice. This resulted in a true prognostic experiment. Based on the DARPA steering committee's suggestions, we changed the selection metric from a percentage to a fixed number: 52 units. In Slices 1, 2, and 3 we now try to pick the best 52 units, representing 20%, 8% and 6% of the fleet, respectively.

The most difficult experiment (Slice 3) also produced the most encouraging results. Using the best single heuristic (Non-Peer) resulted in a performance plateau around 37% (Table 5). Using a peer-based approach and evolving the selection criterion for each slice, we were able to correctly identify 63% of the units that lasted the longest. This is superior to the non-peer and random selection performance, as shown in Table 5.

Table 5. Selecting the Best Performers for the Next Pulse

	Selection Performance		
Slice	Evolved Peers	Non-Peer	Random
1	48.1%	32%	20%
2	55.8%	37%	8%
3	63.5%	37%	6%

Finally, we studied the impact of not updating the peer similarity model after optimizing it for Slice 1. As shown in Figure 5, by Slice 3, the performance deteriorated to near random. This reinforces the importance of not only investing effort in the right representation and reasoning model, but also into the ability to maintain it over time.

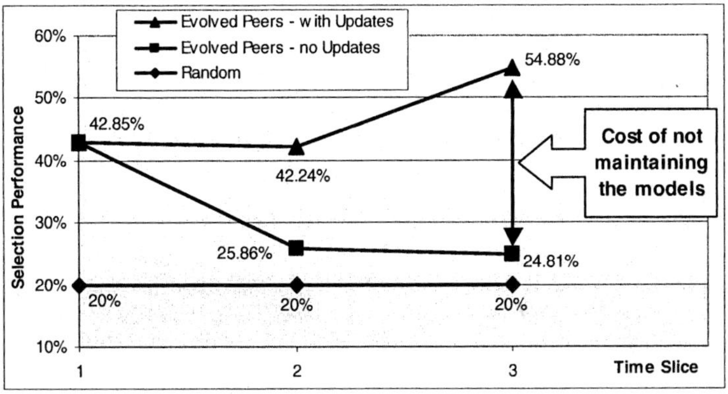

Fig. 5. Decline in Selection Performance Due to Lack of Peer Similarity Model Maintenance

7 Conclusions

For DARPA, the motivation of these experiments was to test if equipment readiness could be computed with relatively sparse deployment history. This required a specialized data set derived from actual equipment operation, one that GE was able to provide by drawing on the breadth of its transportation operations. The results show that the physical analogy of 'equipment peers' holds promise as a way to incrementally reason from experience. We believe this is a key contribution of this work.

From the beginning, CBR has effectively relied on analogy to position itself as a reasoning approach. The notion of a case base of 'objects' and 'entities' rather than experiences was intriguing to us. Peer groups forming and disbanding over the lifecycle of the fleet was a natural extension of the analogy. Maintenance of the criteria for peer identification was critical to this task, given the dynamic nature of the domain.

Directions for future work include experimenting with fleets with a mix of long and short track records, and better understanding how a unit's own track record should be integrated with the estimates provided by its peers. We also plan to test this approach on data from different kinds of vehicles, including aircraft and medical imaging equipment.

Acknowledgements

This work was funded by DARPA, through contract CACI 621-04-S-0031. The authors acknowledge the help of Drs. Norm Sondheimer, Al Wallace, and Peter Will, members of the DARPA Steering Committee, and GE Rail who provided us with the data sets and domain knowledge that were indispensable for the model generation and validation.

References

Aggour, K.S., Pavese, M., Bonissone, P.P., and Cheetham, W.E. 2003. SOFT-CBR: A Self-Optimizing Fuzzy Tool for Case-Based Reasoning, *Proceedings of the 5th International Conference on Case-Based Reasoning*, Springer-Verlag, pp 5-19

Berndt, D.J. and Clifford, J. 1996. Finding patterns in time series: A dynamic programming approach, *Advances in Knowledge Discovery and Data Mining*, American Association for Artificial Intelligence, pp 229-248

Fritsche, L., Schlaefer, A., Budde, K., Schröter, K., and Neumayer, H.H. 2002. Recognition of Critical Situations from Time Series of Laboratory Results by Case-Based Reasoning, *Journal of the American Medical Informatics Association*, vol. 9, no. 5, pp 520-528

Goldberg, D.E. 1989. Genetic Algorithms in Search, Optimization and Machine Learning, Addison-Wesley Longman Publishing Co., Inc.

Holland, J.H. 1992. Adaptation in Natural and Artificial Systems, MIT Press

Jaczynski, M. 1997. A Framework for the Management of Past Experiences with Time-Extended Situations, *Proceedings of the 6th International Conference on Information and Knowledge Management*, ACM Press, pp 32-39

Jang, R. 1993. ANFIS: Adaptive-Network-Based Fuzzy Inference System, *IEEE Transactions Systems, Man, and Cybernetics*, vol. 23, no. 3, pp 665-685

Leake, D.B. and Wilson, D.C. 1998. Categorizing Case-Base Maintenance: Dimensions and Directions, *Proceedings of the 4th European Workshop on Case-Based Reasoning*, Springer-Verlag, pp 196-207

Leake, D.B. and Wilson, D.C. 1999. When Experience is Wrong: Examining CBR for Changing Tasks and Environments, *Proceedings of the 3rd International Conference on Case-Based Reasoning*, Springer-Verlag, pp 218-232

Ram, A. and Santamaria, J.C. 1997. Continuous Case-Based Reasoning, Artificial Intelligence, vol. 90, pp 25-77

Schlaefer, A., Schröter, K., and Fritsche, L. 2001. A Case-Based Approach for the Classification of Medical Time Series, *Proceedings of the 2nd International Symposium on Medical Data Analysis*, pp 258-263

Smyth, B. 1998. Case-Base Maintenance. *Proceedings of the 11th International Conference on Industrial and Engineering Applications of Artificial Intelligence and Expert Systems*, vol. 2, pp 507-516

Varma, A. and Roddy, N. 1999. ICARUS: design and deployment of a case-based reasoning system for locomotive diagnostics, *Engineering Applications of Artificial Intelligence*, vol. 12, no.6, pp 681-690

Witten, I.H. and Frank, E. 2000. Data Mining: Practical Machine Learning Tools and Techniques with Java Implementations. Morgan Kaufmann Publishers

Zhang, Z. and Yang, Q. 1998. Towards Lifetime Maintenance of Case Base Indexes for Continual Case Based Reasoning. *Proceedings of the 8th International Conference on AI Methodologies, Systems and Applications*, pp 489-500

CCBR–Driven Business Process Evolution

Barbara Weber[1], Stefanie Rinderle[2], Werner Wild[3], and Manfred Reichert[4]

[1] Quality Engineering Research Group, Institute of Computer Science, University of Innsbruck – Technikerstrasse 21a, 6020 Innsbruck, Austria
Barbara.Weber@uibk.ac.at
[2] Dept. Databases and Information Systems, University of Ulm, Germany
rinderle@informatik.uni-ulm.de
[3] Evolution Consulting, Innsbruck, Austria
werner.wild@evolution.at
[4] Information Systems Group, University of Twente, The Netherlands
m.u.reichert@cs.utwente.nl

Abstract. Process-aware information systems (PAIS) allow coordinating the execution of business processes by providing the right tasks to the right people at the right time. In order to support a broad spectrum of business processes, PAIS must be flexible at run-time. Ad-hoc deviations from the predefined process schema as well as the quick adaptation of the process schema itself due to changes of the underlying business processes must be supported. This paper presents an integrated approach combining the concepts and methods provided by the process management systems ADEPT and CBRFlow. Integrating these two systems enables ad-hoc modifications of single process instances, the memorization of these modifications using conversational case-based reasoning, and their reuse in similar future situations. In addition, potential process type changes can be derived from cases when similar ad-hoc modifications at the process instance level occur frequently.

1 Introduction

For a variety of reasons companies are developing a growing interest in aligning their information systems in a process-oriented way to provide the right tasks to the right people at the right point in time. However, when automating business processes it is extremely important not to restrict users. Early attempts to realize process-aware information systems (PAIS) have been unsuccessful whenever rigidity came with them [1,2]. Therefore, a flexible PAIS must allow authorized users to deviate from the pre-modeled process schema if needed (e.g., by dynamically inserting, deleting or moving process steps). In addition, the PAIS must be quickly adaptable to changes of the underlying business processes, e.g., due to business process reengineering efforts or the introduction of new laws [3,4,5].

In the ADEPT project we have developed a next generation process management system (PMS) that satisfies these needs. On the one hand, the ADEPT PMS offers full functionality with respect to the modeling, analysis, execution,

H. Muñoz-Avila and F. Ricci (Eds.): ICCBR 2005, LNAI 3620, pp. 610–624, 2005.

and monitoring of business processes [1,3,6]. On the other hand, it provides support for adaptive processes at both the process instance and the process type level. Changes at the instance level may affect single process instances and be performed in an ad-hoc manner, e.g., to deal with exceptional or unanticipated situations [1]. Process type changes, in turn, can be applied to adapt the PAIS to business process changes. In this context, concurrent migration of hundreds up to thousands of process instances to the new process schema may become necessary. ADEPT allows to perform the respective migrations on-the-fly while preserving process consistency and system robustness [3,6,7].

In practice, process type changes are often driven by previous ad-hoc adaptations of individual process instances. Usually, similar or equivalent changes of a larger number of process instances indicate the need for adapting the process type (i.e., the process template) itself [8]. For example, in a patient treatment process an additional lab test activity has been inserted for a significant number of process instances; in order to better reflect the real-world process, a process schema evolution should then be initiated to create a new process template version which includes this additional activity (cf. Fig. 2). So far, ADEPT has not adequately dealt with this fact and has not considered the reuse of information about previous ad-hoc changes. In particular, it has not maintained semantic information about these changes (e.g., their reason and context). Thus, it has been the responsibility of the process designer to identify frequently applied changes and to adapt process types accordingly.

By contrast, CBRFlow [9] enables users to apply process instance changes in a more intelligent way. Particularly, it allows to document the reasons for a process instance change and to reuse information about previously performed ad–hoc changes when defining new ones. For this conversational case-based reasoning (CCBR) [10] is used. So far, focus has been put on ad–hoc changes of single process instances whereas process type changes have not yet been considered. In order to provide comprehensive change support a PAIS must capture the whole *process life cycle* and all kinds of changes in an integrated way.

In this paper we provide such an integrated approach, which combines the concepts and methods offered by ADEPT and CBRFlow: On the one hand, the combined system provides a powerful process engine, which supports all kinds of changes in one system. On the other hand, it enables the intelligent reuse of process instance changes and the derivation of process type changes from the collected information. The added value offered by this integration is shown in Table 1.

Table 1. Benefits from Integrating ADEPT and CBRFlow

	ADEPT	CBRFlow	ADEPT+CBRFlow
process instance changes	+	+	+
reuse of process instance changes		+	+
process type changes	+		+
deriving process type changes			+

Section 2 provides background information, Section 3 discusses issues that arise when trying to derive process type changes from cases. In addition to the resulting evolution of the business processes the corresponding case-bases evolve over time as well. This important issue is covered in Section 4. Section 5 discusses related work and Section 6 closes with a summary and an outlook on future work.

2 Background

In this section we provide background information regarding process management and case-based reasoning (CBR) as used in our approach.

2.1 Process Management

For each business process supported (e.g., booking of a business trip or handling a medical order) a *process type* T has to be defined. Formally, such a type is represented by a *process schema* S of which different versions may exist. In Fig. 1, for example, S and S' correspond to different schema versions of the same process type T (thus reflecting the evolution of T).

In the following, a process schema is represented by a directed graph, which defines a set of *activities* – the process steps – and the control flow between them.[1] In Fig. 1 process schema S consists of 6 activities: for example, activity `Admit patient` is followed by activity `Make appointment` in the flow of control whereas `Prepare Patient` and `Inform Patient` can be processed in parallel. Formally:

Definition 1 (Process Schema). *A process schema S is defined by a tuple (N, E) where N denotes the set of activities and E the set of control edges (i.e., precedence relations) between these activities.*

At runtime new process instances can be created and executed based on schema S. Similar to Petri Nets, the execution state of a particular process instance is captured by a marking function $M = (NS, ES)$. It assigns to each activity n its current status $NS(n) \in$ {NOT_ACTIVATED, ACTIVATED, FINISHED} and to each control edge its marking $ES(e) \in$ {NOT_SIGNALED, SIGNALED}. For the top most process instance $I_\nu^{(1)}$ in Fig. 1, for example, activity `Admit patient` has already been finished and therefore its outgoing edge is marked as SIGNALED. Activity `Make appointment`, in turn, is currently activated, i.e., offered to users for execution in their worklists.

Usually, a process instance I is executed according to the control flow defined by its original schema S. As motivated in Section 1, however, users may have to deviate from the original schema (e.g., by adding new activities or by

[1] In this paper we restrict our considerations to schemes with sequential and parallel activities. Our approach, however, considers more complex control structures as well (e.g., conditional branchings, loops, and synchronizations between parallel execution branches). Details of the process meta model used can be found in [1,6,7].

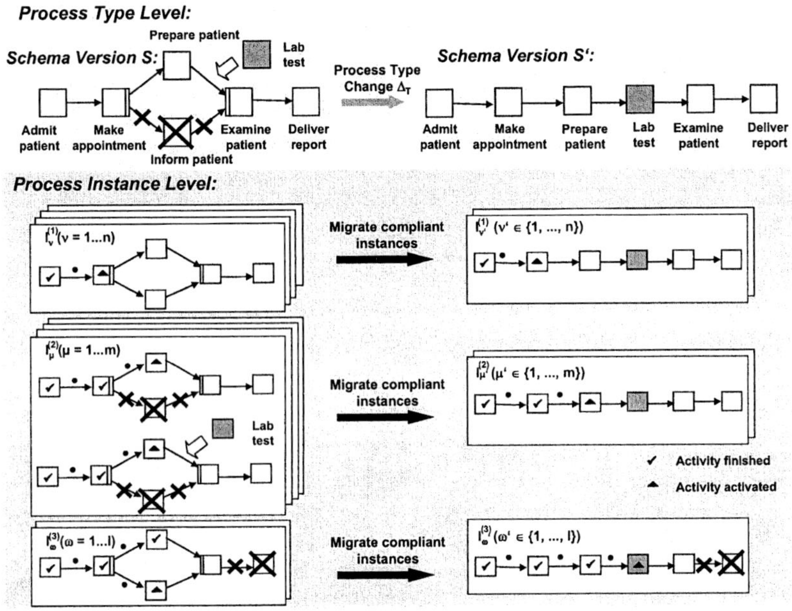

Fig. 1. Migration of Process Instances – Clinical Example

deleting existing ones). For this reason, we must distinguish between two basic classes of process instances, those that still follow their original schema and those that have been individually modified during runtime. In the following, we call instances of the former class *unbiased* and those of the latter one *biased*. Correspondingly, a biased instance I cannot solely be characterized by its original schema S and marking M, but must also capture the sequence of ad-hoc changes $\Delta_I = (a_1, \ldots, a_k)$ applied to it so far. Generally, several ad-hoc changes may have been applied to a biased instance I at different points in time.

For example, consider Fig. 1: Process instances $I_\nu^{(1)}, \nu = 1 \ldots n$ are unbiased. By contrast, process instances $I_\mu^{(2)}$, $\mu = 1 \ldots m$ and $I_\omega^{(3)}$, $\omega = 1 \ldots l$ are biased since their current execution schema deviates from their original schema S. Instances $I_\omega^{(3)}$, $\omega = 1 \ldots l$, for example, are biased due to the dynamic deletion of activity `Deliver report`. Formally:

Definition 2 (Process Instance).
A process instance I is defined by a tuple (S, Δ_I, M) where

- *$S = (N, E)$ denotes the process schema I was originally created on.*
- *$\Delta_I = (a_1, \ldots, a_k)$ comprises the instance-specific sequence of ad-hoc modifications which have been applied to I so far (i.e., changes transforming the process schema S, instance I was created from, into the current execution schema $S_I = S + \Delta_I = (N', E')$). Thereby $a_i = (op, s, paramList)$ denotes an operation $op \in OP$ which operates on a schema subject s (i.e., activities*

Table 2. *A Selection of ADEPT Change Operations**

Change Operation *op* **applied to Schema S**	**Effects on Schema S**
	Additive Change Operations
serialInsert(S, X, A, B)	insert activity X into schema S between the two directly connected activities A and B
parallelInsert(S, X, (A))	insert activity X into schema S parallel to activity A
	Subtractive Change Operations
deleteActivity(S, X)	delete activity X from schema S

*A detailed description of all change operations supported by ADEPT can be found in [11,12].

or edges) using parameters paramList. OP is the set of change operations provided by ADEPT, a subset of these operations is given in Table 2.
- *M =(NS, ES) reflects the current marking of I. It assigns to each activity* $n \in N'$ *its current status NS(n) and to each edge* $e \in E'$ *its marking ES(e).*

2.2 Case-Based Reasoning and Learning Processes

Case-based reasoning is a contemporary approach to problem solving and learning. New problems are dealt with by applying past experiences – described as cases – and by adapting their solutions to the new problem situation [13]. Thus, CBR contributes to incremental and sustained learning: Every time a new problem is solved, information about it and its solution is retained and therefore immediately made available for solving future problems [14].

Conversational CBR is an extension to the CBR paradigm, which actively involves users in the inference process [15]. A CCBR system can be characterized as an interactive system that, via a mixed-initiative dialogue, guides users through a question-answering sequence in a case retrieval context. Unlike traditional CBR, CCBR does not require the user to provide a complete a priori problem specification for case retrieval, nor requires him to provide knowledge about the relevance of each feature for problem solving. Instead, the system assists the user in finding relevant cases by presenting a set of questions to assess the given situation. Furthermore, it guides users who may supply already known information on their initiative. Therefore, CCBR is especially suitable for handling exceptional or unanticipated situations that cannot be dealt with in a fully automated way.

In our approach a case *c* represents a concrete ad-hoc modification of a process instance *I* which can be reused by other instances. It consists of a textual problem description, a set of question-answer pairs, and a solution part (i.e., the action list). The question–answer pairs describe the reasons for the ad-hoc change and the action list comprises the change operations (and related context information) applied to *I*.

Definition 3 (Case, Case–Base).
A case c is a tuple (pd, $\{ q_1an_1, \ldots, q_nan_n \}$, sol, freq) where

- *pd is a textual problem description*
- *$\{ q_1an_1, \ldots, q_nan_n\}$ denotes a set of question-answer pairs*
- *$sol = \{ a_j \mid a_j = (op_j, s_j, paramList_j),\ j = 1, \ldots, k\}$ is the solution part of the case denoting a list of actions (i.e., a set of changes that have been applied to one or more process instances; see also Def. 2)*
- *$freq \in \mathbb{N}$ denotes the reuse frequency of case c*

A case–base $CB = \{ c_1, \ldots, c_m\}$ is defined as a set of cases.

3 Deriving Evolutionary Process Changes from Cases

Fig. 2 illustrates our approach: it shows how CCBR is used to perform ad-hoc changes of single process instances (cf. Section 3.1) and how it triggers process type changes if the same or similar ad-hoc changes happen over and over again (with respect to instances of a given process type; cf. Section 3.2). Fig. 2 also indicates that the evolution of a process schema may require the concurrent migration of the associated case-base (cf. Section 4).

As already mentioned, new instances can be created based on a given process schema and then be executed according to that schema. If required, authorized users may deviate from the pre-modeled process schema during runtime at the level of single process instances. They apply CCBR to retrieve knowledge about previous ad-hoc changes. In addition, they document the new change and collect information about the reasons which required the respective ad-hoc deviation. This information is then immediately available for future reuse in similar situations. Finally, if a case is frequently reused (i.e., the same ad-hoc change is often applied to instances of a particular process type), case usage may exceed a predefined threshold. In this situation, the knowledge engineer is notified about the potential need of a process type change. He can then take action, e.g., by adapting the process type and migrating the case-base.

3.1 Performing Ad-Hoc Changes Using CCBR

Integrating ADEPT and CBRFlow offers promising perspectives: It allows for ad-hoc modifications at the process instance level in a correct and consistent manner, it facilitates the memorization of these modifications using CBR techniques, and it provides for reusing respective cases in similar, future situations. The underlying CBR cycle [14] can be described as follows:

Adding a New Case. Whenever a user wants to apply an ad-hoc change at the process instance level and no similar cases can be found in the CCBR system, she adds a new case $c = (pd, \{q_1an_1, \ldots,\}, \text{sol}, 1)$ to the case-base. The user enters this case by briefly describing the current problem, by entering a set of question-answer pairs describing the reasons for the ad-hoc deviation, and by specifying the actions to be taken from the list of available change operations.

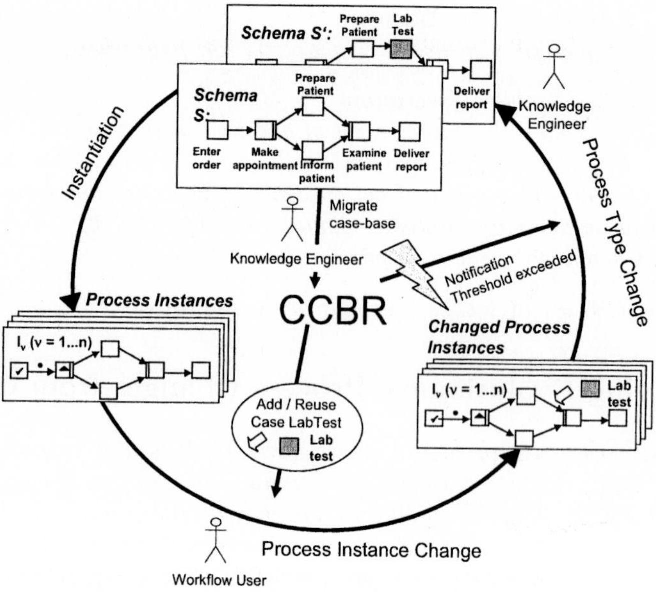

Fig. 2. Deriving Evolutionary Process Changes from Cases

Question-answer pairs can be entered by either selecting the question from a list of previously entered questions (i.e., reusing questions from existing cases) or, when no suitable question is already in the system, by defining a new question and giving the appropriate answer. Depending on the permissions of the user and the current state of the process instance (i.e., which activities are currently performed) only a subset of the ADEPT operations may be applicable. The user selects the desired change operations $op_1, \ldots, op_p$ and the subjects $s_1, \ldots, s_p$ they operate on (e.g., activities and control edges). In addition, she provides the parameters for each selected operation. Finally, the case is retained and thus immediately made available for future reuse.

Retaining a Case. Unlike CBRFlow [9], our approach stores cases not relative to the location in the process graph where the ad-hoc modification occurred (e.g., relative to an activity), but in reference to the process schema itself. There is one case-base version for each process schema version S, as they might be relevant at different locations in the process. For example, the insertion of a particular activity (e.g., order lab test) might become necessary at different points in time during process execution.

Case Retrieval. For case retrieval the CCBR approach as described in [10] has been adapted. When deviations from the predefined process schema become necessary the user initiates case retrieval in the CCBR component. The system then assists her in finding already stored, similar cases by presenting a set of questions. Users can directly answer any of the displayed questions (in arbitrary order) or additionally apply a filter to the case-base by specifying an operation *op* as well as the subject s on which the operation is supposed to operate. Filtering is done by selecting values from predefined lists and by ignoring those cases that do no match the filter criteria (i.e., that do not have the selected operation and subject in the actions list); only the remaining cases are presented. Formally:

Definition 4 (Filtered Case–Base). *Let $CB = \{c_1, \ldots, c_k\}$ be a case–base with $c_i = (\ldots, sol_i, \ldots)$ $(i = 1, .., k)$ and $sol_i = \{(op_j, s_j, \ldots)\}$ $(j = 1, .., m)$ (cf. Def. 3). Then the filtered case-base CB_{filter} can be determined as follows:*

$$CB_{filter} = \begin{cases} \{c_i \in CB \mid \exists (op_j, s_j, \ldots) \in sol_i : op_j = op \wedge s_j = s\} & if A \\ \{c_i \in CB \mid \exists (op_j, s_j, \ldots) \in sol_i : op_j = op\} & if B \\ CB & otherwise \end{cases}$$

whereby

- *A: user has specified change operation $op \in OP$ and subject s*
- *B: user has specified change operation $op \in OP$*

The system then searches for similar cases by calculating the similarity for each case in the case-base CB_{filter}. It then displays the top n ranked cases (ordered by decreasing similarity) and their reputation score, which indicates how successfully each case has been applied in the past. Similarity is calculated by dividing the number of correctly answered questions minus the number of incorrectly answered questions by the total number of questions in the case. Formally:

Definition 5 (Similarity). *Let $c = (pd^c, QA^c = \{q_1^c an_1^c, \ldots, q_n^c an_n^c\}, \ldots)$ be a case of case–base CB and $Q = \{q_1^Q an_1^Q, \ldots, q_m^Q an_m^Q\}$ be a query against CB. Then sim(Q, c) denotes the similarity between Q and c. Formally:*

$$sim(Q,c) = \frac{same(Q,c) - diff(Q,c)}{|QA^c|}$$

whereby

- *$same(Q, c) = |QA^c \cap Q|$*
- *$diff(Q, c) = |\{q_i^c an_i^c \in QA^c \mid \exists\, q_j^Q an_j^Q \in Q$ with $q_i^c = q_j^Q \wedge an_i^c \neq an_j^Q;\ i = 1,..,n;\ j = 1,.., m\}|$*

Case Reuse. ADEPT supports different kinds of ad-hoc changes which, for example, allow users to skip activities, to change activity orders, or to insert new activities [1]. In particular, the system ensures that ad-hoc changes do not lead to unstable system behavior[2] or to inconsistent instance states. When an exceptional or unexpected situation occurs, the user is assisted in selecting the desired change operations and in setting the change context (e.g., the predecessors and successors of an activity to be inserted) accordingly.

Generally, change definition requires user experience, in particular if the intended change requires concurrent adaptations (e.g., when deleting a particular

[2] None of the guarantees (e.g., absence of deadlocks, correctness of data flow) which have been achieved by formal checks at buildtime are violated due to the change.

activity, data-dependent activities may have to be deleted as well). Therefore, the reuse of existing knowledge about previous ad-hoc changes is highly desirable. When a user decides to reuse an existing case, the actions specified in the solution part of the case are forwarded to and carried out by the ADEPT change engine. The reuse counter is increased and a work item is created for evaluating the ad-hoc change later on to maintain the quality of the case-base.

When the reuse counter exceeds a certain configurable threshold the knowledge engineer is notified about the potential need to perform a schema evolution (cf. Section 3.2). Altogether, the reuse of existing ad-hoc changes contributes to hide as much complexity from users as possible.

Ensuring Quality Through Case Evaluation. The accuracy of the cases in the case-base is crucial for the overall performance of a CBR system and consequently for the trust users have in it. When cases are not added by the knowledge engineer but by end users, evaluation mechanisms are needed to ensure quality of the cases in the case-base.

Therefore, similar to Cheetham and Price [16], we propose to augment the CBR cycle with the ability to determine the confidence in the accuracy of individual solutions. However, for CCBR systems the accuracy cannot be determined automatically as the semantics of the question-answer pairs are, unlike in traditional CBR systems, unknown to the system. For this purpose we apply the concept of reputation from e-commerce where such systems are used to build trust among strangers like, for instance, in eBay's feedback forum [17]. There, each positive feedback on a transaction increases the reputation score of a seller, while each negative feedback results in a decrease. In our approach, we use the concept of reputation to indicate how successfully a case has been reused in the past, i.e., how much it has contributed to the performance of the case-base, thus indicating the degree of confidence regarding the accuracy of this case. Like in eBay, users are encouraged to provide feedback when adding or reusing a case. For this purpose, a new work item representing an optional feedback task is automatically created and inserted into the worklist of the user who entered or applied the case. She can then rate the performance of the case either with 1 (positive), 0 (neutral) or −1 (negative), and may optionally specify an additional comment. The reputation score of a case is then calculated as the number of distinct users who gave a positive feedback minus the number of those who gave a negative feedback. Negative feedback usually results in a notification of the knowledge engineer (see below).

During case retrieval the CCBR system displays the overall reputation score together with a table of the totals of each rating in the past 7 days, the past month, and the past 6 months to the user. Upon request the user can read all comments provided in the past and decide whether the reputation of the case is high enough for her to have confidence in its accuracy.

Case Revision. Negative feedback results in a notification of the knowledge engineer who can then revise the case or decide to deactivate it (no deletion is allowed to foster traceability).

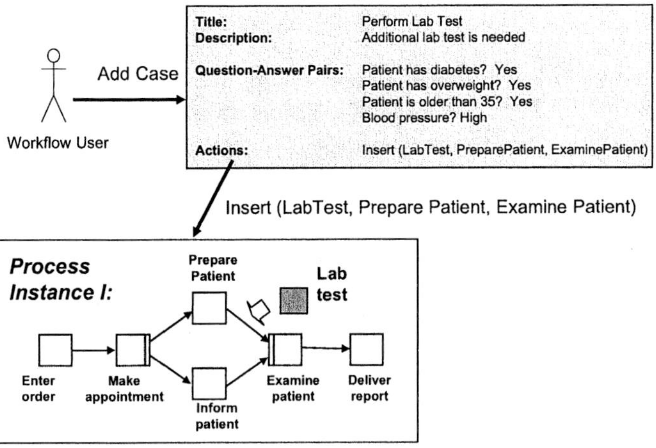

Fig. 3. Adding a New Case to Insert a Process Step

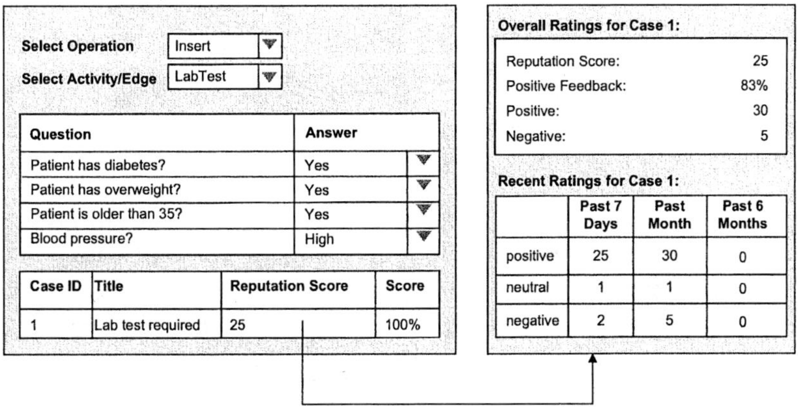

Fig. 4. Retrieving Similar Cases

Example. To illustrate the above concepts we provide a simplified medical example. As depicted in Fig. 1 the examination of a patient usually takes place after a preparation step. During the examination the physician recognizes that the patient suffers from diabetes and he detects several other important risk factors. Therefore, the physician decides to request an additional lab test for the patient to be performed after activity `Prepare patient` and before activity `Examine Patient`. As the system contains no similar cases, the physician enters a new case describing the situation and the action to be taken (Fig. 3). ADEPT then checks whether the insertion of activity `Lab Test` is possible for the respective process instance, and - if so - applies the specified insert operation to that instance. The latter includes updating the instance markings and user worklists. If, for example, `Prepare patient` is completed and `Examine Patient` is activated, this activation will be undone (i.e., respective work items are removed from user worklists) and the newly inserted activity `Lab test` becomes immediately activated. In any case, the newly inserted activity is treated like the other process steps, i.e., the same scheduling and monitoring facilities exist.

When talking with another diabetic patient some time later, the physician remembers that there has been a similar situation before and initiates the CCBR sub-system to retrieve similar cases. As he still remembers that he had performed an additional lab test, he selects the `Insert` operation as well as the `Lab Test` activity to filter the case-base. He then answers the questions presented by the system, finds the previously added case, and reuses it (Fig. 4). Of course, the physician could also directly answer any of the presented questions without selecting an operation or an activity first (e.g., when he doesn't remember a similar previous situation).

3.2 Deriving Process Type Changes

When the usage of a particular case exceeds the specified threshold value (i.e., based on the frequency the case was reused, cf. Def. 3), the system sends a notification to the knowledge engineer. He may then initiate a process type change in order to derive a new version of the process schema. For this purpose he may directly apply the change operations captured by the respective case; alternatively, he can adapt the case's operation set (e.g., by only considering a subset of it).

When a new process schema is released future instances can be created from it. However, the challenging question is how to treat already running process instances, i.e., instances that have been derived from the old process schema version. Particularly for long-running processes, it is crucial that respective instances can be migrated to the new process schema version if desired (cf. Fig. 1). In this context ADEPT first checks whether these instances are *compliant* with the new process schema or not. Compliant means that the process schema change can be applied to the instance in its current state so that it can be smoothly re–linked to the new schema, i.e., *migrated* to it without causing inconsistencies or errors (e.g., deadlocks). Then the set of compliant process instances is divided into unbiased and biased instances. The former can be directly re–linked to the new schema. For each instance its marking with respect to the new schema version is automatically determined. For biased process instances further correctness checks are necessary, e.g., regarding structural correctness (for details see [12]). Finally, all compliant process instances are running according to the new schema version whereas non compliant process instances remain running on the old schema. An example is given in Section 4.

4 Migrating the Case-Base

Assume that the frequencies for reusing certain cases exceed specified thresholds (cf. Section 3.2). For instance, as illustrated in Fig. 5 the specified thresholds for reusing case c1 ($freq = 51$) and c5 ($freq = 60$) are exceeded, thus triggering a

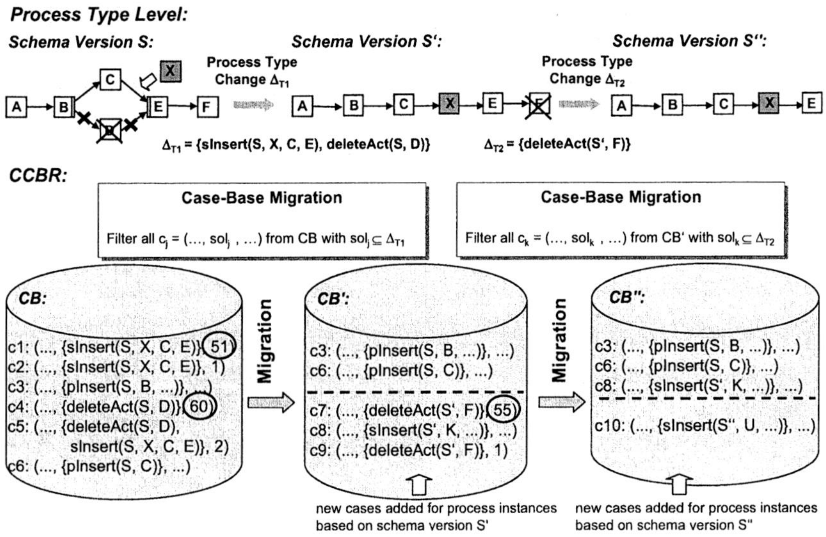

Fig. 5. Migrating the Case-Base

process type change. The knowledge engineer is informed and decides that the respective instance changes serialInsert(S,X,C,E) (sInsert(S,X,C,E) for short) and deleteActivity(S,D) (deleteAct(S,D) for short) should be pulled up to the process type level. He derives a new process schema version S' by applying process type change Δ_{T1} = {sInsert(S,X,C,E), deleteAct(S,D)}.

This process type change is accompanied by the migration of compliant process instances to the new schema version S', whereas non-compliant process instances remain running on the old schema version (cf. Section 3.2). In addition, the challenging question is, which cases of the previous case-base CB (on S) shall be valid for process instances of S' as well. This consideration becomes necessary as the solution part of certain cases may be covered by a process type change Δ_T. Therefore the respective cases are no longer needed. In our approach, only cases whose solution part is not reflected in the process type change Δ_T are migrated to CB'. By contrast, cases whose solution part is a subset of Δ_T are omitted. Formally:

Definition 6 (Case-Base Migration). *Let $CB = (c_1, \ldots, c_k)$ be a case-base stored for process instances running according to process schema S. If then process type change Δ_T transforms S into another process schema S' the new version CB' of CB can determined as follows:*

$$CB' = CB \setminus \{c_i = (\ldots, sol_j, \ldots) \in CB \mid sol_j \subseteq \Delta_T \ (j = 1,..,m)\}$$

In the example depicted by Fig. 5, cases c1 and c4 that initiated the process type change, as well as case c2 and c5 are already covered by the new schema version S'. Consequently, the new version CB' of case-base CB is built by migrating only cases c3 and c6. Of course, new cases may be added to CB' due to ongoing ad-hoc changes of instances based on S'. Again, the migration of this case-base will become necessary if another process schema migration takes place later on. In our example, type change Δ_{T2} = {deleteAct(S',F)} is triggered by case c7 which exceeds a certain frequency $freq$ (55). The resulting case-base CB" is shown in Fig. 5.

5 Related Work

This paper is based on the idea of integrating PMS and CCBR. In related work CBR has been applied to support process modeling [18,19], to the configuration of complex core processes [20], to the handling of exceptions [21] and for the composition of Web Services [22]. All of these approaches apply traditional CBR, to our knowledge there are no other approaches relying on CCBR.

Related work also includes adaptive process management. Existing approaches either support ad-hoc changes at the process instance level or schema modifications at the process type level (for an overview see [3]). Except for ADEPT [12] none of these approaches considers both kinds of changes in an integrated manner. In particular the full life cycle support using CCBR techniques has not been addressed so far. Though CBRFlow [9] fosters the reuse of ad-hoc changes, it has not yet considered process type changes. This gap is closed by the integration of ADEPT and CBRFlow.

AI planning, especially mixed-initiative case-based planning (e.g., NaCoDAE/HTN [23], MI-CBP [24], SiN [25] and HICAP [26]) can be seen as complementary to our approach as we primarily focus on the execution of processes and not on modeling or planning. Process management approaches rely on a predefined process schema (i.e., plan) that is instantiated during run-time in high numbers. In contrast, in AI planning the user is supported in generating a new plan for every new problem situation, which prevents the problem of having to change other running instances of the same plan. Other than in AI planning our meta-model supports complex control flow constructs (e.g., conditional branching, loop backs, and synchronizations between parallel execution branches).

Process-based knowledge management systems are suitable for knowledge intensive workflows and are often used to provide additional process information to the user in order to support them during the execution of activities (e.g., DECOR [27], FRODO TaskMan [28], KnowMore [29]). FRODO TaskMan extends the approach taken in KnowMore by supporting integrated modeling and enactment of weak workflows. Like our approach, FRODO TaskMan allows instance level modifications of the workflow during run-time, but does not support process type changes. Additionally it supports working with an incomplete process schema due to its late modeling capabilities.

6 Summary and Outlook

The integration of ADEPT and CBRFlow offers promising perspectives. It results in a new generation of adaptive process technology, which facilitates and speeds up the implementation of new as well as the adaptation of existing processes. Both, the capability to quickly and correctly propagate type changes to in-progress process instances as well as the intelligent support of ad-hoc adaptations will be key ingredients in next generation PMS, resulting in highly adaptive PAIS. Currently, we are working on the implementation of a prototype that combines the methods and concepts provided by ADEPT and CBRFlow. Future research will include the evaluation of this approach in different application settings, like healthcare processes and emergent workflows (e.g., in the automotive domain). Our future research will include the extension of the presented approach towards agile process mining, i.e., fostering to start with a simple, incomplete process schema and then learn from the living processes to evolve the schema over time.

References

1. Reichert, M., Dadam, P.: $ADEPT_{flex}$ - supporting dynamic changes of workflows without losing control. JIIS **10** (1998) 93–129
2. Jørgensen, H.D.: Interactive Process Models. PhD thesis, Norwegian University of Science and Technology, Trondheim, Norway (2004)
3. Rinderle, S., Reichert, M., Dadam, P.: Correctness criteria for dynamic changes in workflow systems – a survey. Data and Knowledge Engineering **50** (2004) 9–34
4. Casati, F., Ceri, S., Pernici, B., Pozzi, G.: Workflow evolution. Data and Knowledge Engineering **24** (1998) 211–238
5. v.d. Aalst, W., Basten, T.: Inheritance of workflows: An approach to tackling problems related to change. Theoret. Comp. Science **270** (2002) 125–203
6. Rinderle, S., Reichert, M., Dadam, P.: Flexible support of team processes by adaptive workflow systems. Distributed and Parallel Databases **16** (2004) 91–116
7. Rinderle, S., Reichert, M., Dadam, P.: On dealing with structural conflicts between process type and instance changes. In: Proc. BPM'04. (2004) 274–289
8. Rinderle, S., Reichert, M., Dadam, P.: Disjoint and overlapping process changes: Challenges, solutions, applications. In: Proc. Int'l Conf. on Cooperative Information Systems (CoopIS'04). LNCS 3290, Larnaca, Cyprus (2004) 101–120
9. Weber, B., Wild, W., Breu, R.: CBRFlow: Enabling adaptive workflow management through conversational case-based reasoning. In: Proc. European Conf. on Cased based Reasoning (ECCBR'04), Madrid (2004) 434–448
10. Aha, D.W., Breslow, L., Muñoz-Avila, H.: Conversational case-based reasoning. Applied Intelligence **14** (2001) 9–32
11. Reichert, M.: Dynamic Changes in Workflow-Management-Systems. PhD thesis, University of Ulm, Computer Science Faculty (2000) (in German).
12. Rinderle, S.: Schema Evolution in Process Management Systems. PhD thesis, University of Ulm, Computer Science Faculty (2004)
13. Kolodner, J.L.: Case-Based Reasoning. Morgan Kaufmann (1993)
14. A. Aamodt, E.P.: Case-based reasoning: Foundational issues, methodological variations and system approaches. AI Communications **7** (1994) 39–59
15. Aha, D.W., Muñoz-Avila, H.: Introduction: Interactive case-based reasoning. Applied Intelligence **14** (2001) 7–8
16. Cheetham, W., Price, J.: Measures of solution accuracy in case-based reasoning systems. In: Proc. European Conf. on Case-Based Reasoning (ECCBR'04). LNCS 3155, Madrid (2004) 106–118

17. eBAY: Feedback Forum. (2005) http://pages.ebay.com/services/forum/feedback.html.
18. Kim, J., Suh, W., Lee, H.: Document-based workflow modeling: a case-based reasoning approach. Expert Systems with Applications **23** (2002) 77–93
19. Madhusudan, T., Zhao, J.: A case-based framework for workflow model management. In: Proc. 1st Int'l Conf. on Business Process Management (BPM'03), Eindhoven (2003) 354–369
20. Wargitsch, C.: Ein Beitrag zur Integration von Workflow- und Wissensmanagement unter besonderer Berücksichtigung komplexer Geschäftsprozesse. PhD thesis, Erlangen (1998)
21. Luo, Z., Sheth, A., amd J. Miller, K.K.: Exception handling in workflow systems. Applied Intelligence **13** (2000) 125–147
22. Limthanmaphon, B., Zhang, Y.: Web service composition with case-based reasoning. In: Proc. of 15th Australasian Database Conf. (ADC'02), Australia (2002)
23. Muñoz-Avila, H., McFarlane, D., Aha, D., Ballas, J., Breslow, L., Nau, D.: Using guidelines to constrain interactive case-based htn planning. In: Proceedings of the Third International Conference on Case-Based Reasoning, Munich (1999) 288–302
24. Veloso, M., Mulvehill, A., Cox, M.: Rationale-supported mixed-initiative case-based planning. In: Proceedings of the Ninth conference on Innovative Applications of Artificial Intelligence, Providence, Rhode Island (1997) 1072–1077
25. Muñoz-Avila, H., Aha, D., Nau, D., Breslow, L., Weber, R., Yamal, F.: Sin: Integrating case-based reasoning with task decomposition. In: Proc. IJCAI-2001, Seattle (2001) 99–104
26. Muñoz-Avila, H., Gupta, K., Aha, D., Nau, D.: Knowledge Based Project Planning. In: Knowledge Management and Organizational Memories. Kluwer Academic Publishers (2002)
27. Abecker, A., et al.: Enabling workflow-embedded OM access with the DECOR toolkit. In Dieng-Kuntz, R., Matta, N., eds.: Knowledge Management and Organizational Memories. Kluwer Academic Publishers (2002)
28. Elst, L., Aschoff, F., Bernardi, A., Maus, H., Schwarz, S.: Weakly-structured workflows for knowledge-intensive tasks: An experimental evaluation. In: Proc. 12th Int'l Workshop on Enabling Technologies. (2003) 340–345
29. Abecker, A., Bernardi, A., Hinkelmann, K., O. Kühn, O., Sintek, M.: Context-aware, proactive delivery of task-specific knowledge: The KnowMore project. Int. Journal on Information Systems Frontiers **2** (2000) 139–162

CBR for Modeling Complex Systems

Rosina Weber[1], Jason M. Proctor[2], Ilya Waldstein[3], and Andres Kriete[4,5]

[1,2,3] College of Information Science & Technology, Drexel University
[4] School of Biomedical Engineering, Science and Health Systems, Drexel University
[5] Drexel and Coriell Bioinformatics Initiative, Coriell Institute for Medical Research
{[1]rw37,[2]jp338,[4]ak3652}@drexel.edu,[3]sainet@snip.net

Abstract. This paper describes how CBR can be used to compare, reuse, and adapt inductive models that represent complex systems. Complex systems are not well understood and therefore require models for their manipulation and understanding. We propose an approach to address the challenges for using CBR in this context, which relate to finding similar inductive models (solutions) to represent similar complex systems (problems). The purpose is to improve the modeling task by considering the quality of different models to represent a system based on the similarity to a system that was successfully modeled. The revised and confirmed suitability of a model can become additional evidence of similarity between two complex systems, resulting in an increased understanding of a domain. This use of CBR supports tasks (e.g., diagnosis, prediction) that inductive or mathematical models alone cannot perform. We validate our approach by modeling software systems, and illustrate its potential significance for biological systems.

1 Introduction

This paper explores the contribution of the CBR methodology for the modeling task, particularly when the system (e.g. biological, organizational, computational) to be modeled is complex i.e., not well understood or not easily accessible. We envision using CBR to recommend a model to a previously unknown system based on its similarity to previously recorded systems and their adopted models. *Modeling* is the task concerned with creating a description of a system with the purpose of understanding or predicting its functioning and/or effects. When data is available, models can be created with inductive methods. When theory is available, models can be created with mathematical methods. When neither is available, we propose reusing models through CBR. The role we propose for CBR in the modeling task is one of an aggregator or manager of data and knowledge pertinent to the case-based recommendation of models – not as an alternative to inductive or mathematical models.

This paper's intended contribution is to propose an approach to assess similarity between complex systems and between inductive models, and to demonstrate that a suitable inductive model can be recommended to represent a system on the basis of the system's similarity to other systems. As a result, CBR can be used as the underlying methodology for reasoning with complex cases, whose problems are complex systems and whose solutions are their models. This use of CBR will allow

H. Muñoz-Avila and F. Ricci (Eds.): ICCBR 2005, LNAI 3620, pp. 625 – 639, 2005.

the performance of tasks such as prediction and diagnosis; but even more importantly, it will leverage the understanding of the systems it will model.

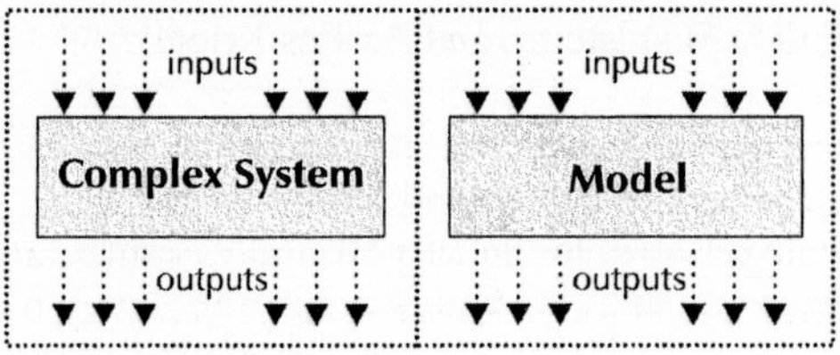

Fig. 1. Models represent complex systems

The CBR methodology can combine knowledge from different sources into one aggregated reasoning task to propose a solution. When domain knowledge is incorporated into the design of a case base that recommends models to represent complex systems, it represents a potential advantage over selecting models without domain knowledge. Determining the quality of a model also requires domain knowledge. Therefore, when a model is proposed and its suitability is revised and confirmed, the case base learns a new case and measures of quality of how a model represents a system can be verified (i.e. confirmed or rejected). Besides the individual power of one more case to improve a future recommendation, this new case becomes a new (properly positioned) piece of the puzzle, allowing a better understanding of the domain, and potentially advancing the field. The ability to assess similarity between complex systems and between inductive models is critical to allow the combination of domain knowledge with the manipulation and understanding of complex systems.

Recommending models for systems that are not well understood or not easily accessible encompasses uncertainty. This uncertainty is associated with the suitability of a model to describe a system. After each confirmed solution, the enhanced understanding of the domain problem is expected to result in reduced levels of uncertainty.

The significance of the approach described in this paper is illustrated by its applicability in modeling software programs and biological systems. Both in software engineering and in bioinformatics, modeling methods used are mathematical or inductive, but neither can be leveraged into a system-wide understanding of the role of models and their interplay with the environment. The conception of a computational approach that benefits from the power of inductive modeling and also takes advantage of analogical reasoning has the potential to drastically improve the performance of tasks such as prediction and diagnosis, and even enhance the understanding of these systems.

1.1 Two Target Problems: Software Programs and Biological Systems

We describe the problems of modeling software programs and biological systems because they are sufficiently similar so that one can serve as a proof of concept for the other. We have already implemented the first one, modeling software programs, and we use it to understand research challenges and test strategies to address them. The second problem seems more significant because of its potential benefits to human health.

Both software programs and biological systems process inputs to produce outputs. In software programs, *inputs* and *outputs* are the terms used to describe the values entered and results from programs' computations. An individual's biological system receives inputs from the environment (e.g. nutrition) and produces as a result health outcomes. In fact, a reasonable explanation for the functioning of cells and genes is that they follow programs to produce an outcome like processed data. Both problems are complex systems that require system modeling. In both problems, the essence of the modeling task is to represent input-output analysis (Fig. 1). Given the suitability of using artificial neural networks to model input-output analysis, they are chosen to model both software (e.g. [18]) and biological systems (e.g. [14]).

The problem we focus on in the software engineering domain is to model software programs with the purpose of generating test cases for software testing. This may be useful because it is easier to manipulate a model than it is to manipulate a real and complete program and because the entire program's details may not always be available. The model can be built inductively by the analysis of randomly generated inputs and the corresponding resulting outputs [18].

In biology, we focus on modeling an individual's biological system with the purpose of predicting health outcomes based upon dietary inputs. This can improve medical understanding, helping individuals predict and achieve desired health outcomes. The model is necessary because it is impossible to submit each individual to different inputs to study what the outputs would be. The model can only be built by comparing and combining models generated with data from other individuals and partial data from the target individual. This is where a computing platform requires analogical reasoning for the modeling task: *to help find a quality model to represent an individual, it is necessary to assess genetic similarities to make use of biological assumptions* (e.g. twins may have similar susceptibility to environment). Consequently, a reasoning platform to model biological systems has to be able to manipulate inductive models and assess similarity between them.

There are uncertainties in both systems. We may know the programming language and we may be able to infer how a program might have been written; but even if we have the code, it is not clear how to use it to define good test cases for its testing. In human biological systems, we may know the genetic constitution of an individual and may have the expression of genes from blood cells and some other accessible organs, but there is always uncertainty with respect to the remaining cells as long as the human individual is alive. Gene expression varies with age [21][23], so even if we know the current expression of genes in some cells, there is uncertainty as to what the expression will be in the future.

Improvements in software testing methods can be significant. The cost of poor software testing is estimated to reach up to 60 million US dollars annually [11]. In the domain of biology, the recent availability of the human genome and knowledge of pathways has created a demand for computing solutions to understand the behavior of molecular processes. This is an area with potential high payoffs in human health but where data is still expensive or impossible to obtain. It is therefore necessary that these computing solutions are able to leverage existing data to support, manipulate, complement, and explain phenotypical and medical facts. These same computing infrastructures can recommend testing methods to support high quality software.

In Section 2 we describe a case-based platform applied to model software programs. Section 3 proposes our approach to overcome the main obstacle to apply CBR: *what makes a system similar to another such that we can reuse their models?* This approach is validated in Section 4. It is then used as the basis to design a second platform, which we discuss in Section 5 to model biological systems. Section 6 discusses related work and Section 7 presents concluding remarks and future work.

2 CBR for Modeling Software Programs

The application we describe here models software programs with the purpose of generating test cases. The current application integrates a case-based framework [22] into a system (CI-Tool) [4] that uses computational intelligence methods (e.g., inductive [11][18]) to generate test cases. Although CBR itself does not perform the modeling task, it creates cases to improve the overall quality of the system [22].

We limit our presentation of the software program modeling system to one inductive method: artificial neural networks (ANN). The elements we discuss when representing cases with ANN are also present when using other inductive modeling methods. Fig. 2 depicts the modules of the software program modeling system. A data mart retains data and functions, managing the communications between the modules. A software program is the input to the system; the ANN module creates an inductive model for it. The individual case base is dedicated to storing cases where problems describe features of software programs, solutions describe elements of an ANN, and the outcome describes the accuracy of the ANN as a model of the software program. Elements of an ANN include its configuration parameters (e.g. learning rate, training dataset, pruning accuracy). We assess model quality based on the evaluation of the ANN training. Our model's accuracy is obtained through the average error rate between the expected outputs and actual output with the final weight matrix.

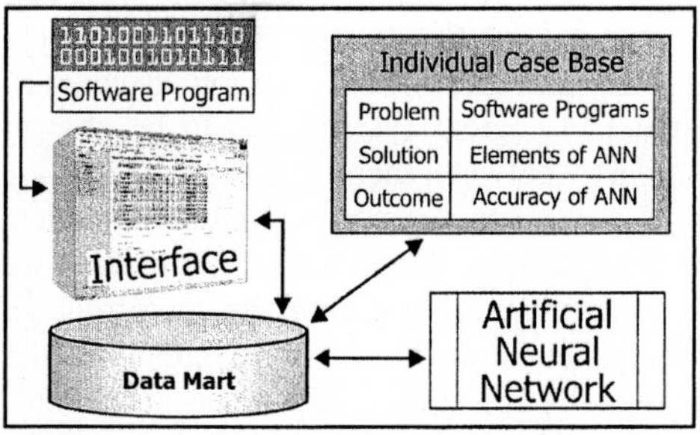

Fig. 2. Software Program Modeling system

There are two problems when using inductive models like ANN as part of case representation; they both stem from the presence of random functions in the computation of ANN. One problem is that one parameter configuration can produce more than one accuracy score. In order to ensure we use values that are sufficiently representative, we train each ANN ten times, using the same training data, and use the average accuracy.

The second problem is that multiple parameter configurations can produce similar accuracies, making it impossible to guarantee one parameter configuration to be optimal. To address this problem, we adopted the notion of a configuration of *good quality*. Starting from the default parameter configuration defined in the CI-Tool [4][18], we evolve configurations with a genetic algorithm [16]. We refer to the configuration resulting from this process as being of *good quality*.

The purpose of the CBR module is to recommend the reuse of an ANN for modeling previously unknown software programs. Here is where the challenges become apparent. In order to reason, the case-based reasoner has to be able to assess the similarity between different software programs and between different ANN models.

3 Strategy to Overcome Challenges for Using CBR

The CBR system for modeling software programs has revealed the most important challenges for using a CBR platform to support such a modeling task. First, because the system we want to model is not well understood, how can we determine what makes one system similar to another? Second, how can we assess similarity between inductive models such as ANN? In other words, if we do not understand the cases well, *how can we find similar solutions for similar problems*?

To allow the case-based platform to recommend a model to describe a new (previously unknown) problem (i.e. system), it may seem that we need to first identify similar problems. However, if we find similarity between problems, we would not know which similar elements are relevant for making two problems amenable to be solved with the same solution. Therefore, we need to first identify similar solutions. Once similar solutions are identified, that is, solutions that would require minimal adaptation to be reused by another problem, we can assume that there may be similarity between problems that have been solved with similar solutions. The main challenge we focus on is to learn what makes one problem similar to another, such that the solutions can be reused.

The first step of our approach is to cluster existing problem-solution pairs (cases) based on features of the *solutions*. Note that for these problems the same exact solution may not appear in more than one case. Once the cases are organized in clusters, the second step is to identify the subset of *problem* features that support these clusters. If we find these features, then it means that they can be used to guide similarity between problems whose solutions can be reused. The final step is to use these features to define the similarity measure across cases. We base our strategy on three assumptions.

Our *first assumption* is that similar solutions can be recognized by individual similarities between elements (i.e. features) of a detailed representation for the solution. Therefore, if the solution is an inductive model, two solutions are similar if the majority of their representational elements are similar; and they are dissimilar otherwise. In an ANN, for example, some of these elements are the values assigned to parameters in its training (e.g. number of epochs). Note that these elements do not assess how well the inductive method models the system. These elements are exclusively the ones that will be used in the reuse step of the CBR cycle.

Because it is important to define similarity and dissimilarity of solutions; in the absence of domain knowledge, we chose an unsupervised learning method to group solutions based on the values of their elements: clustering. Clustering is a well-known method to organize data elements in groups based on attribute values that describe the elements. It produces a set of clusters that group elements that are similar to each other within the same cluster and dissimilar to elements in different clusters.

Our *second assumption* is that, for the task in question, similar problems are the ones that share similar solutions. The first step produces clusters of cases based on the similarity of the solutions. However, to employ the CBR paradigm, we need to determine what makes *problems* similar so that we can reuse their solutions. Hence, the second step is to identify the subset of problem features that support these clusters.

We propose to perform the second step with discriminant analysis (DA). DA is a statistical method that defines boundaries that separate the data into categories to analyze the predictive value of a set of independent variables. Stepwise DA is a variation that initially considers all of the independent variables (our problem features), but removes those that do not make a significant contribution to the overall predictive ability, including those that are closely correlated with other variables. In short, it determines the predictive features from the problem descriptions and eliminates non-predictive features.

Our *third assumption* is that we can use the discriminant functions produced by the DA to assess the similarity between a new, unseen problem and the previously recorded problems. The discriminant functions describe the location of features with respect to each cluster. The rationale of using these functions for similarity is to assess how similarly localized features of a target case are to the features of each of the previously recorded candidate cases. There is always one fewer function than the number of clusters, so if there are 5 clusters, each tuple will be a vector of 4 discriminant function values. The selection step indicates the most similar case by finding the closest tuple using Euclidean distance. This step yields the best matching case, whose solution (i.e. model) we can reuse to describe the target problem (i.e. system). It is important to note that reusing inductive models is not trivial. In fact, we do not reuse the exact model, but the strategy (i.e. parameter configuration) adopted in the most similar case.

4 Validation

In this section, we evaluate the hypothesis that our approach to similarity assessment can support the recommendation of a model to a previously unknown problem with an accuracy that is as high as the accuracy of the models recorded in the case base. That is, it should, on average, produce accuracy that is not significantly lower. We use two metrics for the comparison: $\text{Accuracy}_{\text{ORIG}}$ is the average original accuracy of the models recorded in the case base; $\text{Accuracy}_{\text{CBR}}$ is the average accuracy obtained with the parameter values recommended with our CBR approach.

4.1 Dataset

This study uses twenty-one (21) software programs that constitute our cases. We have identified 23 features to describe these problems. Note that domain knowledge does not indicate what makes two programs similar for the purposes of recommending an inductive model for them. Thus, we include all the features we could determine and expect the approach to indicate the relevant features. Table 1 shows 4 out of the 23 problem features used in the study and values for these features in three software programs T01, T02, and T03. The solutions for these 21 cases were obtained with the system described in Section 2; the quality of the solutions is substantiated by the method in [16]. The solution features consist of elements of ANN such as configuration parameter values and the dataset used for the training. Cases also have an outcome, which indicates the resulting accuracy of the ANN training.

Table 1. Subset of features for three software programs

Features	Testbed	T01	T02	T03
Problem Features	No. of Input Variables	3	5	4
	No. of Program Variables	0	1	0
	Highest Max of Input Variables Range	1000	10	25000
	No. of Conditionals	1	0	0
Solution Features	Training Accuracy	91	91	94
	Pruning Accuracy	93	91	90
	Learning Rate	0.48	0.54	0.47
Outcome Feature	Accuracy	93.4%	90.3%	86.8%

4.2 Methodology

Our methodology is to employ leave-one-out cross validation (LOOCV) across the 21 software programs. At each iteration, the 20 remaining cases are clustered based on linearly normalized solution features, using hierarchical clustering with squared Euclidean distance as the similarity metric. Then, we perform stepwise DA on the problem features to obtain the set of coefficients that describe each cluster. We apply these coefficients to the feature values of all 21 cases (20 known cases and 1 target) to compute tuples to assess their similarity and obtain the closest case. The values used to configure the ANN in the closest case are reused to train a new ANN for the target problem. We use these parameters to train ten ANNs to compute the $Accuracy_{CBR}$. Note that we use the same training data for these ten runs that we use for the ten runs to compute $Accuracy_{ORIG}$.

4.3 Results

The results support our hypothesis that our approach can recommend a model that is as accurate as the models originally recorded in the case base 71.4% (15 out of 21) of the time. Table 2 shows the distribution of accuracy comparisons using ANOVA between our two metrics $Accuracy_{CBR}$ and $Accuracy_{ORIG}$ for the 21 cases. We define significance at $p < 0.05$, and present the averages (Avg) and standard deviations (SD) of the p values for each category in Table 2.

Table 2. Summary of accuracy comparisons

Performance of $Accuracy_{CBR}$	No. of Cases	% to 21	Avg p	SD p
$Accuracy_{CBR}$ is significantly higher	2 Cases	9.5	0.001	0.001
$Accuracy_{CBR}$ produces no significant difference	13 Cases	61.9	0.329	0.224
$Accuracy_{CBR}$ is significantly lower	6 Cases	28.6	0.002	0.002

4.4 Discussion

The consistency of the results indicates that our approach can support the use of CBR to recommend inductive models to represent complex systems. Indirectly, they indicate our assumptions (Section 3) were sound. In this discussion we attempt explore the validity of our approach and investigate ways of improving these results.

The DA identified 13 problem features that contributed to the similarity calculation in every iteration of the LOOCV, and 6 more that were used in fewer than half. Of the 171 possible pairs of these features (each of the 19 features compared symmetrically with the 18 others), only 23 pairs showed any significant correlation at $p < 0.05$, and these were primarily between the infrequently used features. This shows that the features are independent, so the discriminant functions are reliable for the overall validation.

Our choice for the clustering analysis revealed satisfactory results. We confirmed it by observing that the data in our dataset had natural groupings, making it amenable to clustering. The evidence is that for 18 (85.7%) of the LOOCV iterations, the clusters obtained with 20 cases were identical (except for the presence of the target case). In the 3 (14.3%) iterations when they varied, only one or two cases changed clusters. There were five stable clusters identified, and these were confirmed using other distance metrics as well as *k*-means tests for 3 through 7 clusters.

Our choice for the discriminant analysis to capture the relative importance of the features and use it for similarity assessment also proved to be satisfactory. DA is a way to represent the organization of features in the discriminant space in respect to the clusters. Thus, our approach implies that not only the clusters but the relative position with respect to a cluster are relevant for similarity assessment. For 20 (out of the 21) iterations, the reused case (the closest according to our approach) was originally a member of a different cluster than the target case for the iteration. This indicates that clusters could not have been used as outcome classes and that the success of the approach also depends upon the relative position of each case in relation to the cluster.

In order to further investigate the use of clusters, we applied gradient descent (GD) and extracted the relative importance of the features for the entire case base, using the clusters to measure classification accuracy. The results generated a case base that produced an accuracy with LOOCV of 14.3%, i.e. only 3 times the most similar case received the correct classification. In addition, only 3 times (for different cases) the results with the GD weights coincided with the closest case recommended by our approach.

We wanted to employ an algorithm that could reveal a subset of features (and possibly their relative weights) that could be used in the entire case base for similarity assessment. Such results would contribute new knowledge to the domain. In our dataset, for example, we would be able to indicate how to compare two software systems to reuse software testing approaches. However, at least with our dataset, there was no subset of features that could justify the reuse of models with the same accuracy as our proposed approach.

Another potential source of improvement is the refinement of the reuse step. In this study, we did not contemplate the second closest case as a candidate for reuse, and a brief analysis showed the second closest case would have improved our results.

The similarity between solutions could have also been explored by using extracted rules as an explicit representation of the ANN. On examination, there was no correlation between rules and the resulting accuracy. The rules are the ANN's restatement of the problem, but they do not necessarily reflect their quality.

Finally, we believe that the two iterations where the recommended model produced accuracy significantly higher than the one previously recorded indicate that our approach can also be used to improve the quality of model recommendation. That is, not only CBR may be indicated as an alternative when data is not available, but it may also be used to find highly suitable models. This supports our ultimate goal for our case-based platform to increase our understanding of modeling complex systems.

5 Case-Based Platform for Modeling Biological Systems

The diagnosis-prediction task can realize the Nutrigenomics and e-diagnosis dreams. Nutrigenomics is the field that interfaces nutritional environments with genetic and cellular processes [9]. E-diagnosis [10][26] is concerned with bringing quantitative biological information into the problem of medical diagnosis. The goal of the prediction task is to successfully determine which model accurately describes a human individual so that health outcomes, such as the diet-regulated influence of genes on chronic diseases [9][15], can be predicted based on this individual's genetic constitution and diet. Thus, diet and other forms of intervention can be designed to specifically meet each individual's genetic needs and to personalize recommendations to guarantee health outcomes. Imagine a simple exam at the time of birth to establish environmental and nutritional boundaries a child should stay in order to guarantee a long and healthy life.

Our genetic constitution interacts with the environment to either predispose or protect us from disease. The interplay of these two factors is most obvious if one compares cancer incidences in different countries [1]. Only specific genetic diseases show a clear and strong genetic background due to genetic mutations. Otherwise, the interplay between DNA and environment can be ranked according to the amount of genetic influence; e.g. the following conditions are sorted from most genetic to most environmental influence: psoriasis, depression, schizophrenia, diabetes, asthma, cardiac condition, cancer, and multiple sclerosis [7]. Environmental factors can be divided up into two components: 1) nutrition, treatments like drugs, air quality, and presence of toxins; and 2) lifestyle, like activities that impact metabolism, amount of sleep, stress, etc.

Recently, for the first time, a relationship between stress and the impact on the genetic constitution itself was reported [8]. However, it is important to notice that even normal aging has an effect on the genetic constitution and gene expression [21][23]. Changes are not consistent between individuals and may vary most at mid-lifespan [12], giving rise to a difference between chronological and biological age. Genetic changes, on the other hand, impact biological organization, e.g., immune system, respiratory system, mental abilities, bone structure. As a consequence, these changes, on whatever level of organization they occur, determine the interaction between the individual and the environment and shift with age.

The problem of modeling biological systems in order to support tasks such as diagnosis and prediction must consider genetic information, and it must be able to capture both how genes are influenced by the environment and how changes in gene expression impact an individual's health. In practice, given a partial description of a target individual, the goal is to fit a model (which could be created from a combination of models) that can accurately predict the individual's health from the environment to which the individual is exposed.

Table 3. Cases in case-based modeling platform

case		individual K			individual M			individual N		
problem	De-facto age	35			58			35		
problem	nutrition	chemicals x,y,z			chemicals p,q,r,s,t,u,v,x,y,z			chemicals x,y,z		
problem	genotype	TGGGGACACCTCGCCTGC			TGGGGACACCTCTCCTGCAC			TCAGGACACCTCGCCTGCAC		
problem	gene expression	AA80AB20			AA80AB80			AA80AB20		
problem	health	BP 120x180	BMI 40		BP 120x150	BMI 26		BP 120x180	BMI 40	
outcome solution	models	1	2	n	1	2	n	1	2	n
outcome solution	accuracy	.6	.85	.15	.5	.65	.15	.3	.3	.5

Legend: BP=blood pressure; BMI=body mass index

For example, we would like to predict the health of individual K. The available information for individual K is a description of his interaction with his environment, with detailed proportions of nutrients, chemicals (e.g. drugs), and toxins; his genetic constitution through his DNA; his tissue, gene product expression profiles and blood clinical chemistry; and a description of his health through biomarkers and medical evaluation. The black area in Table 3 represents a case for individual K, who is 35 years old and obese.

Obtaining an accurate model for K's biological system will allow us to diagnose the causes for his obesity by determining the relationship between environmental and lifestyle parameters on one end and molecular constitution and physiological capabilities on the other end. It will be possible to prescribe a personalized strategy based on the predictive ability of such a model. The confirmation of the model's suitability will increase the overall understanding of biological systems.

A case-based platform for modeling biological systems has one crucial distinction from the software program system described in Section 2. Software programs can be easily modeled because it is possible to randomly generate inputs for training the inductive method as many times as necessary for a reasonably accurate model. With living biological systems, it is not typically feasible to submit the required amounts of inputs to observe changes in outputs. Sometimes it is possible to do it partially, or in varying scales, and targeting different systems (human, animal, or cellular). Modeling human systems is especially problematic because there are health risks, limited number of human subjects, uncertainty in intervention commitment, and it requires a long term for observance of outcomes. It is easier to conduct experiments with animals (e.g. mice), but tailoring results for humans is bounded by the different biological structure of the different species. It is possible to use human cells, but studies with a subset of cells lose the interaction with the rest of the body. Therefore, instead of one model to describe the biological system of an individual, we propose a case-based platform that will incorporate a series of models (Table 3), obtained from different sources (e.g. partial genetic data from the individual, other individuals, animal cells), to represent potential ways of describing an individual's biological system. This adds complexity to the CBR cycle, as a series of solutions are needed when acquiring cases and the reuse step has to contemplate the suitability of potential models before a solution can be proposed.

In order to determine a model to describe individual K, we first have to assess the similarity between K and other cases in the case base. Those candidate cases from the case base are described with a series of models and their corresponding estimated qualities to describe each biological system (M and N in Table 3). Let us now suppose that individual M resulted with a high similarity score when compared to K, whereas individual N obtained low score. The reuse step would examine the nature of the models in order to assess their potential viability. Thus, not only the similarity between individuals would be used for the basis of reuse, but also the suitability of the models based on how the models were obtained. We use the similarity between inputs used to obtain the model and the individual's inputs as indicators of the expected accuracy of the model.

For individual M, let us assume $Model_1$ was obtained from a study with mice, like the one in [17]. This study used as inputs a portion of knockout mice (i.e. mice that had some genes *turned off*) and obtained as outputs different responses to polyunsaturated fatty acids. The small accuracy estimated for $Model_1$ stems from the fact that the source data was obtained from mice. Let us assume that $Model_2$ was built using human cells, such as studies described in [2]. This study has associated the lack of some specific chemicals, let us call them chemicals *p*, *q*, *r*, *s*, with an output of DNA damage. The higher accuracy for $Model_2$ originates from the fact that the model used human cells and that chemicals targeted by the study were also present in M's nutrition.

The reuse step would examine $Model_1$ and would balance the fact that the model was built for mice and K is human. Additionally, it would assess if there is domain knowledge to correlate low gene expression in K (AA20) with knockout genes in the mice population, which would cause to increase the accuracy of $Model_1$ for K to .6. For $Model_2$, K and M are genetically similar and therefore $Model_2$ would be potentially a good model for K. However, the chemicals used as inputs in $Model_2$ match the chemicals that are absent in K's nutrition, suggesting that if $Model_2$ is a good fit then the DNA damage might be present in K, increasing the accuracy for the model in K to .85. This is further corroborated by K's surface features, which include a BMI of 40 – severe obesity. K's solution is shown in the gray area in Table 3.

The high accuracy of $Model_2$ to describe K can be used to support the diagnosis that K has DNA damage due to the lack of chemicals *p*, *q*, *r*, *s* in his nutrition, and the DNA damage could be responsible for K's inability to process fatty acids, making him obese. The reuse step in this case allows us to better understand how to fit models to humans and a revision step (e.g. confirming a recommendation) after observing a patient along the years can potentially improve the understanding of such biological system.

This is how case-based reasoning can contribute and improve results compared to inductive or mathematical models alone. The contribution of CBR for this task is that it combines knowledge from different sources into one reasoning that enables a solution otherwise not feasible. This is where the ability to assess similarity between partially described systems and inductive models pays off: *we can use domain knowledge supporting similarity between different problems in order to assess the quality of a model to represent one of the problems (i.e. systems).* To implement such a platform in practice the approach introduced in Section 3 is required, because it allows us to manipulate and assess similarity between systems and models that are not well understood.

6 Related Work

The CBR platform described in Section 5 reflects an ongoing trend to unite different computer science approaches to biomedicine [24]. Biological data abounds. Projects have been started to establish databases to organize such data. For example, the UK Biobank is a long-term project to start at the beginning of 2006 to gather information on the health and lifestyle of 500,000 volunteers [25]. CBR can become an essential methodology to analyze this data.

The problem of retrieving similar cases when the target problem is incomplete due to missing feature values was investigated in [6]. This work differs from ours in that their problems are sufficiently understood to design a similarity measure. Our problems are not well understood to design a similarity measure using conventional methods.

The most extensive analysis of neuro-CBR integrations [13] proposes a hierarchy for their description. When interpreting our use of ANN as an integration of the ANN technique into the CBR methodology, it could be categorized as chain-processing. CBR is the main processor and the ANN is responsible for a preprocessing (ANN models are trained for case acquisition) and a post-processing step (new ANNs are trained for reuse).

One aspect of our approach resembles the philosophy of the work discussed in [19], where authors propose an integration of ANN and memory-based learning. They argue that memory-based learning allows them to reuse the memory of the training instances used to train the ANN – what is never done with ANN, because inputs are discarded after the network is trained. The similarity is that we use ANN training data to help determine the suitability of potential models to represent a complex system (Section 5).

Notable CBR systems limit the biological information in their problem descriptions to the use of biomarkers. For example, blood pressure and blood clinical chemistry are used in ALEXIA [5]; and chemical compounds are represented in [3] to predict carcinogenic activity. These applications neither model individuals' biological systems nor reason at the genetic level.

7 Concluding Remarks and Future Work

We proposed an approach to assess similarity between complex systems and between inductive models. We have demonstrated that an inductive model can be recommended to represent a system on the basis of the system's similarity to other systems. This illustrates how CBR can contribute to the modeling task when systems to be modeled are not well understood. Our approach represents an important step towards a learning platform that benefits from the combination of CBR and inductive modeling. Such a platform has the potential to enable unprecedented understanding of complex phenomena.

Biological data is usually partial and incomplete; different studies are pieces in a complex puzzle that humans are not capable of understanding. A case-based platform for biological systems would aggregate partial data into a lazy learning paradigm, where each new iteration would help increase the understanding of biological systems.

7.1 Future Work

This paper demonstrated the suitability of CBR for solutions that consisted of neural networks. We plan to test our approach using other inductive methods, i.e. info-fuzzy networks [11] and also with mathematical models.

We implemented the reuse step in our approach without considering the potential usefulness of the second closest case. A brief examination revealed this alternative may be useful to improve the accuracy of the 6 cases where the accuracy from the CBR recommendation in the LOOCV was lower than previously recorded data for that case. Our approach revealed that 13 features were consistently included in the DA functions, whereas the remaining 10 were consistently excluded. We plan to use these features in an attempt to help assess adaptation needs to reuse a solution of better quality, similar to adaptation-guided retrieval [20].

We also plan to test different variations of algorithms like the backward strategy removing one problem feature at a time and then confirming the clustering until one set of features for the entire dataset supports the clustering. This will probably require the elimination of some outliers, and a bigger dataset.

Finally, we plan to explore rule sets generated by each run of the ANN in order to learn more about what features make some rule sets more successful than others. This could help us predict the quality of the model without having to apply it.

Acknowledgements

The authors would like to thank Dr. M. Last, Dr. A. Kandel, and T. Barr for their continuous support in different stages of our work. Thanks R. J. Upadhyay for his help in developing testbeds. Dr. R. Weber and J. M. Proctor are supported in part by the National Institute for Systems Test and Productivity at USF under the USA Space and Naval Warfare Systems Command grant no. N00039-02-C-3244, for 2130 032 L0, 2002.

References

[1] Alberts, B., Johnson, A., Lewis, J., Raff, M., Roberts, K., Walter, P.: Molecular Biology of the Cell. 4th edn. Garland Publishing, New York (2002)

[2] Ames, B.N.: DNA Damage from Micronutrient Deficiencies is Likely to Be a Major Cause of Cancer. Mutat Res. 475 1-2 (2001) 7-20

[3] Armengol, E., Plaza, E.: Relational Case-based Reasoning for Carcinogenic Activity Prediction. Artificial Intelligence Review, 20, 1 - 2 (2003) 121 - 141
[4] Barr, T.: Architectural Overview of the Computational Intelligence Testing Tool. In: Proceedings of the Eighth IEEE International Symposium on High Assurance Systems Engineering. IEEE Computer Society, Los Alamitos (2004) 269- 270
[5] Bichindaritz, I.: Memoire: Case Based Reasoning Meets the Semantic Web in Biology and Medicine. In: Gonzalez Calero, P.A., Funk, P. (eds.): Case-Based Reasoning Research and Development. LNAI, Vol. 3155. Springer, Berlin Heidelberg New York (2004) 47-61
[6] Bogaerts, S., Leake, D. B.: Facilitating CBR for Incompletely-Described Cases: Distance Metrics for Partial Problem Descriptions. In: Gonzalez Calero, P.A., Funk, P. (eds.): Case-Based Reasoning Research and Development. LNAI, Vol. 3155. Springer, Berlin (2004) 62-76
[7] Chakravati, A., Little, P.: Nature, nurture and human disease. Nature. 421 (2003) 412-414
[8] Epel, E.S., Blackburn, E.H., Lin, J., Dhabhar, F.S., Adler, N.E., Morrow, J.D., Cawthon R.M.: Accelerated Telomere Shortening in Response to Life Stress. Proc. Natl. Acad. Sci. 101 49 (2004) 17312-5
[9] Kaput, J., Rodriguez, R.L.: Nutritional Genomics: the Next Frontier in the Postgenomic Era. Physiol. Genomics 16 (2004) 166-177
[10] Kriete, A., Boyce, K.: Automated tissue analysis – a bioinformatics perspective. Methods Inf. Medicine 1 (2005) 32-37
[11] Last, M., Friedman, M., Kandel, A.: The Data Mining Approach to Automated Software Testing. In: Proceedings of the Ninth ACM SIGKDD International Conference on Knowledge Discovery and Data Mining. ACM Press, New York (2003) 388-396
[12] Lu, T., Pan, Y., Kao, S.Y., Li, C., Kohane, I., Chan, J., Yankner, B.A.: Gene Regulation and DNA Damage in the Ageing Human Brain. Nature 429, 6994 (2004) 883-91
[13] Malek, M.: Hybrid Approaches for Integrating Neural Networks and Case-Based Reasoning: From Loosely Coupled to Tightly Coupled Models. In: Pal, S.K., Dillon. T.S., Yeung, D.S. (eds.): Soft Computing in Case Based Reasoning. Springer Verlag, London (2001) 73-94
[14] McFarlane, A.C., Yehuda, R., Clark, C.R.: Biologic Models of Traumatic Memories and Post-Traumatic Stress Disorder. The role of neural networks. Psychiatr Clin North Am. 25, 2 (2002) 253-70
[15] Park, E.I., Paisley, E.A., Mangian, H.J., Swartz, D.A., Wu, M., O'Morchoe, P.J., Behr, S.R., Visek, W.J., Kaput, J.: Lipid Level and Type Alter Stearoyl CoA Desaturase mRNA Abundance Differently in Mice with Distinct Susceptibilities to Diet-Influenced Diseases. J Nutr. 127, 4 (1997) 566-73
[16] Proctor, J. M., Weber, R.: Systematically Evolving Configuration Parameters for Computational Intelligence Methods. Submitted to the First International Conference on Pattern Recognition and Machine Intelligence (PReMI'05) (2005)
[17] Ren, B., Thelen, A.P., Peters, J. M., Gonzalez, F.J., Jump, D.B.: Polyunsaturated Fatty Acid Suppression of Hepatic Fatty Acid Synthase and S14 Gene Expression Does not Require Peroxisome Proliferator-Activated Receptor-α. J. Biol. Chem. 272 (1997) 26827–26832
[18] Saraph, P., Last, M., Kandel, A.: Test Set Generation and Reduction with Artificial Neural Networks. In: Last, M., Kandel, A., Bunke, H. (eds.): Artificial Intelligence Methods in Software Testing. World Scientific (2004) 101-132

[19] Shin, C. K, Park, S. C.: Towards Integration of Memory Based Learning and Neural Networks. In: Pal, S.K., Dillon. T.S., Yeung, D.S. (eds.): Soft Computing in Case Based Reasoning. Springer Verlag, London (2001) 95-114

[20] Smyth, B., Keane, M.T.: Experiments on Adaptation-Guided Retrieval in Case-Based Design. In: Veloso, M., Aamodt, A. (eds.): Proceedings of the 1st International Conference on Case-Based Reasoning. LNAI, Vol. 1010, Springer, Berlin (1995) 313-324

[21] Thomas, R.P., Guigneaux, M., Wood, T., Evers, B.M.: Age-Associated Changes in Gene Expression Patterns in the Liver. J Gastrointest Surg. 6 3 (2002) 445-53

[22] Weber, R., Wu, D.: Knowledge Management for Computational Intelligence Systems. In: Proceedings of the Eighth IEEE International Symposium on High Assurance Systems Engineering. IEEE Computer Society, Los Alamitos (2004) 116-125

[23] Welle, S., Brooks, A.I., Delehanty. J.M., Needler. N., Thornton, C.A.: Gene Expression Profile of Aging in Human Muscle. Physiol. Genomics 14, 2 (2003) 149-59

[24] Wiemer, J., Schubert, F., Granzow, M., Ragg, T., Fieres, J., Mattes, J., Eils, R.: Informatics United: Exemplary Studies Combining Medical Informatics, Neuroinformatics and Bioinformatics. Methods Inf. Med. 42, 2 (2003) 126-33

[25] Wright, A., Carothers, A.D., Campbell, H.: Gene-environment interactions – the Biobank UK study. Pharmacogenomics J. 2 (2002) 75-82

[26] Zhao, L.P., Gilbert, S., Defty, C.: E-Diagnosis Using GeneChip Technologies Proceedings of the Fourth International Conference on Advances in Infrastructure for e-Business, e-Education, e-Science, e-Medicine on the Internet. CD-ROM. (2002)

CBE-Conveyor: A Case-Based Reasoning System to Assist Engineers in Designing Conveyor Systems

Fei Ling Woon, Brian Knight, Miltos Petridis, and Mayur Patel

University of Greenwich, School of Computing and Mathematical Sciences, London SE10 9LS, UK
{f.woon, b.knight, m.petridis, m.patel}@gre.ac.uk

Abstract. In this paper, we address the use of CBR in collaboration with numerical engineering models. This collaborative combination has a particular application in engineering domains where numerical models are used. We term this domain "*Case Based Engineering*" (CBE), and present the general architecture of a CBE system. We define and discuss the general characteristics of CBE and the special problems which arise. These are: the handling of engineering constraints of both continuous and nominal kind; interpolation over both continuous and nominal variables, and conformability for interpolation. In order to illustrate the utility of the method proposed, and to provide practical examples of the general theory, the paper describes a practical application of the CBE architecture, known as *CBE-CONVEYOR*, which has been implemented by the authors. Pneumatic conveying is an important transportation technology in the solid bulks conveying industry. One of the major industry concerns is the attrition of powders and granules during pneumatic conveying. To minimize the fraction of particles during pneumatic conveying, engineers want to know what design parameters they should use in building a conveyor system. To do this, engineers often run simulations in a repetitive manner to find appropriate input parameters. CBE-Conveyor is shown to speed up conventional methods for searching for solutions, and to solve problems directly that would otherwise require considerable intervention from the engineer.

1 Introduction

Numerical models can provide useful advice to engineers in many fields. They are often designed to simulate the behaviour of physical processes in a forward time direction. Generally, engineers will specify inputs $I = (I_1, I_2, \ldots, I_k)$, and the model will calculate outputs $\underline{O}=(O_1, O_2, \ldots, O_l)$, where $\underline{O}$ is a function of I. However, engineering problems are often not straightforward applications of such models. Engineers often require a model that can be queried in an inverse fashion. For example, a designer may want to know what inputs produce desired outputs. Also, they often want to add constraints to outputs, searching for the right inputs. In addition, there may be other physical constraints on inputs; engineers want to explore what alternatives they can use to produce a given output. To solve these inverse or constraint problems, we often have to resort to running the numerical model

H. Muñoz-Avila and F. Ricci (Eds.): ICCBR 2005, LNAI 3620, pp. 640 – 651, 2005.

repeatedly: running the model, looking at the results and changing the inputs accordingly for another run. In effect, the engineer is astutely generating cases from the numerical model.

Experimental data is often collected by engineers in order to assist in their design task. This data is often more reliable than the modeled data, covering all possible experimental scenarios. However, it is also sometimes much more expensive to produce. In contrast, numerical models can be used to generate databases which may then be tested for accuracy of prediction. A database model of the processes may be represented by a set of stored predicates: $P(I_1, \ldots, I_k, O_1, \ldots, O_l)$. Such a model can be queried flexibly using Structured Query Language (SQL), specifying either inputs or outputs, and constraints. However, such a model also suffers from some disadvantages:

- It can be a very large database, particularly if k and l are large, or if high accuracy is required.
- Queries using SQL can often give null results if the database is kept small.

The motivation of this study is to use a Case-Based Reasoning (CBR) system generated using a numerical model as a flexible query engine for engineers. One of the advantages of using CBR is that in engineering fields there is usually a great deal of regularity in numerical models; one would expect fine detail to be well represented by some adaptive process such as interpolation. This would allow a great reduction in case base storage. Also, CBR retrieval is more amenable to usability questions than is SQL, giving cases ordered by closeness to input criteria; it will always give answers, and they can be ordered according to user needs.

A number of researchers have used case-based reasoning (CBR) and machine learning techniques to improve the usability of numerical models. Cheetham and Graf [3, 4] describe a CBR tool that helps users to select a subset of the allowable colourants for colour matching in plastics. The CBR tool was shown to be cost saving and to increase the colour matcher productivity. Schwabacher *et al.* [12] invented a case-based system based on induction learning for the numerical optimization setup of engineering designs. Results show that inductive learning can improve the speed and the reliability of design optimization. Kalapanidas and Avouris [6] have given an account of a prototype, NEMO, built using a CBR approach combining heuristic and statistical techniques to support short-term prediction of NO_2 maximum concentration levels in Athens, Greece. The NEMO classifier can give fast prediction for the likelihood of an occurrence. It is robust to noisy data. However, there is no evidence of a general CBR architecture proposed to improve the usability of numerical models.

The motivation of this paper is two-fold: First, in Section 2, we discuss the general architecture of a CBR – Numerical model system, to be used in the engineering domain. We look at the advantages and characteristics of this general architecture. In what follows, we term this architecture and domain as "*Case Based Engineering*" (CBE). There are several problems which we encounter in attempting to set up a generally flexible query tool. Ideally, we need to allow an engineer to assign a variety of queries for the search. These can contain both inputs and outputs, and contain either continuous or nominal values. In Section 3 of this paper, we discuss each of the problems of interpolation which we encounter in such a domain, and give a solution based upon the interpolative method proposed previously by the authors [8, 9].

In Section 4 we provide the background information of the pneumatic conveyor model, and in Section 5 we present the findings of a completed practical development known as CBE-Conveyor. This is a CBE system to assist engineers in the design of pneumatic conveyor systems. The application is used to exemplify the general approach, and to show examples of the general problems discussed in Section 3, and their resolution. We conclude in Section 6, with a summary and indications of future work.

2 The General CBE Architecture

In this section, we show how CBR can be used as a flexible query engine to assist engineers to solve inverse or constraint problems. Ideally engineers would like to be able to express their problem constraints without worrying whether the variables are inputs or outputs. Sometimes they need the right inputs for given outputs; sometimes they know some inputs and some outputs. For example, in the conveyor problem the engineer may only have certain bend types available for a design. This is expressed as a constraint on inputs. They may also need to be certain that not too much small particle dust appears in the output receiver: this is a constraint on outputs. The CBE architecture proposed here is designed to handle constraints of this type, allowing the engineer to define any constraints over the unified input and output space.

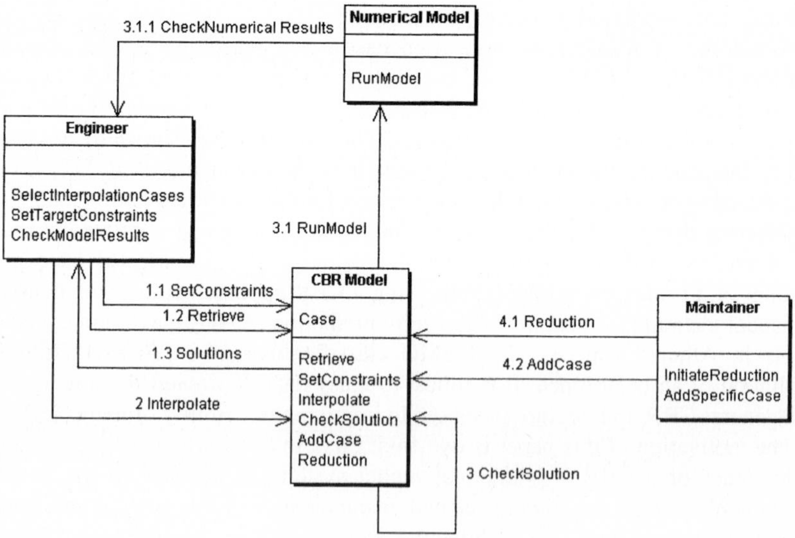

Fig. 1. The diagram for the general CBE architecture

Before examining the special problems we encounter in CBE, we first describe the collaborative CBE architecture, between the engineer, CBR system and numerical model. We also include the case base maintainer as a separate agent in the overall architecture. These agents work together by sharing individual knowledge and expertise to solve inverse and constraint problems.

Fig. 1 is a UML collaboration diagram showing the interactions between these agents. The sequence of steps in a typical query session is as follows:

1.1 The engineer defines a set of constraints over input-output space defining the problem.

1.2 The CBR model retrieves cases near to the problem definition.

1.3 The CBR model presents a list of useful cases to the engineer. The engineer can examine these cases, and possibly redefine the problem if the initial definition was not complete, or was incorrect in some way. There is also an opportunity for the engineer to select some of the retrieved cases manually for the next phase (adaptation). This would be useful in situations where the engineer needs to have more 'hands–on' control of the whole retrieval process.

2. The engineer requests the CBR model to perform interpolation on a retrieved set of cases. The retrieved set may be that selected by the engineer, or simply the k nearest neighbours. It has also been shown in [9] that interpolation can work better on diverse sets. The interpolation phase needs often to be able to deal with nominal values, and to handle a variety of constraints. It also has to make sure that the interpolation set is conformable for interpolation; sometimes two solutions, though close in the problem space, are not at all close in the solution space and should not be used for interpolation. We examine these problems of interpolation later, in Section 3.

3.1 The adapted solution produced by the CBR system has values for all inputs and outputs. It is now possible to run the model against the inputs, and verify the outputs.

3.1.1The Simulation results are then presented to the engineer who can decide whether the solution is acceptable. It may well be that they may need to return to Step 1.3 and select a different set for adaptation. In situations where there is a large difference between the modelled and adapted solution, we have the possibility to add the new modelled case to the case base. The addition of a new case will give reason to return to Step 1, and the session can continue with the new case base.

There are also two interactions shown in the collaboration diagram separate from those described above, which involve the case base maintainer. These are:

4.1 Generation of the initial case base. This must depend upon the dimensionality of the problem space, and the cost of model generation. For fast models and low dimensionality, we can simply produce a regular dense database. However, for high cost, long run time models of high dimensionality (for example computational fluid dynamics models), the case base would of necessity be sparse, and we would have to rely on the effectiveness of the interpolation scheme.

4.2 Subsequent maintenance of the case base such as the addition or removal of cases is managed by the Case Base Maintainer, which may utilise case reduction schemes co-operating with the numerical model.

3 Elements of the CBE Architecture

In this section we examine in detail some of the special issues that arise in the design of a working CBE system. These are mainly due to the need of the engineer to search and interpolate over the whole input – output space. This entails two main problems, which we discuss here. The first problem is the definition of constraints, over mappings which are not necessarily one to one. The second problem is to do with the handling of constraints and interpolation over nominal values.

3.1 Constraints and Interpolation

Constraints of interest in CBE are of two main types: real and nominal. Real constraints are expressible as f(x) > 0, and are usually handled by adding a derived attribute a = f(x) to the cases, and using a prohibitive similarity measure for cases with a< 0. Nominal value constraints occur, for instance, when equipment or methods are not available to the engineer, so that these must be eliminated from the search for reasons of practicability.

Numerical models are generally deterministic in nature, so that $\underline{\mathbf{O}}$ is given as a single valued function of $\underline{\mathbf{I}}$. However, the inverse problem cannot be assumed as single valued. As in Fig. 2, there may be several solutions to a given query where outputs are specified. For 1-NN retrieval (i.e., *k*-Nearest Neighbour (k-NN) where k=1, [5]), this gives little problem, since the multiple nearest cases may be ordered as equal for the user to select. However, for k-NN, it is not desirable to interpolate between cases which are not close in the input domain. Also, problems which are close in the problem domain are not necessarily close in the solution domain. Bergmann *et al.* [1] have also addressed this problem in that the similarity of cases in the problem space does not always correspond to the usefulness of the cases in

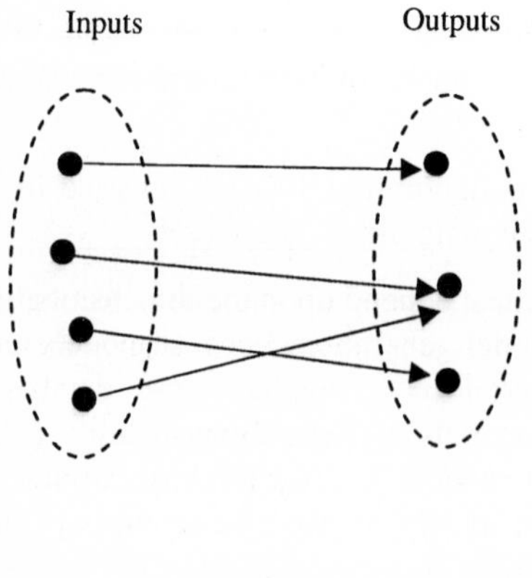

Fig. 2. Direct problem (single-valued solutions)

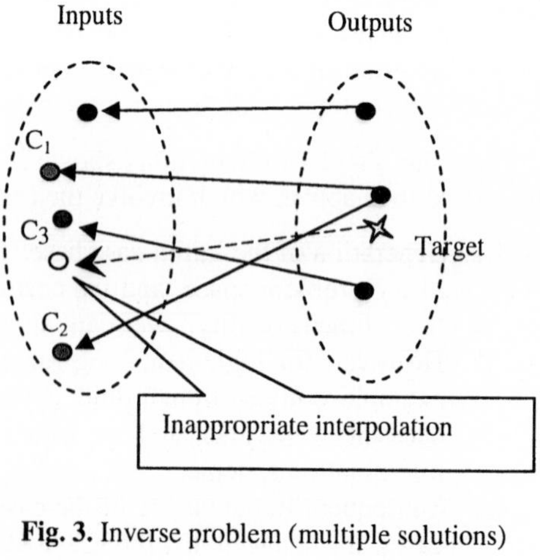

Fig. 3. Inverse problem (multiple solutions)

solving the problem. The approach to this problem which we take here is to perform adaptation on the cases that are close in the unified (problem: solution) space. Fig. 3 shows an inappropriate interpolation (adaptation using C_1 and C_2) and also shows that there is a much more relevant case (i.e., C_3) to a given target (in the input space) which may be a better candidate case than C_2 in adaptation.

In this paper, we view cases which are close in the unified space as "*conformable for interpolation*". This is an important concept for interpolation, since it determines whether we can usefully interpolate over a set of cases, as we shall see in Section 5. Informally, we define:

A set of cases is conformable for interpolation if the cases are near in unified space.

Near cases in the problem domain which are not close in the solution domain will not be close in the unified domain. These cases are not conformable to interpolation. In Step 2, where interpolation is performed, we make the restriction that the whole interpolation set must be conformable to interpolation.

Of course, to implement the conformability criterion we have described, we need to define a similarity metric over the whole input – output space. The standard method used for defining similarity metrics is the weighted sum method [10]. There are several ways of defining metrics in solution space. These include the use of cluster centre distances [16], attributes independent of problem space [9], Value Difference Metric [13] and definition by a human expert. Wilson & Martinez give an account various distance functions' definition in [15].

The second problem which we face is the handling of nominal values in constraints and interpolation. In the conveyor example discussed below, two attributes are nominal in nature: the bend type, and the angle of the bend. These also happen to be values the engineer is searching for in a typical query. For example, they may want to know what bend type is best for a given output size distribution of particles. According to Step 2 of the scenario in Section 2, this means we should interpolate to find the bend type from a set of cases. This requires interpolation over nominal values. In addition, the engineer will often want to express the fact that she/he only has certain bend types available. We need to be able to express this available list of types as a constraint that the interpolation can take into account.

Campbell and Chatterjee [2] have proposed a method for interpolation over nominal value, which assumes a natural ordering. The ranking of nominal values is based on a linear distance metric derived from the ordering. However, their approach cannot take account of a general metric defined over the output space. In addition, it is not obvious how to incorporate nominal constraints when using a system like this.

The problem of the interpolation over nominal values may be approached by the Generalized Shepard Nearest Neighbour (GSNN) method proposed by the authors [8, 9]. This method handles generally defined metrics over the solution set. The method has the extra advantage that it is able to handle nominal constraints. GSNN works by evaluation of the minimum of a function as follows:

Generalised Shepard Nearest Neighbour Algorithm

$$\hat{f}(x_q) \leftarrow \arg\min_{y \in Y} \sum_{i=1}^{k} w_i d_y^{\,2}(y, f(x_i)) \tag{1}$$

Where

$$w_i \equiv \frac{1}{d_x(x_q, x_i)^p}$$

Here the minimum is taken over the set Y of nominal values. This property makes GSNN very suitable for handling nominal value constraints. All we have to do is to subject the set Y to be constrained to the desired set of nominal values. For example if only some bend types are available, these will form the set Y. Hence by using GSNN, we are able to handle both continuous and nominal constraints.

4 Illustrative Example: The Pneumatic Conveyor Model

The pneumatic conveyor design problem is part of the Quality in Particulate Manufacturing (QPM) initiative funded by the UK EPSRC Innovative Manufacturing Initiative for Process Industries. Degradation of powders and granules during dilute phase pneumatic conveying is a problem that has existed for a long time. Degradation refers to the breakage and surface damage of particles during transport and handling. One of the major industry concerns is to investigate how parameters such as air velocity, loading ratio, the angle of the bend and etc. affect particle degradation. Such knowledge is of great use in the design of conveyors. Research [7, 11, 14] shows that conveyor design has critical effects on the particles degradation.

4.1 Engineering Problems of the Conveyor Design

In this problem, there are four input parameters: velocity of air, bend type and bend angle; the output is the particle size distribution at the outlet (see Fig. 4). The engineer's task is to determine suitable input parameters so that there will not be too much dust formed particles.

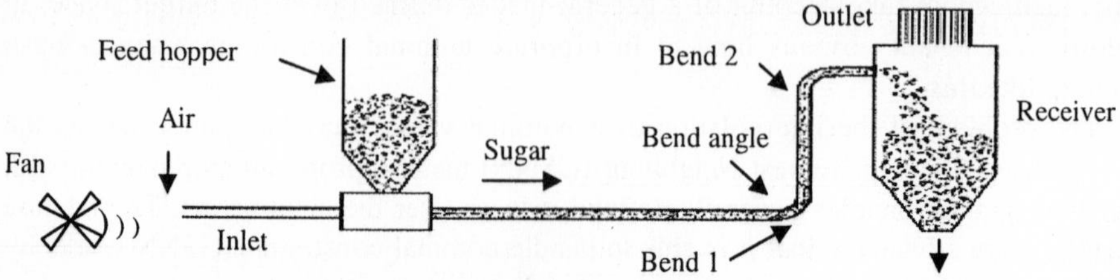

Fig. 4. The schematic diagram of a sample pneumatic conveyor

Fig. 4 shows the schematic diagram of a sample pneumatic conveyor. Particles are fed into a hopper and being transported to a receiver using a pneumatic conveyor. In this example the transported particulate is sugar. Engineers can specify the fan speed, bend angle and bend type.

5 Development of CBE-CONVEYOR

In CBE-CONVEYOR, cases are represented by the predicate:

$$c = (Out\_1, \ldots, Out\_6; VairIn, BendType, BendAngle, In\_1, \ldots, In\_6)$$

where *Out_i* means the fraction of particles at the outlet in size range *i*, *In_i* means the fraction of particles at the inlet in size range *i*, where i=1, 2, ..., 6. *VairIn* is the air velocity. Bend type and angle are nominal values.

The similarity metric between a target case and cases in the case base is computed using the standard weighted sum method. For continuous domains such as air velocity, the distance between two points is normalized by the range value. For a nominal domain such as bend type, the distance metric is provided by a human expert, experienced in the construction and use of the various bend types.

We now use the conveyor example to illustrate the problems outlined in Section 3. For convenience of exposition, we leave out the values of In_1,..., In_6, which were kept constant in the example. First we consider interpolation over nominal values. Table 1 shows two cases selected for interpolation to find Bend type and bend angle for a given target. The target outputs are Out_1 = 24 and Out_6= 3.85.

Table 1. Two cases selected for interpolation

Two cases selected for interpolation						
Distance	**Case Id**	**Out_1**	**Out_6**	**VairIn**	**BendType**	**BendAngle**
0.0047	67	24.09	3.90	14.28	Tdrum	70 deg
0.0052	151	24.16	3.84	14.28	ShortRadius	70 deg
Interpolated value						
0.003	-	24.12	3.87	14.28	Btee	70 deg
Model solution						
0.003	-	24.13	3.86	14.28	Btee	70 deg

Table 1 shows the interpolated solution given by GSNN. Notice that the bend type is neither of those in the interpolation set. Finally Table 1 shows the modelled case, which confirms the accuracy of the interpolation.

Next we consider an example of a nominal constraint. We use the same example as above, but this time we add the constraint that only bend types: LongRadius, ShortRadius and Tdrum are available.

Table 2. Two cases selected for interpolation

Two cases selected for interpolation						
Distance	**Case Id**	**Out_1**	**Out_6**	**VairIn**	**BendType**	**BendAngle**
0.0047	67	24.09	3.90	14.28	Tdrum	70 deg
0.0052	151	24.16	3.84	14.28	ShortRadius	70 deg
Interpolated value, where bend types are constrained to {LongRadius, ShortRadius, Tdrum}						
0.0038	-	24.13	3.87	14.28	Tdrum	70 deg
Model solution						
0.0047	-	24.09	3.9	14.28	Tdrum	70 deg

In this case, GSNN has constrained the search to the available bend types. It should be noticed that the solution is further from the target than for the unconstrained search.

Finally, we show an example of a multi-valued mapping. In this example, the engineer wants to achieve an output where the fraction of the largest particles is 6 times the fraction of the smallest particles. The derived attribute *Out_1/Out_6* is accordingly added to the cases, and we search for cases close on this attribute. This is a good example of a multi-valued mapping, since there can be cases with a wide diversity of inputs which can produce this output ratio. But, as is shown here, it is not acceptable to interpolate from these at random. First, we must check for conformability.

Table 3. A retrieved set searching for Out_1/Out_6 = 6

Distance	CaseId	Out_1 / Out_6	VairIn	BendType	BendAngle
0.1063	98	6.1063	19.49	LongRadius	45 deg
0.1328	80	6.1328	12.52	Tdrum	90 deg
0.1769	67	6.1769	14.28	Tdrum	70 deg
0.1951	116	5.8049	14.28	LongRadius	80 deg
0.2024	103	5.7976	15.96	LongRadius	65 deg
0.2079	38	6.2079	12.52	Btee	90 deg
0.2451	158	5.7549	14.28	ShortRadius	80 deg

Table 3 shows the result of a query subject to a constraint: Out_1/Out_6 =6. As we see, the first two cases are not conformable to interpolation. Although they are close to the target Out_1 / Out_6, they are not close at all in the whole space, including VairIn, Bend type and bend angle. In Table 4, we show the interpolated result based on these two cases. We see that the modelled result shows the interpolation has failed. Indeed the interpolation is worse than either of the cases used for the interpolation.

Table 4. Non Conforming set: cases 98 and 80

Interpolated solution					
Out_1/Out_6	**Out_1**	**Out_6**	**VairIn**	**BendType**	**BendAngle**
6.2328125	23.934	3.84	12.52	LongRadius	45 deg
Model solution					
10.17	27.26	2.68	12.52	LongRadius	45 deg

In Table 5, we show that the interpolation based on cases 80 and 67 is far better. Although these two cases are further from the target than the previous set, they give a much better interpolation result. This verifies the approach to conformability that we have adopted in this project.

Table 5. Conforming set : 80, 67

Interpolated solution					
Out_1/Out_6	**Out_1**	**Out_6**	**VairIn**	**BendType**	**BendAngle**
6.0328125	23.166	3.84	12.83	Tdrum	80 deg
Model solution					
6.0431	22.299	3.69	12.83	Tdrum	80 deg

6 Conclusion

In conclusion, the solutions to the problems inherent in the discipline of Case Based Engineering presented in this paper may all be seen as consequential to one central idea: that we should regard the case base holistically as a unified problem + solution space, and define a similarity metric over the whole unified space. If the metric is defined as the weighted sum of similarity over attributes, then the attribute set should cover the whole unified space, and should include continuous and nominal attributes.

The problems of CBE that are addressed in the paper are: flexibility of query forms, interpolation, multi-valued case mapping, and constraints. The first of these problems is to allow the engineer to specify queries over the whole space (in effect defining his/her own problem space). This provides prime motivation for adopting the unified space approach. However, this approach also impacts on the solution to the other problems, and gives an interesting insight into the 'similarity assumption' in the traditional view.

The second problem of CBE is that of interpolation. For many engineering problems, interpolation can provide a powerful adaptation method, improving the accuracy of solutions considerably. The problem which arises here is that many interpolations will be over nominal values. We need an interpolation method that will give the nominal value that minimizes the distance to target in the unified space. Such a method (GSNN) has been developed previously by the authors [8], In fact, since GSNN work depends only on similarity metrics, it works equally well on nominal-valued attributes and on real-valued attributes. This is an important feature for CBE, since many numerical models will include nominal parameters, particularly in their set-up definition.

The problem of multi-valued problem → solution mappings arises in conjunction with interpolation over several cases. In a deterministic numerical model, we can assume that the problem → solution mapping is many → one. However, because CBE gives the engineer the freedom to define his/her own problem and solution space, we can only assume that it is many → many. How do we determine which cases are compatible when we are interpolating? Once again, we can use the concept of unified space to solve this problem. Using k nearest neighbours for interpolation, we know that they are all near in the problem space. In order to be sure that they are conformable for interpolation, we require that they are also near in the solution space. Hence we define a set of cases as conformable for interpolation if they are near in unified space.

This question is closely related to the well known '*similarity assumption*' which posits that near cases in the problem space are also near in the solution space. This assumption may be re-formulated in unified space as 'near cases in the problem space are conformable for interpolation' (i.e., also near in the solution space). The similarity assumption in this form seems to be too restrictive for CBE, with its emphasis on dynamic problem:solution separation; we therefore prefer to examine the conformability dynamically as well, selecting only cases near in the whole unified space for interpolation.

References

1. Bergmann, R., Richter, M. M., Schmitt, S., Stahl, A., Vollrath, I., Utility-oriented Matching: A New Research Direction for Case-Based Reasoning, Proceedings of the 9th German Workshop on Case-Based Reasoning, GWCBR'01, Baden-Baden, 14.-16. März (2001)
2. Chatterjee, N., Campbell, J. A., Adaptation through Interpolation for Time Critical Case-Based Reasoning. Lecture Notes in Artificial Intelligence, Vol. 837: published by Springer-Verlag, 1st European Workshop, EWCBR-93, Kaiserslautern, Germany, November (1993) 221-233
3. Cheetham, W., Benefits of Case-Based Reasoning in Color Matching, Proceedings of the 4th International Conference on Case-Based Reasoning, ICCBR-01, Vancouver, BC, Canada, (2001) 589-596.
4. Cheetham, W., Graf, J., Case-Based Reasoning in Color Matching, Proceedings of the 2nd International Conference on Case-Based Reasoning, ICCBR-97, RI, USA, (1997) 1-12.
5. Cover, T. M., Hart, P., Nearest Neighbour Pattern Classification, IEEE Transactions on Information Theory, 13, (1967) 21-27.
6. Kalapanidas, E., Nikolaos, A., Short-term Air Quality Prediction using a Case-Based Classifier, Environmental Modelling & Software, 16, (2001) 263-272.
7. Kalman, H., Attrition of Powders and Granules at Various Bends during Pneumatic Conveying, Powder Technology, 112 (2000) 244-250
8. Knight, B., Woon, F. L., Case Base Adaptation Using Solution-Space Metrics, Proceedings of the 18th International Joint Conference on Artificial Intelligence, IJCAI-03, Acapulco, Mexico (2003) 1347-1348.

9. Knight, B., Woon, F. L., Case Base Adaptation Using Interpolation over Nominal Values, Proceedings of the 24th Specialist Group on Artificial Intelligence (SGAI) International Conference on Innovative Techniques and Applications of Artificial Intelligence, Research and Development in Intelligent Systems XXI, Cambridge, UK (2004) 73-86.
10. Kolodner, J., Case Based Reasoning, Morgan Kaufmann Publishers; ISBN: 1558602372; (November 1993).
11. Chapelle, P., Christakis, N., Abou-Chakra, H., Tuzun, U., Bridle, I., Bradley, M. S. A., Patel, M. K., Cross, M., Computational model for prediction of particle degradation during dilte phase pneumatic conveying. Modelling of dilute phase pneumatic conveying, Advanced Powder Technology, 15 (1), (2004) 31-49.
12. Schwabacher, M., Ellman, T., Hirsh, H., Learning to Set Up Numerical Optimizations of Engineering Designs, Artificial Intelligence for Engineering Design Analysis and Manufacturing, 12 (2), (1998) 173-192.
13. Stanfill, C., Waltz, D., Toward memory-based reasoning, Communications of the ACM, Vol. 29, (1986) 1213-1228.
14. Weinberger, C. B., Shu, M. T., Helical Gas—Solids Flow II. Effect of Bend Radius and Solids Flow Rate on Transition Velocity, Powder Technology 48 (1986) 19-22
15. Wilson, D. R., Martinez, T. R., Improved Heterogeneous Distance Functions, Journal of Artificial Intelligence Research, 6 (1997) 1-34.
16. Woon, F., Knight, B., Petridis, M., Case Base Reduction Using Solution-Space Metrics, Proceedings of the 5th International Conference on Case-Based Reasoning, ICCBR-03, Trondheim, Norway (2003) 652-664.

Author Index

Lecture Notes in Artificial Intelligence (LNAI)

Vol. 3632: R. Nieuwenhuis (Ed.), Automated Deduction – CADE-20. XIII, 459 pages. 2005.

Vol. 3626: B. Ganter, G. Stumme, R. Wille (Eds.), Formal Concept Analysis. X, 349 pages. 2005.

Vol. 3625: S. Kramer, B. Pfahringer (Eds.), Inductive Logic Programming. XIII, 427 pages. 2005.

Vol. 3620: H. Muñoz-Avila, F. Ricci (Eds.), Case-Based Reasoning Research and Development. XV, 654 pages. 2005.

Vol. 3607: J.-D. Zucker, L. Saitta (Eds.), Abstraction, Reformulation and Approximation. XII, 376 pages. 2005.

Vol. 3596: F. Dau, M.-L. Mugnier, G. Stumme (Eds.), Conceptual Structures: Common Semantics for Sharing Knowledge. XI, 467 pages. 2005.

Vol. 3587: P. Perner, A. Imiya (Eds.), Machine Learning and Data Mining in Pattern Recognition. XVII, 695 pages. 2005.

Vol. 3584: X. Li, S. Wang, Z.Y. Dong (Eds.), Advanced Data Mining and Applications. XIX, 835 pages. 2005.

Vol. 3581: S. Miksch, J. Hunter, E. Keravnou (Eds.), Artificial Intelligence in Medicine. XVII, 547 pages. 2005.

Vol. 3577: R. Falcone, S. Barber, J. Sabater-Mir, M.P. Singh (Eds.), Trusting Agents for Trusting Electronic Societies. VIII, 235 pages. 2005.

Vol. 3575: S. Wermter, G. Palm, M. Elshaw (Eds.), Biomimetic Neural Learning for Intelligent Robots. IX, 383 pages. 2005.

Vol. 3571: L. Godo (Ed.), Symbolic and Quantitative Approaches to Reasoning with Uncertainty. XVI, 1028 pages. 2005.

Vol. 3559: P. Auer, R. Meir (Eds.), Learning Theory. XI, 692 pages. 2005.

Vol. 3558: V. Torra, Y. Narukawa, S. Miyamoto (Eds.), Modeling Decisions for Artificial Intelligence. XII, 470 pages. 2005.

Vol. 3554: A. Dey, B. Kokinov, D. Leake, R. Turner (Eds.), Modeling and Using Context. XIV, 572 pages. 2005.

Vol. 3539: K. Morik, J.-F. Boulicaut, A. Siebes (Eds.), Local Pattern Detection. XI, 233 pages. 2005.

Vol. 3538: L. Ardissono, P. Brna, A. Mitrovic (Eds.), User Modeling 2005. XVI, 533 pages. 2005.

Vol. 3533: M. Ali, F. Esposito (Eds.), Innovations in Applied Artificial Intelligence. XX, 858 pages. 2005.

Vol. 3528: P.S. Szczepaniak, J. Kacprzyk, A. Niewiadomski (Eds.), Advances in Web Intelligence. XVII, 513 pages. 2005.

Vol. 3518: T.B. Ho, D. Cheung, H. Liu (Eds.), Advances in Knowledge Discovery and Data Mining. XXI, 864 pages. 2005.

Vol. 3508: P. Bresciani, P. Giorgini, B. Henderson-Sellers, G. Low, M. Winikoff (Eds.), Agent-Oriented Information Systems II. X, 227 pages. 2005.

Vol. 3505: V. Gorodetsky, J. Liu, V. A. Skormin (Eds.), Autonomous Intelligent Systems: Agents and Data Mining. XIII, 303 pages. 2005.

Vol. 3501: B. Kégl, G. Lapalme (Eds.), Advances in Artificial Intelligence. XV, 458 pages. 2005.

Vol. 3492: P. Blache, E. Stabler, J. Busquets, R. Moot (Eds.), Logical Aspects of Computational Linguistics. X, 363 pages. 2005.

Vol. 3488: M.-S. Hacid, N.V. Murray, Z.W. Raś, S. Tsumoto (Eds.), Foundations of Intelligent Systems. XIII, 700 pages. 2005.

Vol. 3487: J. Leite, P. Torroni (Eds.), Computational Logic in Multi-Agent Systems. XII, 281 pages. 2005.

Vol. 3476: J. Leite, A. Omicini, P. Torroni, P. Yolum (Eds.), Declarative Agent Languages and Technologies II. XII, 289 pages. 2005.

Vol. 3464: S.A. Brueckner, G.D.M. Serugendo, A. Karageorgos, R. Nagpal (Eds.), Engineering Self-Organising Systems. XIII, 299 pages. 2005.

Vol. 3452: F. Baader, A. Voronkov (Eds.), Logic for Programming, Artificial Intelligence, and Reasoning. XI, 562 pages. 2005.

Vol. 3451: M.-P. Gleizes, A. Omicini, F. Zambonelli (Eds.), Engineering Societies in the Agents World V. XIII, 349 pages. 2005.

Vol. 3446: T. Ishida, L. Gasser, H. Nakashima (Eds.), Massively Multi-Agent Systems I. XI, 349 pages. 2005.

Vol. 3445: G. Chollet, A. Esposito, M. Faundez-Zanuy, M. Marinaro (Eds.), Nonlinear Speech Modeling and Applications. XIII, 433 pages. 2005.

Vol. 3438: H. Christiansen, P.R. Skadhauge, J. Villadsen (Eds.), Constraint Solving and Language Processing. VIII, 205 pages. 2005.

Vol. 3430: S. Tsumoto, T. Yamaguchi, M. Numao, H. Motoda (Eds.), Active Mining. XII, 349 pages. 2005.

Vol. 3419: B. Faltings, A. Petcu, F. Fages, F. Rossi (Eds.), Constraint Satisfaction and Constraint Logic Programming. X, 217 pages. 2005.

Vol. 3416: M. Böhlen, J. Gamper, W. Polasek, M.A. Wimmer (Eds.), E-Government: Towards Electronic Democracy. XIII, 311 pages. 2005.

Vol. 3415: P. Davidsson, B. Logan, K. Takadama (Eds.), Multi-Agent and Multi-Agent-Based Simulation. X, 265 pages. 2005.

Vol. 3403: B. Ganter, R. Godin (Eds.), Formal Concept Analysis. XI, 419 pages. 2005.

Vol. 3398: D.-K. Baik (Ed.), Systems Modeling and Simulation: Theory and Applications. XIV, 733 pages. 2005.

Vol. 3397: T.G. Kim (Ed.), Artificial Intelligence and Simulation. XV, 711 pages. 2005.

Vol. 3396: R.M. van Eijk, M.-P. Huget, F. Dignum (Eds.), Agent Communication. X, 261 pages. 2005.

Vol. 3394: D. Kudenko, D. Kazakov, E. Alonso (Eds.), Adaptive Agents and Multi-Agent Systems II. VIII, 313 pages. 2005.

Vol. 3392: D. Seipel, M. Hanus, U. Geske, O. Bartenstein (Eds.), Applications of Declarative Programming and Knowledge Management. X, 309 pages. 2005.

Vol. 3374: D. Weyns, H. V.D. Parunak, F. Michel (Eds.), Environments for Multi-Agent Systems. X, 279 pages. 2005.

Vol. 3371: M.W. Barley, N. Kasabov (Eds.), Intelligent Agents and Multi-Agent Systems. X, 329 pages. 2005.

Vol. 3369: V. R. Benjamins, P. Casanovas, J. Breuker, A. Gangemi (Eds.), Law and the Semantic Web. XII, 249 pages. 2005.

Vol. 3366: I. Rahwan, P. Moraitis, C. Reed (Eds.), Argumentation in Multi-Agent Systems. XII, 263 pages. 2005.

Vol. 3359: G. Grieser, Y. Tanaka (Eds.), Intuitive Human Interfaces for Organizing and Accessing Intellectual Assets. XIV, 257 pages. 2005.

Vol. 3346: R.H. Bordini, M. Dastani, J. Dix, A.E.F. Seghrouchni (Eds.), Programming Multi-Agent Systems. XIV, 249 pages. 2005.

Vol. 3345: Y. Cai (Ed.), Ambient Intelligence for Scientific Discovery. XII, 311 pages. 2005.

Vol. 3343: C. Freksa, M. Knauff, B. Krieg-Brückner, B. Nebel, T. Barkowsky (Eds.), Spatial Cognition IV. XIII, 519 pages. 2005.

Vol. 3339: G.I. Webb, X. Yu (Eds.), AI 2004: Advances in Artificial Intelligence. XXII, 1272 pages. 2004.

Vol. 3336: D. Karagiannis, U. Reimer (Eds.), Practical Aspects of Knowledge Management. X, 523 pages. 2004.

Vol. 3327: Y. Shi, W. Xu, Z. Chen (Eds.), Data Mining and Knowledge Management. XIII, 263 pages. 2005.

Vol. 3315: C. Lemaître, C.A. Reyes, J.A. González (Eds.), Advances in Artificial Intelligence – IBERAMIA 2004. XX, 987 pages. 2004.

Vol. 3303: J.A. López, E. Benfenati, W. Dubitzky (Eds.), Knowledge Exploration in Life Science Informatics. X, 249 pages. 2004.

Vol. 3301: G. Kern-Isberner, W. Rödder, F. Kulmann (Eds.), Conditionals, Information, and Inference. XII, 219 pages. 2005.

Vol. 3276: D. Nardi, M. Riedmiller, C. Sammut, J. Santos-Victor (Eds.), RoboCup 2004: Robot Soccer World Cup VIII. XVIII, 678 pages. 2005.

Vol. 3275: P. Perner (Ed.), Advances in Data Mining. VIII, 173 pages. 2004.

Vol. 3265: R.E. Frederking, K.B. Taylor (Eds.), Machine Translation: From Real Users to Research. XI, 392 pages. 2004.

Vol. 3264: G. Paliouras, Y. Sakakibara (Eds.), Grammatical Inference: Algorithms and Applications. XI, 291 pages. 2004.

Vol. 3259: J. Dix, J. Leite (Eds.), Computational Logic in Multi-Agent Systems. XII, 251 pages. 2004.

Vol. 3257: E. Motta, N.R. Shadbolt, A. Stutt, N. Gibbins (Eds.), Engineering Knowledge in the Age of the Semantic Web. XVII, 517 pages. 2004.

Vol. 3249: B. Buchberger, J.A. Campbell (Eds.), Artificial Intelligence and Symbolic Computation. X, 285 pages. 2004.

Vol. 3248: K.-Y. Su, J. Tsujii, J.-H. Lee, O.Y. Kwong (Eds.), Natural Language Processing – IJCNLP 2004. XVIII, 817 pages. 2005.

Vol. 3245: E. Suzuki, S. Arikawa (Eds.), Discovery Science. XIV, 430 pages. 2004.

Vol. 3244: S. Ben-David, J. Case, A. Maruoka (Eds.), Algorithmic Learning Theory. XIV, 505 pages. 2004.

Vol. 3238: S. Biundo, T. Frühwirth, G. Palm (Eds.), KI 2004: Advances in Artificial Intelligence. XI, 467 pages. 2004.

Vol. 3230: J.L. Vicedo, P. Martínez-Barco, R. Muñoz, M. Saiz Noeda (Eds.), Advances in Natural Language Processing. XII, 488 pages. 2004.

Vol. 3229: J.J. Alferes, J. Leite (Eds.), Logics in Artificial Intelligence. XIV, 744 pages. 2004.

Vol. 3228: M.G. Hinchey, J.L. Rash, W.F. Truszkowski, C.A. Rouff (Eds.), Formal Approaches to Agent-Based Systems. VIII, 290 pages. 2004.

Vol. 3215: M.G.. Negoita, R.J. Howlett, L.C. Jain (Eds.), Knowledge-Based Intelligent Information and Engineering Systems, Part III. LVII, 906 pages. 2004.

Vol. 3214: M.G.. Negoita, R.J. Howlett, L.C. Jain (Eds.), Knowledge-Based Intelligent Information and Engineering Systems, Part II. LVIII, 1302 pages. 2004.

Vol. 3213: M.G.. Negoita, R.J. Howlett, L.C. Jain (Eds.), Knowledge-Based Intelligent Information and Engineering Systems, Part I. LVIII, 1280 pages. 2004.

Vol. 3209: B. Berendt, A. Hotho, D. Mladenic, M. van Someren, M. Spiliopoulou, G. Stumme (Eds.), Web Mining: From Web to Semantic Web. IX, 201 pages. 2004.

Vol. 3206: P. Sojka, I. Kopecek, K. Pala (Eds.), Text, Speech and Dialogue. XIII, 667 pages. 2004.

Vol. 3202: J.-F. Boulicaut, F. Esposito, F. Giannotti, D. Pedreschi (Eds.), Knowledge Discovery in Databases: PKDD 2004. XIX, 560 pages. 2004.

Vol. 3201: J.-F. Boulicaut, F. Esposito, F. Giannotti, D. Pedreschi (Eds.), Machine Learning: ECML 2004. XVIII, 580 pages. 2004.

Vol. 3194: R. Camacho, R. King, A. Srinivasan (Eds.), Inductive Logic Programming. XI, 361 pages. 2004.

Vol. 3192: C. Bussler, D. Fensel (Eds.), Artificial Intelligence: Methodology, Systems, and Applications. XIII, 522 pages. 2004.

Vol. 3191: M. Klusch, S. Ossowski, V. Kashyap, R. Unland (Eds.), Cooperative Information Agents VIII. XI, 303 pages. 2004.

Vol. 3187: G. Lindemann, J. Denzinger, I.J. Timm, R. Unland (Eds.), Multiagent System Technologies. XIII, 341 pages. 2004.